HELIOTYPE REPRODUCTION
FROM
A DAGUERREOTYPE PORTRAIT OF THEODORE PARKER,
TAKEN AT THE AGE OF THIRTY-NINE.

THEODORE PARKER:

A BIOGRAPHY.

BY

OCTAVIUS BROOKS FROTHINGHAM.

BOSTON:
JAMES R. OSGOOD AND COMPANY,
(LATE TICKNOR & FIELDS, AND FIELDS, OSGOOD, & CO.)
1874.

Boston:
Rand, Avery, & Co., Stereotypers and Printers.

PREFACE.

THE friends of Theodore Parker's ideas, as well as the lovers of his person, thinking that his day was not done, but was rather about to break, have long wished that he might be introduced to a new public by a new biography. The "Life" by John Weiss, written as soon as possible after Mr. Parker's decease, and published in 1863, for obvious reasons failed to command the attention it deserved. Being issued in two large volumes, it proved to be too heavy for general circulation, besides being too costly for general purchase. Another drawback to popular favor was found in the space given to letters and discussions, which, however interesting in themselves, and however important as contributions to thought, had the effect of blurring the outline of his individuality. But a disadvantage more serious, perhaps, than either of these, was the publication of the work at a time when the destinies of the nation hung on a thread, and the crowding events of the war pushed into obscurity nearly all memories, and allowed the public eye to rest only on such men as the combat made famous.

The clearing-away of the war-cloud displays once more the figure of Theodore Parker as one of the nation's true prophets, and at the same time reveals a country prepared in some degree to receive the best results of his thought and experience. In the hope that these results may be appreciated better than hitherto, this memoir is written. The author's aim has been simply to recover and present the person of Mr. Parker with all simplicity, omitting some details which Mr. Weiss's valuable biography will supply to the more searching student, and making prominent the mental and moral traits which concern the miscellaneous public.

The present biographer, in addition to the materials that were placed in the hands of Mr. Weiss, has been intrusted with many private letters and personal reminiscences, which enable him to fill out his picture with more delicate touches. From old sources and new it has been his delightful task to extract the qualities of the man in such a way, that the records, literary and historical, may reveal, and not cumber or cloak, his form. Should the portrait be unfaithful or inadequate, the artist alone will be at fault.

Or rather let me say, should it be unfaithful; for inadequate it must be in the judgment of many, and chiefly of those who knew Mr. Parker most intimately. There was more in him than any one mind, even the most candid and sympathetic, could see; and there was much in him that few, if any, were ever permitted to see; the private journal, to which he committed his most secret thoughts, containing many things of deep significance as illustrations of his interior life, which could not with the least propriety be published, even when their meaning is clear, and which often need interpretation. None of them exhibit qualities inconsistent with a very noble character; but some of them point to secret recesses of feeling which cannot be uncovered.

A few months before his death, to an intimate friend who put a question in regard to his literary executor he said, "If any one writes my life, I think it will be George Ripley: he, better than any one, understands my philosophy, and what I meant to do." — "But the *personal* life," said the friend: "who will write that? When one has achieved such a character as yours, we long to know what elements have been wrought into it." — "That life," he answered with deep emotion, "cannot be written. I have been asked to employ these few remaining months in preparing an autobiography. But it must be written in tears of blood, if at all." It never was written; and only so much of the interior life as a plain record of thoughts and actions exhibits can be disclosed. That will be quite enough for those who did not know him well: it will be all that is desired by those who did.

O. B. F.

NEW YORK, October, 1873.

CONTENTS.

THEODORE PARKER.

CHAPTER I.

BIRTHPLACE AND PARENTAGE.

A STRANGER, visiting the place where Theodore Parker passed his early years, did not find it attractive. Exploring the neighborhood on a fair spring-day, he asked a man who was mending the road where Theodore Parker was born. The man leaned on his spade, stared at the traveller, looked puzzled, and replied, "Dunno." — "Are you a new-comer here?" — "No, sir: lived here, man and boy, nigh on to forty year." — "Are there no Parkers about here?" — "Yes: there's tew lots on 'em." — "I wish to find the *old* Parker place," said the stranger. "Older'n creation, both on 'em," was the reply. "The *Captain* Parker place is the one I want." — "They run to cappens," was the exasperating rejoinder: "but I guess you had better take that 'ar road to the left, and go about a mile; then turn down a lane, and at the end there's a monnerment that must be set up for Cappen Parker." The traveller, obeying the direction, found the monument that preserves the great preacher's memory.

This incident tells many things: the limited influence of a great man's name; the power of association to glorify ordinary spots; the absence of neighborly feeling in rural populations; and the crudeness of society within ten miles of the great city. What the tourist found on arriving at the place of his quest was much the same as what the boy whose name led him thither used to see. There was the old bell-tower, which had rung out the alarm on the eve of the battle of Lexington, and had done humbler service since as a workshop; the broad stone ledge behind the house remained; meadow, orchard, wood, were unchanged; the ash-tree planted by Theodore — which showed its grief at his death by bearing but one crop of leaves instead of the two it displayed during his life — still held its place; the double-headed pine, that seemed a wonder, was as much as ever a feature in the landscape: but the old house was gone.

That was a hundred years old when Theodore saw the light; having been built in 1710 by his great-grandfather, John Parker, who, with children and grandchildren, came to Lexington (then called Cambridge Farms) from Reading. John Parker was a grandson of Thomas, who came to America in 1635 in a vessel fitted out by Sir Richard Saltonstall, with whose family he was connected by marriage. He settled in Lynn; received, as one of the earliest settlers of the town, forty acres of land; and was made a freeman the year after landing. In 1640 he removed to Reading, was one of seven who founded the first church there, and there died in 1683. He was a man of character. His descendants were also serviceable in their places; doing their part as land-surveyors, councilmen, adjudicators of claims, teachers, militiamen, drill-masters, lieutenants, and captains. They had the fighting-temper in them, and made themselves felt in hard battle. Hananiah, the only grandson who did not come with John to Lexington, — a lad of eighteen, — was serving in a Massachusetts regiment engaged in Virginia.

If we trace the family across the water to England, we

find its roots deep down in the soil. Thomas came, perhaps, from a Lancashire stock, which was early transplanted to Yorkshire, where some of them still live in a stately mansion-house of the time of Queen Elizabeth. The first who bore the name in England was a Norman, Johannes Le Parkerre. He followed William the Conqueror, and was keeper of the royal parks; whence his name, variously spelled Parkerre, Parkre, Parchour, Parker. The name occurs frequently in history in different connections. Seldom good Churchmen, they were scattered much at the Reformation. Some were executed under Queen Mary; some were Puritans under Cromwell. But others were true to the royalist party; lost their lands in consequence, and regained them when the king "came to his own again." The Parkers in England now are commonly Churchmen and Tories. The religious and political traditions of the family are mixed. The non-conformist blood, Puritan and Quaker, found its way into the New World.

Theodore's grandfather, John Parker, born 1729, was a marked man. He was a sergeant in the French and Indian war, and present at the capture of Quebec. A parishioner of the Rev. Jonas Clark, who had done his share in rousing the people to indignation against the British claims, he was ready for war when the time came; answered at once the summons to resist the British at Lexington; was present himself, though suffering from illness, which exposure developed into a fatal disease; drew up his troop of seventy men; bade every man load his piece with powder and ball; ordered them not to fire unless fired upon; but added, "If they mean to have a war, let it begin here." At the battle of Lexington, Captain Parker took from a grenadier the weapon which, along with his own light fowling-piece, guarded the door of Theodore's study while he lived, and now hangs in the Massachusetts Senate Chamber.

The people of Lexington were, like the country people

of New England generally fifty years ago, industrious after a homely and unenterprising fashion, but not specially thrifty. Their land was poor, their toil hard, their wealth small. Literary and social advantages were scanty. There were no lectures, clubs, or associations for culture. A small library contained three or four hundred volumes, chiefly novels, biographies, books of travel, with a few popular histories. About a dozen volumes, light reading for the most part, were added yearly. The cost of a share was ten dollars. The library stood near by the meeting-house, nearly three miles off from the Parker residence: hence the custom of exchanging books on Sunday. While some went to the library for books, others went to Dudley's tavern, which was also hard by, to talk politics, tell stories, and drink. The drinking habits of the period were pure and simple. Instead of being apologized for, they were commended on social and on sanitary grounds. Drink was regarded as the poor man's food, the laboring man's strength. It was introduced on sacred occasions as a thing of course. One of the earliest recorded instances of its disuse at funerals seems to have been at the house of Mr. Parker, on the occasion of his grandmother's death.

There was but one meeting-house in the village, the minister of which was a Unitarian. The people, to a very large extent, shared his opinions. In fact, the germs of the later more cultivated rationalism were sprouting in these New-England communities. The doctrines of the Puritan theology had lost their hold on an unimaginative people; and with them the fervors of the evangelical spirit had declined. The sinfulness of human nature, the need of redemption, the deity of Christ, the atoning efficacy of his blood, the necessity of inward renewal by the grace of God, the worthlessness of morality, the everlastingness of future punishment, the consciousness of acceptance, the immanence of Christ in the Church, the eternity of bliss for believers, were all more or less thoughtfully rejected by men whose sober lives had settled down into prose, and whose experience suggested little of mystery. The preaching lacked inspiration: even the prayers were didactic. The best of the clergy were men of letters, rarely prophets: the worst were neither. Churches were closed to Whitefield before Theodore Parker was born. The seats of culture dreaded the influence of the famous preacher of revivals; the clergy encouraged the laity to frown down extravagant views; the sacraments had lost their charm; the mystery had departed from the communion; baptism was rarely administered; heads of families were commonly church-members, the younger people seldom; family prayers were infrequent; grace before meat was unusual; the clergyman was respected as a man of education; the sabbath was observed punctually; the Bible was read; but the soul of the Protestant faith had fled.

The parents of Theodore Parker shared the spiritual life of their time, — the father holding the rational views with something more than the usual positiveness of conviction, the mother with something more than the usual depth of feeling; while both added to them a good deal more than the average weight of character. John Parker, born Feb. 14, 1761, was a good specimen of the New-England countryman, — a "quiet, thoughtful, silent, reading man, of strong sense, of great moral worth, reliable, honorable; worked every day and all day; kept good discipline in his family; governed easily; taught his children to speak the truth; always had a book in his hand in the evening." This is a grandson's testimony. His son described him from memory as a stout, able-bodied man, plain and solid. He could endure cold and heat, abstinence from food and rest. A skilful farmer, he was prevented by want of means from making costly improvements on his land; but he had, perhaps, the best peach-orchard in Middlesex, and adopted nearly all the improvements in farming that had proved valuable. The farm-work, however, he left mainly to his boys, while he pursued his own occupation of mill-wright and pump-maker in the shop: for, like his father and grandfather before him, he was an ingenious mechanic, and worker in wood; expert in making and repairing, as men need to be in a new country, where one must do the work of many. He put brains into his work; originated new methods; "made his head save his hands."

Of course, he had little education, and no culture; but of the raw material of mind he possessed a good deal: he was fond of intellectual things, read such books as he could reach, pondered hard questions, and turned over in his mind the higher problems in ethics and metaphysics. He was a fair arithmetician; understood something of algebra and geometry. He was interested in works on political economy and the philosophy of legislation. Books of history, biography, and travel, engaged him; but his thoughts occupied themselves most eagerly with speculative philosophy, metaphysical and moral, in the current literature of which he was well versed. It is interesting, in view of Theodore's passion for natural objects, to know that his taste also belonged to his father. He watched the heavens, and made himself acquainted with the movements of the stars. He was an observer of plants too, and flowers, and had laid up some store of information in natural history. It is needless to add, that this man was no hearty lover of poetry: he had too much understanding, and too little imagination. He read books of poetry, as he read any books he could lay hands on; but the range of his reading throws doubt on his taste. One who can read, without strongly-declared preference, authors so various as Milton, Dryden, Shakspeare, Pope, Trumbull, and Abraham Cowley, cannot be credited with fondness for the poetic art.

Mr. Parker had a strong mind. He thought for himself, and passed judgment on authorities. Neither Paley nor Edwards was to his liking, — Paley because "he left us no conscience:" Edwards probably for many reasons; among others, perhaps, because he left us no will; for will was a strong feature in the Parkers. He was an avowed Unitarian before Unitarianism as a system was preached, and a stout Federalist when there were but four besides himself in the whole town. Though averse to controversy, naturally silent and reserved, he had a gift of speech; could argue forcibly and talk well on occasion, even with something like eloquence. His diligent study of the Bible made him formidable in theological debate. He had faith in mind; took a practical interest in the town school; was satisfied with none but good teachers; and gave thought to the intellectual and moral training of his children.

He was an upright man, — just, fearless, humane; often called on to arbitrate in disputes, administer estates, and assume guardianship of orphans. He was a friend of peace, well-mannered and companionable, with a streak of humor that would occasionally break into mirth, but never passed the bounds of propriety. No profanity escaped his lips. His towns-people had a saying, "John Parker has all the manners of the neighborhood."

The mother, the daughter of a well-to-do farmer, was as remarkable in her way as the father was in his. Her maiden name was Hannah Stearns. Her son describes her as "a handsome woman, of slight form, flaxen hair, blue eyes, and a singularly fresh and delicate complexion; more nervous than muscular." She had a family tendency to consumption, which increased the mildness and amiability of her disposition. Her education was inferior to her husband's, her mind less positive and independent. She lived more in her feeling and imagination, which kept their freshness amid the homely routine of domestic life, and through the cares belonging to a large family. Her temperament was poetical, though rather fanciful than imaginative. Her favorite reading was the Bible and Hymn-Book; but ballad poetry gave her great delight, and her mind was stored with passages of beauty from English literature. She was fond of romantic stories of adventure among the Indians, some of which were printed in books, while many others floated about in the form of legend. A fine memory enabled her to repeat these wild tales, and to carry about with her such literary stores as she had. The duties of a large and exacting household — many children and no servants — afforded little leisure for mental cultivation; but what she had was improved. Her husband's habit of reading aloud in the evening kept her supplied with food for thought.

She was of a loving disposition towards those about her, tenderly watchful of her children, thoughtful of the aged, kind, and, as far as her means allowed, generous to the poor. Her rigid economy helped her in this. She was religious with the natural religion of the good heart. Her beliefs came to her through feeling rather than through reflection: they were not so much opinions as sentiments. She was no theologian: the doctrines of the Calvinistic creed, which her strong-minded husband rejected as irrational, she rejected as monstrous, having no reasons to give for her aversion that were so cogent as the aversion itself. The heart was its own witness; conscience was the oracle of God in the breast; gratitude and trust were interpreters to her of the ways of Providence. With the simple feeling of a gentle spirit that comprehends more than it apprehends, and clings where definition is impossible, she knew the Deity as an omnipresent Father, the joyous and loving Soul of all things, animating nature and enlightening mind, filling the world with tides of energy that were as vast as the ocean, and bright as the rivulets. She, too, seems to have been silent; a woman of few words, either of conversation or devotion: her prayers were secret. In the moral culture of her children she took great interest, which she expressed, not in doctrinal teaching or incessant precept, but in wise counsel and sympathy as occasion came up.

This information respecting his parents comes from Theodore himself, — an affectionate, grateful, and revering son, who loved to speak of his parents; scarcely ever failed to record in his busy journal the anniversaries of their birth or death, and never made such record without dropping the tenderest words on their memories. If it be objected that filial love glorified the parental qualities, it must be granted that filial love is the best interpreter of them. Affection transfigures, it is true; but then affection understands. We cannot trust the insight of love when it is passionate; but we can rely on its judgment when it is calm, like that of a noble man on those who gave him birth.

From this slight sketch it is plain that the roots of Theodore Parker reached down deep, and spread out wide. Their fibres coiled round sturdy qualities; their suckers found out hidden fountains of water. The stock was vigorous, and could be counted on to produce, under favorable conditions, a style of character at once robust and beautiful, rich in some of the strongest, and attractive in some of the sweetest, elements of mind and heart. Whatever else the Parkers may have had or been defective in, they had force of will, strength of understanding, power of moral purpose, steadfastness, and independence. Some had humor, some remarkable intellectual thirst, one at least a curious knowledge of Eastern tongues: all had courage and endurance. The combination of qualities in this father and mother — the one so serious, intelligent, helpful, toilsome, sincere; the other so tender, earnest, trustful, and deep-hearted — contained a prophecy of rare ability and worth. The fruit from such a tree ought to be rich. These prophecies do not always come to fulfilment. How far they did in this case will be seen as the story goes on.

CHAPTER II.

HOME AND BOYHOOD.

THEODORE PARKER was born on the 24th of August, 1810. He was the youngest of eleven children, — the tenth being five years older than he. One died in infancy: the rest, none of them distinguished, lived to be useful men and women. All but three had a decided fondness for literature, read the best books they could get, and copied the portions that most interested them. The oldest had gone away from home when the last was born; but enough remained to fill the house. John Parker was poor when he married, and he never became rich. "When he married Hannah Stearns," says Theodore in a fragment of autobiography, "he went back to the original homestead to take care of his mother, while he should support his handsome young wife and such family as might happen. It was the day of small things: he wore home-made blue-yarn stockings at his wedding, and brought his wife home over the rough winding roads, riding in the saddle his tall gray horse, with her upon a pillion. The outfit of furniture did not bespeak more sumptuous carriage: the common plates were of wood; the pitcher, mugs, teacups and saucers, were of coarse earthenware; while the great carving dishes were of thick, well-kept pewter. The holiday service 'for company' was of the same material. Yet a few costly wine-glasses were not wanting, with two long-necked decanters, a few china teacups and saucers of the minutest pattern, and — the pride of the buffet — a large china bowl. Besides, the young bride could show patchwork bedquilts and counterpanes, and a pretty store of linen towels, and a tablecloth of the same, white as the snow, and spun, wove, and bleached by her own laborious hands; and her father raised the flax, which her brother pulled and rotted, and broke and swingled, and hackled and combed. Hannah made their work into linen."

"In my earliest childhood," the autobiography goes on to say, "the family at home consisted of my father's mother, more than eighty at my birth, — a tall, stately, proud-looking woman. She occupied an upper chamber, but came down stairs to dinner, — other meals she took in her own room, — and sate at the head of the table, on the woman's side thereof, opposite my father, who kept up the Puritan respect for age, — always granting it precedence. She busied herself chiefly in knitting and puttering about the room; but passed the Sundays in reading the large Oxford quarto Bible of her husband, bought for the price of more than one load of hay delivered up at Boston. She had also the original edition of the Puritan Hymn-Book printed at Cambridge, which was much in her hands. She read the newspapers, — the 'Columbian Centinel,' which then appeared twice a week; but common mundane literature she seldom touched. It was a part of my childish business to carry the *drink* to my venerable grandmother twice a day, — at eleven, A.M., and four, P.M.: this was flip in cool weather, and in spring and summer was toddy or punch: the latter was, however, more commonly reserved for festive occasions.

"The neighbors about us were farmers: a shoemaker lived a mile off on one side, and a blacksmith within two miles on the other. These were generally, perhaps universally, honest, hard-working men. They went to meeting Sundays, morning and afternoon. 'Their talk was of bullocks, and they were diligent to give the kine fodder.' In their houses, generally neat as good housewifery could make them, you would find the children's school-books; commonly a 'singing-book' ('Billings's Collection,' or some other); perhaps a hymn-book; and always a good quarto Bible, kept in the best room; sometimes another Bible, inherited from some Puritan ancestor: these, with an almanac hung in the corner of the kitchen-chimney, made up the family library. Perhaps a weekly or semi-weekly newspaper was also taken, and diligently read. Two families, not far off, were exceptions to this poverty of books: I now think of no more. Yet now and then the life of some great thief like Stephen Burroughs, or some pirate or highwayman, would show itself. In other parts of Lexington, — 'on the great road,' or 'in the middle of the town,' — perhaps there was a better show of books. I only speak of my immediate neighborhood."

The family, as has been stated, were poor. Their means were very slender. The land was small and unproductive, the tillage necessarily inexpensive. The soil was running out. The products were corn and potatoes, beans, vegetables, and apples. The most valuable crop was peaches: sometimes as much as a hundred dollars' worth were sold. The meat was bought, and not seldom the vegetables. The chief income was derived from the shop; but that was not much: a rigid economy was required to meet the daily needs. Mr. Parker had become surety for a brother who failed, and his portion of the farm was sold to pay the debt. The family expenses were increased by sickness. The taint of hereditary disease was aggravated by the unwholesomeness of the situation; and it was rare that one or more of the household did not require medical treatment. This reduced the means of living to a very scanty sum, and left no margin for the commonest luxuries. Theodore had, as a child, a dangerous attack of typhoid-fever which threatened his life, and at another time a severe dysentery; but his boyhood was generally healthy. The household could not afford to harbor unproductive consumers: all the able-bodied members were drafted for toil. When scarcely more than a child, Theodore, with a companion hardly, it would seem, more competent than he, was sent to Boston market with the peach crop; and, long before his strength was adequate to such tasks, he was employed in the laying of a stone wall, the strain of which, he used to say afterwards, was a permanent injury to his constitution. The skill acquired in the use of tools, and implements of husbandry, was no compensation for this excessive labor; nor was the physical strength obtained any suitable reward for the unnatural exertions by which it was won. The out-door life was good; but the conditions of it were bad. The causes of much of the ill health that darkened and depressed the years of manhood may be traced to these laborious days of childhood, to which so many have ascribed the apparent strength of his constitution.

But to return to the autobiography and the childhood. "As the youngest child, it may be supposed I was treated with uncommon indulgence, and probably received a good deal more than a tenth part of the affection distributed. I remember often to have heard the neighbors say, 'Why, Mis' Parker, you're sp'ilin' your boy! He never can take care of himself when he grows up.' To which she replied, she hoped not, and kissed my flaxen curls anew.

"Among the earliest things I remember is the longing I used to feel to have the winter gone, and to see the great snow-bank — sometimes, when new-fallen, as high as the top of the kitchen-window — melt away in front of the house. I loved, though, to run in the snow barefoot, and with only my night-shirt on, for a few minutes at a time. When the snow was gone, the peculiar smell of the ground seemed to me delicious. The first warm days of spring, which brought the blue-birds to their northern home, and tempted the bees to try short flights, in which they presently dropped on the straw my provident father had strewn for them about their hive, filled me with the deepest delight. In the winter I was limited to the kitchen, where I could build cob-houses, or form little bits of wood into fantastic shapes. Sometimes my father or one of my brothers would take me to the shop, where he pursued his toilsome work; or to the barn, where the horse, the oxen, and the cows were a perpetual pleasure. But when the snow was gone, and the ground dry, I had free range. I used to sit or lie on the ground in a dry and sheltered spot, and watch the great yellow clouds of April that rolled their huge shapes far above my head, filling my eye with their strange, fantastic, beautiful, and ever-changing forms, and my mind with wonder at what they were, and how they came there.

"But the winter itself was not without its in-door pleasures, even for a little fellow in brown homespun petticoats. The uncles and aunts came in their sleighs full of cousins, some of whom were of my own age, to pass a long afternoon and evening, not without abundant good cheer, and a fire in 'the other room,' as the humble parlor was modestly named. They did not come without a great apple, or a little bag of shag-barks, or some other tid-bit, for 'Mis' Parker's baby;' for so the youngest was called long after he ceased to merit the name. Nay, father and mother often returned these visits, and sometimes took the baby with them; because the mother did not like to leave the darling at home; or perhaps she wished to show how stout and strong her eleventh child had come into the world."

The child did not increase in beauty as he increased in years. They who remember him in his young days describe him as rather under the usual size, clumsily made, ungainly and inactive, but as arch and roguish in disposition. The bashfulness, and sense of awkwardness, he probably recovered from; but the ungainliness of movement remained with him always.

The thirst for knowledge appeared in him early; but neither so early nor so surprisingly as his consciousness of right and wrong. Two or three interesting examples of this he recalls from his childhood: "In my fourth year, my father had a neighbor, Deacon Stearns, come to kill a calf. My father would not do it himself, as other farmers did. I was not allowed to see the butchery; but, after it was all over, the deacon, who had lost all his children, asked me whom I loved best. 'Papa.'—'What! better than yourself?'—'Yes, sir.'—'But,' said my father, 'if one of us must take a whipping, which would you rather should have the blows?' I *said* nothing, but wondered and wondered why I should prefer that he should have the blows, and not I. The fact was plain, and plainly selfish, and, it seemed to me, wicked. Yet I could not help the feeling. It tormented me for weeks in my long clothes." Another instance must not be omitted, though it has been often quoted for its striking beauty: it is told at the close of the "Autobiography." "When a little boy in petticoats, in my fourth year, one fine day in spring my father led me by the hand to a distant part of the farm, but soon sent me home alone. On the way I had to pass a little 'pond-hole,' then spreading its waters wide. A rhodora in full bloom—a rare plant in my neighborhood, and which grew only in that locality—attracted my attention, and drew me to the spot. I saw a little spotted tortoise sunning himself in the shallow water at the root of the flaming shrub. I lifted the stick I had in my hand to strike the harmless reptile: for, though I had never killed any creature, yet I had seen other boys out of sport destroy birds, squirrels, and the like; and I felt a disposition to follow their wicked example. But all at once something checked my little arm, and a voice within me said clear and loud, 'It is wrong.' I held my uplifted stick in wonder at the new emotion—the consciousness of an involuntary but inward check upon my actions—till the tortoise and the rhodora both vanished from my sight. I hastened home, told the tale to my mother, and asked what it was that told me it was wrong. She wiped a tear from her eye with her apron, and, taking me in her arms, said, 'Some men call it conscience; but I prefer to call it the voice of God in the soul of man. If you listen and obey it, then it will speak clearer and clearer, and always guide you right; but if you turn a deaf ear, or disobey, then it will fade out little by little, and leave you all in the dark and without a guide. Your life depends on your heeding this little voice.' She went her way, careful and troubled about many things, but doubtless pondered them in her motherly heart; while I went off to wonder and to think it over in my poor childish way. But I am sure no event in my life has made so deep and lasting an impression on me." The grateful man tells this story to show "the nice and delicate care she took of my moral culture." But it shows with equal clearness the child's moral sensibility, not rare, we may hope, at that tender age, but certainly rare associated with so much thoughtfulness, curiosity, and sincerity. Not that the feeling came, but that it became reflection, and deepened into character, is the remarkable thing.

The religious sentiment was as quick in germinating as the moral, and had the same conditions in its favor. The father was a religious man of the grave, earnest sort, without much emotion. He went to church, taught his children the Ten Commandments, encouraged their learning hymns, and would have them say their prayers when they went to bed: but he read the Bible with his understanding; omitted, toward the close of his life, the grace before meat; and in his old age, when too deaf to hear the preacher's sermon, staid at home and read novels. The mother had a sweet, fresh, instinctive devoutness. She belonged to "the church," and had the children duly christened in presence of the neighbors. Theodore's turn came when he was about two years and a half old, he being the last and the pet child. The occasion was made impressive by a larger concourse of friends than usual. The ceremony was by sprinkling or touching the forehead with water. The child prefigured the man, not by the idle wail so common at these rituals, but by an outspoken protest, grounded in apprehension, possibly, rather than in reason, but sufficiently emphatic to be remembered. A child of two years and a half could hardly have speculated about the ceremony he was undergoing, or intelligently wanted to know what it all meant, or for what purpose it was done: but the "Oh, don't!" was something more than a cry of fear; there was character in it; it revealed the spirit that afterwards made the man protest against so many things, on the ground that they did not stand in reason.

But if the sharp, challenging disposition was thus forward, the devout tendency was in no way behind. "Religion," he said in a sermon quoted by Mr. Weiss, "was the inheritance my mother gave me in my birth, — gave me in her teachings. Many sons have been better born than I: few have had so good a mother. I mention these things to show you how I came to have the views of religion that I have now. My head is not more natural to my body, has not more grown with it, than my religion out of my soul and with it. With me religion was not carpentry, something built up of dry wood from without; but it was growth, — growth of a germ in my soul."

At an age when most children are amusing themselves with their first fairy tales, he was capable of "spiritual experiences." He was not seven years old when the doctrine of everlasting damnation plunged his soul in anguish, which made the hours of one night, if no more, so wretched, that for years he could hardly think of the horror without shuddering. But such passages were not frequent, nor did they last long. There is no evidence of morbid tendency at this time; none of severe inward conflict. His nature, if sensitive, was buoyant, and soon surmounted the mental difficulties that came in his way. The inherited predisposition to consumption may occasionally have caused a lassitude of feeling; the hardness of his lot may a little further have depressed his animal spirits: but his mind was not self-tormenting. Whenever the man recalled his childhood, the recollection was pleasant. "However it may be with the natural man," he used to say, "the natural boy has no fear of God." "I have swam in clear, sweet waters all my days," he told the Progressive Friends. "From the days of earliest boyhood, when I went stumbling through the grass 'as merry as a May bee,' up to the gray-bearded manhood of this time, there is none but has left me honey in the hive of memory, that I now feed on for present delight. When I recall the years of boyhood, youth, early manhood, I am filled with a sense of sweetness and wonder that such little things can make a mortal so exceedingly rich." Mr. Parker's hilarious humor was of a spontaneous and racy flavor, that could hardly consist with a morbid temperament; and this humor displayed itself in his earliest years. The elements of his being were healthy; the struggles were incidental, and served to make the healthfulness robust. A great capacity for sorrow does not imply an ever-present fact of sorrow. That the capacity was there will be plain enough as the career flows on; that the fact was present too, and often, admits of no doubt: but no melancholy cast prevented the natural wholesomeness from vindicating itself, and coming out easily victorious over foes that held no ground in the citadel, but only stormed the outer walls.

The school-days began early, when the boy was barely six years old. The plain district schoolhouse was a mile distant by the road, but was brought nearer by a short cut across the fields and over the brook. It was kept by one teacher at a time, in summer and in winter: twelve or fourteen weeks in winter, from December; four months, or sixteen weeks, from the middle of May to the middle of September, in spring and summer. In seed-time and harvest the children could not be spared; nor could money be spared to maintain a teacher the full year. The summer school was kept for the smaller children, whose services were not required on the farm. Theodore attended only in winter from his seventh or eighth year. The summer teacher was commonly a woman. Mary Smith, or "Aunt Pattie" as she was called, was the first who had charge of our young friend's instruction. The male teacher whose name is first mentioned was John Hastings. He is not highly praised, either as scholar, teacher, or disciplinarian, by one of Mr. Parker's contemporaries; nor had he any vivid recollections, in after-life, of his distinguished pupil. But Theodore remembered him; and one evening in Brooklyn, after a lecture, the old teacher was heartily greeted by the speaker whom he had been listening to for the first time, and was wittily reminded of an incident in their school-relations which had quite escaped his memory. Hastings tells the story, adding that it was enjoyed by a good many loiterers besides himself. The rage among the boys, it seems, was for pop-guns, — an instrument made usually of a quill, and loaded with a piece of potato: the pushing in of a rammer at the larger end of the tube compressed the air, and the potato came out at the small end with a report loud enough to startle a large room. It was a harmless weapon, the bite whereof was in the bark. Theodore procured from his elder brother a pop-gun of uncommon caliber, and carried it to school. The weapon being new and untried, the hush of the school-room tempting, and the master's back suggestive of opportunity, the experiment on sound was then and there hazarded. In an instant, all heads were raised; the master faced about with inquisitive eyes: but at that instant no boy was studying so hard as Parker; he was devouring his book! The success of the first experiment inspired a second: but this time the master looked up a second too soon; the culprit was detected in the very act. There was a challenge, a summons, a reprimand; the weapon was confiscated, and order was restored.

The New-England district schools were not graded: the scholars were of all ages, from five to twenty. The teachers were young men from some neighboring college, who eked out their expenses by teaching in vacations, and for as much longer as the authorities permitted, or their necessities required. The instruction was never systematic, and almost always thin. The amount accomplished depended, in greatest measure, on the capacity and interest of the instructor: and neither was apt to be great; for the work was undertaken by raw minds half furnished, and was done incidentally, as a make-shift, by young men who had no thought of making teaching their profession. The compensation was small, — twenty-eight dollars a month, the teacher boarding himself. Little besides the elements was attempted. No regular instruction was given in the arts of composition or declamation. The books in use were Murray's English Grammar, Adams's Arithmetic, Whelpley's Compend of History; for advanced classes, Blake's Philosophy, Comstock's Chemistry, Colburn's Algebra, Playfair's Euclid, Blair's Rhetoric.

In 1820, William Hoar White, afterwards a Unitarian minister, then a student in Brown University, twenty-five years old, succeeded Mr. Hastings, and produced a beneficial change in the school. Theodore was then old enough to interest him; and he never ceased to be grateful to the firm, kind, sympathetic friend who led him on past the prescribed line of study, and started him in Latin and Greek. White taught two winters. Theodore felt his loss severely; but it was made good by his successor, George Fiske, also a student of Brown University, who taught three winters. Both these young men were procured by Mr. Parker, who was acquainted with relatives of theirs in Lexington. To these two men the volume on "Theism and Atheism" was dedicated in 1853, "with gratitude for early instruction received at their hands." Mr. Fiske brought some books from the college library that made him doubly welcome to the juvenile student.

This desultory kind of teaching went on ten years for about three months each winter, and two summer terms,—equivalent to something like three years of continuous instruction; though not as effective, by any means, as three years of continuous instruction would have been. At the age of sixteen he went for a single quarter to Mr. Huntington's school, called the "Academy," at Lexington. This costly indulgence—the expense, we are informed by the letter of a friend, was four dollars—was afforded by the lad's self-denial in foregoing the accomplishment of dancing, which the boys and girls of his age were cultivating, in view of social festivities that were the ruling passion about that time. Between the culture of the two extremities, Theodore, on consideration, chose that of the head. At the Academy he pushed his studies into algebra, and extended his acquaintance with Latin and Greek. At the age of seventeen he began to teach himself.

When he was a little boy, an incident occurred that made a deep impression on him. He was on his way to school, trudging alone across the fields. Suddenly he was accompanied by an old man with long white beard and a patriarchal aspect, who talked with him on the way, told him what a bright boy might do and be, making his heart burn with strong emotion, and then disappeared as unaccountably as he came. Theodore often alluded to this adventure in after-life in a manner that betrayed a half-superstitious belief in the visitation. Who the person was, he could not guess: no inhabitant of the neighborhood; he knew them all. No stranger had been seen in the quiet village. Be he who he might be, the meeting fell in with the boy's early consciousness that he had a destiny. Was it the consciousness that made the meeting significant?

The boy was distinguished as a scholar by his thirst for knowledge and his memory. Both were remarkable. He read miscellaneously and every thing. He was always studying, in school and out. Mr. White set evening lessons: Theodore learned them, and wanted more. He had extra studies, and was not satisfied. In the summer noons, when the other hands indulged in a siesta under the trees, he refreshed his mind with books. The winter mornings were too short, and domestic duties left him no leisure; but the winter evenings and the summer mornings were long, and the hours were faithfully used. No boy in the school could match him either in quantity or quality of performance. But one pupil approached him; and that one was a girl, Marianne Smith by name. The extent of his reading was astonishing. Whatever Mr. Fiske could lend, whatever the social library would afford, he devoured. The father brought home nothing that the boy did not appropriate. If the cautious parent put a volume away on a high shelf, judging it for some reason unfit for youthful eyes, the eyes espied it, and the hands reached it the instant the workshop absorbed the parental form. Every thing was fish that came into his net. Before he was eight he had read Homer and Plutarch (in translations of course), Rollin's Ancient History, — a common book, — and all the other volumes of history and poetry that circumstances afforded. Books of travel and adventure were welcomed, and assimilated too; for his parents made him give an account of every volume he read before he could have another. At the Academy he went through Colburn's Algebra in three weeks. Nor were his studies confined to books. The stars interested him; the trees, the shrubs, the flowers of the neighborhood, the plants in cultivated gardens he visited, the foreign fruits he saw in the Boston market, the husks and leaves that came wrapped about bales of merchandise, tea-chests, and packages from distant parts of the world, attracted his attention. The formation of the hills, their direction and slope; the minerals, rocks, stones that lay about, or that were brought from a distance, — excited his curiosity. The means of satisfying it were few. A copy of Evelyn's "Sylva," and Morse's large Geography, did not go very far; but they told something, and a persevering sagacity did what was done beside. His memory — an inheritance from his mother, which he treasured and kept bright by diligent care — held fast whatever the rapacious mind received. He had his mother's aptitude for committing verses; could repeat a song from hearing it once, the Sunday hymn while the minister read it. He could carry several hundred lines in his memory, so as to recite them at a sitting. In mature years, when his mind was burdened with stores, he could appropriate as many as a hundred and fifty lines of blank-verse after a single reading. It was his custom, when walking with a companion, to recite from poems like Wordsworth's "Excursion" till his friend begged for mercy. He had the political events of the country at his tongue's end while yet a schoolboy; and talked so intelligently about them, that the political gossips of the town, assembled in Dudley's Tavern, drew him out for the sake of hearing his opinion. The gift of expression came to him as readily as the gift of acquisition. The disease of verse-making attacked him when he was eight years old. His first composition on the "starry heavens" disappointed his teacher, Mr. Fiske, by being too short. He was an impassioned declaimer; spoke with much applause, at a public exhibition, a piece from Scott's "Marmion;" and showed the power of mimicry that afterwards made him so amusing and so formidable by impersonating a Catholic priest in some juvenile theatricals.

Such lads are commonly more popular with their teachers than with their comrades. This was hardly the case with Theodore. His kindness, and love of fun, disarmed the jealousy his superiority might have excited, and overcame the awe his gravity would naturally inspire. It cost him no effort to be sportive. In play-time he could play with the most frolicsome, after a hearty, robustious manner that was a little too much for some of his companions. He was never graceful, — never, in fact, any thing but uncouth; but he was never tyrannical. He loved fair play: the bullies found him a formidable opponent. We do not hear that he had intimates; there was too much of him for that: but we do not hear that he had enemies. If he was conscious, as he must have been, of remarkable force of character, he did not make others cruelly sensible of it. In the last year of school he was much respected, and had great influence among the boys. They came to him for explanations of difficult points, and referred their disputes to him.

The testimonies to his moral character are all of one tenor. He was modest, pure, single-minded, frank, and true. If Theodore Parker said a thing, it was believed by young and by old. A quick, eager temper would have led him astray into acts of violence, if he did not have it under habitual control: but it could not have betrayed him into vicious indulgence; for there was no taint of sensuality in him. His thoughts were busy with literature; his appetite was for knowledge: his warmth of feeling came to re-enforce the steadfastness of his conscience, not to weaken it. He was open and unselfish. The bent of his nature was towards nobleness. In the humbler virtues of toil and economy his whole life was a school. He wanted more books than his father could give him; and to work for them was the only way to obtain them. His father supplied him with his first Latin grammar: the Latin dictionary he paid for with the proceeds of a whortleberry excursion when he was twelve years old. The well-worn volume had its place in the noble library in Boston, which, but for the purpose displayed on that whortleberry expedition, would have had no existence. It was a humble tome; but it was the corner-stone of the structure.

His career of teaching began at seventeen. The first winter, that of 1827, he took charge of the district school in Quincy; the second, in North Lexington; the third, in

Concord; and the fourth, in Waltham. Farmers spared their boys in the winter, reckoning that their labor was about equivalent to their board; but in summer, if they went away from home while under age, they must pay the wages of a substitute. This he did. When he left home finally, two years before his majority, he hired a cousin to do his work. During the two years previous he worked himself like a field-hand on the farm, digging, ploughing, haying, laying stone-wall, helping his broad-shouldered father in his shop, mending wheels, repairing wagons, making pumps, doing miscellaneous jobs in wood-work, with as much conscience as he studied, if with less joy. He worked as if toil was his whole occupation; he studied as if study was his whole delight. The book was always near to fill up the crevices of time. There were precious moments in the morning. If the evening was occupied, he extorted an hour or two from the night. Rainy days were godsends.

At seventeen, militia duties began; and in these he was as active, prompt, and efficient as in all the rest. There was always a touch of the warlike spirit in him. The two guns in his Exeter-place library were no vain symbols. The military reputation of the ancestor who was at Lexington Common, and chafed under inaction at Bunker Hill, was dear to his heart. Life was a warfare, the outward symbols whereof were as significant as they were to the apostle, who charged his followers to put on the breastplate of righteousness, and to take the sword of the Spirit. He rose to rank in the company: clerk he certainly was, perhaps lieutenant: whether he rose to higher authority is less certain.

With all this, Theodore added much to the social life of the household. His talk was copious and entertaining, his jokes telling, his fun exuberant. His affectionateness ran over to the domestic animals: he had names for the cows; he made the cattle hold imaginary conversations together; rendered the habits of the dumb creatures into parables, thus adopting them into the life of the home.

Of his early teaching little record is preserved. That he worked hard at his calling need not be said. Every spare hour that could be snatched from the day was devoted to his own studies. At Waltham a young woman wished to learn French. He knew nothing of the language, but, obtaining the necessary elemental books, soon mastered the rudiments, and became learner and teacher at once. In North Lexington his monthly salary was twenty-five dollars, out of which he paid his substitute at the farm, met his board-bill, and provided himself with clothing (it did not cost much): the rest went for books, which he bought at second-hand prices. There was in Waltham an impression, that, as a teacher, he was unreasonably exacting in his requirements, and absolute in his discipline. It is quite possible: his faith in human capacity was always large; his anticipations were always sanguine. What he demanded of himself he expected from others, and drew out if he could. Schoolboys are seldom grateful to the master who sets long lessons, and insists on correct recitals: even school committees are willing to pass over defects that promote a pleasant state of feeling among the boys and girls.

One summer day, in August, 1830, — the day before his birthday, — he went away, telling no one whither he was going. His father had given him leave of absence from morning till night. He walked to Cambridge, was examined, passed examination, walked home, and told his father, lying in his bed, that he had entered Harvard College. If the old man wondered in the morning where his son was going, he wondered more at night on learning where he had been. "But, Theodore, I cannot afford it." — "Father, it shall cost you nothing. I will stay at home, and keep up with my class." And this he did for a year, working on the farm as usual, pushing on his studies perseveringly, and only going to Cambridge to be examined. The course at Harvard was not, fifty years ago, what it is now; and Parker found no difficulty in distancing his class in the appointed curriculum, besides doing a vast deal of miscellaneous reading in general literature. Being a non-resident, and his own tutor, he paid no tuition-fees, and was not entitled to a degree. Four years later, he might have had one by paying the arrears of tuition; but that was beyond his means. He was not enrolled among the regular Harvard graduates until 1840, when the degree of A.M. was conferred upon him, as a mark of honor, at the instance of men who thought it a shame that so distinguished a mind should be unrecognized. The point required urging; for the quality of the mind was not altogether such as Cambridge approved; and some were unwilling that so pronounced a rationalist as he was coming to be thought should be an acknowledged son of Harvard College.

That day in August was never forgotten. The recurrence of its anniversary is found frequently recorded in the journal, always in tender, grateful words, accompanied with expressions of thanksgiving and prayer. Five months before he reached the year of manhood he went away from his father's house, his own guide and master, — left it, as in primitive times sailors took leave when starting on a long voyage. The home grew dearer to him every year, — dearer while its inmates lived, dearer still when they lived no more. His heart was always there, his mind often, his presence less and less frequently. He could always revert to it with satisfaction: its lessons he had not to unlearn; its influences he had not to overcome. The memory of father and mother was inexpressibly dear to the last. In his days of ambition and fame, he confessed to himself, and made no secret to anybody, that the best in him was due to those who gave him birth, and to the hardship in which he was nurtured.

CHAPTER III.

TEACHING AND STUDY.

ON the 23d of March, 1831, Theodore Parker went to Boston, as an assistant teacher in a private school, at a salary of twelve dollars a month and board: it was afterwards raised to fifteen dollars, and the increase dated back to the beginning of his service. His worldly goods were contained in a great wooden trunk covered with painted cloth. Eleven octavo volumes and a few twelvemos constituted his library. He was set to teach more than he knew; but, as he never undertook to teach what he had not learned, he made up by toil what he lacked in resources. The toil was fearful. Mathematics, natural philosophy, Latin, French, Spanish, must be kept fresh, or learned newly, and — except with incidental aid from a professed teacher in mathematics, Mr. Francis Grund — by his own solitary efforts. Yet, even at this rate of enforced speed, he distanced duty, adding another language (German) to his store of tongues, and perfecting his acquaintance with those he had. This winter he wrote his first lecture, on Poland, and read it in Lexington. The subject was one of great popular interest at the time, as much as that of Greece or Hungary afterwards. He studied ten or twelve hours a day, — the school required six; from May to September, seven. It was too much: he lost twenty-eight pounds of flesh in three months. He had never learned the art of husbanding his health:

no friend warned him against the consequences of close confinement, insufficient food, broken sleep, excessive strain of faculty; and even his great strength felt the exhaustion. Signs of weakness and despondency appeared thus early: he was laying the basis for the chronic ill health that was such a drag on his after-life. He knew it when too late, and tried by resolute efforts to recover the lost ground; made rules for himself, and did his best to observe them: but the mistake, once committed, could not be repaired; nor could the habits, once contracted and becoming inveterate, ever be wholly abandoned.

He needed air and exercise; but he needed society even more. His disposition was genial: he loved people, he craved friendship, and had not even acquaintances. Recreation he could not afford had he desired it. Nothing broke the monotony of his brain-work, which went on with such pitiless power, that faint and incidental symptoms of paralysis showed themselves from time to time in sensations of numbness and pricking, the purport whereof he did not understand. Even religion, his never-failing supporter, came to him at this period in its least attractive shape. He must needs make a study, and not a refreshment, of that too. He chose that time of all times for attending the pulpit ministrations of the famous Lyman Beecher, then in the height of his popularity,—the most powerful and one of the most uncompromising preachers of orthodoxy in New England, then in the full tide of popularity, battling fiercely against "Unitarians, Universalists, Papists, and infidels." He had come to Boston to crush Dr. Channing and the new heresies. Parker went through one of his protracted meetings, "listening to the fiery words of excited men, and hearing the most frightful doctrines set forth in sermon, song, and prayer." The result of it was, that he lost all the little respect he had for the Calvinistic scheme of theology,—a result, we surmise, that was worth far less than it cost, and was no compensation for the delight and strength the new dispensation would have given him. There was no danger of his respecting the Calvinistic theology too much, and there was danger of despondency in his own heart.

If he could have laid by money for his future plans, which began to embrace a course at the Cambridge Divinity School, it would have been a consolation. But from a salary of fifteen dollars a month, during the first five months of which he supplied a man to work in his place on his father's farm, — his father demurred, but Theodore insisted, — not many dollars could be saved by the severest economy; and his vision of systematic preparation for the ministry, as it faded away into more distant future, left an additional faintness in his spirit.

Fortunately, his life in Boston lasted but a twelvemonth, till April, 1832. He went thence at once to Watertown, at the suggestion, probably, of relatives who lived there, and opened a private school. There the heavens began to brighten to him.

The school was opened in the south part of the town, in a room that had been before used by a Mr. Wilder for a similar purpose. It was on the second floor of what once was a bakery. The part beneath was occupied as a storehouse by Nathaniel Broad, who lived on the spot, and with whom the young teacher boarded. It was in every respect a comfortable, convenient, and pleasant place, at least after the handy tenant had spent some of his carpentry skill on it. He was his own attendant and porter. In winter he sawed, split, and brought up the wood for the stove, made the fire, and at all seasons put the room in order for the scholars. They came satisfactorily, on the whole. He began with the two sons of Mr. George Robbins. Others dropped in one by one, till the school in the first year numbered thirty-five. Subsequently it increased to fifty-four. The charge was not high, — five dollars a quarter; but, rather than turn a deserving boy or girl away because the modest fee could not be paid, he would take the applicant gratis, and bestow as much care on the beneficiary as on the rest. To one girl he gave the value of his instructions for a year and a half, and then begged his successor to allow her to continue her studies with him. Social questions were not as clear to his mind as they were afterwards. A colored girl applied, and was admitted by the teacher without misgiving: he knew no distinction of persons; but the parents of his other pupils did. They made objections, prophesying injury to the school; and the black inmate was dismissed. It was not a generous thing to do: on the contrary, it was a shabby thing. The young man confessed it afterwards with mortification, and made ample amends to her persecuted race; but it was pardonable in a youth who had lived in the seclusion of thoughts, whose conscience had never been touched by the wrongs of the negro North or South, and who regarded race merely as he would any other disturbing element. Had it occurred to him that a principle was involved in the transaction, he would have seen the school dwindle away to nothing sooner than have yielded. The boys gave him society: he made companions of them, shared their sports, invited their confidence, gained their affection, and used the influence he acquired to shape their characters for after-life. Five or six of them were fellow-lodgers with him at Mr. Broad's. With these he took particular pains, correcting their habits, observing their manners, and seeming to feel a genuine concern for their moral welfare. The exercises of the school were opened with prayer; grace was said before meat, in a simple and impressive way, no doubt; and the boys felt the contagion of a pure, reverent mind.

He was a live teacher, with an insatiable hunger for knowledge himself, a keen appreciation of its value to everybody, a high sense of personal duty as an instructor of it, and a faith apparently boundless in the capacity of fresh young minds to take it in. The lads who came to him from public schools were at first dismayed at the studies he expected of them; but he kindled the fire while he fed it with fuel, so gently persuading and skilfully stimulating the faculties, so clearly explaining and so dexterously leading along, that the backward and reluctant followed at length. He had a way of making the scholars answer their own questions, and remove their own difficulties, such as only complete masters of their art possess. The text-book was never substituted for intellectual activity: it was mind to mind as much as possible. Manuals of natural theology he strongly objected to, on the ground that they forestalled inquiry, and raised doubts before the time. If he used such at all, he used them as provocatives of thought; but he preferred discarding them. He had other ways of teaching natural theology, — by suggesting natural religion. This he did by casual comments and reflections, lessons drawn from the day's reading, appeals to feeling, or to the intuitive perceptions of right and wrong. He made the trees, flowers, birds, and animals his texts as he rambled with the boys in the woods. The mind stored with information on natural objects overflowed with half-meditated, half-unpurposed interpretations of the beauty and use of the world of little things, and illustrated by scores of pretty facts the ethics of boyish life. Religion was the first interest with him: he was unhappy if he could not make his schoolboys feel its power and charm.

He insisted on order, but hated to enforce it. In one or two instances he was obliged to speak harshly in reproof; but only in one or two. The discipline of the school was secured by rational kindness, which made the pupils happy in obedience. Backed by his weight of character, the rule of love, which is apt to degenerate into an ineffectual sentimentalism, acquired a sweet stringency that was sufficient for ordinary purposes. His love was a power.

The life in Watertown was more wholesome in many ways than the life in Boston. There was air and light, and the direct contact with Nature. In summer there were long afternoon and morning walks. Every Saturday he walked to Cambridge, and to Charlestown for instruction in Hebrew. The botanical researches were pursued. There was companionship too. Mr. and Mrs. Broad were plain people, but kindly: he was attached to them. On Mr. Broad's death, the young teacher found employment for heart and hand in the service he was able to render his widow in doors and out. As the labors of the school became less onerous, he had leisure and disposition for society. His cousins in Watertown were intelligent, sympathetic, friendly people. His uncle was a man of remarkable dignity and sweetness, of an easy breadth of mind that Theodore enjoyed heartily. Gradually their circle became his: good men and women welcomed him to their homes. Mr. Weiss, who has lived in Watertown himself, and can speak from knowledge, dwells tenderly on the names of eight or ten families, some of them of wealth and culture, where he was intimate, and where his intimacy is cherished in the form of affectionate memories and dearest discipleship. They are associates in thought with Mr. Parker still. The intimacy of two years continued for many, and was an education to him as well as to them.

In Watertown Mr. Parker met two persons whose influence was felt on his whole future. Rev. Charles Briggs of Lexington had given him a letter of introduction to Convers Francis, Unitarian minister to the First Parish; and by its means he gained access to a noble library, a spacious and richly-furnished mind, and a heart warm to every lover of truth and friend of "the humanities." Mrs. Francis was kindness itself combined with elegance, and a passion for flowers which Theodore shared. Mr. Francis was one of those rare men whom too few appreciate: a liberal scholar in the best sense of the phrase; learned without pedantry;

open to the light from every quarter; an enormous reader of books; a great student of German philosophy and divinity, as very few at that time were. The newest criticisms and speculations were on his table and in his mind. He was absolutely free from dogmatism, — the dogmatism of the liberal as well as the dogmatism of the conservative. The students at Cambridge, when he afterwards became professor in the Divinity School there, found fault with him for being too "all-sided," — *non-committal*, they called it, — understanding neither his respect for their minds, nor his reverence for the truth. He was a conscientious, natural eclectic, with as few intellectual prejudices as it is well possible to have. His lectures and sermons were full of suggestions, opening out lines of thought in every direction, eminently useful, but eminently unsatisfactory to such as wanted opinions formulated for filing away. It was a happy, cordial, cheery mind, with extensive prospects from all the windows, — just the mind for one like Theodore to bask in the light of. Now, for the first time, he had the intellectual atmosphere it was a delight to inhale. The Sunday sermons revealed a sunny firmament over a rich world. The week-day talks made the steps familiar with fresh paths and fields of literature. Here were books without stint; here was a friendly interpreter and a sympathetic inquirer. In the two years he was in Watertown, Mr. Parker incurred an immense debt to this high-minded scholar, who had an answer to his questions, and an inexhaustible patience in listening. The debt was increased in later years, and no part of it was ever forgotten.

Intimacy with Mr. Francis brought Theodore into relations with the parish. He became superintendent of the Sunday school. He would not have been himself if he had not formed a Bible-class; nor would he have been himself if he had taught in the usual way. He was peculiar, however, chiefly in his method. His views were as yet too unformed to be a basis for instruction. He was a Unitarian who lived quietly within the confines of his sect. Among the teachers in the Sunday school was Miss Lydia D. Cabot, the only daughter of John Cabot of Newton: she resided with an aunt in Boston, but was boarding in Watertown under the same roof with him. An attachment growing up between them, they plighted troths, and in due time became husband and wife. The passion of love awoke a new being within him. "I have a new pleasure in the discharge of my duties. I love my books the more, my school the more, mankind the more, and even, I believe, my God the more, from loving you." "It has been in other time than this my highest pleasure thus to pass my time, thus to spend my nights, in 'high concord with the God-like past;' to collect my own thoughts, and search for new. But now I find a *new* pleasure, which, with a louder, sweeter voice, speaks to the heart, and tells another tale."

The happy letters of that period are before me; the tenderest passages, meant only for private eyes, being omitted. The dates are very near together. The writer's frankness in pouring out the contents of his mind will entertain the reader, yet betray no confidence. Here are a few extracts: —

WATERTOWN, NOV. 21, 1833.

I have read the Life of Milton: it contains only seventy-four pages; so I finished it Monday night. Dr. Channing, in his Review, has given him praise with too much liberality; and Johnson has, as usual, loaded him with asperity. Still I presume Johnson has the most truth on his side. Milton was a giant, and so was Johnson; but one was a celestial prodigy, the other a mere earthly Antæus. I am glad you advance so well in Homer. Somebody says, "Homer is the only royal road to poetry." I think so.

DEC. 5, 1833.

Whist is an innocent amusement; and I know no law, divine or human, which imposes an unpleasant sanctimoniousness on ministers' wives. I take but little pleasure, I confess, in such amusements, — a satisfactory reason for *my* abandoning them; but it is a reason that should influence *nobody* else.

Nov. 14, 1833.

You speak of "poor, weak woman." Weakness and strength are only comparative terms. To speak absolutely, nothing is strong but Him who is strength itself. But a woman *comparatively* weak! Turn over the pages of history, and read what she has done. Who is it that excites the giant spirits of the world to run their career of glory? and better, far better, and nobler too, who carries joy and peace to the fireside of the poor and the peasant? . . .

I have made very good progress in logic, and find it much more *interesting* than I expected. I shall always be delighted, encouraged, and excited to greater efforts, by your inquiries into my studies.

Dec. 27, 1833.

Why should we not suppose all the stars, and all the planets supposed to belong to each, to be inhabited? They are the work of an infinite Being, who had infinite wisdom, power, and goodness, and an infinite space to exert itself in; and, if we suppose all inhabited with various orders of animals like the tribes of common earth, what a noble universe we have to contemplate! . . .

I do not suppose Moses or Joshua, or even Solomon himself, knew this, or ever thought of it. Nobody in their age had such ideas. The prophets were illuminated with light from on high; but it was to rebuke idolatry, reprove oppression, and excite to virtue: and of Christ himself we may say, that though he must have known this, yet he came to teach religion, to console affliction, and to excite mankind to virtue, not to teach astronomy.

Jan. 15, 1834.

I shall probably finish "Waverley" and "The Antiquary" this week. You know what a task it commonly is to read novels, and will perhaps be surprised to find I have hardihood enough to attempt one. Do you recollect the Rev. Mr. Blattergowl in "The Antiquary"? What a "woful example" Sir Walter held up for the admonition of prosing parsons!

JAN. 22, 1834.

I have been this afternoon to examine a school, which afforded me a walk of somewhat more than two miles. . . .

Sawed wood half an hour this morning. As you will see, I have not been without exercise; that is, exercise of the body, which, St. Paul says, "profiteth little:" my mental exercise has been reading sixty-six pages of German, and *almost* all the Reviews. Sunday night, read Scripture of course, and other *good* books. . . . A little in Byron has been read. He was a wicked poet, and a wicked man. His striking, his graphic descriptions enchain the mind, and the melody of his verse recurs continually to one's ears; but the heart of the thoughtless is in the mean time corrupted. Miss Martineau says Scott has done more to extirpate vice from the world than any preacher in England. It is perhaps true; and she might have added, that no philosopher (!) who denied his God, no epicurean who struck at the distinction of good and evil, has done so much to corrupt the hearts of youth, to stagger the minds of the giddy, as this misanthropic Lord Byron.

FEB. 27, 1834.

Mr. Francis called here yesterday, and lent me the necessary books: so I have commenced the great study, — the criticism of the New Testament; and with the little which has been yet explored of it I am not only pleased, but highly delighted. It is, as you know, a subject on which the noblest minds that philosophy has enlightened have been busy these thousand years, and without exhausting the boundless subject. . . .

I have been to examine a school this afternoon. This is the last of my service as school committee; and glad I am.

FEB. 26, 1834.

I consulted Mr. Francis about going to Cambridge soon and joining the present junior class. He thought it a good plan, and gave me letters of introduction to Mr. Ware. I have walked to Cambridge this afternoon, and seen all the faculty. Have resolved to make the attempt: so I shall finish school-keeping on the 1st of April, and remove to Cambridge, take a room at the Hall, and commence study. . . .

Diligence and patient application will enable me to accomplish by next commencement all that the class will by that time have completed; and no disadvantage will be incurred by thus commencing. I shall study alone all the class has yet attempted; and, if I stay at Cambridge, can hear Mr. Palfrey's lectures. . . .

Nothing is too much for young ambition to hope, no eminence too lofty for his vision, no obstacle too difficult for his exertions, and no excellence unattainable. Patience, perseverance, prayer, have done something already; and when we consider that sincere desires are never neglected, and real endeavors never unassisted, we need not despair of making some approaches at least to the eminence Mr. Palfrey now occupies. Would not this be truly delightful? No situation can be more honorable, no task more pleasant, no prospect more celestial, than that of a virtuous, faithful clergyman. . . .

I have finished "Childe Harold," and am better pleased with it than with "Don Juan," because it contains more soberness of thought, with less of blasphemy and immorality. There is less fire in Harold than in the other hero, but less rage, folly, and madness.

MARCH 13, 1834.

. . . The story of the witch of Endor is quite curious, and has served to perplex many of the best commentators. But it can be explained without any thing supernatural being supposed.

I do not think Saul saw Samuel: the witch only pretended to see him, and gave the answers as if Samuel himself were actually present. It deserves notice, too, that nothing new is told, — nothing which Samuel had not declared while alive. . . .

Many consider all the Psalms of David as inspired. But do they all breathe the good and merciful spirit of the Lord? If we view them as works of inspiration, they appear inconsistent with the character of God; but if we regard them as only the odes of a pious king, who yet had all the frailties of a man, they must be pronounced excellent, though often savoring of a revengeful spirit.

MARCH 26, 1834.

. . . Much in this world is ruled by a power we cannot control; but much also is left completely in our own power. Fate cannot prevent our being *good:* it may forbid us to be great. Let us, then, build our castles upon goodness, not greatness; upon the esteem of the virtuous, not the admiration of the giddy.

Perhaps this is the last letter I shall ever write you from this place, since school closes in a week.

There was another, a very long and singular one, — about the strangest kind of a love-letter ever penned. It is taken up chiefly with an imaginary conversation between a horse and a goose, in which each sings his own praises, and celebrates the glories of his race. Then the pleasant epistles run on till marriage ends the correspondence, — a strain of moral reflection, criticism, notes on books, remarks on persons, accounts of walks and talks, drolleries, bits of sentiment, rhapsodies, interspersed with poems "to his mistress' eye-brow," — fresh, buoyant, various, with but one or two passing touches of sorrow, which yet hardly deserves so expressive a word, and with sparkles of gladness shining through them all.

The two years in Watertown were eventful years both of joy and labor. The achievements in scholarship were amazing. In spite of school-teaching and school-examinations, social intercourse, visits to Mr. Francis, communions with Miss Cabot, he gives us his word that he pursued the study of Latin and Greek authors, the most of Cicero, Herodotus, Thucydides, Pindar, Theocritus, Bion, Moschus (the last four of which he translated), and Æschylus. He wrote for his Sunday-school class a history of the Jews, which still exists in manuscript; pushed his studies in metaphysics, taking up Cousin and the new school of French philosophers; began the study of Hebrew, walking, as before said, to Charlestown to meet Mr. Seixas, a Jew; and entered on the study of theology. Besides all this, the German poets Goethe, Schiller, Klopstock, had a share of his attention, and the works of Coleridge engaged a portion of his thoughts. An occasional novel by Walter Scott, or a poem of Byron, beguiled the leisure moments.

His studies ran into the early morning. The landlady kept the lamps well supplied; but there was no oil in his lamp when the day broke.

To leave Watertown cost him pain. His boys loved him, and concerted a surprise for him in the shape of a silver cup, with ceremony of presentation-speech by Master Briggs. The testimonial of affection was more than Theodore could bear; his tears, whether of joy or grief, being always near the surface. A few moments of retirement were necessary to regain sufficient command of himself to dismiss the school.

CHAPTER IV.

DIVINITY HALL.

Mr. Parker went to Cambridge Divinity School in April, 1834, — three months before the close of the junior or first year of his class, — and remained there two years and a quarter. He had saved up a little money from his teaching, — about one hundred and fifty dollars; having spent some two hundred dollars in books while at Watertown, and clothed himself besides. The expenses of the Hall were not heavy, — sixty-six dollars annually for tuition, and care of room; one dollar and ninety cents a week for board in "commons." This last expense he tried to save by boarding himself at half a dollar a week on dry bread, — a course that he was wise enough to abandon for a boarding-house so far off that he must needs get exercise in going to and from his meals. A successful application for assistance from the beneficiary fund gave him from a hundred and ten to a hundred and fifty dollars more. Teaching, first one boy, then two, then two young girls in addition, brought a moderate accession to his income. He was countenanced in his habits of economy by his fellow-students; for nearly all who came to study theology were poor. The wretched custom of boarding themselves, which meant eating crackers or other food that needed no cooking, was not uncommon. There was no refectory at the Hall: the college commons were half a mile off. Divinity students are apt to be touched by a flavor of asceticism from ancient traditions; but economy was the main consideration.

Divinity Hall is a long brick building, that stands at some distance from the street, and is approached by a pretty shaded avenue. It contains rooms for the accommodation of students, — small, but convenient and pleasant, — recitation-rooms, a pleasant chapel, and a scanty library. The college-library was open to the students, and was, as it is now, the main resource for scholars who travelled out of the beaten path. In front of the hall a broad green made an excellent play-ground. In the rear were the outbuildings, residence of janitor, and so forth: behind these were pretty woods. The professors lived in the neighborhood, — Dr. Palfrey at the end of a continuation of the avenue; Mr. Norton, not then a professor, on a handsome place across the fields behind; Mr. Ware in a modest house just beyond the entrance-gate.

Few divinity students have the polished air of young gentlemen. Parker was no exception to the rest in his unformed appearance; his long, thick hair; his dress, neat, but carelessly worn. But, in other respects, he was remarkable.

"My first and unchanged feeling," says C. A. Bartol, "was of his exuberant life, restless ambition to excel, and an honesty that knew not how to lie. The ruddy face; firm and eager grasp; the manner nothing if not natural; either a complete retreat into himself, or unmistakable evolution to draw the enemy's fire; the smile, frank as spring and sweet as summer, or ready to curl with biting scorn; no maiden's blushing cheek more ingenuously modest, and no graduate's tongue from the college, whose privilege was not his, more ingeniously acute. I remember him, in the theological debates, sitting still in his seat, and tying noiseless knots in his handkerchief, every one of which, he told me, meant some argument for which he had a reply. Afterwards I see him, as he stood before a marble statue, called

'The Genius of Love,' by Horatio Greenough, in my parlor, in earnest admiration, but with no pretence. Perhaps his emotion helped him to hew that other statue of tranquil fervor in his soul, of which, in his 'Discourse of Religion,' he speaks; and doubtless the knotted silk, in the sham-fight of abstract questions, was *practice* preliminary to the woven whip-lash he was to lay on all the hypocrisies, iniquities, and superstitions of Church and State."

There were about thirty students at the Hall when Mr. Parker joined the school. His own class consisted of eight, of whom four are still in the ministry: one of them, Abiel Abbot Livermore, is president of Meadville Theological School in Pennsylvania. Of the rest, one lives in seclusion in Salem, having early left the ministry; another is editor of "The Journal of Music" in Boston,—the foremost musical critic there; a third is an artist, poet, and man of letters. It is a little singular, that, of so small a class, so many should have retired from the profession. The studies the first year were in Hebrew, the criticism of the New Testament, the evidences of Christianity. There was, once a week, an exercise in extemporaneous speaking, and an exercise in declamation. On Friday evening the whole school assembled in the chapel for free debate on some given theme, generally of a social character. Interest in questions of concern to humanity at large was promoted by the "Philanthropic Society," which held meetings once a fortnight. At these meetings a committee appointed for the purpose presented a report on some large subject, like "Intemperance," "License-Laws," "The Wages of Women:" the members joined in the discussion. The whole school listened to a lecture on Saturday morning on the composition of sermons. The senior class showed how much they had profited by the instruction by preaching in the chapel on Sunday evenings, professors and students attending. The religious interests of the school were provided for by daily services of prayer in the chapel, a general religious meeting on Thursday evening, and such private exercises as the students might hold among themselves. Opportunity for practice in some of the departments of ministerial work was afforded by the different Sunday schools in the neighborhood, where the young men took classes, or acted as superintendents; and by the State Prison in Charlestown, whither the more earnest and sympathetic repaired on Sunday morning to teach and help morally the inmates.

Here was duty enough to occupy all the hours. Theodore threw himself into it with his whole might. He had come there to work; and work he did, at whatever invited. It is quite credible that he studied fourteen hours a day: even his astonishing force of concentration and acquisition required no less for what he undertook. A companion at the school remembers that "we all looked upon him as a prodigious athlete in his studies. He made daily acquaintance with books which were sealed books to many old biblical scholars, and, to us youngsters of the school, were scarcely known even by name. He would dive into the college-library, and fish up huge, venerable tomes in Latin and Greek, and lug them up to his room, and go into them as a boarding-school girl would go into a novel. We soon saw what his extraordinary capacities were of reading and retention. He literally devoured books. The rapidity of his reading was something wonderful. Great things were prophesied of him; but it was supposed he would be little more than a scholar,—an extraordinary book-worm. None guessed that he was ere long to be one of the most remarkable men of the day in more ways than one; that the immense fund of learning he was laying up was but his arsenal of weapons with which later he was to do battle for pure, unadulterated Christianity."

Yet at that very time his power of speech and of moral feeling was attracting attention. He was the best debater, though not the best writer, in the Hall; always speaking vigorously, and to the point, with an independence of thought, an enthusiasm of manner, and a freshness, that gave promise of greater pulpit power than he at first displayed. He liked real themes and real talk. He missed none of the exercises that tended to equip him for his office; was devoted to his class at the State Prison, preferring to deal with genuine cases of moral need, and showing uncommon ability to interest unpromising subjects. He was social too, as mere book-worms are not; running into his classmates' rooms for a chat or a gambol. He had as little dust on the surface of his mind as the airiest of them all: none flushed quicker with indignation, none broke out more boisterously into mirth.

The same genial reporter first quoted, C. P. Cranch, says, "His temperament seemed one charged full of electricity, so that he was literally *snapping* at times with sparks of fun and satire. After the long hours of close study in his library, his mind would indulge itself in the most boyish and playful rebounds. He had the keenest appreciation of the humorous and the ludicrous. In his sportive and satiric veins he would throw off the most amusing conceits and pasquinades. His satire was chiefly directed against the theology and social *shams* of the day. His sallies of wit loved to take a pictorial shape. Had he possessed a talent for drawing, he would have been a Hogarth. This Rabelaisian trait would twinkle continually in his eyes, and lurk about the corners of his mouth. It was, however, always tempered and subdued by a becoming deference to his office of teacher and clergyman.

"I remember a whimsical and original joke of his at the Divinity School. It was a play of animal spirits, a practical jest, a protest and a satire combined. Two or three of us divinity students — I remember John Dwight was one — were in full musical blast at something — fluting or singing, I forget which — in one of the rooms of Divinity Hall. Immediately opposite was Parker's room.

He was evidently engaged in much more serious study, and more in the line of his future profession, than we were. Still we were quite unaware of our disturbing him, or we should have sunk our music to a *pianissimo*, or adjourned it to another place or hour. Theodore had, however, borne it some time without protesting. Presently there was a peculiar 'movement' in the entry, just outside our door, executed upon a peculiar and by no means musical instrument, — a sort of *obligato ad libitum* bass, — thrown in as an accompaniment to our strains. On opening the door to ascertain the nature of these strange sounds, there was Theodore, who had left his folios of the Latin fathers, had rushed into the cellar, and brought up a wood-horse, saw, and log of wood, on which he was exercising his vigorous sinews — see-saw, see-saw — to our utter discomfiture and amusement. As for Theodore, he barely smiled."

The "Common-Place Book" contains a page of original puns, which indicate that his brains could at times leave him as completely as they ever leave the professors of that peculiar kind of witlessness. If the jokes were strictly original, they might be excused; but some of them bear traces of very remote antiquity. Their execrableness alone commended them, perhaps; and their venerableness attested their merit.

Such a man could not be a bookworm: still his bookish achievements were most remarkable. Only by transcribing the journal, commenced in 1835, could any idea be obtained of the extent of his researches The folio pages are crowded with lists of books read or to be read, — analyses, summaries, comments on writers of every description, in every tongue. Only to name them would be a fatigue, — Eichhorn, Herder, Ammon, De Wette, Paulus, Philo, the Greek historians, the fathers of the Church, the Greek and Latin poets, Plato, Spinoza, the Wolfenbüttel Fragments. The succession is bewildering; but there is the record in the private journal, the veracity whereof cannot be disputed, — a record showing acquaintance not with the names of the books merely, but with the contents. In two months, November and December, 1835, the names of sixty-five volumes are given as having been read in German, English, Danish, Latin, Greek, reaching all the way from "Peter Simple" to Bouterwek and Rosenmüller. One of them was Dr. Channing's "Essay on Slavery;" the first seed, perhaps, of the tree that spread so widely in ten years. The seed fell upon good soil; for Theodore, though generally indifferent to party politics, held liberal opinions from the first. He never approved of slavery or defended it, or was silent when others spoke in its favor. Dr. Francis in Watertown observed that.

His power of getting at the secret of a language was wonderful. Hebrew he taught to a class of collegians; and during Dr. Palfrey's absence in New Orleans, in 1836, he took the professor's place as Hebrew instructor at the Hall. His studies in languages were not always pushed very far; a taste sometimes sufficed; but the taste detected the quality of the speech. Some of his studies in comparative philology are curious. In the list of languages from whose literature he drank deeper or lighter draughts we find Italian, Portuguese, Spanish, Dutch, Danish, Swedish, Icelandic, modern Greek, Chaldee, Arabic, Persian, Coptic, Ethiopic, Russian. "The Swedish language is easy, and I expect to get much amusement and instruction from it. The Danish presents more difficulties than Swedish; and I shall not study it extensively, but soon make it give place to some other." The Russian he dropped, being unable to master the sounds of the language. Later in life he mastered it so far as to become acquainted with the dialect that is used by the priests. President White of Cornell found him as well booked in Russian affairs as he himself, who had been studying them on the spot for months. A friend found him, one day in later life, poring over the grammar of the Mpongwe tongue, a dialect of Africa. The German furnished him the richest materials for thought in theology, philosophy, criticism, and poetry. His own English speech was not neglected. The journal bears traces of serious work on the Anglo-Saxon alphabet, and on the derivation of Celtic and Gothic tongues. One page of "The Common-Place Book" gives a comparative table of characters in Phœnician, Hebrew, Etruscan, Greek, Latin, Runic, Irish, Thibetan, and two others whose names are illegible.

To deal with such materials, one's tools must be in good condition. He was wont to whet his memory on a huge chart, covered with dates set down in irregular order, which he had posted on his door. Here are canons of self-discipline that he made for himself. They are printed as they stand; though one or two of them are for the privacy of his own eye, and must be read as the secret thoughts of a man in his closet: —

I. Physical.

1. Avoid excess in meat and drink.
2. Take exercise in the air at least three hours a day.
3. Always get six hours' sleep. (To this is added in pencil, as an afterthought, "More is better: seven hours certainly; eight hours very often, and always would be more suitable and proper.")

II. Intellectual.

I. Explore a subject when curiosity is awake. Sometimes this is impossible. Note the subject in a book, and examine as soon as possible in this manner: —

1. By finding out what I really know upon the subject.
2. Obtaining clear and distinct notions in some way.
3. By stating in words the result of my study, and repeating till it has made a deep impression. Sometimes write them in this book.
4. If historical, settle the time; writers who related it; their character.
5. The cause.
6. The effect.

II. *Keep the mind obedient to the will,* so as to be independent of external affairs. This cannot be completely effected, but may be, in a great measure, by the use of certain *intermedia;* viz., words of poets, &c.

III. Moral.

I. Preserve devoutness by, —

1. Contemplation of Nature;
2. Of the attributes of God;
3. Of my own dependence.
4. By prayer at night and morn, and at all times when devout feelings come over me.

II. Preserve gratitude by reflections on God's mercies to me, —

1. In giving blessings unasked;
2. Answering prayer.

III. Restrain licentiousness of imagination, which comprehends many particulars that must not be committed to paper, lest the paper blush.

That last touch shows the sincerity of the man. None but the purest ever make such entries. But for that whisper in the confessional, it would never have been suspected that tainted fancies ever surprised him, so utterly blameless was his life, so strange to his lips was the sound of an impure word, so alien from his frank blue eyes was the most fleeting look suggestive of indelicacy. His moral feelings were strict to austerity. Even his religious sentiments had a tinge of Puritanism in them.

To a nephew he writes in 1834: "One thing in your letter did displease me: I mean the unholy manner in which you quoted words of sacred writ. Such use of Scripture, you know, is inconsistent with the Christian spirit; and you will only need to have its bad tendency pointed out to avoid it in the future." To the same, a month later: "Do you attend Mr. Barry's (Unitarian) church constantly? Are you yet a member? If not, I do not accuse you: yet I think it is the duty of every one to employ all the means of religion within reach; and this is certainly a powerful one. It is not an end to be obtained: it is one of the means to promote spiritual-mindedness and true piety. Perhaps you think keeping the law, and being merely a good moral man, is religion: I think not. Do not think I mean to reproach you. It is only my intention to *warn.*" Again, a few weeks later, to the same nephew, so near his own age that he prefers to address him as "friend:" "So a man is a Christian, it makes little difference whether he is a Calvinist or Lutheran, Papist or Protestant. We all know that each sect contains in its instructions enough of pure and vital Christian advice to insure our salvation, so far as this depends upon ourselves or our fellow-mortals. . . . I am glad you find delight in worshipping where you do. I hope God will hear your prayers, and always grant you happiness in your belief, which I will never exhort you to change; though every conscientious man would prefer all his friends to be of his own persuasion." In a subsequent letter of this intimate correspondence he says, "I do not suppose you mean to say that religion is some *one thing*, state, or feeling, which comes to you in a moment, when you had no conception of such a thing before; but that it is love to God, and good will to men, which gradually arises in the heart, and which goes on constantly increasing. . . . Remember, there is no standing still in religion. If you are not going forward, you are falling backward. Strive for greater eminence in religion. Labor to be more constant in prayer, more exact in self-watchfulness, more perfect in your outward conduct. But, above all, strive, watch, pray, to be more pure in heart. This is the one thing needful. So far as you fail of this, though you attend all the meetings in the country, and pray with the force of a martyr, — nay, though you die a martyr, — you fail of religion; you come short of the requirements of Christianity. . . . Do not forget charity for men's opinions, defects; yes, for their crimes. Do not slight and scorn a man because you think he is less religious than you." In December of the same year (1834) he writes further: "I attended Dr. Beecher's six-days' meeting in Boston some three or four years ago. I confess I derived much advantage from it; but it was too harsh a remedy for gentle souls. Neither Christ nor his apostles ever drove lambs into the fold. A storm drives, every now and then, a ship to land; but how many perish in the waters!" The letter goes on: "If it is a man's duty to be devout in prayer, it is no less so to be devout in business. God never commanded us to be charitable and kind an hour in the morning and a little time at night, and suffered us to be peevish and revengeful all the rest of the day. We are not to keep one day holy, and defile all the rest."

Two more short extracts from the letters to this nephew, Mr. Greene, will give a sufficient notion of his religious mind at this period. The first is dated Nov. 14, 1835. "By religion I mean . . . total obedience to the will of God in all things, the most trifling as well as the most important. This is the religion of the apostles, the religion of Christ. . . . Its points are self-distrust, meekness, *cheerfulness*, *joy*, *faith*, love. If any man on earth has cause to be joyful, it is the Christian." The date of the second extract is June 11, 1834: "I consider a man's duty to be this, — *to do the most good and the least evil possible.* But how is this to be done? To whom is this to be done? A man of tolerable intellect, and of little education, quite late in life *becomes religious;* feels an earnest desire to 'do good,' to 'benefit mankind:' so he leaves his business, and, half educated as he is, becomes a preacher. Now, the man's motive may be the best possible; his desire to 'do good' may be worthy of angels: but he entirely mistakes the means of assisting man. He actually retards the growth of religion, and *puts back the truth*, good as his heart is."

Now for his theological opinions. In 1833, as we learn from a letter to Mr. George T. Bigelow, he is inclined to be sarcastical on the subject of scepticism; and in a long, strenuously-underlined epistle, caricatures the rationalizing process, by stating doubts in regard to the career and even the existence of Christopher Columbus, though still declaring, that, in his judgment, doubt arising from the spirit of free inquiry is preferable to faith founded on prejudice. "Ignorance is not devotion, or the mother of devotion; and faith which is not founded upon reason is not *faith*, but *folly*." But he was very slow in applying to the ordinary Unitarian creed of his youth the results of his study. Immediately on going to Cambridge, he writes to his nephew, Mr. Greene, as follows: "I believe there is *one* God, who has existed from all eternity, with whom the past, present, and future are alike present; that he is almighty, good, and merciful; will reward the good, and punish the wicked, both in this world and the next.

"This punishment *may be* eternal. Of course I believe that neither the rewards nor punishments of a future state are corporal: bodily pleasures soon satiate; and may God preserve us from a worse *punishment* than one's own conscience! I believe the books of the Old and New Testaments to have been written by men inspired by God for certain purposes; but I do *not* think them inspired at *all times*. I believe that Christ was the Son of God, *conceived and born in a miraculous manner;* that he came to preach a better religion by which men may be saved.

"This religion, as I think, allows men the very highest happiness in this life, and promises eternal felicity in another world. I do not think our sins will be forgiven because Christ died. I believe God *knows* all that we shall do, but does not *cause* us to do any thing. I do *not* believe in total depravity, or that Adam's sin will be imputed to us.

"I believe, if a man leads a good and pure life, he will

be accepted with God. I believe prayer to be an especial duty man owes to himself. God is not to be benefited by the paltry homage man can give him; but *we*—we are benefited by it. I think reading the holy Bible, attending church, prayers, professing religion, and pious conversations, are all means of religion. . . . I think sins in the heart as bad as sins of the hand. . . . This will, perhaps, be sufficient to show the grand leading features of my belief." In 1835, when Mr. Orville Dewey delivered the Dudleian Lecture, Mr. Parker made note of it in his journal thus: "It was the best, perhaps, I have ever heard, though upon the least interesting part of the evidences of revealed religion; viz., 'Miracles.' He removed the presumptions against them. The objections were not only met, but overturned."

But the active mind is at work. Here is one of the first signs of it in the journal, Nov. 2, 1835:—

"Tertullian I have always looked upon with considerable jealousy, and believe he introduced more heresies and ridiculous doctrines into the Church than almost all the other fathers, not excepting Austin (Augustine). He first introduced the notion that faith and reason contradict each other naturally. He thought faith which contradicted reason was most acceptable to God. Everybody knows he thought the soul material, &c.: he thought it was *sky-blue.*

"I am heart-weary and reason-weary of these same doting fathers. They have sense; but it is like some worthy's wit,—'a grain of wheat in a bushel of chaff.' I shall soon be done with them, however; for the present, at least. One of the greatest proofs of the darkness of the monastic ages is the folly-admiration bestowed on these same nonsense-writers.

"Origen was not a good Hebrew scholar; and of course his principles of interpretation were bad. He did the Church an essential service by his deep philosophy and eloquence. . . .

"Jerome loved glory rather than truth; was superstitious; and an introducer of important errors, both in doctrine and interpretation. He was not a profound scholar in Hebrew, or even in Greek. He tasted of theology, rather than exhausted it. He wrote his books in great haste. Yet many good things, they say, can be gleaned from his *seven folios*.

"St. Augustine, we all know, introduced more errors into the Church than any other man. Many of his doctrines fly in the face both of reason and virtue, to extinguish the eyes of one, and to stifle the breath of the other."

"Nov. 17, 1835.—Finished De Wette's 'Commentary on the Psalms.' . . . He is a fearless critic; and a critic should fear only one thing,—a *falsehood*. He treats the Messianic interpretation of the Psalms as a mere chimera; which it is, in my humble opinion."

The following passage from the journal shows that all this free-thinking is beginning to have its effect on special beliefs:—

"I do not doubt that Jesus was a man 'sent from God,' and endowed with power from on high; that he taught the truth, and worked miracles: but that he was the subject of inspired prophecy I very much doubt. Does he ever say so? Admitting he did, may we not suppose that he was ignorant of the truth of this matter? Was it necessary for him to know how much inspiration was meted out to the ancient prophets? I suppose him inspired by God immediately for a certain purpose. Could he not accomplish it without understanding the sources whence the ancient writers drew their doctrines?

"But, rejecting this, why should he not accommodate himself to the state of the public mind? . . . I know the above would appear like blasphemy to many divines; but I must stand by my own master, not by another *man*. My confidence in the divinity of Christ's character, of the truth, the sufficiency, of his doctrine, depends not at all upon prophecies or visions or dreams.

"Had the prophets only their authority to build upon, they would not have been believed. They spoke the words of ancient and notorious tradition; but I find no mention of their divine inspiration."

He finds stories of virgin-births in the legends of India, Persia, Greece, though he draws no inference from them;

doubts whether Luke, "whose Gospel we do not now question in general, could, as a foreigner lately converted to Christianity, transmit credible accounts of the juvenile history of Christ;" and is more solicitous to glorify the spiritual powers of Jesus than to defend his miraculous birth.

The condition of Mr. Parker's mind is best revealed in the pages of "The Scriptural Interpreter," a small magazine designed for easy family instruction, commenced in 1831 by Ezra Stiles Gannett, then the colleague of Dr. Channing, but abandoned by him on account of failing health. In 1835 it came under the charge of Mr. Parker and two of his classmates. They continued the publication, writing the great part of it themselves, till it closed in 1836. The largest contributor of the three was Mr. Parker. He wrote constantly and frankly, reporting the results of his studies in biblical interpretations; those being the matters he was most interested in. His articles display fairness and honesty, but give no evidence of peculiar boldness, and no sign whatever of rashness either in speech or thought. The papers have not the intellectual glow of speculative controversy, nor the tingling charm of genius: they are rather dry and dull, plodding industriously along over the rough ground of criticism that lay between the accepted Unitarianism of the period and the new views that had not yet been avowed, if they had been revealed. De Wette, Eichhorn, Astruc, and scholars of the moderate school of rationalism, supplied the material. The Authenticity and Construction of the Pentateuch, the Composition of the Psalms, the Dates and Ingredients of the Books of Isaiah, the Nature of Prophecy, the Meaning of the so-called "Messianic Prophecies," were the topics handled. Theological points were scarcely discussed; principles of philosophy were neither applied nor debated; the themes dealt with were rarely exhibited in their general aspects; the question between naturalists and supernaturalists, involving the miracle controversy which raged so fiercely a few years later, was not touched. There was nothing that should have disturbed a calm mind. Mr. Parker himself demurred at accepting the positions taken by Hengstenberg and other critics of the rationalistic school. He thinks that De Wette makes the prodigy of the withered fig-tree easier of credence by suggesting that the blasting did not follow immediately on the curse. "Gabler undertakes to show that a revelation is not possible, which seems utterly unphilosophical." To Ammon's argument that Moses could not have written the Pentateuch, because that shows a finished language, he replies, "All that may be true; but I do not believe it." Goethe's remark on the Hebrew Scriptures is quoted admiringly: "They stand so happily combined together, that, even out of the most diverse elements, the feeling of a whole still rises before us. They are complete enough to satisfy, fragmentary enough to excite, barbarous enough to arouse, tender enough to appease." "Delany believes in the universality of the Deluge; as who does not?" The arguments of those who held that the laws commanding the extirpation of the Canaanites could not have been inspired by Jehovah were not quite convincing, though plausible: "It must be remembered, the nations to be extirpated were exceedingly vicious and corrupt; and, if suffered to remain, would doubtless have led away the Jews from their better faith. If nations are by the divine permission visited with earthquakes and pestilences, why may not the sword be employed for similar purposes?"

The absence of discrimination in this extract, which places war and earthquake on the same footing; the assumption that Jehovah did send both pestilence and war; the quiet non-distribution of leading terms, — should have indicated that as yet nothing was to be feared from the audacity of a heedless intellect. But some did fear. Angry subscribers sent in their warning protests against the destructive criticism that was unsettling one passage, book, prophecy, after another, till the pious Christian had nothing left to stand on but what was in common with the Deist. "Are the theologians at Cambridge determined to break down the prophecies, and make our blessed Saviour and his apostles impostors and liars?" was the cry of the sentinels on the walls of Zion. Eminent divines shook their heads; were grieved that such an article had been written. The writer was dimly sorry for the uproar he did not understand, but went on, step by step, apparently seeing as little as anybody else the end toward which he was tending, and preserved, both by his mental fearlessness and his spirituality of faith, from any apprehension of danger. His confidence in the truth, and in the honest mind's power to apprehend it, was simple and entire. "Who dares say that the man who will adhere to God's truth is rash? and who will deny the presumption of one who dares depart from it?" This noble unconsciousness kept him safe, but made him, in the eyes of sectarians, unsafe.

The time had not come for him to bring his mental integrity to bear.

Possibly one reason for the slowness with which revolutionary ideas took possession of the future "heresiarch" may have been the literary spirit that at this period controlled him. His reading was by no means confined to books of theology and criticism. He enjoys Dante and Tasso. Goethe begins to interest him, as he did all his life. After perusing Mrs. Austin's "Characteristics of Goethe," he writes, "I always feel my flame growing dim after such reading: it awakens a sense of dissatisfaction in the bosom that does not down at a moment's bidding. The translatress intends to place Goethe in a favorable light; but she does not succeed, in my opinion. I regard the great German literature-giant as not a little selfish: indeed, was not his whole character based on this feeling? What are we to think of the man who shuts himself in from all knowledge of human misery? What did he ever do for the cause of man? Voltaire could be benevolent and patriotic: when was Goethe so? I am, however, but little, nay, not at all, read in his works; so forbear to judge. Heaven send it may not be true!" A page or two farther on the criticism softens: "I have a better opinion of the giant of Germany since reading this book ('Wanderjahre') than before. An enemy of Christianity could by no means have written that description of the School of the Three Reverences, which terminates in reverence for one's self." And again: "Who can say that Goethe was ignorant of religion, after having read 'The Confessions of a Fair Penitent'?"

In a correspondence with Miss Susan Burley, a woman of remarkable literary acquirements, he comments on the characters of the "Jerusalem Delivered," mentions with enjoyment the "sweet little wild witch-stories" of Tieck, and is curious about editions of Dante. His original repugnance to novel-reading is overcome. The journal has a page and a half of appreciative comment on "Tom Jones," which he wonders could have escaped him so long. On another page he writes, "I have just read 'The Linwoods,' a very interesting novel; which shows the woman, however. I think it will do good. Much good may it do in correcting the tone of society, which I regard as villanous just now!" "Bubbles from the Brunnen" he finds a delightful book; the "Gesta Romanorum" interest him, but one volume is enough; the "Robin-Hood Ballads" carry him off into a dissertation on "Volk-Songs;" Ritson's "Fairy Tales" amuse him; "Peter Simple" is not at all to his taste; Bowring's "Poetry of the Magyars" tempts him to make extracts; Longfellow's "Pilgrimage beyond the Sea" is a pleasant after-dinner book; Heine's "Germany" startles him, — "The writer must be a man of genius, and can be no other than a misanthrope and a not-Christian." The list is interminable: Southey's "Doctor," "Memoirs of Oberlin," Toulmin's "Life of Socinus," — all food is nourishing to the hungry mind. He comes across Bulwer's "Rienzi,"—"a fine work, full of beauty, truth, and nobleness. There is rather too much of it." In December, 1836, he falls in with "Pickwick." Moore's "Lalla Rookh" pleases him: "I have not lately been so much delighted with any poem as with this little treasury of sweets. It is full of the East, redolent of its citron-groves and spices, and glows with its fervid sun and burning soul."

After this the transition is not so violent as it would be from the Greek and Latin fathers to floods of verses from his own pen. This favorite amusement of young students was indulged in freely. The titles will sufficiently indicate their character: "To L—a," "Moral Beauty," "A Vision," "Midnight," "Gratitude," "Prayer," "Winter," "An Evening Hymn," "To Sadness," "Two Songs," "Eternity," "A Serenade," "Reflections at Midnight," "Absence," "Midnight Musings," "Spring," "The Complaint of a Lover," "The Stars," "To a Little Flower," "Morning Hymn," "The Rising Moon," "The Setting Star," "Stanzas," and so on,—sonnets and songs and meditations, in various moods, easy-going, often melodious, more often sentimental. The author thought them worth committing to his journal; but it would be hardly worth while to print them here. A specimen, however, must be given. The selection would be easier were the pieces fewer, or were any distinguished by special merit of sentiment or expression.

EVENING HYMN.

The chiming of the evening breeze
  That plays among the boughs;
The ripple of the purple seas
  As Night her mantle throws;
The unveiling of each timid star
That sheds its beauty from afar,—
All these have voices for mine ear.

All nature cries, great God! to thee;
  And I will raise my voice,
Uplift my feeble minstrelsy,
  And bid my heart rejoice.
Thy sun sheds glory in his light;
Deep darkness praises thee by night:
But 'tis thy Spirit makes delight.

Great God! accept the humble praise
  A heart sincere would bring:
My heart's own anthem 'tis I raise,
  My soul's desire I sing.
Glory to thee, all gracious Lord!
For thou dost every gift afford,
And gladd'st my spirit with thy word.

It is not very good; yet it is one of the best. Mr. Parker had not the poetic fire; though he knew what it was. In a letter to Miss Cabot, dated March 14, 1836, he says, "I would I had that 'dangerous gift,' as some call it, but which Milton terms the 'divine gift,'—the power of the true poet. He possesses such a spring of ever-living water in his own deep and noble soul, that continually gushes up to his breast, and wells out in all his life. Who can fail to admire that profound enthusiasm with which the true poet regards all nature? Nay, all that lives and moves, or merely *is*, has for him a deep and permanent charmingness. Go where he will, he sees Beauty; for she dwells in his own breast, and diffuses her sweet influences over all his eye rests upon."

His best poems are religious; and the finest of these are the sonnets addressed to Jesus, whose name never failed to kindle his enthusiasm. The first was written in December of this year.

"Jesus, there is no dearer name than thine,
  Which Time has written on his endless scroll:
Nor wreaths nor garlands ever did intwine
  So fair a temple of so vast a soul.

Ay, every angel set his glowing seal
  Upon thy brow, and gave each human grace,
In a sweet copy heaven to reveal,
  And stamp perfection on a mortal face.
Once on the earth, before dull mortal eyes,
  Which could not half thy sacred radiance see,
E'en as the emmet cannot read the skies, —
  For our weak orbs reach not immensity, —
Once on the earth wert thou, a living shrine,
Where dwelt the good, the lovely, the divine."

The "sentiments" and apothegms scattered up and down the pages of the Journal and Common-Place Book disclose the earnestness of his mind: —

"Faith is collective energy."

"By action of the soul the 'formless and void' becomes 'very good.'"

"Had there been no monsters to subdue, there had been no Hercules."

"Love is the perfect action of the whole soul."

"Egyptian bondage brings Egyptian darkness."

"Nothing dries so soon as tears."

"He that has a principle is inspired."

"Religion is the highest form of love."

"Wealth injures talent more than poverty. Under gold hills and thrones perhaps many a spiritual giant lies buried."

"Liberty is justice secured."

"The soul, like the magnetic needle, ever trembles for an embrace with God."

"Necessity the strongest; time the wisest; man the greatest."

"There is a Solomon in every stupid man, a devil in every saint."

"Artolatry (bread-worship), — that of these times, which invert the old order, and turn God into bread, not bread into God."

"Faith must present her credentials before she rules Reason."

"If you dare not say what you think, soon you will dare say what you do not think."

"Reason acknowledges no useless or dangerous truths."

"If this world were all, a heart were a sad gift."

"If teachers disclose truth as fast as God reveals it to them, there is no danger."

"A new truth can never do so much harm as an old error."

"God and truth are always on the same side."

"Man may say what is heresy; but God only can tell who is the heretic."

"Philosophy is the love of wisdom; Christianity, the wisdom of love."

"Great minds mould things to thoughts: little minds mould thoughts to things."

"A single seed is the result of all the suns that ever shone."

"The faculty of love is the measure of great souls."

"Laughter of fools is like the crackling of thorns under a pot, which they cannot heat, only begrime."

"Climbing plants are always weak."

"Avoid that society in which it is dangerous to speak, and painful to be silent."

This vein of moral earnestness crops out on almost every page. A passage from Plato suggests this comment: —

"What is it proper for the ignorant to suffer from the wise? Learning. What, then, is due from the good to the bad? Hurt? Not at all. Goodness is due them. Is a man bad: the good shall teach him goodness. Penal legislation now-a-days has all the effect of the purest injustice in driving the half-guilty to increased crime, and in making doubly deep the hatred of the revengeful. I doubt not the angel of humanity will beat with her golden pinions all prisons to small dust."

One brief note intimates that he had no fondness for general society: "A ball at Dr. Bowditch's: quite a large party. This balling is tedious business to me. A walk of four miles in and four miles out alone, in a terribly cold night, is no joke." He takes kindly to vacations, however: —

"I have passed the vacation (winter of 1836) delightfully; never more so. Time has flown by on silken pinions. I have been at Boston most of the time; and to see one's dearest of all friends every day, and a thousand times every day, is heart-ravishing. Have been to Salem. Saw all the lions of the place, from the 'murder-house' to 'Deacon Giles's Distillery.' I have made calls, and spent evenings abroad, almost without end. Indeed, I have completely reversed the old order of the day; so that to be at home is the exception, as it formerly was the rule. . . . I have been up to Watertown, and staid some considerable time with my uncle and cousins and with Dr. Francis, and have made a new acquaintance: I mean Mr. Bradford. I met him at Mr. Francis's, and walked to Boston with him: not a little delighted with the man."

This certainly shows a genial spirit. That same winter he lectured in Concord, and passed part of an evening with Mr. Emerson — "truly a most delightful man" — and his wife. "He once said of her, that she was the 'soul of faith.' Of course her life is *faith put in action;* and what more noble can be said of any one?"

In the month of April, 1836, the generosity of a friend gave him the pleasure of a trip to Washington, through New York and Philadelphia. Nothing occurred of note. In Washington he goes to the chambers of Congress; listens to the debate on the bill "for preventing the circulation of incendiary papers" at the South; hears Mr. King and Mr. Calhoun; sees the "little magician" gliding round, clapping men on their shoulders, and shaking their hands, — "very artful and naughty" looking; sees Clay, tall and homely, walking about in a dignified manner; notices the negroes as matter of course, and remarks, "They are a queer set, these negroes: some of them are very merry, dancing and capering about on the sidewalk as if they had nought to do but dance. I saw two negro lovers walking arm-in-arm, cooing and billing as if they could not restrain their joy in one another's presence. Why should *color* prevent them?"

In this man, clearly, there are deeps of power waiting to

be stirred. The angel has not descended to trouble the waters: he is expected. "What a strange life is this of mine! How remarkable appears the course I have run when I look back on it from the present moment! Verily 'there's a Divinity that shapes our ends, rough-hew them how we will.' I wonder what the Almighty Parent designs for me. Where wilt thou, O Father! cast my lot? I would not seek with prurient curiosity to invade the mysterious cabinet of futurity; but I must confess that I am by no means indifferent to the future which shall be appointed me. But I trust I shall be resigned to the will of Omnipotence. At the worst, even, there will be enough to do: this is some consolation to one who loves activity, and would fain be useful to his fellows.

"Opportunities for practical usefulness are always offering themselves to the seekers; one, too, so singularly blessed by Heaven as I, can carry with him another element of felicity, — a companion, whose brave heart *mirrors back my own* from its *celestial depths.* May the Lord send his blessing upon us wherever we are!"

On June 17, 1835, he writes to Miss Cabot, "Let us imagine our happiness in some new station we are to occupy: we shall see a thousand delights which now refresh our whole soul only by their images, — the shadows which they cast before them; and, when they shall *really* come, we shall be all ready to receive them, and welcome them to our company like old guests. . . . It is delightful now to imagine myself a minister, to recount the duties of the station, and consider all the ways of performing them, and the glorious satisfaction of seeing God's work prosper in my hand. I turn to a home, — a home of beauty, of affection, of love; to a home where all noble feelings are cherished, and all jarring interests and strife excluded. . . . Calamities may fall upon that home, — they come upon all men; each country has its own storms; but, if it is built on the rock of holy affection, it will stand. The floods may pass over it: they can never shake its fixed foundation."

His sermons in the Divinity School were dry and scholastic to a degree that provoked reproof from the professor, to Theodore's great chagrin. Their dulness was a surprise. His first public preaching in the village church was a disappointment. "I felt much embarrassed; though perhaps it did not show forth. To say the truth, I did not feel the sermon as much as I usually do; for the hour usually spent in preparing for the service was consumed in 'doing the agreeable.' May God in his mercy grant me power to improve in this holy duty! May I go on from strength to strength, increasing continually in godliness and wisdom, and thus show forth pure and holy Christianity in my life no less than in my teachings! O God! wilt thou help me to become more pure in heart, more holy, and better able to restrain all impetuous desires and unholy passions? May I 'put down every high thing' that would exalt itself against the perfect law of God! Help me, in the intercourse of life, to discharge my duties with a more Christian-like fidelity; to love thee the more, and those with whom I am to deal."

"Visitation Day" was a "day of trembling." The services in the morning "went off" well. His own subject was "Gnosticism," for which he had read Neander and Matter, and had held conversations with the professor, from which he came away with an unpleasant impression of the wise man's want of candor, not to say insight. "The exercises of the afternoon "dragged heavily." He was displeased with a certain D.D., who remarked that he had no denominational character, but was an *eclectic.* "No man can thus set himself free from his contemporaries, and feel none of their influence. He may, indeed, withdraw himself from their meetings, and refuse to co-operate with them; but to attempt to retire from all sympathy with them is silly, and to pretend to have done it is preposterous."

His preparation at the Hall is finished. "Two years and three months have passed speedily and pleasantly away. God has prospered me in all my studies; and I am now ready to go forth, but not without dread and fear. What an immense change has taken place in my opinions and feelings upon all the main points of inquiry since I entered this place!

"I ask for thy blessings, O most merciful Father! upon all my labors and studies. Keep me from sin and from every harmful error."

CHAPTER V.

THE CANDIDATE.

On leaving the Hall, Theodore allowed himself a short vacation; but it was Milton's "idle vacancy" now. The relish for this kind of indulgence was gone. "The two weeks past have been spent in loitering about, idling away time, and living at ease; now strolling about with Lydia, and now picking cherries and flowers alone. By the way, I have found a flower that wants a name in Dr. B.'s book. I have thus loitered about, doing almost nothing; not profiting morally, religiously, or even intellectually, and perhaps but little in body, considering that I am getting bad habits of early retiring, late lying, and general indolence. So much for my state of repose. Blessed be these *iron* times! — there is something for man to *do;* and, still more, something for him to *think.*

"Suppose not, my dearly-beloved book, that I felt no pleasure in thus passing time. I am not so cold-hearted as to wander among the gardens of the Graces with no sense that riots, and no soul that thrills. Nay, my heart has been warmed by the sweetest — I had almost said, the noblest — impulses; but it does not advance me in the journey of life as I would wish to move. It does not allow my soul to unfold its wings in this fledging-place and trial-ground, and prepare for the lofty and dangerous flight when it must 'sail with uplift wing' against tempest and storm. I have sterner deeds to *do*, greater dangers to *dare*. *I must be about my work*."

It was customary for young preachers, after leaving the school, to try their powers in friendly pulpits of older men before dashing into the broad "vineyard of the Lord" which was waiting for reapers. Theodore made his first venture in the desk of his old friend Dr. Francis, at Watertown, on July 24, after wrestling with doubts, hopes, fears, for a month previous. "Not only by day, but in the deep watches of the night, have painful visitations come over me. Well, Heaven be praised that I have *once* preached to a real *live* audience, to *feeling* beings, and those my very friends and neighbors!

"I am resolved to cast forth my seed-corn into the ever-busy working universe, that it may bring forth as the Lord pleases. With him is the result, not with me."

His themes on this occasion were, "The Necessity of a Heavenly Life," and "Religion a Principle and Sentiment," — vital topics both, bespeaking less the bookworm than the prophet, and vitally treated, if we may accept the opinion of his hearers. The preacher says, "I have heard enough of *compliments*, which come from partial judges." The next Sunday he preached for Mr. Putnam in a large and full house, with a success that surprised those who had heard only of his prodigious feats of learning.

The trials of the candidate were now upon him: he must carry his wares to the public market. After a brief experience as a peddler of gospel goods, he writes thus in October to his class-mate Livermore, who had been happy in finding an early settlement: "I rejoice that you are already so fortunate as to escape from the perils of candidating. I have long looked forward to this period of my life as one full of difficulties, unpleasantness, and dangers; and experience has taught me — dearly enough — that not a tithe of the real evil was anticipated. To say nothing about the bodily ills which attend this nomadic life of a minister, there are intellectual evils of no common magnitude, and difficulties in the way of true spiritual culture which are truly frightful. All of us are so far creatures of time and space, and therefore accessible to pleasant sights and agreeable sounds, that we all have some private spot, or at least some chosen time, when the tide of feeling sets afresh in the heart; when, by virtue of long 'use and wont,' our souls mount upward, and soar straight into the region of 'open vision' without an effort. Now, how are we not debarred of this privilege? We are actually driven, by force of circumstances, away from these 'fountains of living water,' and compelled to hew out for ourselves 'broken cisterns which hold no water.' But I will not weary you with a detail of those evils, which, I bless God, you have escaped."

His first extended experiment was one of four weeks at Barnstable, a seaport town on the south side of Barnstable Bay, supported mainly by fisheries and a coast trade. He goes down in the "neat little schooner 'Sappho,'" on a smooth sea, with favoring wind. "Gracefully the little vessel cut the wave." There were about twenty passengers, mostly ladies; two young people of rude bearing, who ate lemons and pickled limes, and who gave him an orange; and three pretty girls, two of them sisters of the Rev. Mr. Greenwood. Their father was with them, — "an intelligent and agreeable old gentleman," with whom he soon came to an understanding. There was but one cabin, which had to serve as lodgement and lounging-room, during the evening and night, for the whole party. "The ladies went down about half-past eight; for it was cold. Soon after nine I descended, feet foremost, — perpendicularly almost. They had gotten into their several berths, and there were lying, the curtains still undrawn. I sat rather awkwardly, and chatted and laughed with them, who did not seem at all disturbed by the peculiarity of the scene. By and by I, too, crept into a crib, — a lady above me, another at my head, and a third at my feet. I had the *poet's* corner. All night there was a noise, — some getting up, others getting down; roisterous fellows carousing; children crying, and mothers attempting to quiet them. Sleep went up the hatch-way, but did not find good quarters, and so came in with me, and staid till nearly five, A.M."

At Barnstable he has pleasant quarters at Mrs. Whitman's, a lady of prepossessing appearance and manners. On Saturday he looks up two or three of the leading men, presents his credentials, and takes a view of the town. "The houses are generally small, — many of only one story, or one and a half, — are usually shingled instead of being clap-boarded, and are not always painted: many are still of the dark hue of the tarnished wood. Some are yellow; others green or red; a few are white. There are some pretty places. The road winds at a little distance from the shore, and the houses are built at irregular intervals along its sides. There is a pretty hill back of the house, which affords a good prospect in all directions." On the whole, he concludes that the town is not, perhaps, so well adapted as some others to a cultivation of æsthetics, but that ethics can be well enough studied. Nevertheless, he tries the Muse: —

"Day's weary portals softly close,
And slow the sun retires;
And Night his dewy mantle throws
On Earth's decaying fires.

'Tis sweet, my love, when day is o'er,
And hushed each jarring sound,
To turn and think of thee once more:
It makes my heart rebound.

A quicker beat now fires my heart;
My thoughts now swifter glow" —

But Barnstable is no better adapted to poetry than to æsthetics; and suddenly the enraptured strain ceases.

He presently suspects the place to be spiritually dead. The people do not seem willing to talk on religious subjects. Still he hopes to do some good. The four private and three public schools suggest an occupation. He begs Miss Cabot not to hang the leaden collar of "Be careful and not do too much" about his neck. He walks eight miles a day, makes new acquaintances, and becomes interested in the doings and feelings of the people. He ascends the hill daily for a breeze and a view; makes excursions to a pretty pond about four miles distant with Mr. Drew, the schoolmaster; goes to tea-parties at Capt. Bacon's and elsewhere; attends funerals; and feels a sort of mental crystallization going on within him. Slight attacks of home-sickness will visit the young minister; but they decrease as he gradually gets acquainted with the inanimate creation, — the trees, hills, rocks. He finds several new species of flowers; makes a beautiful collection of salt-crystals; the cows and pigs afford him entertainment. The qualities of the people improve on closer acquaintance. He finds them not only agreeable, but intelligent; and begins to think there is more religious feeling than he had hastily surmised.

The open pulpit troubled him at first. The people sat within a table's width of his chair, and looked in upon him as if they would eat him up. The house was good, easy to speak in. He felt somewhat awkward at the beginning, but made an effort, and not only delivered the written word, but "added much that was better and more searching, extemporaneously." The people were exceedingly attentive, and showed their interest by coming out in the afternoon even better than in the morning. The best people called on him, — Dr. Tuck, Dr. Mack, Col. Underwood, Mr. Choate, Deacon Monroe. Nobody spoke to him about the sermon; but Mr. Reed — "Squire" Reed, cousin of the Hon. John Reed, Register of Probate "and several other things" — said to Mr. Whitman of one of his discourses, that it was the greatest sermon he ever heard. Parker had the common weakness of ministers, — that of thinking his best sermons the least appreciated. The people did not listen well to his labored discourse; "belike they did not understand it, which was my fault, not theirs:" but when the "preachment had little thought, and as little originality," they were all attention. The babes wanted milk.

The Sundays were pretty full; so were the week-days. There were visitings, social parties, a fishing-excursion, trips to Yarmouth, Hyannis, &c. Dr. Tuck took him to a meeting of the "Charitable and Benevolent Society," where the subject under discussion was the abolition of capital punishment. A theological point that came up brought him to his feet, and he spoke in favor of the abolition. All this we learn from his letters to Miss Cabot, full of pleasant gossip about things and people, walks, talks, rambles, explorations, "jactations," and dejections, the whole of which we would copy if the limits of this biography did not forbid.

Meeting with practical men does the young student good. This he confesses in a letter to his classmate Silsbee, dated Barnstable, Aug. 21: —

"How disqualified we are for contact with the real world I felt when first shown a real live man; and when brought to speak with him I was utterly at a stand, and scarcely knew what to say. Thus, indeed, we come away from our three-years' studies at Divinity College with some little knowledge of science, literature, philosophy, peradventure some small inklings of theology and metaphysics, nay, even a little knowledge of the science of things in general, and with beards on our chins, but with no other marks of manhood. Now, I maintain, that, besides a great deal of knowledge, one needs as much skill to make it of any use to him.

"This art of things in general I hope I have made some little advance in since I came to Barnstable. Indeed, it seems to me I have *grown* in this regard, so that I can really talk to men as if I were also a man, and not a student merely. A mere student is a sort of *homunculus*, an animal not treated by Pliny, except incidentally, when he speaketh of the war they once carried on against their arch enemies the cranes."

The following encouraging record in the journal was set down about this time: —

"It seems that I have gained much light within during the short stay I have now made in Barnstable: it seems as if the wire had touched the chaotic liquid, and crystallization had begun. Seasons occur in the course of one's moral and intellectual history when the work of years seems to be effected in a few hours. It seems to me that Nature wears a new aspect, and life has got a new meaning, since I came hither. Well, if I have learned any duty more clearly, may Heaven be praised therefor!"

A visit to a Methodist camp-meeting at Eastham interested him. He and his companion went in a vessel, which was cast away on a sandy neck of land. Theodore noted the peculiar formation of the hills on the neck, the lighthouse, the mountain-cranberries, a glutinous kind of fish, the conical shape of the sand-mountains, the lines of the beach, the ship's regulator, and a great many other things. Arriving at the camp-grounds, his curiosity was all alive. "One tent was full of negroes, who were more vehement than their white brethren. There was occasionally a touch upon slavery: who wonders at it? . . . The women, I noticed, were always the most noisy. Some of them were in *hysterics*, I should say, and should explain it on well-known physiological principles. They said it was the *Spirit.* How strangely men mistake the flesh for the Spirit! A twitching of the nerves is often mistaken for inspiration. I was much struck with the cold indifference of one young woman, who sat very quietly munching gingerbread while all the process of 'bringing in' was taking place around her. . . . I always noticed that the least learned were the most violent, — had most of the 'Spirit of the Lord,' as they said." The camp-ground presented a striking scene. There were sixteen large tents arranged in a semicircle about the pulpit, some of them containing more than a hundred people. The woods behind were all alive. The description, which is too long to copy, contains nice touches of humor, — the hideous-looking hay-cart; the queer carriages, drawn by oxen or horses, as happened to be convenient; old Capt. Brown, no stockings nor shoes on his feet, no jacket or vest, pantaloons rolled up to his knees, carrying one of the passengers on his back to the cart; the snuff-colored man; the major who had had three trades and three wives, — one for each trade. The two comrades walked back to Barnstable, thirty miles, by the sandy road.

But, great as was the social activity, the mental activity was even more remarkable. The dozen or so of books he brought with him were soon exhausted. He writes to Miss Cabot, "The air of the place braces my whole soul: I could devour a whole library in a week. I think I should write three new sermons a week all the time I am here; but I have only enough of my favorite paper for two more, and I forbear." Among the books mentioned in the journal as in course of reading are Ackerman's "Christliches in Plato;" Schelling's "Lectures on Academic Study," which he finds fault with as being too subjective; Jahn's "Vaticinia Messiana," which seemed fundamentally unsound in assuming the inspiration of all the writers of the Old Testament; Schmidt's "Mysticismus der Mittelälter." But the most significant thing he undertook was the translation of De Wette's "Introduction to the Old Testament." How quietly, yet with what forebodings, he announces the beginning of this great task, which was destined to be a monument of his own industry, a test of his courage, and a mighty inauguration of his career! —

"THURSDAY, Aug. 11. — Finished another sermon on 'The Law of the Spirit of Life in Christ Jesus.'

"Began to translate De Wette's 'Einleitung in das Alte Testament.' I cannot tell what will be the result of this. I shall leave that for another time to determine. Meanwhile I will go on translating it quietly, as I wish, without interrupting important studies."

On Monday, Aug. 28, his engagement being ended, he took leave of his friends in Barnstable "with many a sigh, and certainly with many a wish that I shall soon return to them." They wanted him to stay longer; but he declined. His books were exhausted: he was, for the time, satisfied with the Barnstable life; and he longed, as lovers will, for the society of his heart's mistress.

In the months of September and October his letters report him as enjoying the autumn scenery, and as interesting congregations in Northfield and Greenfield, — charming towns, where, however, he would not care to reside as minister. We hear of him also at Portland, Lowell, Billerica. West Roxbury has been suggested to him, and Concord presents attractions. In September he comes across Emerson's "Nature:" criticises it, of course; finds fault with its excess of idealism, but is delighted with the overflowing beauty and truth. "Blessed is the man who stoops and tastes of them! He erects himself in new vigor and freshness, and becomes a man divine." The correspondence of this period is remarkable for freshness and playfulness, showing the healthiest state of feeling on all subjects. Read these words to his friend Silsbee: "Is not friendship one of the wells of the desert, where the pilgrim cools his parched lips, reposes for the time, and starts afresh in his life-journey? Love is the well that stands by his cottage-door. It is there in winter: it freezes not. It is there in summer: the drought never makes its waters abate. It hath ever a pleasant flavor upon the palate, and a grateful, life-giving influence on the whole inner man. I trust you will soon find this healing water, and, though 'the well is deep,' will draw an abundant supply."

Here is a day in Northfield: "Rose at seven; shaved and dressed; looked at the newspaper; read the books of Nehemiah, Esther, Solomon's Song, first twelve chapters of Isaiah, in English; wrote part of a sermon; finished a hundred and fifty pages of Allan's 'Life of Scott,' two of Herder's 'Briefe.' Dinner. Read in various books; walked two or three miles; found a queer plant; gathered about a quart of chestnuts; noticed the peculiar position of some stratified rocks. Dr. Hall dropped in, and asked me to ride. Took tea. Mr. Nevers called; staid two hours at least. Called with Mr. Allen at Dr. Hall's; ascended Mr. Pomeroy's mountain." There is no mental sickness here.

In November he is at Barnstable again for three Sundays, with a plentiful supply of books and papers to brighten the gloomy autumnal days. The people are glad to see him; his old friends are cordial; the church fills up, though there is no fire in it, and no means for making one. Chairs have to be brought in to accommodate the comers. The audience is attentive as ever, listening so eagerly, that, when a good thing is said, their faces look like "fires new stirred." They wanted to give him a "call;" though some were doubtful, suspecting the soundness of his views. A meeting was arranged for the purpose; but he, hearing of the intention, prevented it. "I wish I could divide myself, give them a part, and take the rest up to some other place. But one cannot give away half a mind any more than half a heart; and a church is, doubtless, as jealous as a damsel. I shall not let them give an invitation to me. I am no *coquette* among parishes."

At Barnstable he receives intelligence of his father's death.

BARNSTABLE, Nov. 11, 1836.

I received your letter, my dear Lydia, as I never fail to do, with unspeakable pleasure and satisfaction; but if the outside gave me pleasure, and the inside told me what I had long expected, yet I cannot deny that the intelligence found me unprepared. I have, as you know, long expected the death of him who is now no more; yet I had fondly put off the day of his departure: and, when the event was told me, my grief and sorrow were tenfold greater than I had expected. One never knows when his armor is strong enough for the conflict. We know that our friends must die, and join the companions of their youth. If they are old, we think that it may come soon; and, if they are feeble and sick at the same time, we fear that we must soon wend on our pilgrimage without their kindly aid. All this compels us to prepare; but, when the dreaded event actually takes place, all our resolutions, our expected resignation, and our imagined strength, disappear like frost-work in the sun. I do not mourn for my father's sake, but for my own. He goes to meet his friends, to see again his wife, his fathers, and his children: no doubt it is a pleasant meeting. They may pity his long delay on the earth, and rejoice now that he has put off the mortal to put on the immortal.

After I read your letter, and sat silent and lonely by my own fire, I could almost see his fathers of other days, the wife of his youth, and his children and long-separated friends, pressing gloriously around him to press him once more to their hearts. Their shout and song of welcome still ring in my ears. But, as I said, I lament not for him: he has no sigh to stifle, no tear to wipe away. But how *can* I, who have been cradled in his arms, fed by his hands, blessed by his prayers, and moulded by his tender care, — how can I forbear lamenting, now he's gone?

But enough of this. We shall yet meet; and I will no longer weary your soul with the bitterness of mine. He has gone! let *us* say no more about it. And now I entreat you to say nothing upon that subject in your letters, nor when we meet. A thousand circumstances will bring it all up before me again and again. Do not let us multiply them without need, nor foolishly turn away from them when they occur naturally: for the valley of tears, when dwelt in, hath a poisonous influence on the soul; but, if only occasionally passed through, it is full of "healing waters," and fountains of strength.

The journal of the 8th of November contains touching reflections on the same event, and pictures the scene of the re-union in the other world. As often as the anniversary came round, it was tenderly remembered. Years did not weaken the sentiments of gratitude he cherished for his father. In heavy and dark days, when the battle raged about him, and friends fell off, and his heart trembled, the record is passionate with feeling: the strong man seems to stretch out his arms to the revered shade, and to hide his face in the consoling bosom. Something of the same emotion was excited by the recollection of any of his kindred, — brothers and sisters whom he had scarcely known, uncles and cousins whom he had hardly more than heard of. The power of the root is strong in him: the ancestral fibre never loses its hold. He had a plan of exploring in England the remotest nooks of family association, and of placing some memorial on the grave of every ancestor in America. They were blood of his blood: it was a pride for him to remember that he was blood of theirs.

It is interesting to note that already, away off at the Cape, the young war-horse smells the coming battle afar. Mr. George Ripley had written an article on Martineau's "Rationale of Religious Inquiry," in "The Christian Examiner," that had roused the ire of an eminent ex-professor in the Divinity School at Cambridge; and the ex-professor had replied in "The Boston Daily Advertiser," rebuking the bold young writer in imperious terms. The reviewer replied the very next day. Theodore speaks his mind in a letter thus: —

"This coming out in the print, and denouncing the writer of an article which appeared soberly and unostentatiously in a periodical with which Mr. N. had nothing to do, is ridiculous. A man writes something which differs a little from what Prof. N. believes, and, forsooth, he must come out 'with his sign manual,' and tell the good people of the land he does not think so! What if he does not? Is he the people? *Will all truth perish with him?* . . .

"The last time I saw Mr. R., I suggested that the first one who lifted a hand in this work would have to suffer; and I wished to push some old veteran German to the fore-front of the battle, who would not care for a few blows: but he thought there was no danger."

This was the first gun in a long battle.

The only incident set down in the list of events during this dismal month of November is a visit to an Indian settlement about twelve miles from the town. The poverty, squalor, smoke, and stench of the only real wigwam of the settlement, the talk of the old squaw, need not be detailed. The poor hag had seen trouble; she said her children were dead: "But she had found the only comfort which the savage receives from the white man: it peered out from under a bench in the shape of a *jug of gin!*" The quick glance of the future reformer detects the yet covered path his manly foot is to tread.

The last month of the year was spent in Salem with the family of his classmate Silsbee. He filled the pulpit of the "East Church," though not as a candidate. The cultured and friendly old town offered him its choicest hospitalities. The Silsbee family was large in more senses than one. The brightest and most amiable of women and the heartiest of men were members of it in near or remote connection; and their social circle embraced the elegance, wit, and brilliancy of the city. Parker saw the best people, and "did more talking than the whole family of the patriarchs during their apocryphal journey over the waters of the flood." Miss Burley lived there with her sparkling and beautiful nieces, — ready for all conversation, and very delightful in literary talk, — Mr. and Mrs. Frederick Howes also, and his classmate Samuel P. Andrews.

"I have been as happy as Adam was before he was turned out of paradise; nay, I mean that I was much happier. . . . By the way, woman is often abused by modern writers because good Mother Eve did not throw the apple in the serpent's face, instead of being wheedled into eating it. But, if it had been offered to her precious spouse, he would not have stood there shall-I-shall-I-ing, but would merely have said, 'Apples, indeed! so early! thank ye, Mister Snake!' and would have eaten it without thinking of conscience. Now, the sons of this biped pique themselves upon being men, not women!

"Kings say they reign by divine right, and impiously stamp 'Rex, Dei gratiâ,' upon innocent copper: but woman is the only monarch that can justly use these words, and she may, — 'I am a woman *by the grace of God*.' She alone rules by divine right."

The mental exercise was as vigorous and various as ever. There are schemes of lectures on Heine, Spenser, the Use of Nature; Notes on Public Instruction among the Romans; a Study on English State-Trials; a Careful List of Public Documents in England; an Account of the Different Rolls from the Earliest Time; Dates of the Doomsday Book, and Memoranda of the Libraries where such Antiquities are stored; Summaries of Statistics in regard to the Social Condition of Germany; Births and Deaths in Prussia; Number of Pupils in the Universities; Longevity of the Professors; Proportion of Soldiers to the Population in Europe; Pay of Officers; and so forth. Damiron's "Cours de Philosophie" shares with "Jacob Faithful" the leisure hours. He transcribes into the journal a number of Latin monkish hymns; apothegms and parables have their place also. His fun overflows in a ponderous squib, — "History and Spirit of Coxcombry or Puppyism, in its Origin and Development; from the Night-Book of Gottesgute von Thiergarten." The subject is laid out in divisions, — Puppyism in the Pulpit, Puppyism of the Press, Puppyism of the Parlor; and through all this flows the uneasy stream of verse, not clearing itself, alas! as it flows.

Studies in theology go ominously on. The origin and composition of the Pentateuch is under consideration. To this date belongs the following schedule of labors to be undertaken:—

I. Sundry questions in theology:—
   1. What is the extent of known supernatural revelation made to man?
   2. What is the foundation of the authority of Jesus Christ?
   3. What is the meaning of faith in Old and New Testament?
   4. How is Christ more a Saviour than Socrates?
   5. Why did the world need a Saviour?
   6. What has been his influence?
   7. Is Christianity to be a universal religion?
   8. What is the foundation of religion in man? the design of miracles? the pretence of them in other religions?

II. Questions in Scriptural criticism and exegesis:—
   1. The authenticity of the beginning of the Gospels of Matthew and Luke. The miraculous conception.
   2. The resurrection: why was the body of Christ raised? why "carried up"? How is the resurrection of matter proof of the immortality of spirit? Is not the material resurrection of the body of Jesus Christ unspiritualizing?

The questions in theology are preceded by questions in ethics, less systematically drawn up, but suggestive of his moral drift:—

1. The connection between the understanding and the will.
2. Foundation of the idea of duty.
3. Foundation of the idea of God.
4. The limits of duty.
5. Subjective consequences of doing or of omitting duty.
6. Liberty and necessity.
7. Why is man placed in life?
8. How great is the difference in the value of the various means afforded to attain the end of life? What state best fitted

thereto? Are outward means of any avail? How much? (Compare the condition of a Carolinian slave and the son of a Boston merchant, or a New-Zealander with a citizen of Massachusetts.)

In close connection with these questions are noble thoughts from Plato, and devout prayers for help to lead a consecrated life:—

"Give me an understanding heart; let me not only know, but feel, that my duty, my nature, my destination, demand continued labor and earnest action.

"Give me rest for my soul. Help me to control impetuous passions, to rule my own spirit, to attain a sublime command over all appetite and desire, bringing every thought into subjection to the law of my being."

The cast of Mr. Parker's religious philosophy comes out in a letter to his friend S. P. Andrews, written Jan. 3, 1837, from Northfield, where we find him preaching:—

"Bowen has written a piece in 'The Examiner' on what think you? Why, on Emerson's 'Nature.' Pelion upon Ossa is bad; Jew upon Bacon: but Bowen upon 'Nature' caps the climax. He has given transcendentalism '*sich a lick*,' that it is almost dead. Kant, Fichte, and Schelling appeared to me in a vision of the night, and deplored their sad estate. 'Transcendentalism is clean gone,' said Kant. 'Verdammt!' said Fichte. 'What shall we do?' exclaimed Schelling. They could not be appeased."

In February he is at Greenfield, the birthplace of his friend George Ripley. An accident (he was thrown from a sleigh, and had a narrow escape from serious hurt) disabled him with cold and headache much of the time; but his letters are charming specimens of intelligent prattle about people and scenery. The air inspires him; the cool wind from the north braces his frame; and the sight of mountains and great trees and wide meadows refreshes the inner man not a little. The aspect of Nature in winter is a delight to him: "In the country there is a tale in every thing; and every little object in Nature hath its beauty to please by, and its moral to instruct with. Indeed, the country is a great 'system of divinity;' while the city is but a commercial dictionary, a 'ready-reckoner,' or a 'cook-book.' A single walk along the banks of the Connecticut or among the hills, or a moment's listening to the kine's soft music, has taught me more than Mr. Emerson and all the Boston Association of Ministers." The parish is not, on the whole, attractive: the services are held in a court-room, and the spirit of the place is not congenial with his. There were then only about two thousand people in the town, and there were five societies, — a sign of sectarian activity and religious lethargy that was not encouraging. There were agreeable features about the place; and he felt that he might go farther, and fare worse: but his heart was not drawn to it. The prospect of other places was more tempting. But for his desire to be married, he would have preferred remaining unsettled a year longer to staying in Greenfield, remote from the active centres of thought. The smallness of the salary did not repel him: he was used to poverty, and was willing to accept it on the bidding of duty. But as long as other men could satisfy the people as well as he could, or better, and one who was already spoken of was comparatively indifferent to salary, he turned his face elsewhere.

The fact is, he was becoming weary of the candidate's aimless life, in which no seed was watered, no field tilled, no harvest reaped. He wanted continuous, energetic work. As far back as the previous October, he had said to an intimate friend who had misgivings in regard to the ministry, "I should have been much less surprised at finding self-doubt in my own bosom, for I have still much 'unreclaimed blood;' and though I love the ministry of Christianity with all my heart and mind, yet I have an affection for silent vigils, and there is a pulse in my heart that sometimes beats wildly for the stir and noise and tumult and dust of the literary course." On the 15th of February he writes to the same correspondent, Mr. S. P. Andrews, —

"Sometimes, Samuel, I fear lest I have missed it capitally in becoming a minister; that as a lawyer, in other departments of thought and action, I might have been more useful, and, at the same time, free from a certain restraining bond (invisible, but strong as Fate) with which convention has tied up every minister withal. I do not ever think of deserting a ministry which would dignify angels, and has been honored by the Son of God himself. No: I never think of that; for I deem it writ down in my duty to preach the gospel, come of it what will. And although some of my dearest expectations have been disappointed, still I shall 'bear up, and steer with upright wing right onward, nor bate one jot of heart or hope.' Yet sometimes the thought comes mightily upon me, 'Thou hast mistaken thy calling.' Yet think I still there is no employment so noble on the earth as the faithful attempt to give a loftier action to humanity, to make men unfold the natures God has given them, and to lead them to be whole men, with no part wanting, and not merely miserable halves and quarters of men, as they mostly are, cultivating only a part, and that the meanest part, of their natures. It sometimes makes my heart bleed to think of the men whom the world calls 'happy' and 'great,' but whom I call miserable and little, so much so as never to have suspected their misery and littleness. Now, if I could remove this frightful state of things, and show men wherein true strength lies, and divert them from *bubble-hunting* all their days, then gladly would I labor, spending and being spent. But when I consider how vast are the obstacles to be removed, how deeply rooted is the evil, how strongly supported by men's most active principles, and how hotly it is encouraged by the force of the senses and the wild intoxication of gold and ambition, and that to all this I can only oppose the 'foolishness of preaching,' rendered still more 'foolish' by the foolishness of the preacher himself, by his consciousness of ignorance, of sinfulness, and of weakness, I think the attempt almost a mad one. It is an attempt to try to beat down Gibraltar by throwing figs at it. Now, it is mathematically demonstrable that the rock might be beat down by throwing figs; for a force *infinitely small*, when put forth for an infinite time, will overthrow any finite obstacle, be it never so big: but who would attempt such a work? One sole thing encourages me; to wit, I know that one who keeps God's 'law of the Spirit of Life,' and puts forth his might manfully in obedience thereto, be his might never so little, — be it less than mine even, — has for his friend and ally and co-worker the entire almightiness and perfect virtue of God as much as he who obeys the laws of matter brings the whole weight of the earth to bear upon his wheel or lever: and in such a cause, with such a coadjutor, it is nobler to be conquered, dragged at the wheels of the enemy, yea, trodden to dust by his followers, who shout aloud, '*Great is Mammon of the Yankees!*' than to engage in any other warfare. Therefore I shall go on. Consequences I have nothing to do with: they belong to God. He will take care of all consequences. To me belongs only duty. Come what will come, I shall do it. All that I have give I to the one cause, be it little or much."

Wherever Mr. Parker preached, he was received gladly: in most places he was invited to stay. This was the case at Waltham and Concord and Leominster; but the attractions of West Roxbury gradually prevailed over the rest. It was a quiet country place; the salary was meagre, — six hundred dollars; the society was small, and composed, for the most part, of plain people: but the town was near Boston and Cambridge, and it promised leisure for work he had set his heart on. Mr. Francis at Watertown, and Mr. Stetson at Medford, were not far off. The position was suggested to him four or five months before this. He had preached there several times; and when the invitation came, on May 23, it was accepted. He was anxious for a seat of activity, and full of schemes for the execution of which uninterrupted days and nights were needed. The translation of De Wette's "Einleitung in die Bücher des Altes Testaments" was finished on the 20th of May. It must be diligently revised; notes from various writers are to be

8

added, essays and dissertations to be appended: it will be a work of years yet. He must have a home, — a home at once. How eagerly he longed for it, how glowingly his heart dwelt on it, these extracts from letters tell: —

To S. P. Andrews.

SALEM, March 16, 1837.

. . . With regard to my marriage and the "happy day," thereof I can only say that probably matters will be brought to a crisis about the 20th of next month. With regard to my feelings in approaching that moment, you may imagine them. They are not homogeneous, but of a widely different and various character. Sometimes the fear predominates; but usually hope rules the balance. I look to matrimony as the completion of man. One cannot be a *whole* man until married, but a pitiful fraction thereof merely, a manikin. I look forward to marriage with reverence.

I promise myself much happiness. How soon my hope will be destroyed no one can say. From the character (both of mind and heart) of Miss C. I have every thing to hope, and nothing to fear.

To the Same.

BOSTON, April 23.

. . . The tree of life still stands in paradise, though Adam and Eve be cast out, and Cain murders Abel. So sometimes I console my spirit when I deem that all my present felicity may in a moment turn into dust, bitter dust, or at least vanish like the momentary rainbow. So, indeed, it may be. Sad presentiments sometimes spread their shadows over my path; but I know that two souls made one by love, and *realizing* that union, can laugh at time and space, and live united forever. Besides, Death is only a kind angel with severe countenance, who comes to bless, though with sighs and tears. . . .

The above was written three days after his marriage. The journal celebrates the wedding-day with exuberant verse and tender prayer, accompanied by a "*Codex Matrimonianus*" in Latin, which is inserted here, Englished, to show with what conscientious feeling he entered on the relation which so many assume lightly: —

"Since, by the will of God, a wife is to be given me, it is becoming that I prescribe for myself rules and laws. Therefore, by God's help, I here resolve, promise, and bind myself steadfastly to observe the following regulations: —

1. Never, except for the best of causes, to oppose my wife's will.
2. To discharge all services, for her sake, freely.
3. Never to scold.
4. Never to look cross at her.
5. Never to weary her with commands.
6. To promote her piety.
7. To bear her burdens.
8. To overlook her foibles.
9. To love, cherish, and ever defend her.
10. To remember her always most affectionately in my prayers: thus, God willing, we shall be blessed.

"April xx., MDCCCXXXVII."

The ordination took place June 21, 1837. Mr. Francis preached the sermon; the prayers were by Chandler Robbins, Mr. Cunningham, and Henry Ware; the charge by Caleb Stetson; the right hand of fellowship by George Ripley. John Pierpont and John S. Dwight wrote hymns for the occasion. Dr. Francis warned the young man not to neglect his studies. Henry Ware prayed, "May his fondness for peculiar studies never divert him from doing Thy work!" Both admonitions he resolved to heed.

CHAPTER VI.

WEST ROXBURY.

MR. PARKER's situation at "Spring Street"—for so the place was called—is best described in a few extracts from letters to his classmate Silsbee: "We have a clever house, a fine garden, a good horse. I am at the head of a family of seven souls, 'to be, to do, and to suffer' for them all: no little care. I have become as practical as Stebbins's ideal man; always carry a rule and compass in my pocket; all my 'talk is of bullocks,' pigs, grapes, strawberries, and other things which perish in the using. . . . Our neighbors are pleasant: about fifty or sixty families are in the parish; one hundred to one hundred and fifty worshippers; the people good, quiet, sober, church-going,—capital listeners, none better; so much so, that I tell my friends I think my parishioners are as much blessed in preaching as those of even Dr. Channing: for what is wanting in preaching they make up in listening; which is not the case with the doctor's people, they depending altogether on him. The Sunday school grows under my hand; and once in two weeks I have a teacher's meeting, whereat I explain Bible, which is far better for me and them than all preachment: for I aim at the heart and conscience not less directly than when in the pulpit; and, since there is no formality, the matter goes home, I trust. I preach abundant heresies, and they all go down; for the listeners do not know how heretical they are. Nay, I preach the worst of all things,—transcendentalism, the grand heresy itself, — none calling me to account therefor, but men's faces looking like fires new stirred thereat." Besides this, pastoral visits, which were no ceremonial thing with Mr. Parker; visitations of schools, always a deep concern; professional duties, baptisms, funerals, and the like, — justify him in calling himself a busy man. The reading goes on as usual. The De Wette is progressing; Jacobi, Henry More, the Life of Apollonius of Tyana, Bulwer's "Athens," Fichte, Coleridge, Descartes, are in exercise during midsummer. Spinoza, Gesenius, Ovid, Seneca, are in prospect. There is reading in Homer almost every day. An engagement is made to translate Ammon's "Fortbildung des Christenthums," four volumes octavo: this in July, a month after ordination! "Old studies prosper, — metaphysics, theology, criticism: all that used so much to delight and instruct us flourishes and grows apace in my new situation. Thoughts high as heaven and profound as the centre of the earth sometimes visit me in my loneliness. Then, too, the smiles of love cheer and encourage me."

Of special value was the society he found at West Roxbury, — a small but choice circle of elegant, graceful, cultivated people, used to wealth, accomplished in the arts of life, of open hearts, and, better still, of humane instincts, who lived in such near neighborhood, that a path from Mr. Parker's gate led directly to their gardens and welcoming doors. The fine grounds of Mr. George R. Russell lay adjacent to his own modest domain; and adjoining those again was the estate of Mr. Francis G. Shaw. In both families he was at home on the heartiest terms. All there were his friends, faithful and sympathetic. To be with them was always delightful and refreshing; for they had literature and art, an intelligent interest in public affairs, a high tone of sentiment, and that rich flavor of character which distinguishes people well bred. It was a new world for Theodore, born and bred in poverty, inured to toil, conversant with few persons to whom the world brought bloom and aroma. These were idyllic days, — golden hours spent on lawns, or under verandas, or in the sweet-scented hay-fields, with youth and beauty and wit, and literary enthusiasm, and social merriment. Discussions of the newest book, the last poem, lecture, speech, the freshest speculation, did not take him from study, but relieved the pressure thereof by entertaining the jaded mind.

The neighboring farms had dear and intimate friends, whom he neglected no opportunity of seeing: old friends were never forgotten; new ones were continually added. His heart had room for as many as could feast in it; and his hospitality was as big as his heart. The "prophet's chamber" usually held a guest, whose stay was encouraged; the pleasant study, with flowers looking in at the windows in summer, and the sunlight streaming through the glass in winter, had room for friends as well as for folios, and resounded with the noise of laughter many times when Cranch, with the power of a skilful caricaturist, put Theodore's grotesque fancies on paper, or Francis greeted with loud mirth the fantastical descriptions of some brother-minister from the host's rollicking mind. The fun was exuberant to wildness, but hurt nobody: it was the irrepressible overflow of a nature that could not contain its glee. It had even its earnest, its pathetic side, — the humanity of humor. If there was any thing that Parker enjoyed, it was "taking off" pretenders; but such laughter was near akin to tears. He had a quick eye for qualities. Beauty and joy interested him; but goodness interested him more. "Opposite my house," the journal says, "lives a poor woman. Her husband labors on a farm at a short distance from his home, and receives wages. They have five children, the oldest probably not more than ten years old. The family is entirely dependent on the earnings of the husband. A strange family came into the village, — a Mr. Wallace, with his wife and two small children. They were still poorer than the first; and, to add to their distress, Mrs. Wallace was sick with a pulmonary consumption, and 'very low,' as we say in the country. Now, this good woman finds out Mrs. Wallace, sees her condition, pities her sufferings, and goes to help her. She takes home the little child, lest it disturb the mother by its cries; carries home the soiled linen, washes and irons it. She sits with her by day and night. Mrs. ——, the wife of my orthodox brother, came in to visit her, prayed with her, and frightened the sick woman badly by telling her her time was short; asking her if she ever read her Bible, &c. It made her almost insane for two days. When she slept, a weight seemed to oppress her head: she saw frightful visions, pined for her child, and has been rapidly growing worse. I make no comment."

The absorbing study of this period was the literature of the Bible. The Egyptian and Phœnician alphabets have attractions for him; ancient inscriptions and coins, Carthaginian, Persian, amuse him; the Orphic poems have a share of his time; Meiner's book "On the Doctrine of the One God," Staüdlin "On the Morality of the Drama," fall under his notice: but the Bible literature leads all the rest. The works of Paulus, a great name in rationalistic interpretation, and of G. L. Bauer, who wrote on the "Mythology of the Old and New Testaments," are on his table. Mr. George Ripley, one of the earliest students of the new German criticism and philosophy, live of mind and warm of heart, lent him Eichhorn's "Urgeschichte," and a great many volumes of rationalism besides. Schleiermacher's essay on Luke was one of the most suggestive of these. The famous work of Strauss, the "Leben Jesu," he was already acquainted with. The journal mentions at some length a fragment of a work in Greek on "things incredible," written by one Palæphatus. It was an attempt to resolve the Greek mythological stories into ordinary transactions: as, for example, the horses of

Diomedes devouring their master signifies the expense of cultivating horses, which eat up the substance of the people; Lynceus' piercing sight into and through the ground referred to the discovery of the use of metals; the bull that carried off Europa was a Cretan named Taurus; the hydra that Hercules attacked was a town defended by fifty archers; Niobe's loss of her daughters, and erection of a statue to their memory, suggested the fable of the weeping marble; Scylla was a swift piratical craft that infested the sea about Sicily. "I have been a good deal amused, and perhaps instructed, by the book. How the priests must have exclaimed against the 'impious' book on the day of its appearance! Such books do good. I wish some wise man would now write a book on 'things incredible,' or 'vulgar errors,' and show up the absurdity of certain things commonly believed on the authority of old Jews: to be plain, I mean the Old-Testament miracles, prophecies, dreams, miraculous births, &c."

But the student did not jump hastily at conclusions: he read carefully, and pondered long, feeling his way step by step. He detected the shortcomings of Strauss's mythical theory, and exposed the feebleness of Paulus's common-sense explanations. "There is one objection to the assumption of myths in the New Testament; viz., they belong *to unhistorical times.* Some think myths may exist even in a literary people. For a long time, there was no written account of Jesus Christ: tradition enlarged in the Jewish style; hence much was added to the New Testament. We are not to suppose men sit gravely down, saying, 'Come, let us make us a myth:' they were formed gradually. Some suppose there are only philosophical myths in the New Testament; others, only historical. Schleiermacher calls the history of the temptation a parable. Bauer thinks there are myths in the New Testament coming from the Old Testament: such are some of the stories of the youth of Jesus, angels coming to him, &c. Yet no man can justly believe in myths in the New Testament who does not deny the fact that it was written by contemporaries or eye-witnesses." All of which shows an undecided mind, and indicates, moreover, that his interest in such questions was, thus far at least, rather literary than professional. The serious bent of Mr. Parker's mind was practical. Matters of exegesis did not stir his blood unless they were associated with issues which affected human relations: then they became watch-words and battle-cries. This time had not come; and he read, re-read, considered, commented, in a scholar's temper, with a serene mind. Such studies did not even occupy his thoughts to the exclusion of others of a directly opposite kind. In the very thick of them we come across statistical tables of population and commerce in Massachusetts. Two pages of the folio journal are devoted to a well-considered estimate of the comparative advantages and disadvantages of banks! Compare several of his schemes of work: —

THINGS TO BE DONE THIS WEEK.

1. Finish two sermons.
2. De Wette.
3. Jacobi.
4. Fichte (Ethik).
5. Duty *vs.* inclination.
6. Commence the account of Moses.
7. Begin the translation of Ammon's "Fortbildung Christenthums."

WORK TO BE DONE THIS WEEK.

1. Plant the other side of the brook.
2. Sow the garden-vegetables.
3. Plough the new land.
4. Plant the old alleys.
5. Visit Mr. Keith and Chapin in evening.

6. See about the Sunday school.
7. Get the benches for the vestry.
8. Ask Mr. Ellis to be superintendent.

Here is work laid out for a month:—

1. Continue the translation of Ammon.
2. Continue the study of Plato.
3. Read Tasso and Dante.
4. Iliad.
5. Greek Tragedies.
6. Aristophanes.
7. Goethe's Memoirs.

The work of a year is projected with the same deliberation:—

1. Finish the translation of Ammon; and publish, if possible.
2. De Wette.
3. Course of study on the New Testament.
4. Course of study on the Old Testament.
5. Progress in Syriac.
6. Danish and Swedish.
7. Finish Plato.
8. Continue the study of Greek writers.
9. Dante and Tasso.
10. Spanish Ballads.
11. Commence the *ideal* work.

Such a man as this is certainly in no danger of becoming a "man of one idea."

The tide of life with him seems to be at its flood in the summer and autumn of 1837. Early in the winter, vapors gather in the sky; though from what cause is not apparent. Writing to his friend Andrews in December, he says, "You stated, in that little bit of paper which you call a letter, that you detected something in my bearing which argued that there was unhappiness, at least discontent of some sort, in the wind. I admit its existence in a greater extent than you imagine; but of the cause, *not a word!* Let rumor tell you: *I shall not,* — not even to you. You may think I talk lightly: so I do now; but there are times when I feel heavily. I always knew that I had trouble enough in store; but I never thought it would come in the present shape." About a month later, he puts down the following in the private journal: "I have lost many things; but the greatest was hope. Days there have been when I saw nought else to freshen my eye, weary with looking over the dull waste of my early life. Tired with labors, I have laid down my books beside me, the lamp at summer midnight burning low, all else silent in sleep. Hope visited me. She sat beside me; trimmed my lamp. In her sublime presence I grew calm, composed myself to her majestic features.

"Years have passed over me: Hope never deserted me. Now where is she? She is not all gone. I see her, but not on the earth: she is above. She shall never again fade out of my sight; for she stands on the Rock of ages.

"I often ask myself what I am doing with my one talent; and can only reply, that I deem myself well-nigh wasting it, — preaching to an audience of seventy to a hundred and twenty souls; going about talking tattle with old women; giving good advice to hypocrites; and scattering here and there, I hope, a corn that will one day germinate and bear fruit. Oh, could I be satisfied that I am doing even this last! If I deemed it certain that any word of mine would ever waken the deep inner life of another soul, I should bless God that I am alive and speaking. But I will trust. I am sometimes praised for my sermons. I wish men knew how cold those sleek speeches are. I would rather see one man practising one of my sermons than hear all men praise them." After a visit from Dr. and Mrs. Francis in the summer of 1838, he takes himself to task again. "I have not been in so good spirits as usual to-day: indeed, for a whole fortnight, and that in the most beautiful season of the year, I have been as good as dead." But nothing of this despondency appears in his letters. They are full, fresh, and joyous, without exception, abounding in expressions of sympathy with his friends, and showering merriment on all the incidents that occur. The exhaustion was temporary. The most incidental contact with a cordial fellow-creature revived him. Intellectual intercourse was delightful; but human intercourse was dearer. The hunger of his heart was even more eager than the thirst of his mind. In writing to his intimate friends, he puts them in his debt all the time, not only by the number, but by the length and fulness of his letters, which crowd big sheets of paper with the outpouring of his mind.

There was in Boston an informal association, or club, which met at irregular intervals, generally in the rooms of Mr. Jonathan Phillips, to discuss the living questions of the day, whether religious, political, social, or philosophical. Dr. Channing often came in. George Ripley, Charles Follen, Bronson Alcott, Frederic H. Hedge, Wendell Phillips, and others eminent in the world of thought, appeared with more or less regularity. The journal has notes of meetings at which Mr. Parker was present. They are interesting on many accounts.

"THURSDAY, Feb. 8, 1838. — Went at evening to Mr. Phillips's room at the Tremont House to attend a meeting of the 'Friends.' This is my third meeting with them. The first evening, the question of the progress of civilization was discussed with great power of thought and richness of eloquence, especially on the part of Dr. Channing and Mr. Ripley. The conclusion in which all rested was this: 'That a real vital progress had been made by society since the creation, especially since the time of Jesus Christ; but that certain disadvantages attended this progress: actions passed at an unreal value; vanity, love of show, — in short, all forms of selfishness, — were more common than in other days.' This was a Socratic meeting. Dr. C. is the Socrates. Had the conversation of this evening been written out by Plato, it would equal any of his beautiful dialogues.

"The next Wednesday we spoke upon Mr. Emerson's lecture; and this led to a discussion of the personality of God. It was thought Mr. E.'s doctrines were dangerous; that he denied the personality, which is, practically speaking, to deny the existence, of the Deity. Mr. Ripley accused him of maintaining that God was only an idea formed in the mind of the individual, and then projected into omnipresence. It is the idea of power, love, &c., without any substance to which these attributes belong. I take it, Mr. E. merely denies the materiality of God; though some of his expressions, if taken singly, would almost justify the construction Mr. R. puts upon them. Another charge was that of pantheism; a charge so vague, that every thinking man is liable to it. Certainly one expression of his is on the high road to pantheism: 'The universe, being perfectly beautiful, exists by its own laws, and needs no outward cause.' But this sentence occurred in a connection which belied such construction.

["Touching the personality of God, what do we mean by the term? Personality cannot exist without will. Suffer all my faculties to remain as they are, but annihilate the will, I am no longer a person, an individual: I cannot say 'I:' a fagot of powers has taken the place of I. There are attributes, but no substance to which they belong. How, then, can I conceive of God without personality? But is will the only essential of personality? The question is difficult. I conceive of God as a being easy of access, full of tenderness, whose character is summed up in one word, — Father. Now, the idea of God's *will* unites all these attributes into a being. Here, then, are the attributes of God united with a substance, — the will. What is the essence of God? I know not what is the essence of myself: I cannot tell. The idea of God is no more mysterious than that of *self:* that of the divine personality is as clear as that of human personality. Men have always perplexed themselves in meditating on this subject. They have come to this conclusion: 'He is past finding out.' This is variously expressed by the thinkers of different ages and countries. 'Search not after the

9

essence of God and his laws,' says the old Veda. God is 'Unrevealed Light,' 'the Ineffable,' 'Incomprehensible,' the 'Primal Being,' say the Gnostics. 'The most real of all beings,' says Plato, 'himself without being.' So the mystic can only say 'I am,' 'He is.']

"Mr. Alcott talks of the progress of God, — the Almighty going forward to his own infinity, progressively unfolding himself: an idea to me revolting. Mr. H. utters oracles to the same effect.

"This last evening we discussed the condition of women, especially in the conjugal relation; our apparent coldness towards relatives, its causes, consequences, and remedies; our want of local attachment; want of amusements: yet the new state of things was deemed better than the old.

"Before attending this meeting, I went to Dr. Channing's, staid a couple of hours, and took tea. His conversation was truly delightful, — rather of the nature of discussion. I felt there was a broad common ground between us, notwithstanding the immense superiority of his elevation. We spoke of Dr. Walker's lectures on philosophy. Dr. C. thinks the lecturer approaches very near materialism himself. I. He speaks of thought as putting the brain in action, as the digestive force moves the stomach, and the hepatic the liver. Now, the digestive force, acting by the stomach, secretes chyme; the hepatic force, acting by the liver, secretes gall; but thought, acting through the brain, secretes — what? Not thought. Again: the hepatic and stomachic force is physical: why not also the cerebral force? And then where is the spirituality of men? II. He says the attributes of matter — such as solidity, divisibility, extension, attraction — are totally unlike the attributes of spirit, — thought, feeling, &c.; but he (Dr. W.) *does not show that there is not a common substance in which both inhere.* [This admitted, the essence of matter and of spirit is the same: all matter is spirit, and all spirit is matter.] III. He says the difference between man and the animal is this: man has spiritual powers, existing for *their own sake;* animals similar powers, existing, not for their own sakes, but for the sake of their bodies. Man thinks. Why? That he may think; beasts, that they may be fed. Beast never says 'I;' has no personality. Dr. C. agrees with this. [But how can it be known? Can we enter the consciousness of the horse, and learn that he never separates himself from all other creatures, and has no self-consciousness ?] We see reason in brutes, not conscience, not religion. Hence they are mortal.

"Dr. C. thinks no injustice done to brutes by their mortality, but acknowledges the difficulty attending it."

These extracts show the drift of speculation in New England thirty-five years ago, before the modern school of Darwin and others came up. Thus boldly did thinking men form and express opinions among themselves, having no fear of each other. There was an admirable freedom combined with an equally admirable modesty. Theodore listens and thinks, as courageous as any, but, perhaps, with something less of the gravely intellectual spirit that entertains ideas apart from their sentimental, moral, or social relations. He hears that Mr. Francis is reading a book by one Richter, a German, who denies the immortality of the soul. He is surprised to learn that some ministers of the gospel are disposed to agree with him. Yet he has no feelings of acrimony, he falls into no hysterics, but asks his friend to lend him the book when he has done with it, unless somebody else wants it more. Mr. Parker shows his hand this spring in an article printed in "The Boston Quarterly Review" for July on Dr. J. G. Palfrey's "Lectures on the Jewish Scriptures and Antiquities." The paper handled the matter under discussion with a freedom that many thought disrespectful. The writer declares that his own hair stood up when he thought of what he had written. He is accused, as he was so often afterwards, of being sarcastic; to which he replies thus to the friend who made the charge: —

To William Silsbee.

West Roxbury, Nov. 27, 1838.

You think there is sarcasm. I do not think that is too strong a word; though I never intended any thing like it. I hate sarcasm; yet am, perhaps, sarcastic. I wished to indulge in a little harmless pleasantry; but I fear the dean would not share in the mirth he excited. You think I indulge in the ludicrous vein too much: such is my propensity, no doubt. But how ought things to be treated? Light things lightly, grave things gravely, ridiculous things ridiculously. I must think ridicule has its place, even in criticism. E.g.: Suppose Mr. Poyer should write a book on the miracles of the Saviour, attempting to explain them as the result of animal magnetism: a critic might show the attempt was not successful; and show also how ridiculous it was to make the attempt, and represent the Saviour as filling the five thousand with a fancy they had eaten, and letting them go off under that impression.

To my mind, William, there is something strange and startling in the assertion, that man has been so constituted, that he can, by the use of his faculties, on condition of obedience to their laws, achieve all the wonders of science, and take the dimensions of the planets, their where-abouts and their what-abouts, and yet never be able, by the use of his highest faculties, — I mean the *spontaneous religious sentiments* (which Jacobi sometimes calls faith, sometimes reason and conscience), — and by obedience to their laws, to learn religious truth, and to be certain it was *truth* he learned, and not error. Is it not most of all important for man to settle the questions of Deity, to possess religious truth and religious life? Has God, so bountiful in bestowing other powers, given him none to discover these truths, the most important, the most necessary? When the little (the carnal and temporary) is so abundantly provided for, would the spiritual and eternal be neglected? If I were told (by an angel from that planet) that the inhabitants of Uranus differed much from us, that they had seventy senses to commune with the outer world, with my present views of God I should say with confidence, then must they have seven hundred internal senses to commune with God, and should expect him to add seven thousand! Is it not the case, William, that, while the Almighty takes such bounteous care of all little things that no animal can be found in utmost height or utmost deep, all of whose wants are not *perfectly satisfied*, — none found wandering up and down, seeking rest and finding none, — he lays most stress on the most important of his works; giving to man, e.g., such uncontested superiority, — reasoning, social, æsthetic, religious, and moral powers? . . .

I am better satisfied of religious and moral truth than of any thing besides. My eye roams to the stars, and returns to the frost on my window which reflects their light; but the perception only startles me with its beauty. I can doubt the existence of stars and frost-work; but in religious truth I doubt nothing. The spirit affirms. In science I have a root of truth: in common matters, where the senses reach, I have only opinions. I keep their laws; but they *can* give nothing more. In morality and religion I have TRUTHS of which I am perfectly certain. Why is it? Because they have been told me? But for any one of these one thousand sensual opinions, which are nothing worth to me, — *vox et prœterea nihil*, — fleeting opinions, I have a fountain within me whence to draw infinite supplies of religious and moral truth. Did miracles open the fountain? Did they create it? The dean says there is no such. . . .

Next you ask if I think a man can attain to all religious truth without revelation. No, no, no! to none at all. But how comes the revelation? It is a revelation in consciousness, made on the single condition that man lives by the "law of the Spirit of Life," and always made when the condition is fulfilled. I take it that all truth is revelation (though, as there are different modes of truth, so there are different degrees of revelation made to different men), and that all revelation is strictly in conformity with the law of our being, and in conformity with the *highest* powers and laws. I am dependent upon God for all things. I have no wisdom without him. In him I live and move, &c. To be without him — i. e., to be *carnally-minded*—is spiritual death, — death to the truth. So, William, I believe no man discovers truth without a revelation. So the truth is not *man's*, but *God's*. Did you ever say, "That is *my* truth"? But I believe revelation is always made *through* and *by* the laws of the Spirit, and not in a foreign way. Now, I cannot think the revelation of Moses or of Jesus different *in kind* from that of Numa or Socrates, but infinitely *in degree*.

But the truth flashes on the man. You have felt such revelations. We labor upon a thought, trying to grasp the truth: we almost have the butterfly in our hand, but cannot get it. Again we try: it will not come. We walk, sit, pray: it will not come. At last, in some moment, it flashes on us; the crystals form in a moment; the work is all done. Whence came it? I

9*

do not know. It is in these burning moments that *life* is lived: the rest is all drudgery, beating the bush, planting and weeding and watering; this is the harvest-hour. These hours are few to any man, — perhaps not more than two in a week; but yet all the real thought of the man is compressed into these burning moments. The Methodist dates his *new birth* from them: the Orthodox are attempting to reproduce them in four days' meetings, &c. The mystic is united to God in these moments. Paul was caught up to the second heaven. Now, I believe God is the fountain of truth, which overflows from him into all minds that lie low in his power, wishing to feed these minds of theirs in wise passiveness. But how this influence comes I do not know. I know nothing about the manner in which my soul is connected with God: I only know the fact. It is a matter of experience. My faith is greater than myself. Conscience, the religious sentiment, settles truths which I am only to obey; for I have no control over them.

Now a word upon miracles. I believe most heartily the miracles of the New Testament, in the Gospels and Acts. Some of them I should explain as natural events; such as Paul's conversion, Peter's liberation, perhaps the death of Ananias (I doubt on this), Paul's wonderful visits from the angels: I do not think of any others but the gift of tongues. Now, I do not see reason for believing *any* of the *miracles of the Old Testament.* The evidence does not satisfy me: the occasion is not worthy of them; the consequence is nothing. All old nations claim similar miracles (you remember those in Livy and the Greeks), which rest on similar evidence. If any one of the miracles (of the Old Testament) rested on sufficient evidence, I would believe it. Besides, this is to be remembered, — the Orientals never made a sharp distinction between the natural and the supernatural: you see this in the story of the sun and the moon standing still; and often in the Psalms and historic books they would represent matters as miraculous which were not so. They do the same now. . . .

I would say the same of Christian miracles. They relate to the history, but not to the doctrines, of Christianity. Prove to me that they never took place, that there never was a Paul or John or Jesus, and I will still prove that Christianity is true: it was true before Jesus Christ; for it is older than the creation.

It is true still. In a word, its truth or falsity has nothing to do with the accompanying miracles, I fancy. It makes no difference whether Socrates taught in a surtout or a scarf, by day or by night: his teaching was false or true by *itself.* I do not see how the *doctrines* of Mosaism involve historical questions.

West Roxbury, Aug. 10, 1838.

. . . I have never had a summer of more delightful study than the present; never found more satisfaction in theological and philosophical pursuits. I have solved many questions which have long perplexed and troubled me; and have grown, in some small measure, calmer than of old time. Tranquillity is one of my *attainable* but unattained virtues. Some of my inquiries have been historical, others critical; but philosophy has given me most delight this season. I do not say that the greatest questions are yet solved, or ever will be. They stand now like fire-breathing dragons in my path: I cannot drive them away. But, though they often heat, they never bite me. Mr. Francis says, in expressing his despair of philosophy, "It is better to give it all up, and study the facts of Nature with Kirby and Spence, and White of Selborne."

Who can do it if he would? The sphinx will have an answer, or you die. You must read the riddle. Love of philosophy may be "the last infirmity of noble minds;" but I will cling to it still. You ask what effect my speculations have on my practice: you will acquit me of boasting when I say, the most *delightful,* — better than I could hope. My preaching is *weak* enough, you know; but is made ten times more spiritual and strong by my views of nature, God, Christ, man, and the Sacred Scriptures. In my religious conversation, I tell men religion is as necessary as head to the body, light to the eye, thought to the mind. I ask them to look into their hearts, and see if it is not so. They say I tell them the doctrines of common sense; and it is true.

Questions are often asked on heretical points. I had to tell a man the other day that Paul was overtaken by a thunder-cloud in his Damascus journey, &c. He said it made it all plain. I tell men that Moses and the writers of the Old Testament had *low* views of God, — the best men could have in those times: they understand it, and believe the New-Testament account of

God. In regard to Christ, they see a beauty in his character when they look upon him as a man who had wants like theirs, trials, temptations, joy, and sorrows like their own, yet stood higher than the tempter, overcome in every trial.

They see the same elements in themselves; but some of them almost despair of his elevation of character. I can tell them that even he has not exhausted human nature; that what is not *behind* them is *before* them; that a future is better than a past; and that they, by a faithful use of their powers, may yet be, in another world, as far before Jesus as he is now before them. I dwell mainly on a few *great* points: viz., the nobleness of man's nature; the lofty ideal he should set before him; the degradation of men of this time, their low aims, and worthless pleasure; on the necessity of being true to their convictions, whatever they may be, with the certainty, that, if they do this, they have the whole omnipotence of God working for them, as the artist brings the whole power of the river to turn his wheel. Also I dwell on the *character* and *providence* of God, and the exactness and beauty of his laws, natural, moral, and religious. My confidence in the Bible is increased. It is not a sealed book, but an open one. I consider there are three witnesses of God in creation. 1. *Works of Nature:* these do not perfectly reveal him; for we cannot now understand all its contradictions. 2. The words of our fellow-men. This confirms all the wisdom of all the past. It includes the Sacred Scriptures. Parts of it differ vastly *in degree* from other writings, but not in *kind.* 3. *The infinite sentiments of each individual soul.* Now, I lay stress on the first, but more on the second, and still more on the third: for a man may have just as bright revelations in his own heart as Moses or David or Paul, — I might say, as Jesus; but I do not think any man ever has had such a perfect God-consciousness as he.

But Paul says the spirit searches all things, even the "deep things of God;" and I dare not fancy it can never go beyond the writings of the Old Testament. I find nothing in the Gospels that can ever perish. Paul mistook sometimes, Jesus never: men no more understand his words than they can do his miracles. "Be perfect as God." Do they know what this means? No, no! My confidence in the gospel is immeasurably increased. I see that it has meaning, profoundest meaning, in its plainest figures. "He that is greatest among you shall be your servant." What meaning! It will be understood a thousand years hence, not before. But I see the gospel is human, but infinitely almost above present humanity. I feel bound to communicate my views just so fast and so far as men can understand them; no farther. But, if they do not understand them when I propound them, the fault, I think, is mine, and not theirs. I often find it difficult to make myself understood; for I doubt much you could find a more ignorant set in the State than my congregation of one hundred and twenty. But there are some twenty who are intelligent; all are *moral;* and I *respect* them *all.* There is but little *religious* life among them. My predecessor had little, and could not, poor man! impart what he did not possess. We will have a long talk upon these points; for you know the pen is dull and cold, while the tongue is nearer the heart. My heart and my hand go together like two turtle-doves, who perch on the same bough, and eat of the same food, and drop water in one another's beaks. My religion warms my philosophy, and my philosophy gives strength to my religion. You know I do not boast in all this.

The finest spirits come about him; among the rest, William Henry Channing, — "a most delightful man, full of the right spirit; a little diseased in the region of consciousness, but otherwise of most remarkable beauty of character; full of good tendencies, of noblest aspirations; an eye to see the evils of society, a heart to feel them, a soul to hope better things; a willingness to endure all self-denial to accomplish the end whereto he is sent; not covered by thickest wrappages, which rather obscure his worthy uncle, whom I venerate perhaps too much."

The intellectual event of the summer was Mr. Emerson's celebrated "Address" before the graduating class of the Cambridge Divinity School.

"THURSDAY, July 15. — After, as usual, preaching, Sunday-schooling, teachers' meetinging, &c., wife and I went over to Brookline, and proceeded to Cambridge to hear the valedictory sermon by Mr. Emerson. In this he surpassed himself as much as he surpasses others in a general way. I shall give no abstract, so beautiful, so just, so true, and terribly sublime, was his picture of the faults of the Church in its present position. My soul is roused; and this week I shall write the long-meditated sermons on the state of the Church and the duties of these times."

To George E. Ellis, then in Europe, he writes, Aug. 7, —

"You know Emerson was to preach the sermon before the class. I heard it. It was the noblest of all his performances: a little exaggerated, with some philosophical untruths, it seemed to me; but the noblest, the most inspiring strain I ever listened to. It caused a great outcry; one shouting, 'The Philistines be upon us!' another, 'We be all dead men!' while the majority called out, 'Atheism!' The dean said, 'That part of it — as I apprehend — which was not folly was downright atheism.'"

Later he writes to the same correspondent, —

"I sent you Emerson's address to the divinity students. It has made a great noise. Mr. Norton opened the cannonade with a broadside aimed at Emerson, Cousin, Carlyle, Schleiermacher, Shelley, and a paper called 'The Western Messenger.' This provoked several replies, — one of singular beauty from Theophilus Parsons; one from the iron pen of Brownson, in 'The Post;' and one from J. F. Clarke, in defence of the article in 'The Messenger.' Ministers preached on Emerson's sermon. Henry Ware delivered a sermon on the personality of God, which, it is said, Emerson denies; and the students of the Divinity School come out, cap in hand, and say, '*Peccavimus omnes*,' the last class in particular, and request Henry Ware to publish his sermon, which is said to be a very good one, and to the point. Brownson writes a fierce review in 'The Quarterly;' which, after all, is rather good than bad, though it contains some severities. Chandler Robbins speaks mildly, as his manner is, of the whole affair, and calls the vulgar rant of denouncing Emerson a 'vulgar clamor' and 'the popular roar.' A. N. is indignant thereat; and this very minute I have read a fourth article of his, in this morning's 'Advertiser,' on Emerson, in which he says infidelity and atheism have been long preached by the Unitarian ministers, — not by all, but by some few. All this makes a world of talk. It is thought chaos is coming back: the world is coming to an end. Some seem to think the Christianity which has stood some storms will not be able to weather this gale; and that truth, after all my Lord Bacon has said, will have to give it up now. For my part, I see that the sun still shines, the rain rains, and the dogs bark; and I have great doubts whether Emerson will overthrow Christianity this time."

The air is filled with "wild views." The same letter continues: —

"Simmons was ordained last Tuesday at Dr. Channing's, as evangelist, to go to Mobile. Bellows preached the sermon; Dr. Follen gave the charge, Ripley the right hand; Walker read the Scriptures; Henry Ware made the prayer. All was quite transcendental, except Mr. Ware's part, which, of course, was savory enough without transcendentalism. The sermon is described as being particularly 'liberal;' the preacher maintaining that goodness is goodness in a heathen; that an Esquimau would not be turned out of heaven if he were a good and religious man; and that a true and sincere prayer, though offered to an idol, would go to the right place, for the only God would take it. The discourse alarmed and shocked the more backward of the brethren; but the younger-hearted were not disturbed.

"The other day they discussed the question in the Association, whether Emerson was a Christian. G. said he was not, and defended his position; rather poorly, you may suppose. J. P. maintained he was an atheist. But nobody doubted he was a virtuous and most devout man, — one who would enter heaven when they were shut out. Of course, they were in a queer predicament: either they must acknowledge a man may be virtuous and yet no Christian (which most of them thought it a great heresy to suppose), and religious, yet an atheist (which is a contradiction, — to be without God, and yet united to God), or else affirm that Emerson was neither virtuous nor religious, which *they could not prove.* J. W. and N. L. F. thought he should be called a Christian if he desired the name. Some of the ministers think we need to have certain 'fundamentals' fixed for us all to swear by, lest the new school among the Unitarians should carry the whole body up to the height of transcendentalism. It is notorious that the old Unitarians, in the days when there was fighting for the faith, had no such fundamentals. It is quite evident there are now two parties among the Unitarians: one is for progress; the other says, 'Our strength is to stand still.' Dr. Channing is the real head of the first party: the other has no head. Some day or other there will be a rent in the party: not soon, I trust, however."

From all this it will be seen that Mr. Parker's interest in his profession was sincere. He was a minister; and nothing that concerned his ministry was indifferent to him. But he interpreted his ministry in a large way, and occupied himself with a hundred matters which seemed but distantly related to his calling. All literature in his eyes was sacred literature; all facts were divine facts. Scattered up and down the pages of the journal are curious studies into the mysterious phenomena of nature and life,— unaccountable cures, presentiments, previsions, stories of second-sight, incidents old and new illustrating the connection between things visible and things invisible. To the last of his life he was gleaning accounts of prophecy and miracle. His reading was literally universal in its range. He takes up Chapman the poet, Herrick, Wither, Drummond, Wotton, Flecknoe,—from whom he copies verses,—Surrey, Suckling: no matter who; there is honey for him in every flower. He bursts into such glee on hearing of More's poems from Dr. Francis, that two men working in the garden think him crazy. The early Christian Hymns, the Milesian Fables, "Cupid and Psyche," Campanella, biographies of Swedenborg and others,—these were his mental recreations. Richter he read, but says little about. Goethe always interested him: "I shall not dare attempt a *mécanique celeste* of Goethe. The greatness of the subject appalls me. My plummet will not fathom his deeps, nor will my telescope reveal all his far heights. He is so vast and so many-sided, I am puzzled, lost in the labyrinth of the man. The 'Farbenlehre' strikes me with amazement. I looked for a fanciful work, full of ingenious theories, — conclusion before the fact, and even against the fact; but, instead, the work is compact, systematic, vigorous. It overthrows my old notion of colors. In my notice of Dwight's translation of his poems, I shall speak of Goethe only as a poet, and confine myself mainly to his lyrics, 'Reinecke Fuchs' and 'Hermann and Dorothea.' The last is my especial favorite." But he cannot get over the moral defects of the great German: "Goethe is an artist, not a man. . . . His patriotism seems quite low: there is no warm beat out from his heart. . . . Goethe never seems to have looked on men as brothers. Most men have a technical standpoint from which they survey the world. Ministers look on men as things to be converted; kings, as things to be ruled. Goethe viewed them, first, as things to minister to his pleasure; second, as objects of art. 'Go to, now,' says he; 'let us make us a poem.' His perfect artistic skill is wonderful. In his finished works there is scarce any thing in bad taste. . . . He talks of self-renunciation and the like, but never practises it."

Through these sunny fields of literature the torrent of severer study ploughs its way on. Hume, Gibbon, Robertson, are trifles; Schleiermacher, Bouterwek, Baur, Hegel, Laplace, Leibnitz, are more serious. Bopp's "Vergleichende Grammatik," Karcher's "Analecta," Meiner's "History of Religions," Rimannus' "History of Atheism" (Latin), are samples of the solid reading. The books he has not within reach, — Abélard, for instance, and Averroës, — he stretches out his hand, and obtains from afar. Wilkinson and Rossellini are familiar to him. Hesiod he comments on minutely. No book is mentioned without some notice of its contents and a critical remark, which proves it to have been read. Plato is a constant companion. The only notice of Shakspeare we find is of the Sonnets, which delight him with their glow of feeling. Is it wonderful that this man now and then fainted, and fell into moods of sadness?

"Thursday, Friday, Saturday. — unwell the first, and sick the two last, of these days. Have had no thoughts, save on Saturday night, when a real gush from the heavenly fount ran through the dusty bed of my brooklet. It gives life; and a sermon is already getting forward through its quickening influence. The critique on Goethe has grown into shape, and sundry flowers for my picture-poem have begun to unfold; but the headache still lingers, —

'Though often took leave, yet seemed loath to depart.'

"What a fool I am to be no happier! I have enough of the outward of life (bating some few sorrows known only to myself); am engaged in congenial employment. I should be much happier, — pshaw! I should be much *nobler*. Let happiness happen as it may: it is an accident, not the essence. Let me be more *manly*, *true*, simple, Christian. I am not doing my work: I am too idle; too much afraid of the world.

"This week has been entirely wasted. One *good hour* of thought a week is all I will ever ask. Then all the growth is effected: the rest is only digging and watering and pruning and lopping. I have had more than one, — one on Monday, and one to-night. Yet I have *done* but little."

The special causes of this occasional despondency are not disclosed. There was no serious ill-health: his habits were regular, simple, wholesome. In the pleasant weather he was much out of doors, planting and trimming in his garden. He took long walks, visiting Boston and the neighboring towns on foot; doing his ten, fifteen, and twenty miles a day without fatigue. In summer his pedestrian exploits would have tasked the vigor of any but a very strong man. He once journeyed from New York to Boston on foot, making about thirty miles a day. He walked easily through the White-Mountain region, ascending Mount Washington from the Notch and back the same day; and betimes the next morning started off for Franconia. His mirthfulness, the natural overflow of animal spirits, the sparkling wit and frolic merriment of his near friends in West Roxbury, the variety of his studies, the diversion of the lightest literature, — for Bulwer's novels, and Longfellow's romances, and Marryatt's tales, were in his hands, — saved him from the oppression of overwork. He mingled freely with people; was no solitary; and the people with whom he had most to do were simple-hearted, plain, homely folks, whom he met on the warm ground of a common humanity. He was not morbid: there was not a touch of the morbid element in his constitution. The cries that broke from him, like those voiced above, came partly from his heart, and partly from his soul. He was a hungry man, — hungry for knowledge, and hungry for affection. The hunger for knowledge could be appeased by books: of them there were enough, and they never failed him. The hunger for affection was less easily satisfied. Wife, friends, lovers, failed to provide bread enough for him. His thirst for confidence and sympathy of the genuine manly sort was literally insatiable.

"At home nominally; but, since wife has gone, my home is in New Jersey. I miss her absence — wicked woman! — most exceedingly. I cannot sleep or eat or work or live without her. It is not so much the affection she bestows on me as that she receives by which I am blessed. I want some one always in the arms of my heart to caress and comfort: unless I have this, I mourn and weep. But soon shall I go to see the girl once more. Meantime, and all time, Heaven bless her! I can do nothing without Lydia, — not even read."

The fear that he was to be childless was exceedingly bitter to him. The children of his friends he treated as if they were his own, — petted them, gave them endearing names; but they were not his own, and they only increased the sense of vacancy in his heart.

But deeper than this, even, was the feeling of baffled aspirations which came to torment him in his hours of suspended effort. He was not hungry for fame or power or riches; but he was hungry for attainment; and the more he attempted, the less he was satisfied with his accomplishment.

But these moods of depression were comparatively few. Such passages as those quoted above occur, perhaps, a dozen times in all the volumes of the journal; and they are followed by words of strength that seem to rebuke them. On the same page with these, as if written with the same stroke of the pen, is one of his sketches of work for the week: —

1. Write a sermon, and finish one not completed.
2. Finish Goethe's "Farbenlehre."
3. Baur's "Gnosis."
4. Do something to Ammon.
5. Critique, — Hebrew Lexicon.
6. Begin Augusti's Einleitung to A. T.

His enjoyment of his literary friends was intense, and it was continual. He had long and frequent talks and walks with George Ripley, deriving fresh vigor from that cheerful, buoyant, accomplished mind. Mr. Ripley was one of his great stimulators, as Dr. Francis was, perhaps, his chief support, in matters of pure erudition. "George Ripley and his wife came to our house Friday, and staid until the next Friday. We were full of joy and laughter all the time of their visit." His conversations with Dr. Channing on the sabbath, the New Testament, the character of Jesus, the mythical theory, the morality of the Gospels as compared with that of the best heathen, were suggestive. Channing was in some respects the more, in others the less, conservative. He rather shocked Theodore by his doctrine that conscience must be educated, — an idea which Theodore ridiculed, holding to the infallibility of conscience, and maintaining that it will always decide rightly, if the case is fairly put before it, and old habits have not darkened its vision. Channing even went so far as to question whether we needed an infallible guide, — whether such a guide would not be rather a disadvantage than otherwise; but, in regard to the gospel morality, he was inclined to think that his friend did less than justice to Christianity. He was persuaded that the character of Jesus was different *in kind* from his own; he accepted the Bible miracles as distinct in genus from those of other nations or books: in all which opinions Parker dissented emphatically from him. In other words, Parker was a pure transcendentalist, Channing only a partial one. There were discussions with Mr. Alcott on the comparative merits, aims, and work of Dr. Channing and Mr. Garrison. George Bancroft cheered him with his brave confidence in the popular desire for spiritual truths. Convers Francis was a fountain of living water. He walked to Andover to see Moses Stuart, the famous "orthodox" professor; found him "full of talk and anecdote, very uncouth in his manners, broad in his mind, and free in his spirit, but crude with undigested learning and mixed beliefs." He even called on Mr. Norton, who always received him coldly; and, failing to find communion of heart, paid a tribute to the neatness of his mental operations and the perfect order of his papers.

The event of 1839, in the Unitarian world, was Mr. Norton's address to the alumni of the Divinity School on "The Latest Form of Infidelity," a performance which revived the war between the old and the new schools. "Is it not weaker than you ever fancied?" Theodore writes to Miss Peabody. "What a cumbrous matter he makes Christianity to be! You must believe it is authenticated by miracles; nor that only, but that this is the only way in which it can be attested. I doubt that Jesus himself could be a Christian on these terms. Did you notice the remarkable mistranslations of the German passages? They are such as no tyro could make, I should fancy. It will do one good work: it will present the subject to the public mind; and now we may have a fair discussion." To Mr. Silsbee he writes, "Ripley is writing the reply to Mr. Norton. It will make a pamphlet of about one hundred pages octavo, and is clear, strong, and good. He will not say all that I wish might be said; but, after we have seen that, I will handle, in a letter to you, certain other points not approached by Ripley. There is a higher word to be said on this subject than Ripley is disposed to say just now. But a long controversy will probably grow out of this: ink will be spilled on both sides, and hard names called in the excess of Christian charity that usually attends religious controversies. I find no men among the Unitarian ministers who like the address: even Dr. Parkman thinks it weak. But some of the lay brethren think the matter fixed; that Mr. Norton has 'done transcendentalism up.'"

The points that Mr. Parker wished presented were fundamental. How does man attain to religion? whence get the essential truth thereof? What is meant by a revelation? Is revelation necessary in order to a vital and sufficient religion? Has the revelation been made to all nations, or so that all nations have had an opportunity to become acquainted with it? Is Christianity a peculiar revelation, or the perfection of all previous revelations? These points he proposed to open in a pamphlet by "Isaac Smith." The pamphlet was written and published, but under another title: "The Previous Question between Mr. Andrews Norton and his Alumni moved and handled in a Letter to all those Gentlemen, by Levi Blodgett." And a very admirable tractate it was for clearness, pith, and point. Planting himself on the ground that man has a spiritual nature endowed with original capacity to apprehend primary religious truth directly, without the mediation of sacrament, creed, or Bible, he stood outside and above the controversy that raged about him. His faith, being intuitive, was unassailable by historical doubt or literary criticism. Every thing might go, — Old Testament, New Testament, miracles, ordinances, formularies: he was safe. On the question of literary criticism his mind was far from clear; but he was content that it should be so. He would answer questions as well as he could when they came up; but he would not fret if they were unanswered. He would not timidly thrust them aside, nor would he rashly jump at conclusions that were not warranted by his discoveries. He was deeply, almost passionately, concerned that people should not rest their beliefs in God, duty, immortality, on external evidence; that they should trust in the revelations that come to their own souls: but there his concern stopped. He made no war on opinions as such, but on the principles relied on to justify opinions, and on the spirit in which opinions were held. Men might believe, if they would, in the Bible, Hebrew and Christian; in the miraculous birth and peculiar nature of Christ; in the incarnation, the transfiguration, the resurrection. He would not molest them, provided they believed, first of all, in the soul of course: being thus justified in thinking freely, he thought freely; being privileged to use his intellect, he used it.

To Dr. Francis.

"It seems to me most of us set a false value on the writings of the New Testament. We take them to be our standard of life and doctrine; and yet probably *no learned and free Christian thinker believes all that is contained in any writer of the New Testament.* Two evangelists evidently believe the miraculous conception; all, perhaps, credited the popular notions about 'possessions.

Matthew, Mark, and John do not say a living *dove* descended on Jesus; but Luke does say it. Can there be any doubt the first three evangelists supposed that *words were spoken in an articulate voice* announcing his acceptance with God? Certainly there can be no doubt that they, and the *Saviour himself*, as well as Paul and Peter, misunderstood passages of the Old Testament, and misapplied them. No doubt Paul thought he saw 'angels.' I don't believe Luke thought the Damascus journey a natural affair, or that Paul thought it was less than miraculous. Peter and John need not be mentioned, and still less the Epistle to the Hebrews; for in all these the incongruities are more remarkable, perhaps, than in the other parts of the New Testament. Now, if the New Testament is a standard of life and doctrine to you and me, we are bound to believe these statements (if possible). But we *do not believe them*. This is all right; but the people believe them, or think they *must* believe them, which is still worse. Now, as you said the other day, how different the Bible as you studied it at home from the Bible as your parishioners listened to it at church! Is it necessary there should always be this *clerical view*, and this *laical view* so different from it? Would not the people be *better*, *wiser*, and *holier* if they were emancipated from this stupid superstition which now hangs like a millstone about their necks? It seems to me, if the true *inspiration* of the New Testament was understood, if men could read it as they read Plato or Seneca (not that the New Testament is not incomparably superior to them), they would be more enlightened and inspired thereby. I take it, the main difference between us and the Orthodox is not respecting the doctrine of the Trinity, or total depravity, or the fall, or election (for we all agree near enough on these points, and believe in 'God the Father,' in revelations *in* man, which is the *Son*, and in revelations *to* man, which is the Holy Spirit, &c.), but in respect to the Scriptures. The Orthodox place the Bible above the Soul; we, the Soul above the Bible. They tell us, that, when you and I were born, all revelation was at an end, all the capital prizes of humanity withdrawn before our time. When we go up to the bar of God, and ask for our mite, they say, 'You have Moses and the prophets: hear them.' In short, they say, 'The canon was closed before you were born: you are to study its letter, to get out its spirit; that is all.'

We do not believe this statement. Is revelation at an end? Is the Bible better than the soul? The Hindoo says that of his *Veda;* the Mohammedan, of his *Koran.* But, if the Christian says so, he *dies;* for Christianity is the religion of freedom. So the fact that we always take texts from the Bible, read its *good* passages, and pass over its *objectionable* clauses, and allegorize, or put a higher sense to passages, tends to mislead men as to the true nature of the book. Do not suppose I have any disposition to undervalue the Bible: I only want the people to understand it as it is. I remember talking with old Mr. John Richardson about the Bible once. He said he had recently read the first part of the Old Testament again: and *he was sorry he had read it, because he could not believe it; and, before, he thought he believed all.*

"Let any sober man read De Wette's 'Biblical Dogmatics,' and he will be astonished to see how many doctrines are taught in the Bible which enlightened men cannot believe. I must think, that by and by, centuries hence, the Old Testament will be dropped out from the Church: then the New Testament will follow, or only be used as we now use other helps. I can't but wish, with you, that Jesus had written his own books; but even then they must have contained some things local and temporary."

To the Same.

MARCH 22, 1839.

. . . Is not this plain that the New Testament contains numerous myths? Certainly the book of Acts has several, — Paul's Damascus journey; Peter's delivery from prison; Paul's shipwreck; the story of the ascension; of the miraculous gift of tongues. We can explain all these things naturally; but did the compiler of this queer book explain them in this way? What right have we to use a different system of exegesis from that we apply to the apocryphal Gospels and every other writing? Not the smallest. But we cannot believe the literal statement of Luke: so we attempt to save his credit, and invent a system of interpretation for the purpose. But, in the same manner, we could make the story of John Gilpin an allegorical history of the origin, progress, and perfection of Christianity.

The Gospels are not without their myths, — the miraculous conception, the temptation, &c. Now, the question is, Where are they to end? Who will tell us where the myth begins, and the history ends? Do not all the miracles belong to the mythical part? The resurrection—is not that also a myth? I know you will not be horror-struck at any doubts an honest lover of truth may suggest; and certainly I see not where to put up the bar between the true and the false. Christianity itself was before Abraham, and is older than the creation, and will stand forever; but I have sometimes thought it would stand better without the New Testament than with it.

CHRIST.

From the Journal.

"How much do we idealize him? Very much, I suspect. I look on the Christ of tradition as a very different being from the ideal Christ. The latter is the highest form of man we can conceive of,—a perfect incarnation of the Word; the former a man, perhaps of passions not always under command, who had little faults and weaknesses that would offend us. He must have been fatigued at times, and therefore dull. His thoughts came like mine: so he was sometimes in doubt, perhaps contradicted himself, and taught things not perfectly consistent with reason; or, at best, gave utterance to crude notions. From the nature of the case, he could not do otherwise. Thought is life generalized and abstract: it comes, therefore, only as we live. So, from year to year, and day to day, Christ must have generalized better as he lived more. His plans evidently were not perfectly formed at first: he fluctuates; does not know whether he shall renounce Moses or not. He evidently went on without any plan of action, and, like Luther at the Reformation, effected more than he designed. At first, perhaps, he meditated simply a reform of Mosaism; but finally casts off all tradition, and starts a fresh soul.

"His power of miracle-working is an element of the soul; we find it in all history: it is a vein running through all history, coming near the surface of life only in the most elevated characters, and in their raptest states of mind. So the central rocks only crop out in mountains. We all feel this miracle-power ideally (Alcott says *actually* likewise, and perhaps he's right: I can feel something of it, supposing it is what Emerson calls demoniacal influence). Jesus, a greater man than ever lived before or since, lived it actually. His miracles, therefore, were natural acts; not contrary to outward nature, but above it. To man they were *natural;* to the mass of matter, *supernatural.* So he can raise the dead, multiply loaves, walk on the sea.

"His inspiration I can understand still better. There can be but one *kind* of inspiration; it is the intuition of truth: but one *mode* of inspiration; it is the conscious presence of the Highest, either as Beauty, Justice, Usefulness, Holiness, or Truth, — the felt and perceived presence of Absolute Being infusing itself into me. . . .

"Christ, I fancy, was one of the greatest souls born into the world of time, and did also more perfectly than any other man fulfil the conditions of inspiration: so the Spirit dwelt in him bodily. His was the highest inspiration, his the divinest revelation. But this must be said of actualities, not of possibilities. It is folly, not to say impiety, to say God cannot create a greater soul than Jesus of Nazareth. Who shall attempt to foreshorten God, and close the gates of time against him, declaring that no more of his Spirit can be by any possibility incarnated? Jesus was cut off at an early age, the period of blossom, not fruitage. . . .

"The Christ of tradition I shall preach down one of these days to the extent of my ability. I will not believe the driving beasts out of the temple with a whip; the command to Peter to catch a fish; still less the cursing the fig-tree, and the old wives' fable about the ascension."

PAUL AND CHRISTIANITY.

From the Journal.

"What would have been the result if St. Paul had not been converted on his Damascus journey? Take the life of St. Paul out of the Christian Church, and how much is left? Would Christianity have sunk down into a Jewish sect, like that of the Essenes? or would it, by its inherent might, have created a Paul? How he shot above James and Peter and the others, save only John! . . . What if Christ had been born in Kamtchatka: we should have heard nothing of him. Why, then, may there not have been other Christs? . . .

"The first Christian writings were Paul's Epistles. In his time there were no Gospels. I doubt strongly that Paul knew any thing of the Christian miracles, or the miraculous birth of Jesus, or his temptation, or prediction of his death. Had he known the facts (?), would he have alluded to them?"

THE EARLY CHRISTIANS.

From the Journal, 1841.

"All I read of them convinces me more of their noble character, aim, and life. But I see their limitations. They were superstitious, formal; at least, after the middle of the second century, and perhaps also in the apostles' times: the letter burdened them; but they were full of the noble, manly spirit. Their ascetic doctrines of marriage, dress, amusement, education, I dislike vastly. They laid too much stress on baptism, the eucharist; giving the latter to men to keep at home, carry in their pocket, &c.; gave it to little children just after baptism; put it in the mouth of dead people, and the like.

"But how they died! How they prayed! How they lived! We cannot yet afford to criticise these men. Certainly they were not gentlemen; but they were *men*. The wonder is, that, *being* so much, they *saw* no more."

HERETICS.

From the Journal.

"They began very early: indeed, we find them in the times of the apostles. In Jesus you are in the *pleroma* of light: step into the apostles, it is already evening, and the light is behind you; take another step, and you are in fathomless darkness. Heretics have always been treated as the worst of men. Imaginary doctrines have been ascribed to them, — immoral ceremonies. They have been charged with sins of the blackest dye. . . . Jerome says the heretics, even if they lead blameless and beautiful lives, have only the image and shadow of virtue. Tertullian chides Marcion, after the fashion of Dr. South, with his God who is not to be feared; and asks him why, if he does not fear God, he does not go to the theatre and bawdy-house, and game and drink. Philastor and Augustine censure some heretics who would think the planets, sun, moon, and stars were worlds, because they denied the resurrection of the flesh. . . .

"Nothing will ever save us but a wide, generous toleration. I must tolerate and comfort my brother, though I think him in error, though I know him to be in error. I must tolerate his ignorance, even his sin; yes, his intolerance. Here the only safe rule is, if some one has done you a wrong, to resolve on the spot never to do that wrong to him or any one else. It is easy to tolerate a man if you know he is a fool, and quite in the wrong; but we must tolerate him when we know he is not a fool, and not altogether in the wrong."

From the Journal, April 1, 1839.

"I have just finished a review of Strauss for 'The Examiner.' I could not say all I would say from the standpoint of 'The Examiner,'—for this is not allowable,—but the most the readers of that paper will bear. If the editor is shabby, as he was a few days ago, he will 'decline the article,' ungrammatical as it may be. I have written it, however, at his request, and with no small labor. The reading of sixteen hundred pages like this is something; and then, to consider the study of the books of Ullman, Tholuck, and the 'Streit Schriften,' it makes up a good deal of work."

From the Journal, Sunday, Aug. 1.

"Was at home. Communion in the morning. This rite becomes less and less to me. I would gladly abandon it; for it troubles me. Leave the elements, and give me a meeting for prayer, conversation, or preaching, not the amphibious thing we have now. I confess the rite was never much to me. The time spent alone would always have been the more profitable. Could it be possible, this should be my plan,—to have a meeting in the evening for religious conversation, and prayer (if needful) at private houses; and bread and wine might form part of the entertainment. I cannot but think Christ would be astonished at these rites. But let this go: it warms the hearts of pious women, we are told."

Though these opinions were expressed chiefly in the journal and in private letters, Mr. Parker's published writings were guarded, and his sermons were mostly practical and religious. Towards devout prejudices he was very gentle, not from lack of courage, but partly from distrust in the finality of his views, partly from fear of going too fast for his hearers, and partly from his deeper interest in essential ideas than in casual criticisms. The spirit of his beliefs appeared in sermon and prayer. He said nothing in public he did not believe: he was careful that his people should not be justified in ascribing to him beliefs he did not entertain. But he waited the bidding of conscience before telling all he knew, or thought he knew, about the Bible. Two discourses on the Scriptures remained unpreached in his drawer for two years, biding their time for delivery. When the time came, the preacher found the people more than prepared for their contents. At this period, Parker was no image-breaker: indeed, he never was, unless he saw that the image concealed the god.

Still an evil opinion of him got abroad. Pulpits began to be closed against him; ministers declined to exchange, a sign of fellowship withdrawn.

From the Journal, November, 1840.

"I have solicited an exchange repeatedly with Y——g; could not get it: with B——tt; with Dr. P——n. To ask either of these men again would be a dereliction from Christian self-respect. So let them pass. I feel no ill-will towards any of them. I will try G——tt soon, for the experiment's sake; and so with the others, excepting ——, with whom I wish no exchange for moral reasons. Their answer decides my course for the future. Let us see! I should laugh outright to catch myself weeping because the Boston clergy would not exchange with me!"

Before it fairly came to this, his position was so well understood, and he was so generally regarded as a man suspected, that letters of sympathy, encouragement, and friendly warning, came to him. The following letter shows how he received such communications: —

To Miss E. P. Peabody.

"Touching my becoming a martyr, as you and Miss Burley conjecture, I think I should have no occasion for the requisite spirit, even if I had that article in as great abundance as John Knox or John Rogers. I have precious little of the spirit of a martyr: but, inasmuch as I fear no persecution, I fancy I can 'say my say,' and go on *smoothly;* but if not — why, well, I can go *roughly.* I trust I have enough of the spirit always to speak the truth, be the consequence what it may. It seems to me men often trouble themselves about the consequences of an opinion or action much more than is necessary. Having settled the question that an opinion is *true*, and an action perfectly *right*, what have you and I to do with consequences? They belong to God, not to man. He has as little to do with these as with the rising of the sun or the flow of the tide.

"Doubtless men said to Galileo, 'Your system may be true; but only think of the consequences that follow! What will you do with them?' The sage probably replied, 'I will let them alone. To do duty and speak truth is my office. God takes care of consequences.'"

To the Same.

"I thank you most profoundly for the kind and seasonable advice touching the matter of prudence; but you cannot fancy I have any desire to set the world on fire by promulgating heresies. I have not the *furor divinus* which impels some of the *young* men to vent their crude conceptions, to the injury, perhaps, of themselves and the public. Prudence, in the common sense, is a vulgar, sneaking virtue, which bids a man take care of his meaner interests, though at the expense of all that is noble in action or divine in contemplation. But Christian prudence is a different thing. It is a wise forecasting of results; a foreseeing consequences in their *causes*, and preparing to meet them when they come. Mr. Alcott would no doubt rejoice to say that *prudentia* was only *pre-videntia;* and so it is.

"I have only one consolation for all evils; and that is, an absolute faith that it is all right, that it will one day produce the best possible influences over me, and that then I shall see how foolish I have been to complain. All of us mourn over many failures: favorite schemes are dreamed out, only to fail soon as we attempt to realize them. By and by the cloud breaks away, and we see it would have been worse had they succeeded. It must be so in all cases. 'May Heaven refuse to grant half of our prayers' was a wise petition of some old sage. There can be no such thing as absolute evil; and from the standpoint of Omniscience, when the *whole* appears as it is, there can be no *semblance* of evil. This is all the comfort I have for any sorrow, or for all sorrows: therefore I can say with old Henry More,—

> Lord, thrust me deeper into dust,
> That thou mayst raise me with the just.'

"Is it possible, however, for any one to have a faith so deep, so active, so perfect, that all sorrows can be borne as cheerfully as blessings are enjoyed? It may be possible for some to reach this state; but only for a few; certainly not for me. You have by nature a deep and active faith, which spontaneously overflows, and, like the sacred waters of the Nile or Ganges, makes all around it green and fruitful."

If these passages express confidence, they also betray sorrow. Though endowed with a sanguine temperament and a stout heart, Mr. Parker had an immense capacity for suffering, which all his power of accomplishment could not deaden or suppress. The cry was the more agonizing for not being heard. He did care more than he thought he did for the fellowship of his ministerial brethren; for they were his brethren in a ministry which he loved, and could not bear to see desecrated by sordid considerations. To lose his companionship and his confidence at once was a severe blow.

CHAPTER VII.

THE FERMENT OF THOUGHT.

It was a remarkable agitation of mind that went on in Massachusetts thirty years ago. All institutions and all ideas went into the furnace of reason, and were tried as by fire. Church and State were put to the proof; and the wood, hay, stubble — every thing combustible — were consumed. The process of proving was not confined to Boston: the whole State took part in it. It did not proceed from Boston as a centre: it began simultaneously in different parts of the Commonwealth. It did not seem to be communicated, to spread by contagion, but was rather an intellectual experience produced by some latent causes which were active in the air. No special class of people were responsible for it, or affected by it. While in Boston the little knot of transcendentalists — Channing, Ripley, Margaret Fuller, Emerson, Alcott, Francis, Hedge, Parker — were discussing the problems of philosophy at the Tremont House and elsewhere, the farmers in the country, and plain folks of Cape Cod, were as full of the new spirit as they, and were reaching, though from the opposite region of common sense, the same intrepid conclusions. It was a time of meetings and conventions for reforms of every description. A man of the people like Theodore Parker, utterly free from conventionality, knowing no distinctions of persons, equally at home with learned and simple, interested in what Epictetus calls the "bare man," was sure to be on the spot where any thing of practical moment was taking place. The journal contains a long account — eight closely-written folio pages — of a convention held in Groton in August of 1840. It is too long to be copied in full here, as Mr. Weiss has done in his biography; nor would the importance of the occasion justify the occupation of the required space: but so characteristic an example of the mental condition of the time must not be passed by.

The call for the convention was issued by Second Adventists and Come-outers, — two very unlike classes of people, except in the one particular of being rude and uneducated. The former we know about: the latter had no distinguishing tenets, but held opinions of every radical type, taking their name from the mere circumstance of their having "come out" from the regular churches. The distance to Groton from Boston was about thirty miles. An expedition thither on foot was proposed; the original company being Ripley, Parker, and a new friend of theirs, E. P. Clark. They picked up Cranch at Newton, and walked on to Concord; stopping, as they went along, to refresh themselves at a farm-house, or rest a moment by the way-side, but trusting to the talk to shorten the way. At Concord they called on Mr. Alcott; got a word of admonition from old Dr. Ripley (aged ninety), who charged them not to become "egomites," or *self-sent men;* and then repaired to Mr. Emerson, "who looked as divine as usual." With him they took tea. The next morning the party, increased by the addition of Alcott, trudged on to Groton. Some little reconnoitring was required before Mr. Hawley, the herald of the convention, could be found. When discovered, he proved to be a young man of about four and twenty years, of pleasant countenance, but unprepossessingly so, Mr. Parker thought. "Brother" Hawley introduced them to Brother Himes of Boston, Brother Myrick of Cazenovia, Brother Russell, and others whose names were unremembered.

On inquiring what was to be done at the convention, the reply was negative and unsatisfactory. The two questions *not* to be discussed were, 1. What constitutes a Christian? 2. What constitutes a Christian church? Brother Jones was to hold forth that night on the second coming of Christ in 1843. The discourse would be very interesting, no doubt; but 1843 was still in the future: there might something be transacted in the mean time. So the party of travellers adjourned, and enjoyed a talk by themselves. The convention had interesting features, from the mere circumstance of its wildness and fanaticism; but the most interesting were the people themselves. There was Joseph Palmer, "a man with a meek face, and a fine gray beard six or eight inches long, clad in fustian trousers and a clean white jacket." He had been a butcher; but had renounced that calling, partly from the conviction of the wrongfulness of eating flesh. His face was pleasantly touched with enthusiasm: Alcott found him full of "divine thoughts." He wore his beard because God gave it to him, doubtless for some good end. Joseph spoke to this effect in the convention: "If you are here to discuss the Church of Antichrist, I have nothing to say; for I know nothing of that. But I know something of the Christian Church. You have said a good deal about getting into the Christian Church, and about getting out of it. Now, there is but one way of getting out of the Church, — that pursued by Judas, also by Ananias and Sapphira. No man, save himself, can put one out of the Church. Now, I will tell you how to get into the Christian Church. Christ said to the young man who asked how to obtain eternal life, 'Sell all that thou hast, and give to the poor.' If he did that, he was saved. Now, if he was saved, he was a Christian, of course, — a member of the Church of Christ. Why, then, do you make such a talk about the way to become a Christian? It is perfectly plain. There is not a girl here twelve years old who cannot understand it." For himself, he had thought out all that had been said in the meetings long ago, when he lay in a dungeon for conscience' sake.

B. W. Dyer was a young man of about twenty-five, a farmer, and a minister as well. He had little book-learning, but deep thoughts. When Alcott asked him about Christ, he said, "Truth is Christ, and Christ truth." He expected salvation from the inward Christ; in short, by becoming the Christ. Here was a rude farmer, who had found the same well-spring that had quenched the thirst of the learned Ralph Cudworth and many a profound mystic besides. His theory of inspiration was, in substance, that set forth in "The Dial." Paul and Peter were inspired; but so were others, — some more, some less. His idea of death and the resurrection was strictly apostolic. He believed that they who possessed the entire truth, who were the Lord's own, would never die, but would be spiritualized, and caught up into the air. Another personage Mr. Parker christened "Mantalini," from his close resemblance, in whisker, dress, watch-chain, and drawl, to the illustrious character in "Nicholas Nickleby." He was an Englishman; had been a Baptist, then a Universalist, afterwards a member of the legislature, and was then a preacher. In his affected, "dandiacal" manner, he compared the Christian Church to Samson going down to Timnath and slaying a lion; a remark which provoked our friend Theodore to the satirical rejoinder, that, when Samson went down to Timnath and slew the lion, he had not been shorn by Delilah, but continued true to his vow of austerity. The covert allusion to soap-locks and other effeminacies was lost on "Mantalini," who, when the meeting was over, congratulated the grim humorist on his interesting speech, with nearly all of which he heartily agreed.

Nickerson and Davis were two preachers among the "Come-outers," — "two as rough-looking men as you would meet in a summer's day; but their countenances were full of the divine." Their hands, their dress, their general air, showed that they belonged to the humblest class in society.

Mr. Bearse was a plain Cape-Cod fisherman, — a skipper, probably, — of bright, ruddy, cheerful countenance. He spoke briefly, gesticulating in a manner distressing to Brother Hawley, and to this effect: "I see about in the land many little Babels of sectarian churches, as you call them. Now, I see you wish to pull down these little Babels; to take the combustible materials of which they are made, and erect one great Babel, into which you may enter. You are in a fair way; and, if this is not confusion of tongues already prevailing, I don't know what confusion is." Brother Hawley was not rejoiced. Presently Mrs. Bearse, a "sister to live" as they called her, arose and spoke, her husband cheering her on. She stated meekly and beautifully — this Cape-Cod saint — her religious history, her connection with an Orthodox church, then with a Freewill Baptist church, and her persecution in both. "Now," she said, "the Lord has set me in a large place." "Her remarks showed plainly that she spoke from the divine life. I afterwards talked with her, and saw how divine her heart appeared, and her countenance also; for she has one of the fairest faces I have seen for many moons."

The opinions of the "Come-outers" were found to coincide in many respects with those Mr. Parker had arrived at by his own trained reflection. The Christian ordinances they esteemed highly: "They are our *daily work.* We do not count a rite better than any other act. If our heart is right, whatever we do we shall do for the glory of God. Baptism we think little of," said Mr. Nickerson, "and therefore seldom administer it." — "But," said Mr. Bearse, "sometimes a brother wishes to be baptized; and, if the Spirit moves me, I baptize him, or some other does it. We don't think it necessary for the minister to do this: any one into whom God puts the desire may do it."

The Lord's Supper they held in light estimation; rarely administered it, and never except one was moved to it by a spontaneous action of the divine feelings. The last time it was administered was at Sister Nancy's house. Several had met one evening to worship; and Brother some one said, "The Spirit moves me to eat the Lord's Supper." Whereupon Sister Nancy went to the cupboard, brought forth bread and wine, placed it on the table, and the brother sat down and ate and drank. "All our meals," they said, "are the Lord's Supper, if we eat with a right heart. He that eateth, eateth to the Lord; and he that eateth not, to the Lord he eateth not."

Whoever wished to join their company did so without ceremony. No questions were asked about his creed; he subscribed to no confession; set his name to no paper; was free to come and go. In case of difficulty between one of the society and a member of another church, some of the brethren went quietly and settled the dispute according to the apostolical method, and so successfully, that they were sometimes asked to mediate in matters of controversy outside of their own body. Should one come to their meeting who did not believe in Christ or the Bible, or even a God, they took him by the hand, bade him welcome and God speed in a good course. Should such a one offer to speak in meeting, they heard what he had to say; and, if he could convince them, they were ready to be convinced.

They had no rules for worship: each prayed as he was moved, in words or silently. As they talked with their new acquaintances, Joshua Davis felt moved by the Spirit to pray; knelt down, and poured out his petition "with beauty and great earnestness."

Their ministers declared that they were ministers of silence no less than of speech. They never spoke except when moved thereto; and each spoke as moved, without restraint; "for it took the whole Church to preach the whcle gospel."

They had no church-edifices: all houses where good and pious people lived were Lord's houses; all days well spent, Lord's days. Since one day had been set apart by custom, they met oftener then than on other days when labor prevented; but the true worship was a divine life during the week, — a life of humility, justice, and mercy. Thus they prayed without ceasing; thus their life was a continual sacrifice.

Their ministers might or might not be educated. They had no ordination, and received no salary: they worked like others for their living, owing no debts but the debt of love; making their own wants few, that they might have something to give to them that were in need. Joshua Davis was a working-man, who, over and above the time given to labor for his bread, visited troubled and dying people as a "physician of souls." Yet he managed to give away out of charity, in one year, a hundred dollars. They counted their calling sacred; but no more so than any other; no more so than that of the humblest sister, though she were but six years old, who made herself useful. They recognized no distinction between sacred and profane things where the heart was holy. Some of the ministers lived up to a very high calling. This very Joshua Davis rose the year round at four o'clock, and was heard often before daylight at his devotions, which were at times so fervent as to disturb the household; in which event he would go out to the barn, and give voice to the passion of his prayer.

They used the Bible as a help to godliness. "Men worship the Bible," said Mr. Bearse to Mr. Parker, "just as the old pagans worshipped their idols. This is just as truly idolatry as that false worship was. The Bible is a *Scripture of the Word*, not the Word itself; for the Word is never written, save in the living heart." Books of a mystical character were used among them, such as Law's "Serious Call," "Spirit of Prayer," "Christian Perfection," Scougal's "Life of God in the Soul of Man," George Fox's "Journal." Jacob Boehme's more simple and practical treatises were not unknown to them. They held that men were inspired in proportion as they had received the truth; and they received the truth through obedience.

Mr. Parker made a long speech at the convention, to the general approval of the audience, in which he set forth in direct and simple language his idea of the original Christianity as it lay in the mind of Jesus; described the early departures from it; traced the rise of the ecclesiastical and sectarian spirit; portrayed in vivid colors the actual condition of the Church; and more than hinted at the radical reforms that were necessary, if the religion was to vindicate its claim to be the savior of mankind. "What is the Church now?" he asked. "St. Paul said, 'Where the Spirit of the Lord is, there is liberty.' But where the spirit of the Church is, there is slavery. The Holy Spirit says, 'Be a true soul; live a divine life.' The Church demands a *belief*, and *not* a divine life. The best men come to her, and find no life, no power." Thus he sums up his impressions of the convention:—

"1. I am surprised to find so much illiberality amongst the men who called the convention. They were not emancipated from the letter of the Bible, nor the formality of a church. They simply wish to pull down other sects, to make room for their own, which will probably be worse than its predecessors.

"2. I am surprised and enchanted to find these plain Cape-Cod men and numerous others, who have made actual my own highest idea of a church. I feel strengthened by their example. Only let it be united with high intellectual culture.

"3. I am surprised to find many others who have emancipated themselves from the shams of the Christian Church, and now can worship God at first-hand, and pray largely and like men.

I don't know that I have got any new ideas: but certainly my confidence in my old ideas has been deepened; for I see they may be made actual.

"This convention effects nothing directly by its long string of resolutions; but it does much indirectly. It sets the ball in motion, which will go far before it stops."

If it was a bold thing to attend a convention of "Come-outers" at Groton, it was a bolder thing to be one to call a convention in Boston for the consideration of questions concerning the sabbath, the ministry, and the church. It was held in Chardon Street, Nov. 17. Few acts so damaging to reputation could be done. The risks of inundation from all kinds of radicalisms were very great: it was striking a blow at the heart of the holiest respectabilities, and offering a large opportunity for unruly spirits to disport themselves. "All my friends after the flesh, and some of my friends after the spirit, regretted that I had any agency in calling the convention. Lamson, a beautiful soul, doubts the convention; fears bad use will be made of truth: *nous verrons.* Dr. Channing also doubts the propriety thereof, since it looks like seeking agitation: here, again, we shall see. I have my own doctrines, and shall support them, think the convention as it may. I look on the Church as a body of men and women getting together for moral and religious instruction, on the minister as a moral and religious teacher, and on Sunday as a day set apart from work and common secular vocations. All of them are human institutions, but each valuable; I would almost say, invaluable."

The convention met, discussed, and dissolved, having brought to pass no very great result.

From the Journal, Sept. 23.

"Went to Boston to attend the Non-resistant Convention. Don't agree with them entirely, but like their spirit and upward tendency. Like not their formula of 'No Human Government.'

12

Think circumstances render it needful sometimes to take life. If a man attack me, it is optional on my part to suffer or to resist; but, should he attack my wife with the worst of purposes, why should I suffer the wicked to destroy the righteous, when I could save her by letting out his life? I should deprecate the issue being tendered; but, if it were tendered, I have little doubt which course would be revealed to me as the true one."

The time, however, for enlisting in special reforms had not yet come to Mr. Parker. General questions interested him now rather than particular ones. The condition of society at large weighed heavily on his mind. Like all thoughtful men who lead secluded and bookish lives, — we may say, in proportion as they lead secluded and bookish lives, — he was interested in the problem of evil. The separate problems of evil present themselves chiefly to those who live in cities. In his sweet country village, books supplied the chief materials for speculation on the ills of society. The writings of St. Simon, Victor Considerant, Charles Fourier, and others of the various schools of socialism, were becoming known in America, and their doctrines were already creeping into our speculations. Albert Brisbane's pamphlet, in part a reproduction of Fourier, had attracted attention. It pointed out the vices and miseries of modern society, and proposed to cure them by reconstructing society itself from the foundation, on new principles, resting on a new philosophy of human nature. Mr. Parker reads, ponders; thinks the book will do a great deal of good. The "phalanx" does not appear to him more improbable than a city may be presumed to have seemed to Abraham. The portrayal of the evils of society strikes him forcibly: he is glad to see the case stated boldly.

From the Journal.

"Brownson has recently written an article on the laboring-classes calculated to call the philosophic to reflection. He thinks inherited property should be given up; that the relation of master and servant, employer and employed, should cease; that the priest is the chief curse to society. This makes a great noise. The Whigs, finding their sacramental idea — money — in danger, have come to the rescue with fire-brands and the like weapons. Fearful lest the article should do harm, they trumpet forth to the people those doctrines, which, if left alone, would come only to scholars. I like much of his article, though his property notions agree not with my view. Yet certainly the present property scheme entails awful evils upon society, rich no less than poor. This question, first, of inherited property, and, next, of all private property, is to be handled in the nineteenth century, and made to give in its reason why the whole thing should not be abated as a nuisance.

"Society now rests on a great lie. Money and service have much to answer for. Can one man serve another for wages without being degraded? Yes; but *not in all relations*. I have no moral right to use the service of another, provided it degrades him in my sight, in that of his fellows, or of himself; yet personal service is connected with this degradation."

In a note on Murphy's "Science of Consciousness," he remarks, "This book is but a straw on the stream; but it shows which way the current sets; and God knows what will be the end of this awful movement. Heaven save us from an English reign of terror! . . .

"The same question must be passed on in America. Property must show why it should not be abated; labor, why it should exempt so many from its burdens, and crush others therewith. It is no doubt a good thing that I should read the Greek Anthology, and cultivate myself in my leisure, as a musk-melon ripens in the sun; but why should I be the only one of the thousand who has this chance? True, I have won it dearly, laboriously; but others, of better ability, with less hardihood, fail in the attempt, and serve me with the body. It makes me groan to look into the evils of society. When will there be an end? I thank God I am not born to set the matter right. I scarce dare attempt a reform of theology, lest I should be in for the whole; and must condemn the state and society no less than the church."

From the Journal.

"Ripley dislikes the customs of property, — a father transmitting it to his son; but I see no way of avoiding the evil. The sin lies deeper than the transmission of property from getter to enjoyer. It lies in the love of low things, and in the idea that work degrades. We must correct this notion, and then all is well; and, before that is done, to hew down the institutions of property, and cut the throats of all that own lands, would do little good. How the world ever came into such a sad state it is difficult to conjecture: how it is to get out of it is impossible to foretell."

From the Journal.

"Mrs. R. gave me a tacit rebuke for not shrieking at wrongs, and spoke of the danger of losing our humanity in abstractions. Many remarks of hers sank deeply into me."

From the Journal.

"I have lived long enough to see the shams of things, and to look them fairly in the face. 1. The State is a bundle of shams. It is based on force, not love. It is still feudal. A Christian State is an anomaly, like a square circle. Our laws degrade, at the beginning, one-half the human race, and sacrifice them to the other and perhaps worser half. Our prisons are institutions that make more criminals than they mend: seventeen-twentieths of crimes are against property, which shows that something is wrong in the state of property. Society causes crimes, and then hangs the criminals. 2. The Church is still worse. It is a colossal lie. It is based on the letter of the Bible and the notion of its plenary inspiration. It is the hospital of fools, the resort of rooks and owls. The one thing it does well is the baptizing of babies."

In August of 1840 Mr. Parker went to New York and visited the "Tombs," which he thus describes: "It is a large block of buildings, embracing a whole square, and comprising a court-house, jail, and yards. It is a very magnificent and imposing edifice in the old Egyptian style. The taste which would expend all that architecture on a building so loathsome as a jail is most wretched. Shame that the disgrace of society should be thus arrayed in costly dress, and made to flaunt before the public eye! I went into the court-house to see 'justice' administered. A negro was on trial in the Court of Sessions for abusing his wife. It seemed to me the place was well called 'Egyptian' from the darkness that covered over justice there; and 'Tombs,' for it appears, as all our court-houses are, the sepulchre of equity. How can it be 'justice' to punish as a crime what the institutions of society render unavoidable? How could any thing better be expected of the poor wretches daily brought up to that court, exposed, naked as they are, to all the contamination of corrupt society?

"This poor negro, on trial for a crime, showed me in miniature the whole of our social institutions. 1. He was the victim of Christian cupidity, and had been a slave. 2. From this he had probably escaped by what was counted a crime by his master; or else was set free by charity, perhaps desiring to cover up its own sins. 3. He was cast loose in a society where his color debarred him the rights of a man, and forced him to count himself a beast, with nothing to excite self-respect, either in his condition, his history, or his prospects. Poor, wretched man! What is life to him? He is more degraded than the savage; has lost much in leaving Sahara, and gained infamy, cold, hunger, and — the white man's mercy — a prison of marble. Oh, what wrongs does man heap on man!"

George Ripley, one of the strongest pulpit-speakers in Boston, was so pierced and wounded by the sense of social abuses, that, in full sympathy with a noble wife, he left his profession, impatient with the "foolishness of preaching," sold his fine library at auction, and, gathering together all that he had, inaugurated the enterprise of associated mind and labor at Brook Farm. The experiment was tried in a spirit of deep sincerity, as an effort to carry out in some degree the ethics of the Sermon on the Mount, by restoring natural and primitive relations between man and nature, and between man and man. Neither the founder nor his coadjutors were disciples of any particular teacher of socialism, though some of them were acquainted with French writings on the subject. The views of Fourier were understood but partially through translators and interpreters: few accepted his system as a whole. The spirit that animated him was abroad in society; but the opinions he formed at the suggestion of that spirit were more congenial with the French than with the English or American mind. The problem of Brook Farm was the practical reconciliation of labor, capital, and culture, by mutual participation in toil and its results. This is not the place to give an account of an undertaking, which, from obvious causes, did not prosper either as a financial speculation or as a social scheme, but which brought together for a short space of time a remarkable company of men and women, most of whom have since been distinguished in letters, and gave to all who were concerned in it an amount of pleasure they never could have obtained otherwise, and never will recall without feelings of hearty satisfaction. The story of Brook Farm is a story which the cultivators of it delight to tell over to their friends. Will not one of them adequately tell it to the public?

The grounds were, by a short cut across the fields, not more than a mile from Mr. Parker's house. The spirit never moved him to take part in the enterprise. He was too absorbingly interested, it may be, in the theological reform he was pushing, to throw himself with force into any scheme for the regeneration of society; or perhaps the instinct of practical utility which he followed made such schemes seem visionary. But he was a frequent visitor, and a keen inspector of the movement. The social freedom there was a delight to him; the conversations were a lively joy; and no one relished more than he the fine ironies of cultivated ladies bending over the wash-tub, of poets guiding the plough, or of philosophers digging potatoes. His faith in the undertaking may have been small; but his entertainment with it was immense. It is probably from the circumstance that the experiment took so little hold of his mind that there is no more notice of it in the journal. His enjoyment was on the spot.

Parker's faculty of getting fun out of serious things in which he felt a truly deep concern, and at which even he did his share of work, is shown in the way he pleasantly laughed at "The Dial," a magazine for literature, philosophy, and religion, which was begun in 1840. He wrote for it faithfully, putting into it some admirable articles on literature, theology, and ecclesiastical affairs; yet, in a letter to a friend, he can speak of it thus: —

To Dr. Francis.

DEC. 18, 1840.

Apropos of "The Dial:" to my mind it bears about the same relation to "The Boston Quarterly" that Antimachus does to Hercules, Alcott to Brownson, or a band of men and maidens daintily arrayed in finery, "walking in a vain show," with kid mitts on their "dannies," to a body of stout men in blue frocks, with great arms and hard hands, and legs like the Pillars of Hercules. If I were going to do the thing in paint, it should be thus: I would represent a body of minute philosophers, men and maidens, elegantly dressed, bearing a banner inscribed with "The Dial." A baby and a pap-spoon and a cradle should be the accompaniment thereof. The whole body should have "rings on their fingers, and bells on their toes," and go "mincing as they walk," led by a body of fiddlers, with Scott's Claude Halcro "playing the first violin and repeating new poetry." This body of the excellent should come out of a canvas city of Jerusalem set upon a hill. On the other hand should come up a small body of warriors looking like the seven chiefs before Thebes, and swearing as they did, with just about as modest devices on their shields. They should be men who looked battles, with organs of combativeness big as your fist. They should be covered with sweat and blood and dust, with an earnest look and confident tread. "Sonorous metal blowing martial sounds" should encourage them. At their head should stand "Orestes Augustus Brownson," dressed like Daniel, with Goliath's sword in one hand, and that giant's head in the other. Would not this make a picture?

This muscular mind was impatient of amateur performances: he had a keen eye for the deficiencies of people who put themselves forward as reformers of the world, but were themselves unreformed. His admiration for Miss Margaret Fuller was qualified. Here is the mildest judgment on her from the journal: "Miss Fuller came Saturday. She has outgrown Carlyle. Well, I am glad: I wish the world had outgrown him. She thinks Carlyle inferior to Coleridge (doubt this much); that the latter will live, and the former be forgot. Miss Fuller is a critic, not a creator, not a seer, I think. Certainly she is a prodigious woman, though she puts herself upon her genius rather too much. She has nothing to do with God out of her. She is not a good analyst, not a philosopher." Character was uppermost with him. The moral element was decisive: it is the apparent absence of it that staggers him as he contemplates the system of nature. Read this from the journal: —

"There are many things in nature which are utterly incomprehensible to me. They are contradictions rather than exceptions. I mean such facts as the following: Alligators devour their own young till they are too large: how frightful this is! how unlike the rest of God's creation! Volcanoes and earthquakes I can understand: they do not puzzle me. Squirrels castrate one another. I have often shot young and old males deprived of a part of their generative organs. I have seen two old squirrels seize a young one half grown; and, one holding the wretch, the other plied his sharp teeth, and emasculated him. What does all this mean? This is a sad symbol of what man does. Mr. Alcott's theory accounts for it better: viz., the world is the product of all men: so long as men do such things, some animals will do likewise."

This was penned before Darwinism was in vogue, or the new doctrine of evolution, which contents itself with tracing the development of life, leaving interpretations to the future. "Mr. Alcott's theory" has a flavor of the old orthodoxy, which ascribed the fall of nature to the fall of man; a theory that would be less vulnerable if the fall of nature had succeeded the fall of man, instead of preceding it, as for the most part it does. It is hard to believe that the fall of man was heavy enough to shake in pieces and disjoint the order of creation which had existed several hundred thousand years before he came; unless indeed, by making the whole planet reel, he jostled out of place every thing upon it. This ancient theory Mr. Parker discarded when he thought of it; and he had no other to put in its place. He could only observe: that he did. He noted the cruelty of animals towards one another, — the barbarity of the cat to the mouse, which she tortures before eating; the abortions of nature, — the monsters, calves with three heads, human fœtus consisting of only a head, and the like; the robbery which the bald eagle commits on the fish-hawk, the lion on the jackal, the wolf on the fox; the want of natural affection, — wasps destroying their young, bees killing drones, &c., birds driving other birds from their nests and then appropriating them, ants enslaving other ants; the sins against nature committed by numerous animals, — the dog, for instance; the disgusting practices of apes, frogs, and fishes; things that suggest a dark element in the creative cause of the world, or imply that matter has some qualities which the Deity cannot control.

But the philosophy of dualism he will not accept: it seems to him inconsistent with common sense.

He is not without suspicion of a law of development. He marks the anticipations or prophecies which a lower class of beings afford of the next higher, — the toes in the horse's hoof; the fingers beneath the skin; the singular man-likeness of certain monkeys; the resemblance to human limbs noticed in some plants, as the orchis and lady's-slipper: but the clew is not continuous enough to lead him far; and he sets these things down as curious facts, which puzzle, but do not torment.

"If we look scientifically at these things, and attempt to classify as in other cases of scientific examination, shall we conclude the world is governed by an infinitely wise and good Being?

"I. Notice the immense physical evils occasioned by war, slavery, oppression, like that of the Turkish rulers, of the rich barons; the horrible mutilations, cruelties, &c., that take place, even in these days; the evils of sickness and poverty, that are without fault of the sufferer.

"II. Note the exceeding low state of morals in all lands, in the United States, even in Boston; how unchristian men are; yet Christianity is only absolute humanity. Note the selfish spirit, money-getting, ambition, intemperance, ignorance; yet this is probably one of the most favored peoples. Take the richest class in Boston: how do they stand when tried by the absolute standard?

"Note still further the prevalent vices in other countries, — licentiousness in Italy, Germany, and France. We may say the sin in each individual is slight: perhaps there is no sin in the matter; for personal sin is violation of conscience. So it may be an absolute sin, viewed from the point of pure justice or right, and not a personal sin. Still the consequences are the same: 1. The physical evils that follow the violation of material law. 2. The degradation of the individual, so that conscience is cast down, and all but extinguished.

"Consider the *superior activity of evil over good.* Vice

spreads with rapidity, virtue slowly. Notice the extreme sufferings of individuals.

"Now, in estimating these matters, my own faith says there is a perfect system of *optimism* in the world; that each man's life is to him an infinite good: of course, all his physical evils must be means of progress; all his vile acts, likewise, unavoidable steps in his course to happiness. But, to legitimate this in the court of the understanding where all other truths are legitimated, I find difficult. Faith has nothing to do there. I will imagine a person who claims that all things work together for good, and suppose myself to reply to the arguments I should bring in such a case. I should not know how to answer him: I should appeal solely to faith for my own satisfaction."

Thus sincerely he faced the problems, presenting the difficulties in their most formidable shape. He had, however, a constitution which turned away naturally from the repulsive side of creation. A single flower affected him more deeply than a blasted forest; a beam of light gave him a joy that many cloudy days did not dispel. He was so sensitive to beauty, that ugliness, though of hundred-fold bulk, scarcely seemed to reach him. The tender plant growing from a bed of rotted leaves justified the pile of decay; the violet lifting up its blue eye from the cold damp ground more than excused the ground. Had his temperament been less buoyant than it was, his heart must have fainted; for no spectral optimism would have availed against the terrible realism of his thought.

To Miss E. P. Peabody.

DEC. 18, 1840.

At different stages of life I have been amazed at the power and the wisdom that are involved in the creative act; but of later years, as I look more through the surfaces of things, — or, at least, try to do so, — it is the beauty and *loving-kindness* of God that strike me most. I think, with you, that we can apprehend the creative moment through love, and through that alone. It is this that solves all the mystery. It cares little for the details of the work, but tells us at once, "Out of the depths of infinite love God drew forth the world. O mortal! whoever thou art, thank God that thou art born, and take courage; for thou also art a child of infinite love, and all of the past is working in thy behalf: so fear not. What though you weep a little as you scatter the seed, and the cold rain of spring drenches and chills you: from this very field you shall fill your bosom with sheaves of satisfaction." To me, this thought, this feeling, is enough to wipe the tear from my eye at any time. It is infinite counsel and infinite comfort. It has been adequate for all the trials I have yet found, and I trust it will help me "till the world ends." I often wish I could impart this same feeling to others; but the attempt always reminds me of the truth in Plato: "It is of all things the most difficult to find out God, and impossible to communicate him to others." Yet it has come to me with little *conscious* difficulty. I sometimes try — yes, it is the object of my preaching — to lead all to this same "watch-tower in the skies:" but they tell me, "Look at the evil, the wretchedness, the sin of the world, the wrongs 'that patient merit of the unworthy takes'!" as if I could not see them all, and feel some of them. I wish you would tell me, my dear Elizabeth, some better method of doing this: you are the all-sympathizer, and must know how to do *this* kindly office also. Prithee tell me how you would go to work to "*create a soul* under the ribs of death," and give this confidence to one who lacks it still.

To impart his faith he finds difficult. When others suggest their doubts and fears, he often stands dumb, praying internally for them, and hoping that time will bring them repose. But for his own part, however much his heart may be wrung, the serenity of his soul is unbroken. The following passage on death is taken from a letter: —

"How few of us are there that are bound to the mortal by ties so strong we would not willingly see them severed at almost any time! Even those who reluct a little at the thought of death are usually unwilling on their friend's account, not on their own. Death is always a blessing to him who dies: the man ceases to be mortal. I cannot look on this change which takes place in the animal system with that terror wherewith some men regard it. To me it is a change which is always made for the better, — an important change, it is true; but it is no more to a man than the change from the infant's 'long-clothes' to the 'frock and trousers' of the boy.

"I understand, therefore, why *Swedenborg* found men in the other world who had forgotten all about their death; in a word, did not remember they had ever died. Perhaps most men do not remember any thing about their change from 'baby-clothes' to the boy's dress. Why need they think any more about death, or fear it any more? I have not forgotten all about my change of dress. I remember that I cried, and struggled most lustily against the new dress; and, when my legs were squeezed into their new envelopes, I was so ashamed, that I went into the fields to hide myself. I doubt that I should complain half so much if Death were to come with the new suit, and tell me to lay aside my old rags, and put on the new clothes.

"Are we not foolish in talking about preparing to die? Our business is to live. He that is prepared to live, and *fit* to live, is fittest to die: is he not? To wear well the one suit is to prepare well for the next. I am sometimes disturbed by the canting talk one hears about preparing to die. I want to live; for the soul never tells you or me that we shall die. The senses die; and so death is an affair of the senses, — too sensual a matter for wise men to concern themselves much about."

I cannot more fitly close this chapter, or the thoughts it contains, than with the prayer written out in his journal at the close of the year. Such words of supplication close all the years. Prayer was as natural to Theodore Parker as breathing: it was breathing, — the deep inspiration of his soul, as he stood at the "eastern window of divine surprise," and caught the breeze from the "mountains of the dawn." It is not often pleasant to come across written prayers in a private diary; but his seem like the efflorescence of what went before.

PRAYER.

"O thou Spirit whom no name can measure, and no thought contain; thou to whom years are as nothing, and who art from

13

everlasting to everlasting! I thank thee that my life still lasts from year to year. I thank thee that my cup is full of blessings. But I would bless thee still if thou didst fill my cup with grief, and turn my day into night. Yea, O God, my Father! I will bless thee for whatever thou shalt send. I know it is all very good. I bless thee that thou art still very nigh me; that thou speakest to my heart from year to year. Thou kindlest my faith; thou quickenest my love; thou castest down my fear. When my father and mother forsake me, thou wilt take me up. O my God! bless me still this coming year. Be not afar off. May I never become false to thy gift! Let my eyes be open, my heart true and warm, my faith pure and heavenly. May religion dwell in the inmost sanctuary of my heart; let it be my daily life! And, wherever the years shall find me, may I do my duty without fear, and so live on, lying low in thy hand, and blessed by thy goodness! Amen."

CHAPTER VIII.

THE UNITARIAN CONTROVERSY.

IT has by this time been made clear that Mr. Parker was not a rash innovator either in doctrine or in practice. He was as far from that as it was possible for a man to be whose steps take hold on new paths at all. By sentiment, affection, association, practical bent of mind, he was conservative, not destructive. He had no disposition to break the bruised reed, or to quench the smoking flax. He loved the church, the ministry, the brethren. Though swift in reception, he was deliberate and cautious in creation. He took time in coming to conclusions, and waited his opportunity. Bearing testimony "in season and out of season" was not his way. He would be sure before he made up his mind; he would be sure before his intimate friend knew that his mind was made up. All things considered, it is surprising that his old opinions gave place so reluctantly to new ones. What he believed was too strongly rooted in his tenacious mind to be pulled up by even a strong hand at the first effort. Like Luther, he clung to the faith of his youth as long as it would allow. In the Divinity School, although he had talked much with Mr. Francis, and read many a book of a rationalizing tendency, he was old-fashioned in his opinions for a Unitarian. The elder ministers were his admiration. His relation to Miss Cabot brought him into familiar acquaintance with Mr. Ripley, afterwards his bosom-friend, who was importing the latest books in German philosophy and criticism, and reading them with eager interest. They were freely lent to the young student, to whom all literature was manna from heaven, and in whose warm veins all honest thought made blood. The books were, with hardly an exception, unorthodox, in most cases vehemently so; and, being learned and strong, they naturally modified the student's mind. Parker had never identified literature with faith, however closely he may have held them associated; and so, without serious misgivings, he suffered the literature of religion to undergo inevitable changes. His views of scripture, of miracle, prophecy, apostolical and other infallibility, became altered from month to month, as matter of course. Truth to him was truth.

But these books contained a good deal besides criticism: they contained philosophy of a new school. The re-action against the philosophy of sensation, supported by the authority of John Locke, and pushed to extremity by David Hume, — a re-action which began with Kant in the last century, and continued through Fichte and Schelling, — had carried before it the living mind of Germany. The great names in literature became great through its inspiration. Richter, Goethe, Schiller, were its prophets; Schleiermacher and Herder were its apostles; Staüdlin and Ammon, Gabler and Wegscheider, were its theological expositors; Strauss and De Wette assumed it. The doctrine of intuition, that truth is disclosed immediately to the reason or the soul, took place of the doctrine of sensation, that truth is revealed by mediation of book; and the authority of all outward instrumentalities, church, bible, creed, was tacitly repudiated before a single scripture was doubted, or a single miracle denied. The vessels of dogma, rite, ceremony, church, were not scuttled until the spiritual freight they carried had been transferred to the spiritual nature, there to be secure from hidden reef or sudden tempest. In England the transcendental movement was represented by Coleridge, who was a student of Schelling. Thomas Carlyle came later, with reproductions of Jean Paul and his own tremendous preaching against shams in church, state, and society. France took the work in hand according to her genius, not with philosophic profundity or critical acuteness, but with neat faculty of generalizing and explaining, — Victor Cousin, and Jean Philibert Damiron, and Benjamin Constant, and Theodore Simon Jouffroy, each after his own manner, and in his own department, vindicating the competence of the human reason. The writings of these men, especially of Cousin, Jouffroy, and Constant, were known here in the original, or through translations by George Ripley and William H. Channing. America had a prophet and seer all its own, beholding and announcing the same great vision on this side of the water, Parker's admiration of whom was early and boundless. "The brilliant genius of Emerson," he says, "rose in the winter nights and hung over Boston, drawing the eyes of ingenuous young people to look up to that great new star, 'a beauty and a mystery,' which charmed for the moment, while it gave also perennial inspiration, as it led them forward along new paths and towards new hopes."

The new philosophy commended itself to Parker at once, like his mother's milk. Religion had always been a spiritual thing with him from his childhood, never a formal or doctrinal thing. He never knew what it was to be converted from the philosophy of sensation to the philosophy of intuition. As a boy, he was a transcendentalist without knowing it. When he became a man, he was a transcendentalist on conviction. Then reason legitimated what he had always felt: the piety of the heart became the philosophy of the intellect. His only task was to remove from the new spiritual temple, which was rising in beauty, the rubbish of former edifices that once stood on the same ground; and this task he performed with great cheer, presuming on the copious gratitude of his generation for the work performed.

But the Unitarians were not in a mood to be thankful for such service. They, with very few exceptions, looked on their work as done. They had proved, to their own satisfaction at least, that the dogmas of Trinity, Deity of Christ, Vicarious Atonement, Total Depravity, and Everlasting Damnation, were unsupported by Scripture, and they were in the main content. Precisely what was supported by Scripture they did not undertake specifically to declare; but that whatever was accepted must be accepted on the authority of Scripture, they did not question. "To the law and to the testimony!" was their cry. In textual criticism they showed themselves skilful; but behind the text they did not go. The genuineness and the authenticity of the New Testament, the plenary authority of the apostles, the supernatural origin and divine mission of the Christ, the inspiration of the prophets, the validity of miracles as credentials of the Messiah and his officers, were accepted truths. The Unitarians were, almost to a man, disciples of John Locke, — professors more or less, probably less, intelligent of the philosophy that the great religious ideas — God, immortality, duty — were given to the world through external revelation imparted by men inspired for the purpose, written in "sacred books," and authenticated by signs and wonders. Half a dozen minds, perhaps, had distinctly outgrown this position. Dr. Channing was outside of it so far as the fresh vigor of his moral sense revolted against the conventional ethics of his sect, and his aspiration after a nobler humanity transcended the dull level of respectability where the Unitarians as a party stood; but he seems never to have been a complete transcendentalist. The Wares were full of evangelical piety, and were honest-minded as men could be; but they were neither deep students nor bold adventurers into new fields of speculative thought. A few scholarly men of fine literary culture read the German and French books; entertained their minds with the new thoughts; took an intelligent interest in them; accepted in their libraries the conclusions of Herder, Schleiermacher, Gabler, De Wette; but felt no call to announce their discoveries, lacking the moral earnestness, or the faith in the people, or the sense of professional duty, or the vitality of interest, that the reformer's task demanded. Among the ablest and most accomplished were some, who, from the constitution of their minds, could not take a side. As students, thinkers, men of letters, they had their opinions, and rather startling ones, too, in some cases; but, as clergymen, they considered it their office to repeat the traditions and teach the received theology in the most reasonable form.

The sect, as such, was torpid. It was respectable, and wished to remain so. It had put off its armor, and flung itself down on the grass, and was unwilling to be disturbed. Its piety was low: the sermon had become a moral essay; the hymns were didactic; the prayers were dry; the passion for holiness had cooled down to a sense of propriety. The creative period of the movement had passed; and the apathy was the deeper as the stir had been shallower. When Luther parted from Romanism, he was in the open sea, with the great winds blowing and the mighty waves tossing about him; but, when the Wares and Buckminster and their compeers left Protestantism, they were comfortably near shore, and soon tethered quietly to the wharf. The Unitarians were about as complacent a set of Christians as ever took ship for the kingdom.

In parting from Protestantism, Theodore Parker, on the contrary, believed himself to be slipping his moorings, and going out into the open sea, — the deep sea of truth. A man of complete integrity, an undivided nature, all of one piece, he could make no practical distinction between man and minister, scholar and preacher, man of letters and man of duty. All his thoughts were beliefs; all his beliefs were convictions. The nice discrimination between opinions of the library and opinions of the pulpit was unknown to him. Already his outspokenness had made him suspected as a disturber of the peace: he had received warning letters; had been called "infidel;" brethren had been prevented from exchanging pulpits with him by "ill health," "home engagements," "frequent absence from their desks;" but no open rupture had taken place, neither party being aware how wide the gulf had become.

The revelation was made on the now famous occasion of the ordination of Mr. Charles C. Shackford at South Boston, on the 19th of May, 1841. Mr. Parker preached the sermon, on "The Transient and Permanent in Christianity," from the text, "Heaven and earth shall pass away; but my word shall not pass away."

It was a memorable sermon. Though written in a week of languor; though regarded as poor by the preacher, and pronounced by a friend to whom it was read before delivery to be the weakest thing he had ever done; though loose in structure, redundant in style, and shadowy in definition, — it was a remarkable discourse, the more effective from the faults, that were such to the critical hearer alone. The gorgeous amplitude struck the popular imagination; and the moral earnestness that throbbed in the speaker's heart, and thrilled to his fingers' ends, made itself felt like the presage of a revolution. Not to be a moment compared, as a work of art, with Emerson's exquisite chant three years before, as a manifesto it was vastly more significant. The opening passage sounds an alarm: —

"In this sentence we have a very clear indication that Jesus of Nazareth believed the religion he taught would be eternal; that the substance of it would last forever.

Yet there are some who are affrighted by the faintest rustle which a heretic makes among the dry leaves of theology: they tremble lest Christianity itself should perish without hope. Ever and anon the cry is raised, 'The Philistines be upon us, and Christianity is in danger!'" On this hint the discourse proceeds, gathering volume as it goes on, and ploughing a furrow that was not to be mistaken, through the whole ecclesiastical domain. A few sentences will explain the effect the sermon produced:—

"Jesus felt his words were for eternity; so he trusted them to the uncertain air: and for eighteen hundred years that faithful element has held them good, distinct as when first warm from his lips. Now they are translated into every human speech, and murmured in all earth's thousand tongues, from the pine-forests of the North to the palm-groves of Eastern Ind. They mingle, as it were, with the roar of the populous city, and join the chime of the desert sea. Of a sabbath morn they are repeated from church to church, from isle to isle, and land to land, till their music goes round the world. These words have become the breath of the good, the hope of the wise, the joy of the pious, and that for many millions of hearts. They are the prayers of our churches, our better devotion by fireside and fieldside, the enchantment of our hearts. It is these words that still work wonders to which the first-recorded miracles were nothing in grandeur and utility. It is these which build our temples and beautify our homes. They raise our thoughts of sublimity; they purify our ideal of purity; they hallow our prayer for truth and love; they make beauteous and divine the life which plain men lead; they give wings to our aspirations. What charmers they are! Sorrow is lulled at their bidding. They take the sting out of disease, and rob adversity of his power to disappoint. . . .

"Looking at the word of Jesus, at real Christianity, the pure religion he taught, nothing appears more fixed and certain. Its influence widens as light extends; it deepens as the nations grow more wise. But, looking at the history of what men call Christianity, nothing seems more uncertain and perishable. . . .

The stream of time has already beat down philosophies and theologies, temple and church, though never so old and revered. How do we know there is not a perishing element in what we call Christianity? Jesus tells us *his* word is the word of God, and so shall never pass away: but who tells us that *our* word shall never pass away; that *our notion* of his word shall stand forever? . . .

"For centuries, the doctrines of the Christians were no better, to say the least, than those of their contemporary pagans. The theological doctrines derived from our fathers seem to have come from Judaism, heathenism, and the caprice of philosophers, far more than they have come from the principle and the sentiment of Christianity. As old religions became superannuated and died out, they left to the rising faith, as to a residuary legatee, their forms and their doctrines; or, rather, as the giant in the fable left his poisoned garment to work the overthrow of his conqueror. . . . The stream of Christianity, as men receive it, has caught a stain from every soil it has filtered through; so that now it is not the pure water from the well of life which is offered to our lips, but streams troubled and polluted by man with mire and dirt. . . . On the authority of the written Word, man was taught to believe impossible legends, conflicting assertions; to take fiction for fact, a dream for a miraculous revelation of God, an Oriental poem for a grave history of miraculous events, a collection of amatory idyls for a serious discourse 'touching the mutual love of Christ and the Church.' They have been taught to accept a picture sketched by some glowing Eastern imagination, never intended to be taken for a reality, as a proof that the infinite God spoke in human words, appeared in the shape of a cloud, a flaming bush, or a man who ate and drank, and vanished into smoke; that he gave counsels to-day, and the opposite to-morrow; that he violated his own laws; was angry, and was only dissuaded by a mortal man from destroying a whole nation. . . . What was originally a presumption of bigoted Jews became an article of faith which Christians were burned for not believing. . . . Matters have come to such a pass, that even now he is deemed an infidel, if not by implication an atheist, whose reverence for the Most High forbids him to believe that God commanded Abraham to sacrifice his son, — a thought at which the flesh creeps with horror; to believe it solely on the authority of an Oriental story, written down nobody knows when or by whom, or for what purpose; which may be a poem, but cannot be the record of a fact, unless God is the author of confusion and a lie. . . . Modern criticism is fast breaking to pieces this idol which men have made out of the Scriptures. . . . Men have been bid to close their eyes at the obvious difference between Luke and John; the serious disagreement between Paul and Peter; to believe, on the smallest evidence, accounts which shock the moral sense and revolt the reason, and tend to place Jesus in the same series with Hercules and Apollonius of Tyana. . . . Men who cry down the absurdities of paganism in the worst spirit of the French 'free-thinkers' call others infidels and atheists who point out, though reverently, other absurdities which men have piled upon Christianity. So the world goes.

"Almost every sect that has ever been makes Christianity rest on the personal authority of Jesus, and not the immutable truth of the doctrines themselves, or the authority of God, who sent him into the world. Yet it seems difficult to conceive any reason why moral and religious truths should rest for their support on the personal authority of their revealer, any more than the truths of science on that of him who makes them known first or most clearly. . . . To judge the future by the past, the former authority of the Old Testament can never return. The ancient belief in the infallible inspiration of each sentence of the New Testament is fast changing, — very fast. One writer, not a sceptic, but a Christian of unquestioned piety, sweeps off the beginning of Matthew; another of a different church, and equally religious, the end of John. Numerous critics strike off several Epistles. The Apocalypse itself is not spared, notwithstanding its concluding curse. . . . If it could be proved that the Gospels were the fabrication of designing and artful men, that Jesus of Nazareth had never lived, still Christianity would stand firm, and fear no evil. . . . The history of the Christian world might well be summed up in one word of the evangelist, — 'And there they crucified Him.' . . . Measure Jesus by the world's greatest sons, how poor they are! try him by the best of men, how little and low they appear! Exalt him as much as we may, we shall yet, perhaps, come short of the mark. But, still, was he not our brother?

the son of man as we are? the Son of God, like ourselves? . . . Who shall tell us that another age will not smile at our doctrines, disputes, and unchristian quarrels about Christianity, and make wide the mouth at men who walked brave in Orthodox raiment, delighting to blacken the names of heretics, and repeat again the old charge, 'He hath blasphemed'? . . . In an age of corruption, Jesus stood and looked up to God. There was nothing between him and the Father of all. And we never are Christians as he was the Christ until we worship as Jesus did, with no mediator, with nothing between us and the Father of all. . . .

"Already men of the same sect eye one another with suspicion and lowering brows that indicate a storm, and, like children who have fallen out in their play, call hard names. The question puts itself to each man, 'Will you cling to what is perishing, or embrace what is eternal?' This question each must answer for himself. My friends, if you receive the notions about Christianity which chance to be current in your sect or church solely because they are current, there will always be enough to commend you for soundness of judgment, prudence, and good sense, — enough to call you Christian for that reason. But, if this is all your religion, alas for you! The ground will shake under your feet if you attempt to walk uprightly and like men. You will be afraid of every new opinion, lest it shake down your church; you will fear, 'lest, if a fox go up, he will break down your stone wall.' If, on the other hand, you take the true Word of God, and live out this, nothing shall harm you. Men may mock; but their mouthfuls of wind shall be blown back upon their own face. . . . And alas for that man who consents to think one thing in his closet, and preach another in his pulpit! God shall judge him in his mercy, not man in his wrath. But over his study and over his pulpit might be writ 'EMPTINESS;' on his canonical robes, on his forehead and right hand, 'DECEIT, DECEIT!'"

Imagine words, of which these are the fewest possible specimens, spoken on a public occasion, from a pulpit filled with ministers, to an audience composed in considerable degree of clerical people! That it was listened to as quietly as it was, that only one man went out, that the other participants in the exercises made no immediate protest, is the wonder. But, if the shock was not felt instantaneously, it was felt soon.

The opinions themselves advanced by the preacher were not new: many half entertained them; more were dallying with them in an amateur way; a few held them in their studies as literary speculations, but breathed no whisper of them out of doors. These were the first to take alarm. As birds who have been sailing pleasantly before the gentle wind hurry to covert when the air becomes agitated and the black storm comes up, so these excursionists crowded back into the shelter of the walled town when they saw the dust-cloud on the road before them. The most forward made most speed to retrace their steps. One gentleman, a doctor of divinity, but a man of letters rather than a theologian, a radical in literature, but a conservative in sentiment and usage, who once had said to him, that if Strauss had written a small book, in a single volume, in a popular style, he would have about done the thing for historical Christianity; who on another occasion, when asked how he reconciled the conflicting accounts in the four Gospels, replied, "I don't try to reconcile them; you can't tell where fact begins or fiction ends, nor whether there is any fact at all at the bottom;" who on yet another occasion, when asked what he thought of Cousin's "Atheism," answered, "I don't know whether he believes in a God or not; but I know that he has the ethical and religious spirit of Christianity, and is a Christian;" who yet once more, when challenged on his belief in the prophecies of the Old Testament, responded, that he did believe them true prophecies, but only as every imperfect thing is a true prophecy of the perfect, — this gentleman, when the question was no longer one of literature, but one of custom and institution and social tranquillity, left the ranks of the pioneers, and fell back upon the old guard. He had gone out for a pleasant reconnoitre: he was not prepared for battle. The less distinguished felt quite at liberty to retire with the leaders, and fully justified in throwing an occasional stone from behind the breastwork. Man after man on whom Parker had reckoned for countenance was found wanting in the hour of need.

Boston rang with the controversy. The daily press took it up with such intelligence as it possessed. Here, before me, are clippings from the newspapers, preserved by Mr. Parker himself, who detected the hand of friend or enemy in the fluttering columns. "The Daily Advertiser" and "Evening Transcript" had communications from instructed pens, handling the matter with thoughtful discrimination. "The New-York Herald," then as now, trusting in the plenitude of its theological wisdom, passed final verdict on the merits of the controversy, and predicted the result. The religious papers, being more nearly concerned,—the "liberal" papers more especially,—did their best, probably, to be charitable; but the proverbial bitterness of family quarrels found constant illustration in their issues: it was not possible to repress the rancor engendered by disappointment, mortification, chagrin, wounded partisanship, and broken associations. The writers seemed all to use steel pens. The words "infidel," "scorner," "blasphemer," were freely bandied about. Parker's name was rarely spoken, except in connection with Voltaire, Paine, and other high priests of unbelief. His piety was called sentimentalism; his professions of faith, hypocritical; his learning, second-rate; his genius, apparent only in his rhetoric. Friendly writers were hardly more than apologetic: hostile writers alone forbore to practise the virtue of moderation.

The effect of the sermon on the preacher's ecclesiastical relations was felt instantly. One after another of the "brethren" cancelled exchanges that had been agreed on, making the usual transparent excuses for postponement. In July, the list had shrunk to twelve names; and of those twelve, only a portion stood faithful. The pressure that was brought to bear, both on the part of clergy and laity, against those who exchanged pulpits with the heretic, was greater than any but truly honest men could stand. Many were the revolvings and resolvings in ministerial breasts. "Is he willing to exchange with Mr. Parker?" "Would he, if asked, exchange with Mr. Parker?" were questions raised in church-committees when discussing a candidate. "What shall I do if Parker applies for an exchange?" was the question which the young minister anxiously put to himself. To exchange pulpits with Parker became the test of faith. The minister of a secluded parish where Parker's face was unknown might quietly treat his people to a sermon from an eloquent stranger whom they never suspected to be the arch-heretic; but, in the vicinity of Boston, these clandestine indulgences were impossible. A proposition to exchange from Theodore Parker made the heart sink, as the water in wells sinks at the coming of the earthquake. "Will your husband exchange with me next Sunday?" asked the proscribed man of the wife of one of his oldest friends. "I know he would with pleasure, but am quite confident that he has already made an engagement." — "Ought I to exchange with you?" said to him one of his neighbors, a man of unusual popularity and courage. "You know best," answered Parker. "But some of my people will be offended if I do." — "Very well," rejoins Parker; "let it go, then: I don't press the matter." — "But what would you do in my case?" said the pondering brother. Parker answered, "I should think freedom of thought and speech worth defending at all risks, and should make a matter of duty of the business; or, if I thought it of no value, I should say so." The argument was not conclusive. The exchange was not effected. The brother shared the prevailing opinion that the pulpit was not the place to vindicate freedom of thought and speech.

When Convers Francis was deliberating whether or no to accept the theological professorship at Cambridge, the authorities there advised him, "under the circumstances," to cancel an existing engagement to exchange with Mr. Parker in Watertown. One strong and noble man in Boston, who disagreed heartily with Parker's theological opinions, spoke of them in print as "shallow naturalism," described Parker as "the expounder of negative transcendentalism," in contrast with Mr. Emerson, who represented positive transcendentalism, and pronounced his system at once "ignorant and presumptuous," did, later, when the controversy was at its fiercest, announce to his congregation his intention to exchange with Mr. Parker, on the ground that difference of opinion did not justify breach of fellowship; that Parker was a Christian man and a devout minister; and that intellectual liberty was too precious to be sacrificed to a point of criticism. The announcement caused a flutter; the deed caused more; but the minister's avowal of motives partially disarmed consequences.

There were curious scenes at the meetings of the Boston Ministerial Association. The vexed question was the exchange with Parker. How far ought difference of opinion to prevent ministerial exchanges? That question were easily answered if taken alone; for Parker had himself carefully confined the difference of opinion to matters of learning and criticism. The man who said that every member of the Association, while he continued to be a member, had a right to claim an exchange from any and every other on the ground of fellowship, touched that point fairly; but the same man, a college-mate of Parker's too, confessed the secondary importance of the point by admitting that he would not exchange if asked, because influential men in his congregation would be offended. It was suggested, that, if any member of the Association held views distasteful to the majority, he should withdraw: no one recommended that such a one be expelled. One frankly advised that the Association be broken up. The discussion was made ridiculous by a remark from the clerical wit of the body, that, if a minister had a comical twist in the face, that was reason enough for declining an exchange with him. There were but two or three men — there were two or three — who never failed to bear their testimony to the Christian character and essential Christian faith of Parker. Their names cannot be mentioned; for the humility that was ever their characteristic would be hurt thereby. They were always present when courage was demanded, but absent when praise was bestowed. So let it be now.

The story of sectarian diplomacy is not pleasant; but it must be told, that the true position of things may be understood.

The journal, under date of Jan. 23, 1843, gives a full account ("to be printed in 1899, as a memorial of the nineteenth century") of a meeting of the Association at which Mr. Parker was present by particular request, for the purpose of conference on matters of ecclesiastical concern. To print it as it stands would be unprofitable and in bad taste: the pith of it is given here in illustration of the ecclesiastical spirit of thirty years ago. The attendance was large, with a fair representation of both sides. After an early tea, the embarrassing business began with the customary disclaimers and apologies, and gracious devices for smoothing the way. Then the chairman, a man of culture and a gentleman, opened the debate by charging that Mr. Parker's book was, first, "vehemently deistical," using the word in the worst sense; and, second, subversive of Christianity as a particular religion.

The book referred to was the "Discourse of Matters pertaining to Religion," published in the spring of 1842. It contained the substance of five lectures delivered in

Boston during the previous autumn. In preparing them for the book form, the author considerably enlarged them, adding at the same time an over-abundance of notes, chiefly of reference, but preserving the brilliant, popular style of the chapters. The volume has passed through four editions, is probably the best known of Mr. Parker's writings, and has exerted a wide and excellent influence. From time to time, instances of its converting power come up. A Western judge put it one Sunday into the hands of an idle, thoughtless youth, who was looking about for a pleasant Sunday time-killer. He took it reluctantly, — never, he said, having been able to read a religious book in his life, — and went with it to his room. By evening he had read it half through, and wished to keep it longer. A religious book like that he had never seen. If that was religion, he liked it. Some days after, the young man came to the judge, and said, "Will you sell me that book? I want to own it." — "No," said the judge: "I won't sell it to you; but I will give it to you." And the youth went off with the book, grateful. Years went by. The young man became prominent as a politician. A benevolent institution of the State needing patronage, which his friends were indisposed to give, he stood up and said, "You ought to give it. The institution is worthy of all assistance. I have been there, and examined it; and, if there are any Christian people in the world, the managers of that institution are Christians." Through his influence the aid was obtained. About the same time, his old friend the judge met him, and asked how he got on with his religious studies. "Oh, bravely! I have that book now: it has been lent ever so many times, and read till it was read almost to pieces. I have had it strongly bound in leather to preserve it." In the preface to the first edition, the author wrote, "It is the design of this work to recall men from the transient shows of time to the permanent substance of religion; from a worship of creeds and empty belief to a worship in spirit and in life. If it satisfy the doubting soul, and help the serious inquirer to true views of God, man, the relation between them, and the duties which come of that relation; if it make religion appear more congenial and attractive, and a divine life more beautiful and sweet, than heretofore, — my end is answered. I have not sought to pull down, but to build up; to remove the rubbish of human inventions from the fair temple of divine truth, that men may enter its shining gates, and be blessed now and forever." The language of the preface found comment in the incident above narrated.

This was the book that the chairman at the meeting of the Boston Association pronounced "vehemently deistical," and "subversive of Christianity as a particular religion." The preface had then been written. It is fair to add, that the incident just narrated had not occurred. But this is a digression. We must return to the meeting, where Mr. Parker is under examination. The chairman having opened the discussion, the next who took up the word, after expressing agreement with the chairman in regard to the character of the book, submitted that they were not met for theological discussion, and tried to confine attention to matters personally at issue between Mr. Parker and the Association to which he still belonged. This was the important thing. Mr. Parker's opinion concerned them no more than another man's, except as he was connected with an ecclesiastical body which they helped compose, and for the character of which they were responsible. Mr. Parker had been guilty of conduct unbecoming a member of the body, inasmuch as he had said and printed things reflecting on the conduct of the brethren.

Against this accusation Mr. Parker defended himself by protesting that he had never felt an ill-natured emotion, nor uttered an ill-natured word respecting them, on account of their withholden fellowship; that he put his own interpretation on events as the rest did, but had never wittingly disregarded truth, or violated propriety. Touching the doctrines of his book, he did not see how they could fairly be called "deistical;" for deists, if he knew any thing about them, denied the possibility of direct inspiration from God; whereas he not only admitted the possibility of such inspiration, but claimed inspiration for all men in proportion to their quantity of being and the amount of their spiritual obedience. If he was a deist, he made a new class, whereof he was the sole constituent member, and which all others excluded. The other assertion, that his book was subversive of Christianity, surprised him still more; for he had supposed it to be full of most essential Christianity. Christianity was one of three things: first, it was less than absolute religion; or, second, it was equal to absolute religion; or, third, it was absolute religion and something more. The first none of them would admit; the second he maintained; the third expressed their belief. If, therefore, they would specify what peculiarity Christianity added to absolute religion, would "point out the precise quiddity" that made absolute religion to be Christianity, they would do a great service to the unlearned. Would the chairman be good enough to instruct him? That there was no curl of the lip, or gleam of deadly import from the steel-gray eyes behind the spectacles, at this moment, the reader may believe if he will. The chairman reminded the questioner that catechising was not in order.

Mr. Parker's personal affair with the Association was then taken up. In "The Dial" of October, 1842, he had published a remarkably plain-spoken, not to say caustic article, reviewing the proceedings of an ecclesiastical council that was called to adjust the relations between the Hollis-street Society and the Rev. John Pierpont, its pastor, accused of conduct unbecoming a clergyman in persistently remaining and preaching on topics exceedingly distasteful to an influential portion of his people, more especially the vice, crime, and sin of manufacturing, selling, and promoting the consumption of intoxicating liquors. In his review, Mr. Parker had spoken of the "result in council" as a "Jesuitical document," thus reflecting on those who drew it up. The members of that council were prominent members of the Association. The charge was produced at length with much vehemence of manner. Mr. Parker had held up the council to the scorn and derision of mankind; had represented the members of it as a set of hypocrites and double-dealing knaves; had done his best to weaken their influence and ruin their character; with much more of the same sort: to all which the accused replied, that what he had written he had written, and for that was answerable; that for other men's interpretations of what he had written he was not answerable; what they charged he was at liberty to disclaim. To an accusation, that, in a sermon on the "Pharisees," he had meant to "take off" the Association, he replied, that, as the sermon was written a whole year before any trouble began, such an intention could not be imputed. So the debate went on from one point to another, to nobody's satisfaction.

The talk came back to the book and its doctrines. Mr. Parker asks for the peculiarity of Christianity as a religion. "It consists in a recognition of the authority of Christ as authenticated by miracles." Mr. Parker replied, that, admitting the miracles (for argument's sake), he did not see how they made to be true or binding what was not so already, or how they increased the obligation to be true and dutiful. For his part, he had no philosophical objection to miracles (in his definition of them), but only demanded more evidence for them than for common events. He was by no means certain of the genuineness of the Gospels; and, if he were, could not take what was there recorded as literally true. "We have heard enough!" exclaimed one of the examiners. "It is plain that Mr. Parker is no Christian; for Christianity is a supernatural and miraculous revelation." — "That may be," replied the defendant; "but that is the point to be proved. Nobody accuses me of preaching less than absolute morality and religion. If they can exist without Christianity, what is the use of Christianity?" — "But plainly Mr. Parker is no Christian. We cannot hold ministerial intercourse with a man who denies the miracles." — "Ah!" said Mr. Parker, "that is not the trouble: that is but a matter of theological opinion, at the best. The difference began before the Hollis-street Council, before 'The Discourse of Religion:' it dates back to the South-Boston sermon. I have some curious letters on that theme which one day may be published. I was at first surprised at the effect that sermon had on the Unitarian ministers. I looked round to see who would stand by me in the pulpit; and, in general, I have not been disappointed. In two persons I have been disappointed, — grievously disappointed."

Chandler Robbins, a sturdy conservative, but a resolute peacemaker, and the kindest of men, hereupon interposed, and said, "Since Mr. Parker finds the feeling against him so general, *I think it is his duty to withdraw from the Association.*" This touched the practical point. Approving voices joined in. Mr. Parker hurt their usefulness, compromised their position, &c.: he should withdraw at once. But this Mr. Parker had no mind to do. They had put him on his mettle, had waked the reformer in him, and must allay the spirit as they could. For his own part, he assured them, were he alone personally concerned, he would retire with pleasure; but a matter of much graver concern, even the right of free inquiry, was at stake. His retirement would be taken as a concession from him, and would be cited as a triumph for them: and, in that view of the case, his duty was to stay; and stay he would so long as the world lasted.

Here was a new dilemma. The chairman said, "Were this a body of free inquirers, and not an association of Christian brethren, I should withdraw myself." — "Why, then, ask me to withdraw?" said Parker. "Dr. Freeman was for many years a member of the Association, disagreeing with the rest so much in opinion, that they never exchanged with him." — "The case is not in point," was the rejoinder: "Dr. Freeman was not alone in being a Unitarian among Trinitarians." — "Indeed! Did *they* say so?" — "Besides, the difference between Trinitarians and Unitarians is a difference *within* Christianity: the difference between the Association and Mr. Parker is a difference between Christianity and no Christianity." — "But that is the very point in question. What *is* Christianity? and what is it that puts Mr. Parker outside of it?" — "We do not deny that you are a Christian man, but only that your book is a Christian book." — "But the man belongs to the Association, and not the book; and, besides, what is it that makes the book unchristian?" — "But, Mr. Parker, were you not a member of the Association, you certainly would not, with your known opinions, be admitted. Now, either you have changed your opinions since you came in, or you concealed them when you entered. Whichever be the case, you should withdraw." — "When I entered, my opinions were not asked, nor was I required to promise always to retain such as I held. If I do you an injury, you have the remedy in your own hands, and can pass a vote of expulsion at any time. It is a new thing to make miracles the Unitarian shibboleth of Christianity. A few years ago, it was said in the Association that 'Christianity once rested on two great pillars, — Jachin and Boaz, prophecy and miracles. Dr. Noyes knocked down Jachin; and George Ripley, Boaz: yet Christianity stood.' If I remember right, it was the chairman who said that." — "True," said the chairman. "I do recollect something about Jachin and Boaz: but I did not say I was one of them who said Christianity did *not* rest on the two; still less did I say that George Ripley had knocked the miracles down."

There was more talk to the same effect. At length Bartol spoke warmly in praise of Parker's sincerity; and Gannett, in his glowing, earnest way, responded; and Chandler Robbins chimed heartily in. This was too much for the tender-hearted iconoclast. He burst into tears, shook hands with R. C. Waterston, the host, and went out. In the entry he met the chairman, who had left the room a minute before. The kind, courteous gentleman, whose professional animosities, however vehement, did not strike deep, shook him cordially by the hand, and hoped to have a visit from him soon. So the matter ended. The sharp arrows fell harmless to the ground; the flushed faces became placid; the angry looks died away. Two days after the meeting, Mr. Parker received the following letter, which shows how one good man felt: —

From Chandler Robbins.

WEDNESDAY, Jan. 25, 1843.

MY DEAR FRIEND, — From the moment when you left the secretary of the Association on Monday evening, my heart has been yearning to unbosom itself to you. I felt most deeply the delicacy and the hard trial of your situation, and am constrained to say that you sustained yourself nobly. It would have been unjust to you to have been less frank than we were; and yet I fear that *my* frankness seemed ungenerous and unfriendly. I knew not what I ought to say in my struggle between the love I do most truly bear towards you, and the desire that the whole truth of your position relative to the Association should be clearly understood, and that you should be fully informed concerning all the matters which the Association had in consideration respecting you and itself. I grieved that you left just as I had begun to give a declaration of my individual opinions and sentiments; for I feared that I had been the cause of inflicting a wound, which my tongue should cleave to the roof of my mouth before it should intentionally give. Yet, after you had gone, I could more freely pour out those friendly and most affectionate sentiments, the flow of which would have been narrowed and restricted by your presence. And this I *did*, and felt better for having made a "clean breast:" indeed, I could not have gone to my rest that night if I had not. I am sorry, my dear friend, that we differ so much in our opinions on theological questions. I am sorry that a brother whose feelings and whose motives I so much esteem and love should feel under the necessity of publishing doctrines, that, in my opinion, are inconsistent with faith in Christianity as a special revelation, and in Christ as "the anointed of God,"—doctrines whose avowal necessarily prevents an interchange of pulpits between us. But this is all I have against you. Against you? no, between us, I mean, as a bar. All the other charges (those relating to the Hollis-street Council and the rest), however grave they may be held by others, do not weigh a feather's weight with me. I don't believe that you have said aught in malice against your professional brethren; and, when I hear any of these attempting to make out a case against you on such grounds, I have not the least sympathy with them.

It may be, my friend, that you are in advance of us all in theological knowledge, and nearer to the clear mount of truth; and that the interval that separates us in this journey of immortality is the true gulf between us. It may be that your soul is purer and more virtuous than ours, and that this moral superiority lifts you out of the reach of our sympathy, and gives you a vision of the spiritual world which our medium of view is too dark to allow us to discern. Or, my brother, it may be that you have speculated too boldly; that an intensely active intellect and much learning have carried you beyond the safe foundations of the eternal Word; and that you have as far to return, as we to advance, before we can come to stand together on the Rock of ages. There are questions which abide the solution of the all-exposing hours and the judgment of the Spirit of light. I do not wish to attempt to answer them. I only wish to regard you without "a beam in my own eye," while both of us shall be seeking humbly yet earnestly after "the truth as it is in Jesus." I hope that both may have more and more "of the spirit of Christ;" that, like him, we may be true children of the Father, and true brothers of mankind.

I cannot satisfy myself with this expression of my state of feeling towards you, being a sad bungler in the use of set forms of speech. I wish my breast had a window: I would go to you and sit in silence whilst you looked into it, if you would take the trouble to survey all its images which are associated in any manner with you.

Believe me your sincere friend,

CHANDLER ROBBINS.

To Rev. Chandler Robbins, Boston.

PLYMOUTH, Sunday Morning, Jan. 27, 1843.

MY DEAR FRIEND, — I thank you truly for your kind note of Thursday last; thank you for your sympathy; thank you, too, for the caution you give me. I can live with no sympathy but that of the Infinite, and his still small voice saying, "Well done!" but when sympathy, human sympathy, comes, it is truly welcome. You mistake a little the cause of my tears the other night. It was not a hard thing said by yourself or others. All might have said such as long as they liked: I would not have winked at that. It was the kind things said by Bartol and Gannett, and what I knew by your face you were about to say: it was this that made me weep. I could meet argument with argument (in a place where it is in order to discuss "the subjects" of a theological book which is talked of), blow with blow, ill nature with good nature, all night long; but the moment a man takes my part, and says a word of sympathy, that moment I should become a woman, and no man. If Pierpont had been present, I should have asked him, at the beginning, to say no word of defence of me, but as many of offence as he liked. I felt afraid, at first, that a kind thing might be said earlier in the evening, and am grateful to the "brethren" that they said none such till late. But to leave this painful theme.

I knew always the risks that I run in saying what was hostile to the popular theology. I have not forgotten George Fox, nor Priestley; no, nor yet Abélard, nor St. Paul. Don't think I compare myself with these noble men, except in this, — that each of them was called on to stand alone; and so am I. I know what Paul meant when he said, "At my first answer no man stood with me:" but I know also what is meant when a greater than Paul said, "Yet I am not alone; for the Father is with me." If my life ends to-morrow, I can say, —

> "I have the richest, best, of consolations, —
> The thought that I have given,
> To serve the cause of Heaven,
> The freshness of my early inspirations."

I care not what the result is to me personally: I am equal to either fate, and ask only a chance to do my duty. No doubt my life is to be outwardly a life of gloom, and separation from old associates (I will not say friends). I know men will view me with suspicion, and ministers with hatred: that is not my concern. Inwardly, my life is and must be one of profound peace, of satisfaction and comfort that all words of mine are powerless to present. There is no mortal trouble that disturbs me more than a moment; no disappointment that makes me gloomy or sad or distrustful. All outward evil falls off me as snow from my cloak. I never thought of being so happy in this life as I have been these two years. The destructive part of the work I feel called on to do is painful, but is slight compared with the main work of building up. Don't think I am flattered, as some say, by seeing many come to listen. Nothing makes a real man so humble as to stand and speak to many men. The thought that I am doing what I know to be my duty is rich reward to me: I know of none so great. Besides that, however, I have the satisfaction of knowing that I have awakened the spirit of religion, of faith in God, in some twenty or twenty-five men, who, before that, had no faith, no hope, no religion. This alone, and the expression of their gratitude (made by word of mouth, or made by letters or by a friend), would compensate me for all that all the ministers in all the world could say against me or do against me. But why do I speak of this? Only to show you that I am not likely to be cast down. Some of my relations, two or three hundred years ago, lost their heads for their religion. I am called to no such trial, and can well bear my lighter cross.

Perhaps I ought to say, that if the Association think I compromise them, and injure them, and hurt their usefulness, they have the remedy in their own hands, and in one minute can vote me out of their ranks. At that I will never complain; but, so long as the world standeth, I will not withdraw voluntarily while I consider rights of conscience at issue. I think, too, that, when I shall have more leisure (as I shall in a few weeks), I shall attend the meetings more frequently than heretofore. To withdraw voluntarily would be to abandon what I think a post of duty.

Excuse this long letter, and believe me

Truly your friend,

THEO. PARKER.

This was noble on both sides, and generous. But Theodore Parker knew now that he must stand alone; and he accepted the situation. Alluding to the bitter things written and said, he records in the journal, "All these things are disagreeable to me; but they must be. I can stand alone. I know the stake I laid down, and am not unwilling to pay the forfeit. I doubt not I shall be forced to leave the pulpit in this way: the clergy will refuse to exchange with me. I shall not be willing to write a hundred sermons a year for a hundred and twenty people (half children); so shall leave it for something else. I shall leave the calling if an opportunity occurs, but never the deep love I feel for it, nor ever neglect an opportunity to utter my word, and pray with men." To a friend he writes, —

"I feel it is a great work which I have undertaken. I know, that, so far as the ministers are concerned, I am *alone*, — ALL ALONE. But I have no ambition to gratify, and so neither fear the disgrace, nor covet the applause, they can give me. If I can speak the truth plainly to honest and earnest men, it is all I ask. The result is with the God of all; and you and I have no cause to fear. I have received the ready sympathy of intelligent and religious laymen, and confess that it makes me feel strong."

To Dr. Francis.

FEB. 14, 1842.

MY DEAR FRIEND, — It is a great while since I had a letter from you; and I confess the fault is my own. But now, as I can do nothing else, and, besides, want to write to you, I will do so. It is not often I have an hour for such a purpose; since to write two sermons a week, and spend five days of the week in other matters, and get no sabbath on Sunday, though it may do well with stronger heads, yet goes hard with mine. I never cared much for the sympathy of other men, and never less than now; but, once in a great while, I feel it is not altogether pleasant to stand alone, to be viewed with suspicion and hatred. Blessed are those men who can take things as they find them, and believe as the mob believes, and sail in the wake of public opinion. I remember you said a year ago, "He that defies public opinion, like the man who spits in the wind, spits in his own face." It is so. Better men have found less sympathy than I. I do not care a rush for what men who differ from me *do* or *say;* but it has grieved me a little, I confess it, to see men who think *as I do* of the historical and mythical matter connected with Christianity, who yet take the stand some of them take. It is like opening a drawer where you expect to find money, and discovering that the GOLD has gone; only the copper is left. This has been my fate very often. I put my finger on *a minister*, and "he ain't there." Somebody said the ministers were a very selfish set: I fear there is some little truth about it. Some think, and even say, they are glad at what has been done, and glory in freedom of thought, and all that sort of thing; but it is all TALK, TALK, TALK.

To Dr. Francis.

JUNE 24, 1842.

MY DEAR FRIEND, — There is one thing of some consequence to me, — though of little to you, — of which I want to say a word or two (I am not complaining of any one, nor writing a jeremiade to grieve you). The experience of the last twelve months shows me what I am to expect for the next twelve years. I have no fellowship with the other clergy: no one that *helped* in my ordination will now exchange ministerial courtesies with me. Only one or two of the Boston Association, and

15*

perhaps one or two out of it, will have any ministerial intercourse with me. "They that are younger than I have me in derision." Well, *quorsum hæc spectant?* If I stay at Spring Street, I must write a hundred and four sermons a year for about a hundred and four people. This will consume most of my energies, and I shall be in substance *put down*, — a bull whose roarings can't be stopped, but who is tied up in the corner of the barn-cellar, so that *nobody hears him;* and it is the same as if he did not roar, or as if he were muzzled. Now, this *I* WILL NOT DO. I should not answer the purposes of life, but only execute the plans of my enemies, — of the enemies of *freedom of mankind.* I must confess that I am disappointed in the ministers, — the Unitarian ministers: I once thought them noble; that they would be true to an ideal principle of right. I find that no body of men was ever more completely sold to the sense of expediency. Stuff them with good dinners, and freedom, theology, religion, may go to the Devil for all them. I believe the abolitionists and temperance-men are *half* right when they say, "*The Church is a humbug;*" and the *other half* of the right is, "*the ministers are ditto.*" Now, freedom of thought and speech are either *worth preserving*, or *they are not worth preserving.* If the ministers think the *second* (as their life shows they do), let them say it plainly and manfully, that the public may no longer look to those clouds without rain: if they think the *first*, then something must be done.

Now, I am not going to sit down tamely, and be driven out of my position by the *opposition* of some, and the neglect of others, whose conduct shows that *they* have no love of freedom except for themselves, — to sail with the popular wind and tide. I shall do this when obliged to desert the pulpit because a free voice and a free heart cannot be in "that bad eminence." I mean to live at Spring Street, perhaps with Ripley. I will study seven or eight months of the year; and, four or five months, I will go about and preach and lecture in the city and glen, by the road-side and field-side, and wherever men and women may be found. I will go eastward and westward, and northward and southward, and make the land *ring;* and if this New-England theology, that cramps the intellect and palsies the soul of us, does not come to the ground, then it shall be because it has more truth in it than I have ever found. I am perfectly free of two things, — of FEAR and AMBITION. What I have seen to be false I will proclaim a lie on the housetop; and, fast as God reveals truth, I will declare his word, come what may come. It grieves me to the very soul of my heart's life to think of leaving the ministry (which I *love* as few *ministers* love it) and this little parish; but, if duty commands, who am I to resist? If you have any word of advice to give me, I shall be glad; and, in the mean time, rejoice in the new field of usefulness opening its harvest to you. I hope you will teach the young men to be valiant, and fear not.

Parker was brave; but, as has been said already, he was tender, with an immense capacity for suffering. He could battle long and well; but to battle alone cost him dear. He wanted love; and they from whom he had the best right to expect it failed him. He speaks of "impudent letters" from gentlemen in his profession who had been friendly. One or two of his old personal intimates changed their manner. That Mr. Andrews Norton should receive him coldly was not strange; but, when one who had been to him a bosom-friend made him a visit which deserved to be spoken of as "the most painful I ever received from any man," the bitterness went to his soul. Those who called themselves his admirers and lovers had a singular faculty of remembering his severe words, and forgetting his grand ones: the spirit of excessive righteousness came upon them. Of the three that abide, charity seemed so immeasurably superior to faith and hope, that they stung the poor sore soul with admonitions against sarcasm, warnings from bitterness, beseechings to bear in mind the Christian law of love, till it is wonderful the high-strung nature did not become wild. That he was able to answer such letters as sweetly as he did is a testimony to his patience that should weigh something against the biting indignation his kind censors deplored. It is so easy for people to forgive their neighbors' enemies!

From the Journal, June, 1842.

"I have done nothing for a month; been stupid beyond measure; was never in such a state before. Never knew till now the sadness of that perpetual disappointment of hoping, hoping, hoping, and finding nothing come of that hope. But I submit. I think I should complete the drama of my life well by dying next autumn, after the book is ended; but can't tell if it will then end. External sadness is in store for me, no doubt; but the light is all bright and beautiful within. I feel somewhat as Luther in that sad period of his life. . . .

"Few would mourn at my departure. Some few souls who know me as I am would find a few tears in their eye, but wipe them soon (such is the nature of man); others who have heard my word with joy would look for another: but the many to whom my name has come would rejoice at my fall, that the churches might have rest for a season. Why am I spared? I know not: not for what I enjoy. I asked but little from Heaven: that little I have not. I am disappointed, but not soured; still cheerful. My smiles are few, but heartfelt. Let me but finish the work now in my hands, that my past life may have its fruits on earth, I will embrace death. I know not wherefore I am spared. There are some living that I cling to as to angels: these it were sad to leave. But"—

The death of Dr. Channing awakens a similar strain. To a friend he writes, Oct. 5, "Dr. Channing is dead. He died at Bennington, Vt., of the typhus-fever, on Sunday afternoon. You know, as all do, that no man in America had done so much to promote truth, virtue, and religion as he. I feel that I have lost one of the most valuable friends I have ever had. I have known him well, and have been blessed by his counsels and liberal sympathy. His mind was wide, and his heart was wider yet. I know not what we shall do without him: but there are good men still left; though never, it seems to me, could he be so ill spared. Well, he has done a good work. I am glad that he has lived thus long, and glad that he has gone to his reward."

The journal betrays a sadder mood: "I have to-day heard of the death of Dr. Channing. He has fallen in the midst of his usefulness. His faculties grew brighter as age came on him. No man in America has left a sphere of such wide usefulness. No man since Washington has done so much to elevate his country. His life has been spent in the greatest and best of works. A great man and a good man has gone home from the earth. Why, O my God! are so many left when such are taken? Why could not I have died in his stead?

"To-day was the funeral of Dr. Channing. There was a strange combination of men to perform the services of the burial, — two of them bitter enemies, two others differing heaven-wide from the doctor. It made me feel disagreeably to see them in the pulpit to speak of Dr. Channing, — men whom I have heard mock at and deride the excellent man. But strange things meet in this world."

Still he had the great consolers which never fail, — "Nature, full of God. It is new to me each year. Then there are my studies, the prospect of usefulness, endeavors to promote the public virtue." Work, the greatest of consolers, does not desert him. His lectures in Boston and elsewhere cost him great labor. The toil on De Wette's "Introduction to the Books of the Old Testament" was not ended till the summer of 1843, having cost a world of toil, as well as more time and money than he could afford. His mind teemed with literary projects: schedules of industry fill pages of the journal. Studies in primitive Christianity; studies in church-history; studies in the development of doctrine; studies in the dynasties of Egypt, — the dismal chronicles of conjectural kings; studies in mythology, — Persian, Semitic, Christian; studies in philosophy, — Bacon, Leibnitz, Plato, — occupy his severer days. In hours of comparative leisure, the poets of Greece — Tyrtæus, Anacreon, Sappho, Orpheus, and Pindar — come to his side. In profounder moods of meditation, his companions are

La Motte Fénelon, Madame Guyon, and John Woolman, in whose sober, deep piety his soul finds repose. Translations from the German of mystic hymns reveal the still longings of his spirit for the infinite peace. His life was getting stormy on the surface; but below reigned the perpetual calm.

That he was able to preserve the even balance of his opinions attests the depth of his conviction. He would not be driven to extremes, or tempted to associate himself with views that lay invitingly adjacent to his own. The cool abyss of pantheism must have looked attractive to his fervid faith. The glowing diction of his books roused something more than a suspicion that he had plunged into that shoreless sea. But he writes to a friend, "I am no pantheist, nor ever was. I am no more troubled by pantheism or by anthropomorphism than at noonday the evening and morning twilight trouble me. The whole difficulty comes of attempting to get a logical and definite conception of God; but neither the head nor the heart will subsist on abstractions." He was accused of depreciating Jesus. To another friend he writes, "It seems to me, that, if we *always* obeyed the law God has written on our hearts, the decisions of reason, of conscience, and of faith, would be as infallible in their action as the instinct of the bee and the law of gravitation now are. But no man is in this state. We are not one with God as Christ was: so we are in doubt and fear. The best and wisest now feel this the most deeply. *Jesus alone felt none of it.*" He was called an enemy of Christianity. The journal testifies thus: "Christianity is a field on which may be raised the strangest crops,—wood, hay, and stubble, wheat and beans. The soil remains, the crop varies. . . . The time is coming when men will wonder quite as much at the Christianity of the nineteenth century as we wonder at that of the ninth century. . . . Christianity is progressive, because it is not *positive*, but natural: therefore Christianity is the hope of the world, the desire of all nations." He is blamed for making rash and hasty generalizations; yet his letters to learned correspondents show how long and carefully he still entertained questions that his philosophy might have been pardoned for answering on *à priori* grounds,—such as the primitive condition of man on the planet, the descent from one or from many stocks, the order and law of human development, the rank of succession in the series of religious stages. No suspicion of Darwinism, or of any other theory of evolution, seems to have entered his mind. It was urged against him that he impatiently discarded miracles; but his refusal to sweep away stories of miracle on general grounds of theory, his discrimination between different classes of marvels, and his curious studies in the literature of the supernatural,—some of them very recondite, and all of them perfectly ingenuous,—refute these insinuations. His name was constantly associated with that of Thomas Paine; he was tauntingly spoken of as Paine's disciple and successor: but when Mr. Horace Seaver invited him to take part in the celebration of Thomas Paine's birthday, Jan. 30, 1843, Mr. Parker sent the following reply:—

West Roxbury, Jan. 14, 1843.

Dear Sir,—Your favor of the 11th instant came in my absence from home; and I now hasten to reply to the invitation you offer me. With the views I entertain of Mr. Paine's character in his later years, I could not, consistently with my own sense of duty, join with you in celebrating his birthday. I feel grateful, truly so, for the service rendered by his *political* writings, and his *practical efforts in the cause of freedom;* though with what I *understand* to be the spirit of his writings on theology and religion I have not the smallest sympathy.

I am, respectfully, your obedient servant,

Theo. Parker.

Horace Seaver, Esq.

There has been no intimation, during all these years, of failing or impaired vigor, except in the beginning of a letter to Dr. Francis, written from St. John's in August, 1842; and there he merely says that he has gone down East for his health. The journal of Jan. 1, 1841, reports him as dull and in low spirits, but "well in body, temperate in meats and drinks." But the autumn of 1843 found him so much spent from anxiety and toil, that a voyage to Europe was recommended. His great work, the De Wette, was done and issued: other subordinate work was completed or dropped. He had passed through a critical passage in his career, and had reached a point in his professional life at which pause and retrospect were desirable. Anxious to survey his work from a distance, to give his mind rest by letting in a flood of new associations, to compare the ideas and institutions of the Old World with those of the New, to see some of the men whose thoughts had nourished him, and to visit some of the places which had been so long venerable to his imagination, he accepted with gratitude the bounty which made the year's vacation possible; and on the 9th September, 1843, set sail in the ship "Ashburton" for England, and put the Atlantic Ocean between himself and his past.

To those who review now the period just covered, it is a surprise that there should have been so much feeling on so small occasion. Mr. Parker's slight unpleasantness with a score of gentlemen in Boston hardly justifies so much animosity on one side, or so much sorrow on the other. By the side of Savonarola's deadly fight with Pope Alexander, or Luther's grim battle with Rome, the Unitarian controversy looks paltry indeed. The shedding of ink was copious; but it depleted only inkstands, and it blackened only paper. The sighs and wailings were uncalled for; weak; almost, it may be thought, childish. But Theodore Parker was no sentimental milksop: he was a brave, firm man, who, when tested, proved himself possessed of heroic qualities. He could face jail, and even gibbet: steel he could have met with tougher steel. But no such fierce provocatives stirred his blood, or made the involuntary tears caused by the stings of insects an impertinence. Savonarola and his peers were driven back on their moral grandeurs, shut up in the citadel of their souls: they had at once the support and the consolation of their own heroism. Parker had none of this stimulus: unbuffeted and unchallenged, he had nothing to do, and nothing to bear. His friends weakened him, and his foes did not strengthen. He fainted because there was nothing to fight.

Then, it must be said, he believed that a second reformation, more radical than Luther's, was at hand; another conflict "between old systems and the Word," in which the soul was to be on one side, and Protestantism backed by Romanism on the other; and he believed himself called to be a leader in the struggle. In the proscribed body of Unitarians, the advanced guard of liberalism, disciples of reason, friends of culture, he naturally expected to gain allies and supporters. To find them blind and heedless, if not false, was a bad omen for the cause of truth, a sad revelation of the adversary's might, and a bitter presage of coming woes. What the Unitarians said or did was of small moment, in itself considered; but, as indicating the temper of Christendom, it was profoundly significant. It told the new Luther that he was to stand literally alone; and it told him this, not in tones that thrilled the blood, but in smooth accents which betrayed the lack of spiritual virility in the speakers, and implied the disbelief of it in the protestant, who had not even the comfort of being assailed. This was the situation as he viewed it. The view may have been mistaken, distorted, distempered; but it was honest: and they who can share it by an effort of imagination will not condemn as unmanly the personal sorrow, or the evil forebodings it brought with it. To a mind so exercised there is no medicine like travel in the great world of Europe, which quiets while it strengthens souls like his ; for there, while many things are a-making, many things are made. The world's judgment is written large in the world's history; and monuments of victory proclaim the final success of what seemed once to be hopeless struggle.

CHAPTER IX.

EUROPE.

Mr. Parker's year in Europe was no holiday trip for sight-seeing: it was a serious pilgrimage. His object was, not to kill time, but to improve it; not to evade work, but to prepare for it. He took mind and conscience with him; had a clear notion of what was worth seeing, and a sense of his own deficiency, which was likely to make him receptive of the best things. No more intelligent or loyal American ever went abroad. But the Old World was to him a new world to be explored for treasure that his own continent did not possess. On the fly-leaf of his European journal is a pencil-drawing of the little village church in West Roxbury, put there, it would seem, as a symbol and a remembrancer, to keep before him the simplicity of his vocation in presence of the rich cities and superb cathedrals he was to visit. On other leaves are lists of things to be seen in different cities, — in England, matters relating to his own and his wife's ancestors; points in New-England history and biography to be looked up in the herald's office; the Cudworth Papers in the British Museum; Lord Howe's monument in Westminster Abbey: in London, the houses of Johnson, Franklin, Newton, and Milton; the London University; "see Hallam and Hennell; ask Dickens about the writer on American newspapers in 'Foreign Quarterly Review:' in Germany, examine the schools in Saxony and Prussia, the Herrnhütter Establishment: in Switzerland, *ascend Mont Blanc.*" These hints strike the key-note.

The pilgrimage begins in New York, where he is detained three days, "The Ashburton" waiting for a wind. The bad weather does not keep him housed. He visits Lydia Maria Child, soon after known as the brilliant writer of "Letters from New York;" and passes hours with Isaac T. Hopper, for whom he expresses the warmest admiration: "I have never seen a man who charmed me so much as a thoroughly Christian gentleman. He is fearless, kind, industrious, frugal, and as true to moral principle as the needle to the star. I can never tell half the veneration I feel for him. It makes me strong to see him." In company with John Hopper he explores the wicked haunts of the city; goes to Palmo's on Broadway; spends an hour at the "Five Points;" inspects the "Tombs," and gets no better impression of the justice administered there, but a pleasanter one of the sanitary condition of the prison; attends church at St. Paul's, and thinks the service unaffecting, "fussy." On the 9th the party go on board ship, accompanied by a few friends, who leave with them a fragrant blessing of peaches and flowers. The shore of America floats away in the sunset. "My friends are behind; but ONE is with me to whom my mortal weal and woe are united. I often think I ought never to return; yet perhaps I shall. Be this as Heaven appoints."

Mr. Parker was a thorough landsman. He did not like the sea, nor the sea him; but no sickness could repress his indomitable energy. Books failing, he tries thinking; plans courses of sermons; lays out schemes of professional work, projecting his past labors into the future, with difficulty detaching his tenacious mind from its associations. He is disturbed by the cruel distinction between the cabin and the steerage and forecastle, — a hundred and sixty poor wretches in the steerage with almost no comforts, and thirty in the cabin living in luxury. "As the lion in the wilderness eateth up the wild ass, so the rich eat up the poor." One of the earliest entries in the journal thus expresses the spirit in which the pilgrimage is undertaken: "I am now to spend a year in foreign travel. In this year I shall earn nothing, neither my food nor my clothes, nor even the paper I write on. I shall increase my debt to the world by every potato I eat, and each mile I travel. How shall I repay the debt? Only by extraordinary efforts after I return. Those I design to attempt." Then he maps out a comprehensive scheme of labor, and commits it to paper, as if to make sure of fidelity to his vow.

The voyage of twenty-five days ended at Liverpool. The business before him began at once. We cannot attempt to tell what he saw; for he saw every thing there was on the surface, and much that lay beneath. His was a busy journal. It contains no fine writing, but records of places and people visited, and copious memoranda for thought. His route varied from the usual track (there was no beaten track then) just enough to take in a few spots of historical interest rarely visited by ordinary tourists. Liverpool and Manchester are prodigies to him of wealth and power. At Chatsworth he notices the "Christus Consolator" from which the familiar print was taken. He gathers acorns from the ditch at Kenilworth, and plucks ivy from the walls of Leicester's pride. At Warwick he admires the Vandykes and Holbeins; the picture of Charles I. on horseback; the portraits of Strafford, Ignatius Loyola, John Locke. At Stratford he copies curious inscriptions on tomb and chapel-wall; one of which should be given here, if the combination of old English and modern hieroglyphics did not make exact transcription hopeless. At Oxford, wonders in quick succession astonish him,—the venerable buildings, the halls, pictures, and, above all, the books. In the Bodleian Library, not satisfied to be a gazer, he must be a reader too; and has a quiet little time with William of Ockham. The journal leaps from Oxford to Paris, plunging into the latter city with a devouring appetite which nothing can satiate. He calls a cabman, who proves to be a good fellow, takes compassion on his ignorance of the place and the language, and points out to him every thing of interest. (That was a time when an American was a curiosity and an object of reverence.) His first destination was the Sorbonne, to present a letter to Victor Cousin, — the Sorbonne in the daytime, the Opéra Comique in the evening. He admires the nobleness of the ancient churches, — Notre Dame, the Panthéon, St. Sulpice, St. Étienne du Mont, — notes the curious non-observance of the Sunday, copies the queer names of the streets, marks the thrift and intelligence of the working-people. No public building is passed by. He looks in at the Morgue; rambles about among the old book-stands on the quays. The great gallery of the Louvre overpowers him with its glory. There he sees the Venus of Milo, which he thus speaks of in connection with the Venus de Medici in Rome: "The *toy woman* came to her perfect flower in the Medicean Venus: that is all she is, — woman as a plaything, a bawble woman, voluptuous, but not offensive directly to the conscience. It is only after much reflection that you say, 'Get thee behind me!' But the Venus of Milo is a *glorious human creature*, made for all the events of life. Imagine the Venus de Medici as a mother, as a sister, as a wife to some rich man, and his fortune perished! Pah!"

He has time to peep into lecture-rooms, and take notes of lectures on all sorts of themes, from mysticism to mineralogy, from the philosophy of Descartes to the first movements of life in the zoöphyte. In the Jardin des Plantes he hears a lecture from Isidore Geoffrey St. Hilaire on "Vultures," which contained interesting facts. He takes lessons in French, and practises writing the language by describing in that tongue Père la Chaise and other places of interest. Reading, theatres, walks about the city, occupy the leisure-hours. From the prayer-book in use at the Oratoire he copies the following remarkable version of the twenty-third Psalm:—

"Tu m'es si bon que par ta Providence
Parfums liqueurs, j'ai tout en abondance:
Tant de douceurs accompagnent ma vie,
Que mon bonheur est digne d'envie;
Et tu feras que dans ta maison sainte
Je passerai tous mes jours en ta crainte."

Hôtel de Cluny, Porcelain Factory at Sèvres, Musée d'Artillerie, Palais de Justice, Hôtel de Ville, Hôtel des Invalides, Bibliothèque Royale, the Gobelin tapestry, St. Germain des Près, Palais des Beaux Arts, École des Beaux Arts, St. Denis, Versailles, each calls forth its appropriate emotion; while the procession of eminent men that pass before him is too long to enumerate.

He liked to haunt the Boulevards and the borders of the Seine, and recall the great events of French history; seeing in the foreground the gay multitude, in the background the awful events of times past,—the rivers of steel which once ran through the streets; the blood which soaked down, and dripped into the catacombs. He stood on the site of the old Tour de Nesle, scene of mad revelry and murder; remembered the Palais de Thermes as the place where the soldiers hailed Julian emperor, and where the "Apostate," so called, lived all winter without fire, save once or twice in a brazier; found where Abélard's house used to be.

He went to the very roots of the old city. The Parini of Cæsar's time came back. "The word 'par' is the same as 'bar,' I take it, and meant the *limit* between two great and hostile tribes of Celts. So the Parini were the borderers, the frontier-men, of old time, and had their stronghold on the island in the Seine with its two wooden bridges." Next came the Paris of Julian's time, next the Paris of the Merovingians, then of the Carlovingians. He gets at the curious fact, that the foundation of Notre Dame contains remains of an old Roman temple, with an inscription still on the stones. He must have been a tired man, when, after twenty-six days of this work, he took leave of the city, and set off by diligence for Lyons.

At Lyons, "the city of massacres," he goes into the cellar where Polycarp "preached the gospel of Christianity when it cost something to be a Christian;" stands on the very grave of Irenæus; sees the bones of the Christian martyrs piled up in a large vault; and in those memories forgets the "Boston Association, the heroes of the Thursday Lecture, and the trials, dangers, and sufferings of Brothers —— and ——." Avignon comes next in order. There was the Palais des Papes, — convent, palace, prison, and castle in one. He stands (with what emotions!) in the secret chambers of the Inquisition; sees the holes where the instruments of torture were put up, the fireplace for heating pincers, the dungeon where heretics were starved to death; and recovers the failing consciousness of his identity in gratitude that those hideous days are past, and in resolve that the future shall be worthy of its opportunity. A day was more than enough for Arles; and the most engaging thing about Marseilles was the view of the sea. Genoa then opens to him her princely gates, and welcomes him to romantic memories and delicious art: it is a sadness to break away from it, and sail even by the "Charlemagne" to Leghorn. From Leghorn, two horses took him in a coach over the level, cultivated country, where women carried piles of fire-wood on their heads, and walked barefoot, in order to save their coarse hob-nailed shoes, to Pisa. Here the Duomo, Baptistery, Leaning Tower, Campo Santo, call forth due notice, and the beggars due comment; but here he finds other curious things, — paintings, relics, historical sites, which travellers do not commonly know enough to ask about.

Pisa introduces the pilgrim to Florence, the fascinations of which are so engrossing, that he stays there ten days without making a record in the journal. There is the San Marco, full of reminiscences of Savonarola. There is the Medici Chapel with Michael Angelo's "Day and Night," the tower of Galileo, the cathedral, the baptistery, the seat where Dante contemplated the beautiful bell-tower. There are the great churches on which architects and artists had lavished their genius. There is the Santa Croce, where the illustrious Florentines are buried, the exiled and persecuted sleeping in peace at last. There are the miracles of art, — the works of Raphael, Titian, Del Sarto; the Apollo, the Laocoön, both of which rather disappointed him at first; the great portraits, Julius II., Leo X.; the Fornarina, which surpassed his expectation; the Seggiola, — "What a painting! God in heaven, what a painting!" There is a famous library too, the Laurentian, with treasures of literature. What is there not in Florence for one with Parker's eyes? But Florence, too, must be left. He returns to Leghorn, and takes vessel for Naples. Of course, nothing of interest is omitted. He ascends Vesuvius, and goes so near the crater, that he is in danger from the masses of melted stone which fall continually. A few of the smaller pieces hit him on the shoulder. Baiæ, Puteoli, Pozzuolo; the places "where the old Romans revelled in their Titanic lust, poisoned one another, framed plans or conspiracies which affected the welfare of the world;" the spots where Cicero had his villa, where Horace wrote his poems, where Pollio fattened fish for his table with refractory slaves, where Virgil, by tradition, was buried, — all these he visited. But here, as everywhere, he made a study of the town itself, the population, taxes, cost of living, statistics of traffic, &c.; having an eye for the humanity in the streets, as well as for the art in the galleries. Herculaneum and Pompeii interested him so much, that he made a diagram of them. At the theatre only, he went to sleep.

From Naples to Rome by diligence, — a tiresome drive, with lumbering vehicle, jaded horses, clumsy conductor, and frequent delays from trivial causes. The most beautiful part of the scenery was passed in the night. The early morning gives sight of Gaëta, the ugly cattle on the Pontine marshes, the desolate Campagna, the wretched people, the dirty villages. As the day wears on, the classic spots, one after another, appear. He is on the great road which Hannibal and Fabius Maximus and Sylla travelled with their armies. On either side the plains had been battle-fields. Cæsar and Pompey and the triumvirs had taken their turn of victory and defeat on these vast wastes. The traveller has Horace in his hand, and follows the poet in his description of the spots passed. Along the Appian Way, in sight of the mounds that covered fine villas of wealthy nobles, past tombs and aqueducts, they roll on from Albano, and come within view of Rome. The gate was passed at half-past three o'clock on a March afternoon. Close by famous buildings they drove to the Dogana. In an hour's time, after applying in vain at seven public-houses, lodgings were found at 70 Via del Babbuino, — two pretty little rooms on the street, first floor, and one in the rear, for twenty dollars per month, service included. It was the 20th of February. Rome was in the height of its glory and gayety. It was carnival-time. The party took a coach, and "rode round to see the nonsense. *Mem.* — The beggars in the midst of this festivity, their hideous deformity, crippled, &c. Gave half a paul to one. Beggars are sad enough objects at all times: on a festal day what shall we think of them? Men throw flour at each other, and the rich spoil the coats of the rich with what would have gladdened the heart of the beggars. 'Whatsoever ye would that men should do unto you.' Ah! this is the place where Paul was beheaded. They would crucify Christ if he were to come here or to Boston. God bless men! they can't crucify Christianity. In the evening L. and I went to the theatre, — the everlasting Polichinello."

This homebred rustic has an eye for art. In the Vatican, the palaces, the churches, he picks out the gems, and yields to them the homage of unfeigned admiration. The beauty of the Apollo Belvedere comes to him now. The Laocoön, which disappointed him in Florence, holds him by its wonderful spell of suffering. The silence of the agony impresses him as it does everybody; but everybody does not get at the artist's secret as he does. The point that Lessing makes so admirably in his famous essay — that the marble description of a *cry* would be fatal to a work of pure art — occurs to Parker, who makes no allusion to Lessing, and probably had never seen his essay. Michael Angelo's "Moses" is to him a wonderful thing: "He looks as if he could compile or devise laws to hold a nation for thousands of years, and seems armed with the deep insight into causes which marks the philosopher, and the ready faculty to grapple with effects that makes the practical leader." Michael Angelo is his master. Raphael now and then disappoints, as in the "Galatea;" Domenichino seldom meets anticipation; Leonardo and Titian surprise him in their greatest paintings by their perfect accomplishment and subtle feeling. There must be a *soul* in work, if he is to be pleased. In architecture, the simple grandeur of the temple is more impressive to him than any magnificence of style, or sumptuousness of decoration.

But it is as a Christian minister, after all, that the pilgrim sets himself to study Rome. The Christendom of fifteen centuries is there. The most imposing part of living Christendom is there also. He is there for a few weeks: he must not miss his opportunity. Well equipped with learning, well furnished with understanding, singularly endowed with candor and ingenuousness, with a scholar's reverence for the past, a wise man's charity for the present, a philosopher's trust in the future, a disciple's humility, a reformer's earnestness, he addressed himself to the task of studying the religion of Rome. One of his first expeditions was to the Coliseum; and thus his impressions are recorded: "It is more perfect than I feared. It has now been consecrated to keep it from the devastations of the barbarians of modern Rome. At the entrance is a cross, with a sign-board which promises forty days' indulgence to all who will kiss the cross. In the very centre of the amphitheatre is another cross with another direction, — that he who kisses that shall have plenary indulgence for two hundred days. If Seneca or Cicero were to come back, he would think the world had made little progress in the *theory* of religion, whatever had been done in the practice of it. Sometimes a monk preaches here. What recollections come up! — the gladiators, the wild beasts, the Christians, the emperors, the armies; Rome fallen; the new Rome, and that, too, fallen. Oh! one could move the stones by preaching here. I could not help looking at the place professionally, and thinking it would be a fine place to preach *Parkerism* in."

The churches are a study, — St. John Lateran, famed for the twelve great councils held there. "In the church is the table on which Christ and the twelve took the last supper. Here, too, are the heads of St. Paul and St. Peter. Here, also, we saw the actual well of Samaria between two pillars from Pilate's house in Jerusalem; the stone on which the soldiers cast lots for Christ's vesture; the pillars between which Pilate stood when he told the people to take the Christ and crucify him; the column that split asunder at his crucifixion (it is split asunder quite uniformly the whole length; it is about a foot in diameter, and ten feet long); and four columns supporting a slab which shows the exact height of Jesus, — just six feet; and not far off is the Santa Scala, a flight of twenty-eight marble steps, which Jesus descended when he went to be crucified. It is not lawful for any one to walk up them: penitents ascend on their knees. We saw several going up; but they are poor folks, for the most part. At the head of the stairs is a chapel, containing a picture of Jesus when twelve years old, painted by St. Luke, — the only one from that artist.

"Went to St. Peter's, the cupola, the ball, and all that is commonly seen here. The Inquisition near by, with four or five hundred inmates. The guide says they are not put to the torture in these days; but they never come out again, and are never seen any more or heard of." Santa Maria Maggiore: "Exceedingly rich, but not imposing; not a religious architecture. It seems to me the modern Unitarians would like this style. It is clear, actual, the work of logical and demonstrative heads, wholly free from mysticism. The fragments of Christ's cradle are preserved here; and the miracle of the snow that covered the Esquiline Hill on the 5th of August, 352."

CATACOMBS. — "Went to the catacombs in the vicinity of St. Ignese, a little way out of the city. Entered the chapels with the little caves on each side, each large enough for a single body. These once contained the ashes of the martyrs. In some of the chapels the ceiling was covered entirely with paintings. There was the *Good Shepherd;* here *Christ preaching*, though but a child; here the *Hebrew youths in the flames;* here *Daniel in the lions' den;* here the whole *story of Jonah*, emblematic of the death and resurrection of Christ; and here the *miracle at Cana*, the symbol of transubstantiation, and many more.

"I am confirmed in my opinion, that, long before Constantine, the Church had departed from the ideal simplicity of the primitive state so often contended for by Protestants. Indeed, I am now more than ever persuaded, that, as Christ gave no form, the first one used by the apostolic churches was much less simple than we fancy. I shall never forget the impression left on my mind by this visit. Yet, as I walked about here, I could not but think how easy it must have seemed, and have been too, to bear the cross of martyrdom. The recollection of Christ, of the apostles, the certainty of the prayers and best wishes of men of earth, the expectations of heavenly satisfaction, — all would conspire to sustain the spirit, and make the man court, not shun, the martyr's death.

"Father Marchi, a priest who has devoted his life to the study of the catacombs, went with us, and explained every thing; showed us curiosities without stint relating to the early Christians; bottles of dried blood of the martyrs; instruments of torture; images of Christ, of the Virgin, &c. I saw proofs enough that some of the alleged 'corruptions of Christianity' date back to 107 A.D. The worship of the Virgin can be traced nearly as far; that of the invocation of saints for the dead, quite to that very year. I think you find the ceremony of saying mass, as at present, pretty distinctly traced back to the beginning of the second century. In the chapels of the catacombs are frescoes, painted in the second century (at the latest, in the early part of it), representing the miracle of Cana in such conjunction with the saying of mass, that it shows a distinct allusion to the transformation of the bread and wine into the body and blood of Christ; at least, they say so."

On Ash Wednesday he visits the Sistine Chapel to see the pope celebrate mass in presence of the cardinals and other church dignitaries. "The music was fine. The ceremony did not impress me at all. It brought to my recollection Him of Nazareth, whose picture hangs over the altar. I remembered what he said of the temple, of the chief priests, &c. The whole filled me with compassion, and drew tears from my eyes. Is it always to be so, and in Christian Rome, by the head of the Church? The ceremony of kissing the pope's hand or foot, the kneeling before him, and burning incense, and all in the name of the *carpenter's son* at Nazareth, — it is quite too bad. I honor the learning, the zeal, the devotion, the humanity, there is in the Catholic Church; but this nonsense is too much for me. As if God laughed at the whole, there was the awful fresco of Michael Angelo representing the Last Judgment; and here, too, was Aaron, with the Hebrews worshipping the golden calf; and Moses in indignation, breaking the tables he had just received! There is no irony like that of Nature." The music rarely fails to touch him; the ceremony never succeeds. As the pope blesses the palms, he compares the violet dresses of the cardinals with the garments that were once stripped off the peasants' backs, and laid beneath the ass's tread. The passionate music of Allegri's "Miserere" will not drown his spiritual remonstrance against the haughtiness of the assembly; and as, standing on the *piazza*, he looks at the illuminated dome of St. Peter's, "like a story from the 'Arabian Nights,'" the mendicants in the square suggest the number of the "honest poor for whom no candle burns all the year."

Still he has a heart of charity. At St. Peter's he hears the sweet music at vespers, and smells the incense: the music, "the perfection of music, — it would stir the heart of a statue to hear it. The children were gathered together (i.e., a *few* children) to be instructed. Half a loaf is better than no bread; and I make no doubt the essentials of Christianity are inculcated."

He was presented to the pope, who stood in the simple dress of a monk, with his back against a sort of table, and talked a little about the state of Rome, the English language in America, the famous polyglot cardinal at the Propaganda. He looked kindly on the visitors, made a sign, and they withdrew.

Mr. Parker made serious efforts to understand the religion of Rome, not from the monuments only, or the ceremonies, the superstitions, and the dumb-shows, but from the men who interpreted and administered it. He visits under the best guidance the College of the Propaganda, where men of every nation, tongue, and complexion, are instructed in the faith, and prepared to proclaim it to all lands in their own speech; and he visits the Industrial School for Poor Girls; the Conservatory of the Virgin of Sorrow, founded by Cardinal Odescalchi. Letters of introduction make him acquainted with men eminent in the Church for piety, goodness, and learning; with Dr. Grant, Bishop Baggs, Father Glover, Cardinal Acton. Bishop Baggs and Father Glover favor him with long conversations on the doctrines and institutions of the Church; he not disputing with them, but questioning, to be sure of understanding their position. "I feared that I might have sometimes done them an injustice; but I think I have not. I have found them universally kind, perfectly free from cant. They don't draw down the corners of their mouth, nor talk through their nose, nor roll up the whites of their eyes, and say 'O-o-o-o!' There is much about the Catholic Church that I always liked, — its music, architecture, paintings, statues. Besides, there is a long list whom I truly reverence enrolled on its calendar. The Church is democratic (in the good sense) in appointing its saints. None are made saints except for *personal* qualities; not for wealth or birth or power, but goodness. What if they do pray *to* the saints, as the Protestants say? or *through* them, as *they* say? The true God, I take it, would as lief be called St. Cecilia as Jehovah; and a true prayer must be acceptable to the true God. I told a Jesuit father so the other day: but he said that was an *odious doctrine;* it justified idolatry.

"The Catholic Church practically, I think, cultivates the feelings of reverence, of faith, of gentleness, better than the Protestant churches; but I can't think it affects the conscience so powerfully, and I know that at present it does not appeal to the reason or practical good sense. While Bishop Baggs says, '*Out of the Catholic Church is no salvation*,' he adds, '*but none is damned except for his own fault; and many may be in the soul of the Catholic Church who are not in its body*.' God only knows who. I wish I could think better of the priests here.

"It is difficult to say what is the present condition of the Catholic Church: they are certainly making great exertions to extend their faith in all parts of the world. The present pope is a pious and excellent man, I should judge,—one that fears God, and loves mankind; believing himself fallible as a man, but infallible as head of the Church; and his character has had an influence on the Church. I should be sorry to see the Catholic Church fall now; for which of the Protestant sects could take its place? Perhaps it will outlive them all. If I wanted to convert a fop to Christianity, I would send him to Rome; but, if I wanted to put a philosopher in the Catholic Church, I would send him anywhere but to Rome."

It is the custom of young people, on the eve of their departure from Rome, to drink from the Fontana di Trevi. The last night Theodore Parker was there, he walked out to the aqueducts (it was full moon); took a last look at the Coliseum, where on a former midnight he had seen an owl light on the cross, and hoot; viewed for the last time the Capitol, the columns, and bade them all farewell: perhaps he thought never to see them again, but was grateful for the sight once in his life. The next day (Thursday, the 11th of April), at one o'clock, the diligence passed the Porta del Popolo, crossed the Milvian Bridge, and travelled over the old Flaminian way toward Bologna.

On the 20th he is in Venice. "Venice is a dream of the sea. Occidental science and Oriental fantasy seem to have united to produce it. A pagan Greek might say that Neptune, drunk with nectar and Aphrodite, slept in the caves of the sea, and dreamed as he slept: Venice is the petrifaction of his dream. The sun colors curiously the walls of her palaces and churches: it seems as if their wealth had run over, and stained the walls. What a history was hers! what a destiny in the economy of the world! Who that lived in the time of the second crusade could ever have fancied her present lot? Yet who knows that her ports shall not again be full of the wealth of the East, and merchants from afar traffic with her? Let canals and railroads do their work, and she may live again."

From Venice by rail to Padua, and thence by diligence to Vicenza; thence by vetturino to Verona; from Verona over the Brenner Pass to Innsbrück, — the lovely, romantic town, surrounded by picturesque mountains, where the wolves could then be heard by the villagers talking together at night. He takes time to see the twenty-eight colossal statues of royal persons, in bronze, that surround the tomb, surpassingly rich in carving, where the Emperor Maximilian was not buried. From Innsbrück to Munich, of which small mention is made. From Munich to Regensburg; the funny little towns on the way being "done" in ink on the pages of the journal, there being no better use for the space. From Regensburg by *dampf-schiff* on the Donau to Passau and Lintz, the same industrious but not artistic pen making caricatures of the ugly faces on the boat. The curious would not be much enlightened in regard to the scenery on the Danube by these sketches. At last, on Tuesday the 7th, at about seven o'clock in the evening, he is at the "Golden Lamb" in Vienna. The city struck him as the most frivolous city in Europe, — elegant, easy, heartless: only St. Stephen's seemed to redeem it; and that belonged to another age. "All the mediæval cities are serious: even the Paris of the middle age is serious, almost sad-looking; but the modern Paris is far less frivolous than Vienna. For Vienna there is no life of science, art, literature, or commerce; only politics and pleasure." But he enjoyed the pictures in the gallery of Count Esterhazy and the Royal Gallery, — the Murillos, Raphaels, Peruginos, Paul Veroneses. The famous Correggios he admired less. The journal mentions nothing of this; only the music of Strauss, which seemed singularly suited to the city. Twelve years afterward he advised friends in Vienna not on any account to miss the paintings, mentioning the particular gallery in which his favorites hung; but the music of Strauss impressed him as more congenial to the place, — "rich, rhythmic, graceful:" it reminded him of Paul Veronese's pictures, "examples of a joyous festivity of well-bredness." The drive from Vienna to Prague had few incidents, though the blithe pencil made its quaint observations on the page of the journal. Prague was interesting. The ancient city, type of the middle ages; the Jews' quarter; the venerable Hebrew burial-place; the antique synagogue, the walls whereof are black with grime, because to clean them might erase the name of God, supposed to be inscribed somewhere on the stone; the monumental bridge; the grotesque legends of St. John Nepomuck; the palaces; the Wallenstein Fortress; the Black Tower and the White Tower; the queer streets; the odd churches, saturated with the superstitions of hundreds of years; the memorials of Huss and Jerome and the religious wars, — got hold of Parker by his faculty of veneration. He bought some Hebrew books in a Jewish bookstore surprisingly cheap. He could have bought the complete Talmud in twelve volumes, large paper, a fine copy, for forty gulden. Twelve days are all he can spare for Dresden: but there are Raphael's divine "Madonna," and Titian's "Tribute Money," and Veronese's "Marriage of Cana," and Holbein's "Virgin," and the Dutch masters; and there in the

"Green Vaults," more interesting than the jewels, interesting to him as those are, are the ring and drinking-cup of Martin Luther, and the crucifix of John of Bologna. On the evening of April 18 he is in Berlin.

"Do you know," he writes to Dr. Francis, "what sort of a place Berlin is? No? Imagine a sandy plain forty miles square, with one or two nasty rivers trying to get through it, but doubtful all the time that they had taken the right way; in the centre of this plain, and on the banks of the most doubtful of the rivers, imagine a great number of brick houses covered with stucco, and a few churches, and so forth, of the same material; then imagine one street sixty or seventy feet wide and two miles long, with another street two hundred feet wide and one mile long, having four rows of lime-trees in it, a foot-walk in the centre, and two carriage-ways, one on each side; then add some hundreds of other streets, all straight, — and you have a conception of Berlin. For the moving part of it, imagine a thousand hackney-coaches, the drivers with cows' tails on the top of their caps, a hundred private carriages, four hundred drays for beer, a hundred and fifty carts and wagons for other business, thirty thousand soldiers, sixteen hundred and fifty students, a hundred and eighty professors, a king, Baron Von Humboldt, and two hundred and seventy thousand others; imagine the king with a belly like Uncle Tom Clarke, the students with mustachios, the professors lecturing on *Dagesh lene*, the king 'counting out his money,' Baron Von Humboldt sleeping on his laurels, and the two hundred and seventy thousand smoking, walking, weaving, making pipes, and getting dinner, — and you have an idea of the *personale* of Berlin."

The days here are given up to literary matters, hearing lectures, visiting celebrities, studying the institutions of government, the habits and morals of the people, inspecting schools, collecting statistics of education, and such like.

A day in Potsdam, — to most travellers, much the most agreeable feature in a short sojourn in Berlin, — for some reason, gave him no satisfaction: he counted it a day wasted. Sans Souci was not to his taste. Of the Museum he hardly says a word; of the music and musicians, who gave lustre to the flat city, not a word: but of the scholasticism of the place there is much. Hengstenberg and Twesten and Marheinecke and Vatke and Michelet and Boeckh and Schelling, — he heard them all, each in his own department of philosophy, history, antiquities, or philology. Hegelianism was in the ascendant. Here is a characteristic description of a lecture by a young disciple of the school (Werder) on *Logik:* "The point at issue was *Bestimmtheit* (the definite ground or substance of thought). He got into a great passion and a desperate fix with his *Bestimmtheit,* trying, as I dimly gathered, to discover the *Ur-Bestimmtheit* (the fundamental foundation). He said in *Bestimmung* there was *Daseyn* (being) and *Réalité.* Hereupon a fat, chubby student, with cheeks like one of your classmates, evidently his ma's darling, tried hard to conceive the difference; but, after numerous ineffectual attempts, gave it up in despair. Then said the professor, 'In Daseyn there is Etwas real, und Anders' ('something real, and something else'). Now, 'Etwas ist durch und durch Etwas, und nicht Anders: Anders ist durch und durch Anders, und nicht Etwas' ('The something is through and through something, and not the else: else is through and through else, and not the something').

"He got into quite a dithyrambic mood upon this; put his finger on the organ of individuality, then laid it alongside of his nose, then flourished it in the air. It is no easy thing to go down to the profound of Hegelism. You must take off your *Sinnlichkeit* (corporeity), which is all of many men; then lay aside your *Vorstellungen* (notions), which is, with most men, like plucking Æsop's jay;

then take off your *Begriff* (conception); then you are 'far too naked to be ashamed.' In short, you are an *Urmensch* (primitive man), a *blosse Geist* (pure spirit). You have then the proper 'alacrity in sinking:' you go down, down, down, and learn that *Seyn* is equal to *Nichtseyn*."

The most interesting of his studies in Berlin were those on the civil and social condition of the state and people. These were at once comprehensive and minute. They are too long for insertion here, even if lapse of time and the social changes of the last generation did not considerably diminish their value for us. But it is interesting to know that Theodore Parker, on the spot, did not put a high estimate on the moral state of the Germans. The ancient reputation for chastity which Tacitus gave the women, was not, according to his observation, sustained by facts. The statistics of the consumption of beer and ardent spirits proved that intemperance was a prevailing vice, — not the intemperance that maddens, but the intemperance that muddles. He estimated, that, in Prussia alone, from forty to forty-five million gallons of distilled spirits was consumed yearly; while the consumption of beer was something enormous.

The ride by rail to Wittenberg through a beautiful country was a great delight, and Wittenberg itself was pure satisfaction. His steps led him directly to Luther's grave in the Schlosskirche. Opposite was the grave of his friend, the illustrious Melancthon; and near each were paintings of the men, said to be by Cranach. "Luther is sadly spread out, and looks hard." The church contained the pulpit in which Luther sometimes preached, and the chancel where stood the tombs of the electors, Frederick the Wise and John the Steadfast. In the church, copies were for sale of the ninety-five theses which Dr. Martin Luther, on Oct. 31, 1517, at the Eve of the Festival of All Saints, nailed to the door of the Schlosskirche. Theodore bought one on the spot, and inserted it at the appropriate place in the journal. "What a change from then till now! Where shall the work end?" At night he walked in front of the church, lost in meditation. "The evening star looked down; the soft air fell upon my head: I felt the spirit of the great reformer. Three centuries and a quarter, and what a change! Three centuries and a quarter more, and it will be said, 'The Protestant Reformation did little in comparison with what has since been done.' Well if THIS work be of God."

He went to Luther's house; saw the very room where he used to write and think and work; the stove which he devised himself, with its reliefs representing the four evangelists and other scriptural characters; the seat at the window where he sat and looked out at the evening sky; the table at which he took his meals, and studied with Melancthon and the rest. The books (he had not many) were gone. Other rooms contained curious relics,—a beer-jug, a glass cup, some embroideries from the hand of Catherine Bora, impressions of his seal. Outside the walls was the spot where Luther burned the Papal bull. It was railed round, and planted with shrubbery. A young oak grew in the midst of it: the old oak under which the bold deed was done had been hewn down in the Seven-Years' War. The monument was visited, of course. On a pedestal of polished granite ("I regretted the *polish*"), beneath a Gothic canopy of cast-iron, stood the bronze figure of Luther in his preacher's robes, with his Bible in his arms. "A grand figure, large, manly, with that peasant's expression, but full of nobleness and commanding faith." Below was the inscription:—

> "Ist's Gottes Werk, so wird's bestehen
> Ist's Menchen Werk, wird's untergehen."

To the Rathhaus, the church-steeple, wherever Luther had been or might have been, this true disciple of

Luther went, drinking in the great German's soul all the time.

At Halle he heard Erdmann defend Schleiermacher from the charge of pantheism; saw Tholuck, and heard him lecture; went to the house of Gesenius, the great Hebrew scholar, walked in his garden, plucked a leaf from the vine that grew over his window, and paid a visit to his grave.

At Leipsic he went about with Dr. Flügel to see old Hermanns, whom he heard talk about German scholars, and lecture; and dropped a tear on the grave of Charles Stearns Wheeler, an excellent American scholar, and a beautiful spirit, who went to Leipsic to study and to die. At Lützen he saw the stone where Gustavus Adolphus died, and the Rathhaus where his body lay. At Weimar, the city of Wieland, Herder, and Goethe, he had the poor satisfaction of viewing the outside of Goethe's house. At Erfürt he remembered the cloister where Luther, when a monk, paced up and down, and the monastery where he took his vows. At Gotha he admired the fine gardens that beautified the town. At Eisenach he went out early to the Wartburg, where Luther lived and worked in seclusion. "Saw the very room where he toiled in translating the Bible, the table he wrote on, the spot on the wall where he threw the inkstand at the Devil. The blow must have been a hard one; for it knocked off the plaster, and left the ink on the stone itself. But relic-hunters must not be critical. Here is the closet he used, studded all over with thick-headed nails; the chapel where he used to preach 'justification by faith,' and 'hatred to the pope.' This was his Patmos. It is a fine position. You see a great ways from the Wartburg." At Frankfort the Jews interest him, and he puts down thoughts on the religious condition of Germany. At Heidelberg there were learned men to see, — Schlosser, Ullman, Umbreit, Hävernik, Delitzsch, Paulus, Creuzer (men whom he knew well by their books), Gervinus, a young man since so famous in the philosophy of history, and from this moment one of Theodore's warm friends. After Heidelberg comes Carlsruhe, then Stuttgart. There was Thorwaldsen's statue of Schiller, and, in plaster then, Dannecker's beautiful statue of the Christ, which J. P. Lesley calls the noblest image of the Christ in the world. Parker admires its grandeur and purity, but thinks it a little *transcendental.* At Tübingen, Ewald and Baur were the great figures, — the former the wonderful historian of the people of Israel, the latter the founder of the historical school of New-Testament criticism. He had long talks with both, besides hearing them lecture. The conversations were not fluent; for Theodore had not the gift of tongues in great profusion; but he contrived to get at the heart of some important matters. Baur was a prodigy of learning. "How many hours a day do you study?" asked his visitor. "*Ach! nur achtzehn*" ("Only eighteen"), replied the old man. The American never touched that mark even in his best days; but he did what the German did not, — he spent much time in adapting the results of his mental toil to the people, and in putting them into plain working shape for social uses. The Tübingen giant was aghast at the idea of taking the general public into his confidence: it was the American's effort and pride to do so. The German lived in his library to a great age: the American died in the prime of his years.

At Bâle he saw, as was natural, a great deal of De Wette; walked with him; dined with him; visited under his guidance the curiosities of the place. At Berne he enjoyed the society of the Follens, kindred of the good Charles Follen, so affectionately remembered at home. From Berne he had his first view of the Alps. "The solid mountains seemed clouds, not at all to belong to the earth." It was in Berne, too, that his wife earned her name of "Bear," or "Bearsie," from her delight, not unshared by her husband, in Bruin, the tutelar deity of the city, enshrined in his capacious pit. At Lausanne there is a cathedral, an old castle, Gibbon's house, and fine scenery. At Geneva, memories of Calvin and Servetus, of Rousseau and Voltaire, crowd upon him. "Went into Voltaire's house: saw his study, sleeping-room, all just as he left it. The furniture is of the plainest character. From this little room he made kings and popes tremble." There were no great exploits at Chamouni: only the Montanvert and the Mer de Glace. The stay there was short. Martigny, Vevay, Fribourg, Lucerne, came in rapid succession. The heroic legends find their place here. At Zurich he heard Hitzig lecture on certain points of Hebrew syntax: "Quite entertaining, as might be expected." He also heard Oken lecture on "Amphibia:" "A little man, with an enthusiastic face, forty to fifty years old; lectures with great rapidity. Not many pupils for this course." At Schaffhausen, Schenkel is the object of chief interest. Retracing his steps to Bâle, the traveller, who seems to be in a hurry, judging from the note-book, pushes on to Strasbourg. There the cathedral is the prominent feature. He mounts the spire as high as the police permit. Mayence, Wiesbaden, Biberich, Ems, Coblentz, — no notice of any thing but the scenery. In Bonn he tried to see Bleek, but found him not at home. Presented his letter to Nitsch; but he could read no English. They talked, however, not much to the American's delectation: for the professor was narrow, cold, and dry; was surprised to learn that the Unitarians existed without a common confession of faith. He spoke of Strauss as *ganz und gar unchristlich.* What he was at *heart* he did not know: his life, he confessed, was pure.

He admires, as all do, the Cathedral of Cologne, but does not believe in finishing it. "The day of building grand churches is over. Ours is not a believing age, but an investigating one. Better days will come, when a nobler civilization shall incarnate its thoughts, and, without oppressing the poor, rear temples to God most high." The pictures of Rubens in the Cathedral of Antwerp were disappointing. The descending Christ "is a man, not a dead God." Liege and Aix-la-Chapelle awaken thoughts about the Catholic Church.

"What is to become of the Catholic Church I neither know nor care much. I have little fear that it will bring back the middle ages, while the philosophy of the age, the entire spirit of the times, is against it."

At last he gets back to England. The journal becomes more and more sketchy and illegible: much of it is in pencil, as if the pilgrim became impatient as the time for returning home drew near. In London he sees Carlyle, Sterling, Hennell (whom he finds more negative than positive in his religious views), and others of eminence; tries, without success, to get a publisher in England for the translation of De Wette; hears William J. Fox preach about the Jews, and is introduced to him after sermon. "He may be the best man in London; but his face is unfortunate." Of course, the round of sight-seeing in London is performed with energy; but few impressions of it are recorded in the journal. A scant page is given to Cambridge, and that contains nothing of significance. In Liverpool he finds Martineau, and talks with him about "promiscuous things."

The days were doubtless fuller than the journal. The "promiscuous things" would have appeared weighty to anybody else; for Mr. Martineau was not one to dwell on trifles, and Mr. Parker never wasted the rare moments of opportunity. At Cambridge he fell in with an English scholar whose special pursuit was Aristotle. He could boast that he knew Aristotle by heart. His visitor had read Aristotle, and was ready enough for discussion on his philosophy; but that topic exhausted, as it was at length, Parker introduced the name of Plato. The Englishman had read Plato, but only once. So the Yankee, who perhaps had read him once also, but remembered him, descanted copiously on Plato, analyzing the separate Dialogues, and setting forth his views over against those of Aristotle. Perhaps he called that " talk about promiscuous things."

The journal of Sept. 1 has this record: " Sunday, after a most prosperous and felicitous voyage of twelve days, completing the quickest passage ever made, I reached home, saw the household, William Whitney, the blessed Russells, — all the four little and live plants in bed, — and Squire Cowing. Who shall tell my joy at returning? who the rapture with which I saw old friends?

" I really believe that my enemy *hath left me;* at least, *for a season.* I can't tell the gratitude I feel for that."

This enemy was the trouble in his head, which had pained and alarmed him from time to time in his travels. His health had not been uninterrupted. He was ill in Florence, and again in Rome, with symptoms in the side which were distressing; but his apprehensions he kept to himself.

From Florence, in January, he wrote to his friend Dr. Francis, " I have now had five months to consider my own position. I feel all its melancholiness, the severity of the task laid on me: but I feel, too, that I must *on, on;* that the time of rest will never come in my day, and for me; but, so long as I live, that I must war against the false gods, and their priests as false. I have done little hitherto: if health continues, I may, perhaps, do somewhat. I am grateful for this opportunity to pause in the middle of my course, and see where I am going. I have done wrong things, no doubt; but, the more I think of it, the more the general tendency of my path seems to me the true one, and the less do I feel an inclination to turn away or to stand still." Whether his subsequent travels in Italy, Germany, Switzerland, altered his mind, we have now to see. The year in Europe had been a great privilege and a great delight. He had seen the past face to face, and could fill it in as a strong background to sustain his present, and throw into relief his future. It had been a year of consolation, which he felt the need of; and of experience, which he also felt the need of. The effect of it was visible ever after in the rich fund of memories it supplied, but more palpably still in the solid groundwoık of conviction on which he built.

CHAPTER X.

THE CONFLICT RENEWED.

THEY who imagined that Theodore Parker would return from Europe a submissive member of the Boston Association, with changed views and altered purposes, deceived themselves. He came back with every opinion and every determination more than confirmed. He had surveyed his position from a distant point; he had viewed it under all lights; he had examined the institutions of Christendom in the places of their power; he had talked with high priests of the Papal Church in Rome, with Protestant ministers and theologians in London, Oxford, Berlin, Heidelberg, Bâle, Zurich; he had attended lectures from the most eminent professors in philosophy; he had studied the working of ecclesiastical and doctrinal systems; he had noted the signs of the times in the speculative, social, and moral world; and the result was a deeper conviction than ever of the justness of his own method, and the correctness of his own conclusions. He felt himself, more than before even, a reformer, — one who was commissioned along with many others to lead a new religious movement, as significant in its time as Protestantism was when it appeared. His beliefs were not imported: they were the native product of his own mind and experience. They were felt before they were formulated. As a boy, almost as a child, his sense of the reality, the immanence, the infinite perfection, of God, had been profound; his assurance of the soul's personal immortality was beyond necessity or reach of argument; his reverence for the moral law, as voiced by his private conscience, was habitual and deep. He seems never to have doubted on these three points; and they were the cardinal points of his religious faith. Subsequent study and reflection hardened the feeling into faith, and the faith into formula, but added nothing essential to the substance of belief. To give expression to these three great verities, to make them seen in their beauty, appreciated at their intrinsic value, and accepted as vital principles in private and public life, was his ruling passion. He proposed as the great object of his labor to prove by wide historical survey that the leading races of man gave the sanction of their thought to his three fundamental positions; and he made a multitude of very interesting and close studies in the subject,— studies conducted, not as a partisan or a controversialist, but as a philosopher, in a spirit of singular candor. He read the best literatures; he gleaned industriously from all fields; nay, he ventured on all tests. The writings of atheists and materialists were as familiar to him as the writings of believers. He knew Feuerbach as well as Cudworth, Vogt and Moleschott as intimately as Fichte and Sintenis. He was eager to talk with the German professors at home and abroad about the New Hegelians and their strange views. Some of his fastest friends were disbelievers in his theological opinions, able and eloquent men too: he was glad to confront their minds with his own, and so to test his faith. From every encounter he came out with stronger conviction.

The sermons preached in West Roxbury after his return were charged with positive faith, larger, broader, more earnest, than had come from him before. The negative side of his theology was presented incidentally, that the affirmative side might be made more prominent. He disturbed what he considered rubbish, that he might reveal the temple; he removed the shanties of the workmen, that the people might behold its open doors. He had no objection to the belief in miracles, provided their importance was not exaggerated, or their function misconceived. He was willing that people should believe in prophecies, if they would not regard them as demonstrations of truth. As has been repeatedly said, a score of notes on the pages of the journal show how deeply interested he was in the forecasting power of the human mind, and how little disposed he was to put limits to it. He had no wish, apparently, to reject any thing that was of active service in the cause of religion. What he did reject was thrust aside simply because it stood in the way of direct appreciation of religious truth. He wanted that, and could not be satisfied that any should be contented with less.

But for the unwise passion of Mr. Parker's opponents, the former controversy might not have been renewed. He might have remained at West Roxbury, a devoted parish-minister, a diligent student and writer, comparatively unknown in the religious world outside of Boston, and unfelt as a power beyond the confines of his sect. His enemies did for him what his friends never would have done; what he might never have done from his own ambition. In November, 1844, Rev. John Turner Sargent, minister of the Suffolk-street Chapel in Boston, — a mission-chapel under the charge of the Benevolent Fraternity of Churches, — invited Mr. Parker to exchange pulpits. Had Mr. Sargent been an independent congregational minister, responsible to his society alone, his action would have made no great stir; but being, as it were, the agent of an association, the Executive Committee of the Benevolent Fraternity felt themselves compromised. They took alarm; called a meeting immediately; deliberated; passed resolutions; framed a remonstrance, which was sent to each of the ministers at large; and addressed an earnest letter to the transgressor of ecclesiastical proprieties. The case was interesting. Mr. Sargent was a valued minister among the poor. His family contributed largely to the erection and embellishment of the chapel where he preached. He spent freely of his private property for the people under his charge, and was untiring in his labors in the lower parts of the city. His family had wealth and influence. His personal character was above suspicion: no shadow of reproach clouded his name. A devoted, upright, self-denying man, he went out into the alleys and streets of Boston, gathering together the poor and the forsaken, and forming a society which prospered under his ministry, and became strongly attached to him. He was never openly accused of preaching in his pulpit, or believing in his study, the opinions which made Mr. Parker obnoxious: indeed, he disclaimed intellectual sympathy with them in the letter he wrote to the remonstrating committee. But all this availed nothing. He had exchanged with the arch-heretic; he justified the act; he would make no promise of future obedience to his superiors; and the resignation that self-respect dictated was accepted. The ministry to the poor lost its best man; an excellent pastor was taken from service he seemed made for, and eventually from the calling for which he had shown himself eminently fitted, because the Unitarian body had not courage to stand by its own principle.

The case made a great sensation. Letters and replies, arguments and counter-arguments, criminations and recriminations, came out in newspaper and pamphlet. The "orthodox" struck in, jubilant and sarcastical. The secular journals took the matter up once more, and thrashed the vacant straw with lively flail.

The excitement was at its height when Mr. Parker, still a member of the Ministerial Association, took his turn in preaching the Thursday Lecture at the First Church in Chauncy Place, on Dec. 26. The Thursday Lecture was an ancient institution, inaugurated in the early days by one of the fathers of the First Church, who preached it at first himself, and afterwards invited his brother-ministers in Boston and the vicinity to participate with him. For many years it was a famous institution, and went by the name of "the great and Thursday Lecture." But, thirty years ago, it had fallen sadly from its primeval glory. The galleries were empty, the lower pews nearly so. A score or two of venerable women glided silently in at the hour of eleven, and took their seats, well provided with bottles of *sal-volatile* against the probable effect of the discourse. Here and there a country clergyman, drawn by legendary associations or personal regard for the victim in the desk, showed a resigned face in the shadow. The choir was extemporized for the occasion, and made music of an extraordinary quality; the handiest amateur being drafted to play the organ, a son of the minister of the First Church commonly doing arduous and unremunerated duty at the bellows. The sacrifice lasted a painful hour. There was no enthusiasm among the brethren for the honor of court preacher. Substitutes were eagerly sought, and volunteers were rare. It was long since a sinner had been awakened on Thursday forenoon: the sinners had ceased to expect awakening, and staid away. None came but saints, and these came not with jubilant feet.

It was another scene when Theodore Parker spoke. The pews, above and below, were crowded early. The tardy comers had to stand in any spot they could find; the pulpit stairs were occupied; the volunteer singers had not even their "loft" to themselves. Strangers who had scarcely heard of the Thursday Lecture were there: the old *habitués* did not know the place. The venerable old ladies were in the minority. Scent-bottles were uncalled for. The preacher's theme was, "The Relation of Jesus to his Age and the Ages." It was not a great sermon; it was loose, rhetorical, and unsatisfactory in almost all respects: but it was glowing, earnest, sweeping, with immense rush, the negative aspects of it completely hidden behind the gorgeous ascriptions of praise to Jesus. The audience listened with various emotions. Simple and straightforward though the sermon was, it stirred the most opposite feelings, and provoked the most discordant comment. It was printed; but even then the disputation over it did not cease. Theodore Parker had made, perhaps, the most kindling affirmative statement about Jesus that had ever been made from that pulpit; and yet his making it there was construed as a new offence, that must not on any account be repeated. The discussions were warm. To expel Mr. Parker from the Association was a step that could not be ventured; and he declined to withdraw. At length, after many revolvings and resolvings, a device was hit on. The minister of the First Church still held the matter in his hands. Originally, it was his lecture: at his invitation only, others shared with him the privilege of delivering it. He had now but to fall back on first principles, to return to the original arrangement, cancel the invitations which had been so long out that they were held to be rights, issue new ones to the proper men, — omitting the wrong man from the list, — and the knot was cut. The minister of the First Church, acting on the hint, took the matter into his own hands, summoned all but Mr. Parker to his side, and the "stream of tendency" was so far checked. The device was ingenious, but not handsome. The ungodly called it a trick. The divine powers did not think it noble; for, not long after, "the great and Thursday Lecture" was discontinued.

Precisely one month after the lecture, Rev. James Freeman Clarke, pastor of the Church of the Disciples in Boston, against the wishes of his chief parishioners, — two of whom, Benjamin H. Greene and John A. Andrew, called on Mr. Parker to represent the feeling, having in vain remonstrated with Mr. Clarke, — after giving due notice to his people the Sunday before, exchanged pulpits with Mr. Parker, disavowing all sympathy with his heresies, but performing what he considered a duty of Christian fellowship. The hall, Masonic Temple, was crowded, notwithstanding that some of the regular congregation staid piously away. Mr. Parker brought the most innocent sermon he had, a very innocent sermon indeed, on "The Excellence of Goodness." It ought to have satisfied the most timid people that he was not dangerous; but it did not. There was a secession from the Church of the Disciples in the direction of Rev. R. C. Waterston, the minister of Pitts-street Chapel, as Mr. Sargent had been of Suffolk-street. Mr. Waterston, in a long letter disapproving of Mr. Sargent's course, had thrown himself into the current of the popular sentiment, which took him from his humble mission-chapel, and bore him to a handsome stone church in Bedford Street. But the under-current was with Mr. Parker, after all. The tide soon began to ebb: the new society, having no special ground of being, diminished and disappeared.

The reformer was now practically excluded from the churches of Boston: the pulpits, one and all, were closed against him with an emphasis like that of the slamming of doors. At this juncture a company of gentlemen met on Jan. 22, 1845, and passed a single resolution, —

> "That the Rev. Theodore Parker shall have a chance to be heard in Boston."

A commodious hall was obtained, — the Melodeon. It occupied the ground now covered by the Boston Theatre; and on Feb. 16 — a cold, wintry day, the air thick with bitter rain, the streets full of snow — the ministry in Boston was begun, with much misgiving on his part, with sanguine expectation on the part of his friends, who saw the gold drop into the crucible, and remembered the text which prophesied the fine result of that process. But the preacher had courage, if he had distrusts. In his journal he writes, at date Jan. 16, 1845, "I pray God for the permanency of my ability. I feel that I have a great work to do: I think I shall not fail in it. I have no fears for myself; but it is a little painful to see the condition of others. I would I had the presence of two men: then would I be two ministers, — one here, and one in Boston." In a letter to his young friend, Joseph Allen, he says, "You say your professional function is different from mine. That may be true; but mine has been, hitherto, to endeavor to lay the foundation of my religious teachings so deep that nothing could move or shake it. I never scruple, nor ever will, to remove out of my way any rubbish that I come upon, and to declare the rubbish is one thing, and the Rock of Ages a little different, nay, quite another thing. I never regarded my function as negative, except in a small degree. I would pull up the weeds, and give them to the pigs; then plant the corn for men and pigs too."

A conference with a committee of the Boston Association of Ministers was fruitless of any good result. It was kindly in temper, but revealed no common ground of professional action, and closed even less satisfactorily than the famous interview between Paul and the Judaizing apostles which the Romish Church dignifies with the name of the First Council. His feeling about the Unitarians is pungently expressed in the following short extract from a letter to S. J. May: "The Unitarians are getting shockingly bigoted and little. Their late meetings were windy. They went to ventilate their narrowness. Yet how contemptible must be a sect who only deny the divinity of Christ, — affirming a denial, — their life the development of a negation! Anniversary-week had painfully little of the Channing; much of the Norton, bating his scholarship; more of the ——, — specious, superficial, and worldly. The Universalists are more humane than we: they declare the Fatherhood of God, and do not stick at the consequences, — *everlasting happiness for all men.* I think they are the most humane sect in the land. They had an address on temperance, one on slavery, one on war, delivered before their ministers on anniversary-week. Think of that, we whose 'mission it is to be silent about slavery,' and I suppose about war, intemperance, and all other sins that everybody has a mind to! Do tell the youngsters to be men, — not merely dawdling ministers, with no more —— than a pack of cards. They never will ask me to preach to them, and I hope they won't; but I rejoice in your opportunity to teach them how to love the unlovely, and to overcome evil with good."

The advent to Boston was signalized by the following letter, which effectually terminated a long discussion, and with it Mr. Parker's connection with the Unitarians. If he expected a formal reply to it, he was disappointed. But probably he intended it only as a published manifesto on his own part, which might or might not call forth a counter-manifesto from the opposite party, but which, whether it did or not, would remain a standing challenge to the churches. Such it was, indeed, — a challenge that has never been fairly accepted.

A LETTER TO THE BOSTON ASSOCIATION OF CONGREGATIONAL MINISTERS TOUCHING CERTAIN MATTERS OF THEIR THEOLOGY.

GENTLEMEN, — The peculiar circumstances of the last few years have placed both you and me in new relations to the public and to one another. Your recent actions constrain me to write you this public letter, that all may the more fully understand the matter at issue between us, and the course you design to pursue. You are a portion of the Unitarian body, and your opinions and conduct will no doubt have some influence upon that body. You have, I am told, at great length, and in several consecutive meetings, discussed the subject of my connection with your reverend body. You have debated the matter, whether you should expel me for heresy; and by a circuitous movement, recently made, have actually excluded me from preaching the Thursday Lecture. I do not call in question your motives; for it is not my office to judge you: neither do I now complain of your conduct, public or private, towards me during the last three years. That has been various. Some members of your Association have uniformly treated me with the courtesy common amongst gentlemen; some also with the civilities that are usual amongst ministers of the same denomination. Towards some of your number I entertain an affectionate gratitude for the good words I have heard from their lips in my youth. I feel a great regard for some of you, on account of their noble and Christian characters, — virtuous, self-denying, pious, and without bigotry. I cherish no unkind feeling towards the rest of you: towards none of you do I feel ill-will on account of what has passed. I have treated my opponents with a forbearance, which, I think, has not always been sufficiently appreciated by such as have had the chief benefit of that forbearance. However, I hope never to be driven, either by abuse from an opponent or by the treachery of a pretended friend, to depart from the course of forbearance which I have hitherto and uniformly pursued. But since you have practically taken so decided a stand, and have so frequently discussed me and my affairs among yourselves, and have at last made your movement, I think it important that the public should have a distinct knowledge of your theological position. I am searching for truth, however humbly; and I suppose that you are as desirous of imparting to others as of receiving from Heaven. Therefore I shall proceed to ask you certain questions a good deal talked of at the present day, to which I venture to ask a distinct and categorical reply. But, by way of preliminary, I will first refresh your memory with a few facts.

Until recently, the Unitarians have been supposed to form the advance guard, so to say, of the Church militant; at least, they have actually been the *movement-party in theology*. It may hurt the feelings of some men now to confess it; but I think it is true. As such, the Unitarians have done a great work. As

I understand the matter, this work was in part *intellectual;* for they really advanced theological science, both negatively by the exposure of errors, and positively by the establishment of truths: but in greater part *moral;* for they declared, either directly or by implication, the right of each man to investigate for himself in matters pertaining to religion; and his right also to the Christian name if he claimed it, and by his character seemed to deserve it. They called themselves "liberal" Christians, and seemed to consider that he was the best Christian who was most like Christ in character and life; thus making religion the essential of Christianity, and leaving each man to determine his own theology. They began their history by a denial of the Trinity, — a doctrine very dear to the Christian Church, of very ancient standing therein, common alike to Catholics and Protestants; a doctrine for centuries regarded as essential to the Christian scheme; the fundamental dogma of Christianity. For this denial they encountered the usual fate of the movement-party: they were denied Christian fellowship, and got a bad name, which they keep even now. I am told that they are still called "infidels" by the Trinitarian leaders; and that, you know, gentlemen, is a term of great reproach in the theological world. It has been asserted, I think, in some Orthodox journal, that the lamented Dr. Channing — whose name is now, perhaps, praised by your Association oftener than his example is followed — undoubtedly went to hell for his sin in denying that Jesus of Nazareth was the Infinite God. Gentlemen, these things happened not a great many years ago. I do not wonder at the treatment the Unitarians have received, and still receive, where they are not numerous and powerful: for the Trinitarians maintain that no one can be saved without a belief in certain doctrines of their theology; which very doctrines the Unitarians stoutly denied, and in public too. The Orthodox were consistent in what the Unitarians then regarded as persecution, and, I doubt not, would have used the old arguments, — fagots and the axe, — had not the laws of the land rendered it quite impossible to resort to this ultimate standard of theological appeal, which had been a favorite with many of the clergy for more than fourteen centuries. The Unitarians complained of that treatment as not altogether Christian.

But now, gentlemen, it seems to me that some of you are

pursuing the same course you once complained of; and, if I rightly apprehend the theology of your learned body, — of which, however, I am not quite sure, — without the same consistency, having no warrant therefor in your theological system. I say nothing of your motives in all this; nothing of the spirit in which some of you have acted. That matter is beyond my reach: to your own master you stand or fall. In 1841 I preached a sermon at South Boston at an ordination. That was soon attacked by the Rev. Mr. Fairchild, and numerous other clergymen of several denominations equally zealous for the Christian faith. Since that time, most of you have refused me the ministerial courtesies commonly shown to the ministers of the same denomination. And yet, gentlemen, I think these courtesies are not, in all denominations, withheld when one of the parties has a moral reputation that is at least ambiguous. Only five of your number, I believe, have since exchanged with me; though comparatively but few members of other Unitarian associations have departed from their former course. I do not complain of this: I simply state the fact.

Now, gentlemen, there is one matter on which you will allow me to pause a moment. The Fraternity of Churches is, I suppose virtually, though not formally, under the direction of certain members of your Association. Now, that Fraternity has virtually expelled from his office a minister engaged in a noble and Christian work, and performing that work with rare ability and success. You have thus expelled him from his place simply because he extended ministerial fellowship to me in common with ministers of several other denominations. The case of Mr. Sargent is peculiar, and I must dwell a moment on a few particulars respecting it. If I rightly remember, his family contributed largely to the erection and embellishment of the chapel out of which he is expelled. He has himself spent freely his own property for the poor under his charge, and has been untiring in his labors. No shadow of reproach attaches to his name. He is above suspicion of immorality; but, on the contrary, is distinguished beyond his fellows by the excellence of his character and the nobleness of his life. A righteous and a self-denying man, he went out into the lanes and highways of Boston gathering together the poor and the forsaken, and formed a society which prospered under his ministry, and became strongly attached to him. And yet, gentlemen, some of you have seen fit, knowing all these circumstances, by demanding of him a pledge that he would never exchange with me, to drive away from the field of his labors and the arms of his parish this noble man, solely because he extended the usual ministerial fellowship to me; and yet I still continue a member of your Association! I think he has never been accused, perhaps not suspected, of preaching in his pulpit, or even believing in his study, the peculiar doctrines of my own theology, which are so obnoxious to some of you, and apparently reckoned worse than a grave moral offence. It may be said that Mr. Sargent was minister over a *vassal church*, and the Fraternity were his *feudal superiors;* and this seems to be true. You will say, furthermore, that the Boston Association, as a whole, is not responsible for the acts of the Fraternity; and this is doubtless the case: but, as I think some of its members are accountable, to them let the above remarks apply. I pass to another matter.

The Unitarians have no recognized and public creed. It used to be their glory. At the Theological School in Cambridge I subscribed to no symbolical books; at my ordination I assented to no form of doctrines, neither church nor council requesting it. When I became a member of your learned body, no one asked me of my opinions, whether orthodox or heterodox: no one even demanded a promise that I should never change an opinion or discover a new truth! I know well, gentlemen, that I differ, and that very widely, from the systems of theology which are taught, and from the philosophy which underlies these systems. I have no wish to disguise my theology, or to shelter it beneath the authority of your Association: let it stand or fall by itself. But still I do not know that I have transgressed the limits of Unitarianism; for I do not know what those limits are. It is a great glory to a liberal association to have no Symbolical Books, but a great inconvenience that a sect becoming exclusive should not declare its creed. I cannot utter the *shibboleth* of a party till I first hear it pronounced in the orthodox way. I shall presently proceed to beg you to point out the limits of scientific freedom, and tell the *maximum* of theological belief which distinguishes you from the "orthodox" on the one side, and the *minimum* thereof which distinguishes you from the "infidels" on the other side.

Gentlemen, you refuse me fellowship; you discuss the question, whether you shall expel me from your Association; and you actually, though indirectly, prohibit me, as I understand it, from preaching "the great and Thursday Lecture." Gentlemen, I wish to know distinctly the ground you take in this matter. It is not altogether plain why you put yourselves in your peculiar attitude towards me. Mr. Sargent is expelled for granting me ministerial fellowship. He was an accessory after the fact in my alleged heresies, and being but a vassal of the Fraternity, and therefore within their power, is punished, while the principal of the mischief is allowed to go unscathed; and other clergymen who exchange with me, but have no feudal lords, retain their places as before. Here the issue is obvious; and Mr. Sargent is expelled from his pulpit for *positive misprision of heresy*, if I may make use of such a term. Of course the same doctrine excludes him from his pulpit and the Association. But I am told that Mr. Pierpont was quite as effectually excluded from the actual fellowship of your Association as even myself; for, while three of the city members of your Association have continued to extend ministerial fellowship to me, — Mr. Pierpont, Mr. Sargent, and Mr. Clarke, — only three, — Mr. Gannett, Mr. Sargent, and Mr. Clarke, — if I am rightly informed, have extended that fellowship to him since the time of the famed Hollis-street Council! Yet I think he is guilty of no heresy, — *theological* and *speculative* heresy I mean; for, in practical affairs, it is well known that his course is the opposite of that pursued by most of his brethren in the city.

Still more: at a conference I had with the Association a little more than two years ago, the chairman of the Association — the Rev. Dr. Parkman — declared that my main offence was not my theological heresies: they would have been forgiven and forgot, had it not been for an article I published on the Hollis-street Council (printed in "The Dial" for October, 1842), in which, as he alleged, I "poured scorn and contempt upon the brethren." Yet others charge me with heresies, and on account thereof, I am told, actually deny my right to Christian fellowship from them, and even my title to the Christian name.

In this intricate confusion, gentlemen, you will probably

see the necessity of saying a word to put all things in a fair light, that I may know on what point you and I are really at issue. Notwithstanding the remarks of the Rev. Dr. Parkman, I am still inclined to the belief that the charge of heresy is the main charge; and as you have had the field of controversy entirely to yourselves these several years, and as yet have not, as a body, made a public and authorized statement of your theological belief, I must beg you to inform me what is *orthodoxy* according to the Boston Association. The orthodoxy of the Catholic Church I know very well; I am not wholly ignorant of what is called orthodox by the Lutheran and Calvinistic churches: but the ORTHODOXY of the Boston Association of Congregational Ministers is not a thing so easy to come at. As I try to comprehend it, I feel I am looking at something dim and undefined. It changes color, and it changes shape: now it seems a mountain; then it appears like a cloud. You will excuse me, gentlemen; but, though I have been more than seven years a member of your reverend body, I do not altogether comprehend your theology, nor know what is orthodox. You will do a great service if you will publish your Symbolical Books, and let the world know what is the true doctrine according to the Boston Association of Congregational Ministers. I have defined my own position as well as I could, and will presently beg you to reply, distinctly, categorically, and unequivocally, to the following questions. Gentlemen, you are theologians; men of leisure and learning; mighty in the Scriptures. Some of you have grown gray in teaching the world; most of you, I think, make no scruple of passing judgment, public and private, on my opinions and myself. It is therefore to be supposed that you have examined things at large, and been curious in particulars; have searched into the mysteries of things, deciding what is true, what false, what Christian, and what not; and so have determined on a standard of doctrines which is to you well known, accessible, and acknowledged by all. Some of you can sling stones at a hair's-breadth in the arena of theology. You are many, and I am standing alone. Of course I shall take it for granted that you have, each and all, thoroughly, carefully, and profoundly examined the matters at issue between us; that you have made up your minds thereon, and are all entirely agreed in your conclusions, and that on all points: for surely it were not charitable to suppose, without good and sufficient proof, that a body of Christian ministers — conscientious men, learned, and aware of the difficulties of the case — would censure and virtually condemn one of their number for heresy, unless they had made personal investigation of the whole matter, had themselves agreed on their standard of orthodoxy, and were quite ready to place that standard before the eyes of the whole people. I beg that this standard of Unitarian orthodoxy, as it is agreed upon and established by the authority of the Boston Association, may be set before my eyes and those of the public at the same time; and therefore, gentlemen, I propose to you the following

QUESTIONS.

Class I. — Scholastic questions relating to the definition of terms frequently used in theology: —

1. What do you mean by the word "salvation"?

2. What do you mean by a "miracle"?

3. What do you mean by "inspiration"?

4. What do you mean by "revelation"?

Class II. — Dogmatic questions relating to certain doctrines of theology: —

5. In questions of theology, to what shall a man appeal? and what is the criterion whereby he is to test theological, moral, and religious doctrines? Are there limits to theological inquiry? and if so, what are those limits? Is truth to be accepted because it is true, and right to be followed because it is right, or for some other reason?

6. What are the conditions of salvation, both theoretical and practical? and how are they known?

7. What do you consider the essential doctrines of Christianity? What moral and religious truth is taught by Christianity that was wholly unknown to the human race before the time of Christ? and is there any doctrine of Christianity that is not a part also of natural religion?

8. Do you believe all the books in the Bible came from the persons to whom they are, in our common version thereof, ascribed? or what are genuine and canonical Scriptures?

9. Do you believe that all or any of the authors of the Old Testament were miraculously inspired, so that all or any of their language can properly be called the *Word of God*, and their

writings constitute a miraculous revelation? or are those writings to be judged of, as other writings, by their own merits, and so made to pass for what they are worth? In short, what is the authority of the Old Testament? and what relation does it bear to man, — that of master, or servant?

10. Do you believe the law contained in the Pentateuch, in all parts and particulars, is miraculously inspired or revealed to man? or is it, like the laws of Massachusetts, a human work in whole or in part?

11. Do you believe the miracles related in the Old Testament? — for example, that God appeared in a human form, spoke in human speech, walked in the garden of Eden, ate and drank; that he commanded Abraham to sacrifice Isaac, and made the verbal declarations so often attributed to him in the Old and New Testament; that Moses spoke with him "as a man speaketh with his friend;" that the miracles alleged to have been wrought for the sake of the Hebrews in Egypt, the Red Sea, Arabia, and Palestine, and recorded in the Bible, were actual facts; that the births of Isaac, Samson, and Samuel, were miraculous; that Balaam's ass spoke the Hebrew words put into his mouth; that God did miraculously give to Moses, and others mentioned in the Old Testament, the commands there ascribed to him; that the sun stood still as related in the Book of Joshua; that Jonah was swallowed by a large fish, and, while within the fish, composed the ode ascribed to him? And do you believe all the miracles related in the Books of Daniel, Job, and elsewhere in the Old Testament?

12. Do you believe that any prophet of the Old Testament, solely through a miraculous revelation made to him by God, did distinctly and unequivocally foretell any distant and future event which has since come to pass? and, in special, that any prophet of the Old Testament did thereby, and in manner aforesaid, distinctly and equivocally foretell the birth, life, sufferings, death, and resurrection of Jesus of Nazareth, so that Jesus was, in the proper and exclusive sense of the word, the *Messiah* predicted by the prophets, and expected by the Jews?

13. What do you think is the meaning of the phrase, "Thus saith the Lord," with its kindred expressions, in the Old Testament?

14. Do you believe that all or any of the authors of the New

Testament were miraculously inspired, so that all or any of their language can properly be called the *Word of God*, and that their writings constitute a miraculous revelation? or are those writings to be judged of, as other writings, by their own merits, and so made to pass for what they are worth? In short, what is the authority of the New Testament? and what relation does it bear to man, — that of master, or servant?

15. Do you believe the Christian apostles were miraculously inspired to teach, write, or act, with such a *mode*, *kind*, or *degree* of inspiration as is not granted by God, in all time, to other men equally wise, moral, and pious? Do you think the apostles were so informed by miraculous inspiration as never to need the exercise of the common faculties of man, and never to fall into any errors of fact and doctrine? or are we to suppose that the apostles were mistaken in their announcement of the speedy destruction of the world, of the resurrection of the body, &c.

16. What do you think is the nature of Jesus of Nazareth? Was he *God*, *man*, or *a being neither God nor man?* And how does he effect the salvation of mankind? In what sense is he the Saviour, Mediator, and Redeemer?

17. Do you believe that Jesus of Nazareth was miraculously born, as it is related in two of the Gospels, with but one human parent; that he was tempted by the Devil, and transfigured, talking actually with Moses and Elias; that he actually transformed the substance of water into the substance of wine; fed five thousand men with five loaves and two fishes; that he walked on the waters; miraculously stilled a tempest; sent demons out of men into a herd of swine; and that he restored to life persons wholly and entirely dead?

18. Do you believe that Jesus had a miraculous and infallible inspiration different in *kind* or *mode* from that granted to other wise, good, and pious men, informing him to such a degree that he never made a mistake in matters pertaining to religion, to theology, to philosophy, or to any other department of human concern; and that therefore he teaches with an authority superior to reason, conscience, and the religious sentiment in the individual man?

19. Do you believe that it is impossible for God to create a being with the same moral and religious excellence that Jesus had, but also with more and greater intellectual and other facul-

ties, and send him into the world as a man? or has Jesus exhausted either or both the *capacity of man*, or the *capability of God?*

20. Do you believe, that, from a state of entire and perfect death, Jesus returned to a state of entire and perfect physical life; that he did all the works and uttered all the words attributed to him in the concluding parts of the Gospels after his resurrection; and was subsequently taken up into heaven bodily and visibly, as mentioned in the book of Acts?

21. Do you believe, that, at the death of Jesus, the earth quaked, the rocks were rent; that darkness prevailed over the land for three hours; that the graves were opened, and many bodies of saints that slept arose and appeared to many?

22. Do you believe that Jesus, or any of the writers of the New Testament, believed in and taught the existence of a personal Devil, of angels good or bad, of demons who possessed the bodies of men? and do you yourselves believe the existence of a personal Devil, of such angels and demons? In special, do you believe that the angel Gabriel appeared to Zacharias and to the Virgin Mary, and uttered exactly those words ascribed to him in the third Gospel?

23. Do you believe that the writers of the four Gospels and the book of Acts never mingled mythical, poetical, or legendary matter in their compositions; that they never made a mistake in a matter of fact; and that they have, in all cases, reported the words and actions of Jesus with entire and perfect accuracy?

24. Do you believe the miracles related in the book of Acts? — for example, the miraculous inspiration of the apostles at Pentecost; the cures effected by Peter, his vision, his miraculous deliverance from prison "by the angel of the Lord;" the miraculous death of Ananias and Sapphira; the miraculous conversion of Paul; that diseased persons were cured by handkerchiefs and aprons brought to them from Paul; and that he and Stephen actually, and with the body's eye, saw Jesus Christ, an actual object exterior to themselves?

25. Do you believe that Peter, in the Acts, correctly explains certain passages of the Old Testament as referring to Jesus of Nazareth, his sufferings, death, and resurrection; that Jesus himself, — if the Gospels truly represent his words, — in all cases, applies the language of the Old Testament to himself, in its

proper and legitimate meaning? Was he never mistaken in this matter? or have the passages of the Old Testament many meanings?

26. Do you think that a belief in the miraculous inspiration of all or any of the writers of the Old Testament or New Testament; that a belief in all or any of the miracles therein mentioned; that a belief in the miraculous birth, life, resurrection, and ascension of Jesus; that a belief in his miraculous, universal, and infallible inspiration, — is essential to a perfect Christian character, to salvation and acceptance with God, or even to participation in the Christian name? and if so, what doctrine of morality or religion really and necessarily rests, in whole or in part, on such a belief?

27. Do you believe that the two ordinances — Baptism and the Lord's Supper — are, in themselves, essential, necessary, and of primary importance as ends, valuable for their own sakes? or that they are *helps* and *means* for the formation of the Christian character, and therefore valuable only so far as they help to form that character?

28. Do you think it wrong or unchristian in another to abandon and expose what he deems a popular error, or to embrace and proclaim an unpopular truth? Do you count yourselves, theoretically, to have attained all religious and theological truth, and to have retained no error in your own creed, so that it is wholly unnecessary for you, on the one hand, to re-examine your own opinions, or, on the other, to search farther for light and truth? or do you think yourselves competent, without such search or such examination, to pronounce a man an infidel, and no Christian, solely because he believes many things in theology which you reject, and rejects some things which you believe?

Gentlemen, you have yourselves constrained me to write this letter. I write to you in this open way; for I wish that the public may understand your opinions as well as my own. I beg you will give your serious attention to the above questions, and return me a public answer, not circuitously, but in a straightforward, manly way, and at your earliest convenience. I have at various times, as distinctly as possible, set forth my own views; and as you have publicly placed yourselves in a hostile attitude to me, as some of you have done all in their power to disown me, and as they have done this partly on account of my alleged heresies, it is but due to yourselves to open the gospel according to the Boston Association, give the public an opportunity to take the length and breadth of your standard of Unitarian orthodoxy, and tell us all what you really think on the points above mentioned. Then you and I shall know in what we differ: there will be a clear field before us; and, if we are doomed to contend, we shall not fight in the dark. I have invited your learned attention to matters on which it is supposed that you have inquired and made up your mind, and that you are entirely agreed among yourselves, and yet that you differ most widely from me. I have not, however, touched the great philosophical questions which lie at the bottom of all theology, because I do not understand that you have yourselves raised these questions, or consciously and distinctly joined issue upon them with me. Gentlemen, you are men of leisure, and I am busied with numerous cares; you are safe in your multitude of council, while I have comparatively none to advise with. But notwithstanding these advantages, so eminently on your side, I have not feared to descend into the arena, and, looking only for the truth, to write you this letter. I shall pause, impatient for your reply; and with hearty wishes for your continued prosperity, your increased usefulness, and growth alike in all Christian virtues and every manly grace, I remain, gentlemen,

Your obedient servant,

THEODORE PARKER.

WEST ROXBURY, March 20, 1845.

Mr. Parker's arrangement with his Boston friends contemplated a Sunday-morning service at the Melodeon for a year; the pulpit at West Roxbury being temporarily filled by substitutes, he still having his residence there, and maintaining pastoral relations with the people. The Boston preaching was regarded as an experiment; but it was so prosperous, that, before the year had elapsed, a permanent settlement was decided on and effected. On the 13th of December, 1845, an invitation from the Boston Society to become their minister was accepted. On the 3d of January, 1846, the position at West Roxbury was resigned in a tenderly-worded letter, and the new relation taken up. Signal success had attended the preaching at the Melodeon. The hall was filled every Sunday morning with earnest listeners, humble people in the main, but intelligent, eager, determined; who came for spiritual food, and were sure to get it. They flocked together, individual men and women, from the four corners of the ecclesiastical world; some from the "outer darkness" of the world non-ecclesiastical. The circles of fashion were not largely represented; but the thoughtful, sensitive, and humane were there in numbers. The seekers, doubters, reformers, were conspicuously present. It was such an audience as the preacher liked. It made him feel that his office was no sinecure, his work no child's play, but a battle; but it made him feel, too, that he was surrounded by fellow-laborers and fellow-soldiers. The attraction and the inspiration were mutual. The people looked up to the preacher; the preacher looked into the faces of the people; and both were cheered.

The installation took place on Jan. 4, 1846, according to the strictest congregational usage, the society themselves taking the pastor of their choice. The ceremony was of the simplest. There was no charge, the minister's good conscience being deemed sufficient pledge of his fidelity; no address to the people, they having already listened to the voice of their own heart, and being disposed to follow it; no right hand of fellowship, a hundred hands with souls in them being outstretched to give the pastor welcome. The minister preached his own sermon, and prayed his own prayer: none could do it better. The chairman of the committee made a short statement of the measures taken in founding the society, and calling Mr. Parker: then the "exercises" went on. The preacher announced as the subject of his sermon, "The Idea of a Christian Church." Let us catch at least the spirit of it; for it struck the key-note of his subsequent ministry. He took no text, but began as if he meant business, and had no more than time enough for it.

The Church was defined as "a body of men and women united together in a common desire of religious excellence, and with a common regard for Jesus of Nazareth, regarding him as the noblest example of morality and religion." "Its essential of substance is the union for the purpose of cultivating love to God and man; and the essential of form is the common regard for Jesus, considered as the highest representation of God that we know." "It is not the form, either of ritual or of doctrine, but the spirit, which constitutes a Christian church. Christianity, to be perfect and entire, demands a complete manliness, — the bravest development of the whole man, mind, heart, and soul. It aims not to destroy the sacred peculiarities of individual character: it cherishes and develops them in their perfection." "A Christian church should aim to have its members Christians as Jesus was the Christ, sons of man as he was, sons of God as much as he." "If Jesus were ever mistaken, — as the evangelists make it appear, — then it is a part of Christianity to avoid his mistakes, as well as to accept his truths." "It is Christian to receive all the truths of the Bible; all the truths that are not in the Bible just as much. It is Christian also to reject all the errors that come to us from without the Bible or from within the Bible." "It is only free men that can find the truth, love the truth, live the truth. As much freedom as you shut out, so much falsehood do you shut in." "To think truth is the worship of the head; to do noble works of usefulness and charity is the worship of the will; to feel love and trust in man and God is the glad worship of the heart." "Christianity should be represented as human, as man's nature in its true greatness." "The members of a Christian church should be mindful of one another; they should bear one another's burdens; they should advise and admonish one another: the strong should help the weak, the rich the poor."

"The Christian Church should have an action on others

out of its pale; should live to see its truths extend; should be a means of reforming the world after the pattern of Christian ideas; should bring the sentiments, ideas, actions of the times to be judged by the universal standard; should measure the sins of commerce, the sins of the State, by conscience and reason, by the everlasting ideas on which alone is based the welfare of the world. A Christian church should be a society for the promotion of true sentiments and ideas, for the promotion of good works. It should lead the movement for the public education of the people."

"Here are the needy, who ask for justice more than charity. Every beggar, every pauper, condemns our civilization. Whence come the tenants of our almshouses, jails, the victims of vice in all our towns? Why, from the lowest ranks of the people, from the poorest and most ignorant; say, rather, from the most neglected. What have the strong been doing all this while, that the weak have come to such a state?"

"Does not Christianity say *the strong should help the weak?* Does not that mean something? Every almshouse in Massachusetts shows that the churches have not done their duty; that the Christians lie lies when they call Jesus Master, and men brothers. Every jail is a monument, on which it is writ in letters of iron that we are still heathens: and the gallows, black and hideous, the embodiment of death, the last argument a 'Christian' State offers to the poor wretches it trained up to be criminals,—it stands there as a sign of our infamy; and, while it lifts its horrid arm to crush the life out of some miserable man whose blood cries to God against Cain in the nineteenth century, it lifts the same arm as an index of our shame." "Is that all? Oh, no! Did not Jesus say, 'Resist not evil with evil'? Is not war the worst form of that evil? and is there on earth a nation so greedy of war, a nation so reckless of provoking it, one where the war-horse so soon conducts his foolish rider into fame and power? Is that all? Far from it. Did not Christ say, 'Whatsoever you would that men should do unto you, do you even so unto them'? And are there not three million brothers of yours and mine in bondage here, the hopeless sufferers of a savage doom, debarred the civilization of our age, the barbarians of the nineteenth century, shut out from the pretended religion of Christendom, the heathens of a Christian land, the slaves of a Christian republic? The Rock of Plymouth, sanctified by the feet which led a nation's way to Freedom's large estate, provokes no more voice than the rottenest stone in the mountains of the West. The Church is dumb, while the State is only silent. While the servants of the people are only asleep, 'God's ministers' are dead."

"In the midst of all these wrongs and sins, amid popular ignorance, pauperism, crime and war, and slavery too, is the Church to say nothing, do nothing, nothing for the good of such as feel the wrong, nothing to save them who do the wrong? If I thought so, I would never enter the Church but once again, and then to bow my shoulders to their manliest work, — to heave down its strong pillars, arch and dome and roof and wall, steeple and tower, though, like Samson, I buried myself under the ruins of that temple which profaned the worship of God most high, of God most loved. I would do this in the name of man; in the name of Christ I would do it; yes, in the dear and blessed name of God."

"The Christian Church should lead the civilization of the age. It will be in unison with all science; it will not fear philosophy; it will not lack new truth, daring only to quote; nor be obliged to sneak behind the inspired words of old saints as its only fortress, for it will have words just as truly inspired, dropping from the golden mouths of saints and prophets now. A church truly Christian must lead the way in moral enterprises, in every work which aims directly at the welfare of man. There was a time when the Christian churches, as a whole, held that rank. Do they now? Oh, no! — not even the Quakers, perhaps the last sect that abandoned it. A prophet filled with love of man and love of God is not therein at home. I speak a sad truth, and I say it in sorrow. But look at the churches of this city: do they lead the Christian movements of this city, — the temperance-movement; the peace-movement; the movement for the freedom of man, for education; the movement to make society more just, more wise and good; the great religious movement of these times? Not at all."

"Christianity is humanity. Christ is the son of man, the manliest of men; pious and hopeful as a prayer, but brave as man's most daring thought. He has led the world in morals and religion for eighteen hundred years, only because he was the manliest man in it, the humanest and bravest man in it, and therefore the divinest. He may lead it eighteen hundred years more. But the churches do not lead men therein; for they have not his spirit, — neither that womanliness that wept over Jerusalem, nor that manliness that drew down fire from heaven to light the world's altars for well-nigh two thousand years."

"There are many ways in which Christ may be denied: one is that of the bold blasphemer, who, out of a base and haughty heart, mocks, scoffing at that manly man, and spits upon the nobleness of Christ. There are few such deniers: my heart mourns for them. But they do little harm. Religion is so dear to men, no scoffing word can silence that; and the brave soul of this young Nazarene has made itself so deeply felt, that scorn and mockery of him are but an icicle held up against the summer's sun. There is another way to deny him; and that is to call him Lord, and never do his bidding; to stifle free minds with his words; and, with the authority of his name, to cloak, to mantle, screen, and consecrate the follies, errors, sins, of men. From this we have much to fear."

"In our day, men have made great advances in science, commerce, manufactures, in all the arts of life. We need, therefore, a development of religion corresponding thereto. Let us have a church in which religion, goodness towards men, piety towards God, shall be the main thing. Let us have a degree of that suited to the growth and demands of this age. Its prayers will be a lifting-up of the hearts in noble men towards God, in search of truth, goodness, piety. Its sacraments will be great works of reform, institutions for the comfort and culture of men. If men were to engage in religion as in commerce, politics, arts; if the absolute religion, the Christianity of Christ, were applied to life with all the might of this age, — what a result should we not behold! We should build up a great State, with unity in the nation, and freedom in the people; a State where there was honorable work for every hand, bread for all mouths, clothing for all backs, culture for every mind, and love and faith in every heart. Truth would be our sermon; works of daily duty would be our sacrament. Prophets inspired of God would minister the Word, and Piety send up her psalm of prayer, sweet in its notes, and joyfully prolonged. The noblest monument to Christ, the fairest trophy of religion, is a noble people, where all are well fed and clad, industrious, free, educated, manly, pious, wise, and good."

Brave words are common in ordination-sermons, but seldom are prophetic of brave deeds. In this case they were. The minister of the Twenty-eighth Congregational Society meant to carry out, if possible, what he foreshadowed. In a letter to Joseph H. Allen in 1849 he says, "Our church in Boston attend a little to the humanities in an ecclesiastical sense; not much, for we are poor. We have a Committee of Benevolent Action, who are the almoners of the society. Twice a year we take up a collection for the poor. Once a fortnight the committee meet in the season from October to May, and consult about cases, &c.

They keep a record of their doings, and are eminently useful. They find places for men, women, and children; and the blessing of such as are ready to perish falls upon them. Besides that, the members of the society are almost all engaged in some of the great reforms; e.g., antislavery, temperance, prisons, &c. But we have no organized ecclesiastical action in these matters; I wish we had: but I have not time for all things of that sort. I once hoped to have a committee on each of these topics, to report annually to the society the condition of each of these reforms. Then such as liked one, and not another, could work in their own way. But perhaps this is better done as it is; each man connecting himself as he sees fit, without any ecclesiastical organization about it." The Sunday school was not successful, although he always attended personally, and talked pleasantly to the children, telling them a story or a parable. Sunday schools rarely prosper in cities; never, probably, in intelligent congregations that choose to teach their own children, and improve their Sunday leisure in their own way. The Saturday-afternoon class for young women did better. The women manifested even an unusual desire to be considered young: mothers and daughters sat side by side like sisters. The minister excluded none. He wanted the minds, not the years. He welcomed all to the best he had, and introduced all to the best they had themselves, with singular skill and delicacy drawing them out to speak. He found, on trial, that the least severe and systematical method was the best; but he never allowed the conversation to run into gossip or inane generalities. The subjects were large and various, but were made pointed and kept vital by the pastor's watchful mind, which made every question keen, and every answer pertinent. The tone of seriousness was never lost. "Mr. Parker," said one of the less astute and sensitive of the company, "what is that feeling which makes one person so devoted to another that she will cling to him through every thing, even drunkenness?" — "*I cannot tell you.*" — "But you believe in it; do you not?" — "*Indeed I do.*" He took great pleasure in these meetings; was at much pains to be present; and would hurry home from lecturing expeditions in order not to miss them. They were continued for several years, and covered important fields of thought, ethical, social, and religious. The question of education in its varying aspects occupied a whole winter; the capacities and duties of women came in for their share of consideration; right habits of reading and listening were inculcated; the importance of thoroughness and exactness was urged on the young in regard to their mental operations; the influence of sickness, misfortune, calamity, on character, were subjects discussed.

The public Sunday-afternoon discussions proved unmanageable through the presence of the arch-fiend who goes about in the plausible guise of prophet, reformer, or saint, and lifts up a shrill, inopportune voice, to the discomfiture of chairman and listeners. He is deaf to argument and entreaty. The voice of the presiding officer has no subduing spell. The policeman alone is potent to expel the intruder; but the apostle of the free spirit stultifies himself by an appeal to force, and Mr. Parker was compelled to retire to private quarters.

To organize a society in a city is never easy. There are too many occupations; the workers are all overworked in other ways; the parish method is loose and slow; things worth doing are best done in detail, by individuals active in their own places; the main direction and impulse come from the minister, who feels it to be an encumbrance and a waste of effort; the machinery is out of all proportion to the achievement; the ropes creak, the pulleys groan. The best-intentioned pastor confesses at length that the effort of combining the various elements of his society for social purposes is more exhausting than profitable. If anybody could make such operations successful,

Theodore Parker could; but he boasted of no triumph. He was invited to Boston as a preacher. The public were interested in his theological opinions. His friends wanted his thought on religious themes. His battle with the churches had made him famous. The hall was opened as an arena for intellectual conflict, not as a room for conference-meetings, or an apartment for a Sunday school. He might be a pastor in many ways, a teacher in private as much as he would; but before the world he stood as a prophet, the inaugurator of a new religious movement, the preacher of a new reform, in the line of Luther's, but deeper.

The society was not rich. Radicalism and riches have not yet formed alliance: a generation ago, the connection was exceedingly loose. The following note tells a story common enough on one side, not so common on the other: —

BOSTON, Oct. 30, 1847.

MY DEAR SIR, — Last Sunday I learned that the financial condition of our society was neither prosperous nor hopeful; indeed, that we are four hundred dollars in debt. I think I can help you a little in this difficulty, though not much of a business-man; and accordingly I propose, that, for the year 1848, my salary should be, not two thousand dollars, but sixteen hundred. I can easily make up the other four hundred dollars by some other labor, and then the church will not be burthened. I beg you to present this proposal to the rest of the committee as one cheerfully made on my part, at the same time asking them *not* to mention it to other members of the society.

Believe me, dear sir, truly your friend,

THEO. PARKER.

To the Treasurer of the 28th Congregational Society.

This might have been the first, but it was not the last time that the devoted minister took less than was offered. The clerical calling is rarely lucrative. With him it was impoverishing; for it cost him a good deal more than it brought him, even in money. Had he been a hireling priest, he would have kept nearer the flesh-pots. But the Master he followed rated hireling shepherds among thieves and robbers.

This chapter may close with the well-known sonnet, which presents the standard he aimed at, and conveys the spirit in which he meant to labor: —

"Dear Jesus, were thy spirit now on earth,
Where thou hast toiled and wept a world to win,
What vast ideas would sudden come to birth!
What strong endeavors 'gainst o'ermastering sin!
Thy blest beatitudes again thou'dst speak;
And, with deep-hearted words that smite like fire,
Wouldst thou rebuke the oppressors of the weak.
But, turning thence to prophets that aspire,
How wouldst thou cheer the souls that seek to save
Their brothers smarting 'neath a despot's rod;
To lift the poor, the fallen, and the slave,
And lead them all alive to worship God!
Bigots wouldst thou refuse that hindering stand,
But send thy gospel-fraught apostles conquering through the land."

CHAPTER XI.

THE PASTOR.

In January, 1847, Mr. Parker removed from West Roxbury, where he had been living till now, to Boston. A house in Exeter Place — a little court, so near to Essex Street that his yard was adjacent to that of his friend Wendell Phillips — was provided for him. The upper floor was thrown into one room for a library. In this house he lived till his last sickness took him away: there his widow resides still, though the quiet of the spot is invaded by business. The household consisted of himself and his wife, "whose domestic name is Bear, or Bearsie, and who, as usual, is nearly the opposite of her husband, except in the matter of *philanthropy;*" a young man by the name of Cabot, one and twenty years old, an orphan, brought up by Mr. and Mrs. Parker from childhood, and treated by them as a sort of nephew; and Miss Stevenson, "a woman of fine talents and culture, interested in all the literatures and humanities." The entire house was given to hospitality. The table always looked as if it expected guests. The parlors had the air of talking-places, well arranged and habitually used for the purpose. The spare bed was always ready for an occupant, and often had a friendless wanderer from a foreign shore. The library was a confessional as well as a study: this room, airy, light, and pleasant, was lined with books in plain cases, unprotected by obtrusive glass. Books occupied capacious stands in the centre of the apartment; books were piled on the desk and floor. There was but one table, — a writing-table, with drawers and extension-leaves, of the common office-pattern. A Parian head of the Christ, and a bronze statue of Spartacus, ornamented the ledge: sundry emblematical bears, in fanciful shapes of wood or metal, assisted in its decoration. The writer sat in a cane chair: a sofa close by was for visitors. A vase of flowers usually stood near the bust of Jesus. Flowers were in the southern windows, placed there by gentle hands, and faithfully tended by himself. Two ivy-plants, representative of two sisters, intwined their arms and mingled their leaves at the window-frames. Every morning he watered them, and trained their growing tendrils.

Mr. Parker's feeling for flowers was as delicate as his knowledge of them. In the country they were his companions, in the city his joy. He would never allow his flowers to be thrown away because they were faded. The drooping or shrivelled petals falling off to give place to the seed-vessel were as beautiful to him in idea as the unfolding or ripened bud. Standing one day in his drawing-room at a table covered with the earliest spring-flowers, — flowers which bloomed in his parlor simultaneously with their unfolding in the sheltered nook of field or wood, — a lady took up a bunch of hepaticas, saying it was one of her favorites. "Why?" he asked: "it has no perfume." "But think where it grows," she replied: "out of the dead leaves of the past year." He started a little; an emotion passed over his face: but he said nothing. The hepatica had a deeper root in his affection after that. A vase of flowers stood on his pulpit, — the wild flowers in their season, cultivated flowers always, — placed there by friends in the parish. Their beauty and fragrance crept into sermon and prayer. Having thus served in the worship of the morning, they went in the afternoon to the chambers of the sorrowing and the sick to fulfil the other divine duty of love. His love for the wild flowers was almost a passion: he watched for their annual return, and knew where, for miles around, he should find their first blooming. Every year he went to Lexington to gather the earliest violets on his mother's grave. In plucking wild flowers, he always refrained from taking many from one locality, lest he should injure the future growth; and there were friends of his to whom he would not betray the haunts he well knew of some of the shyest kinds, lest they should exercise on them their propensity for gathering a great quantity. He appreciated the gift of flowers. The friend who had always been responsible for those on the pulpit sent to New York, when he was to sail thence for Havana, an order for a bouquet to be placed in his stateroom. From Nassau, where the steamer touched for a few hours, he sent back to her a pencilled note, enclosing a Nassau rose: —

"Next week I hope to hear the whippoorwill, and see bobolink; to walk to my old haunts in the woods, and gather my old and favorite flowers, — the *arethusa*, *side-saddle*, and *lady's-slipper*, not forgetting the little dear *polygalla*. Dear me, how much the woods and meadows of Spring Street have been to me! Well, let me learn yet more. Thou, Father, art nearer me in the woods, the fields, than elsewhere. I see why men need their conferences and prayer-meetings in the city, while in the country they are an interruption."

The following sonnet is from the journal: —

TO ONE WHO SENT ME FLOWERS ON CHRISTMAS DAY, AND I KNEW NOT WHENCE THEY CAME.

Dear child unknown, there came thy Christmas-flowers,
A bloom exotic 'mid December's snow,
Cheering my heart yet more in these glad hours,
When nought abroad save piety dares blow.
And yet, my friend, amid a heavier snow,
A sweeter flower thyself hast been to me.
'Mid other storms, and in a wintrier woe,

My flower-glad eyes were satisfied with thee.
Thy comfort brought into my bosom glee,
Yea, confidence and trust thy look did lend,
When else in vain I sought tranquillity.
Thus daughter, sister, mother, wife, and friend,
To one long nursed in grief's perplexity,
Little know'st thou what healing cheer thy words could send.

DEC. 27, 1849.

Thus with the humblest creatures the pastorate began; but it did not cease with them.

MAY 19, 1848.

It has been one of the beautiful days we sometimes have in May. It is summer come in without ringing at the door. The thermometer says 90° in the shade; yet all the morning the weather was perfect. Oh, how bright the sky was! and so deep the blue! Then the grass on the Common was so green, and the children so happy, and the dogs so delighted with their swim in the Frog Pond! It did me good to see such a day. I feel in love with all creatures on such a day: and such as I love most, I feel quite tender to; I long for their presence. For, when I have any thing so good as existence to-day, I want to share it with all I love.

In the winters of heavy snow he kept a little corn-crib in his library, and regularly fed at the window-sill the city pigeons deprived of their street-food. They soon found where breakfast was to be had, and flocked daily to the window; while he, with delight, watched them as they cooed and quarrelled, and hustled each other, and sidewise nodded through the pane at him. At table, in a summer boarding-place, a thoughtless mother told how merry her little boy was over a grasshopper in the kitchen, which was making ineffectual struggles to escape from a string by which she had fastened it to the table for the child's amusement. A blush of indignation and pain passed over his face as she spoke. The next moment he was out on the grass, watching his rescued captive as it skipped away. Friend he was of the insect, and of every thing else that needed a helper.

He was a providence to fretful children in the railway-cars with his bag of sugar-plums, and to elder children without number. From his eighteenth year, says one who knew him well, there was never a time when he was not giving to some young person the means for education. Many a youth struggling into college or through it felt the pressure of his strong uplifting arm, often without knowing whence the help came. Those of his parish in West Roxbury he stimulated to study by giving them his precious time, correcting their attempts at composition in the most attractive way. "Don't write about nightingales, my child: listen to the robin and the blue-bird in our fields." Young girls without means of obtaining a superior education, while there were no State normal schools within reach, received his instruction, often when his busy brain was overtasked with study and care. Nor did he wait for their application, but with exploring kindness sought out those whom he could help, and gave aid in a spirit so brotherly that it could not be refused. The president of Harvard College had a standing request to let him know of any deserving youth whom a little money would help. He counted it a privilege to pay the bills of an incipient scholar. No devotion to his studies ever led him to disregard an appeal for assistance, from whatever quarter. He never seemed to feel that there he had any rights which man, woman, or child, black or white, was bound to respect, but voluntarily tied himself hand and foot, and laid himself smiling on the altar of self-sacrifice. Just as he might be pouring out upon the paper the full flow of his thoughts, a tap at the library-door, answered by the ready "Come!" would bring in some unknown visitor. The pen was quietly dipped into the sponge-cup; the India cane-chair slipped round from the desk to the sofa, where the comer was invited to sit; while the genial "What can I do for you?" uttered as quietly as if no torrent had been checked in its course, put the two into harmonious relations.

And what a multitude came to him with their private affairs, domestic and personal! A young Scotchman with a general letter "to some Christian minister in America," seeking employment in his handicraft, is told that the man most likely to help him lives at No. 1, Exeter Place. The Methodist minister from the country, seeking literary help, receives it abundantly. A husband and a wife, each without the other's knowledge, come to seek counsel in mutual estrangement, and learn long afterwards whose wise advice it was that made them friends again. The man of culture and wealth who would not be seen at Music Hall goes to its preacher for consolation in his hour of affliction. Young people with noble aspirations and stifling surroundings look to him for guidance to congenial activities. The selfish intruder with private axe to grind; the ripe scholar, wishing to verify a quotation from a classic; the well-meaning revivalist, who would pray with him then and there for his immediate conversion, and was courteously permitted to try; the bully, who, believing himself aimed at in a public speech, ascended the stairs breathing vengeance, knocked at the door with the cane he intended using on the person of the occupant, but, forgetting his wrath in the calm presence, went subdued away; the doctor of divinity, wise and revered, wanting to see the man who had done such true work in the temperance cause; the young clergyman soliciting his aid in recovering a faithless husband whose desolated wife was sure that Mr. Parker could reach the delinquent; anxious mothers seeking counsel about their children from the man whose lifelong grief was his childlessness; public men to consult him on the moral bearings of their official action; chairmen of committees needing a skilful pen to write their reports; the fugitive slave hastening to a way-station, or perhaps a terminus of the "underground railroad;" a friend, bringing the first hepatica or the latest fringed gentian for the writing-table; a little pet to play an hour with the toys in "Parkie's" bureau, put there for the children's amusement; a Baptist clergyman with a polemical manuscript to be revised for the press; a young aspirant for literary fame, with verses to be criticised, or a paper whose eager craving for a magazine he was expected to satisfy, — these are authentic cases of visitation, specimens of whole classes of visitants, against whom he never shut the door. They consumed the time, but never seemed to exhaust the patience, of this most hospitable of minds. He had enough of that for the maiden's peevish complaint, for the enthusiast's dream of a new religion, for the Millerite's vision of the second coming, and for the fanatic's howl over the sins of society; and, before the infliction was at the foot of the first flight of stairs, the swift pen had taken up the unfinished sentence, and was speeding along the page as if there had been no pause in its work. He was the universal pastor, the shepherd of the forsaken sheep. A company of friends had planned a journey to Dublin, N.H., for the man overworked and sick; but as he sat at dinner on Sunday, the day before the starting, a black woman, poor of course, and a stranger, came and asked him to attend the funeral of her child on the Tuesday. He let the journey pass without hesitation, abandoned it, and did as the suppliant desired. He visited prisons, and comforted such as were under condemnation.

The writer of this biography has received fresh testimonies to his kind thoughtfulness; the following, for instance, from a young student, son of his valued friend, S. J. May: "Established in Cambridge, he at once extended to me that friendship father and mother valued so much, and made me familiarly welcome in his quiet, pleasant home, and conscious that he was watching over me with an unintrusive fatherly care. He constantly inquired as to my progress in study, discussed matters on which I was engaged, and advised me both in reference to them and to the homelier subjects of my health and comfort. I can hear him coming down stairs, with his tread so firm yet light, two steps at a time, from his study, humming or whistling some little quiet strain; and then came his hearty hand-shake, and sweet smile, and cordial greeting, in that voice with something suggesting gruffness, yet so gentle as to be musical. There was never a kinder voice.

"His meals used always to be exceedingly simple and light. But I remember, that, when he discovered I had planned a system of diet too meagre, he remarked it, and gave me good counsel in regard to more generous food. So, discovering that I was sleeping, for economy's sake, on a husk mattress, he stopped me one evening as he was going up stairs, thrust into my hand a bill, and charged me to go at once and get a hair mattress. Every year, knowing that my father's means were small, he sent a considerable check to me to help pay my college-bills. I believe he did the same for more than one of the young men in college, whom he had taken likewise under his fatherly care.

"The first Christmas after I entered college, I found a package waiting for me at a friend's office. It contained a costly dictionary of mythology and biography, with only this line: 'Dear Jo, this book is from one who loves your father very much, and hopes to like you equally well. So be a good boy.'

"Of all influences whatever which have tended to develop in me the *religious* sentiment, the influence of his character, preaching, and prayers, was altogether and peculiarly pre-eminent; it stands out in my consciousness distinct from all others; and it was the influence of character, of which preaching and prayers were only the expression."

A young girl who had listened to Mr. Parker, being about to leave home alone for the first time in her life to take charge of a district-school in Pennsylvania, called with her father to say good-by, and thank him for what he had done for her. Taking from the table at his elbow the volume of "Ten Sermons," then recently published, he wrote her name with his own, and his good wishes for her; then, with a kiss and a blessing, sent the maiden happy away.

A young woman called on the preacher to borrow a sermon, a passage whereof had pleased her especially. He was not at home. Two days afterward, she met him. He had returned her call, and, not finding her in, had left a book for her. He now lent her Herbert's "Poems," which he was preparing to edit. Subsequently he corresponded with her, sent books to her into the country, and gave her the use of his library when she was in the city, requesting her to send him abstracts and criticisms of the books she read, and descriptions of the people she met.

The correspondence with this lady, covering a period of eleven years, would make an interesting collection of itself. Her letters must have been brilliant, if, as he said of them, "They are as good as Bettine's to Goethe, without the lies."

The long arm befriended people across the sea. The refugee from Germany or Switzerland saw his beckoning hand. The foreign scholar was indebted to him for shelter and employment. He exerted himself to find publishers for unrecognized works, and to make good terms for needy authors who had no name. The exile knew where to come for help of all kinds. Purse, mind, heart, were all open. He had no theories that prevented him from observing the apostolic precept, "Bear ye one another's burdens." The strong man helped the weak in the human way until social science should find a better. Such notes as the following are not infrequent in the journal: —

ADVENTURES OF A DAY.

"After attending to numerous little matters belonging to new housekeeping, I sat down to complete my sermon; and there came, —

"1. A black man — a quite worthy one — for some pecuniary aid. He is a trader in new and second-hand clothes. Borrows money sometimes. Commonly pays one-fourth of a cent a day on a dollar, — ninety-one per cent a year; sometimes one-half of a cent, — equal to a hundred and eighty-two per cent a year. I could not help him, being myself out of money; but will do what I can.

"2. An Orthodox minister from Ohio, seeking for aid to erect a free church in his State. He wants five thousand dollars. He seems a good man, pious in my sense of the word, and moral too. With him was another man from the same place, who said little.

"3. Came a clergyman to talk about the Zoroastrian doctrine of the immortality of the soul, and to get Oporin's 'De Immortalitate Mortalium' which I had imported for him. *Mem.* — He will have the 'Dabistan.'

"4. Silas Lamson, with his full beard and white garments. He has two machines which he wished me to look at. They are to facilitate spading, ploughing, &c. He wants to get them before the Exhibition at New York.

"5. Mrs. M—— was here relative to Ned and the medicine we sent him yesterday.

"6. Greeley Curtis, just from Rome, and now for California, came. I have not seen him in several years. He worked his passage to and from Italy, and will work it famously through the world. A brave, good fellow.

"7. Dear Mrs. Russell came at five, and staid till nine. She consecrated the first introduction of the gas into the house: so the light of the house and the light of the heart burns at the same time. We took tea by the gas for the first time; lighted the parlor and kitchen therewith, and study."

How did such a man find moments for the books that every steamer brought him from England, France, Germany? He appropriated their contents as if by an instinct. Chatting, he cut the leaves of the thick octavo, turning them over slowly one by one. The book is laid down, with the paper-knife. "You have not read it, surely!" — "Try me, and judge." He was never caught tripping. The play of the mind went on in separate strata, as it were, each department of thought following its own lines with undisturbed serenity, and leaving its broad trail as it proceeded. The feelings never interfered with the working of the strong mechanism. The powers that received and the powers that distributed had a perfect understanding; so that, while the master was temporarily absent on lighter business, the obedient faculties performed their duty. It was as if the man had a double consciousness, — one outside of him, and one inside; the one chatting in the street while the other toiled in the office: but neither contradicted what the other said.

"O thou great Friend to all the sons of men,
Who once appeared in humblest guise below
Sin to rebuke, to break the captive's chain,
To call thy brethren forth from want and woe!
Thee would I sing. Thy truth is still the light
Which guides the nations groping on their way,
Stumbling and falling in disastrous night,
Yet hoping ever for the perfect day.
Yes, thou art still the life; thou art the way
The holiest know, — light, life, and way of heaven;
And they who dearest hope and deepest pray
Toil by the truth, life, way, that thou hast given;
And in thy name aspiring mortals trust
To uplift their bleeding brothers rescued from the dust."

CHAPTER XII.

THE PASTOR. — SPECIMENS OF CORRESPONDENCE.

THEODORE PARKER tended flocks on distant hills. His correspondence shows the extent and the delicacy of his care. The copied letters and notes of all kinds, which are but a portion of all he wrote, are contained in seven bound volumes of quarto size, and number nine hundred and forty-eight. Besides these are piles of manuscript epistles to intimate friends, — to one, ninety letters and fifty-three notes; to another, thirty-nine letters, long, and full of various matter. The correspondence with one dear friend in Europe covers three hundred pages folio. In addition to all this, private notes in great numbers were sent in response to the present biographer's call. And these are but a part; for many were not kept at all, many were lost, and many are held back from all eyes but those to which they were sent. They are of every conceivable description, and of every measure of length. Some are treatises on politics, theology, social ethics, philosophy, agriculture; and some are notes of three lines: but, whether long or short, they contain the writer's peculiar quality. Each had a purpose, and accomplished it. They were written to statesmen, politicians, governors, senators, presidents, men of letters, clergymen, scholars, men of science, historians, teachers, farmers, trades-people, boys at school, girls at home, friends in sorrow. The five minutes before dinner or bed, the spare half-hour on a railway-train, between the finishing of one book and the opening of another, were used in this cordial way. When his intimates were absent, it was his custom to send them almost daily some word of greeting, always bright, often humorous, never other than affectionate. They lie before me now, scores of these hurried missives, in queer hieroglyphics of pen or pencil, often quite illegible to unfamiliar eyes, but never so to the sensitive feeling; for the lovingness burns through the shapeless words, and communicates itself. If these papers could be printed, — he in his simple-heartedness saw no reason why they should not be, — they would do much more than convince the world that Theodore Parker was one of the tenderest hearts that ever beat, the truest of friends, the most sympathetic of men; they would illustrate the beautiful mission of letter-writing, the loving ministries of note-paper, the sweet uses to which the spare moments of the busiest day may be devoted, the possibility of making the pen the vehicle of pure feeling, just sufficiently weighted with thought not to be evanescent.

Of course, in a volume of these limited dimensions, to print many letters in full is impossible. The biographer's wish is to present Theodore Parker, not his literary remains; and this will best be done by giving specimen-letters, and portions of letters, so as to exhibit him in his several relations to men and women. Those who desire to read many important letters in full are referred to the biography by Mr. Weiss, whose selection is as admirable as it is copious. That I should in some instances print the same letters that he did is necessary; for we both have sought the most characteristic ones: but whereas he took such as were most interesting in themselves, either on account of the subject or the treatment, the present biographer has chosen such as best illustrated the texture and breadth of the writer's sympathies. We will begin with the most personal and private, — the pastoral epistles, as they may well be called.

To David A. Wasson.

BOSTON, June 14, 1857.

MY DEAR MR. WASSON, — Please tell me what pecuniary means you have for your journey to Europe. Perhaps my wife and I can add our two mites thereto. Tell me how you are, and when you sail.

Faithfully yours,

THEODORE PARKER.

BOSTON, Oct. 26, 1857.

MY DEAR WASSON, — How glad I am to know you are safe back in New England once more! I have not ceased to think of you since you left us last May, looking so sick, and yet trying to be so determined. Tell me all about *yourself*: that is the matter of interest now. How well are you? *Where* are you sick? What are the symptoms? What treatment do you receive? Where shall you pass the winter? Tell me all.

Shall I send you fifty dollars now, or a little later? It shall be just as you like. At all events, I *shall* send it.

Thanks for the kind interest you take in me. I shall prize Dr. Wilkinson's prescription, and never look on the pretty flower the plant bears without thinking of him. When you write, thank him kindly from me for his affectionate concern for me. I think I am now doing pretty well. I can work with about half of my former powers. Have a trouble in my side, but hope to *outgrow* it (!) My brothers and sisters died at about my age; yet I think I shall go round the "Cape." Give yourself no concern about *me*: take thought for *yourself*. German will do you good if you take it in *moderate doses*.

My wife and Miss Stevenson both send their love to you and yours.

Faithfully,

THEODORE PARKER.

BOSTON, Dec. 5, 1857.

MY DEAR WASSON, — Here is a check for fifty dollars, which please accept with the best good wishes of Mrs. Parker and myself. Let us know how you are in these days. Please ask your two excellent doctors if electricity would not help you. Love from Mrs. Parker and Miss Stevenson.

Yours truly and hastily,

THEODORE PARKER.

Rev. Friedrich Münch.

WEST ROXBURY, Oct. 12, 1846

DEAR SIR, — Your letter of Sept. 23 has just come to hand. I thank you for the frankness with which you speak about religious and theological matters, and rejoice most heartily in your desires and efforts to restore rational Christianity, which is the only *real* Christianity. I shall be happy to serve you in any way that is possible. I think your book had better be published at Boston. If you will send me the manuscript, I will do all in my power to find a publisher, and make no doubt that I shall succeed: if I cannot, I will return it to you without cost. But I think the book would *sell* better, and sooner find a circle of readers, if you should write a little account of yourself, telling where you were born, educated, &c. It might be brief as the biographical articles in the "Conversations Lexicon." I think you need not hesitate to send the manuscript by mail. The postmaster will tell you how to send it with the least expense. Then, if there be any profit from the sale, I will take charge of it, and send the money to you. . . . I knew Dr. Follen very well. *His* wife is a relative of my wife. She has long been my parishioner, neighbor, and friend. I saw some of Dr. Follen's relatives — a brother at Zurich, and a sister at Berne — a few years ago, and prize them highly. I rejoice to find that you are laboring in the great field of rational Christianity, and welcome you as a brother. I have myself written a little book on that theme. If you were not so distant, I would send it to you: as it is, I send only a couple of sermons, which will show you my *Standpunct* and that of the church which I have gathered together in Boston. The *Unitarians* as a body have done a great work already: they have fought against the old Orthodoxy (so called), against *total depravity*, the eternal damnation of men, and the like. Some things I think they have done wrong: much they have failed to do. Now a new *Richtung* begins to show itself; but it finds small favor with the mass of Unitarian *clergy*, though much with the people. This new tendency, I think, is to do much good. It aims at ABSOLUTE RELIGION, the Christianity of Christ; takes the Bible as a helper, not as master. I know none in Germany who *exactly represents this tendency.* De Wette, perhaps, comes the nearest to it; but he *keeps back a good deal,* I fear, and does not speak out clearly. A merciless warfare is waged by the *Philisterei* of the old party in the new school; but it is fought with very *dull* weapons, though *poisoned* ones. . . . When you write, address me, if you please, at *West Roxbury, Mass., near Boston.*

Believe me truly your friend,

THEO. PARKER.

To Dr. Fock.

BOSTON, June 27, 1851.

MY DEAR SIR, — I received your letter of the 27th of May a fortnight ago, and immediately made inquiries to see what can be done for you if you should come to America. It will be difficult for you to find a suitable employment. If you were a blacksmith, a carpenter, a fiddler, or a beer-house keeper, you would succeed well enough. But America is not a good country for a theologian or a philosopher. We have many colleges in America; but all but one are in the hands of Calvinists, who would be afraid of you: they would fear your philosophy and your freedom of thought. I think it would not be easy to find a position in any of them. One college (*Universität*) is in the hands of the Socinians (Unitarians), — Harvard College, at Cambridge, near Boston; but there is no place vacant there. Still I may be mistaken about some of the colleges in the *western* parts of America. If you come, we will do all that we can for you; but I am a very unpopular man, and must therefore work for you in secret. My theological opinions, and my opposition to American slavery, have made me so hateful to many here, that *it would not be wise in you to mention me as one of your friends.*

I have lately seen Herr Edouard Pelz, a German who was driven from Leipzig by the police. He has been in prison in Prussia for his writings: he has written many little works. He has been two months at New York, and edits a literary journal. He thinks, if *you have money enough to support yourself for a year, that your success is certain.* At Boston there are ten thousand Germans, with three or four churches, — one Catholic. At New York there are sixty thousand or seventy thousand, and in the suburbs of New York (*Vorstädten*) thirty thousand or forty thousand more: so there are not many places in Germany where you will find so many Germans as these. If you desire to come to America, you had better land at New York, and not Boston. It will give me pleasure to be of service to you in any way, and I will do all that I can to help you if you come; for I sympathize most deeply with you and with your unhappy country in her great trial. I would recommend you to write to my excellent friend Dr. J. G. Flügel, American consul at Leipzig, who will give you advice as to the mode of getting to America. At New York, when you arrive, if you will visit Mr. Rudolph Garrigue (No. 2, Barclay Street, under the Astor House), bookseller, he will give you information about the Germans in New York. Please let me know, if you decide to come, in what *ship* you embark, and at what *time:* then I will do all that I can to aid you, and may, perhaps, secure you some friends. But your first year must be a hard one. You do not mention that you have a wife: if not, your condition will be more fortunate; for a man alone can endure much.

Believe me faithfully your friend,

THEODORE PARKER.

To Prof. Felton.

BOSTON, June 19, 1851.

DEAR SIR, — I am well aware that it is not according to the etiquette of gentlemen that I should write you a note like this, after all that you have publicly written about me; but as I never entertained any unkind feelings towards you, and never doubted that you were as faithful to your own conscience as I was to mine, I do not feel that I am doing a wrong to you or myself in writing what follows. Of course, you will do as you like about attending to it.

I left a long letter (from Dr. Lobeck to me) with Dr. Walker to hand to you (for I did feel some scruples in calling upon you at your house), hoping you would take an interest in a brother Grecian. His "Book of Ionic Questions" speaks for itself, and I think you have seen that. Can you help the poor man to any place where he can get bread for himself, his *liebliche Frau* and *drei Kinder?* It is a hard case, and one that touches my heart most tenderly. I wish you would inform me if you can do any thing for him; for I shall write him soon as I can ascertain what he can do here.

Truly yours,

THEO. PARKER.

To Mr. and Mrs. John Bigelow, Medford

FRIDAY, Feb. 6, 1852.

MY DEAR GOOD FRIENDS, — How much I rejoice with you in the *fine healthy little boy*, the little immortal left in your mortal arms! I rejoice with you with all my heart, and thank you for letting me know of this new advent, thus making me a partner in your happiness. I was almost afraid — you had lived so long in Exeter Place, and been so near a neighbor to us — that your silver-wedding might be like ours, when it shall come, — the rejoicing of only *two*.

It is my lot to have no little darlings to call my own; yet all the more I rejoice in the heavenly blessings of my friends. The thing that I miss most deeply in coming from Roxbury to Boston is the society of my neighbors' little children, whom I saw several times a day, and fondled, and carried, and trotted, and dandled in all sorts of ways, as if they had been my own.

Well, God bless the life that is given, and the life that is spared, and the life that rejoices in them both!

I thank the new mother for remembering an old friend at *such* an hour: so give her my most affectionate greetings, and believe me

Happily yours,

THEO. PARKER.

To William Sturgis, Esq.

BOSTON, Nov. 31, 1855.

DEAR SIR, — Fourteen years ago this month, I delivered a course of lectures on matters pertaining to religion in Boston. A few minutes before I began to speak, while I felt such agonies of embarrassment and fear as I hope never to know again, you came and sat down beside me, and strengthened me. I have been thankful ever since; and now beg you to accept the volume which accompanies this note, with the grateful regards of

Yours truly,

THEO. PARKER.

To J. B. Parker.

BOSTON, April 28, 1853.

DEAR JOHN, — The house will be a nice thing. It is well to own the house you live in, but not dwelling-houses in general. But there are several things to be considered. There is, 1st, The insurance, which is not much at the Mutual; 2d, The cost of annual repairs; 3d, The fact that the house wears out in perhaps a hundred years, so that you consume one per cent of the principal a year. All this is to be considered; but you pay for these in the shape of rent to some other man, who considers all this when he makes up the rent. I hope you will buy a nice house, such as you like, with sun *in the kitchen.* A house on the south side of the street is worth much more than one on the north. You want the *sun* in the back part. Love to all.

Truly yours,

THEO. PARKER.

To Mrs. Martha P. Dingee, York, Penn.

BOSTON, June 27, 1856.

MY DEAR MARTHA, — I don't know what to advise Charles. It seemed to me a little rash on his part to take a farm so early in life, with so little acquaintance with the country and its ways; but I suppose he knew better than I. I don't like to advise him at such a distance, with so little knowledge of the facts. But one thing I am sure of, — if he goes back to Lexington, *he will do nothing, and, ten years hence, will be driving some other man's milk-cart for eighteen dollars a month, with no chance of any better fortune before him for life.* I trust he will not waste his time and money in a visit; and also that he will not *return to live here.* It seems so cowardly and unmanly to give up defeated! The Illinois Company makes good offers; but, if I were he, I think I should take government land at a dollar and twenty-five cents the acre, as so many thousands do every year. But I should work for others till I had two things, — 1st, a little experimental knowledge; and, 2d, a little ready money. You see the Illinois Railroad Company will sell land for five dollars an acre on credit, or four dollars for cash. It is so with every thing. Let him work a few years on wages, and *save his money,* and then he can buy land when he will. He can lay by from a hundred to a hundred and fifty dollars a year, — say a hundred and twenty-five dollars. Here, then, is the state of the case if he puts the money out at interest, seven per cent: —

1857 earns and saves	$125.	Puts at interest.				
1858 " " "	125.	Interest	$8.75	equal	$133.75.
1859 " " "	125.	"	9.36	"	143.11.
1860 " " "	125.	"	10.01	"	153.12.

Then on the 1st of January, 1861, he will have $554.98 of *his own earnings and savings.* With that he can buy land where he likes, and he will have such experience as enables him to *buy nicely.* He has made a bad experiment: he must be wiser next time. But to return to Lexington would be a yet worse experiment: he might as well go into partnership with "Bije Perry" at once, as general loafer.

I am glad to see that Charles has improved in his *spelling;* but he still seems to think it a severe task to write a letter, and so only does it at rare intervals. I see no reason why he should not become a thriving man.

Now, with many and the kindest regards for *yourself and yours,* believe me

Affectionately your uncle,

THEODORE.

To George C. Cabot.

BOSTON, Aug. 24, 1858.

MY DEAR GEORGIE, — Have not seen the old gentleman for a whole month! Never away from him so long since 1848! I was quite sorry not to find you the last day I went in town, but was glad to hear such good things from my wife. Mr. F—— pays you a large salary. I hope you will be sure to earn and deserve it all. I have always made it a rule to earn a little more than I was paid for. But the difficulty with young men often is to *keep and save* what they actually receive. Have a good care of that. You know your fortune depends on your earning and saving. If I know you, I think you are a very good young man. I don't know any immoral habit that you have, and I hope I shall never hear of any. You have an excellent opportunity to acquire a reasonable fortune. If you conduct well, and save your money, by the time you are five and twenty you will be able to marry some suitable young woman whom you love and who loves you. I don't know who it is: perhaps you do not yet, but will find out in due time. I am glad you are staying at Mr. Thayer's to take care of the house and the girls. I trust you will prove worthy of the confidence they place in you. Innocent young people can have a good time together when the unworthy must not be trusted. It is my birthday. I am forty-eight years old! — more than twice as old as you. When you are as old, I hope you will be a better and more useful man. I shall be at home next Thursday afternoon, I think; but am not quite sure.

Affectionately yours, T. P.

WEST ROXBURY, April 17, 1846.

MY DEAR LITTLE NIECE, — I thank you for your note asking my advice; and will give it, as you ask me. I would advise you by all means to do just as you think proper and right. But, if you were I, you would go without any hesitation. The advantages for you are very great. To go amongst strangers is one of the best things which could happen to you. You will see a beautiful country, new forms of society, and a whole set of new things. It will give you new ideas, make you more of a woman, and be an exceeding great help to you. You know the proverb, "Home-keeping youths have ever homely wits;" and there is a great deal of truth in it. I hope you will go. Surely you will, if you have any spirit of enterprise in you; and I think you have a good deal of it, and hope to see more. Don't be afraid of getting out of the reach of your mother's apron-strings. You can walk alone now, and it will do you good to walk alone. You may feel a little homesick for a week or so, but will soon *find* new friends, or *make* them. Write me as soon as you make up your mind, and tell me when you shall go. If possible, I will go there with you, see you comfortably settled and fixed down, and will then as now wish you all manner of pleasant things: so believe me

Truly your affectionate uncle, T.

A Friendly Letter of Advice.

BOSTON, Feb. 2, 1853.

DEAR SIR, — I do think you did wrong to be married under such circumstances. I think it was not wise to leave —— for a wider field, when no wider one was in sight; and you left a certainty for an uncertainty. It seems to me it would not be a very difficult thing for a hearty young man, with good abilities and good courage and a good heart, to pay off a few hundred dollars, or a few thousand dollars even, if he is industrious and economical. I don't wonder at the feeling you speak of in ——. I hope you are not going to break poor ——'s heart with sorrow, disappointment, and chagrin. She is your wife: you are bound to treat her more tenderly than yourself; to sacrifice your own personal predilections for her. You say she must have a husband whom she can *admire* and be *proud* of. It is for you to give her such a husband; to make such a husband for her out of yourself. It is not manly in you to be out of employment. There is a deal of work to be done in the ministry, in the Unitarian ministry: there was never such a time for a real living man to do a manly work. It is much easier now than ten, or eight, or even six years ago. There are more parishes vacant, looking for earnest and religious men. There was never a time when idleness in a minister was such a stigma and reproach. If you have any conscience in you, you will work; if you have any manhood in you, you will work. Not only is there the general call of duty addressing every religious man, but the special call of duty to you as a husband; and this also is the voice of God. You can find an opportunity to preach, I doubt not. Let the new responsibilities of marriage stir you to fresh efforts. I beg you not to put the self-denial on ——, but to take that to yourself. You are young and vigorous. The world is before you, and a noble and religious career of honorable service if you will.

Yours truly,

THEO. PARKER.

WEST ROXBURY, July 10, 1847.

MY DEAR PATIENCE, — I have not had a convenient opportunity to write you before. In your note you do not give me very distinctly to understand why you expect to lose the love and affection of your friends. It seems to me that you may "study the laws of the Spirit," and live the life of the Spirit, without losing the affection, or even the sympathy, of your friends. The laws of the Spirit may be as well studied in one place, or one sphere of life, as another. Living itself affords the material of that study; and the study consists in reflecting on the material thus given. But perhaps you are looking for some new form of activity in which to work. I am no judge of that: you must determine that for yourself. But I hope you will not mistake any transient impulse, which has its origin in some physical derangement, for a serious monition of a lasting duty. I know you will be faithful to your own convictions of duty: my only fear is that you should decide without due deliberation, and without a complete understanding of your own case. Then, of course, the decision will be incorrect, and the result vanity and vexation of spirit. Would not it be well to state distinctly to yourself *what* it is that you wish to do, and *how* you wish to do it? then you will know exactly what you are about, and not "fight as one that beateth the air."

I know you will be true to yourself, but only fear lest you should not always consult your *permanent* self, but only a fleeting emotion of the day or the night. If I can ever be of any help to you, you know it will give me great pleasure to be so. So, dear Patience,

Farewell! T. P.

West Roxbury, Feb. 7, 1845.

My dear Patience, — I thank you for your kind and seasonable letter. It came, as your letters always come, at the right time. I have delayed a little while my reply, because I have been too much occupied to find time to write any letters but the most urgent: so you will excuse my delay with the same charity you have always extended to me.

What you say of the love of God is true and beautiful. I understand your feelings and your experience; at least, I think so. No one can dwell too deeply in the love of God; for it is the noblest sentiment we are capable of feeling; and it leads out to a love of truth, goodness, usefulness, loveliness; for these are among the modes in which we conceive of God. It leads, therefore, in a sound and healthy state of mind, to a life full of truth, goodness, usefulness, and loveliness. But there is always a danger that such as dwell in this sentiment should lose themselves in contemplation; become *dreamers*, not *doers;* and so should be abundant in the blossoms of piety, and yet bring no fruit to perfection; so that, when the Lord comes seeking fruit, he shall find *leaves only*. Now, there is always a strong temptation for a mystical man, and I think still more strong for a mystical woman, to dwell amid the sentimental flowers of religion, charmed with their loveliness, and half bewildered with their perfume, so to say, — a danger lest common sins of the times should not be thought so sinful and injurious as they really are; and lest the man should sit down patient and contented, not heeding his brother's condition, nor helping him out of the ditch into which he has fallen. At a certain stage of religious progress we lose sight of the human element; we look perpetually at the divine; we think God does all; we resign ourselves unconsciously to his will; our own will ceases to be. Many stop there, and stop in outward inaction; then they become one-sided, and at length dwindle. But, if a man goes on, he catches sight of the human again, and does not lose the divine. He serves God consciously, and knowingly lives in obedience to the Great One. He ceases to be one-sided, but loves God with all his UNDERSTANDING and REASON, as well as with all his heart. Then, too, though he loves contemplation none the less, he loves action all the more. The one lives like a worm in the heart of an apple, fattens and grows, and then flies off: the other not only grows and fattens, but comes out, not a moth, but a bee, and visits all the flowers of the garden, culling from all its sweets, but carries off honey for other bees, and builds up the comb, — the residence of future bees that are to rejoice in his labors. We must not only *fly*, but, as we mount up, we must take others on our wings; for God gives one more strength than the rest only that he may therewith help the weak. I hope you will one of these days come and see us, and let us talk with you. I had a very pleasant conference with Mr. Hall the other day. I wish there were more such men in pulpits.

Remember me to your parents and sisters, and believe me, as always,

Truly your friend and brother,

THEO. PARKER.

WEST ROXBURY, Oct. 27, 1845.

MY DEAR PATIENCE, — I did not hear of your affliction until Saturday, or I should have come up to see you instantly. Now I am obliged to go off for some few days: so I fear I shall not see you till next week. I hope you not only sustain yourself with a Christian fortitude, but are able also to comfort your father, whose afflictions are greater than your own, and your sisters, who naturally will look to you for consolation in this hour of sorrow. I know you will be calm, resigned, lying low in the hand of God. I know you will know that all is for the greatest good of her that is gone and those she has left behind. I hope you will be able to cheer hearts which are sadder than your own. They will see more than *patience* in you, I doubt not, even resignation, cheerful acquiescence in the will of the Great One, who always is doing us good, not less when he causes us to weep than when he makes us smile. I beg you to assure your father of my sincere sympathy for him in this loss, and my hope that he will find comfort and peace. Let your sisters see and feel that you are superior to affliction, and you will gradually take away the grief of this sudden wound, and at last heal it. I have time to say no more; for I go presently: so good-by!

Sincerely,

THEO. PARKER.

To Miss Etta M. White, Salem, Mass.

BOSTON, Oct. 12, 1857.

MY DEAR MISS WHITE, — It gave me great pleasure to receive your letter, which I have just this moment laid aside. Thank you for the generous feelings you express to me. Gratitude is one of the rarest as well as fairest of the Christian virtues. But you need not feel so much towards *me*; for it gives me more pleasure to help you a little than it does you to receive the help. Besides, am I not paying an old debt? Your father was one of my earliest teachers. He put me upon the study of Latin when I was a little boy, and took great pains with me. I must not forget that. I trust you will take good care of your health: all your success will depend upon that. Don't sacrifice it even to desire of excellence in your studies. I hope you will take regular exercise in the open air, and be sure to have warm clothing. Salem is a damp, chilly, east-windy place, and, I think, not quite healthy. The more care will be needful on your part.

Where do you go to meeting? Whom do you know at

Salem? When I visit the town, I shall certainly come and see you. If you are ever in Boston, both my wife and I shall be glad to see you at No. 1, Exeter Place.

Believe me faithfully your friend,

THEO. PARKER.

To Mr. Henry A. Wilcox, Mendon, Ill.

MR. WILCOX. BOSTON, Oct. 10, 1856.

Dear Sir, — Your case is a very hard one; but I do not know what advice to give you. It would be in vain to venture to Boston or any of the Eastern towns, where the avenues to all kinds of business are more crowded than with you at the West. I feel the warmest sympathy with you, and trust that patient efforts will secure you the victory in the end. There are several modes which men try to overcome an enemy withal: one is to knock him down; another to talk him down; but I think the manly way is to *live him* down. After a little while, farmers will sow the wheat which gives the largest crop of the best kind of grain, and will not care much by what *name* it is called. If *Hebrew* wheat yields only ten bushels to the acre, and *Heathen* wheat yields thirty of a better quality, the bad name won't keep the wheat from the fields.

It is always pleasant to try and live down the evil name which good deeds bring on a man. You are always sure of the peaceful victory at last.

Believe me yours truly,

THEO. PARKER.

To H. A. Wilcox.

MR. WILCOX. BOSTON, April 15, 1858.

Dear Sir, — I thank you for your kind letter, but fear your others must have miscarried; for I have answered all I have ever received. You may not have received all my replies. I am glad you like farming. It is the most natural, and so the most healthy, of all human employments. Omitting all who die before twenty years of age, the average age of farmers in Massachusetts, at death, is sixty-four; that of printers, thirty-six. After they reach the age of majority (twenty-one), the printers live fifteen years; the farmers, forty-three.

I am not astonished that you find the head saves the hands. A man with a good head and no hands at all can direct the muscles of a thousand men. It is a good profession for one's whole life. I am sorry to find it is no more popular. In Europe it is the favorite employment with a great mass of men. It is not fast enough or noisy enough for the Americans.

I send you a couple of little sermons of mine lately printed, which please accept with the best wishes of

Yours truly,

THEODORE PARKER.

To Mr. James B. Patterson, Dayton, O.

BOSTON, Feb. 28, 1855.

DEAR YOUNG FRIEND, — I am the person whom you met in the cars, and parted from at Albany. I sought you in the cars; but, in the dim light, I failed to find you. I took a good deal of interest in the bright young face, looking so pure and hopeful, and thinking, that, some five and twenty years ago, I was on the same road that you are now. I am sorry that you have met with the "misfortune" you refer to. It certainly casts a shade over a young man's prospect for the moment, not for the day. You have a good start thus far, and seem to have laid the foundation well. It will be no misfortune, in the end, that you must get your own education. It will bring out the deep, manly elements at an earlier period; will make you more thoughtful when you would else have been more gamesome and playful. If you are a teacher, you can find much time to study by yourself. I began to teach when seventeen years old, and continued it for four winters, working at home on my father's farm in the other parts of the year. I always found from eight to ten hours a day for study, besides the work-hours in school. Then I taught a high school for three years more, and kept far ahead of the class in college of which I was a (nominal) member. You can do all that, and perhaps more.

Perhaps it will be well to pursue the same studies you would have taken at college, with the addition of such as belong to your calling as teacher; or you may, perhaps, teach till you accumulate money enough to go through the college at a later date. *No good thing is impossible to a serious and earnest young man with good abilities and good moral principles.*

But, above all things, be careful of *your health.* Your success depends on a *sound body.* Do not violate the laws which God writes in these tables of flesh.

Let me know where you go and what you find to do, and I will write you again when more at leisure.

Truly your friend,

THEO. PARKER.

To Miss Abby M. Parker, Savannah, Ga.

BOSTON, Feb. 6, 1852.

MY DEAR MISS PARKER, — I am truly obliged to you for your kind letter. I am glad you have had the opportunity to visit another land, see other skies, and become acquainted with forms of social life so unlike ours in New England. The longing for home is natural, and painful too, I know very well; but it will not be without good results in years to come. It is a good thing, in the early part of life, to fill the eye with pictures of lovely things, — in the North with our shaggy forests, mountains, &c.; in the South with the varied and beautiful vegetation of tropic-lands; in all countries with the stars, the little flowers, the forms of animals, and the faces of handsome men and women, especially of children. All these things help educate the sense of the beautiful, give delight at the time, and furnish a world of loveliness for the imagination to wander in at other times, when there is no object of delight for the senses, and no special thing to interest the mind. You have the opportunity to add to your store of such things; and the absence of society, of near friends, and of books, will force these things upon your eye, to remain there forever.

I never thought you would like to live at Savannah all your life; but you will return better in health, I trust, and with the happy result of your experience. I shall value the flowers very much which you speak of. I have heard my friends speak of the abundance and beauty of the flowers in your neighborhood. Perhaps you will find it a pleasant thing for yourself to gather a flower from each spot you visit, press it in a book, — putting the date and place in the margin, — and so keep a diary of blossoms as the day-book of your travels. I always do so in my rambles about the world, and find my flower-books the most valuable records.

If you get time, and feel the inclination, I hope you will write me again; for I love to keep my eye on the minds of my young friends when they wander off from me. We have had some things here that would have interested you this winter, — concerts by the *Germanians*, the *Musical Fund Association*, &c., and, best of all, six lectures from Mr. Emerson. The latter you may read some day. Accept my kind and friendly regards, and believe me

Truly yours,

THEO. PARKER.

To M. A. Parker.

BOSTON, May 16, 1852.

MY DEAR MARTHA, — I was glad to receive your letter, which has just come to hand; and quite pleased to find you like your new situation. I am always afraid, in so small a school, you will not have enough to do. It is better to have too much than too little. If you have not enough to do, the mind grows sluggish, and all the faculties deteriorate.

I hope you will improve the opportunity to learn French and drawing. I would do so by all means. In learning to draw, do not confine yourself to *copying prints*, but draw from nature also. Hang up a cabbage-leaf or a burdock, with its side towards you, and draw that; then hang it a little edgewise (so as to see half of its breadth), and then draw again. I think this will help you much.

I think you need society, the acquaintance of educated and refined persons. I would take every opportunity to meet such persons. At York I think you will find many agreeable and instructive persons.

Shakspeare you will find a mine of beauty and of rich wisdom. "Hamlet" it will be worth while to read over twenty or thirty times, till you know it thoroughly, and can repeat all the finest pieces. If you come in contact with a copy of Byron, you had better read that carefully; delightedly I know you will. I tried to get for you a copy of "The Cyclopædia of English Literature" when you went to Pennsylvania; but found none. Some time, when I see you, I will bring it. I shall not attend the Convention this year. I wish I could; but I have so much to do at home, that I have no time for such an expedition this year.

Give my regards to the *Wrights* and the *Townsends*, and believe me truly

Your friend,

THEO. PARKER.

To a Young Woman.

BOSTON, Dec. 14, 1855.

MY DEAR LITTLE MAIDEN, — "The course of true love never did run smooth:" so is it writ in many a history. This particular affair may turn out quite different from what it now appears. There may be ups and downs in a courtship. If there were not a true congeniality between you, it is fortunate *he* made the discovery so early: by and by it would be more painful to break off. But, be the future what it may, of this you are sure, — *the love which filled up the few months with its handsome flowers.* That leaves a mark, like the traces in the rocks of New England, which will never be effaced from the character. I know it is very painful for a young maiden to bear such disappointments, especially for deep-hearted maidens; but there is a source of strength and comfort in the religious faculties within you, which will never refuse supply in time of sorest need. Burnt spots in the woods bear the earliest plants and most luxuriant and most delicate flowers: so can it be with you; so I trust it will be. It will always give me pleasure to see you and hear from you.

Truly yours,

THEO. PARKER.

Extract from a Letter.

AUG. 14, 1859.

. . . I am glad you are busy with work of the house and dairy; that you can make good bread (I think it one of the fine arts), and also good butter. We lived (or staid) ten weeks at St. Croix, and had never a morsel of tolerable bread. There are few American women who can make a decent article: many of them commit the (female) sin against the Holy Ghost continually by transfiguring good meal into bad bread. By famous I meant eminent (which is in your power), not renowned (which is both undesirable, and out of your control). I should rather be eminent for bread and butter than famous for straddling about on platforms, and making a noise in public meetings, and getting into the newspapers, as many women do.

If you can find a school that you suit, and which suits you, I would take it; but, if not, I would make the most of duty which lies about me at home. By and by you will have that opportunity to be loved which you wish for so much, and perhaps in the most attractive of all forms. But I should not lightly esteem the purely affectional love of father and mother for an only daughter, nor cherish romantic nonsense in my head. The river of life is not all foam: indeed, froth is a very small part of it; one, too, which neither waters the meadow, nor turns the mill, nor adds much to the beauty of the stream. Books will enliven the else dull hours of winter; and both strengthen and enrich your mind, if you choose them well. There must be a plenty of intelligent people in ——, of your own age, to afford you the company you need. I see not why you should not be as happy at home as a young maiden need be. The prose of life is quite as indispensable as the poetry, and about twenty times greater in quantity. The apple-tree is in flower a week, in bearing some twenty weeks, and, besides, is still and silent long months, but active all the time. . . .

To the Same.

BOSTON, Sept. 10, 1858.

MY DEAR ——, — Your lot is harder than I fancied; for I thought your occupation was a fixed fact which would continue, and that Theodore's health was mending, and would finally be restored. It is indeed very sad to see a boy thus fade away. It is natural the old should die: it is against nature that the young pass off so premature. Still I see no reason for the foolish melancholy you indulge in, and seem to cherish. I know not how much of it is constitutional, and so beyond your control. Still I fear much of it is wilful, and within your own power: this latter you should check at once, and finally make way with and end. It cannot, perhaps, be done by a direct act of the will, but indirectly by the performance of daily duties. The common wants of life afford the best opportunities for happiness and noble character. Housekeeping, school-keeping, and the like, are the best things for the majority of women: they are as good as grass for cattle. By and by you will find a school somewhere. A common school will not be an unfit place for you to work in. I would seek the highest I was fit for, and put up with the best I could find.

But, for the time, you must, no doubt, stay at home, and do what you can for your little brother. I trust you will find comfort and satisfaction; but it must come out of your own soul. Remember me with kind sympathy to your father and mother, and Theodore too.

Affectionately yours,

THEODORE PARKER.

To W. Silsbee.

BOSTON, Dec. 4, 1848. — Monday morning.

MY DEAR WILLIAM, — I did not know what had befallen you till late on Saturday, or I should have come instantly to Salem, not to offer you my *consolation* (I know how poor and cold that will appear in your case), but to give you my sympathy. How little did I think, when you were last with us, that so soon such an affliction would befall you! But, William, you are a man, and can bear hardness; you are a Christian, and can trust God with an absolute faith. It is not an evil thing that has befallen Charlotte. Oh, no, William! it is a good thing: it is only a hard thing that has befallen you. But why has that come upon you? Is it a thing infinitely evil to you? Surely not. Now you will have tears. I know what tears; I know what grief and rending of the heart. But the tears are not forever: the heart now rent is to be blessed by that very rending. I know there is an ecstasy of grief in spiritual men, finely attuned by religion, which for a time gives an unnatural calmness and a beauty of faith not seen or known before. I never could doubt the Infinite Goodness in times of severest trial. But that ecstasy will not last: there come sore days of emptiness, when we go stooping and feeble, with failing eyes and a hungry heart. That is the great sorrow, the *long* grief. But there is comfort in that period. Your wife will not be lost to you. She will come back to your affections: the kind words you have spoken to her will now return, echoed from the immortal world. The wife will become an angel to cheer you, guide you, bless you. It is not now the mortal woman, failing and imperfect, it is the madonna out of heaven, who will lean down, and look over to help you. In the autumn I have seen a spot in the woods burnt over by some accidental lightning, a roving thunder-bolt falling at random (so it seemed) out of heaven. All was burnt over,—the leaves and the grass; the trunks of trees looked black and ugly: but in the spring tender flowers came up which grew nowhere else in the wood, for the sun came warmest on that blackened earth; fragrant grass grew there; and all summer long it was the greenest and the fairest spot in all that wood. Yes, it was the last spot which the autumnal frost set foot upon. So it is with sorrow-stricken souls. But why do I write as if to *console*? I only wish to offer you the sympathy of one kind heart which bleeds at the arrow so sorely piercing you. I would come and see you to-day; but it is impossible. Perhaps to-morrow; at any rate, as soon as possible.

God bless you, and wipe the tears from your eyes.

T.

WILLOUGHBY LAKE, VT., Aug. 3, 1854.

MY DEAR SANBORN,—Your letter apprises me of the sad fact which I always thought must soon or late come to your knowledge. I know the nature of that treacherous complaint too well. When you were first engaged, I felt about it as you do now. There was a flower as brief as beautiful. Young love sustained her, gave her new hope, new vigor, new strength, and so, doubtless, prolonged the life you loved so fondly. I saw how her friends mistook love for life. But there are cases in which the soul thus deeply stirred pushes the malady aside, and the body lives in triumph. If she recovers, it will be by that medicine.

I have watched your love with great interest, always with trembling. Well, it is a dear and beautiful thing once to love with all the fervor of youth; to love one so worthy of a firm and manly love, so capable of firm and womanly love. Come what may come, so much you are sure of, so much joy of the noble sort given and received, so much life made into character. This attachment has blessed you both. If death must separate the two souls which seem made for each other, I know nothing but religion which can sustain the survivor: that can. The tenderest sympathy of your friends will be freely given you: that will be a little comfort. All the excellences which made you love her will appear more lovely, more excellent, when they are immortal. Your affections will follow her where she precedes. "Where thou diest will I die," you will say; meaning, "Where thou *livest* will *I live.*" But the sweetest, best, of consolations, will come from your realizing sense of the love of God. She takes the step in her progress which we call "death." You had hoped it would not be taken yet, nor separately, but arm in arm, at the same time, you should become immortal together. Alas! the better half of the *treasure* exhales to heaven, and leaves the *earthen vessel* and the widowed soul. But there is a self-sustaining faith which looks even that disaster in the face, and is triumphant.

Do not doubt you shall have my tenderest sympathies in my *holiest hours*. I know too well the touch of suffering: 'tis part of my daily life to try and strengthen others for the cup of sorrow which may not pass from us. You do not yet know what heroic strength there is in the womanly part of manhood. I could wish you might not find it out for many years. But, if you must, then let me say, that he who drinks early at this deep spring has a life in him which common men know not, — other sorrows, other joys, other hopes, other aspirations. Fear not, my brave young friend, God will be with you as with her; and eternity will mend what time so sadly seems to mar.

Come and see us when you return to Cambridge, soon as you can. Let me hear from you. I shall be in Newbury, Vt., in about ten or fourteen days. You and your friends will know best what to do. But you must not think of forsaking Cambridge: that will not save her, and will seriously injure her. Let me know if a little money is needed, and you know it will give me pleasure to furnish it.

Affectionately yours,

THEO. PARKER.

Remember me affectionately and tenderly to A——; but I think she had better not see the letter.

BOSTON, Sept. 5, 1854.

MY DEAR SANBORN, — So the summer and the mortal life went out together. It was pleasant that she passed farther on at such a time, — the day of your souls' nuptials. Tears you will shed; tears you *must* shed: do not try to check them. But you have an angel in place of a wife. I never thought your wedding would be other than it is. But the marriage between a mortal and an immortal has the tenderest influences on the humbler spirit which yet wears the dusty dress of flesh. You will look up.

I know not how to try to console you, but would rather use "words of endearment when words of consolation avail not." But she has gone forward to that higher wedlock, where development and delight not dreamed of here must needs take place. To the intellect, death is nothing, — it is a ferrying over the river, where the yonder banks are fairer than the hither: to the religious part of our nature it is a triumph, a great circumstance and a joyous; but to the affections it is the most cruel of separations.

"Was liebt muss zusammen sein,"

and we mourn bitterly as our dear ones are torn away. But in the burnt spots of our woodland there come up sweet grass and fairest flowers: the tenderest virtues bloom gloriously there.

I see the effect this is to have on your character. I know, as you cannot, how it will stimulate the noblest things in you, making you wise before your time, and giving qualities else not won in many a year. Doubt not that you are remembered in the tenderest communings of my heart, both in its public and its private hours. I did not receive your letter till Monday, but remembered you not less in the opening services at the Music Hall, where I saw only one of your friends, — May. I hope you will come and see us soon as you return this way. In the mean time look to me for any kind offices you need, and believe me one that early learned to suffer, and

Most faithfully your friend,

THEO. PARKER.

To C. A. Bartol.

BOSTON, Dec. 1, 1852.

DEAR BARTOL, — I thank you heartily for your new volume of sermons, which has just come to hand (I received your note at the tea-table). Don't dream that I value or love a man less because he and I differ on questions of geology or theology, or any thing else. I never did, and, I think, never shall. We have lots of errors both (and all) of us, no doubt, but some little truth to cling by, to live with, and (if need comes) to die for at the last. I love to meet all sorts of persons, to live with all sorts of books, and so get a little widened by intercourse with Heathens and Christians, Catholics, Protestants, and Mormons. I am amazed at the intolerance of men. They hate one another for a difference on a question of time in the geological periods of the earth, for a difference in regard to tariff or free trade, to Gen. Scott or Gen. Pierce, to Trinity or Unity, Christianity or Mosaism. It is all wrong. We may ask each man to be faithful to himself, not to another man's self. The same fidelity leads different men to very different conclusions. Was not Beecher honest as Channing, and Blanco White faithful as either of the two? Let us agree to think differently (when we must), and to love one another still.

Truly, as of old,

T. P.

Rev. John Pierpont.

WEST ROXBURY, Oct. 15, 1845.

DEAR SIR, — I called to see you yesterday, but unluckily missed you; and as I shall not, it is probable, have another opportunity to take you by the hand, I will now say a word to you before you leave Boston. None can regret your departure more than I. We have not been much together. You have been busy, and so have I: therefore I have not seen you so often as I could always have wished. But I have always felt encouraged and strengthened by your example, and that long before I had any "troubles" with my theological "brethren." If you had done as the other ministers, had you been as they are, you would not now have been leaving Boston. If you had flattered the follies, and winked at the sins, of the rich, you would have had, not *your* reward (that you have now), but *their* reward: I mean, the reward of the ministers you leave behind. But you have chosen another part, and have YOUR reward, — a little different from theirs. You must go in triumph; for you have fought a good fight and a great one. For nearly thirty years, you have been foremost in all the great reforms of the day which had the welfare of men for their object. You have been fearless and free. If others didn't help you, you thought that was a reason why *you* should work the more. When your valor was called for, you did not turn round to remember your discretion. None of the great moral enterprises of the day would have stood where now they stand, if you had not opened your manly voice in their behalf. Where would *temperance* have been if John Pierpont had been silent? where many other good and noble causes? It is your zeal for the great cause which Jesus died to serve that now has brought you to your present position. Your reward is with you. The confidence that you worked faithfully, and wrought a great work, will go with you, and bless you to the end of your days. Nothing has happened for years so reflecting disgrace on the Boston clergy as your departure from the city under the present circumstances. But what is their disgrace is your glory. Go, then; and may God be with you! For *my* sake, for the sake of *many*, I could wish you were to stay; but it is better you should go. I know you will find work enough to be done, and warm hearts to welcome you in doing it. You leave behind not a few to bless you for your toils, and to pray for your future success and welfare. Your memory will live ever in their affections, and their good wishes will follow you wherever you go. I beg you to accept my thanks for all that you have done, and to believe me ever

Your friend and brother,

THEO. PARKER.

To Mrs. Julia Bridges, Newton Corner.

BOSTON, April 9, 1858.

DEAR MADAM, — I am much obliged to you for the interest you take in my spiritual welfare, and obliged to you for the letter which has just come to hand. I gather from it that you wish me to believe the theological opinions which you entertain and refer to. I don't find that you desire any thing more.

I make no doubt the persons who pray for my conversion to the common ecclesiastical theology, and those who pray for my death, are equally sincere and honest. I don't envy them their idea of God when they ask him to come into my study and confound me, or to put a hook into my jaws so that I cannot speak. Several persons have come to "labor with me," or have written me letters to convert me. They were commonly persons quite ignorant of the very things they tried to teach me. They claimed a divine illumination which I saw no proofs of in them, in their lives or their doctrines. But I soon found it was with them as it is with you: they did not seek to teach me either piety (which is the love of God) or morality (which is the keeping of the natural laws he has written in the constitution of man), but only to induce me to believe their catechism, and join their church. I see no reason for doing either.

I try to use what talents and opportunities God has given me in the best way I can. I don't think it is my fault that I reject the absurd doctrines which I find in the creed of these people who wish to instruct me on matters of which they are profoundly ignorant.

But the Catholics treated the Protestants in the same way, and the Jews and the Heathens thus treated the Christians. I find good and religious men amongst all classes of men,— Trinitarians, Unitarians, Salvationists and Damnationists, Protestants, Catholics, Jews, Mahometans, Heathen. There is one God for us all; and I have such perfect love for him, that it long since cast out all fear.

Believe me yours truly,

THEODORE PARKER.

What flocks of letters like the one that follows would have fluttered over desolated homes had Theodore Parker lived to animate the strong, and console the bereaved, in our great war! And this was written by a dying man. Young Meriam was one of John Brown's little band. The expedition alluded to was the enterprise at Harper's Ferry. The youth had been reported killed.

To Mrs. Eliza F. Meriam.

ROME, Nov. 19, 1859.

. . . Your son has *fallen a martyr in a cause not less holy*, and *much more philanthropic*. He sought to deliver his own countrymen from domestic misrule and oppression incomparably greater than what your fathers fought against. Don't think his young life was wasted and thrown away because the expedition failed of its immediate object: it will help obtain its ultimate object; will strike terror into the hearts of all slaveholders, and so weaken the bonds which now hold the slave. Every victory we rejoice in has been bought with the blood of men. Such as died had mothers and sisters, often wives and children, to mourn the private cost at which the public benefit was bought. To the emancipation of American bondmen you have contributed your first-born son: not a drop of his blood is wasted. He himself is immortal, and has passed to that higher world we shall all enter on before long. He is a gainer by the change; and though his second birth took place in such terrible scenes, and he was delivered from the mortal flesh with such dreadful instruments, not the less does he pass into that glorious life "which eye hath not seen, nor ear heard, nor the heart of man conceived." I know what you lose; but I think of no cause in which I should rather one of my friends would lay down his mortal life. Surely the blessing of men ready to perish will fall on him. Here is your consolation on earth; and, beyond the earth, it will not be long before there is another meeting of souls widowed and orphaned here below. . . .

I know nothing of the details of your son's departure, only what "The Standard" briefly told. The last time I saw him, he came to consult me about another enterprise, which yet looked to the same end, only by means apparently more fearful. I could not fail to honor the motives which prompted him then: not less do I honor him now; nay, far more.

Your family have been always in the first rank of the opponents of slavery, continually making sacrifices for the slave. It is not inappropriate that the crown of martyrdom should be set on one of the members of the same family, — a crown of thorns, indeed, but also a crown of glory. I have been with you in other troubles terrible to bear. I think I know with what religious fortitude you will endure this.

Oh that I were in Boston to give consolation in private, and in public to warn the young and wicked nation against the folly which now threatens to ruin us! I would prove that the slaves have a *natural right to destroy their oppressors*, and that it may be the duty of freemen to help them. This is only the beginning. Nine experiments will seem to fail: the tenth will succeed, and pay for all the previous mistakes. The defeats in the early part of the American Revolution were essential to the great victory at last; part of the battle in which we were conquerors. My dear Mrs. Eddy, accept again my heartiest sympathy: would I had more to offer! Tell your father I shall write him soon as

I have news of the trial and fate of Capt. Brown. God bless you all!

Believe me ever faithfully yours and affectionately,

THEODORE PARKER.

To Dr. Bowman, Edgington, Ill.

DR. BOWMAN. BOSTON, May 22, 1858.

Dear Sir, — I have heard of several cases like that sad one you mention. No man becomes mad in attempts to become honest, truthful, humane, merciful, a good father, husband, brother, &c. What a direful thing is a *false theology!* No wonder men grow mad in attempting to appease a God who damns nine hundred and ninety-nine while he saves but one; a God who is nine hundred and ninety-nine one-thousandths damnatory, and only one one-thousandth beneficent.

But better times are coming.

I send you a few sermons.

Yours truly,

THEODORE PARKER.

To Dr. Bowman, Edgington, Ill.

DR. BOWMAN. BOSTON, Nov. 3, 1856.

Dear Sir, — I have just returned from a tour to your State, and find your pleasant and encouraging letter with four dollars in it. I send the books by express to-day. I am exceedingly glad when I find that I can help a man out of the mire of the popular theology to the firm footing of natural religion.

Please let me hear from you again. I have some sixty letters to write, and must now be short.

Yours truly

THEO. PARKER.

To Dr. Bowman.

BOSTON, Jan. 11, 1858.

MY DEAR DR. BOWMAN, — I thank you for your kind and noble-spirited letter, which I have just read.

I know how difficult it is to make headway against the organized errors of the popular theology. It is so here, where the mass of the people are both more intelligent and more reflecting than in your neighborhood. Yet such is the vital affinity between truth and the nature of man, that there is a continual and obvious progress here. A great change has taken place in the theological opinions of the thoughtful men in New England within ten years. In twenty more, it will be very great.

Still the stationary party becomes more intense in its conservatism, and adopts the course of your Presbyterian friend. At North Woburn, a little town fourteen miles from Boston, a church invited a Mr. Nickerson to be its minister. The council came to ordain the young candidate, and examined him to see if he was sound in the faith. He was right in all points but one: he *did not believe the eternal damnation of babies dying newly born.* The council refused to ordain him, and adjourned for eight weeks, when they will come together again.

The council never asked the young man if he believed in piety and morality, the substance of the religion which he ought to teach; but pressed only the questions of their theology, and insisted on the worst of all. In 1787, Dr. Townsend found that the Spanish physicians knew nothing of the circulation of the blood, and the young candidates for the honor of M.D. were not expected to believe it; but, before admission to practice, they took their oath that they believed the immaculate conception of the Virgin Mary. It was not so ridiculous as the conduct of that council. The method of men of science is this: 1. To accumulate the greatest possible number of facts; 2. To induce thence a general law which is common to all those facts; 3. To deduce other doctrines from that general law; and, 4. To make practical application thereof to such cases as require it: so his doctrine rests on facts, not whims. The ministers' method is to assume an hypothesis to be true on the testimony of nobody knows who, and thence deduce doctrines and apply them. Thus the inspiration of the Bible, the Trinity, the Fall, the Devil, Eternal Damnation, &c., are not supported by the smallest particle of evidence in the world: there is no fact of nature or of human history to support them. Doctors can do a deal of service in the manner you refer to, and sow seeds by the wayside which the fowls of the air will not devour.

I agree with all you say about slavery: only my compassion

falls more on the negro, who is the unwilling victim, than on his masters, who might set him free.

Believe me heartily yours,

THEODORE PARKER.

To Thomas G. Barnard, Esq., Norway, Me.

BOSTON, March 30, 1853.

DEAR SIR, — I thank you for your interesting and welcome letter, which I have just read. It gives me great pleasure to know of such men as yourself, bred by deeply-religious parents in the old forms of religion, yet coming out of bigotry into freedom with a continual increase of piety, and faith in God. I know some men who cast off the old forms of theology and of church service for the sake of getting rid of the restraints of religion. I always love to find one who grows in morality as he advances also in intellectual freedom.

I know many persons whose history is the same as yours. The Methodist Church does a great deal of good. The Methodist minister, poor, badly educated, often quite ignorant, goes amongst men more ignorant than he, and rouses up the religious spirit in their souls, and quickens them with new life. How many thousands of men there are who owe their earthly salvation to the labors of some modest minister of that persuasion! I have great respect for them. But, alas! they bind men in fetters; they make men fear; they drive by terror, while they ought to draw by love; they make too much of a separation between life and religion. Their idea of God is dark and sad; so is their notion of the next life. But when one comes to the conviction that God is infinite, — I mean perfectly powerful, perfectly wise, just, loving, and faithful to himself, — then the great difficulty is over. You do not *fear* God: you love him. You will not seek to shun his laws, but to keep them; and, if you fall away sometimes through the strength of temptation and the weakness of your character, you feel mortified, ashamed, and penitent, and come back full of vigor and resolution anew, and go on your way rejoicing.

I am sorry I did not know you while you were here in Boston, and hope you will continue to grow in all religious and manly excellence.

Truly yours,

THEO. PARKER.

To Robert White, Jun., New York.

BOSTON, March 15, 1853.

MY DEAR GOOD FRIEND, — I should have written you long ago; but, when I came home from New York, I had another of the comforts of Job, which seated itself on my right hand, so that I could not write with it. Some indispensable letters I wrote with the left. You would laugh to see them, but give up the attempt to *read.* Now that is gone, and all its companions, I hope. I was never better than now.

Your old and intimate relative has taken that step in his life which we commonly call death. I doubt not it was a pleasant step for him to take; though painful always it must be for us, the living, to separate from such as go to a higher life. But there are so many beautiful associations which cling to those we love, and come out with all the more beauty when they cease to be mortal, that the departure of a friend is always attended with an exaltation of our spirits, if we have faith in the infinite goodness of the great Father.

There are some men whom I pity exceedingly: —

1. Such as have *no belief in the soul's eternal life*, and look on death as an ultimate fact.

2. Such as only *fear a God*, but do not know the infinite Father (and infinite Mother) of all souls, and so have nothing on which they can perfectly rely.

I meet both classes of men, the latter oftenest; and I pity them most exceedingly. To one the grave is only a deep, dark hole in the ground: to the other it is a hole which leads down to hell.

The popular religion makes death a most formidable enemy, a thing to be shuddered at.

I am amazed at the feebleness of men's faith in God. Death is one step in our progress. Birth was a step once; but birth was a death to one form of being, and death is a birth into another form of being. To die in infancy, youth, or manhood, does not seem after the true course of nature; but to die in old age, —

"Life's blessings all enjoyed, life's duties done," —

that is no misfortune, but a blessing also. My father, when an old man (seventy and seven years old), laid down his weary mortal bones, and was glad to die. We wept over his toil-worn hands and venerable head, which we had kissed so many a thousand times; but we were glad that the dear old man rested from his labors, and went home to his God and our God, — the earthly father to the *infinite Father and Mother.* So shall we all one day be glad to go, and knock with our feeble hand at our Mother's door. "Undo the gate, and let me in," shall we all say, as we go, willing and welcome, to meet her.

I hope you and yours are all well. We send our kindest salutations to you all. My wife and Miss Stevenson admired your daguerrotype, and thought it quite faithful.

Sincerely yours,

THEO. PARKER.

To J. T. Sargent.

WEDNESDAY, Dec. 18, 1844.

DEAR BROTHER, — Thanks for your letter, which I am now *hot* with reading. I will lecture, as you say, sell tickets, and do any thing, for so good a cause. I wish to lecture the time you mention; for I shall preach the Thursday Lecture that day, and so shall save time. Thank you, thank you, for the letter! But you must not leave "those few sheep in the wilderness." With whom *can* you leave them? No, no! Have no superstition about injuring "the cause," or hurting the feeling of the "*Fraternity* of Churches." Take a hall, and preach to such as come. Let the "brethren" fill their chapel as they may and can. Don't budge an inch. I look on this holding as all the *free ground* that is taken in the city: I would fight for it to the last. I don't know what else you may have in view; but I think you can do nothing better, nothing half so good, as to continue and preach to these men you have attached to you. They look to *you* for help in time of trouble. "The *hireling* fleeth when he seeth the wolf coming," &c.; "but the *good shepherd giveth his life for his sheep.*"

Putnam said, yesterday, he did not see the necessity of your resigning. I do, and the necessity of your continuing with your old friends. But what do I say? I have no authority to advise any one, least of all one who knows his duty himself. I only fear that you have a superstition about injuring *the cause;*

while I think you will injure it by deserting the *little ones*, and so causing them to offend.

Believe me most heartily yours,

THEO. PARKER.

A second letter to the same friend, and in the same strain, will not seem too much in illustration of that sentiment, half gratitude and half compassion, which is rare except with the best minds: —

To J. T. Sargent.

WEST ROXBURY, Jan. 30, 1845.

MY DEAR FRIEND AND BROTHER, — I should be very recreant to my own inward promptings if I did not tell you how my heart feels moved towards you of late, and how much I feel grieved at your troubles. For my own I never cared much: they pass by me as the wind. I open a book; I walk in the fields: they fall from me as I shake the loose snow from my hat, and trouble me no more. My dreams are sweet as a boy's, so calm and untroubled! But it gives me great grief and pain that I have unwittingly brought you into trouble. What can I do to help you? I know not. If I were to *write* in your defence, you would say, as Brother Young at Ellis's ordination, "*Non tali auxilio*," &c.; and I should do you more harm than good. It would be regarded as if the *Devil* should come out and defend Job from those excellent "friends" who fastened on him in his misfortunes. I can give you my sympathies: you have those rich and abundant. I can tell you how much I admire your spirit, how much I applaud your courage (the courage of gentleness), your gentleness too (the gentleness of strength). I have not had time to thank you for your noble and manly sermons. They are the true expressions of a noble spirit. They are rich in magnanimity. If any thing had been wanting to place the Fraternity in their true light, it was the publication of the last sermon you preached in the chapel. I feel for you; but I *pity* the Fraternity. I hope I feel contempt for none.

"I pity such as wicked are;
I pity and I mourn:
But the great God hath fashioned them;
And, oh! I dare not scorn."

Your last sermon places you in a fine light before the public. It has the *rhetoric of facts* and the *eloquence of truth*. I know not what are your plans for the future. I feel almost glad that you did not take my advice, and open a new chapel for the poor, and yet still almost sorry you did not. Do you think the Fraternity will adhere to their ground?—adhere to it, and not expel me? That is quite inconsistent. But it was good-natured and manly to appoint the committee they did to confer with me. Though nothing but *good feeling* will come of it, it is worth while to have that *among brethren*. Tell me if you have my "Treatise on De Wette:" if not, it will give me great pleasure to send you a copy.

Believe me most truly your Christian brother,

THEO. PARKER.

P. S. — Give all cheering regards to Mrs. Sargent.

To S. J. May.

OCT. 24, 1853.

. . . I hope you read "The Register" of last week and the account of the Annual Convention. What subjects for discussion! — Have we a litany amongst us? Shall we have one? That is, when the Rev. Mr. Peabody reads, "The Lord delighteth not in the strength of the horse," whether —— —— and —— —— shall respond, "He taketh no pleasure in the legs of a man;" or whether Peabody shall drone away alone to the end of the chapter.

Again: On what terms shall persons be admitted to the communion? i.e., "on what terms" shall an old woman be allowed once a month, in a meeting-house, on Sunday, to eat a crumb of baker's bread, and drink a sip of grocer's wine, which the deacon has bought at a shop the day before?

What if *nobody* at all is allowed to come to the communion? will not Christendom be in just as good case at the year's end? What if everybody eats the *soda-biscuit* (—— thinks that is the "unleavened bread"), and drinks the *wine:* who is the worse for that? Dear me, what a world it is! — drunkenness all round us; covetousness eating the heart out of society; the Fugitive-slave Bill making it incumbent on a man to send back his own mother to bondage; ministers, with kidnappers members of their churches, discussing a litany and the terms of admission to the Lord's Supper! Bless me! if the Nazarene were there at the Worcester Convention, I think he would have made a scourge of large cords, and let loose upon the assembly, till there was such a stampede among the brethren as one does not often see among the reverend clergy. Well, the age is leaving these old boys to their litanies, and their communions, and their miracles. What politician, what philanthropist, what merchant (of any *head* at all), what man of science, cares a pin for all this humbug? Religion rises early every morning, and works all day.

Good-by!

THEO. PARKER.

Please write to me as "Mr.," not "Rev.," &c.

Following this letter, as if it were a postscript, is a note telling Mr. May of two very noble and beautiful actions done by a gentleman between whom and Mr. Parker no love was lost in the fierce times of political strife. The note should be printed but for the necessary mention of private affairs. It is alluded to now as one of the many instances of Mr. Parker's readiness to acknowledge the personal goodness of men whose public course he felt compelled to assail. That he was always successful in rendering this species of charity is not claimed; that he always tried to be cannot be doubted by any who have read his private papers.

To S. J. May.

BOSTON, June 17, 1851.

DEAR FRIEND, — I will try and write so plain that you can read all the words. I write on the anniversary of the battle of Bunker Hill, because I know you were one of the chief contributors to the Monument Fund, and will be pleased to be associated with any battle, — you son of a colonel, you! So much for the time of writing: now for the matter in hand. I have just had a letter from Dr. Otto Fock, professor of philosophy at Kiel in Denmark, who wants to come to America. He is about forty years old, learned and able, but, alas! a republican.

He cannot live in Germany: the police look after him too sharp. Can we do any thing for him here? He is learned and industrious; will *work*. Can we find a place worthy of him? He has written a valuable book,—history of "Socinianismus." Perhaps he might write an "*excellent tra-a-a-ct*" for Father Briggs, or prove that the apostle Thomas was a Unitarian, or, if not Thomas, then at least Jude, or Judas. Besides Dr. Fock, another German doctor of philosophy has written for the same purpose,—to find a home in America. He is a philologian, (Dr. Lobeck from Königsberg), a learned man, librarian of the university at that place. He has written some books, and has been an editor of a *Volksbote* ("People's Messenger"), and is a democrat. Do tell me whether we can do any thing for these noble-hearted men.

I hope you will not let the committee appointed by the ministerial conference go to sleep. We must have the meeting, and do our prettiest to have justice done at it. Perhaps it would be well for you to stir up Brother Hall to greater diligence in this matter; for I fear that evil counsels may yet prevail. With best regards all round, believe me

Yours heartily,

THEO. PARKER.

To S. J. May.

DAY AFTER SECOND PREACHING DAY IN MARCH,
SECOND MONDAY IN LENT, A.S., 1854.

DEAR, BELOVED, AND MOST REVEREND FATHER,—I rejoice that thou art in so good a work as confuting the heretics who dare lift up their voices against the most ancient, most orthodox, and infallible church of the Unitarians. It will be easy to show that the author of the fourth Gospel was a Unitarian, you a member of the Boston Association of Congregational Ministers. This is the way, reverend father: Strike out all after Ἐν ἀρχῇ, and insert our "excellent tracts,"—the apostle John a Unitarian. By a similar process, it may be shown that the apostle Paul was also a Unitarian; nay, likewise, Peter; that the author of the Apocalypse was a non-resistant. It is true, in the text he makes the "Lamb" take charge of an army of two hundred million horse, and destroy one-third part of the human race, and then tread the "wine-press of the wrath of

God," and slaughter men till he make a blood-puddle on the earth two hundred miles wide and three feet deep; and then there is quite a portion of "the rest of mankind" who are pitched down into the lake of fire, whither Death and Hell — Θάνατος and Ἅδης — had preceded them. But all this, O father! is a delusion of Σαθαν, who will deceive the very elect if they do not keep a top-eye open and a bright look-out. The Καινη Διαθῆκη contains nothing but a revelation of the most mild and gentle characteristics of "God and the Lamb:" all else is a delusion of Satan, whom thou wilt put to rout with the army of the aliens.

I send thee, O father! a copy of a little discourse preached by thy son touching the Nebraska matters; and will soon send thee another *adhuc sub prelo sudans*, more befitting thy venerable years; to wit, "A Sermon of Old Age."

Vale, pater dilectissime,

THEODORE.

The correspondent who drew forth the next long letter on a most important subject much discussed at present, and likely to be discussed more still, was one of those estimable men whose spirit always teaches truth, whatever may be thought of their opinions. The contents of the epistle are not, perhaps, striking for originality; but we learn to admire commonplace, when a sorely-vexed man patiently employs them as the only weapons at his command. They illustrate, at least, the excellent quality of the writer's heart, which will not be wearied by any drain made on the hours.

To Robert White, Jun.

BOSTON, Dec. 31, 1849.

MY DEAR FRIEND, — Soon as I received your last letter, I set myself seriously to work to write an answer in detail. But continued interruption for the sake of other duties renders it impossible that I should be able to do this: therefore I will limit myself to considerations of a more general character, which require less time and space, and leave the other matter to be *talked* over some time when we may meet, as I trust we shall;

for a little conversation will do more than a good deal of writing.

I shall take it for granted, that in making man *male* and *female*, providing them with instinctive desires for union, and providing no other way for the perpetuation of the race except by such union, God established marriage in the very nature of man's body. I think the spirit of one sex is as incomplete without the other as the body, and that there is as much a *spiritual* desire for the spirit of the other sex in men and women as a bodily desire for the bodies of the opposite sex, only in most persons it is not so strong. On these two points I think we do not differ.

Now the question comes, Did Jesus Christ intend to forbid marriage to his followers? or, allowing it, did he think celibacy the better state?

Before answering that question, it is necessary to look a little at the state of opinion in the world about him on this matter.

I. The Jews considered marriage necessary and sacred. Celibacy in a *man* was thought impious, in a *woman* disgraceful (see Isa. iv. 1); but afterwards marriage got into worse repute among the Jews, and moralists found it necessary to commend marriage (see, e.g., Ecclus. xxxvi. 24–26; xxvi. 1–3, 13–16, 20–21; xl. 23, and other passages). At length there grew up a sect which abandoned marriage, — the Essenes: they had some excellent ideas, it seems, and had a good deal of influence on the early Christians in many matters.

II. Amongst the heathens, marriage was generally held in esteem; or, at any rate, celibacy was not much allowed or practised. Still it was sometimes practised as a religious duty by a *caste* of men or women: the *vestal virgins* are examples.

In the offering of sacrifices, it seems early to be thought that what was most valuable to men, or most dear, was also the most acceptable offering to God. Hence the fruits of pastoral life (oxen, &c.) or of agricultural life (wheat, fruit, &c.), and not the spontaneous productions of the earth, were the sacrifice. As the organs of generation were of value in keeping the race in existence, and in satisfying the instinct of man, in a fit of religious excitement men mutilated themselves in the name of God (the *priests of Cybele* are examples of this), and others made a vow of temporary or continual chastity.

III. The Hebrews never had a high idea of woman. Man is created for his own sake, woman to be a *help-meet* for him (Gen. ii. 18–24). Man is of *God;* woman only of *man*, and for man. This, also, is Paul's notion (1 Cor. xi. 7, &c.). The common notion of woman in the Old Testament is, that she is a wanton, a drudge, or a shrew. She lost us paradise; her heart is "snares and nets." "Any wickedness but that of woman" was a proverb. Among the heathens there was great wantonness: there was among the Jews, to judge from complaints in the Old Testament, and the numerous words the Hebrew language has for the crime of sensuality.

IV. These things being so, it is not at all surprising that some of the Christians thought it best to cut off that passion altogether, which they found it difficult to regulate; not surprising that they thought they ought to sacrifice their powers of generation, as the vestals or priests of Cybele had done. Especially would this be so among the *rigid* Christians; and the persecutions tended to make them *all* rigid. Still more, if men came from the Essenes to Christianity, would they bring their own notions of marriage with them.

This being the case, I am not at all surprised to find St. Paul speak of marriage as he does. But yet further: the early Christians thought the world was soon to end,—in their lifetime: so marriage was not needful to perpetuate the race. So Paul suffers it for such as cannot do without it; but to him it was a mere *physical necessity*, not at all a spiritual affection, which led to wedlock. I am not surprised to see such language attributed to Jesus as occurs in Matthew, Mark, and Luke. But I do not find reason to believe that Jesus was at all desirous of disturbing the natural order of things in relation to this affair. Still I think such opinions were attributed to him before the fourth Gospel was written; for in that Christ is said to work his first miracle *at a marriage.* It seems to me the author meant to show that Christ sanctioned marriage and the use of wine, of which Christ makes three or four barrels for the occasion. Now, if Christ intended to overthrow and supersede the union of the sexes, I think he would not have left it at all ambiguous, but would have said so with great plainness, speaking as distinctly as he did of the *sabbath* and of the *Jewish institutions,*—fasts and the like. Many of the interpretations of Mr.

Dunlary seem to me mistaken; e.g., his account of "the abomination of desolation" seems to me wholly a mistake: yet in other passages he shows a great degree of ingenuity as well as fairness, and I feel much respect for the man. But you see how much time it would take for me to go over the whole matter, text for text: it would require me to write a great book, which I have not time or health to undertake. I hope you will forgive me for my long delay and neglect: I know you would if you knew the amount of matter which I *must* attend to. Allow me to wish you a happy New Year.

And believe me your friend,

THEODORE PARKER.

To J. B. Parker.

WEST ROXBURY, Aug. 29, 1846.

MY DEAR JOHN, — I told you I despised the study of heraldry: I have yet wasted some little time over Guillim and other writers on that theme. I am quite up to giving any information about the noble family of *Kettles*. The motto is,

"NE CALL THE POT BLACK."

It is a most ancient family. It is related to the *Pots*, the *Skillets*, the *Patty-Pans*, the *Porringers*, and divers other great and noble families in all civilized countries. Lord *Copper-Kettle*, Baron *Stew-Pan*, and his Grace the Duke of *Brass-Kettle*, are all branches of this family: so is that famous champion, Sir *Kettle-Drum*; and he is soon to be elevated to the peerage. The family of *Boilers* is of the same descent, but were for a long time in obscurity, devoted mainly to agriculture and domestic economy. But lately some of the family have entered the marine service, and have done great honor to their family; while others have become famous on land. Lord *Steamboat-Boiler* and Sir *Fizaway-Locomotive* are of this latter class. It is thought this branch of the family will surpass all others. Indeed, some of them have been so elated by success, that they have actually *burst*; and this, by the way, is the great danger to which this family is subject. You will find all about the stock, &c., in Burke's "Peerage" or "Commoners," &c.

What you say of Salem is pretty true, but not wholly. There

are, as I know very well, some noble exceptions to what you state as the general rule.

If you want any books from time to time, let me know, and I think I can procure them for you. But Emmeline tells me you sit up late. Now, that is quite — nay, almost — as bad as lying late. Be sure you will repent it. If your eyes are sore, go to bed; go to sleep. You must mind me. There is no excuse for violating a law of Nature. The laws God wrote on the body are quite as binding as the ten commands which Moses wrote on stone. KEEP THE COMMANDMENTS.

And believe me truly yours,

THEO. PARKER.

To Horace Coolidge, Boston.

WEST NEWTON, Aug. 31, 1852.

MY YOUNG FRIEND, — As you are about commencing the study of your profession, I wish to give you a word of advice. The study and practice of the law has this advantage, — that it keeps the intellectual faculties in a great activity; at least, some of them. And I notice, in general, that lawyers are more eminently intellectual than any other class of men, unless it be men of science and authors by profession. But the law has these disadvantages: 1. That it exercises and develops the intellectual to the detriment of the other and higher faculties; and, 2. That it does not allow a very complete and generous development of the intellect itself, especially of the higher departments thereof, — say the reason and imagination, — but only of the understanding. Most of the lawyers that I have known are examples of this defective and vicious development. Indeed, most of the lawyers that I know make a mere money-getting trade of their profession, and no science at all: so that with them law is not a *liberal* pursuit, only a head-craft; and they are only *mechanics at law*, with little more elevation, and sometimes less, than is law to a handicraft.

I take it you wish to be, first, a complete man, with all your faculties harmoniously developed; and next a complete lawyer, master of your calling, and eminent in it, enjoying, accordingly, the emoluments and honors thereof. So I hope you will take pains to avoid the common evils of the profession, and get a wide intellectual expansion. To help in this matter, there are several things which may be recommended: —

I. One is the *study of metaphysics:* that forces you to look at first principles, and study the laws of Nature and the constitution of the universe, and helps to correct the one-sidedness and partialism of the ordinary lawyer. But there seems to be a sort of repugnance between law and metaphysics. I never knew a lawyer that cared much for that pursuit; and, of all the eminent metaphysicians, I remember no one that was a lawyer. Besides, to prosecute this study with success, or even pleasure, there must be a certain natural inclination that way. If *you* have it, I hope you will continue your interest in metaphysical studies all your life.

II. Next the study of *natural science:* this has a fine effect in widening the reach of thought and the range of observation, and so helps the intellectual development of man. Few lawyers attend to this at all. The same one-sidedness which keeps them from the study of the *permanent-abstract* of metaphysics deters them from the *permanent-concrete* of natural science. So they look on the arbitrary statutes of men, which are only a temporary accident of development, as if they were absolute and fixed, as much as the permanent-abstract or the permanent-concrete mentioned above. A statute is a temporary rule of conduct devised to suit the passing emergency. The metaphysician and the naturalist deal with natural laws, which are the *constant modes of operation of the forces of the universe;* the lawyers deal with those statutes which are the *variables of man;* while the philosopher deals with those laws which are the *constants of God.* But the misfortune of the lawyer is, that he looks on his human variables as if they were as permanent and as absolutely imperative as the divine constants, the laws of matter or of mind. Hence he loses his natural conscience, and gets a fictitious and artificial conscience; loses the *conscience of nature*, and gets the conscience of *Doctors' Commons*, or of the *Old Bailey*, or of the *Supreme Court.* The study of science helps correct this; yet I fear few lawyers care much for science. Judge Parsons was a man of large scientific attainments: John Pickering, also, — a quite uncommon man in many respects, — was quite familiar with the highest results of science. Both of these men were better lawyers, as well as more complete men, for this scientific development. I know a young lawyer who had to manage a case of damages for injury done to cows by water artificially contaminated, who, in preparing for the case, set himself to study the *physiology* of the cow, and so understand the effects of poison upon her. That was the true way for a scientific lawyer to go to work: the rule applies everywhere. But I believe lawyers, in general, have a professional dislike for physics as well as metaphysics. I do not know whether you have any decided natural fondness for science; and, if you have not, I should not look in this quarter for the corrective to the one-sidedness of legal studies.

III. Here is a third thing; viz., the study of human history: I mean (1) the study of *political national history*, — the development of Rome, France, England, &c.; and (2) *universal-human history*, — the development of mankind. Both of these will be of great advantage to you, first as a man, and next as a lawyer. Historical knowledge is of immense importance: its practical application to the purpose of the lawyer is obvious enough. Hence lawyers, though ignorant of physics and metaphysics, are better versed in history than any other class of educated men (excepting professors of that department whose knowledge is a technical affair). But here the vicious development of the lawyer appears again: he attends only to the transient things of history, and not the permanent laws of development; to the *variables of enactment*, not to the *constants of nature*. The study of the gradual evolution of any particular nation, — say the Romans or the Anglo-Saxons, — with its domestic, social, national institutions, will be of great advantage to you. It is not of much importance to know whether Gen. Fairfax charged up hill or down hill, wore a blue feather or a red one, or whether his military breeches were of plush or fustian; but it is of great importance to know what ideas were in his head or in the heads of his opponents and of his soldiers, and what organization those ideas got in the world.

I hope you will study carefully the political history of some of the leading nations, especially of the Roman and Anglo-Saxon: it will be of great advantage to you. But you will be profited by studying also the gradual evolution of mankind from savagedom to its present development. I hope you will study the *history of the legal institutions* (and enactments) of various countries as well as of your own. It is unfortunate that there is no good account of the development of English law. There are much better accounts of the history of the Roman, the German, and the French law, in Latin, in German, or in French. I hope in the course of your life you may become acquainted with all these three. Your acquaintance with German will help you in this matter; for the best book on the historical development of law in England has been written, not in English, but in German. But, in the course of your preparatory studies, I suppose you will not take a very wide range: that will come later, when your wings are grown. I cannot fail to think that a careful study of history will be of great help to you.

IV. The study of *belles-lettres* I suppose I need not speak of: the general stream of custom will carry you thither. But I would not waste my time on mean authors: I would study the masters of poetry before I played with their *apprentices*, and still more before I played with *lackeys* of the apprentices. You see uneducated people waste a whole evening in silly talk about silly men or women. It is still worse for an "educated man" to waste his time on silly books: they are always bad company. The books of *great men* will be good company, — the great poets, English, French, German, Italian, Greek, and Latin; dramatists, moralists, essayists, &c.

The study and practice of the law tend to weaken the moral sense and to quicken the intellectual powers. I trust that your respect for the integrity of your own character, and your reverence for the Infinite God, will keep you from the moral ruin of which the courts present so many examples. You need not fear that you shall suffer as a lawyer for what you gain as a man. A reputation for strict veracity, integrity, and honesty, will be most eminently valuable to you as a lawyer: it will give you the best kind of business of the best men. I am glad you are to study with Mr. Charles G. Loring; for I take it his moral character is loftier than that of any lawyer of his age in Boston: his personal influence will be good, and greatly good. I need not say to you that I think there is no real nobleness of manly character without manly religion, the love of God, and the love of man. I wish you great joy and great manhood in the profession you have chosen, and am

Truly your friend,

THEO. PARKER.

The following familiar letters illustrate the pleasantry of his mind, and his unbounded affectionateness of disposition. As the overflow of his friendliness, they are printed just as they were written.

To Miss ——.

BOSTON, June 6, 1851.

DEAR OLD LADYE, — Now she *shall* have a letter, though she has not yet written me one. I felt grim as a bear all the time I was at Northampton. I don't know why, unless it was the beginning of a certain biliousness, which oranges and rhubarb are to drive away. At any rate, I felt as gloomy as a snake in October. I hope I shall behave better next time.

Well, the world goes on here after the old sort. Wednesday, Mrs. R. came and passed the day with dear old *Mites o' Teants* and *Bits o' Blossoms* too. We had a nice time of it. *Teantie* had her rides in "express-trains," on "Bessie," and the "colonel," and all that; her *dets*, &c. Nay, I tried to find her a Labbit in the toy-shops, but got a *Cochon* instead, which the Mites pronounced to be *a pigh*, and was delighted with Mr. *Cochon*. Blossoms sprawled out his legs, — and *such* legs! — and *purred* and mooed; and, when any thing displeased him, he said, "Waugh" with a deep grunting tone. The children quite eclipsed their mother; but we all had a nice time.

There is to be a Thompson Festival on the 16th of June (he goes off to England the 17th), and you ought to be there. T. will speak an hour by "Shrewsbury clock." We expect a great gathering of the *Simon Pures*. (Here I ought to stop to shoot at my bill with one of Dr. Wesselhoeft's bullets.) There! the association of ideas carries me off to the ship, and J. P. Blanchard, and the sea-voyage he will *enjoy* with Thompson. Well, let that go.

I have finished the Life of Wordsworth, and got a straw hat — manilla — just like the old one raised from the dead; and that is all I have done this week. Wordsworth was a dear old granny, with a most hearty love of mankind, especially of the least attractive portions of it, — *beggars* and *fools*, and Bishop Doane, who he thinks was a great and good man. Wordsworth heard him preach once at London; saw him at his

(Wordsworth's) house, and liked him much. If Wordsworth had lived a little in London, and felt the presence of some one who was manly and differed from him, it would have done him service. He runs in a narrow round of objects, ideas, and sentiments; is humane (and means to be so in his penal sonnets), devout, self-denying, and genial: but he lived too much in solitude, was too much with his worshippers, and limited himself in his reading. He loved his neighbors and their little bits o' blossoms. His domestics he treated in the most Christian way, — like his own sisters. I love the man the more after reading all the twaddle of his letters and talk. He was like Dr. Channing and William Silsbee united. But he was the most self-conscious poet I remember to have read or read of: he knows the anatomy of his own mind as if he took himself to pieces. There was more of *will* in his poetry than you commonly find. Things were so because William Wordsworth would have them so. They grew out of his will more than out of his whole nature. But I love the dear old poetical Betty more after reading his Life than before. You will rejoice in the book, which will wait for you when you return.

Susan has gone home; sister sick; mother ailing. The cat mews at your door, and will not be comforted. He sends you his best *purr-r-r*, to which I have just room enough for mine. Lots of love to all the Hunts and Miss A., and quantities of kisses to the Mites o' Willy. "Bits" can't say *papa;* but "Mites" counts one, two, fwee, four.

WEST NEWTON, Wednesday, Sept. 15, 1852.

POOR OLD LADYE, — Presently after reading the Life and Letters of Byron and Goethe, I read also that of Admiral Robert Blake. You know he was first a Puritan soldier, and held out the town of Lyme against Prince Rupert, and subsequently the city of Taunton (if *city* it were), both in a most extraordinary and successful manner; next he was admiral, and such an admiral! Cromwell on the land was the equal of Blake on the sea. He fought the Dutch, and swept the famous and formidable Van Tromp out of the Channel. He went off to the Mediterranean, and levied contributions on the cities of Italy, Genoa, Leghorn, Rome, Naples, and on Tunis. He humbled the Spaniards in the Old World and the New. A man of not many words;

a compact, resolute man, of the most formidable action. Well, Goethe's and Byron's lives seem little, mean, and trifling, after such a man, and more wicked; for, in all Blake's dreadful slaughters, there was conscience and humanity at the bottom of the man. I should rather be Blake sweeping Tromp out of the Channel for the nation's sake, and (as he thought) for *justice'* sake, than Byron sending for the police to turn the Venetian woman out of his house, or Goethe breaking the heart (so cruelly and wantonly) of pure, good Frederika von Sesenheim. It seems to me less to answer for before man and God. Then the lives of these literary men seem to me intensely *frivolous*, and scarred all over with egotism and selfishness. Goethe wastes how much time in nonsensical study of form, and in vain dramas, *Grosskophtas*, &c.! I felt often a great disgust at the sight of so much *génie* directed to such trifles as he spent much of his time upon. After all, Goethe was less of a man than Voltaire. Both wrought wholly by the pen, — or *chiefly*. Voltaire influenced his own age vastly more than Goethe, and will reach much farther into the future. His influence was better in kind, as well as greater. As a *philosopher*, Voltaire was more, more as a *poet*, and, including prose as well as rhythmic works, more as a *man*. I suppose it would be thought treason to say this; but it is true.

Yesterday afternoon I went over to West Roxbury to see the old familiar places, not the people. So I sat down on the seat under the willow, and went to my old haunts in the woods and elsewhere, and got my favorite flowers in the favorite spots. But it was very sad, very sad, — *this body of* a place after you have been born out of it. It is a little curious that such a man should live in our old house, and drink his wine in my old study, and grow his hunkerism. I should feel uncomfortable to do such things in a place where such different ones had been done. Poor old ladye! When will she come home? House empty, papered, and *varnished*, but, alas! not yet swept.

Boo!

MONDAY NIGHT, Feb. 2, 1852.

DEAR POOR OLD LADYE, — This is the last letter I have the time to write before I get home. To-day I went with Sam Jo May — the best man in this world; and, if there are any better in the *next*, I shall be all the more glad when I get there — to see the Onondaga Indians. Queer folks, these red men! I did not find a squaw fit to bring home, nor a pappoose that I liked. Saw some real Pagan Indians; went into their council-house, church, and several houses. Saw squaws and sawnups and iktashes, and the like; got them to read some Indian books to me to get the pronunciation. Saw the missionary, — a real nice man for the place, with a real nice wife. Sam Jo is at work *on* the Indians, *for* the Indians, and *with* the Indians. He has done a deal for them since he has been here, and will do much more.

Ah, me! I wish I was at home; but home shall I be before long. I think of all the good folks, — when you lie down, when you rise up, when eat dinner, supper, &c. But I have had a nice time; and, though I have had no *great* audiences, I yet have had a good time. To-night I had a fine audience in the city hall. Emerson comes this week, Friday. I give 'em the devil on Wednesday. At Buffalo I saw my "Brother" Hosmer. I did not venture to call on him without his calling on me first: so I only saw him after the lecture. Good-by!

Love to all. I shall take the cars from here Wednesday night at nine or at twelve, and ride all night.

Parker's familiar letters bubbled with humor, running all the way from pleasantry to fun; not always graceful, but always characteristic, sometimes expressing the hilarity of his own mood, and sometimes designed to touch with mirth the moods of his correspondents. In this grotesque way he ministered to his own and to other minds diseased. A few short examples of this must be given in notes and extracts. The dates are of small moment. This note was written on a piece of birch-bark: —

No Place, N.H., Aug. 12, 1853.

My dear S., — I am in such a wilderness, that you will excuse me for writing on such rude material. I peeled it from a tree to-day in order to let you know what a savage country I have wandered into. Last night I lodged with a man who chops wood in the mountains all winter, and drives his logs to market down the river. It is so wild, that we walked twenty miles to-day in a howling wilderness. At one man's cabin we saw the skin of a bear, newly slain, nailed on the side of his house. Another with whom we lodged told us the bears killed six of his sheep last spring; they ate up his apples, and broke the trees down; they devoured his rye and his pumpkins.

You may judge what a dreadful place it is, and so hot that I have bathed *four* times to-day; and still the thermometer is 80° in the shade. Bathing won't bring it down.

I send this by the hand of a valiant young man. I hope the wild beasts will not destroy him. The man who took us in last night had but one daughter, and she is a — wife! Good-by!

Yours faithfully (if I get out of the woods),

THEO. PARKER.

BOSTON, Feb. 3, 1857.

DEAR FRIENDS, — This is to say that I, the undersigned, have removed from the house in Exeter Place, and live miscellaneously, — perambulating, or rather pervehiculating, through space in all manner of directions. That wicked wag Aristophanes personified the Athenians as Demos, who gave his residence as Pnyx, the place of public meetings, — equivalent to people of town-meeting: so I might sign myself as Theodore Parker of everywhere, and no place in particular.

I live in taverns, move in railroad-cars, and have my being in the Music Hall and other places of public speaking. I am not a skylark, but a "wandering voice:" so I get no time to write you all (or singular) the letters I wish. Forgive me now, have patience with me, and I will pay ye all; that is, so far as possibility goes.

Poor little Potamous! such a shining blade, that he seems like to eat up the scabbard. What a pity the brightness could not have been more uniformly distributed over the surface of the whole family! I wish he could exchange places with ——. He *needs* the stimulus which dear Potamous gets too much of, I fear; and Potamousie needs the wet blanket of dulness which hangs round little ——.

Dear me! if I had been born with such surroundings, really I might have come to something. I should have made a spoon, or spoiled (pronounced spilt) a horn. T. P.

BOSTON, April 19, 1856.

. . . The sanguinarias are out at Melrose, the hepaticas at West Roxbury, the Mayflowers where they condescend to grow; columbines are suspected at Concord; saxifrages are in their (little) full glory. You at Rome have cherries of quotable bigness; and grape-vines have grown a foot or more. Did not I leave dear, dear old sunny Italy on the 16th of April, 1844, and turn my face towards the Alps? Shall I ever do the like again?

I hope you got my sermon; and of course you read it to the Pope. I hardly dare ask what he thought of it. I fear he might not think all parts of it quite (Roman) orthodox.

Poor Pope! How are the *hens?* I hope he had eggs enough for Lent, and that there will be chickens in the summer. I send you another sermon, which I fear you had better not read to Pope, nor even to Mrs. Pope. I speak of his Holiness as a mummy. The shabby old fellow, not to send me a cardinal's hat and robes! Why, how can I go to the meeting of the Progressive Friends at Pennsylvania with nothing but my *stove-pipe* on my head, and my *cut-away* on my back? If I had the cardinal's great red hat and the purple robes, how I would sit on the antislavery platform at New York and at Boston in anniversary-week! How the Quakers would fall down and worship the image of the beast, and the great scarlet what-is-it in the Revelation. Dear me! I never saw a cardinal without thinking of the whole book of Revelation and the city of Babylon.

Poor Sumner is worse again. Dear, noble soul! If his pain could be divided amongst us, how soon he would be on his legs! But it is only pecuniary sufferings we can thus alleviate. Poverty is divisible by dollars, not sickness by numbers, not sadness. Good-by! Here's a Mayflower for S. T.

NEWTON CORNER, July 12, 1858.

. . . A little word before I go to bed. Bear is just snuggling herself in. It has become a very naughty Bear, and can't say its catechism till the Hunts come home. It is getting wild again, and heathenish. I don't know what to do with the creature.

Hannah writes to the sixty-seven-years-old mother, and will

tell of the sacrament of the preserved peaches and sponge-cake; and she will tell, likewise, all the news: this is her province. She is a *woman*. But I must tell Frederick May is engaged to Miss Morse of Dorchester. Just the right thing! "Marriage made in heaven." It was a good while coming down, though: that is what all the people say. Fred and Martha came over and told me of it. She sat in the chaise. How happy she *did* look! Dear me! I love to see these lovers. I walk in the public garden at the proper time of day, and delight to look at these birds of *paradise* flying after their *garden of Eden*. They are in heaven for a time. How the most precious joys are also the commonest! It is dear, loving God who fills the earthly cup with such sweet blessings, and pours out so liberally. T. P.

SEPT. 6, 1858.

It is the last Sunday that we shall spend at —— this season: so I shall write a word of a letter to our dear Sarah; and, as I write out of doors on one of the most beautiful days in the year, I think she will excuse the writing with a pencil, and not with a pen. We intend to go to Boston next Wednesday morning with all our worldly goods. It will be pleasant to *touch* the *crockery* once more: we have done no such thing for a long time here: a thick film of Paddy is spread over every thing. I shall also be glad to escape from the everlasting baby, whose life is one continual yell, or squeal, or scream, or screech, or by whatever name the most disagreeable of (*human*) sounds, *except the voice of an ill-natured woman*, may be called. We have had a delightful summer, — fine weather, good health, and all; but I am tired of the leisure, and long to preach again.

Your beautiful book came only a week after my birthday itself. Had it come a week earlier, I could not have received it sooner; for I was absent from Massachusetts. It is a quite charming little book; the only piece of popular song I have in Italian. All the songs are of love and its accompaniments, — youth, beauty, tenderness, &c.; but they are singularly delicate and refined. Yet it is said all come from the mouth of the people. If so, it is a remarkable monument of the national character. It has none of the wonderful richness of fancy and dear human love of common things which appear continually in the English ballads of the people and in the *Volkslieder* of the Germans. Idealization of the common and homely is the characteristic of the æsthetics of the Teutonic mind, including all the people of that great ethnological family. It appears in the Dutch pictures; in Rubens, who yet had a culture quite alien to his nature; and in the noblest of them all, Albrecht Dürer. It comes out, too, in their poetry; most perhaps, of all, in Shakspeare; but how clear in Burns! even in (stately and Latinized) Milton. Of course, this appears in the literature of the people. One day, the Americans, also, will have a national consciousness, and a literature to express it; when the same thing will appear. Now we have none of it in artistic forms, except our *landscapes*, which are real bits of American nature. . . .

Hereupon came the bell for supper: so the rest of this scrawl must be written within doors, and that, too, in Boston itself. Here I have no interruption, — only the hand-organs, and the omnibuses, and the ringing at the door. It is something to be rid of that baby, crying, roaring, bawling, teasing, screaming, screeching, yelling, yowling, yelping, barking, growling, snarling, snapping, squealing, squeaking, mowing! "He is a *nice* baby, mamma's little darling, so he is, isn't he?" But he is also a nuisance. At breakfast, at dinner, at supper, and between all the meals, came the universal baby, — baby in all forms, often *au naturel*, which is the prettiest kind of dressing. But Bear and Hannah have a most feminine delight in all the performances of the aforesaid baby: indeed, I shrewdly suspect they are the (proximate) cause of much of the nuisance he commits.

Here must I make an end of my letter, which it took two days to write, and which was begun in Middlesex, and ended in Suffolk. T.

JUNE 16, 1857.

It is Boston now, twelve, noon; nay, almost one, afternoon. Wind north-east; sky covered with lead-colored clouds; a storm and a holiday coming for to-morrow. There is to be a celebration of the battle. A statue of Gen. Warren is to be inaugurated. Gov. Gardner is to have a finger in the pie. Mr. Everett and Mr. Winthrop, I think, are to do some small chores in the way of speaking at a dinner or elsewhere. And we are to have any quantity of soldiers, (Heaven save the mark!) firemen, &c. Gen. Scott was expected. He was to walk in the procession, — no, to *ride* on an animal as big as the pale horse in West's picture of the Last Judgment, with similar following, I suppose. But his wife is sick in Europe; and so he can't come to Massachusetts. But in his place the "SIRTI" is to walk, preceded by (the skeleton of) old Dr. Warren riding on his mastodon. I only know this: "no other paper has the news." But the penny journals say "Gen. —— will not be in Charlestown on the 17th;" but Sand's circus will be there, and the elephants, &c. So the bears have gone over to Charlestown to celebrate the great battle. Last year, you remember, Mr. —— was to deliver his eulogy on Washington at Cambridgeport on the 12th of June, but got frightened, and did not dare let fly. So, to make it all right with the public, he requested Dr. —— to give him a certificate of ill health, stating that his vocal organs were in such a condition that he ought not to speak. Now, the 18th, Mr. —— is to deliver the long-expected speech, and satisfy Mr. Public, who has been waiting these twelve months. I understand that the president of the "Sirti" is to introduce after this sort: "Gentlemen, a year ago Mr. —— could not address you (state of *vokl orgns*); but now, by the aid of science, and the happy disposition of his nature and his will, he has become *vox et præterea nihil.*"

The "Sirti," it should be remarked, by the way, was the name given to an imaginary society existing in Mr. Parker's brain, consisting of his wild fancies and bad puns. It figures conspicuously in his familiar letters. The letter from which the following extract is taken was written in the summer of 1858, when he was struggling with disease: —

"I, too, have been a traveller. Shall I give you my 'impressions'? At three in the afternoon, left Boston by the railroad for New York; distance two hundred and forty miles. Stop at Framingham, twenty-six miles off. Some of the people reading newspapers, which seems the chief literature of the people. Boys bring round popped corn and peanuts: these seem the chief delicacies of the country. Several persons ate the latter voraciously. (N.B. — The boys seem all to be of the same family, as they all answered to the name of 'Bub.' I had a copy of 'The Boston Directory,' but found no such name in that collection of surnames.) At Worcester, forty-four miles from Boston, found a town of about thirty thousand inhabitants. It has a court-house, jail, meeting-houses, and one enormous hospital for the insane. It contains a hundred and thirty-five inmates, — a large proportion for so small a town. Several of the Bub family visited us again; some with apples and oranges as well as the peanuts; others had candy, and popped corn gummed into balls with molasses. A few bought lozenges. (I think the sale of such articles is confined to the members of this family, — the Bubs. It must be a quite profitable business; for an intelligent gentleman told me one of them would probably be in the Senate of the United States before long, and the other would stand a good chance to be governor of Massachusetts.) The chief business of the taverns seems to be providing for travellers. Many persons crowded about us with the cry, 'Have a *caidj?*' (that is the American name for a coach drawn by two horses.) The word 'caidj,' or 'kaidj,' — for I have not seen it spelt, — is probably derived from the Indians, who, I suppose, had the same kind of vehicle. (*Mem.* — Look in the dictionaries in the Astor Library, and see what tribe of Indians.) Others called out with great violence, '*Temprenceous!*' which seems to be another name for the same thing. But it has not found its way into the dictionaries, more than the 'Bubs' into the directory.

"Apple-trees are getting into blossoms. The buttercups have yellow flowers. There is *red* clover in the fields, mixed with *white;* but the red is the tallest: I suppose it is the native. Mr. Agassiz says *red* is the typical color of the continent: thence *red* men, *red* roses, *red* bricks, *red* combs on the cocks and turkeys (the latter *an American bird*). The cows are *red;* so are the horses; nay, many of the farm-houses. I am told that the *cherries* are also red, the *beets* also, many of the apples, and *all* the *native strawberries*, *cranberries*, *raspberries*, and *barberries*. One gentleman told me there are red lilies, and that all the green blackberries are red before they are ripe.

"The State of Connecticut has but one county, — Barnum County: it extends over all the State, and indicates the morals of the people. Mr. Barnum is the typical American: he is the bright consummate flower of the nation. Men say Mr. Buchanan is but another Barnum. I proposed to a gentleman with a clerical look, if it would not be well to consolidate the prayers of all the churches on Mr. Barnum; after he was converted, get him and Henry Ward Beecher to engineer the *revival* through the United States. He thought, with their help, the Tract Society might be 'saved,' and Mr. Buchanan re-elected in 1860.

"Reach New York quarter before twelve. City lit by gas. Streets are muddy when it rains. (Coachmen cry the same name for their vehicle as in Worcester; viz., kaidj.) Stopped at the Astor House. Enormous spittoons in the rooms. Men sitting with their *feet in chairs.* (*Query.* — Is it to avoid dirtying their boots? or is it a custom derived from the Indians?) There are several churches in New York. I heard the bells strike twelve; and at one went to bed in the uppermost story, with the city-hall clock staring me in the face.

"Here ends the traveller's journal."

GALESBURG, ILL., Oct. 21, 1856.

It is a good old ladye; only it is a good ways off, — twelve hundred miles by the shortest cut. To-morrow night (at Jacksonville) it will be thirteen or fourteen hundred. Don't like it to be so far away. What a country it is out here! Between this place and Chicago there is not a hill fifteen feet high, no undulations, only little ripples of land in this great sea of earth. There are few trees. You go many miles, and find none. The ground, where it is ploughed, is black as coal-dust, and fertile as Egypt. The natural wealth of Illinois exceeds belief. The rapid growth of population, too, seems fabulous, a miracle. Thus, seven years ago, Galesburg had six hundred inhabitants; now about seven thousand. One Judge Hale of Kenosha told me, on the 3d of July, 1835, he was following an Indian path through the Wisconsin Territory, and at night slept with only the sky above and the ground under him. There was not a house within many miles: only one woodsman was just beginning his log-cabin, chopping the trees for it. Last July 3 he went to the same spot (by railroad), and there was the city of Janesville, with nine thousand inhabitants; and he slept in a hotel not ten rods from the old spot where he encamped in 1835!

Quantity is immense out here. Bulk is the word to describe with: quality will come later. Quantity is the great burly brother; quality the nice, dainty little sister; but both of the same father and mother. Babies! — why, they are universal: babies in all the moods and tenses, — babies indicative, subjunctive, potential, imperative, and also infinitive; babies present, imperfect, perfect, pluperfect, and in the first (or obvious) and second (or potential) future; babies in the taverns, in the lecture-rooms, in the meeting-houses; in the cars, babies. Here they are stationary; there locomotive. I no more expect to see a woman without a baby than a man without tobacco. They are not only an "institution," but also a nuisance.

Preached at Waukegan Sunday forenoon, in a public hall, to about eight hundred or a thousand people. Our hymn-book in the desk. I sent them the hymn-books years ago. We had live singing too.

It is a dark day for America; but she has seen dark *years* before. Tories are nothing new. Reading Washington's Life again. I wonder that we ever got through the Revolution, so heedless are individuals of the welfare of the whole, so many are only particular, so few universal or national. There is something radically wrong in our civilization, which leads men to neglect their country. The pulpit is partly to blame; for while it is pounding away all the time on matters of individual, private concernment, — patience, prudence, prayer, benevolence, &c., in its best endeavors, — it seldom touches the great political duties which men owe to man as divine service of God. But politics is the religion of a nation, just as individual daily life is that of Peter and Rebecca. But how few ministers do (or can) look beyond mere individuals — in the "church on church green" and its Sunday school! But it is not worth while to scold men, only to mend 'em.

Love to all. It must be the best old ladye that ever was in all the world.

Good-by! T. P.

TELEGRAPH FROM O. F. — "Meetin 'v Sirti 'n Sexn 'v Theolurgi. *Questyun:* Why did the Lord make the world? *Answer:* Nobodi els cood. Wa'n't none reddi mād: so he done it."

BOSTON, Nov. 7, 1852.

POOR DEAR OLD LADYE, — I had a nice time at Loring's Monday night. Saw Thackeray, — a great, monstrous man, six feet and a half high, with a huge shock of gray hair on his head, spectacles, a large *stumpf nase*, and a long *old* chin. He seemed a little shy. Sumner was there, and looked short beside Thackeray. It was a caution to hear —— "let on" the great men. It would have amused Wendell. Mr. Crowe, son of the "Nightside of Nature," I take it, was there. He is a secretary of Mr. Michael Angelo Titmarsh, and accompanies him from Cornhill to Cairo.

Emerson was here yesterday, full of the sweetest *bonhommie*. Came to ask me to dine with him and Clough — the "Bothie of Toper na Fuosich," you know — and others at the Tremont House on Saturday. Emerson's house is in disorder, and he can't give us treat at Concord, and would not let me give it in our house at Boston. So it is.

Well, I am all sound and round and light and bright; sleep like a *pic;* and have the appetite of a wild roe on the mountains: so I shall soon make amends. I have answered all the letters; and "owe no man any thing," according to the Scriptures. I have even subscribed for "The Daily Advertiser;" and think in time, say a thousand years, I may be an — old man.

Love to all, especially one; to whom also,

BOO!

The pure nonsense often comes at the end of a grave letter, as if to relieve the sadness of his thought; for example: —

WEST NEWTON, June 17, 1852.

DEAR OLD LADYE, — Seventy-seven years ago this day, my worthy grandfather felt a little different from what I feel just now. It was a hot day then; but they made it hotter. I think it will be hot at Baltimore to-day. All Boston believes that Webster will be president. Seven hundred of the Hunkers have gone to Baltimore as outside members of the convention. Things look very ill for the country. If Pierce is chosen, or Webster, I think we shall have Cuba and half Mexico in the next administration. How long this re-action in favor of despotism is to last, I do not know; but it extends everywhere. We shall have slavery in California yet. But one good thing gets established, though a dangerous good, — the South has got the Federal Government to *assume* the control of slavery. One day, they will be very sorry for this.

The whole house is in delicious confusion. We were at Uncle Peter's on Monday. The great oxen are gone into the country to board; but the *Pics* are at home, and receive company. I saw O. F. the other day with his white hat on. He read a paper before the "'Cademy," mathematical section, *on the trisection of the arc*. Who first did it? That was the question. O. F. examined the claims of Archimedes, Zeno, &c. No, 'twarn't they. Who was it? Noah trisected the ark for Shem, Ham, and Japhet. Never was such a family. O. F. recommended that Noah be made honorary member of the Academy.

Boo!

BOSTON, May 18, 1858.

IT IS AN OLD LADYE, — We went to Lexington yesterday, P.M. Emily is to pass away, and that before long. In cold weather she feels pretty well; but in a warm day she wilts like a cut flower. I doubt that she sees midsummer. All the rest are well. The rheumatism alone ought to have been enough to stop me from going to New York; but I fear it would not. I did not like to leave the Ellises in that time of trial. Either was reason enough for not going; but I made public the most *quotable*.

I am afraid you will lose interest in Boston, unless you know the important events of this great town: so I advise you thereof.

The *Daily* has a paper, which was read at the Sirti last night, by Col. S., on "*Stravgnz 'v 'Pinyun.*" Here it is.

Boo!

Nobody misses it. At a "meetin' of the Sirti" last night, the question came up on the antiquity of *omnibuses*. The usual variety of (wise) opinions was entertained. But O. F. decided that they were as old as the time of St. Ambrose, — fourth century. He quoted the well-known rule of that saint, *not* with entire accuracy; for his imagination sometimes supplies his memory with facts, — *In triviis unitas;* i.e., "unity in *things of no consequence;*" for that is what he thinks is meant by *triviis*, — not, as the dictionaries say, the public squares where *three ways* meet: *in cubiculis libertas;* i.e., "you may do what you have a mind to:" and *in omnibus caritas;* i.e., "good manners in an *omnibus*."

BOSTON, Saturday Morning.

DEAR OLD LADYE, — We got into town last night, driven in by Mrs. A., who comes up *from the sea-shore* in such weather as this. Last night I could not coax the thermometer down below 79°, any way we could fix it. Now, at eight and a half, A.M., I dare not look at it, it is so high. Susan is here, quite well. In the midst of the heat, there just came a monstrous African. *Black!* — oh, dear, how black he was! Fat! — bless me, he looked like a barrel (no, a *sugar-hogshead*) of tar, so black, so fat! What an aggravation, with the thermometer at 90° in the shade!

We have now A. He has been studying German; and, as usual, his originality develops itself into new forms: indeed, originality with him becomes imitation (of himself, namely). He has discovered a misprint in Schiller's Frauen. Now it reads, —

> "Ehret die Frauen, sie flechten und weben
> Himmlische Rosen in irdische Leben."

He says, "misprint." Read so, —

> "*Ehet* die Frauen, sie flechten und weben
> *Cottonische Faden in ihre schön* Leben."

That makes sense.

At the last meeting of the "'Cademy" he announced these new things: "Why do men eat meat and bread?" — "Cos they're hungry."

"Why do they eat fruit?" — "Cos they like it."

There never woz sich a fomily az our fomily!

I send a letter of Desor's. The frontispiece represents a *fact*. Bradford was going to disturb a pig, a monster, lying in the road. I remonstrated against stirring him up, and said,

"Pig, pig, lie still, and slumber;" but pig got up, and followed us for ten rods, accompanied by a whole troop of blessed darlings, that cried for their breakfast. So naughty Desor has taken me off in a scrap.

Boo!

Catz came in safe. His arrival was announced in "The Caterwaul and Transcript:" and so, last night, George Ticknor's cat, Sam. A. Eliot's cat, and George T. Curtis's great tom-cat, all came down to welcome him back; and they scolded and quarrelled and spit and fought to their hearts' content. Good-by!

WEST NEWTON, July 19, 1852.

POOR OLD LADYE FORTY-FIVE, — So she has got a comfortable chamber for a particular person never so particular. Well, at the time appointed, — a long time away it is too, — I shall report myself. We shall have room for you here for a little while at the beginning of September; and, after the middle, as much more as you want. I should like most dearly to take some of the walks with you, and some of the drives: the *waltzing*, *polkaing*, &c., I am content to leave to you and the four-wived deacon.

Boarding has its comforts for a few days, but its disadvantages for many days. I think most of the men of great intellectual renown have associated chiefly with men of large intellect and of fine culture: so it was with Socrates, Aristotle, Bacon, Leibnitz, Newton, and the rest of such men. But what is so good for the head, I take it, is rather hard for the heart. Men who have attained a large growth in affection, in justice, in religion, I think have associated with all sorts and conditions of men. I believe one must do so to get this human sort of culture. A baby is better for the heart than a whole academy of philosophers. Martin Luther lived with his *liebe Käthie*, and with all the plain, homely people about his little town: so must all teachers of religion, and all learners thereof, I fancy. It is a deal better to get a whole culture than a half culture. What business would Newton, Locke, Leibnitz, or Kant, have with a baby, or even a wife, or even a woman? Thomas Aquinas, Scotus, and that sort of folks, have a right to a family of books; nc more: their "folks at home" are only folios.

Out here I have got comfort with the cattle; and the old horse knows me, and calls for hay; and I talk with the dumb beast, who is not deaf. He is an excellent creature: and Mrs. L—— says, "E'en his failings lean to virtue's side;" for he wants to go too fast. The great long-horned oxen are pets of mine. The *pic* is one of my favorites also; and I speak to him every morning, noon, and night, and he answers me. Then I throw him nice dainty pigweed and plantains, which he receives with a patient shrug; for eating is "the badge of all *his* tribe."

Here is a nice little boy, — Bubby White. I like him and little Bits o' Blossoms; but he does not begin to compare to Mousie or famous Mites o' Teants. "To-morrow to Clark's Island and pastures new:" so good-night; and night it is too.

We have a young woman here (she is 10+10+5=25) who is on the way to the society of O. M's. She is booked for an O. M. I would not mention her name for the world: she would take my head off, and I should be even worse treated. So don't mention the unpardonable sin to any one. BOO!

Here is a piece of pure nonsense addressed to a lady of fifty, in capital letters, as if for the eyes of a child: —

APRIL FOURTH, 1849.

MY DEAR HAN., — I am now at Ports-mouth. It is a small town close to the sea. Howe and I are at a small house where they take folks in to lodge if they are *good.* The moon shines here just as it shines at home. If you ask the Bear, she will tell you that she thinks it does so in all the world, but is not quite sure of it. We went from Fall River on foot to Tiverton: it was six miles. The land is full of hills and vales, with some brooks. I have seen some flocks of birds: some were black, and some were blue. I heard one of the black ones say, —

"If our dear Han.
Will do all she can;
If she will not be rude,
But will try to be good, —
Some day in the spring
She shall hear the birds sing.
Good lit-tle Han.:
She does all she can."

Well, to-day we mean to go from Ports-mouth to New-port. I hope you will get this note next day, if you will be a good girl. Howe walks on both of his feet. He has got a new cane; and I thought I could not keep up with him if I went on two legs while he had three: so I got me a new cane; and I can walk as fast as he. I went down to the coal-mine last night; but I could not get in. You see, they fear that men will come and spy out the coal; and so they keep dark about it. Here is a steamboat in the bay, and a nice gall in the house. We get on quite well. We have seen a bridge, and some men with a great long net to catch fish. You must be good, my dear Han., and do all that the poor old Bear tells you. Give my love to her; and here is a kiss for Han.

But usually a strain of pathos runs through it: —

JUNE 21, 1849.

MY DEAR HANNAH, — You don't know how sad all things are here without you. Nothing goes well without you. The birds have forgot half their singing; and Lizzy chatters more than ever. Do you know how hot it is here? Mr. Shaw's thermometer rose so high, that it went off out of sight. I suppose you have a buffalo to keep you warm, and wonder how the poor folks at West Roxbury do who have *no* buffalo.

What an unlucky station that is at Monterey! I walked over there to-day at half-past two, P.M. There I was hot as a grasshopper or a kettle of tar. The "spectacles" were fixed, "eyes right;" and I stood there panting like a locomotive, only *redder* in the face, and by went the cars: so I took it coolly, — for it was a cool thing, — and walked home. No Boston this day; no Cambridge yesterday; Cambridge the day before.

You don't know it; but to-day is the twelfth anniversary of my settlement. Chandler Robbins read the Scriptures: this day his new church is sold on account of whom it may concern. Ripley gave me the right hand: now he is the New-York correspondent of "The Chronotype." Whitney, Dr. Gray (illustrious name, *clarum et venerabile nomen*), have both gone. Henry Ware also is gone — to heaven. Not one that took a part in the services — and there were seven of them — remains where he was; and three are dead. Old J. Q. Adams was the delegate from Quincy, and drank the milk that was left in his saucer after he had fished out the strawberries which *he* was lucky enough to get (I got neither strawberries nor milk): he is gone. Mr. Polk, whom nobody ever heard of, has been President, and is really dead. Gen. Harrison, whom nobody ever dreamed of for any thing but drinking hard cider, has been in that bad eminence, and died. Capt. Taylor is not dead; only buried alive as his fathers were before him. And now a fourth man, then as unheard of as a new baby, is President; and I think the worshipful Whigs will one day wish that they had never heard of him, or never touched him.

Not a word from you yet: only think of that! I hope you will take care and keep out of the way of the sea-serpent.

These must suffice as specimens of this man's extraordinary facility, fulness, and variety. They present but a meagre sketch of his sympathetic relations with people. It must be enough to mention that this busy man found moments to write letters to a little boy six or seven years old, living with his parents in Europe; and to print them laboriously with the pen, that the child might be able to spell them out for himself. The temptation is great to print a curiously-elaborate *jeu d'esprit*, in the shape of the biography of St. Gambrinus, sent to his friend Mrs. Apthorp. It occupies, exclusive of the illustrations, four pages of foolscap; and is a pure piece of rollicking fun, — a jolly bubble escaping to the upper air from a deep well of native joyousness, which was not satisfied to play in ordinary fountains of frolic. Miss F. P. Cobbe, who was present when it was opened at Montreux, pronounced it a delicious satire on the illustrated travels and overdone picture biographies of the day. The pictures, fifty in number, were cut out of children's story-books, papers, cheap prints, advertising columns, and pasted on the thin letter-sheet in most amusing order. And this was done in the summer of 1858, when his animal spirits must have been at their lowest point! But the water was never so low in his spring that thirsty souls could not come to him freely in their need for a long draught or a drop of moisture. These heaps of letters, now brown and lifeless, gladdened many a wilderness, and made solitary places sing, when they issued from his exuberant heart. It is enough for us to know that the refreshing tide never failed those who came to it. But, when the spring is dried up, the standing water in the reservoir becomes tasteless.

The letters that follow show the breadth of his sympathies, as the preceding show their warmth.

To E. Desor.

INDIANAPOLIS, IND., Oct. 18, 1854.

DEAR DESOR, — Here I am a thousand miles from dear old sedate Boston. I am on a lecturing-expedition. I am to lecture eleven times, and to preach once, in Indiana, Michigan, Ohio, and Pennsylvania. I have many things to say about the country and the people. I wish I had you to help me observe, and to generalize after the facts are known. The WEST, which I have now visited three times, impresses me much with the *width of all things*. There is a certain *largeness* to every thing, — streams, plains, trees, pumpkins, apples, swine (a hog in Ohio, 1854, weighed, alive, 1,980 *pounds*; another, 2,150), and men. But there is a certain *coarseness of fibre* also noticeable in all things. The wood is coarse-grained; the nuts are big and fat, not nice and sweet; the apples have a coarse texture, all the vegetables, and all the fruits. Did you ever see the fishes of the Ohio? They are the most uncouth-looking monsters I ever saw, save the Roman fishes in the market at Rome, — the CATFISH, an ugly-looking devil, with a face like an owl; the SPOON-BILLED CATFISH (here is a picture of the "Spoon-bill Cat:" he weighed about eighty pounds: his spoon-bill was *two feet eight inches:* he looked like Dr. F——r), looking yet worse; the BUFFALO (an overgrown *sculpin*), the RED HORSE, and the SUCKER. One must be hard pushed to eat one of these wretches. The men look sickly, yellow, and flabby. In Indiana I saw but one rosy-cheeked girl, about eighteen or nineteen. "Were you born here?" — "No, sir: in New Hampshire." — "I thought so." I saw three or four hundred children in the schools at Indianapolis; not a rosy cheek. The women have *no bosoms*, or, as "the professor" would say, "a very imperfect development of the *glandular* formation." They are tall and bony, their hair lank, their faces thin and flabby-cheeked.

What effect is this Western climate to have on the human race? It must check the intensity of the Anglo-Saxon character. The fertility of the soil, the dulness of the air, the general enervating influence of the physical circumstances, must deteriorate the human being for a long time to come. Health is poor; activity small, in comparison with New England. You are right in your estimate of American climate on Europeans. When Dr. F. the pachyderm came here, he weighed 293 *pounds:* he has *lost* 80 *pounds*, — over twenty-seven per cent. But I fear the West deteriorates Americans quite as much. It is too early to undertake to determine the future character of the Westerners; but this is pretty plain, — they will no more have the same energy as the New-Englanders than the Britons have the same as the Norsemen and Danes who went from Scandinavia to England.

There has been a great *baby-show* in Ohio. One hundred and twenty-seven babies were offered for prizes. One received three hundred dollars; one, two hundred dollars; one, one hundred dollars; and, besides, several gratuities were given to others. The prize, of course, was given to the mother. I think Jonathan is the first to offer *prizes to the best baby*. An agricultural society in England, a few years ago, gave twenty-five pounds for the prize ox, and *five shillings* for the *model peasant*. But you will see an account of the baby-show in "The New-York Tribune."

Here the letter suddenly breaks off; but in others the writer reverts again and again to the humanity of the New World. It was not as a speculative philosopher merely, but as a deep lover of his kind, that he watched the shifting problems of his age.

To Prof. E. Desor.

WEST NEWTON, Aug. 9, 1852.

DEAR DESOR, — Your very welcome letter came in due time, and gladdened all our hearts. We were glad to find you were well, and your brother in no worse condition. Of course, he knows nothing of me; yet, as he is your brother, I beg you to present him my best wishes and kind regards. It delighted us all to find that you were received so kindly both at Neufchâtel and at Paris; but I always supposed it would be so, and that your enemies were confined to Cambridge and its hunker neighborhood.

You kindly asked if I would like to have a set of the microscopic specimens which somebody is preparing. I should like them much. If they are sent to M. Bossange, 11 Quai Voltaire, Paris, care of Little and Brown, Boston, they will reach me in safety. Let me know the cost, and I will send it. So if any thing remarkable appears in the way of philosophy, science, or any thing of note: you know how gladly I shall receive it. By the way, you did not give me the address of your friend the German bookseller at Paris.

Now a word about the politics of Europe. It has long seemed to me that France was in its *decadence;* that the phenomena of the Bas Empire are getting reproduced. Just now, there are great families in Europe: 1. The Italo-Greek and their descendants; 2. The Celtic; 3. The Teutonic; 4. The Ugrian, comprising the Hungarians, Finns, Lithuanians, and Lapps; 5. The Turkoman; 6. The Slâves. I take it the Turks will be conquered and subjugated by Russia; that the Ugrians will come also under the same power; and all the Slâves unite in one great, monstrous nation. The effort of the Hungarians, it seems to me, is only that of a nationality about to perish. The Italo-Greek will never rally, I fear: indeed, there is no example in history of an old race becoming young and vigorous again. What is to be hoped for from Greece, Italy, or Spain, the two last not only old, but with the Catholic religion on their backs? The Celtic race will rapidly disappear. The language will not last a hundred years in Scotland, Wales, or Ireland, it seems to me. Facility for intercourse destroys local dialects in Europe, as it prevents their formation in America. France, partly Celtic, partly Italo-Greek, and partly Teutonic (by the Alemanni, the Franci, the Burgundi, mixing with the old Galli or Keltæ), seems likely to fall gradually into the condition of Italy and Spain. Then there are left two great families, — the Teutonic and the Sclavic. In Scandinavia and the Alps, I take it, they will keep up liberal governments, and become progressively more liberal; but in the centre of Europe, it seems to me, this family will continually retreat before the Slâves. Then England, with her immense practical talent, energy, and materialism, seems to me likely to become more and more powerful, more and more liberal. This is a remarkable peculiarity of the Anglo-Saxon race: they never fight for glory, but for gain. France is poorer for all her "glorious" victories: England is richer. Then France covets *old* countries: England covets *new ones.* Look at her possessions now, — Great Britain, Gibraltar, Malta, Greek Islands, a footing in Greece, right of way in Egypt, little bits of land all along the Gulf of Guinea, South Africa (and is now fighting the Caffres, and will soon have all the east of Africa), India, a footing in Siam (and is marching by that route to China), a footing in China, New Holland, New Zealand, a footing in Borneo, multitudes of islands in the Pacific Ocean, Jamaica, Bermudas, half of North America. She has now a hundred and fifty millions of subjects, and is horribly rich and formidably wise. Then there is the Anglo-Saxon American, just like his mother, with the same materialism, the same vulgarity, the same lust for land, and longing for individual freedom. I take it, that, a hundred years hence, there will be only two great factors in the civilization of Christendom; viz., the Anglo-Saxon family (in two divisions, — the Anglo-Saxon Briton and the Anglo-Saxon American) and the Sclavic family. The history of mankind is getting simplified. It would not be surprising if these two tribes, then, should conquer all the globe. In due time, I trust, a nobler race of men will spring up, with higher notions, to establish a higher civilization. We Anglo-Saxons are *Romans of industry,* as the Romans were *Anglo-Saxons of war.* See how we invade nations with our *peddlers* and *workmen!* True, England and America are just alike in this.

I expect a good deal from the Sclavic family. Look at their

great territorial possessions ! — half Europe, half Asia, a big piece of North America. Look at their language, with every sound of all the alphabets of the race except the *th;* at their large heads, the biggest in the world ; at their power in diplomacy, ruling all the courts of Europe for fifty years ! Note the steady advance of the race in territory, in internal civilization, and all art. I think it will not be long before Russia is at Constantinople, and then at Athens. Let England go to Naples, to Rome, to Thebes, and Russia may go to Byzantium and Smyrna.

Well, these are dreams, — only dreams. Poor, short-sighted mortals ! our faculty of prevision is most exceedingly little. Consider that I am dreaming.

Now a word of America. I think Pierce and his Democrats will come into power ; that this will be the aim of his administration, — to divide California into two States (one a slave State), to get another slice from Mexico (slave territory), to make slave States out of New Mexico and Utah, to re-annex Cuba. This re-annexation of Cuba will be the darling object of the administration. It will be popular, 1. With the *people*, who want a *great territory*, just as all the farmers want a great farm. 2. With the CAPITALISTS : the capitalists will like it for these reasons, — they will then have a chance to speculate in cotton stock, and make lots of money. Then there must be a national debt of a hundred million dollars, or more : that will give them, 1. An opportunity to defraud the government in getting the stock. 2. An opportunity for a safe investment of money. 3. A high tariff to protect their manufactures. Then the trade with Cuba will be so much increased, that the merchants will like it ; and Northern gentlemen will like to have estates in Cuba to live on in the winter, and escape taxation by moving thither from Boston, as they now run out into the country on the last of April to escape taxing the first of May. Then the productiveness of the island will be much enhanced if Jonathan gets hold of it.

The great difficulty is on the side of England and Spain. There is a secret treaty, I think, between the two nations (France, also, I think, is a party to it), which guarantees the possession of Cuba to Spain. But, if we can *buy* it of Spain, that nation is quieted. But England desires the abolition of slavery. I take it, the government cares nothing about it; but the people do. Now, it is from the action of England that I have much to hope. I do not believe that American slavery will see the year 1900. If we undertake to get Cuba by violence, the governor of the island has orders *to liberate the slaves at once.* England will not suffer us to keep slaves there without a word against it. I think we shall have a little trouble. "The pitcher is broke that goes oft to the well," says the proverb. If the pitcher of slavery does not get broken, it is not in consequence of *not going* to the well.

I see one of your Swiss-German gentlemen (Louis Vertisch) has written a real German philosopher's book on the geological changes of the earth ("Die jüngste Katastrophe des Erdball:" Brunswick, 1852), in which he maintains that an unknown cosmic mass came in the neighborhood of the earth, and drew away part of our atmosphere. I suppose all the evils in the world, from "Adam's fall to the German revolution," are to be ascribed to the "unknown cosmic mass." I have before me a new edition of "Carpenter's Physiology" (8vo, pp. 1080), which posts up the literature to the year 1851. It is all new except a hundred and fifty pages, and is a grand work. Owen's distinction between a *lover* and a *loved* is there observed. I have read a book of M. Mathieu ("Études cliniques sur les Maladies des Femmes:" Paris, 1848), which contains many things that are interesting,—on hysteria, nervousness, and all sorts of exaltation, clairvoyance, possession, &c. The superior science of the French doctors over the English and American springs in the eyes at once.

Here we have nothing new of any importance. I had a kind, nice letter from "the professor" a few days ago, at Pottsville, making new discoveries in "the infra carboniferous series" "almost daily." Dear, good, kind, feminine soul! we must both meet him at some association of geologists on the planet Jupiter; and "mi brother and I" must have just returned from the planet Leverrier, with specimens of the *matutinal series* of limestone. How pleasant it will be! Well, he is a good soul, and I like him dearly.

Now I must tell you more about the good folks here at Boston, &c. Mrs. Howe and Chev. have just gone to Newport. Howe looks ill, and seems sad: things go not right. Mrs.

Howe sends the kindest regards to the *Stets Lieber-wurdig* in return for yours. "The old count" is at Newport again, railing against Kossuth. "Ugsh!" says he, "have you got the great Kossuth fever?" — "Not even the *great Gurowski* fever," replied some one. A queer fellow, that Gurowski, but, I think, more honest than men judge. Paskevitch gave his word of honor to Gurowski's sister-in-law at Warsaw, that, if he (Gurowski) desired it, all things should be arranged, and he might return with honor. The old count wrote him a violent refusal. "Noh, noh!" said he. Old Füster is actually stouter than ever, but has new pains in the *Beinen* (*Beinsängste*), — "effect of poison." He is no longer the "*mastodon Kalb*" which you used to call him: he is the *mastodon selbst.* He has enough to do in "giving hours," as he used to call it; and now speaks quite well, but rather "sanft," as he says. He still thinks the Boston Germans are *schlechte Kerlen.* He desires me to remember him to you after the most friendly sort. He is one of the kindliest and most womanly-tender souls that ever lived.

We have a new German paper in Boston, "The New-England Zeitung," conducted by Wagner, Domscke, and Schläger: antislavery all through. But just now it has come out for atheism, and denies the immortality of the soul. "Es giebt kein Gott, und keine Unsterblichkeit," is its creed. Miss Stevenson is at Vermont. I go to bring her back soon. Wife sends all manner of love to you. I think you, Howe, and I shall yet make our excursion to the tropics. — Good-by!

Yours,

THEO. PARKER.

To the Same.

BOSTON, Jan. 29, 1853.

DEAR DESOR, — There are two reasons why you could not read my letter of last summer, — 1. You have forgotten your English; 2. You are growing old. But *this* shall be so plain, that, if you put on your spectacles, you shall read it all through. Well, I thank you heartily for your last kind letter, and am much rejoiced that you went to the German scientific meeting, and saw some parts of your native land which I have seen before. I wish I could have been with you. Some time we will journey together all over Germany, and up to the North, "lighting our pipes at the midnight sun." Nay, perhaps we will go down to the equator in America, and see the grandeur of tropic vegetation. Did you see Alexander von Humboldt in your visit to Berlin? I have more curiosity to see him than to see all the *Königen* and *Kaisern* that ever stood on the world. He is a noble specimen of a man. When I was at Berlin in 1844, I had letters to him; but he was not in the city: so I missed the good man. His "Kosmos" seems to me a little over-ripe: the tone is old-mannish; not enough of the *youth of genius* in it.

I suppose Europe will now return to the quiet pursuit of science and literature. "Il n'y aura pas de révolution aujourd'hui." The *gens de salon* at Paris may return to their opera, their *petite comédie*, and their *jolies filles;* the German *Gelehrte* may re-ascend the clouds, and thence rain down new systems of philosophy, *Kritiken der reinen Vernunft*, and the like. It seems as if another Kant was possible now. But I fear that all Continental Europe will fall a prey to what the old count would call CZARISMUS. Liberty is an Alpine plant in the flora of Continental Europe. It grows in Scandinavia and Switzerland; but where else?

In Continental Europe there are four great families of the Caucasian race: 1st, The Celtic; 2d, The Italo-Greek, or Classic family; 3d, The Teutonic; 4th, The Sclavic. The destinies of Europe are in their hands. The influence of Hungary and Turkey is only exceptional, and at this day quite feeble, it seems to me; only restrictive, and not initiatory. Now, for the Celtic family, I expect nothing new or great in the political way. It is only in France that they have any power. In Scotland, Wales, Ireland, they are nothing. The Spaniards, mixed up of Ibero-Basques, of Celts (*Celtiberi*), of Classics, and of Teutons (*Visigothi*), are of no account. Well, in France you are re-enacting the old scenes of the Bas Empire. Paris is the *Byzantium of the nineteenth century.* What can you hope of a people that are the prey of an adventurer, who, in a time of revolution, lands with a tame eagle and a pocket full of debts, a miserable wretch without character or talents, and in two years is emperor of the forty million Frenchmen?

The Classic family is well-nigh dead. They live only by the bones of their fathers, the glorious names of Greece and Rome. Political liberty cannot revive in that worn-out soil.

Then there is left the *Teutonic* and the *Sclavic* family. What do you expect from Germany for the next five hundred years? Will freedom get established there? What will Russia do? I have more hope of the *Sclavonics* than of the Continental Germans. In a hundred years, it seems to me, there will be but two great powers in Christendom; viz., the *Anglo-Saxons* of England and America and the *Sclavonics*. I cannot believe that the Germans or French will stand against these hundred millions of Slâves. America will soon be the citadel of freedom, with three million bondmen in the donjon-keep.

Here in Massachusetts the Whigs have regained the power. The Hunkers are triumphant again to-day: they have elected their governor (Mr. Clifford), and got all the officers. Mr. Everett will probably be the senator. The ministers are worshipping Daniel Webster. The politicians think his opinions are an "amendment to the Constitution:" the clergy think his life one of "the evidences of religion."

We have nothing new in the way of literature or science or art. Stansbury's "Survey of New Mexico" I have for you, and will send it soon, with several things of my own. "The professor" is as happy as surroundings can make him. He has a little neuralgia, and a "slight attack of erysipelas in the nose." The good soul was never happier, and is as wise as the French Institute. I have seen a good deal of him this winter, and love him more and more. He lectured to the Natural-history Society the other day on — what do you think? — on Earthquake Waves. He won the admiration of all that heard him, — such clearness of statement with such nicety of speech!

"Old Füster," as you call him, is often here. Miss S—— kindly teaches him English. His *Bein* is much better, and he has got a new *Rock*. He is a dear good soul, and is translating a little volume of sermons of mine just now published. Dr. C. T. Jackson is fighting for ether, and gets no release from pain by his own discovery. It is not *anæsthetic* to him. The Cabots are both well: I saw them to-day; and they send their best regards to you. Dr. and Mrs. Howe are in fine condition, and send also their kindest salutations. The doctor and I go to New York this day. He is one of the editors of "The Commonwealth," and slashes "The Daily Advertiser" with no mercy. I saw your friend Mrs. John Howe yesterday. She was at meeting, and looks quite well. You don't know how we miss you. We eat the sacramental cheese on the Natural-history Society nights, and think of Desor; and I imitate you, and ask after "Kâtz," &c. Wife and Miss Stevenson send their kindest regards. Do go down to Italy with your brother and see Rome, Pæstum, Vesuvius. Send me the microscopic objects, and tell me the address of that bookseller at Paris. I want some books from him.

Believe me ever most truly yours,

THEO. PARKER.

I have a letter from Siljeström. His wife has a son Hans, and he a book, — "Resa i Förenta Staternia." I shall send him "Mother Goose" for the *Hanschen*. He says Sweden is dull, dull, dull.

My sermon on Webster will be printed in a pamphlet form in a few weeks; and I will send it to you, with sundry other things. Do go to Italy, if your brother is well enough. Send me some early flower in your letter. I value your gentiana much. One of the clergymen said, "There was only one thing above Daniel Webster: that was the Almighty God." There have been more than a hundred and thirty eulogies of Webster printed: only three have found any fault with the man, — May's (at Syracuse), Higginson's (at Worcester), and mine. Write as often as you can conveniently: but do not distress yourself; for I know how many friends there are to claim your attention. Some time or another, I must see you again on this side or the other of the ocean. Good-by!

To Peter Lesley, Philadelphia.

BOSTON, Nov. 15, 1857.

MY DEAR MR. LESLEY, — It did me great good to see your handwriting again; but I fear there is little to be done this year in the way of lecturing, even on *iron*. The lecturers hereabouts complain of no work. Some societies have sent out their circulars, and cancelled the engagements already made; others have "suspended" for this season. The way to make yourself known in that way is to send a line to "The New-York Tribune," and ask it to put your name in its list of lecturers. But I fear little will be done this winter. *Labor stops, and all stops.*

I wish you lived where I could see you often, and talk over matters of science. Since Desor has gone, and now Prof. H. D. Rogers, I am in great want of scientific company. By the way, do you see the attack which Agassiz has made on Desor? It is in a note on page ninety-seven of his "Essay on Classification," so called; which is the general introduction to his contributions to the "Natural History of the United States," volume first, and is just published. He charges Desor with plagiarism from him, Agassiz! I make no doubt that the boot was on the other leg, and that Agassiz took from Desor. But we shall see what the good soul will say for himself: I sent him the passage. I wish you would tell me what you think of Agassiz's essay. Three-quarters of it is on the subject of the "Bridgewater Treatises," chap. i.; the rest on Classification, chap. ii.

I wish you would tell me if Agassiz, in chap. i., removes the difficulty which philosophers find in their way, and which makes atheists of them, so the ministers say. I find more *real atheism* amongst *theologians* than amongst *philosophers*. The former deny the *substance of God* in the world of things and men, and send us off to some phantom which lives (or stays) at a distance, and now and then "intervenes" by a miracle, — this *Deus ex machina;* they are ready to deny his *laws*. But the latter deny the existence of *that God*, and yet admit the *immanent reality* of a power of thought, will, and execution, which fills all space and all time, is ever active, and never needs to "intervene" where he forever dwells.

Mr. Agassiz says there are "not more than six men in the United States who can understand his book, and perhaps twelve or twenty in Europe:" so I suppose it would be presumptuous in a man brought up on Descartes, Bacon, Leibnitz, and Newton, and fed on Kant, Schelling, and Hegel, not to speak of such babies as Plato and Aristotle, to think of comprehending the popular lecturing of this Swiss dissector of mud-turtles (for I take it this chap. i. is only a part of his lectures on the Evidences of Religion in Nature, delivered at Washington, or somewhere else). Agassiz is a man of great talents, great industry. His power of analyzing a clam or a turtle, an echinoderm or a snail, is wonderful; his skill in lecturing, and making the philosophy of fish pleasant to men who only catch and eat them, is beyond all praise : but when he comes to the metaphysics of all science, and the relation of the clam to the Causal Power and Providence of all things which are, I should like to know what you think of him. With hearty regards for you and yours, — those with the incisors, and those with the molars, — believe me

Yours heartily,

THEODORE PARKER.

To David A. Wasson.

BOSTON, Dec. 12, 1857.

MY DEAR WASSON, — Many thanks for your kind and welcome letter. I know how much it cost you to write it; and that dims my joy in reading it. You must not write much. You learned to labor long ago : now "learn to wait." I ate my lunch in the railroad-station, and thought over all Higginson said in defence of the Irish. I like good plump criticism, and need it oftener than I get it. But I think he was mainly wrong, and still adhere to my opinion of the *Celtic Irish*. In other lectures I have showed at length the good they will do our ethnology. When I give this again, I will do so, and name the good qualities of the "gintleman from C a r r r k k" and the poor wretches from Africa.

I take Blumenbach's five races only as *provisional*, — five baskets which will hold mankind, and help us handle them. In respect to *power of civilization*, the African is at the bottom, the American Indian next. The history of the world, I think, shows this, and its prehistoric movement. I don't say it will always be so : don't know.

You and I don't differ, save in words, about the Greeks. In the *emotional* element of religion, I think the Shemites surpass the Indo-Germans ; and the Jews were at the head of the Shemites. (The Phœnician took to trade, and cared no more about religion than a Connecticut tin-peddler, who joins any church for a dollar. Somebody found one of the scoundrels — a mummy now in an Egyptian tomb — who was *circumcised*. He took the religion of the place just as the current coin.) Religious emotion, religious will, I think, never went farther than with the Jews. But their *intellect* was sadly pinched in those narrow foreheads. They were cruel also, — always cruel. I doubt not they did sometimes kill a Christian baby at the Passover, or the anniversary of Haman's famous day. If it had been a Christian *man*, we should not blame them much, considering how they got treated by men who worshipped a Jew for God. They were also lecherous: no language on earth, I think, is so rich in terms for sexual mixing. All the Shemites are given to flesh. What mouths they have! — full of voluptuousness: only the negro beats them there.

The Jews, like all the Shemites, incline to despotism: they know no other government. The Old Testament knows no king but one absolute: the New Testament is no wiser, — if, perhaps, you bate a line or two which Jesus spoke; and they indicate a feeling more than a thought. The New Jerusalem is a despotism, with a LAMB for the autocrat, — a pretty *lamb* too, by the way, who gathers an army of two hundred million horse, and routs his enemies by the Euphrates, and then comes to Italy and kills men, till he makes a puddle of blood two hundred miles wide and three feet deep (see Rev. ix. 16: "And the number of the army of the horsemen were two hundred thousand thousand; and I heard the number of them." And xiv. 20: "And the wine-press was trodden without the city, and blood came out of the wine-press, even unto the horse-bridles, by the space of a thousand and six hundred furlongs"). In the Old Testament, Jehovah is KING, — a terrible king too. He is not a constitutional king, but arbitrary, — "*Thus saith* the Lord." There is no proof of any thing; no appeal to individual consciousness. With the Greeks all this was different; Indo-Germanic, not Shemite. I love the Greeks, especially the authors you name; but, for moral helps and religious emotional helps, I go to that dear Old Testament, for all Æschylus and Sophocles, &c. Do you remember any example of *remorse* in the Greek literature? The Hebrews had a pretty savage conception of God; but he is *earnest:* there is no *frivolity* attributed to Jehovah. He is the most efficient deity of old times, — none of your *dilettanti* gods. Besides, he is wholly superior to the material world; while none of the Greeks or Romans got above the idea, that, in some particulars, it was more than any deity or all deities.

Get well as fast as you can.

Yours,

T. P.

The following needs no introduction: —

To George Ripley.

BOSTON, Sept. 21, 1854.

MY DEAR GEORGE, — I will try and write so that you can read the matter. I have just read your papers on Pierpont and Ralph Waldo Emerson. I think I love and admire Emerson more than you do: so there are some things in the paper which I don't quite agree with. But, in the main, I like it. The spirit is high and generous. It is admirably written. You never wrote better than in the three sketches of "Pierpont," "Ralph Waldo Emerson," and "Andrews Norton." "Yàs, it was wall done. But ugh he lied! He knows he lied!"

There is no shadow in your picture of Pierpont. You once gave me an analysis of Pierpont (and of Sumner at the same time), which I thought was most masterly. You gave the shadow then which both made the picture more artistic, and the noble traits in Pierpont yet more salient. But I like your portrait of Pierpont better than that of Emerson; and I am almost glad that you did not put in the criticisms which you made to me on Pierpont. Just now, considering all that he has done and suffered, it would seem a little ungenerous to be quite just. All pictures must be painted in reference to the light they are to hang in and be looked at. Now, when you come to tell about me, I wish you would make a picture which will make me ashamed of what is ill in me and in my works. I need a thorough criticism from an able hand. It is too much to expect in private; but I should read with great interest a critique which told me of my faults of nature, culture, motive, conduct, aim, and manner. I know I must have made great errors; but I don't see them. I am afraid that the hollow of my foot "will make a hole in the ground," and somebody will one day fall into it. I should like to be criticised as I criticised Emerson; only better. Now, don't let your friendship run away with your judgment: —

"Nought extenuate, and nothing add."

I know you will set down nought in malice. But here are yet one or two things which I want in the picture. I love science in almost all departments, from the most abstract metaphysics to the most concrete application of Nature's laws in the new machine for planing oblique and irregular surfaces, which one of my neighbors put in his shop last week. I love all departments of natural history, and am at home with beast, bird, fish, and insect, and all manner of (phænogamous) plants.

When a boy, I had an intense passion for beauty in every form. I knew all the rare flowers, wild or cultivated. When a little boy in petticoats, I used to lie all the forenoon in June, and watch the great clouds, and see the incessant play of form and color. There was a pond a mile off, whither I used to go a-fishing; but I only caught the landscape. I never fished much, but looked down into the water, and saw the shadows on the other side creep over the water, and listened to the sounds from the distant farms. When I was six or seven years old, there came a perfectly beautiful young girl to our little district-school: she was seven to eight. She fascinated my eyes from my book, and I was chid for not getting my lessons. It never happened before; never after the little witch went away. She only staid a week; and I cried bitterly when she went off. She was so handsome I did not dare speak to her, but loved to keep near her as a butterfly to a thistle-blossom. Her name was Narcissa. She fell over into the flood of time, and vanished before I was seven years old. I loved beauty of form before beauty of color. I wonder if this is usual. You know beauty of sound (not artificial, of music) filled me with ravishment. The winds in the leaves, and the rushing brooks, were a delight from the earliest boyhood till now. Fine little pieces of literary art I culled out in childhood, and committed them to memory. It was no effort: it did itself. Especially poetry was my delight. My sisters had a little bagful of clippings from the newspapers which helped nurse my little soul. They also encouraged me in my transcendental tastes for the beautiful. But hard work and the *res angustæ domi* left but a poor soil for such a harvest. Yet it was hard to tear the tired body from the handsome moonlight or the evening star. Mornings, from before daylight to sunrise, when forced to be abroad, gave an acquaintance with the beauty of Nature at that hour, which was worth more to me than all my night-labors brought to my father. It was poetry to me, even if only a dull horse or heavy oxen were my only companions. The pictures of old times live now in my memory, a never-failing delight in my hours when I am too tired to do any kind of work or to sleep. This hanging-garden is always over me; and I rejoice therein as no Nebuchadnezzar, I fear, ever did.

I love children and hens; all sorts of men; and have the oddest set of intimates you will find any scholarly man to be acquainted with. But I am much less of a practical man than men think. All my ideals of life are of philosophical and literary activity, with a few friends about me, Nature and children. Good-by!

Please send me the parcel I sent you, — the article from Chapman. Send by Adams's Express.

Can this chapter be closed more fittingly than with one of his religious sonnets, addressed to Jesus, as the model of his imitation? The printed letters conspire with the devoted life to show how faithful was the attempt at imitation. If the success of it was incomplete, the effort was never relaxed, nor was the idea ever lowered.

"O Brother, who for us didst meekly wear
The crown of thorns about thy radiant brow!
What gospel from the Father didst thou bear
Our hearts to cheer, making us happy now?"
"'Tis this alone," the immortal Saviour cries:
"To fill thy heart with ever-active love, —
Love for the wicked as in sin he lies,
Love for thy brother here, thy God above.
Fear nothing ill; 'twill vanish in its day:
Live for the good, taking the ill thou must;
Toil with thy might; with manly labor pray;
Living and loving, learn thy God to trust,
And he will shed upon thy soul the blessings of the just."

CHAPTER XIII.

THE PREACHER.

THEODORE PARKER'S fame as a preacher is associated with the Boston Music Hall; for there his greatest efforts were made, and there the crowds listened to his speech. The hall is situated behind Winter Street, and has a double approach, — one from Winter Street, and one from Tremont through Bumstead Place. Its position insures for it a complete seclusion and utter silence from without. It has no architectural exterior for the public eye. The approach to it is not imposing. It was built by subscriptions, collected under the direction of the Harvard Musical Association, at a cost of a hundred thousand dollars for land and building. The design was by an English architect, Mr. Snell, practising his profession in Boston. Before completing his drawings, which were submitted to the first authorities in London, he visited the chief public halls in England, with a view to avail himself of the best experience in acoustic elements. The result was an auditorium admirably adapted to purposes of music, vocal or instrumental, and almost equally well of speaking; pleasantly lighted in the day-time by semicircular windows above the cornice, fifty feet from the floor, and at night by a fringe of gas-burners running along the cornice beneath the windows, round three sides of the room. The ventilation is sufficient, and facility for egress abundant. Two light galleries relieve the monotony of the long walls. The wide platform connected with retiring rooms in the rear, and having behind it a recess for the organ, occupied one end: an ornamental screen of iron concealed the instrument. The speaker's stand was an ordinary movable desk. At musical festivals, or on grand-concert occasions, seats were piled up in ranks, from the centre of the platform backward and sideward, sufficient to accommodate some five hundred persons, in addition to the twenty-seven hundred who were supplied with seats elsewhere, above and below: in an exigency, musical or oratorical, three thousand and more have found accommodation in the room itself. The dimensions, one hundred and thirty feet in length by seventy-eight in width and sixty-five in height, are according to most approved proportions, and satisfy the critical eye, as does also the simple elegance of the decoration.

Mr. Parker's society removed from the Melodeon to their new place of worship on Nov. 21, 1852, with not a few regrets on the part of the early friends, who felt that the family feeling they had enjoyed would be dissipated or choked by the multitude in the vast space, and that intimate relations with the pastor and with one another would be no longer possible. On the 2d of March, 1856, Mr. Parker welcomed his "new colleague" of "majestic brow," and "eyes turned inward and upward,"—the bronze Beethoven, presented to the Association by Mr. Charles C. Perkins. When the great organ was set up, in 1863, the preacher could not give it welcome: he was silent in his Italian grave.

In this spacious temple, dedicated to art, Theodore Parker made his power felt. He grew to the place. The central position commanded a broad view. Standing here, he could be seen on all sides. The multitudinous doorways let in the world: it was the world he wanted. The assembly was, on the whole, the most remarkable that ever gathered statedly within four walls in America; up to that time much the largest, if we except Whitefield's, which was composed of very different people, drawn by a very different attraction. Whitefield's audiences consisted of unintellectual people, sympathetic and passionate; Parker's, of people unlettered and uncultivated in the main, but thoughtful and questioning. Whitefield was an orator and a revivalist, who played with consummate art on the emotions of an excited crowd: Parker was a scholar and a teacher, who addressed the individual understanding and the private conscience. He had no accessories of rite, symbol, ceremony, doctrinal or ecclesiastical mystery. He read the old Bible, but with great freedom; and he read other writings beside. Hymns were sung, but not from collections in general use with Christians. The prayers were expressions of devout feeling, usually of gratitude and longing, on a sober level, personal and tender, but without humiliation, superstition, or the least recognition of dogma at beginning or end. The sermons were grave, solid; seldom less than an hour in length, often more; and were crammed with thought. The preacher took the intelligence of his audience for granted, and often tasked it severely. To listen to him regularly was, indeed, a liberal education, not in theology, or even in religion, alone, but in politics, history, literature, science, art, every thing that interested rational minds.

He had not rhetorical gifts. His eyes were wonderfully clear and searching; but their effect was marred by the interposition of glasses; and his countenance otherwise was not expressive. Neither was his figure imposing, nor his gesture fine, nor his action graceful. He moved but little as he spoke: his hand only occasionally rose and fell on the manuscript before him, as if to emphasize a passage to himself; but his person was motionless, and his arm still. The discourse was read, save on rare occasions or in interpolated paragraphs, in a voice not musical or sympathetic in its ordinary tones, with little training or natural modulation. His audiences were held by the spell of earnest thought alone, uttered in language so simple, that a plain man hearing him remarked on leaving church, "Is that Theodore Parker? You told me he was a remarkable man; but I understood every word he said." He was not like the doctor of divinity who made a point of having in every sermon one sentence that no one in the congregation could comprehend. His rule was, to have no sentence that was above the comprehension of the simplest intelligence. The style was never dry; the words were sinewy, the sentences short and pithy; the language was fragrant with the odor of the fields, and rich with the juices of the ground. Passages of exquisite beauty bloomed on almost every page. Illustrations pertinent and racy abounded; but the steady, methodical movement of thought forbade all attempt to carry the heart in opposition to the judgment.

The audiences were singularly untractable. They did not assemble in the usual churchly fashion, from habit or association, in the mood of reverence, or of regard for the opinion of the world. They came in such garments as they had; sat in such seats as were vacant; went out if they were tired. Some brought newspapers in their pockets, which they read in the few minutes that preceded the preacher's entrance. Some betrayed by their manner that they regarded the prayer as an impertinence; and others that they came for the sermon, not for the scripture or the hymn. The sittings were free: the expenses—which were not heavy, for Mr. Parker was ever greedy of a small salary—were met by voluntary contributions, mostly given by a few devoted friends and steadfast parishioners, who constituted the minister's body-guard, and were relied on for the active organized work of the society. Hence the multitude who heard him from Sunday to Sunday felt none of that peculiar interest, half mercantile, half personal, which goes with the paying of money. No tie held them but that of intellectual and moral satisfaction.

If the preacher's theological opinions, his "heresies," attracted many, they also repelled many. They were so pronounced as to offend conservatives even of the liberal class, yet so sober and reasonable as to fail often of satisfying radicals of an extreme school. Not a few bore them patiently, at first, for the sake of the humanity which they found in Music Hall, and could not find elsewhere. To his heresy Parker owed his "chance to be heard in Boston," but not the hearing he had there. Had he been moderately "orthodox," his following would probably have been larger and more influential. His influence was due to his intrinsic power alone. He is commonly thought of as exclusively intellectual. Never was a greater mistake. His wealth of sympathetic emotion was as remarkable as his wealth of mind. A good man who sat very near him on the platform, and, while living in Boston, heard every sermon he preached there, says, "More than half the time, in his prayer, I could see the tears run down his face before he was done. Two years, on attempting to read on Easter Sunday the story of the trial and crucifixion of Jesus, he could not get through, but, overcome by his emotions, had to sit down, and give way to his tears." The prayers of Sunday, which usually seem a difficulty hard to get over by minister and people alike, were with him a means of drawing far-off hearts to him, and putting them in tune for the sermon. "Is it not sometimes a burden to the preacher to go through the devotional exercises of the Sunday?" asked one of his friends. "Never to me," was the reply. "The natural attitude of my mind has always been prayerful. A snatch of such feeling passes through me as I walk in the streets, or engage in any work. I sing prayers when I loiter in the woods, or travel the quiet road: these founts of communion, which lie so deep, seem always bubbling to the surface; and the utterance of a prayer is, at any time, as simple to me as breathing."

He wrote in a sermon, "When I was a boy, I heard men pray great prayers and deep ones. To me it seemed as if an angel sang them out of the sky, and this man caught the sound, and copied it easily on his own string. I wondered all men prayed not so; that all could not. Before I was a man, I learned that such inspirings come not thus, but of toil and pain, trial and sorrow, — here spread over many days, there condensed into a few; that it was not by gathering flowers in a meadow of June they got their treasures, but by diving deep into a stormy water that they brought up with pain the pearl of the twisted shell." So fervent was his utterance, so natural and human his cry, that the flowers on the table before him colored his devout speech, and the voices of animals blent easily with his own. One Sunday, a terrier-dog, that had strayed into the hall, suddenly, in the midst of the prayer, lifted up a piercing bark. "We thank Thee, O Father of all, who hast made even the humblest dumb creature to praise thee after its own way!" responded the supplicating lips.

He was preaching a discourse, one winter's day, on "Obstacles." Describing the man to whom obstacles are helps, he said, "Before such a man all obstacles will" — at this instant a mass of frozen snow that had collected on the roof came down with a noise like thunder, that shook the building, and startled the audience with a momentary feeling of dismay — "slide away like the ice from the slated roof," said the preacher's re-assuring voice.

This emotion gave a positive flavor to even an unpromising discourse. It disarmed many an invective of its power to wound. In a letter to an intimate friend, written in 1845, he said, "I have sometimes felt disappointed at the expression in some faces as I have spoken; for it showed that they did not always appreciate what I said,

29

just as I did. I will endeavor to avoid leading astray such as are now ready to start in a false direction. It is by no means pleasant to me to write or preach negation. I would rather give light, however thin, than lightning, however sharp. It is painful to me to thunder; but it is sometimes needful. I must now and then say, 'Woe unto you, scribes and Pharisees, hypocrites!' but the burden of my song will be, 'He that doeth the will of my Father,' &c."

He loved to preach: subjects crowded on him faster than he could deal with them. The Sundays were too few rather than too many. Travelling in Europe, three thousand miles from his desk, he delighted in planning sermons that he could not preach. Vacations were short with him: he would have been glad had they been shorter. It was his custom to preach a fresh sermon every Sunday, especially on rainy days; for the people who came out in storms, he said, have a right to the best. When illness, or pre-occupation, or unexpected absence from home, prevented his preparing a new discourse, instead of disguising the old manuscript, he displayed it, herein violating another clerical tradition. But he could not afford to preach many old sermons. It cost him more to keep the new ones back than to write them.

Parker no more *made* his sermons than his prayers: both made themselves: they came in troops, in clusters, in long files, that stretched over months, and even years. He is known to have laid out subjects for four years in advance, and to have adhered to his plan. Groups of sermon topics appear with curious frequency in the journal. There was no conventional limitation of theme. They were on all vital concerns, from those of the soul to those of the kitchen,—religion in all aspects, personal and public; the greater and lesser affairs of the community; social reform in all its branches; the immediate questions of the day, philosophical, theological, ethical, commercial: and each theme was treated according to its own laws and conditions; no pulpit rule being applied to their discussion, no professional bar being erected for their judgment. When the topic demanded extensive research, the materials were collected long, sometimes a year or two, in advance. Careful studies were made, notes were kept, and generalizations from time to time applied to the facts amassed. His discourses on national matters or on themes of deep and wide import, such as "The Merchant," "The Perishing Classes," "The Dangerous Classes," "Great Cities," "The Dangers and Duties of Woman," "Intemperance," "Crime," cost vast labor in compiling statistics, as well as in reflection. They are treatises as well as sermons, at once profound and fascinating. His political discourses, dealing with each crisis as it occurred, are a combination of history, philosophy, and prophecy, that deserves a place in permanent literature; yet they were prepared for exigencies that soon must pass away. There was conscientious work enough in them for a volume. His biographical discourses were models of thoroughness and strength. While preparing his pulpit oration on John Quincy Adams, he reviewed the statesman's whole career; read every speech; analyzed every argument; scrutinized every act; went behind every piece of public policy; and laid out the history so simply, that the least-instructed intelligence could understand it. Before writing the greatest discourse of them all, on Daniel Webster dead, he did more than this: he gleaned from all credible sources information in regard to Mr. Webster's private life and character; probed the secrets of his ancestry; read the principal works of distinguished orators, jurists, and statesmen in England; studied again the orations of Demosthenes and Cicero in order to settle precisely in his mind the rank of the great American as lawyer, statesman, orator, and man.

That wonderful oration — eulogy, litany, arraignment, verdict — was written at a heat. The preparation for it covered weeks, nay, occupied years; for Webster had been one of Parker's idols, exerting on him something like fascination. A few hours of solitary meditation in the country, after the statesman's death, fused the mass of material so completely, that it ran like molten metal into the literary mould. The sentences poured hot from the speaker's heart. The effect in the delivery was prodigious. It was not uncommon for the audience, towards the close of Mr. Parker's impassioned discourses, to lean forward in rapt attention, showing, as he said once, the angels or the demons in their faces. They did so now, listening with breathless intensity; and when he spoke of his mourning for Webster, and cried in a choking voice, "O Webster, Webster! my king, my king! would I had died for thee!" every eye was wet with tears.

This utter fidelity to his calling made Theodore Parker the great preacher that he was; probably, all things considered, the greatest of his generation. He was greater than Newman Hall, who entertains adult thousands with Sunday-school addresses; than Spurgeon, whom five or six thousand men and women flock to hear, but who lacks learning, knowledge of men and things, breadth and poetic fervor of mind, culture of intellect, and delicacy of perception, — an earnest, zealous, toilsome man, powerful through his sectarian narrowness, not, as Parker was, through his human sympathy. He was greater beyond measure than Maurice, Robertson, Stopford Brooke, or any of the new Churchmen; the delight of those who want to be out of the Church, and yet feel in it. He was greater than Channing in range of thought, in learning, in breadth of human sympathy, in vitality of interest in common affairs, in wealth of imagination, and in the racy flavor of his spoken or written speech. Channing had an equal moral earnestness; an equal depth of spiritual sentiment; a superior gift of look, voice, expression, manner; perhaps a more finely-endowed speculative apprehension; a subtler insight: but, as a preacher, he addressed a smaller class of his fellow-men. His was an aristocratic, Parker's a democratic mind. Channing was ethereal, even when treading most manfully the earth; and seraphic, even when urging the claims of negroes: Parker, when soaring highest, kept both feet planted on the soil; and, when unfolding the most ideal principles, remembered that his brother held him by the hand for guidance. Channing always talked prose, even while dilating on transcendental themes: Parker, even when discussing affairs of the street, would break out into the language of poetry. Channing could sympathize with great popular ideas and movements, but was too fastidious to be ever in close contact with the people: Parker was a man of the people through and through; one of the people, as much at home with the plainest as with the most cultured, more heartily at home with the simple than with the polished: hence his word ran swiftly in rough paths, while Dr. Channing's trod daintily in high places.

Few persons, if asked to name the greatest living preacher in America, would hesitate to mention the pastor of Plymouth Church in Brooklyn. Mr. Beecher is undoubtedly a more popular speaker than Mr. Parker was: he is more eagerly sought after, more widely known among the "common people," more potential through his word. Yet Beecher owes much of his popularity to qualities that gave Parker his fame, — to his humanity, his big-heartedness, his feeling for nature, his simplicity, his independence, his humor. But the obstacles he has to contend with are nothing as compared with those that stood in Parker's way: in fact, he has no difficulties at all. He is not a reformer, an innovator, a teacher of new or unwelcome truths, a champion of unwelcome principles. The popular drift befriends him. His equivocal position as minister of an Orthodox Congregational society makes him attractive to both conservatives and liberals. Not being radical enough to shock the former, nor conservative enough to displease the latter, he retains people of all descriptions, much as the English broad Churchman gathers Episcopalians and Unitarians alike into his fold. Such persons as Theodore Parker assembled — persons whom he culled from the unchurched, the unbelieving, the protesting — are a minority in Mr. Beecher's congregation. Such a ministry is not for them: they want more knowledge, more courage, more devotion to reform, more boldness of speculation, more incisiveness of speech, more living vigor of address. Parker, while fully Beecher's equal in humor, wit, vivacity, playfulness, was greatly his superior in wealth of mental resource, in depth of feeling, in force of emotion; and in moral earnestness he was so vastly before him, that the two men cannot be spoken of in the same breath. Beecher is the Spurgeon of America: Parker was its Martin Luther. With a wealthy congregation like that of Plymouth Church, what would not Parker have done for mankind! Beecher entertains the country: Parker instructed and moulded it. The former is an object of interest and admiration: the latter was an object of love and fear. Where the former causes a titillation on the surface of the community, the latter ploughed a deep furrow in its soil.

Judge the men by their printed sermons. The sermons of each are a literature. Who that can read any other books can read Spurgeon's volumes? The reading-power of the cultivated man breaks down in their dreadful slough. Beecher's are dull when taken in quantity, often commonplace, conventional, and verbose, rarely instructive or nobly stimulating. It is easy to believe that they were made on Sunday morning, after breakfast. Parker printed a great deal too much: not a few of his productions are happy in being out of print. But take up any of his volumes containing the sermons he thought worthy of permanent preservation, — the volume of "Ten Sermons" on religion; the "Theism and Atheism," which is made up of pulpit addresses; read the pamphlet sermons on "Immortal Life," on "The Perils of Adversity and Prosperity," "What Religion will do for a Man," "Lesson for a Midsummer Day," "The Function and Place of Conscience," the "Sermon of Poverty," "Of War," "Of Merchants," "The Chief Sins of the People," "The Power of a False Idea,"—and you have many a long hour full of edification, instruction, and delight. They are sermons, always sermons; not essays or disquisitions. Every book began as a sermon. The parenetical character runs through every thing the man wrote, as the moral element ran through the man. As literary productions, they are open to criticism as being diffuse, clumsy with repetitions, overloaded with illustrations; but as sermons intended to reach the conscience as well as the understanding of miscellaneous and heedless auditors, who must have a thought expressed in several forms, and reiterated more than once, in order to catch or retain it, they are almost perfect, and are destined to do a most important work in educating and inspiring thousands whom the preacher's voice never reached; who, perhaps, were not born when he fell asleep. More may be learned from his political speeches and addresses than from many volumes of contemporaneous history. His speculative discourses throw light on abstruse problems of philosophy: his ordinary sermons are rich in practical wisdom for daily life, and will be read when hundreds of sermons now popular are forgotten, and even when the literature of the pulpit has fallen into the neglect it for the most part deserves.

The habitual attendants on Theodore Parker's Sunday teaching will probably assent to all that has been said. His intimate friends and admirers will think it hardly less than the literal truth. There was much fault-finding, of course, on the part of people whose opinions were attacked, or whose prejudices were wounded. There was occasional complaint from parents of worldly mind that the Music-Hall preaching was not wholesome to young men. It was seldom that fair minds objected to the devotional character of the services, though occasionally one did. Dr. S. G. Howe, for instance, told a friend of Mr. Parker that he did not oftener go to hear him because he did not satisfy his religious nature: he preferred the Swedenborgian chapel. The remark wounded Parker deeply. "This is, in reality," he writes in his private journal, "the most painful criticism I ever heard made on my ministry. I never before heard of any one as objecting to my preaching, that it was not religious enough. Several have gone away for various reasons, — these because I preached against war; those because I preached against slavery; yet others because I preached against intemperance and the making drunkards of men; others, again, because I spoke against the misdeeds of the political parties. Some have left me because I did not believe the popular theology, and so hurt their feelings (all that is natural); several more because the place was not respectable, and the audience was composed chiefly of 'grocers and mechanics:' but this is the first that I know of who has gone elsewhere because the preaching was not *religious* enough. But who knows how many have been grieved away by the same thing? 'God help me to know myself, that I may see how frail I am!' Dr. Howe said that other men went down into the deep places of his heart more than I, and gave him a glow of religion which I failed to produce. Prof. Porter accused me of sentimentalism in religion. I did not think that was true of a man that wore a blue frock, and held the plough, and mowed hay, and delivered temperance lectures, and stormed round the land, preaching antislavery, and making such a tumult as I once made; but it was nearer my own judgment of myself than this of Dr. Howe.

"I once loved pleasure; and religion kept me in. I

loved money, even now have a passion for acquisition, and once resolved to accumulate a hundred thousand dollars; but religion forbade me to be rich while the poor needed food and the ignorant to go to college. I love ease; but I don't take it. Religion keeps me at this desk, and sends me to a thousand things, which, even now, I like not to do. I love fame, and for religion I took a path that I knew would lead me to infamy all my life; and, if any thing else ever comes of it, it will be when I am wholly oblivious to all such things. I love the society of cultivated people, a good name, respectability, and all that; and religious conviction has deprived me of it all, made me an outcast and the companion of outcasts, and given me a name more hated than any in all New England. I see men stare at me in the street, and point, and say, 'That is Theodore Parker,' and look at me as if I were a *murderer*. Old friends, even parishioners, will not bow to me in the street. I am cast out of all respectable society. I knew all this would come. It has come from my religion; and I would not forego that religion for all this world can give. I have borne sorrows that bow men together till they can in no wise lift up themselves. But my comfort has been the joy of religion: my delight is the infinite God; and that has sustained me.

"Yet I am glad of the criticism; and, true or not, I will profit by it."

Such an avowal as this in his private confessional indicates a deep and genuine feeling. Neither the sadness nor the complaint was affected. It was true that men looked at him askance, called him bitter names, — "liar," "scoundrel," "wolf in sheep's clothing," — names worse than "infidel," — and that as early as 1845. The epithets did not become milder, the tone gentler, or the gesture feebler, as years went on, and the conflict deepened between the reformer and the "world." The bold preacher who took the Sermon on the Mount at its word, revered the Commandments, loved the Beatitudes, worshipped the eternal law, applied it strictly to every private vice and every social evil; who, knowing no distinction of persons, publicly summoned the most eminent men of Boston, Massachusetts, New England, the nation, before the judgment-seat of Christ, and openly arraigned them for private infidelities and public misdeeds; the prophet who pointed his warning finger at Winthrop, Everett, Webster, Choate, great manufacturers like Lawrence, great capitalists like Thayer,—could not escape the opprobrium that is always visited on the censor of morals. There was no stake for him, no scourge, no jail. It was not necessary for him to take refuge in any Wartburg to elude the ecclesiastical or other hunters for his blood. That old-fashioned persecution, which put men on their mettle, roused their passions, braced them with the proud sense of martyrdom, and steeled them against sharp but momentary physical pain, would have been easier for one like Parker to bear than the icy neglect, the cold shoulder, the averted eye, the sneer that could not be warded off, the shadow of hate that could not be struck with a weapon, the venomous back-biting that no stubbornness of will could beat back. To "battle against flesh and blood" is comparatively easy; for flesh is hard with muscle, and blood hot with flame: but to "battle against the wicked spirits that dwell in the air" makes the bravest faint.

From the Journal.

FEB. 16, 1851.

This is the sixth anniversary of my coming to the Melodeon. I little knew what I had to encounter, nor who would come to help me do the work. I have found Boston worse by far than I expected. I have been disappointed in its intellectual power, in the intellect of its controlling men, and still more in their moral character. But, on the other hand, I have found a power of goodness in quarters where I did not look for it. My confidence in the people, in mankind, is strengthened. My confidence in men of the mercantile profession in Boston is much weakened. I know noble exceptions. But Boston is the metropolis of snobs.

THURSDAY, March 27, 1851.

To me it seems as if my life was a failure. Let me look at it, —

1. *Domestically.* — 'Tis mainly so: for I have no children; and what is a house without a little "mite o' teants," or "bits o' blossoms"?

2. *Socially.* — It is completely a failure. Here I am as much an outcast from society as if I were a convicted pirate: I mean from all that calls itself "decent society," "respectable society," in Boston.

3. *Professionally.* — I stand all alone; not a minister with me. I see no young men rising up to take ground with me, or in advance of me. I think, that, with a solitary exception, my professional influence has not been felt in a single young minister's soul. True, I have a noble parish: that I am proud of with a pride that makes me humble.

WEDNESDAY, Sept. 24, 1851.

The parish committee applied for the Masonic Temple to hold our meetings in for a few Sundays; and, after due deliberation, were refused, on the ground that *it would injure the reputation of the house.* Mr. W. felt badly about it; Mr. A. not. I only looked for this result. There is no indignity that I do not expect, if an opportunity offers for it. All things have their penalty.

TUESDAY, April 27, 1852.

Kossuth came to Boston. I rejoice at his advent here; but none of the rich men appeared in the streets. Old Josiah Quincy was the only distinguished citizen that I saw in public. Many prominent persons closed their curtains, and one would not allow his familv to go to the window.

NOV. 20.

In Boston I have universally been treated with studied neglect, and often with deliberate and premeditated insult. When I left the parish at West Roxbury, I was treated quite ill, and with the design to wound my feelings. I know very well at whose instigation it has all been done, and am not disposed to blame the majority.

The letters abound in similar confessions.

To Rev. Dr. Francis.

MARCH 12, 1852.

. . . I am sorry to hear you complain of your lot. It seems to me you ought to be a happy man, — material wants all met, a useful and respectable position in society, incubating some eggs which the Unitarian hen lays from year to year, warming them into ministerial chickenhood, brooding over some other eggs in the college-chapel, with two children, the respect of the denomination, and not an enemy in the world. Really, my good friend, it seems to me you ought to be happy. Think of me, hated, shunned, hooted at; not thought worthy to be even a member of the Boston Association of Ministers or of the P. B. K.! Not half a dozen ministers in the land but they abhor me; call me "*infidel:*" even you and Lamson would not exchange with me for ten years past. I have no *child*, and the worst reputation of any minister in all America. Yet I think I am not ill used, take it altogether. I am a happy man. None of these things disturb me. I have my own duty to do, and joys to delight in. Think of those poor Germans, *scholars in Boston!* — poor companionless exiles, set down in vulgar, tory Boston, and shivering with cold, yet thanking God that it is not an Austrian dungeon. Why, you and I might have "glorified God in the grass market," if we had lived two hundred years ago, or three thousand miles east of New England. Come, let us be happy. I, at least, have had quite as good a time in the world as I have merited, and daily bless God for favors undeserved.

Of course, a sensitive nature suffers where an insensible one does not feel. Parker's nature was keenly sensitive, and made what others might have regarded as slight affronts malicious insults and studied outrages. Possibly his sensitiveness now and then imagined affronts where none were intended. But he was not suspicious: the morbid taint, if it existed, was very slight. He tried never to entertain a disposition towards others he could not justify; and any one acquainted with the social condition of New England between 1835 and 1860 will find it much easier to believe than to disbelieve that he had excellent grounds for his feeling. Outspoken reformers were treated with disdain. Not only men like Garrison, whom nobody in "society" knew, but men like Phillips, whom everybody knew, were put under the social ban. Charles Sumner, the pet of society, a worshipper at King's Chapel, was outlawed, cut in the streets, avoided, dropped from fashionable visiting-lists, on account of his anti-slavery opinions. Others less courageous, or more trammelled by conventionalities, shrunk from the ordeal, having ventured near enough to feel the scorch of the flame on their clothes. All Dr. Channing's fastidiousness, quietness, strength of family connection and of personal saintliness had failed to save him from personal unkindness and neglect. They did not save him from dislike, suspicion, and ugly comment among his brethren. Dr. Howe, who had lived in Boston for twenty years, most of the time at the head of the Blind Institution, declared that he never received any sign of recognition from the city authorities in the shape of an invitation to any of their festivities. Parker added to the worst offences of these noble men that of theological heresy. He was a Garrison, a Sumner, a Channing, a Pierpont, combined; and he was more offensive to the respectability of Boston than either, because he was an "infidel," and an infidel among Unitarians, who were the ruling sect. He discredited the religion of the churches.

And he did it every week, on Sunday, — not by editing a paper which the nobility never saw; not by making a strong speech on anniversary occasions, or delivering a grand oration on a Fourth of July; but by preaching great gospel-sermons — one every seven days — to two or three thousand people, and having them reported in the daily papers. He was an incessant thorn, a Nessus shirt that could not be pulled off, a dreadful presence that could not be laid. He was felt every time he moved. Even from his silent lips fell rebuke; through his shut eyelids flashed lightnings. He was loved and he was hated, both more than he knew. Fortunately he could always lose himself in his darling books; he could forget himself quite in the bosom of his friends; he could find himself in communion with his Father.

At the close of this chapter a word will not be out of place, though it may not be necessary, touching the intellectual influence of Mr. Parker's preaching. He is commonly thought of in a senseless, traditional sort of way, as a denier, a destroyer of faith. This every positive teacher must be: his "yea" will cast a shadow proportionate to its own substance. Luther had a strong negative side; so did Calvin; so did Wesley; so did Channing. Only the light wisp of vapor causes neither darkness nor chill. The man who departs from accepted opinions puts them away: if he bolts from them, he denies them; if he is expelled by them, he spurns them. To Mr. Parker the truth was an open common, which he trod with stout walking-shoes, no doubt to the offence of the fastidious; but he traversed it on human errands. The occasional hearer of a single discourse might experience a severe shock; could not help it, if he was mentally thin-skinned. The frank preacher spoke his mind. Questions were started to which the casual listener found no answer; doubts were raised which the novice, unable to lay them himself, presumed the speaker unable to quell; the swift thoughts would strike heedless minds at an unfortunate angle, and so wound them that they went limping away to warn their friends against the poisonous tongue. But there was no more positive preacher: by this very sign he was positive. To build up faith on imperishable foundations was his one purpose; to rescue it from earthquake and flood, to transfer it from the howling wilderness to the safe city, to enable it to stand by virtue of the rational laws rather than by force of clamps and buttresses, was the aim of his life. And in this he succeeded. He created five convictions where he unsettled one. He made ten believers for one infidel. They who listened to him statedly felt the ground firmer under their tread from week to week; were conscious more and more of the reality of things unseen, and the validity of intangible hopes. Could it have been otherwise? Conviction must beget conviction: it cannot beget scepticism, unless it be incidentally, in loose and spongy minds. Convictions have roots, and roots must have soil. Parker did his best to fill in the swampy ground before building. If he but partially succeeded in many cases, the fault was not entirely his. He could not choose his audience, nor force them to remain till his work was finished. Hold not the sower answerable for farm and climate.

CHAPTER XIV.

THE REFORMER.

THEODORE PARKER came to Boston as a theological, not as a social reformer; but life in the city brought him into such close contact with misery, crime, and vice, that he could not stand aloof. A reformer by instinct, readily kindled into indignation at the thought of evils he never saw, the daily communication with evil in its concrete forms moved and roused every energy in him. His gravest charge against religion was not its superstition, but its inhumanity.

From the Journal.

"I have sometimes in the woods found the dead body of an eagle, all dry, and yet tenanted by horrid worms, — a fetid, noisome thing. Once it was an eagle, that soared and screamed in its awful heaven, the playmate of the lightning and the symbol of the thunder: now it is carrion. So, too, the traveller in Sahara finds in the desert a camel, all dead, grim, and dried up, only skin, bones, and emaciated muscle, shrivelled by the hot wind of the wilderness. Once it was a ship of the desert, carrying food in his pack-saddle, and water in himself. How the children loved the camel! Now it is all dead and worthless, very noisome, and only supplicating burial; its teeth, long and useless and dry, protruding from its withered lips. But crazy men stood by and told me that the dead camels were still the only ships of the desert, and the thunder of heaven slept in the eagle's claws.

"The clergy leave the errors (lies), follies, and sins of the times alone, and go, first to routine, and second to mysticism.

"They erect sin (which is a fact) into a principle, and teach a *theory of wickedness,* — e.g., declare there is no 'higher law;' justify slavery and fugitive-slave law; praise the sins of men in high office."

In philosophy Parker was an optimist. His faith in the infinite God, "Father and Mother too," made him so.

"Optimism," he says in the journal (January, 1848), "is the *piety of science.* In the world of creatures subordinate to their instinct, there is only enough capacity of pain to insure the preservation of life and limb. Hunger is no evil, but only a stimulus powerful enough to provoke the lion and the sloth to do their work.

"So is it in human affairs. Take the whole world together, the whole race: sin is the provocation to virtue. Take remorse, the subjective and self-conscious evil of sin; take shortcoming, the subjective result, not necessarily self-conscious; take outward evils from slavery, war, intemperance, pauperism, &c., — these, all the sufferings of the human race, are just adequate to waken mankind, and put him about toil for a greater good. Take the evils which come of pauperism now, begging, &c.: all that suffering has this result: —

"1. It stimulates men to toil rather than starve.

"2. It stimulates men to think out a less wasteful mode of life. When that comes, see what more there will be of life and welfare. God is a loving Father, not a fond one who spoils his children."

But Parker was no idle optimist, disposed to sit still and see Providence work up the raw material of evil into beatitude. He believed in conscience as a powerful operative in the celestial factory; in his particular conscience as an important wheel, rod, strap, driving-beam, or what not, in the engine-room; and was mindful to keep it in good working-order. Small faith had he in a Providence that left out man; in a living God who did not care whether his highest attributes in their highest incarnation co-operated with him or not; in a Divine Will that worked underground alone, in chemistry, gravitation, physiology. His God was human, and, through humanity, made himself felt: thus his optimism was an inspiration, not an incubus.

"Men begin and say, 'THE RIGHT.' It seems hard to forget themselves: so they say, 'THE RIGHT AND I.' That serves their turn: so they take another step, and say, 'I AND THE RIGHT.' That does a good deal better; and they end by saying, 'I, WITHOUT THE RIGHT, OR AGAINST IT.' Thus they go to the Devil, and nobody cares how soon. God honors him who says, 'THE RIGHT.'"

I shall sum up in this chapter Mr. Parker's opinions on the leading reforms of his time, collecting passages from letters and journals of different dates; this method being more convenient and more effective than a reference to his views at intervals along his career. The opinions changed little, if at all, in course of years; so that dates are of little value.

THE SABBATH AND SUNDAY.

In 1848 the agitation against the perpetuation of the Hebrew sabbath in Christian society, which had been going on for a good while, broke out in the form of a call for an Anti-Sabbath Convention, written by Mr. Garrison, and signed by many leading reformers, including Mr. Parker. The object in view by him was the restoration of the Sunday to its place as a day of spiritual recreation, improvement, and joy; the abrogation of penal laws that punished as crime innocent, beneficent, and even necessary infringements of the ancient Mosaic institutions; and the extension of freedom of conscience to men of all faiths. The convention met in March, and resulted, as conventions so often do, in a large pamphlet, the most interesting and valuable part of which was Mr. Parker's exhaustive speech on the whole subject, containing essentially the views that were expressed in a sermon on "The Most Christian Use of Sunday," which was preached two months earlier. It was too moderate in tone to satisfy the convention, crowded as it was with radicals of the extremest description, but too advanced in spirit to suit even the "liberal" community of Boston. Nearly two months before the convention, he wrote to Rev. Increase Smith, —

"The *Anti-Sabbath Convention* is not to be an *Anti-Sunday Convention:* not a bit of it. I think we can make Sunday ten times more valuable than it is now, only by abating the nonsense connected with it.

"I have all along been a little afraid of a re-action from the sour, stiff, Jewish way of keeping the Sunday, into a low, coarse, material, voluptuous, or mere money-making abuse of it. But, if we take it in time, we can cast out the Devil without calling in the aid of Beelzebub. The past is always pregnant with the future. The problem of the present is to deliver the past. If the case is treated scientifically, the labor is easy, the throes natural, and the babe is born; but, if the case is not treated scientifically, the labor is long and difficult, the throes unnatural, and the sufferings atrocious. The poor old matron must smart under the forceps, perhaps submit to the Cæsarian operation, perhaps die; and the little monster who thus comes into the world by a matricide is himself in a sad condition, and will have a sad remembrance all his life of the fact that he killed his mother.

"Now, I think that we can deliver the Jewish sabbath of a fine healthy Sunday, who will remember that he comes of a Hebrew stock on one side, but that mankind is his father; and, while he labors for the human race, will never make mouths at the mother who bore him. But, if the matter be delayed a few years, I think there is danger for the health of both child and mother.

"I hope you will come to the convention, and will speak too. I mean to do so; but as I am not a bit of a re-actionist, and share none of the excesses of either party, I suppose I shall be too radical for the conservatives, and too conservative for the radicals, and so be between two fires, — *cross*-fires too."

And so indeed it proved. I copy from the journal the resolutions he prepared for the convention, but which did not pass: —

"1. That it is not our design to weaken the moral considerations or arguments which lead Christians to devote Sunday to worship, and efforts to promote their growth in religion.

"2. That we learn from history, from observation, and all our experience, that the custom of devoting one day in the week to the special work of spiritual culture has produced very happy results.

"3. That we desire to remove such obstacles as now hinder men from the most Christian use of the first day in the week.

"4. That we consider the superstitious opinions respecting the origin of the institution of the Sunday, as a day to be devoted to religious purposes, to form the chief obstacle in the way of a yet more profitable use of that day.

"5. That we should lament to see the Sunday devoted to *labor* or to *sport*; for, though we think all days are equally holy, we yet consider that the custom of devoting one day in the week mainly to spiritual culture is still of great advantage to mankind.

"6. That, as Christians and as men, we lament and protest against all attempts of governments to tyrannize over the consciences of men."

From the Journal.

MARCH 23.

The Anti-Sabbath Convention assembled to-day. It was a more respectable-looking body of men than I expected to see together. Mr. Garrison's call was read, and sounded well. His resolutions were thorough, but had some of the infelicities which have always been distasteful to me.

24th. — Garrison's resolutions passed. I voted *against* some, *for* some, and was silent upon others. My own lie on the table; for after so much objection was made to them by Lucretia Mott, Garrison, Foster, and Pillsbury, I thought it not worth while to disturb the convention with such matters.

The report of the convention contains about all that can be said on the subject, and is richly worth reading.

TEMPERANCE.

The same moderation of opinion that characterized Mr. Parker's views on the sabbath question marked his expressed views on temperance. The studies on intemperance are frequent and minute in the private journal. He made them everywhere, — in Northern and Southern Europe, England, America. The question was interesting to him economically, morally, socially, ethnologically, nationally. He was a temperate man himself, abstaining from wine till his physicians advised it as a medicine. I find this record in the journal, under date of Jan. 26, 1846 : —

> "To-day a man came out from Boston to sign in my presence the temperance pledge. He brought two of them. I handed him a gold pen to write it with, and added mine with his. He keeps one, and I keep the other."

Often in sermons he said tremendous things about intemperance. The "drunkard-makers," as he called the traders in ardent spirits, came in for their share of his blasting invective. The "demon of the still" he warned people against; did his best to paint black and to exorcise. His rhetoric was fearful: "You see men about your streets all afire; some half burnt down; some with all the soul burned out, only the cinders left of the man, — the shell and wall, and that tumbling and tottering, ready to fall. Who of you has not lost a relative, at least a friend, in that withering flame?" John Pierpont, the champion of temperance in the Boston pulpit, had his sympathy to the last; and the people who expelled him from Hollis Street for preaching against the evil by which his wealthy parishioners lived, received at his hands a castigation they neither forgave nor forgot.

But Parker never ceased to be a student of facts, whether they made for a theory or against it. In a long letter, written in 1858 to Dr. Henry I. Bowditch, who had asked him for the results of his observations on consumption, he says, —

"Intemperate habits (where the man drinks a pure though coarse and fiery liquor, like New-England rum) tend to check the consumptive tendency; though the drunkard, who himself escapes its consequences, may transmit the fatal seed to his children.

"I knew a consumptive family living in an unhealthy situation, who had four sons. Two were often drunk, and always intemperate, — one of them as long as I remember; both consumptive in early life, but now both hearty men, from sixty to seventy. The two others were temperate, — one drinking moderately, the other but occasionally: they both died of consumption, the oldest not over forty-five.

"Another consumptive family, living in such a situation as has been already described, had many sons and several daughters. The daughters were all temperate, married, settled elsewhere, had children, died of consumption, bequeathing it to their posterity. Five of the sons whom I knew were drunkards; some, of the extremest description. They all had the consumptive build, and in early life showed signs of the disease; but none of them died of it: some of them are still burning in rum."

The last expression shows that Mr. Parker thought the tendency to consumption no excuse for the intemperance; though he himself drank red wine, and even brandy, when threatened by the same disease. There is no evidence that in the last danger he regretted not having been a sot as a preventive. Physiological questions he kept distinct from moral.

Thus he comments in the journal on the prohibitory law that was passed in Maine in the winter of 1850–51: —

"They have a new law in Maine, passed last winter, which went into operation in May or June. This prohibits the use of all intoxicating drinks except for medical or mechanical purposes. They are now enforcing it with great vigor. It makes the whole State an *asylum for the drunkard.* The principle was long ago acted on, though perhaps not recognized, that the public should seize and destroy things deadly or dangerous to the community. Thus no man is allowed to keep a 'dangerous beast.' In France, and perhaps all countries, the government seizes contaminated meat, &c. Instruments for gambling, for counterfeiting, &c., are also *contraband of peace.* Suspected persons are deprived of arms in war time. All this is of the same principle. In Ohio there is a party — I hope a large one — that will vote for none but *teetotalers.* If Maine can keep her actual law, and Ohio her contemplated one, for a single generation, it will be of immense value to the State.

"The law seems an invasion of private right. It is an invasion, but for the sake of preserving the rights of all. I think wine is a good thing: so is beer, rum, brandy, and the like, when rightly used. I think the teetotalers are right in their practice *for these times*, but wrong in their principles. I believe it will be found on examination, that, other things being equal, men in social life who use stimulants moderately live longer, and have a sounder old age, than the teetotalers. I don't know this, but believe it. I fancy that wine is the best of stimulants. But now I think that nine-tenths of the alcoholic stimulus that is used is abused. The evil is so monstrous, so patent, so universal, that it becomes the duty of the State to take care of its citizens; the whole, of its parts. If my house gets a-fire, the bells are rung, the neighborhood called together, the engines brought out, and water put on it till my garret is a swamp. But, as I am fully insured, I don't care for the fire, and contend that my rights are invaded by the engine-men and their water. They say, 'Sir, you would burn down the town.'"

This is the whole of Mr. Parker's doctrine on this momentous subject. It is not original. In the mouths of some people it would have a fanatical sound on its practical side, and an empty sound on its philosophical; but from his it sounded otherwise. His earnest humanity interpreted both sides; forbade his being cold, forbade his being hot. He looked at the physiological question as a philosopher, at the social evil as a man. The aspect that is conspicuous gains his attention. If the evil alone is conspicuous, he will lay aside the most plausible theory that interferes with the directness of his blow. Each class of facts in its own order; first, that which bears immediately on the moral salvation of men. That he held to be primary; there he had no doubts. Whatever questions might be open to dispute, the question that was not at all in dispute was the question of duty on the part of the strong to aid the weak, of the safe to rescue the perishing, of the wise to teach the simple. Let government represent the conscience and intelligence of the people, and, to his practical understanding, the matter was plain: if the government failed to represent the conscience and intelligence of the people, it was the reformer's office to mend it so that it would. Parker was a *realist;* no *doctrinaire*, no *sentimentalist.* He had no patent medicine or infallible pill: he could not march with a trainband, but was prepared to go from one position on a question to another, as the fortunes of the battle turned; his principle being, to win the battle of humanity on the field of fact. The new fact determined the new attitude.

WAR.

The following extract from a letter to his friend Robert White, written June 8, 1852, declares that Mr. Parker was far from being a non-resistant: —

"In respect to repelling force by force, I should differ from you widely. I respect the conduct of the Friends in this matter also; but I do not share their opinions. I follow what seems to me the 'light of nature.' It seems to me the opinion of Jesus is made too much of in this particular. He supposed the 'world' was soon to end, and the 'kingdom of heaven' was presently to be established. He therefore commands his followers to '*resist not evil;*' not only not to resist with violence, but *not at all.* In like manner, he tells them to '*take no thought for the morrow.*' These counsels, I take it, were given in the *absolute sense* of the words, and would do well enough for a world with no future. The day was 'at hand' when the Son of man should come with power and great glory, and give fourfold for all given in charity, and eternal life besides. But the Son of man (or God) is to use violence of the most terrible character (Matt. xxv. 31–46). Men were not to take vengeance, or even to resist wrong; not to meditate the defence they were to make when brought before a court: all was to be done for them by supernatural power. These things being so, with all my veneration for the character of Jesus, and my reverence for his general principles of morality and religion, I cannot accept his rule of conduct in such matters.

"Yet I think violence is resorted to nine times when it is needless to every one instance when it is needed. I have never preached against the doctrine of the non-resistants, but often against the excess of violence in the state, the church, the community, and the family. I think cases may occur in which it would be my duty to repel violence by violence, even with taking life. Better men than I am think quite differently; and I respect their conscientiousness, but must be ruled by my own conscience, and, till otherwise enlightened, still use violence, if need be, to help a fugitive."

So much for the general principle. Touching the problem of war in particular, he rather skirted the gigantic subject than doggedly attacked it. He was exceedingly curious about war, — the cost of it; the expense of maintaining armies; the waste of life; the effects, physical and moral, on society, whether to stunt and brutalize, or to stimulate and ennoble; the part it played in the progress of mankind; its avoidableness or inevitableness; the amount of guilt implied in it; the value of the virtues it educated. His inquiries extended as far as to the strength of cannon, and the ordinary supply of ammunition kept on hand by government; but no rule was given that covered every special case. No doubt he thought war occasionally justifiable and beneficent, as well as morally inevitable. But the perusal of such a letter as he wrote to Charles Sumner after reading his superb Fourth-of-July oration on "The True Grandeur of Nations" leaves no doubt in regard to the nature of his moral sentiments: —

West Roxbury, Aug. 17, 1845.

Dear Sir, — I hope you will excuse one so nearly a stranger to you as myself for addressing you this note; but I cannot forbear writing. I have just read your oration on "The True Grandeur of Nations" for the second time, and write to express to you my sense of the great value of that work, and my gratitude to you for delivering it on such an occasion. Boston is a queer little city: the public is a desperate tyrant there, and it is seldom that one dares disobey the commands of public opinion. I know the reproaches you have already received from your friends, who will now, perhaps, become your foes. I have heard all sorts of ill motives attributed to you, and know that you must suffer attack from men of low morals, who can only swear by their party, and live only in public opinion. The Church and State are both ready to engage in war, however unjust, if a little territory can be added to the national domain thereby. The great maxims of Christianity, the very words of Christ, are almost wholly forgotten. Few dare move an inch in advance of public opinion.

I thank you with all my heart for so nobly exposing the evils of war, its worthlessness and its waste. The noises made about you show plainly that you have hit the nail on the head. I am glad the "park of artillery" got let off against you.

Laudari a viro laudato is thought of some value; and so it is no small praise to be censured by some men. I hope you will find a rich reward in the certainty that you have done a duty and a service to mankind. I wish a cheap edition might be printed; for I want to scatter abroad fifty or a hundred copies. Would it be possible to print a cheap edition like that of Mr. Mann's noble oration?

I beg you to excuse me for writing you this letter, and believe me

Very respectfully yours, &c.,

Theo. Parker.

The sermon on War, preached Jan. 4, 1846, and the special sermon on the Mexican War, preached June 25, 1848, leave no doubt in regard to the tendency of Mr. Parker's own teaching on this great subject.

CAPITAL PUNISHMENT.

The strong preacher's convictions on this point were spoken without qualification; not often, perhaps, but with emphasis.

From the Journal.

MAY 30, 1845.

Attended the anti-capital-punishment meeting, — nothing remarkable, but as a sign of the times. Soon this sin of judicial murder will be over. (*Mem.* — The remarkable variety of persons: all conditions were represented there.)

AUG. 30, 1850.

To-day, by command of the Governor of Massachusetts, Dr. John White Webster, professor of chemistry and mineralogy in Harvard University, was hanged in the jail-yard at Boston (Leverett Street) at twenty-five minutes before ten o'clock, A.M. This is the second execution in Boston within a very few years; and it is a terrible sin — it seems to me — thus to take the life of a man completely in our power. The laws deal equally with the poor negro and the well-educated and respectable professor; but I think it cannot be long that we shall continue thus to kill men for killing man.

PRISONS.

To Charles M. Ellis.

WEST ROXBURY, Saturday Night, June, 1846.

MY DEAR CHARLES, — I want to trouble you again a few minutes. Can you get for me a copy of the last June Report of the Committee on the City Prisons, Houses of Correction, &c.? Then, too, can you find out how many persons from Boston are sent to the State Prison from June 9, 1845, to June 9, 1846, and the term of their sentences? I want to ascertain this matter very much. Who can tell me the proportion of *second-comers* in the State Prison? You will see the use I mean to make of this information when I print the sermon "Of the Perishing Classes in Boston."

Yours truly but hastily,

THEO. PARKER.

That sermon "Of the Perishing Classes" had the meat of many reports in it, and the soul of a deep and wise humanity. It should be added, that, while denouncing heartily the prison system as barbarous and idiotic, he was not enthusiastic over the substitutes which were proposed for it. When the community glorified the Reform School at Westborough, Mass., he doubted. "The school at Westborough is a school of crime," he said. He expressed himself not sorry to hear that it was burned. This was quite in keeping with his philosophy of reform. The substitution of a plausible evil for an undisguised evil gave him no consolation. The education of humanity was the cardinal point; and that was a deep matter, which good men might blunder about as well as bad men. Amiability did not excuse folly.

WOMAN.

Under this caption I can only hint in general terms at Mr. Parker's opinions on some of the deep questions which most can ask, and few can answer, and none yet can decide, affecting the happiness and well-being of women. That he estimated the native genius of woman as highly as any, ranked her as loftily in the order of humanity, expected as much from her, demanded for her as complete an enfranchisement and as thorough an education, recognized as unqualifiedly her claim to social and civil privileges, anticipated as glorious results from her participation in the active concerns of life, need hardly be said. Evidence could be collected, if need were, from published and unpublished sermons; but here as elsewhere the actual condition of things engaged him more than the possible condition at a future day. He allowed his Utopias to float in the clouds, and occupied himself with digging for foundations on which they could securely stand.

The problem of prostitution interested him much from the earliest day.

BOSTON, April 24, 1852.

DEAR HIGGINSON, — I send you our circular, which will interest your kind heart. Hope to see you soon.

Yours truly, T. P.

The circular asked co-operation in the work of an association that aimed to protect girls whom idleness and vagrant habits led into temptation, and made offenders against the laws. Boys were provided for in parallel emergencies. He wanted a similar care bestowed on girls, — to take charge of them before they became offenders; to take possession of such as were arraigned for crimes; to furnish a temporary home for them in the city, instruction in the means of gaining a living, and places in the country towns of New England for such as needed them. Rev. John T. Sargent consented to act as agent of the association in the courts and elsewhere, becoming bail for such as he thought deserving. Among the names subscribed to the project were Edmund Jackson, Theodore Parker, Hannah Stevenson, and Wendell Phillips.

On a Sunday afternoon in 1854 he is writing to a company of philanthropists to come and devise means to help the poor girls in the streets of Boston who were on the way to the brothel. He is sick too; tormented with rheumatism; laid prone on the sofa. The good work done in New York by Charles Loring Brace interested him exceedingly, especially as it bore on the moral condition of exposed girls. He took at least one journey to New York on purpose to consult with Mr. Brace on his methods and results; and always, when in his neighborhood, made a point of collecting information from that valuable source.

The misery incident to thoughtless marriages oppressed him sorely; and he spoke of them in terms that would give aid and comfort to some modern enemies of the marriage institution, if taken in their bald, literal sense, apart from the earnest moral feeling that lifted all his opinions above the range of low-minded discussion. The following frank letter to Miss Stevenson will answer as well as many notes from the journal to convey one phase of his feeling on this vexed theme:—

WEST NEWTON, August, 1852,
Fourth Vacation Day.

DEAR HANNAH,—Thank you for the nice letter which came Tuesday *für mir selbst allein.* There is nothing in it which I dissent from. The other which I wrote contained some exaggeration, and did not fully represent my own view of the matter. I had been talking with one who—and his wife equally—suffered intensely from a mismarriage, and took rather his view of the matter than my own: at least, the letter partook of the exaggeration of his statement.

About half the people in the world want a husband or a wife for the utility of the thing, for the various modes of marketable utility. The partner is an instrument, a medium for the accomplishment of various purposes. The highest of these is the *attainment of respectability.* The partner is a medium of respectability. The sufferings of these persons are only like the pain of an ill-fitting shoe, or the mortification of a bad bargain, or the discomfort of a hard bed. I have not much feeling for these persons in their connubial griefs.

But when a noble person marries for the noble end, and then finds it is no marriage, there is a horrible suffering; and all sorts of abnormalities of conduct, internal and external, may be expected to take place. The very eminence of morality in New England intensifies the suffering; for elsewhere the connubial *Abschweifungen* are tolerated, and the disappointed persons find some relief, at least abatement, for their long-continued affliction.

Still I must think that the connubial organization is extremely imperfect, and does great injustice on all sides. There is the gross licentiousness of young men, continued by some through all their lives; then the unnatural and involuntary celibacy of so many women, not to speak of conduct that sends many to the madhouse: all of this is unnatural, is *against* nature, and only exists in consequence of the general tyranny which has been so long exercised by the bigger brain over the smaller. There is a radical defect in our organization of the family. In most countries, polygamy is a rough remedy against the involuntary celibacy of women. Among the Catholics, monastic establishments are an organization of celibacy, the voluntary or the involuntary. The celibacy is often, with the Catholic women, against their consent. The organization is voluntary. (A nun is an old maid organized.) In Spain there are now in the several conventual establishments six thousand nuns; in Boston five thousand and fifteen widows, and how many nuns unorganized, involuntary nuns, nuns of the orders of necessity! Now, there will always be noble women who refuse marriage, not from lack of affection or lack of passion, but for other reasons and considerations; and they will have their joy and delight. There will always be unlucky marriages. There is always a margin of miscarriage in all human affairs; but this mighty amount of involuntary celibacy on the part of women, and its consequent suffering, will gradually disappear fast as the idea of her equality obtains footing. When woman has the same rights of mind, body, and estate, recognized by all, that man has, then you will not find five thousand and fifteen widows in Boston, and three hundred and seventy-six widowers.

Dear old ladye, good-by!

From the Journal.

"From psychological considerations, I should think that *monogamy* was the natural law of human nature. I find the same thing shown in the equality of the sexes; and the same conclusion is confirmed by history. E.g., among the negro slaves there is no marriage-form; the whole is voluntary: but separations almost never take place. The same is true of the North-American Indians, — e.g., the Osages, who know nothing of this, — though there is no *law* or *custom* to prevent it. If the whole were more free in social life, I doubt not that marriage would be happier, and divorces more rare. What a deal of prudery is there about the matter here in New England!

"All marriages that I have ever known, or almost all, are fragmentary. If I read aright, a perfect and entire marriage can only take place between equals, or, at least, equivalents. Now, it frequently happens that the parties are vastly unequal, one by no means the equivalent of the other. Hence they are married but partially, and touch only in one point or so. I know a man whose wife has no passion: sentiment enough; but the passional part of marriage is hateful to her. In this point, then, the man is not married. I know many where in soul there is no equivalent; and in *soul* the man is not married. So with intellect, affection, benevolence, &c. A man not mated, or a woman not mated, seeks sorrowing the other half, and wanders up and down without rest. Most men are married only in their philoprogenitiveness or their acquisitiveness, perhaps in their amativeness. Marriage is mainly a discipline to most men: to few is it mainly an enjoyment. A man's courtship often begins after his marriage; and he tries to piece out a wife, — a little here, and a little there. With women the case is worse still. To a sluggish nature this is a slight thing: he wants to sleep, and sleeps. But to a great active soul it must be a terrible curse. A man marries a wife far superior to himself. He cannot carry her. She wants sympathy in the unsupported part, and she must have it. Suppose she does not have it: that part of her nature perishes, and corrupts the rest. If she does have it, then, in that point, her legal husband is not her true one. So it goes."

This is the staple. It is shrewd and commonsensical, but has not the great moral lift that characterizes Mr. Parker's mind. The sorrow and perplexity are too much for him.

Certain aspects of this subject are well treated in letters to Robert White of New York, printed in full by Mr. Weiss. They are interesting, but add little to the hints already given. The discussion is thorough on the lower planes; but it does not ascend to the higher. The spiritual element is somehow wanting. The redeeming feature all through is the faith in God and man, and the brave trust that the race will work its way through the slough to better states.

"This great matter (of divorce)," he wrote to Miss Cobbe in 1859, "I have not touched, for two reasons: 1st, I don't feel quite competent to deal with it, and perhaps never shall, even if I live; and, 2d, things are going on very well without my interference, — perhaps better without it. All the progressive States of America are changing their laws of divorce; and in New England they have altered much in fifty, even in twenty years. The instinct and reflection of the people demand a change. In the new Western States the alterations are very great and rapid. In private I do not share the opinions attributed to me, and have painfully spent much time in attempting to reconcile married people who at first sought a divorce. Yet, out of many trials, I remember but one where the attempt was at all successful. I have small sympathy with men and women who would either make or break a marriage lightly. But I do not think material adultery is the only breach of marriage. I think I once petitioned the Massachusetts Legislature to make habitual drunkenness a ground for divorce, if the aggrieved party desired it. But proper notions of marriage, and so of divorce, can only come as the result of a slow but thorough revolution in the idea of woman. At present, all is chaotic in the relation between her and man: hence the ghastly evils of involuntary celibacy, of unnatural marriage, and of that dreadful and many-formed vice which disgraces our civilization. But we shall gradually outgrow this feudalism of woman."

The problem of woman suffrage was another which Mr. Parker did not work out. The agitation had not come up in his day as it has since; so that the consideration of it was speculative, and therefore lacked vitality. On general principles, he was doubtless disposed to favor the reform. Were he alive to-day, he would probably be one of its leaders. He evidently wished to encourage in others faith in the capabilities, in all noble directions, of woman ; and in conversation occasionally spoke with enthusiasm of the part they would perform in situations now held exclusively by men. In private letters he spoke cordially of woman's efforts at social and civil emancipation. The sermon on the "Public Function of Woman," published in the second series of speeches, addresses, and sermons, was printed by the friends of woman suffrage as a tract powerful in argument and strong in sentiment on their side. It was claimed that he argued woman's equal title to every political right with man. On June 3, 1853, Mr. Parker, with Lucy Stone, Wendell Phillips, and T. W. Higginson, appeared before a committee appointed to revise the Constitution of Massachusetts, and made an earnest appeal for the admission of women to political rights. The meeting, which was significant, was held in the Senate Chamber, Hon, Amasa Walker presiding; still his views were not unqualified. His private faith was a little at the mercy of moods, and of obvious facts which met his eye from day to day. I find the following observation in the journal of 1859 :—

"It is surprising to notice the odds between the talk of men and women, who bear the same relation to mankind and to humankind. The women talk so much more on trifles ; and, when they treat important matters, it is in a comparatively poor and narrow manner. If half the American Senate were women, who should bear the same relation to their female constituents as the men to the male, I think half (perhaps more than half) of the debates would be of a strange character."

But here, as in other cases, his faith in the principle would have proved more than a match for his doubts respecting details of operation. His confidence in the regenerating power of liberty, or of humanity in a condition of liberty, was too entire, and his trust in the future too sincere, to be daunted or dashed by difficulties incidental, perhaps, to a transient phase of social progress. Certain it is that women would have always found in him a champion pledged to defend every one of their natural rights, and loyal to claim every human privilege. He would always have been more than a partisan, but never less than a friend.

SPIRITUALISM.

This, too, is to be ranked among the reforms; for a reform indeed it is, and, as such, was honestly recognized by the candid mind which tried to reckon all movements at their true value. Again and again Parker admitted its worth as an agent in emancipating the human mind. As early as 1854 I find mention of the subject in a letter written to Albert Sanford. His intellect was constitutionally averse, some will say constitutionally powerless, to grapple with matters that bordered on the supernatural; and familiar practical objections occurred to him with force. The ludicrous side was ever obvious. The spirits were never at home when he called; and they never pulled his latch-string, though it always hung out. It was not his way to seek an extramundane cause, if a mundane cause could be conjectured; and, if none could be, his demand that the extramundane cause should justify itself intellectually, inclined him rather to rest in ignorance than to repose in faith. In a word, he never obtained satisfaction. Yet he blamed the scientific men, Agassiz among them, for their unfair methods of investigating the phenomena; rebuked the prigs who turned up their noses at the idea of investigating the subject at all; and took faithful measure of the unbelief in immortality which pronounced communication between the visible and invisible worlds impossible. He admitted to his friend Prof. Desor that Spiritualism does two good things: 1st, It knocks the nonsense of the popular theology to pieces, and so does a negative service; 2d, It leads cold, hard, materialistic men to a recognition of what is really spiritual in their nature, and so does a positive good.

"In 1856," he writes in the journal, "it seems more likely that Spiritualism will become the religion of America than in 156 that Christianity would be the religion of the Roman empire, or in 856 that Mohammedanism would be that of the Arabian populations. 1st, It has more evidence for its wonders than any historic form of religion hitherto. 2d, It is thoroughly democratic, with no hierarchy, but inspiration open to all. 3d. It is no fixed fact, has no *punctum stans*, but is a *punctum fluens;* not a finality, but shows a great vista for the future. 4th, It admits all the truths of religion and morality in all the world sects."

Of Swedenborg, the high priest of Spiritualism, Mr. Parker had not an adoring appreciation. "Swedenborg has had the fate to be worshipped as a half-god on the one side, and on the other to be despised and laughed at. It seems to me that he was a man of genius, of wide learning, of deep and genuine piety; but he had an abnormal, queer sort of mind, — dreamy, dozy, clairvoyant, Andrew Jackson Davisy; and, besides, he loved opium and strong coffee, and wrote under the influence of those drugs. A wise man may get many nice bites out of him, and be the wiser for such eating; but if he swallows Swedenborg whole, as the fashion is with his followers, — why, it lies hard on the stomach, and the man has a nightmare on him all his natural life, and talks about the 'Word' and the 'Spirit,' 'correspondences,' &c. Yet the Swedenborgians have a calm and religious beauty in their lives which is much to be admired."

In August, 1838, after reading a Life of Swedenborg, — probably Hobart's, the first published biography in English (Boston, 1831), — he makes the following note in the journal: —

"It seems written with the most honest intentions, but is not satisfactory to me farther than this: it shows he was a very remarkable man. As to his wonderful deeds, I have no antecedent objection to them; though the evidence is not always sufficient to establish their actuality. If actual, they are of no value to my mind as proof of spiritual inspiration. I cannot believe in his interpretations of the Scriptures, if he were to move mountains.

"There is a little unfairness in giving part of the testimony of Kant, without giving the part against the credibility of Swedenborg."

Parker was, then, acquainted with Swedenborg's story before reading this book. It would have been singular indeed had so extraordinary an intellectual phenomenon escaped him.

To effect a *theological* reform Parker conceived to be his mission. To this the cast of his mind and his passion for books inclined him. He was a student and a thinker, endowed with a prodigious capacity for receiving the thoughts of others, and with a singular power of simplifying them in statement. Though not a philosopher in the technical meaning of the word, he had a vigorous grasp on the moral bearing of ideas, which qualified him to be a leader in the general philosophic world. He treated ideas as if they were living powers, and watched their working with the intense interest of a spectator at a gladiatorial show, or, to speak more accurately, with the absorbing enthusiasm of a master of the games. His faith in the regenerating force of a correct theology was vital. He believed with all his heart, that if the theology of the Romanist and Protestant — in other words, of the "Christian" churches — could be destroyed, and juster views of God, and of man's relations to God, could be substituted for it, society would feel the change in all its departments, from government affairs to domestic service: every wrong would be righted, every mischief removed, every mistake corrected, every sorrow taken away. His interest, therefore, in social reforms, like those mentioned above, was at first incidental to his interest in theology: it illustrated the bearings of his theological idea; it exhibited in concrete form the drift of his speculative spirit; it was an application of his scheme of the universe to the separate concerns of the community.

Thus far, therefore, though his sentiments were those of a reformer, Parker, in the ordinary sense of the word, was not a political reformer. He was not a reformer as Garrison was, or Phillips; as Wilberforce was, or Clarkson, or George Thompson, or John Howard, — men who gave themselves to a particular cause, consecrated time and means and talents to it, fought for it, made sacrifices for it, were ready to die for it. The interest he felt in temperance, peace, education, the abolition of the gallows, the rescue of imperilled girls, did not take him from his study, force him into daily consort with men of affairs, make him discontinue or countermand his orders for foreign books, keep him on his feet day and night, fill his house with children of misery, his hours with efforts to relieve suffering and thwart iniquity, his heart with anxieties for the destiny of his country. The time for this had not come; but it was coming. When it came, it found him ready. His reform of theology meant, at bottom, reform of society; and, if society raised the loudest cry, his ear was open to hear it.

The following sonnet, copied from the journal of 1849, expresses the spirit in which he tried to work: —

"Father, I will not ask for wealth or fame,
Though once they would have joyed my carnal sense:
I shudder not to bear a hated name,
Wanting all wealth, myself my sole defence.
But give me, Lord, eyes to behold the truth;
A seeing sense that knows the eternal right;
A heart with pity filled, and gentlest ruth;
A manly faith that makes all darkness light:

Give me the power to labor for mankind ;
Make me the mouth of such as cannot speak ;
Eyes let me be to groping men and blind ;
A conscience to the base ; and to the weak
Let me be hands and feet ; and to the foolish, mind ;
And lead still further on such as thy kingdom seek."

CHAPTER XV.

THE FIGHT WITH SLAVERY.

THEODORE PARKER never was, never could have been, indifferent to slavery as an inhuman system. His attention was early fixed on it as a blunder in economics, and a blot on American institutions. A sermon on slavery, preached in 1841, and again in 1843, was published. In 1842 he wrote to a friend, "Perhaps you feel a stronger interest than I do in the welfare of Latimer" (a fugitive slave, whose examination was pending, and in whose behalf the abolitionists had asked public intercession from divines), "and of the slaves in general. It must be a very strong one if it is so. But I will not boast of my zeal." It was not, however, till 1845, when slavery became prominent in the national politics, and menaced republican government with overthrow, when men began to talk of the "slave power," that his concern in the matter became engrossing. That year finds him busy with statistics on the general subject. He writes to the historian Michelet for information in regard to a work alluded to by him, as he is preparing an essay on slavery in the Roman empire. The same year he collects facts on slavery in the United States, its introduction and domestication there. The scheme of the "Letter to the Citizens of the United States," published in December, 1847, is drawn up at this time in rough form; books are noted, and materials gathered from all sources, familiar and remote. The "Letter," when finished, was a model of terse composition, throbbing with an earnestness as deep as Garrison's, and animated by a wisdom as calm as Channing's. Slavery had become the one practical question in America, involving all others. It called for practical measures: the practical man rallied all his forces to meet it. In 1848 it was suggested to him that political life would give him a better position than the pulpit. In one of his despondent moods he writes thus in the journal: —

"*May* 19. — Several persons of late, as well as formerly, have talked to me about going to Congress as representative or senator. To which there are two objections. 1. *Nobody would send me.* I don't believe any town in Massachusetts would give me any post above that of hog-reeve; and I don't feel competent for that office: a man in spectacles could not well run after swine. 2. *Politics are not my vocation, nor yet my desire.* I aim to labor for ideas, to set men a-thinking. I feel as if born for a pulpit, if for any thing. If I could be well, — well enough to work, to do a man's duty, — I should be glad. Yet that is not a thing I ever mention in my prayers. I am content, yes, content, to pay the price of violating the laws of the body in struggling for an education; though I knew not what I did."

In a braver mood he saw the advantage of his professional position. He was responsible to nobody, and nobody to him: he was his own master; owned his own mill; built his own dam; could grind as much and as little as he liked. He could speak his own word, in his own way, and in his own time; was the servant of no party, the slave of no machine. He could excite the sentiment and supply the idea for the political reformer to work up for his uses. But he believed in politics, too, as the instituted agency for carrying ideas into effect. He did not stand outside of politics, as the abolitionists did: rather he stood above them, as one who would make them serve his turn. He voted; encouraged voting; counted the actual and reckoned the possible votes; interested himself in the candidates to be voted for; stirred up the enthusiasm of constituencies; marshalled his armies of ballots as a general his myrmidons; all the time ringing out his prophetic call to conscience, and impressing on men the majesty of the eternal law. No disabling scruples respecting the constitutional guaranties of slavery restrained him on the one side; no ethnological doubts respecting the negro's rank in mankind restrained him on the other. He saw democratic institutions — the dream of history, the hope of humanity — menaced with destruction; and he rushed to the rescue, snatching up the most effective weapons that lay near his hand.

A brief sketch of the episodes in the conflict, their dates and characteristic features at least, is necessary to explain his course. The events have passed into history; and, even if they had not, are important here only as illustrating the man, his methods and his spirit.

The annexation of Texas — the first step, as he foresaw, and as it proved, in the march of the slave power towards its goal, the supreme control of the American government — was effected in 1845. By this measure a territory as large as France was added as a slave State to the Union.

The war with Mexico — the first consequence of the annexation of Texas — followed in 1846, and was advocated by the same party that carried through the former measure. The issue of the war increased the reputation of the party, and greatly raised the confidence of the slave power.

The election of Gen. Taylor to the presidency in 1848 confirmed the gains already made, and favored new plots for the feudal usurpation. In 1850 the famous Fugitive-slave Bill was passed, which opened the whole North as a hunting-ground for Southern masters whose slaves had escaped into the Middle and New-England States. Of this bill Daniel Webster was the great Whig supporter. He carried with him the wealth, eminence, and social respectability, of Massachusetts.

The administration of Franklin Pierce gave to the conspirators an opportunity to consolidate their plans, which they diligently made use of, and so openly, that the public sentiment of the North was at last aroused to a sense of the danger.

On the 15th of May, 1854, the Kansas-Nebraska Bill, which had passed the Senate on the 4th, passed the House of Representatives in spite of vigorous opposition from Northern men; and a new episode in the course of events was opened. Neither Territory having the population required for admission as a State, both made haste to stock them with people after their own kind. The "border ruffians" poured in from Missouri, and took violent possession of the strategic points. The emigration societies formed their organizations in the free States, and pushed their bands of pioneers across the Western prairies, fully equipped with implements of civilization, and armed with rifles to defend them. The suppressed war broke out in the new Territories with fury. Outrages of every kind made existence there tolerable to none but combatants. Murders, accompanied by acts of deep atrocity, were of daily occurrence. There was no law, no restraint of custom, no respect for property or person. Re-enforcements were continually coming in to the aid of either party; and, as numbers increased, difficulties accumulated. The condition of things was one of simple anarchy: men went armed; houses were prepared for assault; guards were stationed as in time of war. Nobody was safe.

Prominent among the figures that loomed up in this dreadful time was that of John Brown, the stern man of grim puritanical cast, whose deed of sacrifice closed one epoch of history.

In May, 1856, Charles Sumner delivered in the Senate his famous speech, "The Crime against Kansas," which lashed the proslavery party to frenzy, and brought upon him a brutal assault, on the 21st, by Preston Brooks. The Massachusetts senator dragged his outraged form from Washington to Boston, touching all hearts with pity, filling all souls with indignation, and swelling the party which had determined that the slave power should lose the next battle and be crushed.

But it was not. The battle was fiercely fought between John Charles Fremont and James Buchanan. Buchanan won; and the dominion of evil was strengthened for another term. The tide was not turned till 1860, when the success of Abraham Lincoln checked the slaveholders' advance, but too late for a peaceful solution of the problem. The civil war punished the South for its iniquity, and the North for its complicity.

At every crisis of this long conflict, from the first moment till near its close, Theodore Parker made himself felt. His voice was the loudest; his presence was ubiquitous; his action was prompt. He enlisted for the war, and brought all his forces with him. The importation of books slackened; the folios were dropped; purse and brain were devoted to the one duty of meeting the public emergency. With astonishing assiduity he went through the Northern States, enlightening and rousing the people with ponderous lectures that were orations, sermons, arguments, historical disquisitions, harangues, all in one. His lecturing-field touched the Southern border, and once, at least, lapped over. Thomas Garrett, the famous station-master of the "Underground Railroad," proposed to him to lecture in Wilmington, Del. (a place where the proslavery feeling was particularly acrid); telling him at the same time that the undertaking was dangerous; that he would be exposed to insult, and perhaps to personal violence. The peril was a temptation; and the invitation was accepted with alacrity. A special lecture was prepared for the occasion. On his arrival, posters were out on the walls, of an alarming nature. The hall was filled with excited people; scowling faces confronted him as he entered; there were whispers of tar and feathers in the back-yard. Parker took the stand, and, as quietly as if he were in Music Hall, announced his theme: "Rhode Island and Delaware, the Two Smallest States in the Union." He began by drawing a picture of the two States as regarded natural advantages, — of position, climate, resources, historical and political antecedents, — all so conspicuously in favor of Delaware, that the audience was delighted. Having thus sketched the States as they ought to be, he drew another picture, representing them as they were, — Delaware poor, unenterprising, decadent; Rhode Island vigorous, rich, advancing. Having set the two pictures face to face, the question was raised and answered, "What explains these unexpected results?" With careful array of facts and figures, it was shown how, in the one case, slavery had defeated the promise of Nature; and how, in the other case, freedom had defeated Nature's menace. The lecture was long, serious, and close; but its vast ability, its evident candor, and its unimpassioned tone, kept the audience attentive to the end, and left them deeply impressed. A handsome substitute for the tar-barrel was a vote of thanks. Parker's earnestness disarmed the rancor of those who would listen to him. He spoke as a teacher, not as a partisan. His aim was truth, not victory.

His pulpit rang from Sunday to Sunday with the tones of a Hebrew prophet. He kept his eye on every public man, sounded his trumpet-call in the ears of the lagging, admonished the hesitating, warned the faltering, praised the valiant, instructed the ignorant, denounced the faithless, respecting no persons, but aiming his blows where his blows would fall heaviest. The history of those dozen years cannot be written in this volume: nor need it be; for it is written in books easily accessible; in none more truthfully or vividly than in those of Theodore Parker himself. We are studying now Parker's character, for the sake of its influence on other characters to be trained for other emergencies. Let us try to understand how he worked.

The following letter to George Bancroft shows him willing, if necessary, to break friendship, rather than be faithless to his own soul:—

WEST ROXBURY, Nov. 18, 1845.

DEAR SIR,—I was once in friendly intercourse with the historian of the United States; and the remembrance of that emboldens me to write the following letter to an important member of the cabinet council, which is the actual government of the United States. Once you wrote the history of other men's achievements; I need not say, a noble history of noble men and noble deeds: now you are to *enact* a history, not to write one; to create materials for the future historian. You can add new laurels to such as you have already won, acquiring the imperishable renown of noble words, and deeds as noble; or add another to the list of men whose deeds are words, and words only. I look to you for the noble deeds. I know that most of your political opponents do not expect that; I know that some of your political *friends* expect it no more: but I have obstinately said to both, that I expected the historian of great worth to show a worth fit to be as greatly described. But to come to the point. It is rumored about in this neighborhood, it is the talk in State Street, that you, with others in place, are desirous of a war with England,—a war, too, on account of that wretched business of Oregon.

Now, I cannot believe the talk of State Street to that effect; nor can I believe, spite of "The Union" and its editorials, that the two leading nations of the world are to plunge into a war out of which both are to rise *losers*. I will say with Cicero, *that there never was a just war or an unjust peace*. I write to beg of you—if the thought of war, or even *the thought of that thought*, enters into the councils of the government—to consider that posterity, which awards fame or disgrace to men, will damn into deep infamy that government which allows a war to take place in the middle of the nineteenth century. Yes, posterity will pass a damning sentence on the men who even tampered with the war-spirit so madly active in these half-brutal men who swarm in our parties. I say, too, that this vengeance will fall heaviest on *you*, and that deservedly. You know at what cost war is waged. I don't speak of treasure, not even of blood, but of the confusion it brings into the minds, and hearts too, of men. You know, from the bloody page of history, how war in the latter ages has arrested the progress of man. A war of but a single year between England and the United States, I seriously believe, would retard the progress of man full half a century. I know some men would win a reputation for a few months in the mouths of the vulgar; but I know, and you know, that such fame is real infamy, and will soon appear such even to those men that are the *food for powder*.

There is yet another matter on which I feel constrained to speak: that is the *admission of Texas as a slave State*. As a member of the cabinet, you must have an influence on this matter. As an *historian*, you know that slavery was the corruption of Greece and the undoing of Rome. As a *philosopher*, you know that slavery is supported only by the worst passions of man; that it is this day the *infamy* of the whole nation; that it is the curse of the very South, which clamors for it with such foolish speech; and is the real cause of all the ill feeling between the South and the North; yes, the drug of an evil prophet thrust into the mouth of that fair statue our fathers set up to the Genius of Freedom, — a drug which will rend their work into fragments and ruins. Now I ask if you, George Bancroft, the historian of freedom, are willing to aid in bringing into this republic that province which has restored slavery after poor Mexico had abolished it. You told me once you thought your lecture on Roman slavery was the best thing you ever wrote. I think few men place you higher as an author than I have done; but I confess that I know no passage of your writings that surpasses your thoughts on Roman slavery.

Now, with that before the eye, and fresh in remembrance, if you can allow the introduction of Texas as a slave State at all, still more with that infamous constitution it has adopted; if you can do that, — why, what is your lecture on Roman slavery, what your whole history of freedom, but a piece of brilliant declamation? I love noble words as well as you; but I love deeds worthy of noble words, — love them far better. I prize literary reputation; I don't mean that I aspire to it, only that I place a great author very high in the scale of man: but I would rather posterity should say of me, that, holding a place in the government of the United States, I opposed that government in its scheme of annexing a slave territory big as the kingdom of France, and, in consequence of that opposition, gave up my place in the cabinet sooner than be partner to a horrid wrong, — I say I would rather have posterity tell that of me than say I wrote the history of the United States better than mortal ever wrote before. You will say I am but a poor country minister, with no voice in the Commonwealth, and no knowledge of political affairs. All that is true: none know it better than I know it. But I do know what is *right by the everlasting law of God;* and I do know that the admission of Texas is wrong by these laws. I beg you in this matter not to consult with that mushroom popularity which is gained without merit, and lost without crime; but to act worthy of a *philosopher;* of a man enriched by the wisdom of the past, and full of the culture of a Christian's noble life. If you do so, future generations, ay, the present generation too, will crown your head with the noblest of honors, — the applause bestowed by good men on great and noble deeds. If you do it not, if you falsify your own bravest words, and allow the area of slavery to be extended, thus to be perpetuated, while you lift up no word of manly remonstrance, how can the world help regarding you as a mere declaimer, a poor sophist, who had the art to cheat the vulgar with fine words, and deceive the many lovers of freedom by brilliant pretensions, but was himself words and pretensions, nothing more? If you falsify your own writings, what can you say to me if I burn your books, and then say, "*He and his books are the same thing,* — FINE-SOUNDING WORDS, BUT AT LAST ASHES AND DUST"?

Act only as you have written, and your reputation is secure: a great deal more than that, — you will have done a man's deeds. Men will write on your tomb, "PAR OFFICIO ATQUE OFFICIUM MAXIMUM." That would be a nobler epitaph than this: "*Levis sit terra super terram levem;*" and this is the inscription which justice writes on many a tomb.

What shall I say at the end of such a letter as this? Why, this only, — that it is the strongest proof of friendship and esteem that I could show any man. If you are offended, I shall be sorry for it: not sorry that I have written; not sorry that I expected deeds commensurate with your words; sorry only that I do not find them. But I will trouble you no more, except to say I hope you will be as jealous of your own real honor as I have been; and to add, that, with many good hopes for your welfare and usefulness, I am

Most heartily your friend,

THEO. PARKER.

The dead earnestness comes out again thus: Parker had made a speech at a public meeting, which some of his best friends found fault with, on the ground, it would seem, that it was extreme in statement, and bordering on vulgarity in tone. Thus he replies: —

To Miss Stevenson.

WEST ROXBURY, Sept. 30, 1846.

MY DEAR HANNAH, — I wrote the within letter immediately on reading yours. Since then, two days have passed; and I have thought the matter over a little more carefully; have looked at it *impersonally* as a matter of history. It seems quite otherwise. I am glad it is done; sorry that some things I meant to say were omitted, — things that would have made no man *laugh*, but all men's blood curdle with horror to have heard, — things that would have rung like the blows of a battle-axe on a robber's doorposts. To have said just the words I then said, at that time, may do *me* no honor: I looked for none, want none. It may cover me with disgrace: I care not for that. I am glad I said it; glad I said it *just so.* I went there in a quite unusual mood. I was filled with indignation at the mean, base spirit (so it seemed to me) which led strong men to halt, to *say*, and not do. I felt that I could eat them up, and spit their pitiful ambition out of my mouth. I have little patience with a man who makes a negro's neck a stepping-stone to fame and power. I believe most men sincere. I never ten times in my life accused

33

anybody of hypocrisy. Then I felt there was something a good deal like it, not only in the Democrats and in old Whigs, but where I had not looked for it before. I felt like a Hebrew prophet towards all the doughfaces, new school as well as old. I am glad that I used *low words for scurrilous things;* glad I said the slaveholders who passed political anti-slavery resolutions were "jolly green." I wish I had said, that, though "hell was paved with resolutions," *the antislavery resolutions of political parties at the North were too thin, insincere, and hypocritical to be allowed a permanent lodgement even there.* I *meant* to say that. I wish I had said what I thought of the heart of the real good men of Massachusetts, and what of that for which the demagogues were striving. I wish I had taken up the Whig party, and the Democratic party too, and held up their words and their deeds in the light of God's law, making that blaze into men's minds, and be reflected upon their parties.

If a man called that "a rowdy speech," it was because he had the soul of a rowdy; and, if fifty men said so, it was because there were fifty so ensouled, so animated. I don't want to blame such critics. I must confess the fact, I have seldom risen so high as that night; never thundered and lightened into such an atmosphere. I did not think of such words: they *came;* and I thank God for it. I hope I may never have to speak so again. I know I shall not often; perhaps never. I know how *unusual* the strain was. If a man had told me I should speak so, I should have thought it impossible. But I did greater than I could counsel; far greater than I knew. My caprice, my personal taste, stood in the background; and my nature — the nature of mankind — and honest blood spoke in me, through me. I solemnly think *now* that I spoke more and better than ever before. *Good judges* will not tell you so; but if another man had done as I, and I stood there, feeling as then I felt, *I* would tell you so.

I like your letter much. The wounds of a friend I will bear thankfully, and keep forever the blessed scars thereof. Do so always. I don't want to wait for my foes to tell me my faults. You have an insight, a depth of vision, and a delicacy of soul, far greater than I ever met before, and can help me more than any other one. Don't treat me like a baby or a g-i-r-l, but like a man that loves you best when you beat him.

The letter is marked "Privatissime;" and most private it should have been and was kept long after it was written. But the awful illuminations of the war have made the most fiery words look pale; and we do not wonder now at speech which twenty-five years ago seemed excessive, but which history has proved to have been prophetic. The speech which Providence has justified needs neither excuse nor concealment.

Mr. Parker was fond of formulas, — short, pithy statements of principle, which could be easily remembered, and contained food for meditation long and close. In religion, he summed up his fundamental doctrine in the three points, — *consciousness of the infinite God, of the immortal life, of the eternal right.* These came over as faithfully in the Sunday sermons as the five points of Calvinism in a Presbyterian discourse. In politics, his compact definition of a democracy, as "*government of the people, by the people, for the people,*" recurred with similar constancy. So in the antislavery war he put the whole case in a terse form which neither could be missed nor misconceived: 1. Freedom may put down slavery by due course of law; 2. Slavery may put down freedom by due course of law; 3. Slavery and freedom may draw swords, and fight. These propositions appear in sermon, speech, lecture, letter, with tireless iteration. The speaker started from them, and came back to them continually; developing, illustrating, demonstrating; accumulating facts, arguments, and appeals upon them; using the latest events and the freshest incidents; but making these strong formulas stand up in full view all the time, so as to keep the grand issues steadfastly in mind. The stern repetition of the alternatives, accompanied as it was by keen criticism of men and measures, was an education in history and in ethics.

He had an instinct for men as for principles, and tested them with singular insight and success. He knew a proslavery man under the cunningest disguise, and detected the antislavery disposition with a quick eye, by reason of the moral sympathy which felt farther than it could see. His letters reveal these swift glances into the characters of prominent or ambitious men, who afterward, in almost every case, justified his prophecy; and he was ready either to fan or to tread out the spark, according as it promised to illumine, or threatened to consume. Let who would be faithless, he would be faithful. No man should falter for lack of his encouragement.

To Hon. John G. Palfrey, Washington, D.C.

BOSTON, Dec. 1, 1847.

DEAR SIR, — I took the liberty the other day to send you the first number of "The Massachusetts Quarterly Review," in which you will find a scholarly and able paper on the condition of Greece, from the pen of Mr. Finlay. I did not intend to bore you with a letter; but you force me to that yourself. I do not write for your sake, but my own, and to thank you most heartily for the honest, manly, and brave course you have pursued in regard to Mr. ——, unworthy son of most worthy sires. I hope you will excuse me for saying it to *you*, that I have looked with admiration and delight at your whole course of late years, especially at the manly position you have taken in respect of the matter of slavery. I know what conscience and what courage it demands to do as you have done; but perhaps you do not know what conscience and courage your example is ministering to younger men.

I see your vote censured in the newspapers. The censure shows what degree of freedom is expected of a politician in the Whig party as well as the Democratic. I should count such censure as the highest honor such men could confer. How could you vote for Mr. ——? with what expectation of justice to your country? While I read the censure in the newspapers, I hear the warmest praise of your vote from men whose esteem you would value most highly. I am glad it falls to the lot of a man constitutionally courageous to stand up in the bear-garden of American politics, and show that a man may be in politics, and yet not out of morals. I am only sorry that I do not live in Middlesex to lend you my vote when needed; though I have the satisfaction of having two brothers there who do so. I hope you will have abundant satisfaction for your conduct, which certainly is not less than heroic. And I remain

Yours respectfully and gratefully,

THEO. PARKER.

To the Same.

JUNE 14, 1848.

HONORED AND DEAR SIR, — I hate to trouble so busy a man as you are, but will not trouble you needlessly with apologies or a long letter. I intend, on the 25th of this month, to preach on the Mexican war; and wish to know how much money it has cost, and how many men have perished on the American side in its wickedness. Of course I know the official documents accompanying the President's message: but if you can send me any more information, either by a letter or a document, you will help me much; for I love to know *exactly the truth*. If the President has issued any proclamation of peace, I shall be glad of that, as, indeed, of a copy of the treaty and any thing connected with that. But I will only trouble you by saying with how much and how grateful admiration I look on you and your services, and how heartily I say, *God bless you!*

Respectfully and truly yours,

THEO. PARKER.

Already Mr. Parker's energy in the antislavery cause had made his name familiar in all parts of the country. It had even reached the State of Georgia, from which came long letters, first of rather scornful argument, and afterwards of senseless vituperation, from a Mr. Flournoy. To the first Mr. Parker replied in the following letter, which, though printed by Mr. Weiss in connection with Mr. Flournoy's letter, is reprinted here for the benefit of those who would not otherwise know how patient he was in dealing with even irrational people. The contents of the correspondent's communication may be gathered from Mr. Parker's reply: the vulgarity of its tone is best left to imagination.

To J. J. Flournoy, Esq., Wellington (near Athens), Ga.

BOSTON, Feb. 2, 1848.

SIR, — Your letter of January last has just come to hand; and I hasten to reply. I thank you for your frankness, and will reply as plainly and openly as you write to me. You need not suppose that I have any spite against the slaveholders. I wish them well, not less than their slaves. I think they are doing a great wrong to themselves, to their slaves, and to mankind. I think slaveholding is a wrong in itself, and therefore a sin; but I cannot say that this or that particular slaveholder is a sinner because he holds slaves. I know what sin is; God only who is a sinner. I hope I have not said any thing harsh in my letter, or any thing not true. I certainly wrote with no ill feeling towards any one.

You seem to think that the Old Testament and New Testament are just alike; that Christianity and Judaism are therefore the same: so, as a Christian, you appeal to the Old Testament for your authority to hold slaves. Now look a little at the matter, and see the difference between the Old Testament and the New Testament. The Old Testament DEMANDS circumcision, a peculiar priesthood, the sacrifice of certain animals, the observance of certain fast-days, full-moon days, new-moon days, the seventh day, and the like: it demands them all in the *name of the Lord.* Yet you do not observe any of them. Now, you say, I suppose, that the ritual laws of the Old Testament came from God, but were repealed by Christ, who also spoke by the command of God. If that were so, then it would appear that God had repealed his own commands. You say God could not change: so I say. I do not think God ever makes laws, and then changes them. But if the Bible as a whole, as you say, is the word of God, then it is plain, that, in the New Testament, he takes back what he commanded in the Old Testament. In the Old Testament a man is allowed to put away his wife for any cause, or none at all; but you know that Christ said Moses gave that command on account of the hardness of men's hearts. In Exod. xxxv. 2, 3, it is forbidden to kindle a fire on Saturday (sabbath), on pain of death. In Num. xv. 32, 36, it is said the Lord commanded a man to be *stoned to death* because he picked up sticks on Saturday. Yet I suppose you have a fire in your house Saturday, and Sunday too; and perhaps would not think it wicked to bring in an armful of wood to make a fire on either of those days. Now, I do not think God changes: therefore I don't believe he ever uttered those dreadful commands in the Old Testament. I believe that God has the attributes of universal justice and universal love. Doubtless you will call me an "infidel;" but that makes no odds. I try to be a Christian, but do not begin by discarding conscience, reason, and common sense. I think St. Paul was a Christian; and you know what he says about the law — that is, *the law of Moses* — in the Old Testament.

Now let us look at the case of the negroes. You think the children of Ham are under a perpetual curse, and that the negroes are the children of Ham. The tenth chapter of Genesis treats of the descendants of Ham; but it does not mention among them a single tribe of negroes. I don't think the writer of that account knew even of the existence of the peculiar race of men that we call negroes. He mentions the Egyptians, it is true, and other North-African people; but it is well known that they were not negroes. But even if some of the descendants of Ham were negroes, — though it is plain from Gen. x. they were not, — still that does not bring them under the curse of Noah; for Noah does not curse Ham and all his children, but only Canaan. Now, the descendants of Canaan are mentioned in Gen. x. 15–19. Not one of them was ever an African people: they all dwelt in the western part of Asia, and were the nations with whom the Hebrews were often at war. The Hebrews conquered many of these tribes, seized their country, and often their persons. Many of them fled, and, I think, settled in North Africa: the Berbers, and in part the Moors, are of that race, perhaps; but none of them are negroes.

But, even if the negroes were the children of Canaan, — as it is plain they were not, — what title could you make out to hold them by? It would be thus: Four thousand years ago, Noah cursed Canaan; and therefore you hold one of Canaan's children as a slave. Now, do you think a *man* has power to curse so far off as that? But you will say God gave the curse: well, the Bible does not say so. You say Canaan and his posterity were "constitutionally unworthy;" but you don't know that: on the contrary, the Sidonians, who were the descendants of Canaan, were a very illustrious people of antiquity, a good deal like the English and Americans at this day, and actually held great quantities of the Jews in slavery.

Before you can hold a single negro under that clause in Gen. ix. 25, you must make out, 1. That the negro is descended from Canaan ; 2. That the curse was actually uttered as related ; 3. That it denounces personal slavery for more than four thousand years ; 4. That the curse was authorized by God himself. Now, there is not one of these four propositions which ever has been made out, or ever can be.

My dear sir, I am really surprised that an intelligent man in the nineteeth century, a *Christian man*, a *republican of Georgia*, could seriously rely a moment on such an argument as that. Fie on such solemn trifling about matters so important as the life of two or three millions of men ! For my own part, I don't believe the story of Noah cursing his grandson for the father's fault. I think it all a Jewish story got up to justify the hatred which the Jews felt against the Canaanites.

I know Bryant's book and Faber's, but never use either now-a-days. Bryant had more fancy than philosophy, it always seemed to me. I may be as "confident" as you think me, but don't call myself a learned man ; though I have read about all the valuable works ever written on that matter of Noah's curse.

You ask me if I could not propose some good to be done to the slaves now. Certainly : their marriage and family-rights might be made secure, their work easier, their food and clothing better ; they might not be beaten ; pains might be taken to educate them. But all this is very little, so long as you keep the man from his natural liberty. You would not be happy if a slave ; would not think it RIGHT for a Christian man to hold you in bondage, even if one of your ancestors but fifty years ago had *cursed* you, still less if four thousand years ago. If I were a slaveholder, I would do this : I would say, "Come, now, you are free : go to work, and I will pay you what you can earn." I think in ten years' time you would be a richer man, and in two hours' time a far happier one, a more Christian one.

Dear sir, Christianity does not consist in believing stories in the Old Testament about Noah's curse, and all that, but in loving your brother as yourself, and God with your whole heart.

Do not think that I covet your slaves. No consideration would induce me to become a slaveholder. *I* should be a SINNER (though God grant that you are not one!) for that act. Let me ask you, *While you take from a man his liberty, his person, do you not violate this command,* "Thou shalt not covet any thing that is thy neighbor's"? *Do you not break the Golden Rule,* — "Whatsoever you would that men should do unto you, do ye even so unto them"?

I do not think you feel easy about this matter. What you say about colonization convinces me that you do not believe slavery is a Christian institution; that you are not very angry with me, after all. Do not think that I assume any airs of superiority over you because I am not a slaveholder. I have never had that temptation. Perhaps, if born in Georgia, I should not have seen the evil and the sin of slavery. I may be blind to a thousand evils and sins at home which I commit myself: if so, I will thank you to point them out. I hope you will write me again as frankly as before. I wish I could see Este's book. I will look for it, and study it; for I am working for the truth and the right. I have nothing to gain personally by the abolition of slavery; and have, by opposing that institution, got nothing but a bad name. I shall not count you my enemy, but am

Truly your friend,

THEO. PARKER.

J. J. FLOURNOY, Esq.

To John P. Hale.

BOSTON, Feb. 22, 1848.

DEAR SIR, — I hope you will pardon me for writing you this note. I would not trouble you with it if I did not feel obliged to bear my testimony to you. The slight acquaintance I had with you certainly would not justify me in writing this letter. But a spirit higher than conventional politeness compels me. Your recent vote in the Senate is so noble and heroic, that I cannot be silent. I must thank you for it: I do so in my own name. In the name of many who will not write the gratitude they feel, and in the name of mankind, I thank you. Certainly you have raised my opinion of the human race, when I see you vote in a minority of one. To stand alone in such a case is to stand nobly, left *alone* in the *glory*, but least alone when all alone. Such conduct is worthy of the best men, of the most heroic ages, of the best nations. It does not require much courage to stand up at Thermopylæ or Bunker Hill; not half so much as to stand up in the Senate of the United States, and say you went there to stand alone. Accept, dear sir, my most hearty thanks, and believe me

Respectfully yours, &c.,

THEO. PARKER.

Hon. JOHN P. HALE.

To Hon. Horace Mann.

BOSTON, Nov. 14, 1849.

MY DEAR SIR, — It is time to go to bed; but I cannot go to sleep without thanking you for the noble work you have done to-night. Of the magnificence and eloquence in thought and in speech I shall not stop to speak: they were the smaller beauties of your sermon. I must thank you for the magnificent morality you set before those young men. I think I can appreciate the heroism it required to do so, and speak as you have spoken, on such an occasion, in such a presence, where your words must seem personal to many; no, not to many, but to a few. I know well enough, and you know much more and better than I, how your oration will be received by the men who are looked upon as models, but whose business it exposed, and whose littleness it scathed with terrible fire. But there were many true hearts, in bosoms younger than mine, which beat with yours, and echoed back your words.

I have often been thankful that you are in Congress, — one faithful man, not a slave to the instinct for office more than a slave to the instinct for gold, but a representative of the instinct for justice and for truth. There is one that will long be grateful to you for such words as you have spoken to-night, and the life which made them, not words, but deeds. I beg you to accept my most hearty thanks, and believe me

Truly your friend,

THEO. PARKER.

At this stage of the conflict, Mr. Parker, so far from relaxing his literary efforts, increased them in a way to tax the strength of a strong and leisurely man. His lecturing engagements were making severe drain on his time. His visitors were augmenting in number and urgency. The reading of many books went on inexorably. In addition to this, he undertook the co-editorship, in connection with R. W. Emerson and J. E. Cabot, of "The Massachusetts Quarterly Review," which was designed as an organ for the manly discussion of the momentous questions in science, politics, philosophy, morals, and theology, that interested, or were about to interest, or were worthy of interesting, the American people. He hoped much from such a journal, and tried to induce the ablest men in the country to engage in it. He wanted "a tremendous journal, with ability in its arms, and piety in its heart;" a journal that "would, 1st, Strike a salutary terror into all the ultramontanists, and make them see that they did not live in the middle ages; that they are not to be let alone, dreaming of the garden of Eden, but are to buckle up and work; 2d, Would spread abroad the ideas which now wait to be organized, some in letters, some in art, some in institutions and practical life."

To secure a suitable editor was the prime concern. "We don't want a man of the middle ages, but of the nineteenth century, for our work. I have written a letter to Emerson, asking him to undertake the matter. If he will, it will succeed. He is the better man, if he will take hold. He is a downright *man:* we never had such a jewel in America before. I think him worth two or three of Dr. Channing." Fearing that Emerson would decline, as he did, he wrote to Charles Sumner: "It has been decided in the council of the gods that you must undertake the business of conducting a new review: therefore, O mortal! there is nothing for you to do but to set about the appointed work." But neither was Mr. Sumner obtainable; and practically the charge devolved on Mr. Parker.

The contributors were another anxiety. He must have the best young men of culture and energy, if possible; at all events, the most competent men. He solicits political articles from John P. Hale; and bespeaks a special paper from him, for the first number, on the Annexation of Texas, and the Mexican War. Work is planned out far in advance, as was his custom. The journal has a schedule of contents for three or four numbers after the first. The first was already issued, on the 1st of December, 1847.

No. II.

1. Cabot *vs.* Mill. — Hildreth on Slavery.
2. Ward on Art.
3. James on Swedenborg.
4. Female Education.
5. Howe on Prison Discipline. — Nichols on Ireland.
6. Wilkinson on Central New York.
7. Literary Notices.

No. III.

1. Schwegler. — T. P.
2. Exploring Expedition.
3. Hornitz on Chinese Literature.
4. Furness on Landor.
5. Cabot on Wheaton.
6. Papineau on Canada. — Desor on Squiers. — Cheap Postage. — Barnabas Bates. — Carlyle.

No. IV.

1. Baur on the Gospels. — T. P.
2. Lieber on Humboldt (I.).
3. Pantaleone on Pius IX.
4. Andrew on Thirtieth Congress.
5. Theodore Parker on Dr. Channing.
6. George Lee on the East (Howe will write to him). — Mesmerism.

No. V.

1. Theology in Germany. — T. P.
2. Lieber on Humboldt (II.).

But to propose is one thing: to dispose is another. The writers he had in view did not all meet his expectations. Others came up whom he had not thought of; but few. The labor of all kinds fell chiefly on himself. He did all that he promised, and a great deal more. In addition to the work laid out, he wrote a powerful article on "The Political Destination of America," biographical papers on John Quincy Adams, a careful estimate of Ralph Waldo Emerson's writings, and an exhaustive review of Mr. Prescott's histories, which stirred up the wrath in "select circles." None of his reviews were done on Sydney Smith's rule, — of writing before reading the book, in order to avoid prejudice; but this one was finished with more than even his usual care. Every thing bearing on the subjects treated of was read, — all the contemporary history, every accessible public document (in the original tongue) relating to the times under examination, military and naval statistics, financial reports. The article was not complimentary to Mr. Prescott as an historian. One wonders how the reviewer could have sent it to him with compliments: one wonders not that the historian should have responded by expressing a hope that the public would give the same reception to his criticism that it gave to his theology. In noticing the reviewer's conscientiousness towards his authors, it is worth while to notice the editor's conscientiousness towards his contributors, — not too common a virtue with his tribe.

West Roxbury, June 20, 1848.

Dear Friend, — I like your paper much, and will put it among the critical notices; only I have added a paragraph at the end. If you don't like that, you can strike it out; for I will send you a "proof." The matter lies in a nutshell. The social-compact men think a State can make any law it sees fit; meaning by the State *the people*, or, more commonly, the *bourgeoisie*. Here is their error. They forget that a State *has no right to enact wrong*. Their opponents think a government is divine. It may be the Devil's government: so long as it keeps its legs, it is my duty to obey it.

I suppose you never read Hobbes, nor Mr. Robert Filmer, nor Locke's "Treatise of Civil Government." If you should, you would see that Vinton writes in the interest of tyrants, and not of mankind. He thinks *you must depend on the government*, not it on you; that you must be ruled by an external authority, and he knows nothing higher or better: so he wants an authority in Church and in State. Now, I would as soon trust to the social-compact men as to St. Paul; for he says the powers that be are ordained of God. The power at that time was Nero. I doubt the correctness of your exegesis of the verse. I think you have not sufficiently attended to the historical fact, that Paul was writing to a set of fanatical men at Rome, who thought, that, inasmuch as their Messiah had come, they were set free from all obligation to keep any social laws which *he* had not imposed. I don't believe that Paul at this day would lay down such a general thesis as that; but he *did* lay it down, it seems to me; and surely that text has been a *scripture for despotism* ever since.

This is the sum of the matter. Rights and duties are anterior to all laws or institutions, and always superior to them. Rights and duties are directly from God; while laws are only mediately divine. I wish Vinton had said that; but I don't believe he could, and know he did not mean to in the sermon.

I shall like to exchange with you some time in October. Now my house is shut up in town, and I live here.

Yours heartily,

T. W. Higginson. T. P.

"The Quarterly" lived but three years: thanks to him that it lived so long. The public was not prepared for any thing so thorough or so advanced. Competent and willing contributors were too few; and the political urgency was pressing too hotly to allow the requisite leisure to the chief editor. The year 1850 — the year of the Fugitive-slave Bill — had come, and all superfluities must be dropped. The decks must be cleared for immediate action. Daniel Webster, the potentate of Whig public opinion in Massachusetts, delivered on the 7th of March the speech that forever sealed his doom, and devoted the spring and summer to prodigious efforts to persuade the men of New England to "overcome their prejudices" in favor of freedom. On the 18th of September the bill was passed, and sent to the President for approval. The acting President, Millard Fillmore, a tool in the hands of the slave power, signed it without hesitation, on the advice of Attorney-General Crittenden, a citizen of a slave State.

It was but a virulent revival of an old scheme. A fugitive-slave enactment had been passed in 1793; and under it, in 1842, George Latimer, a slave, was arrested in Boston. "The Latimer Journal," a revolutionary sheet, was published at this time by Dr. H. I. Bowditch, assisted by leading antislavery writers, Mr. Parker being one. What was probably his first antislavery article, in the form of an Eastern allegory, appeared in this journal. Dr. Bowditch, F. S. Cabot, and William E. Channing, as the Latimer Committee, obtained 64,526 names in Massachusetts to a petition for a personal-liberty bill, which was granted by the legislature. This was subsequent to Latimer's release, and intended as a guard against similar attempts at kidnapping. Some years prior to 1850, a Vigilance Committee was appointed at a meeting in Faneuil Hall, called on occasion of the kidnapping of a slave in Boston harbor. John Quincy Adams presided over the meeting. The leading antislavery men of the day were among the members of this committee, whose numbers were subsequently greatly enlarged. Mr. Parker was a member of the executive committee, and, it is said, initiated much of its action.

The new law struck dismay into the hearts of the blacks who had been living peacefully in the Middle and New-England States. The slave-hunters leaped over the border, and prowled about in Northern cities in search of prey. Ignorant, brutal, crafty, insolent, they snatched what they could reach, and laid snares for men and women as superior to them in all human qualities of intelligence, industry, fidelity, and courage, as *they* were superior to Bushmen. When, a few weeks ago, William Craft sat in my parlor, talking over his scheme for an industrial school in Georgia with the air of one accustomed to good society, speaking admirable English, and showing a complete acquaintance with all the conditions of his undertaking, it was hard to believe that he had been pursued as a runaway by a miserable creature who spelt "early" *eirly*, "wait" *wate*, "wife" *wif*, "know" *no*, and "engaged" *inguage*. But so it was. The government decreed the "Christians to the lions;" and the lions did after their kind. The agony and the terror were supreme. Free persons were not safe, even such as never had been slaves. A black man was a black man: his color was a badge of servitude, a *primâ-facie* evidence of chattelhood. If he could produce free papers, and get a commissioner to approve them, all was well; but the commissioner was usually a creature of the government, and too ready to construe appearances against the victim. The hunters' success was naturally greatest in the border States; greatest of any in Pennsylvania: but the best game was farther north; and thither the sleuthhounds sped. It is impossible to tell how many were carried off or seized altogether, — no small number, certainly: but for the vigilance of the antislavery people, it would have been very large.

The old Vigilance Committee was on the alert; and branch committees were formed, wherever there was danger, to warn the blacks, conceal them, expedite their escape if practicable, stand by them with legal aid if arrested, rescue them from the clutch of the pursuers by guile or force if other means failed.

A spy in the United-States marshal's office reported the probable issue of warrants; and rewards were paid for timely information of the official movements. The committee were prepared to resist the execution of the law to the very verge of civil outbreak, but not to go beyond. Their policy was to induce claimants and witnesses, by persuasions or threats, to leave the city; to expel the slave-hunters by all means short of deadly assault: and in the pursuit of this policy they had need of courage as well as discretion; for the infuriated blacks more than once plotted the assassination of their pursuers.

In Boston the panic was fearful; for Boston, as being the hot-bed of abolitionism, was the asylum of the fugitive. Decisive measures were taken for meeting the emergency. Meetings were called, lists of fugitives were made, names of citizens were enrolled, organizations were effected. A printed list of this Boston Committee of Vigilance is before me: it numbers one hundred and sixty-three names. They rose in a short time to two hundred and fifty. The first name on the executive committee was Theodore Parker. Associated with him were Wendell Phillips, S. G. Howe, Edmund Jackson, Charles M. Ellis, Charles K. Whipple. When a special committee was appointed to act in sudden emergencies, Theodore Parker was made its chairman. His whole soul, at this time, was on fire. He was ready for any and all work,— to draw up resolutions, to write placards, to counsel, or to act. Here is his account of the meeting in Faneuil Hall to express the popular feeling in regard to the bill. It is given in a letter to Miss Stevenson, dated the 14th of October.

"You will wish to hear about the meeting last night. It was a *very good one.* Phillips and Apthorp went down with me at half-past six. The galleries were crowded then. At seven there were three or four thousand in the hall. None of the respectability were there, or but few of them; none of 'our family.' C. F. Adams presided; read a neat little speech. Dr. Lowell opened the services with a touching prayer, which carried the hearts of the audience to heaven. It was not non-committal, not *respectable and pharisaic*. Douglas spoke, not very well, but only long. However, the moderation of his tone, the facts he related, and his wit, made it effective on a part of the audience. Then came a long letter from Old Quincy, not interesting except from its authorship. Then Wendell spoke, and never better. He was received with great applause, cheered continually, but once hissed a little when he said that Winthrop had voted right in '*a temporary spasm of liberty*.' He said nothing about disunion or of hostility to the Constitution. Then followed a Mr. Briggs of Ohio, — a tonguey fellow, who told some anecdotes, but made little sensation. He is a low stump-orator apparently; but said, wisely enough, that the audience would probably like best to hear Boston men, and sat down. Then I said a few words; told the people a few stories about the feeling and perils of the blacks now; and put several cases, asking them what they would do if the marshal tried to carry off a man adjudged to be a slave. They answered well, and promised to go with only the arms their mothers gave them, and rescue the slave. I asked them to thank Winthrop for his course in the Senate; and to give Mr. E——, not their hate, &c., but their PITY; which they did. Then Remond spoke; then Douglas again, saying that the directors of the Albany and Syracuse Railroad had forbidden their agents to take any slave on their road in the hands of the officers, but to put him and the officers out of the cars, and to do their best to set the slave free. Then we passed the resolutions, — pretty good ones too. Then Colver spoke, and interrupted the resolutions by adding, that, 'law or no law, Constitution or no Constitution, we will never let a fugitive slave be carried back from Boston.' That, also, was put; and then, at five minutes before eleven, just as Mr. —— was coming forward with a resolution on the *habeas corpus*, I suppose, all adjourned."

The above is but a tame account of a most extraordinary meeting. The packed hall was charged with feeling to which the speakers, all but Phillips and Parker, failed to give expression. Douglas's great ship labored heavily in the stormy sea. Lesser barks could not live in it a few moments, but quickly put back to harbor. The strongest sentiments were most tumultuously applauded. If the slaveholders had been there, they would at once have abandoned all idea of carrying out their purpose.

They were not there, and they ventured.

The excitement in Boston centred in four cases. The first touched Parker nearly. William and Ellen Craft were fugitive slaves of the higher order, from Macon, Ga. He was a joiner, and hired himself of his owner — "a very pious man," "an excellent Christian" — for about two hundred dollars a year. He and his wife had cherished for years the plan of escape. Having saved a little money, they bought, piece by piece, of different dealers, at different times, by stealth, a suit of gentleman's clothes. These Ellen put on. William attended her as her servant; and so they escaped. They lived in Boston, he working at his trade. Parker had known them ever since their coming. They were parishioners of his, respectable, orderly, estimable people. Returning home from Plymouth late in the afternoon of Oct. 25, Parker learned that the slave-hunters were on their track, — one, Hughes or Hews, the jailer at Macon; another, Knight, who knew Craft as a tradesman formerly, and accompanied Hughes as a witness. Their lodgings were at the United-States Hotel. The Vigilance Committee was on their watch. Craft was warned, and was not to be caught by his old friend's polite invitation to show him the sights of Boston, and visit him with his "wif" at the hotel. Ellen was secreted at a friendly house. William consented, unwillingly, to hide at the "South End," — to be smuggled there in a carriage; but presently, and having armed himself, preferred to go about his business, and take care of himself after his own fashion. He told a police-officer that he would rather be drawn and quartered than be carried back into slavery. The hunters had no easy task. Judge Woodbury, a Democrat, having issued warrants of arrest against Craft and his wife, they brought a suit against the kidnappers for defamation of character: they having charged him with being a *thief*, in that he stole the clothes he wore, as well as his own person, when he ran away. The writs were served, and the arrests were made amid no little confusion, the crowd gathering, and muttering ominous threats against the "slave-hunters." On the way to the sheriff's office, Knight declared with emphasis that he had come for William and Ellen Craft, and nobody else; "and, damn 'em! I'll have them if I stay here to all eternity; and, if there are not men enough in Massachusetts to take them, I will bring some from the South. It is not the niggers I care about; but *it's the principle of the thing*." The judge demanded bail in ten thousand dollars, that being the amount of damages laid. There were men in Boston to give it. Who they were is not known; but two persons who were known to be intense negro-haters — one a pettifogger, who had expressed a willingness to see all negroes hanged; the other a packet-agent, who, four years previous, when the United-States Government gave no such permission, had sent back a wretched fugitive who had concealed himself in the brig "Ottoman" from New Orleans, and was discovered almost famished when the voyage was about ended — were on hand, and the prisoners were released. Knight slipped out at the back-door, to the disappointment of the crowd, which had prepared for him an honest welcome. As Hughes entered the carriage which drove him away from the scene, a negro jumped up behind, dashed in the glass, and would have shot the wretch, had not one of the committee dragged him down. The carriage was chased a long distance, till it was out of town.

The Committee of Vigilance instantly held a meeting, and took new precautions. A poster was issued, describing the slave-hunters in graphic and thrilling language, such as was wont to proceed, on occasion, from the minister of the Twenty-eighth Congregational Society. The men were watched. Parker urged the appointment of a committee to attend them all day, keeping them in view from morning till night: he was ready to take his turn. The pastor does not neglect his parishioners. He goes to Brookline, to Mr. Ellis Gray Loring's, to cheer Ellen; to Louis Hayden's, to advise William. "I inspected his arms, — a good revolver with six caps on, a large pistol, twc small ones, a large dirk, and a short one: all was right." On the very day of the bond-giving, the committee met, and voted to visit *en masse*, at six o'clock the next morning, the United-States Hotel, where Knight and Hughes were staying. At the hour appointed, about sixty gentlemen were on the spot, filling the hall-ways, avowing their purpose to watch the kidnappers. Mr. Parker knew their room, and, taking with him a companion, ascended the stairs, stationed himself as a sentry at the door, and paced solemnly up and down; he and his comrade gravely passing one another in the corridor. This continued for some minutes; when the landlord, excited, came, and insisted that they should withdraw. Mr. Parker refused to leave his post without assurance of seeing the men he sought. The landlord promised them an interview in the parlor, and consented — readily enough, it is likely — to rid his house of such obnoxious guests. The interview was held; Mr. Parker speaking for the committee. He addressed them as their sincere friend, who came in the cause of peace, and to secure their safety from the populace. He had not stirred up the excitement. The indignation was spontaneous, natural, and deep, and could not be allayed while they remained in Boston. He represented to them the extreme personal danger in which they stood, the utter hopelessness of their undertaking; and counselled them, for their own sake, to leave town at once. Knight blustered, and Hughes complained; but both the men were a good deal frightened, and took the P.M. train for New York. It was time; for indignation was waxing hot. Their persons were known: they could not leave the hotel unmolested by street-boys, who bestowed on them unsavory names, and required no urging to bestow unsavory things. Had they staid longer, there might have been bloodshed; for the President, so it was rumored, talked of sending soldiers to dragoon the Bostonians into their duty.

The hunters being gone, the Crafts determined to go to England, and requested their minister to marry them by legal form before they went. A certificate was obtained according to the new law of Massachusetts; and, at eleven o'clock in the forenoon of Nov. 7, the ceremony was performed at a colored boarding-house in the city. Before the ceremony, the minister, as was his custom, addressed a few pertinent remarks to the couple, who now, for the first time, entered into the bands of Christian wedlock. He said to them first what he usually said to bridegrooms and brides. Then he spoke to Mr. Craft of his peculiar duties. He was an outlaw. No law protected his liberty in the United States: for that he must depend on the public opinion of Boston and on himself. If attacked by one wishing to return him to slavery, he had a right, a natural right, to resist the man unto death. For himself, he might refuse, if he saw fit, to exercise the right: but his wife depended on him for protection; and to protect her was a duty he could not decline. "So I charged him, if the worst came to the worst, to defend the life and liberty of his wife against any slaveholder, at all hazards." The marriage-rite was then performed. The occasion prompted the prayer. A Bible lay on one table; on another a "bowie-knife," placed there by some person unknown to Mr. Parker. He saw them when he came in, and, the ceremony being ended, took the book, placed it in the man's left hand, and charged him to use its noble truths for the salvation of his own soul and his wife's soul. This done, he took the knife, placed it in the man's right hand with words of equal pertinency, and charged him to use it only in the last extremity; to bear no harsh or revengeful feelings against those who once held him in bondage, or such as sought to make him and his wife slaves even now: "Nay, if you cannot use the sword in defence of your wife's liberty without hating the man you strike, then your action will not be without sin."

The fugitives left the country, bearing the following letter-missive from their pastor to his brother-minister in Liverpool, James Martineau: —

To Rev. Mr. Martineau.

BOSTON, Nov. 11, 1850.

DEAR FRIEND, — I take this opportunity to write you a brief note to interest you in a couple of my parishioners who are about to visit England under quite remarkable circumstances. They are two fugitive slaves, — William Craft and his wife Ellen Craft. Perhaps you have heard their story: if you have not, you will, before long, learn of their wonderful flight from Macon in Georgia to Philadelphia, — a distance of more than nine hundred miles through the enemy's country. The Fugitive-slave Law was passed last September. It is one of the most atrocious acts ever passed since the first persecution of the Christians by Nero. It allows the owner to come to Boston, or send his agent; apply to a commissioner of the United States, who may be a miserable tool of government, and probably will be (certainly he often is, and we have one loathsome commissioner in Boston, if no more); and decide that a certain man is his slave. The commissioner gives the slave-hunter a warrant to seize the slave, and transport him back to bondage. The slave-hunter takes it to the marshal; the marshal makes the seizure; and the poor victim is hurried off to slavery as hopeless as the grave. All this may be done without allowing the fugitive to defend himself; with no inquest by a jury; without the fugitive ever seeing his hunter till he comes with the marshal to put handcuffs on his wrists.

The Crafts have been in Boston nearly two years; are sober and industrious people. She is a seamstress: he is a cabinet-maker. They are members of my parish. But, a few weeks ago, there came a ruffian from Macon in Georgia, by the name of Hughes, — he is a *jailer* at home, — with authority to seize and carry off the two fugitives. He applied to the proper officer, got his warrant, and secured the services of the marshal. All was ready for the seizure; but William armed himself with two revolvers and a substantial dirk, and was ready to kill any one who should attempt to kidnap him. His wife was concealed by some friends, who kept her safe and sound. I will tell you more of her concealment at some future time; but it is not safe now.

The slave-hunters remained in Boston more than a week. There was a "vigilance committee" appointed by a meeting of citizens; and they kept the slave-hunters in a state of disturbance all the time they remained here, and finally frightened them so, that they were glad to sneak out of the city. After the danger was over, Craft's friends thought it was wiser for them to go to England, that you may see what sort of men and women we make slaves of in "the model republic." They need no *pecuniary* aid; but if you will tell their story to your friends, and draw public attention to the fact that such persons are not safe in Boston, you may help the great cause of humanity in a new mode. . . .

I keep in my study two trophies of the American Revolution: one is a musket which my grandfather fought with at the battle of Lexington (April 19, 1775) against the "British;" the other is a great gun which he captured in that battle. He was the captain of the Lexington soldiers, and took the first prisoner, and the first musket taken in war for independence and the rights of man. But now I am obliged to look to "the British" for protection for the liberty of two of my own parishioners who have committed no wrong against any one. Well, so it is; and I thank God that Old England, with all her sins and shames, allows no slave-hunter to set foot on her soil.

I have written you a long letter, when I intended to write only a short note. I am glad to learn from my friend Sargent what a pleasant time he had with you in North Wales and elsewhere. I wish I had been of the party. Remember me kindly to Mrs. Martineau and the children. I know not how many there are now; but there was a houseful of them once. Give my kindest regards to Mr. and Mrs. Thom. I wish you would show him this letter; for I think his great heart will be interested in the case of these poor fugitives. With many and affectionate regards, believe me

Truly your friend,

THEO. PARKER.

If any are disposed to think the scene of the wedding above described theatrical, the accompaniments stagey, and the speech bombastic, — the whole performance in needlessly bad taste, — let them read, in connection with the letter to Mr. Martineau, the following to President Millard Fillmore, written two weeks after the transaction in Boston. If they feel on reading it as others have done, they will understand how the act and the manner of its doing were in simplest accordance with an established state of mind; that no artificial sentiment, no touch of the mock-heroic, entered into it; that every word was an inevitable product of conviction. Only a man terribly in earnest could even meditate such a writing, as only a man terribly in earnest could have done such a deed.

To Millard Fillmore, Esq., Washington.

BOSTON, Nov. 21, 1850.

HONORED SIR, — This letter is one which requires only time to read: I cannot expect you to reply to it. I am myself a clergyman in this city, — not one of those, unfortunately, who are much respected; but, on the contrary, I have an ill name, and am one of the most odious men in this State: no man out of the political arena is so much hated in Massachusetts as myself. *I* think this hatred is chargeable only to certain opinions which I entertain relative to theology and to morals. Still I think I have never been accused of wanting reverence for God, or love for man; of disregard to truth and to justice. I say all this by way of preface; for I need not suppose you know any thing of me.

I have a large religious society in this town, composed of "all sorts and conditions of men," — fugitive slaves who do not legally own the nails on their fingers, and cannot read the Lord's Prayer; and also men and women of wealth and fine cultivation.

I wish to inform you of the difficulty in which we (the church and myself) are placed by the new Fugitive-slave Law. There are several fugitive slaves in the society. They have committed no wrong: they have the same "inalienable right to life, liberty, and the pursuit of happiness," that you have. They naturally look to me for advice in their affliction: they are strangers, and ask me to take them in; hungry, and beg me to feed them; thirsty, and would have me give them drink; they are naked, and look to me for clothing; sick, and wish me to visit them; yes, they are ready to perish, and ask their life at my hands. Even the letter of the most Jewish of the Gospels makes Christ say, "Inasmuch as ye have not done it unto one of the least of these, ye have not done it unto me." They come to me as to their Christian minister, and ask me to do to them only what Christianity evidently requires: they wish me to do to others as I would have others do to me.

But your law will punish me with fine of a thousand dollars, and imprisonment for six months, if I take in one of these strangers, feed and clothe these naked and hungry children of want; nay, if I visit them when they are sick, come unto them when they are in prison, or help them, "directly or indirectly," when they are ready to perish. Suppose I should refuse to do for them what Christianity demands: I will not say what I should think of myself, but what you would say. You would say I was a *scoundrel;* that I was really an infidel (my theological brethren *call* me so); that I deserved a jail for six years: you would say right. But, if I do as you must know that I ought, then your law strips me of my property, tears me from my wife, and shuts me in a jail. Perhaps I do not value the obligations of religion so much as my opponents of another faith; but I must say I would rather lie all my life in a jail, and starve there, than refuse to protect one of these parishioners of mine. Do not call me a fanatic; I am a cool and sober man: but *I must reverence the laws of God, come of that what will come. I must be true to my religion.*

I send you a little sermon of mine (see p. 36). You will find the story of a fugitive slave whom I have known. He is now in Quebec, in the service of one of the most eminent citizens of that city. He is a descendant of one of our Revolutionary generals. Members of my society aided him in his flight; others concealed him, and helped him to freedom. Can *you* think they did wrong? Can you think of the Declaration of Independence, of its self-evident truths, can you think of Christianity, and then blame these men? The Hungarians found much natural sympathy all over the United States, though some men in Boston took sides with Austria; the nation is ready to receive Kossuth: but what is Austrian tyranny to slavery in America? The Emperor of Turkey has the thanks of all the liberal governments of Europe for hiding the outcasts of Hungary; and can you blame these for starting "Joseph," and helping him to Canada? I know it is not possible.

William Craft and Ellen were parishioners of mine. They have been at my house. I married them a fortnight ago this day. After the ceremony, I put a Bible, and then a sword, into William's hands, and told him the use of each. When the slave-hunters were here, suppose I had helped the man to escape out of their hands; suppose I had taken the woman to my own house, and sheltered her there till the storm had passed by: should *you* think I did a thing worthy of fine and imprisonment? If I took all *peaceful* measures to thwart the kidnappers (legal kidnappers) of their prey, would that be a thing for punishment? You cannot think that I am to stand by and see my own church carried off to slavery, and do nothing to hinder such a wrong.

There hang beside me in my library, as I write, the gun my grandfather fought with at the battle of Lexington, — he was a captain on that occasion, — and also the musket he captured from a British soldier on that day, — the first taken in the war for independence. If I would not peril my property, my liberty, nay, my life, to keep my own parishioners out of slavery, then I would throw away these trophies, and should think I was the son of some coward, and not a brave man's child. There are many who think as I do about this; many that say it: most of the men I preach to are of this way of thinking. (Yet one of these bailed Hughes, the slave-hunter from Georgia, out of prison.) There is a minister who preaches to the richest church in Boston: he is a New-Hampshire man, and writes as *any* New-Hampshire politician. He has been impolitely called the "spaniel of King's Chapel," — an amiable, inoffensive man. But even he says he "would conceal a fugitive."

Not five of the eighty Protestant ministers of Boston would refuse. I only write to you to remind you of the difficulties in our way. If need is, we will suffer any penalties you may put upon us; but WE MUST KEEP THE LAW OF GOD. I beg you to excuse this letter; and, with many good wishes for your prosperity, believe me

Your obedient servant,

THEODORE PARKER.

The Committee of Vigilance was not allowed to slumber. The slave-hunters were still abroad. In less than three months, the excitement was renewed by another case of arrest. The fugitive Shadrach was seized, and shut up in the United-States court-room, on Feb. 15, 1851. The next day (Sunday) the prayers of all the ministers and congregations were requested for his deliverance. They were answered before they were put up. Mr. Parker went to Court Square immediately on hearing of the arrest, "intending to make a rescue if possible;" but the rescue had already been effected. The commissioner had adjourned the case; the crowd had left the court-room; the building was closed; the guarded prisoner remained inside. An importunate member of the Vigilance Committee beat upon the door till it was opened to him; the crowd pushed in; and in a moment, before the bewildered officers could recover themselves, the man was lifted up in the arms of his friends, and borne away. There was no noise or excitement: but the rush of the rescuers was too tremendous to be resisted by any but military force; and that would have been dangerous, for preparations for armed resistance had been made. An attempt at rescue would have been hopeless, even had there been time; but there was no time. That very afternoon the man was hurried off on his way to Canada, and saved. Mr. Parker wrote in his diary, "I think it the most noble deed done in Boston since the destruction of the tea in 1773. I thank God for it."

On the Sunday, in addition to preaching in the morning, lecturing in the afternoon on 1 Cor. iv.–vii., making visits, writing notes for a meeting of the Executive (Vigilance) Committee, and attending the meeting, he wrote a poster describing the slaveholders then in the city. It could not have been the following, doubtless from the same hand, but bearing date the 4th of April; but this will serve as a specimen of the bills that were put up in those fearful times: —

PROCLAMATION.

TO ALL THE GOOD PEOPLE OF MASSACHUSETTS.

Be it known that there are now THREE SLAVE-HUNTERS, OR KIDNAPPERS, IN BOSTON, looking for their prey. One of them is called

DAVIS.

He is an unusually ill-looking fellow, about five feet eight inches high, wide-shouldered. He has a big mouth, black hair, and a good deal of dirty, bushy hair on the lower part of his face. He has a Roman nose. One of his eyes has been knocked out. He looks like a pirate, and knows how to be a stealer of men.

The next is called

EDWARD BARRETT.

He is about five feet six inches high, thin and lank; is apparently about thirty years old. His nose turns up a little. He has a long mouth, long, thin ears, and dark eyes. His hair is dark; and he has a bunch of fur on his chin. He had on a blue frock with a velvet collar, mixed pants, and a figured vest. He wears his shirt-collar turned down, and has a black string — not of hemp — about his neck.

The third ruffian is named

ROBERT M. BACON, *alias* JOHN D. BACON.

He is about fifty years old; five feet and a half high. He has a red, intemperate-looking face, and a retreating forehead.

His hair is dark, and a little gray. He wears a black coat, mixed pants, and a purplish vest. He looks sleepy, and yet malicious.

Given at Boston this fourth day of April, in the year of our Lord 1851, and of the independence of the United States the fifty-fourth.

God save the Commonwealth of Massachusetts!

This resolution was not untouched with sadness. His friends the Shaws sail for Europe. He doubts if he ever sees them again. "For I must not let a fugitive slave be taken from Boston, cost what it may justly cost. I will not (so I think now) use weapons to rescue a man with; but I will go unarmed when there is a reasonable chance of success, and make the rescue."

From the Journal.

Feb. 21, 1851.—Continual alarms about the poor fugitive slaves. A reported arrest of a new one; but this turned out to be a false alarm.

1. The case of ——, who concealed —— in his cellar all night.

2. Also the ——, who came and gave information of an attempt about to be made on ——; and he escaped.

3. The confession which —— made to —— about the intentions of the —— and the provisions he made.

4. The strategy of Mr. —— in getting information, and how he does it.

These are sad times to live in; but I shall be sorry not to have lived in them. It will seem a little strange, one or two hundred years hence, that a plain, humble scholar of Boston was continually interrupted in his studies, and could not write his book, for stopping to look after fugitive slaves,—his own *parishioners!*

Saturday, 22d.—Washington's birthday. At home, and very busy with fugitive-slave matters.

Sunday, 23d.—Sermon 618, A.M. Roxbury, P.M. I have not been well these several days.

Monday, 24th.—At Cambridge most of the day: not we' Writing report on fugitive-slave petitions at night.

Tuesday, 25th.—At home, and about antislavery business. P.M. at State House with antislavery committee. Phillips, Sewall, and Ellis spoke. Vigilance Committee at night.

Wednesday, 26th.—Much time on fugitive-slave matters.

The third great slave case, that of Thomas Sims, terminated less happily than Shadrach's, and caused more excitement afterwards than it did when in progress. Sims was arrested on the night of April 3. He drew a knife on the officers, and was arrested as a disturber of the peace; though the arrest caused the disturbance. The writ of *habeas corpus* was refused him. He never saw a jury; but once a judge. The commissioner, George Ticknor Curtis, after a summary examination, gave him up to his pursuers. The poor boy, knowing that his fate was sealed, begged of his counsel one favor: "Give me a knife; and, when the commissioner declares me a slave, I will stab myself to the heart, and die before his eyes. I will not be a slave!" Such a prayer could not be granted. At the dead of night, the mayor of Boston, with his marshal, attended by two or three hundred policemen, armed with horse-pistols, swords, or bludgeons, at convenience, took the victim from his cell, chained, weeping; marched him over the spot which the blood of Attucks had stained; put him on board "The Acorn;" and sent him off to endless bondage. "And this," said the miserable negro as he stepped on board, "is Massachusetts liberty!" A Boston delegation saw him duly delivered to his owner, who had him whipped in the town jail within an inch of his life. This was on the historic 19th of April.

Parker bore his testimony in a sermon which Charles Sumner thanked him for, saying that it stirred him to the bottom of his heart; at times softening him almost to tears; then, again, filling him with rage. "You have placed the commissioner in an immortal pillory, to receive the hootings and rotten eggs of the advancing generations."

To Hon. Charles Sumner.

BOSTON, April 19, 1851.

DEAR SUMNER, — I wish it was the 19th of April, 1775, on which I was writing: the times would not look so bad for Boston. What a disgrace has the city brought on herself! "O Boston, Boston, thou that kidnappest men!" might one say now.

I never had any confidence in the Supreme Court of Massachusetts in case the Fugitive-slave Law came before it. But think of old stiff-necked Lemuel visibly going under the chains! * That was a spectacle! But it all works well. Thank you for your kind words and kind judgments of

Truly your friend, T. P.

The event that could not be prevented had to be commemorated. To the feeling it excited Charles Sumner was in part indebted for his senatorial election.

In May, Mr. Parker had the curiosity to attend the Berry-street Conference, — a meeting at which Unitarian ministers were wont to commune together on matters that affected their theological peace. On this occasion Rev. Samuel J. May of Syracuse ventured to obtrude the vexed question of duty in regard to the Fugitive-slave Law. It had been brought up at the business-meeting of the Unitarian Association, and was refused a hearing. On Wednesday it was brought up again at the Ministerial Conference, and after a good deal of discussion, and not a little diplomacy, was made the subject of special consideration for the next day. Even on Thursday morning, time was wasted in idle preliminaries, as if with the purpose of preventing action. The social position of the city ministers made them unsympathetic with the brethren from the country, who looked at the matter with a more single eye, and were

* Chief Justice Lemuel Shaw, who could only enter his court-room by stooping under the chain which was stretched round the building to keep off the people.

sincerely anxious to hear what the great authorities of the sect had to say. The discussion began at length, in the usual indirect and inconsequential manner, by a brother from New York, who defended Dr. Orville Dewey against the charge of having said publicly that he would send his own mother back to slavery if it was necessary to preserve the Union: questioning, in the first place, the accuracy of the report; in the next place, protesting against the imputation of "worldly motives" on the doctor's part. Next a leading minister of Boston criticised severely the sentiment of one of the body, — that the Fugitive-slave Law "could not be administered with a pure heart or unsullied conscience," contending that it could; and then made two points justifying obedience to the law: 1. That to disobey would involve disobedience to all law. We must either have law without liberty, or liberty without law. Law without liberty was despotism: liberty without law was license. Despotism was bad; but anarchy was worse. 2. Disobedience to the Fugitive-slave Law involved dissolution of the Union; and with the Union went all hope of freedom and human rights.

Mr. Parker spoke amid a silence of suppressed discontent. He regretted that years ago there had not prevailed more of this brotherly spirit which refused to judge men for their "opinions." In regard to the main question, the consequence of obedience or disobedience to the Fugitive-slave Law, he affirmed that in no country on earth was there more respect for law than in New England. Disobedience is unpopular even when the law is. Nowhere were judges more respected than in Massachusetts. So true was all this, that to inform against one's neighbor, if he violated the law of the land, — an act infamous everywhere else, — was commended, for the reason that the people made the laws for themselves, were represented by them, and educated by them. The value of human laws is to conserve the eternal laws of God. So long as laws did this, they should be obeyed. The Fugitive-slave Law did the opposite. It aspired to trample on the law of God. It commanded what nature, religion, and God alike forbade: it forbade what nature, religion, and God alike commanded. Who are they that oppose the Fugitive-slave Law? Men who have always been on the side of law and order, and whose disobedience is one of the strongest guaranties of just law and equitable order. You cannot trust a people that will keep law *because it is law:* you cannot distrust a people that will keep no law but what is just. Obedience to the Fugitive-slave Law would do more to overturn the Union than all disobedience to it the most complete.

As to the dissolution of the Union, if any State wished to go, she had a natural right to go. But what States wished to go? Certainly not New England. Massachusetts had always been attached to the Union; had adhered to it faithfully; had made sacrifices for it. The cry of dissolution was vain and deceitful: none knew that so well as the men who raised it. But suppose that dissolution were the alternative of disobedience: which would be the worse? Is the Union as precious as conscience, freedom, duty? "For my own part, I would rather see my own house burned to the ground, and my family thrown, one by one, amid the blazing rafters of my own roof, and myself be thrown in last of all, than have a single fugitive slave sent back as Thomas Sims was sent back: nay, I would rather see this Union dissolved till there was not a territory so big as the county of Suffolk. Let us lose every thing but fidelity to God. . . . I am not going to speak honeyed words, or prophesy smooth things, in times like these, — our court-house a barracoon, our officers slave-hunters, members of our Unitarian churches kidnappers! I have in my church black men, fugitive slaves: they are the crown of my apostleship, the seal of my ministry. It becomes me to look after their bodies, to save their souls. I have been obliged to take my own parishioners into my house to keep them out of the clutches of the kidnappers: yes, gentlemen, I have been obliged to do that, and to keep my doors guarded by day as well as by night. I have had to arm myself. I have written my sermons with a pistol in my desk, loaded, with a cap on the nipple, ready for action; yes, with a drawn sword within reach of my right hand, — this in Boston, in the middle of the nineteenth century! I am no non-resistant: that nonsense never went down with me. But it is no small matter that would compel me to shed human blood. Still, that could I do. I was born in the little town where the fight and bloodshed of the Revolution began. The bones of the men who first fell in that war are covered by the monument at Lexington. It is 'SACRED TO LIBERTY AND THE RIGHTS OF MANKIND.' This is the first inscription I ever read. These men were my kindred. My grandfather slew the first man in the Revolution. The blood which flowed then is kindred to that which runs in my veins to-day. Besides that, when I write in my library at home, on one side of me is the Bible which my fathers prayed over, their morning and their evening prayer, for nearly one hundred years: on the other side hangs the firelock my grandfather fought with in the old French war, which he carried at the taking of Quebec, which he used at the battle of Lexington; and beside it is another, a trophy of that war, — the first gun taken in the Revolution; taken by my grandfather. With these trophies before me, these memories in me, when a fugitive from slavery came to my house, pursued by the kidnappers, what could I do less than take him in, and defend him to the last? My brother justifies the Fugitive-slave Law; demands obedience to it; calls on his parishioners to kidnap mine, and sell them into bondage forever. He is a 'Christian,' and I am an 'infidel.'

"O my brothers! I am not afraid of men: I can offend

them. I care nothing for their hate or their esteem; I am not very careful of my reputation: but I dare not violate the eternal law of God. You have called me 'infidel.' Surely I differ widely enough from you in my theology. But there is one thing I cannot fail to trust: that is the Infinite God, father of the white man, and father, also, of the white man's slave. I should not dare violate his law, come what would come."

For two months the journal is suspended. He opens it again with the hope, that, for the next five or six years, he may have less to do with social, civil, and political duties, and attend to his function as scholar, philosopher, theologian, and writer. But the fates forbade. He went in his vacation to hear J. F. Clarke preach; but was called out, the sermon just begun, on antislavery business. The Fugitive-slave Law was in force; though the attempts to enforce it were not, for the moment, active. The passage of the Kansas-Nebraska Bill revived them; and the friends of that relaxed no effort to have it executed. Daniel Webster, who had declared resistance to, and even denunciation of, the Fugitive-slave Law, to be "high treason," died at Marshfield in October, 1852; and Parker — who had glorified him from his childhood up to the fatal 7th of March, when the mighty man turned his back on the fine traditions of his younger days, and had then taken his likeness from the place of honor where it stood, kissed it sadly, and put it away where it could not be seen — made the grandest of his pulpit orations on the false statesman's character. They who would know Mr. Parker should read that oration. It was, as has been said, written literally with prayers and tears, in clearest memory of every step in Webster's career; with judgment clarified by comparison of him with the greatest orators of the race, and confirmed by an exact estimate of his deeds and opportunities; with conscience quieted by the contemplation of nature, and exalted by meditation on the eternal law;

and with soul touched by the sorrows and needs of humanity. There is an awful pathos in some of its sentences.

"Mr. Webster stamped his foot, and broke through into the great hollow of practical atheism which undergulfs the State and Church. The firm-set base of Northern cities quaked and yawned with gaping rents. Penn's 'sandy foundation' shook again; and black men fled from the city of brotherly love, as doves, with plaintive cry, flee from a farmer's barn when summer lightning stabs the roof. There was a twist in Faneuil Hall; and the doors could not open wide enough for Liberty to regain her ancient cradle. Only soldiers, greedy to steal a man, themselves stole out and in. Metropolitan churches toppled and pitched, and canted and cracked. Colleges, broken from the chain which held them in the stream of time, rushed towards the abysmal rent. Doctors of divinity, orthodox, heterodox, had great alacrity in sinking. 'There is no higher law of God,' quoth they as they went down; 'no golden rule; only the statutes of men.'

"But spite of all this, in every city, in every town, in every college, and in each capsizing church, there were found faithful men who feared not the monster, heeded not the stamping. In all their houses there was light; and the destroying angel shook them not. The Word of the Lord came in open vision to their eye: they had their lamps trimmed and burning, their loins girt; they stood road-ready. Liberty and religion turned in thither; and the slave found bread and wings. . . .

"The streets are hung with black; the newspapers are sad-colored; the shops are put in mourning; the public business stops; and flags drop half-mast down. The courts adjourn,— even at Baltimore and Washington the courts adjourn; for the great lawyer is dead, and justice must wait another day. Only the United-States Court in Boston, trying a man for helping Shadrach out of the furnace of the kidnappers, — the court which executes the Fugitive-slave Bill, — that does not adjourn; that keeps on: its worm dies not; and the fire of its persecution is not quenched when death puts out the lamp of life."

On the 23d of May, 1854, Charles F. Suttle of Virginia presented to Edward Greely Loring of Boston, commissioner, a complaint under the Fugitive-slave Bill, praying for the seizure and enslavement of Anthony Burns. The warrant was issued the next day. In the evening, Burns was arrested on the false pretext of burglary, taken to the Suffolk-county Court House, and there kept under an armed guard. On the 25th the case came before the commissioner. Burns was brought in guarded and ironed. The claimant presented his documents: his witnesses were on the spot, ready to testify; his legal counsel, S. J. Thomas and E. G. Parker, were ready with their statement. The commissioner had made up his mind, and the case seemed in a good train to be "summarily" disposed of; when Theodore Parker, with a few stanch friends, made his way into the court-room, gained speech with the prisoner, ascertained that it was his wish to be heard, and demanded the right of counsel. Thereupon Richard H. Dana, Esq., asked that counsel be assigned, and a defence allowed; urging the point so strongly, that the commissioner was forced to yield. The hearing was postponed till ten o'clock of May 27. On the evening of the 26th — the mayor and aldermen cheerfully consenting, the mayor even regretting that a previous engagement made it impossible for him to preside — a great meeting was held at Faneuil Hall. Samuel G. Howe called it to order; George R. Russell presided; Mr. Parker, Wendell Phillips, and others made speeches.

The meeting had a general and a special object. The general object was to excite popular indignation; the special object, to aid in a concerted attempt to rescue Burns by an overwhelming and sudden attack on the Court House. The plan of such an attack had been discussed in committee, and had been voted down by the majority, who thought it desperate. Nevertheless, the committee allowed the friends of the project to meet in one of their rooms for the completion of their plans. Mr. Parker favored the assault: Mr. Phillips, it is thought, did not.

The suppressed excitement at the meeting was intense; and nothing occurred to allay it. The resolutions read by Dr. Howe, the speech of John L. Swift, were in the interest of the conspirators. Wendell Phillips threw no water on the kindling flame. Mr. Parker took the stand, purposing to heat the audience red-hot, fuse them together, and, at a given signal, to hurl them into Court Square. He was a powerful platform-speaker, responsive at once and magnetic; and, on this occasion, he rose to a height he never surpassed: his frame quivered with the action of his mind; his voice, in passages, was like the roar of a lion at bay.

"FELLOW-SUBJECTS OF VIRGINIA," he began; "FELLOW-CITIZENS OF BOSTON, then, — A deed which Virginia commands has been done in the city of John Hancock and the 'brace of Adamses.' It was done by a Boston hand. It was a Boston man who issued the warrant; it was a Boston marshal who put it in execution; they are Boston men who are seeking to kidnap a citizen of Massachusetts, and send him into slavery for ever and ever. It is our fault that it is so. We are the vassals of Virginia: she reaches her arm over the graves of our mothers, and kidnaps men in the city of the Puritans. Gentlemen, there is no Boston to-day. There *was* a Boston once: now there is a North suburb to the city of Alexandria. Gentlemen, there is one law, — slave law: it is everywhere. There is another law which is also a finality; and that law — it is in your hands and your arms, and you can put it in execution just when you see fit.

"I am a clergyman and a man of peace. I love peace. But there is a means, and there is an end. LIBERTY is the end; and sometimes peace is not the means toward it. There are ways of managing this matter without shooting anybody. Be sure that these men who have kidnapped a man in Boston are cowards, every mother's son of them; and if we stand up there resolutely, and declare that this man shall not go out of the city of Boston, *without shooting a gun*, then he won't go back. Now I am going to propose, that, when you adjourn, it be to meet at *Court Square to-morrow morning at nine o'clock*. As many as are in favor of that motion will raise their hands." (Many hands were raised: but there came from many voices a cry, "Let's go to-night;" "Let's pay a visit to the slave-catchers at the Revere House;" and a demand was made for *that* question. It was put.) "Do you propose to go to the Revere House to-night? then show your hands. It is not a vote. We shall meet *at Court Square at nine o'clock to-morrow morning*." The conclusion was lame, impotent, and unaccountable. Parker explained it afterwards to a friend by saying that he waited for the signal, and it was not given. For half an hour he had talked against time, had repeated himself, lingered, and finally taken his seat in sheer perplexity.

By some mistake, it would seem, some inadvertency, some delay, the signal was not given at the moment agreed on. Mr. Phillips rose again (this is William F. Channing's account), never cordially assenting to the plan of assault, and now persuaded that a miscarriage had prevented it entirely, and addressed himself to the task of allaying the passion of the confused and frenzied people. Of course, he succeeded: when did he ever fail in a rhetorical effort? The meeting became calm, — fatally so for its original purpose; and at that moment the signal was given at the door by the announcement that an attack was even then making at the Court House. It was too late. The meeting broke up; the multitude streamed forth; but, before the most advanced could reach Court Street, the struggle had begun. Those in the rear of the hall and on the platform could hardly have made their way to the door by the time it had ceased.

The attacking-party did their work promptly and with determination. Mr. Channing, an antislavery man from the beginning, member of the Vigilance Committee, arrived on the spot in time to see the beam which answered as a battering-ram brought from the staircase of the Museum building opposite, and carried across the street, by a dozen men. The heavy folding-doors yielded to the force of the blows; the sound reverberating through the streets, loud enough to be heard a mile off. The bell of the Court House rang an alarm for the police. But two or three minutes were needed to break the door down. It gave way; and the little band of assailants, rushing up the steps, were in conflict with the marshal and his men. A few pistol-shots were fired, a deputy marshal was killed, — though by whom, or by which side, was never ascertained, — and the assailants fell back. They were unsupported, had no reserves, and were not organized for a work of magnitude. The marshal's men fell back also within the building, apparently as much frightened as anybody, and stood on the stairway leading up to the floor where Burns was confined, impotently flourishing their cutlasses in space. The doorway was regarded by both sides as a gate of death. The battered door alone occupied the empty space. At this moment Mr. A. Bronson Alcott walked deliberately up the steps, stood there a moment with habitual serenity, quietly descended, and remarked to a friend, — his voice preserving its even tone, and pausing, as its wont was, between the words, — "Do you not think we are wanted *there?*" The invitation was not accepted; for the police were on the ground. Higginson was badly bruised by clubs, his forehead laid open by a cutlass; others were beaten or arrested; the rest scattered. The whole affair lasted scarcely five minutes. The opportunity was lost. That very night a force of marines was marched over from the Charlestown Navy Yard. In the morning a detachment of troops arrived from Fort Independence. No further demonstration against the authorities was made. The mayor of Boston applied for the aid of the State militia to preserve the order of the town. The militia held the streets, while United-States soldiers held the Court House. The city had the aspect of being under martial law.

Mr. Parker's distress at the result of the night's work was extreme. On hearing that a black man had fired at Marshal Freeman, and narrowly missed him, he wrung his hands, and cried, "Why didn't he hit him? why didn't he hit him?" Sympathy with the fugitives was not confined to the abolitionists. Judges themselves counselled the removal of negroes when practicable. Even official souls were sorely exercised. More than one Massachusetts commissioner, probably, would have done what the wife of George S. Hillard did in the time of the Craft excitement, — shelter the victim of persecution beneath her own roof, — had he possessed that noble woman's courage. The heart of Boston was sounder than its head. The President, Franklin Pierce, showed eager interest in the proceedings, as frequent despatches from Washington testified. By his direction, the adjutant-general of the army repaired to Boston, authorized to call the two companies of United-States troops stationed at New York, if the State force should prove inadequate. Meanwhile the case proceeded against the prisoner, in spite of the ability and zeal with which Messrs. Dana and Ellis managed the defence. At any other time, under any other circumstances, the Virginia claimant would have been baffled; for he failed wholly to make his points. As it was, hopes were entertained of a decision favorable to the prisoner. Offers to buy the man were made: the commissioner himself drew the sale papers. But Suttle, after temporizing and vacillating, braced, probably, by encouraging hints from those high in authority, intimidated, perhaps, by threats from his Southern neighbors, that, if he compromised, it would be the worse for him, refused to close the bargain. The decision was predestinated by the powers that ruled.

As the gloomy days went on, the black man's friends did their utmost to rescue him from bondage, and the North from shame. The vigorous hand which was ready for any work produced placard after placard to rouse the citizens. Seven are preserved, the most pungent of them bearing the Parker mark. The first simply announces, in short, sharp words, the arrest. The second calls on the citizens of Boston to see to it that no free citizen is dragged into slavery without trial by jury. A third summons the "yeomanry of New England" to come and lend the moral weight of their presence, and the aid of their counsel, to the friends of justice and humanity in the city. A fourth brands the insult of employing murderers, prize-fighters, thieves, and blacklegs to aid in executing the atrocious law. A fifth warns the citizens to be on their guard against an attempt to carry off Burns after the commissioner had declared him free. A sixth admonishes to be on the alert against lies and deceit; a story being afloat that Burns had been ransomed. The last, issued May 31, calls on true Americans to be prepared for the worst: "Let there be no armed resistance; but let the whole people turn out and line the streets, and look upon the shame and disgrace of Boston, and then go away and take measures to elect men to office who will better guard the honor of the state and the capital."

No device was neglected that might help defeat the Burns claimant. Steps were taken to have him arrested, and held to bail, as Knight and Hughes had been, for kidnapping. There were blacks desperate enough to lie in wait for Suttle's appearance at the Court House to answer the charge, purposing his assassination; but the scheme came to nothing. It was too late for expedients. Subsequently to the rendition, a portion of the Vigilance Committee organized, armed, and drilled regularly for resistance to the law. A yacht large enough for sea-service was also purchased and equipped. The captain who was put in charge of it said, that, if he had had the vessel in the time of the Sims case, he would have sunk "The Acorn" before she reached her Southern port. Fortunately these preparations were not needed. The Burns case was too costly and too perilous not to be the last; but that case had to be pushed through to the end. All had been done that could be done at that crisis.

The commissioner handed the man over to his claimant; and on Friday, June 2, crowds of indignant people, thronging the sidewalks, filling porticoes and balconies, peering from windows, gazing from roofs, saw the helpless negro in the centre of a hollow square of armed ruffians — themselves guarded by companies of militia, protected by cannon — marched through Court Street and State Street to the wharf. To the least reflecting the scene was impressive. To those who recalled the traditions of the city, the history of that very street; who saw law and liberty writhing beneath the tread of the soldiers, and the soul of civilization itself gasping under the feet of the foes of all society; who knew what it all portended if it went on, and feared the worst, — the scene was as awful as imagination could make it. The Vigilance Committee ordered the streets in the neighborbood of the route of the procession to be draped in black, and the bells of the city to be tolled. This the mayor tried to prevent: when requested to allow it, he refused with vehement stamp of foot. But the committee detailed men for the service, and it was pretty generally done. One of them obtained the key of Brattle-street Church; let in and locked in a friend: so that bell was made to sound a dirge. As a last means of creating confusion, and effecting a rescue, the new fire-alarm was struck just as the procession was about to move. The engines tore down State Street through the lines of soldiers and the crowds of citizens. It is a wonder that people were not killed in the tumult; that blood was not spilled in the fury: but the sudden irruption passed; the lines closed up; and the iron phalanx was unbroken. They who witnessed the scene of removal will never forget it. How one great soul felt, thousands learned at Music Hall on the next Sunday, when "The New Crime against Humanity" was described in words that woke the echoes of history, and sent ominous thunder rolling through the galleries of time.

The tragedy over, the farce began. On June 7, Judge B. R. Curtis charged the grand jury, in substance, as follows: That not only those who were present and actually obstructed, resisted, and opposed, and all who were present leagued in the common design, but all who, though absent, did procure, counsel, command, or abet others, and all who, by indirect means, by evincing an express liking, gave approbation or assent to the design, were liable as principals; and it was of no importance that the advice or directions were departed from in respect to the precise time or place or mode or means of committing the offence. This was aimed at a few individuals; and, under it, indictments were found against Theodore Parker, Wendell Phillips, Martin Stowell, Thomas Wentworth Higginson, John Morrison, Samuel T. Proudman, and John C. Cluer. Parker was arrested Nov. 29. Time for the trials was fixed,—April 3, 1855. A formidable array of counsel appeared for the defence,—John P. Hale and Charles M. Ellis for Mr. Parker; William L. Burt, John A. Andrew, H. F. Durant, for the rest. But the trials did not proceed. Mr. Parker's counsel moved that the indictment against him be quashed. A brief argument sufficed. The Court pronounced the indictments bad, and ordered that against Stowell to be dismissed. The district-attorney, Benjamin F. Hallett, entered a *nolle prosequi* in the other cases; and the whole affair ended. "Well, Mr. Parker," said Commissioner Benjamin F. Hallett, "you have crept out through a knot-hole this time."—"I will knock a bigger hole next time," was the gruff reply.

The result was anticipated. Mr. Parker wrote to his friend Desor, on the 19th of November, that he should not be indicted. He was half sorry; for he longed for an opportunity to make a speech; but, on the whole, was glad of the result, preferring to be rid of the trouble and vexation, and to have the city and state spared the shame. He did not mean, however, that the persecutors should escape. Three or four days after the judge had delivered his charge, Parker's line of defence was marked out, the fortifications sketched, the place of the batteries determined, arms collected. The quashing of the indictments did not disarm him. Opportunity to address the court was lost; but opportunity to address the people remained. The great issue between free institutions and slavery was open, and was likely to remain open. Other trials might be expected. The fortresses of Liberty needed strengthening; and he set about the preparation of that remarkable "Defence," — less a defence than an historical review, and muscular statement of principles, — which has only passed into neglect with a thousand other things because the "God of battles" would endure trifling no longer, and called more terrible servants into the field. The summer of 1855 was devoted to this burning volume of two hundred and twenty pages. It is a monument of historical learning, as well as a thrilling record of events and a stern judgment on men. The portion that concerned himself personally is small as compared with that which concerned his fellow-citizens. They, and not he, were the persons assailed; and the intention was to plant convictions in their minds in a way to last forever. The slave power was ranked with the most arrant of despotisms; its measures were classed with the most infamous deeds of the most infamous times; its servants were numbered with the meanest tools of tyranny.

"Spirits of tyrants," he cries, quoting the language of a sermon preached after the surrender of Sims, — "spirits of tyrants! I look down to you. Shade of Cain, you great first murderer! forgive me that I forgot your power, and did not remember that you were parent of so long a line. I will open the tombs, and bring up most hideous tyrants from the dead.

"Come hither, Herod the wicked! Let me look on thy face. No: go! Thou wert a heathen.

"Come, Nero, thou awful Roman emperor! come up. No: thou wast drunk with power, schooled in Roman depravity. Thou hadst, beside, the example of thy fancied gods.

"Come hither, St. Dominic! come, Torquemada! — fathers of the Inquisition. Merciless monsters! seek your equal here. No: pass by. You are no companions for such men as these. You were the servants of atheistic popes, of cruel kings.

"Come up, thou heap of wickedness, George Jeffreys! thy hands deep purple with the blood of thy murdered fellow-men. Awful and accursed shade! two hundred years thy name has been pilloried in face of the world, and thy memory gibbeted before mankind. Come, shade of a judicial butcher! let us see how thou wilt compare with those who kidnap men in Boston.

"What! dost thou shudder? thou turn back? These not thy kindred? It is true, George Jeffreys; and these are not thy kin. It was a great bribe that tempted thee. Thou only struckst at men accused of crime, not at men accused only of their birth. Thou wouldst not send a man into bondage for two pounds. I will not rank thee with men, who in Boston, for ten dollars, would enslave a negro now. Rest still, Herod! be quiet, Nero! sleep, St. Dominic! and sleep, O Torquemada! in your fiery jail. Sleep, Jeffreys! underneath the 'altar of the church' which seeks with Christian charity to hide your hated bones."

These tremendous words were spoken soberly, by a man quite as ready to have them judged by the laws of truth as by the rules of rhetoric. They who must look at deeds through the imagination; who need the illusion, if not the enchantment, of distance, and therefore credit antiquity with all the great examples of either fame or infamy, — read them as the ravings of a fanatic. But they who looked at deeds, as he did, in the light of absolute righteousness; whose imagination was filled with the shapes of eternity, and therefore knew but one standard, — the supreme law, — read them with awe, as the judgments of a prophet. Mr. Parker was not playing on the passions of his audience; for he deliberately repeated the language four years after it was first uttered, in a book designed to be read. He was not conscious of dealing in exaggerations: he was merely applying the doctrine which he had vindicated against the objections of Dr. Channing years before, — that the individual conscience enunciated the supreme law, or would if allowed to speak. By that doctrine he was justified with all who accept it. The disciples of a different school of philosophy — which studies human nature by other methods, and is disposed to question the accounts of human monsters as well as human paragons — may pronounce his verdicts unjust, on the ground that they disregarded the complexities of motive, and weighed in rude scales the delicate moral qualities which make up character: these men are very far from being moral enthusiasts; they are apt to be moral neutrals, if not moral sceptics. Parker's invective met with small sympathy from the multitude of respectable people who sincerely believed the Union to be in danger from the Northern spirit of liberty, and felt that the return of a few negroes to the State wherein they were born was an evil of infinitely less magnitude; and the personal friends of the judge and the commissioner, who knew them to be amiable, conscientious, and humane gentlemen, — certainly no more inclined to cruelty or conscious turpitude than their neighbors, — hooted at the preacher's arraignment of them as the wildest folly. Mr. Parker may have been wrong in his psychology; but we cannot see evidence that he was malignant in his temper. He had strong moral antipathies; but was, personally, no hater of men. He detested deeds; the doers of them were hateful to him: but, as a man, he felt for them no animosity. True, he never forgot, and he never permitted others to forget, a minister's unfortunate expression of willingness to return a near kinsman to the slavery he might have fled from, rather than imperil the national unity. He pursued certain prominent men of Boston with remorseless severity, holding them up to public scorn, thrusting acts of theirs into people's faces, till they seemed to be congested masses of turpitude. Theirs, however, he regarded as public deeds, which he fastened upon and exhibited for the purpose of riveting attention to principles, not for the purpose of blackening characters. He knew the force of reiteration and emphasis in making things remembered. No man ever tried harder, against a vehement and sarcastic temper, to separate the personal from the impersonal feeling. No man ever tried harder to suppress personal feeling altogether. That he wholly succeeded cannot be claimed; that he occasionally spoke bitterly, even sneeringly, of his "enemies, persecutors, and slanderers," cannot be denied: but he did pray God to forgive them, and to turn their hearts; nay, he himself was singularly ready to forgive on the slightest show of concession, and would do any thing in his power to turn their hearts. Candor must grant this. May not candor grant, besides, that, if he was guilty of unjust judgments, he was led thereto as much, at the very least, by the intensity of his moral feeling as by the passionateness of his native temper? and, if this be so, something may be forgiven him. In these days, excess of conscience is not common. The levelling process, which brings all characters to the same grade, and that a low one, goes on fast: appeals to interest are more frequent and more urgent than appeals to honor: "sentiment" of the exalted kind is not in fashion anywhere: the pure dictates of the moral law are losing their venerableness. Parker did believe in them; demanded that all should believe; threatened woe to all who flouted them. If he dealt in exaggerations, they were grand ones: they were the exaggerations of faith. To them we owe, in part, the power of the faith which at last saved the nation; for, when the civil war came, the value of conscience became clearer. Few then wished that lighter emphasis had been laid on it in previous years. Exaggerations of language sounded faint enough beside the roar of cannon. He who had uttered the boldest prophecy was seen to be the calmest judge. Instead of holding him answerable for sin because he held up to execration ideas and their representatives, men were more disposed to reproach themselves with faithlessness because they had rejected the warning.

The interior history of the slave-struggle proves that Mr. Parker's share in it was large and important. That his soul was in it, was, therefore, a necessity; and the soul of such a man, once roused, does not stop, when turning over the soil of the stubborn fallow-land, to weep over the daisy his iron ploughshare has bruised. To him sin was a sinner; malignity was a man; the Prince of Darkness was a gentleman. If he loaded his rifle with ball, it was because he was a good soldier. Had more such ball-cartridges as his been driven home, the thunder of a nation's guns might have been spared.

CHAPTER XVI.

THE KANSAS WAR.

THE history of the struggle to people Kansas with true children of New England, so as to secure its admission into the Union as a free State, cannot be told here. Mr. Parker has told it so well, that reference to his discourses is sufficient. There is room now only for a succinct account of his own efforts in this new field. From the nature of the case, his personal activity in the fresh emergency was less than in the cases of fugitive-slave hunting in his own parish. Kansas was very far off; and a press of duties kept him in Boston. But, as far as his influence went, it was at the service of the cause. His counsel was valuable, his encouragement, his generosity in giving, and his aid in collecting money.

From the Journal.

APRIL 2, 1856.

Saw the Kansas party go off, Dr. Charles H. Sanborn at their head, — about forty, *nearly half of them women and children.* There were twenty copies of "*Sharp's Rights of the People*" in their hands, of the new and improved edition, and divers Colt's six-shooters also. As the bell rang for the train to move (at five and a half, Providence Railroad), they were singing, —

"When I can read my title clear."

One of the verses would have some meaning: —

"Should earth against my soul engage,
And hellish darts be hurled,
Then I can smile at Satan's rage,
And face a frowning world."

But what a comment were the weapons of that company on the boasted democracy of America! Those rifles and pistols were to defend their soil from the American Government, which wishes to plant slavery in Kansas. Compare the settler from Boston in 1656, in 1756, and then in 1856.

From Letters to Miss Hunt.

SEPT. 4, 1856.

Congress passed the Army Bill without the proviso: so the President can use his money to push slavery in at the point of the bayonet. There is continual fighting in Kansas. You remember Rev. Mr. Nute from Kansas. His brother-in-law, Mr. Hipps, came from Leavenworth to Lawrence, staid a day or two at Nute's, left his sick wife, and started for home without weapons. A ruffian shot him dead, *scalped* him, and then exhibited the scalp in Leavenworth, and said, "I went out for the scalp of a d——d abolitionist, and I have got one." Of course, the government likes this; "The Post" likes it; and the respectability of Boston must say, "Served him right!" You will hear of yet bloodier work in Kansas. Higginson has gone there. But for your visit to Europe, I should have spent my vacation in Kansas. Next summer will probably find me there. . . .

Brooks is drunk all the time now, and is quite cowed down with the reputation for cowardice fixed on him. It is not thought gentlemanly for a Northern man to speak of him in the presence of Southern ladies. Such is the wrath of his friends, that they engaged a mob of rowdies to insult Burlingame, — spit in his face, &c.; and then, if he resisted, *to kill him:* so Burlingame's friends kept him out of the city, not letting him know the news; and he was not there to vote against the Army Bill. . . .

I still think the election of Fremont presents the only chance for a *peaceful* settlement of the ghastly question; but every day I feel less confidence in such a settlement, even with his election. The *wrath of the South* is too hot to allow of a permanent union. I would gladly separate from them to-morrow, were it not that we should leave four million Americans in bonds. Set them free, I would vote for dissolution to-morrow. We could take all north of the Potomac and Ohio, and all west of the Mississippi, and let the miserable rowdies have Virginia, North Carolina, South Carolina, Georgia, Alabama, Missouri, Louisiana, Tennessee, and Kentucky.

From Letters to Mrs. Apthorp.

SEPT. 11, 1856.

Mr. Nute is in the hands of the ruffians. We fear he is *hanged.* The accounts are awful from Kansas. Five persons were shot after they had surrendered. Scalping is as common as with other savages. . . .

We are now in a civil war. I went to a Kansas meeting at Cambridge last night. R. W. E. was expected, but did not come till near nine; others wasting the time before in idle *laughter* and jokes. Yet good things were said. E. was not happy, but said many good things, as always. He would send out the sergeant-at-arms to compel all Americans to return forthwith, lest by and by there be no country left for them. I know not what is before us, but augur evil, — evil, and then triumph.

SEPT. 19, 1856.

Things look better in Kansas. The ruffians have been worsted in some fights. Lawrence is well fortified now; has a fort that will hold a thousand men. Dr. Howe and others raised five thousand dollars one day last week to buy Sharp's rifles. We want a thousand rifles, and got two hundred in one day. Nute is now at large; but the particulars I know not. Lying is common on both sides, I fear: I know "mistakes" are not rare in such times. But the government is backing down. . . .

It is writ down in the bond that Sumner is to go to the Senate: the Know-Nothing Convention at Worcester unanimously passed a resolve to that effect. But we shall see what we shall see.

Sennott says President Pierce is drunk every day. I had intelligence of his being solemnly intoxicated on a most important occasion last May; but now he is gone over, it is said, to cups, and cups only. Really, born rulers are not much worse than the elected.

Gov. Reeder has come out for Fremont: his long letter is in "The New-York Evening Post" of yesterday. Geary's inaugural speech is just telegraphed to us. He demands obedience to the Territorial legislature till its laws are repealed (repudiation by the people is no repeal of the border-ruffian "laws," I suppose); but promises to protect all, without respect of party, and calls on armed bands to disperse, or quit the Territory. He has dignified with the title of "militia" the companies of Southern marauders whom Shannon had furnished with arms, banners, protection, and whiskey, and set to scalp the peaceful inhabitants of Kansas. Things look much better for Kansas. The Emigrant Aid Society has forever prevented it from becoming a slave State; for, if this company had not been at work, the Missourians and others would have flocked in, and made its institutions to suit the South. Now I have no fears of its future.

We had a meeting of women at our house Monday, P.M., and have raised about a hundred and twenty dollars amongst them for clothing for Kansas; and, besides, any quantity of women are at work making clothes for the men.

To Miss Hunt.

SEPT. 21, 1856.

. . . Yesterday I omitted the chapter of St. James as morning lesson, and introductory to a sermon on Franklin, and, instead, read from a new epistle of St. Ephraim (Nute), written a fortnight before in Kansas, and telling of his captivity and cruel treatment. There was an immense audience; seats all full, and men leaning against the wall. Dr. Bowditch came and suggested that a contribution should be taken up at the door. I mentioned it; and now three hundred dollars are in my drawer for Mr. Nute and his fellow-apostles. It was not ten cents apiece for the audience, but a pretty sum for him and them.

To Mrs. Apthorp.

OCT. 6, 1856.

. . . I don't feel so confident of success as a week ago. Even if Fremont be elected, I have terrible fears for the soundness of his advisers' and of his own course. . . . I never took such interest in an election. In 1840, when the nation shook with agitation, I took no part, no interest: there was no idea at issue which I cared a pin for. The nation was tired of being on one side, and wanted to turn over, and did so with much noise. But now there is a great question: we are to decide a programme of principles, which involves a long train of measures, between such prosperity as we have not ever seen and such misery and ruin as we never feared. There is a battle with swords going on at Kansas, with votes all over the land. Kansas is the centre of the continent. Put one foot of the compasses in the middle of Kansas where the Republican and the Snaky Rivers meet, let the other rest on Boston, then sweep the circle round, it touches (or comes close to) Quebec, the middle of Hudson's Bay, the mouth of the Oregon, San Francisco, the city of Mexico, and Havana. Now, the battle between Freedom and Slavery is for the physical heart of America, and, of course, for its limbs; but the actual battle is not less for the spiritual heart of America.

To Miss Hunt.

Nov. 4, 1856 (Night).

It is election-day. We have heard only from Boston and a few towns round about. All the news is good so far. To-morrow, at nine, I will give the result as far as known: so you shall have the earliest (and latest) news.

It is a day not less critical in our future history than the 4th of July, 1776, for the past. This morning there were three alternatives before the nation: 1. The North might put down slavery by a vote, peacefully, yet securely, though step by step; 2. The North might allow freedom to be put down by a vote, peacefully, yet securely, though step by step; 3. The North and South must have a civil war. So it was at sunrise: at sunset there may be only a choice between the two latter,—slavery, or battle. If the North locks horns with the South, I know which is crowded into the ditch. But, in 1776, the worst part of England was in America: so now the worst part of the North is at the South.

To the Same.

Nov. 16, 1856.

I am more than ever of opinion that we must settle this question in the old Anglo-Saxon way,—by the sword. There are two constitutions for America,—one written on parchment, and laid up at Washington; the other also on parchment, but on the *head of a drum*. It is to this we must appeal, and before long. I make all my pecuniary arrangements with the expectation of civil war. I buy no books; have not orders out for fifty dollars, and commonly have at least five hundred dollars on order in all parts of the world.

To Mrs. Apthorp.

Nov. 11, 1856.

. . . This morning, Mr. Rhett of South Carolina is out with a letter to the governor of that great State of three hundred and eighty-five thousand slaves, and two hundred and eighty-three thousand white men, recommending dissolution. South Carolina will nullify at all hazards. Gen. Quattlebum has again taken the field, — of newspapers, — and sheds ink and valor without discretion. I don't believe we shall hold together long. The union is not by internal cohesion, but outside pressure. The hoop which holds these silly staves together is no thicker than a dollar-bill: a drop of blood, nay, a little ink, will weaken it so that all falls to pieces. I doubt that we see ten years without bloodshed. . . . I don't see the immediate future of America: the remote future appears more clear and distinct. This new administration will make its attack on Cuba, I take it. Mexico is falling to pieces; and Jonathan must be there to pick up the fragments. The American Government has refused to give a passport to a colored man, on the ground that he was not a citizen, though born here. I mean to petition the Legislature of Massachusetts to pass a law directing our officials to furnish the colored citizens of Massachusetts with such passports as will be sufficient. . . .

To the Same.

Dec. 29, 1856.

. . . We need Sumner at Washington just now.

"One blast upon his bugle-horn were worth a thousand men."

For the Republicans apologize and explain, and say they "are not an abolition party, not an antislavery party, not opposed to the extension of slavery:" they "only mean to restore the Missouri Compromise." Men talk hopefully about Kansas.

Certainly all is peaceful there at present; but I know the enemy too well.

> "Then most we dread the tempest's wrath
> When most we seem secure."

To Miss Hunt.

OCT. 31, 1857.

. . . Sumner's friends who have seen him think it would be ruinous for him to return this winter. His health is not much better now than when he left Paris, I should judge. I think Sumner is killed, so far as usefulness is concerned: more merciful if the blow had been fatal at once. George Hillard thinks he had better not come back. There will be nothing of any importance done this session, — nothing about Kansas, you know; about Cuba, nothing; nothing about the slave-trade, or Dred Scott decision. If I were in Sumner's place, when Congress came together, I would be *there.* If I could sit but an hour a day, that hour I would be *there.*

I saw old Josiah Quincy in the street to-day. He has a backbone, which, old as he is, sticks out through his great-coat.

To Mrs. Apthorp.

DECEMBER, 1857.

. . . The little class of well-educated men, by falseness to their position, have lost the confidence of the people; and a few men with more conscience, though often with less culture, command the homage of the very crowds which educated hypocrisy in vain attempted to cajole and win. See what reception is given to Beecher and Chapin! — men of not great intellect or great knowledge, but inspired with the progressive spirit of the age, and so standing in intimate relations with the people.

See the success of Sumner and Phillips! the triumph of Emerson, who has a more glorious history than any American of this generation! Prescott has changed no man's opinion. Bancroft has elevated no man. Irving has made men laugh at his fun, and rejoice in the precious beauty which blossoms in his field and his garden: that is all. Webster has connected himself with nothing except hunkerism: his symbol is his plaster bust; but his calf-bound volumes of speeches are as dead as the brass of the Colossus at Rhodes, which an earthquake threw down, and a Jew bought, — a load also for nine hundred camels: he affects no man's opinion. Clay was the tariff, which is now dead, — an obsolete idea, but a curse, while it lived, to the manufacturers who bought it of him. Calhoun was slavery: the greatest sophist the nation ever knew was properly devoted to the worst institution now in the growing world. The dead tariff will soon be buried also, and on top of Henry Clay; slavery will go to the Devil, and take with it the memory of John C. Calhoun, a great sophist, and of many little sophists at the same time: but Emerson has touched the deepest strings on the human harp, and, ten centuries after he is immortal, will wake music which he first waked.

Thus Theodore Parker took into his heart his country's sorrow and need, not sparing himself a pang. He felt the whole situation; let no aspect of it pass him by; but exhausted, so far as it was in him, even the possibilities of agony. The tremendous facts came before him, every one in the fulness of minute detail. The tremendous issues unrolled themselves before his prophetic gaze. He followed every move of the politicians: no trick of the party managers escaped him. He had his eye on every public man; watched with breathless interest each newcomer on the stage; and weighed, in scales that rarely erred, the persons who undertook the control of public affairs. The following letters show the temper of his own mind, and also the view he took of the good citizen's duty: —

To Hon. W. H. Seward.

BOSTON, May 19, 1854.

DEAR SIR, — It seems to me that the country has now got to such a pass, that the people must interfere and take things out of the hands of the politicians who now control them, or else the American State will be lost. Allow me to show *in extenso* what I mean. Here are two distinct elements in the nation; viz., FREEDOM and SLAVERY. The two are hostile in nature, and therefore mutually invasive: both are organized in the institutions of the land. These two are not *equilibrious:* so the nation is not a *figure of equilibrium.* It is plain (to me) that these two antagonistic forces cannot long continue in this condition. There are three possible modes of adjusting the balance, all conceivable: —

I. *There may be a separation of the two elements:* then each may form a whole, equilibrious, and so without that cause of dissolution in itself, and have a *national unity of action*, which is indispensable. Or, —

II. Freedom *may destroy slavery:* then the whole nation continues as an harmonious whole, with national unity of action, the result of *national unity of place.* Or, —

III. *Slavery may destroy freedom*, and then the nation become an integer, only a unit of despotism. This, of course, involves a complete revolution of all the *national* ideas and *national* institutions. It must be an *industrial despotism*, — a strange anomaly. Local self-government must give place to centralization of national power; the State courts be sucked up by that enormous sponge, the Supreme Court of the United States; and individual liberty be lost in the monstrous mass of democratic tyranny. Then America goes down to utter ruin, covered with worse shame than is heaped on Sodom and Gomorrah; for we also, with horrid indecency, shall have committed the crime against nature in our Titanic lust of wealth and power.

I. Now, I see no likelihood of the first condition being fulfilled. Two classes rule the nation: —

1. The *mercantile men*, who want money; and, 2, The *political men*, who want power. There is a strange unanimity between these two classes. The mercantile men want money as a *means of power:* the political want power as a *means of money.* Well, while the Union affords money to the one, and power to the other, both will be agreed; will work together to "save the Union." And as neither of the two has any great *political ideas*, or reverence for the *higher law* of God, both will unite in what serves the apparent interest of these two: that will be in favor of slavery and of centralized power. Every inroad which the Federal Government makes on the nation will be acceptable to these two classes.

II. Then, considering dissolution as out of the question, is freedom likely to terminate slavery? It was thought so by the founders of the Federal institutions and by the *people* at large. Few steps were taken in that direction, — the ordinance of 1787, the abolition of the *African* slave-trade: that is all. For forty-six years, not a step.

III. The third condition is the one now most promising to end the matter. See the steps consummated, or only planned: 1. The *Gadsden* Treaty; 2. The extension of slavery *into Nebraska;* 3. The *restoration of slavery to the free States*, either by "decision" of the Supreme Court, or *legislation* of Congress; 4. *Acquisition of Cuba, Hayti*, &c., as a new arena for slavery; 5. The *re-establishment* of the *African slave-trade;* 6. The *occupancy* of the other *parts* of *North America* and *South America.* When all this is done, there will be *unity of action, unity of idea.* "Auferre, trucidare, rapire falsis nominibus imperium; atque ubi solitudinem faciunt, pacem appellant."

Now, this must not be. *It must not be!* The nation must rouse itself. I have been waiting a long time for some event to occur which would blow so loud a horn that it should waken the North, startling the farmer at his plough and the mechanic in his shop. I believe the time is coming: so I want to have a convention of all the free States at Buffalo on Tuesday, the 4th of July next, to CONSIDER THE STATE OF THE UNION, and to take measures (1) to *check*, (2) to *terminate*, the enslavement of men in America. I wish you would advise me in this matter; for I confess I look to *you* with a great deal of confidence in these times of such peril to freedom.

If you like, I should be glad if you would show this letter to Mr. Chase and Mr. Sumner. Believe me

Respectfully and truly yours,

THEO. PARKER.

To John P. Hale.

BOSTON, May 23, 1854.

MY DEAR MR. HALE, — You have helped me in many emergencies; and I want a little more advice just now. It seems to me that there should be a convention from all the free States on the 4th of July to organize for action against slavery as we have never done before. If this is not done, we are ruined, and the country becomes one great *slave power.* I suggest a convention at Buffalo, Pittsburg, or elsewhere, to consider the present alarming condition of the country, and to take measures (1) to *check* and (2) to *terminate* this matter of slavery. If the South will not let it down gradually, *we* must let *it down by the run*. Please let me know what you think.

Yours faithfully,

THEODORE PARKER.

HON. MR. HALE.

To Charles Sumner.

ST. ALBANS, VT., Feb. 16, 1856.

DEAR SUMNER, — The *petitions* are all going very well. Tell me any thing else to do. I wrote to Sandusky, Milwaukee, Madison, Syracuse, and divers other places, and got the thing started.

Who is to be nominated for President? — by the Democrats, the Republicans?

Don't forget to introduce a bill providing books in all military ports of the United States.

Yours truly,

THEO. PARKER.

Banks's election is the first victory of the Northern idea since 1787.

To H. Wilson.

BOSTON, July 7, 1855.

MY DEAR WILSON, — I cannot let another day pass by without sending you a line — all I have time for — to thank you for the noble service you have done for the cause of freedom. You stand up most *manfully* and *heroically*, and do battle for the right. I do not know how to thank you enough. You do nobly at all places, all times. If the rest of your senatorial term be like the past, we shall see times such as we only wished for, but dared not hope as yet. There is a North, a real North, quite visible now. God bless you for your services, and keep you ready for more!

Heartily yours,

THEO. PARKER.

To Passmore Williamson, Esq.

DUBLIN, N.H., Aug. 21, 1855.

DEAR SIR, — Your noble action and the wicked treatment you receive for it give me the right to address you, though I am an entire stranger. I cannot forbear expressing to you my admiration for your conduct, and the hope that you will continue faithful and undaunted in the jail which the infamous court condemns you to. I wish I could bear a part of the suffering, and so relieve you from a little of that pain; but I can only send you an expression of my heartfelt sympathy, and thanks for your noble manhood. I suppose there must be much more imprisonment and other judicial outrage before the people are wakened from their sleep. May endless blessings be upon you is the wish and prayer of

Yours sincerely,

THEODORE PARKER.

To Charles Sumner, Washington.

BURLINGTON, VT., May 21, 1856.

MY DEAR SUMNER, — God bless you for the brave words you spoke the other day, — and have always spoken, — of which I hear report in the papers! Send it to me in full as soon as you can.

I have been ill (in *head*), and scarce able to do any thing for a month; else I should have written you before now. I am a little better just now; but still my head feels like an apple which has been frozen all winter, and is now thawed out. I am in Vermont, lecturing on the condition of the country. Pierce is in open rebellion against the people: he has committed the *highest* treason against the *people*, the worst form of *lèse-majesté*.

I have long wanted to thank you for your services in that matter of the Danish-Sound affair. It is quite clear that you are right; that the twofold executive — presidential and senatorial — has no more right to annul a treaty than to annul the tariff law, the law against piracy, or any other statute. Why did nobody ever think of this before?

There are three wicked things now going on in the United States: —

1. Exterminating the Indians in Oregon, &c.

2. Filibustering against Central America "and the rest of mankind."

3. Extending slavery into Kansas and everywhere else. Then, I take it, the free-State men will be *immediately* put down, unless Congress comes to their aid. What can they do

— a handful of them, without arms, no officers — against the border ruffians, eight thousand or ten thousand strong, armed by the United States, and officered by the soldiers of our wicked army? Can nothing be done at Washington? Will nothing arouse the people at the North?

Tell me what you think of the candidates for Republican nomination? Here is my list of preferences if I could make the President: —

1. Seward.
2. Chase.
3. Hale.

But I take it none of these could be elected in the present state of affairs. If we come to actual war, Seward would be chosen, I think; but not now, in the present state of things.

Do tell me how far is *Fremont* reliable? God bless you!

Ever yours,

THEO. PARKER.

I shall send you a *speech* before long.

To Hon. John P. Hale, Washington.

BOSTON, May 23, 1856.

MY DEAR MR. HALE, — Do write and tell me how Sumner is getting on. How much is the noble fellow wounded? Give him my most sympathizing regards and *love*. I wish I could have taken the blows on my head, and not he; at least, *half of them*. Will the Senate do nothing about it? Think of the scoundrel Brooks let off on bail of five hundred dollars! I shall go to the State House as soon as the House meets to see if I can stir up that body to any action in the matter.

Yours truly and heartily,

THEO. PARKER.

To John P. Hale.

GALESBURG, Oct. 21, 1856.

MY DEAR MR. HALE, — I'm glad I am not a senator this year. You win your "Hon." pretty dear this season. Stumping is no joke. I heard your opponent this afternoon, — Douglas. He was considerably drunk, and made one of the most sophisticated and deceitful speeches I ever listened to. It was mere brutality in respect of morals, and sophistry for logic, in the style and manner of a low blackguard.

His enemies said he seldom or never did so ill. But there is a good deal of rough power in his evil face. I never saw him before.

I don't know how you think the election will turn out; but I look for defeat. I hope otherwise, but still think so. The battle is not won by our carrying the electoral tickets by popular vote. If Buchanan gets a hundred and forty-eight electors, a million dollars, I think, might be raised to buy the one hundred and forty-ninth. I think there are thirty men in Boston who would give five thousand dollars apiece to see it done. It is the most important crisis in our national history. No presidential election ever turned on such great questions. It is despotism or democracy which the people vote for. I wish the true issue was represented by the banners and mottoes.

Buchanan's friends would bear this in front of all: "No Unalienable Rights to Life, Liberty, and the Pursuit of Happiness;" "The Declaration of Independence a Lie;" "No Higher Law." Then might follow, in historical order, "Slavery in Kansas," "Slavery in Cuba," "Slavery in all the Territories," "Slavery in all the Free States," "Bondage for Niggers," "Bondage for Poor Whites," "Slavery for 'Greasy Mechanics,'" "No Free Schools," "No Free Press," "No Free Pulpit," "No Free Speech," "No Free Man."

If Buchanan is President, I think the Union does not hold out his four years: it must end in civil war, which I have been preparing for these six months past. I buy no books except for pressing need. Last year I bought fifteen hundred dollars' worth: this year I shall not order two hundred dollars' worth. I may want money for cannons. . Have you any plan in case we are defeated? Of course the principles and measures of the administration will remain unchanged, and the mode of execution will be more intense and rapid. God save the United States of America!

Yours faithfully,

THEO. PARKER.

P. S. — I want, before you go to Congress, to borrow your copy of Force's "American Archives;" also I want you to come and dine with me, and see some politicians.

The Kansas war brought to the front a colossal figure, — JOHN BROWN. This would not be the place to tell his story, even if it had not been well told already by James Redpath, and partially by F. B. Sanborn in the pages of "The Atlantic Monthly" of April and July, 1872; but something must be said about him, — enough to throw light on the character of his friends, especially of one of them, — Mr. Parker. That such a person sought Parker, and was trusted by him, is an incident worth pondering over. John Brown was fifty-seven years old when Parker first met him. He had lived in several places; had engaged in several occupations; had experienced changes of fortune; but had remained himself steadfast and unchangeable in character. The State of Connecticut gave him his Puritan blood; Ohio imparted to the boy the influence of her territorial and social breadth; Massachusetts made the young man acquainted with the highest form of free civilization; New York trained the man of middle age for the work he was set to do; Kansas gave him a field of operations; Virginia, a chance for martyrdom. Through the kindness of a kinsman, he was educated at an excellent private school, and purposed entering the ministry; but poverty, and weakness of sight, compelled him to abandon a career for which seriousness of mind, and weight of character, made him peculiarly fit. He was profoundly religious after the old-fashioned Orthodox fashion; had an awful sense of divine realities, and an implicit faith in the divine decrees. The Bible was to him God's word; life, God's gift; eternity, God's recompense. His desire, from the first, was not to live as was unseemly in the presence of eternal law. He turned from the ministry with regret, but like a true Puritan, who knew that the ministry was only one calling out of many, and returned to his original occupation as a tanner; dropping that later to become a shepherd in Ohio, — a pursuit which has had fascinations before for men of high resolves. At the age of forty-six we find him in Massachusetts again as agent of the Ohio sheep-farmers and wool-growers, who, wishing to establish a connection with the manufacturers of New England, selected Springfield as the fittest place, and Brown as the fittest person to have charge of the enterprise. The business promised well at first, and became flourishing; but from various causes, which need not be detailed here, weakened, and at last collapsed. Brown was ruined, and, after three years' residence in Springfield, in 1849 went to the Adirondack region, in Northern New York, there to settle up his wool-business, renew his sheep-raising, and teach settlers in those wild regions how to clear, plant, and farm the land which Mr. Gerritt Smith had offered to give by thousands of acres to such colored people as would accept them and live on them. Not many availed themselves of the gift; but those who did had the benefit of Brown's experience and care as long as he could give them.

During all these vicissitudes he was cherishing in his heart a purpose which to him was as sacred as was ever entertained by man: this was nothing else than the liberation of the slaves of the South. To say that he never lost sight of this purpose is to say little. He chose his occupations, so far as he could, with a view to the facilities they afforded for carrying it into effect; looked out at once to discover the bearing they had on it; and seized every occasion they offered for promoting it. The occupation of shepherd was attractive to him, as promising the means of furthering his designs. As agent of the Ohio wool-growers in Massachusetts, he sounded for information that might help him in his projects; especially making the acquaintance of fugitives from slavery, who might be made useful. Parker says in a letter from Rome, written in 1859, "If I am rightly informed, he has cherished this scheme of liberating the slaves in Virginia for more than thirty years, and laid his plans when he was a land-surveyor in that very neighborhood where his gallows (I suppose) has since grown." Sanborn declares that his object in retiring to the solitudes of North Elba was, that he might there, away from observation, muster and drill a company of men as the nucleus of his army of liberation. The sheep-raiser, the wool-factor, the farmer, the surveyor, was ever the emancipator in disguise. What he engaged in was done with all his ability, as conscientiously as if it had been his ultimate business; but his ultimate business was to set free the captives.

In 1851, being in Springfield on incidental affairs connected with his wool concerns, he assisted in organizing an armed resistance to the Fugitive-slave Bill, then recently passed; and drew up a paper containing articles of agreement, which were signed by forty-four men and women, white and colored, most of the latter being fugitive slaves or their friends. The paper has "words of advice" that ring like the address of a general to his army: —

> "Do not delay one moment after you are ready: you will lose all your resolution if you do. Let the first blow be the signal for all to engage; and, when engaged, do not do your work by halves, but make clean work with your enemies; and be sure you meddle not with any others. . . . Be firm, determined, and cool; but let it be understood that you are not to be driven to desperation without making it an awful dear job to others as well as to you. . . . Hold on to your weapons, and never be persuaded to leave them, part with them, or have them far away from you. Stand by one another and by your friends while a drop of blood remains, and be hanged if you must; but tell no tales out of school. Make no confession."

Nine years later, he himself, driven to bay, observed these directions to the letter; thus showing how profoundly he had meditated, and how sincerely he trusted to them. The articles of agreement exhibited an equal ripeness of conviction. He held himself ready at any hour to inaugurate his grand enterprise, and listened hourly for the call to do it. During the Anthony Burns excitement of 1854, he was with difficulty restrained from going to Boston, and leading an attempt at rescue. No sooner was Kansas fairly opened to emigrants, than his four sons, who had all been schooled in their father's beliefs and imbued with his resolution, left their home in Ohio, and repaired thither to settle. He himself went some months later, having affairs to attend to in Massachusetts not unremotely connected with his ulterior ends. His hour seemed hastening on; and he wanted to sound his allies once more before the struggle came. When he joined his sons in the autumn of 1855, it was less with the design of establishing himself in Kansas as a peaceful colonist than of obtaining a basis for operations against the slave power. He went, not as a civilizer, but as an emancipator; not as a farmer, but as a soldier. None of the Kansas-Committee money went into his hands: he was assisted moderately by friends in New York, but for the rest provided his own commissariat, and conducted the campaign at his private charge. He went alone, having removed his family from Ohio to North Elba; his four sons only being his comrades.

He established his headquarters near the town of Ossawattomie; whither, in the spring of 1856, his other three sons and his son-in-law joined him. The name of the stern old man first became famous from his defence of that town against an assault of the "border ruffians" in August of that year. The name of "Ossawattomie Brown" was known throughout the country. But the grand opportunity did not come then. There was bloody work. One son was slain; another wounded; a third taken prisoner, and made temporarily insane from cruel treatment: all of which intensified his hatred of slavery and its abetters. But the peculiar combination of circumstances his plans demanded, the situation in Kansas did not supply: so he came away in the autumn to make fresh surveys, and to acquire new resources. He came to Boston, and early in January, 1859, presented himself before the secretary of the State Kansas Committee in his office on School Street. There was little need to tell who he was, or to present the letter of introduction from Mr. George Walker of Springfield, who knew him. The fame of the man had gone before him. His appearance was his testimonial. The moral grandeur was self-evident. I borrow the account of Mr. Sanborn, the secretary to whom he presented himself: —

"His aspect and manner would have made him distinguished anywhere among men who knew how to recognize courage and greatness of mind. He was then in his fifty-seventh year, but active and vigorous when not suffering from an ague contracted in Kansas. His figure was tall, slender, and commanding, his bearing military, and his garb a singular blending of the soldier and the deacon. His coat, waistcoat, and trousers were of a brown color, — such as he always selected when possible, — and of a cut far from fashionable. His gray overcoat was of that shape which our soldiers, a few years after, made familiar to all eyes; and he wore a patent-leather stock, which also suggested the soldier of former years. His fur cap was more in keeping with his military overcoat than with the Sunday suit of a deacon, which he wore beneath it. His face was close shaven, displaying the force of his firm, wide mouth and his positive chin. The long white beard which he wore a year or two later, and which nearly all his portraits now show, added a picturesque finish to a face that was in all its features severe and masculine. His eyes were of a piercing blue-gray, not very large, but looking out from under brows

'Of dauntless courage and considerate pride.'

His hair was dark brown, touched with gray, short and bristling, and shooting back from a forehead of middle height and breadth. His ears were large; his frame angular; his voice deep and metallic ; his walk positive and intrepid, though somewhat slow. His manner was modest, and, in a large company, even diffident. He was by no means fluent of speech ; but his words were always to the point, and his observations original, direct, and shrewd. His mien was serious and patient rather than cheerful : it betokened the 'sad wise valor' which Herbert praises : but though it was earnest, and almost anxious, it was never depressed. In short, he was then to the eye of insight what he afterwards seemed to the world, — a brave and resolved man, conscious of a work laid upon him, and confident that he should accomplish it." *

The object of John Brown's visit to Boston was to obtain control of some two hundred Sharp's rifles belonging to the Massachusetts Committee, to enable him to defend Kansas from invasion, and also to *carry the war, if advisable, into the enemy's country.* All that that meant he kept in reserve; perhaps had not settled in his own mind: though it is far more than probable that his Virginia plan was already conceived. He frankly said that whatever was intrusted to him must be intrusted to him unconditionally ; that he could not take orders from any committee, but must act on his own personal responsibility.

Mr. Sanborn, deeply impressed by the aspect and bearing of the man, spoke of him to Mr. Parker, and soon after took him to Mr. Parker's house in Exeter Place. There he met Mr. Garrison. From that moment, it would seem, the Puritan hero made the rationalist minister an adviser and friend; and from that moment Mr. Parker became one of those who helped him with counsel and with money. Brown spent portions of four months in Massachusetts; addressed the State Legislature, urging an appropriation of money to aid the emigrants from the State in Kansas ; and spoke effectively to a large audience in the town-hall of Concord, Mr. Emer-

* The Atlantic Monthly, April, 1872.

son and Mr. Thoreau being among his interested hearers. Wherever he went, he made the same impression. Wherever he told his story, he drew listeners to him, roused their enthusiasm, and gained their faith. Though silent in regard to his ulterior plans and secret purposes, he did not withhold, even from public assemblies, the avowal of his determination to attack wherever slavery was vulnerable, and to take property, or even life, if it were necessary, to set the slaves free.

The Massachusetts Committee gave Capt. Brown undisputed possession of the arms; subject, however, to future dispositions of the committee in Boston; and money was placed in his hands, — not enough, however, to equip and maintain his company of men: and he went back to his home in North Elba, saddened by his partial failure. Before leaving Massachusetts, he expressed his feelings to Mr. Parker in the following remarkable paper, which is pasted on a blank page in the journal: —

OLD BROWN'S FAREWELL TO THE PLYMOUTH ROCKS, BUNKER-HILL MONUMENTS, CHARTER-OAKS, AND UNCLE TOM'S CABINS.

He has left for Kansas; was trying, since he came out of the Territory, to secure an outfit, or, in other words, the *means of arming and thoroughly equipping* his regular minute-men, who are mixed up with the people of Kansas; and he leaves the States with a feeling of deepest sadness, that after having exhausted his own small means, and, with his family and brave men, suffered hunger, cold, nakedness, and some of them sickness, wounds, imprisonment, cruel treatment, and others death; that after lying on the ground for months in the most sickly, unwholesome, and uncomfortable places, with sick and wounded, destitute of any shelter, and hunted like wolves, sustained and cared for in part by Indians; that after all this, in order to sustain a cause (which every citizen of this *glorious republic* is under equal moral obligation to do, and for the neglect of which he will be held accountable to God) in which every man, woman, and child of the entire human family has a deep and awful interest; that when *no wages are asked or expected*, — he cannot secure (amidst all the wealth, luxury, and extravagance of this "Heaven-exalted" people) even the necessary supplies of the common soldier.

JOHN BROWN.

BOSTON, April, A.D. 1857.

The discouragement was natural. For nearly twenty years Brown had cherished his scheme, and been watching his opportunity to carry it into effect. He had devoted himself and his family to it; he had cautiously taken steps to interest in it one or two from whom he might properly expect co-operation; he had engaged as drill-master for his recruits an English Garibaldian whom he found giving fencing-lessons in New York: and now, when the condition of things in Kansas seemed to favor his enterprise, he was crippled for want of a few hundred dollars which would not have been missed by the donors, obliged to discharge his drill-master, and abandon, for the time, his project. He went away with shut lips, divulging to no one, not even to Mr. Parker, the secret design, the disappointment whereof gave poignancy to his grief. But the scheme was still cherished as intently as ever. In September, 1857, he wrote to Mr. Parker that he was in want of some five hundred or a thousand dollars "for secret service, and no questions asked." He had no news to send *by letter*, being suspicious of the United-States mails. He was, in fact, a man gravely suspected. Rewards were offered for him; traitors were lurking; his whereabouts had to be concealed. His letters were sent to feigned addresses. His friends, in corresponding with one another in regard to him, used circumlocutions, and cloaked their meaning under misleading phrases, speaking of their "wool speculation" and the "shepherd." He went to Iowa again and Kansas, busy with his plots.

Whether they would have come out when they did, but

for an unforeseen accident, is uncertain. The discharged Garibaldian drill-master was angry, and made a noise; wrote abusive letters to Mr. Sanborn, Dr. Howe, and Charles Sumner; denounced Brown; charged his friends with bad faith; and threatened to expose the plot of which he alone was informed. He did not actually do this till nearly two years later, a few weeks before the attack was made; but he created uneasiness and suspicion in the minds of some of Brown's friends, which made explanations necessary. Letters written to him, however, did not reach him; for he had again left Kansas, and was setting his face slowly once more towards the East, whence, in spite of his former disappointment, he still looked for aid. Early in 1858 the following letter was sent to Mr. Parker from Rochester, N.Y.:—

ROCHESTER, N.Y., Feb. 2, 1858.

MY DEAR SIR, — I am again out of Kansas, and am at this time concealing my whereabouts; but for very different reasons, however, than those I had for doing so at Boston last spring. I have nearly perfected arrangements for carrying out an important measure in which the world has a deep interest as well as Kansas, and only lack from five hundred to eight hundred dollars to enable me to do so, — the same object for which I asked secret-service money last fall. It is my only errand here: and I have written some of our mutual friends in regard to it; but none of them understand my views so well as you do, and I cannot explain without their first committing themselves more than I know of their doing. I have heard that Parker Pillsbury and some others in your quarter hold out ideas similar to those on which I act; but I have no personal acquaintance with them, and know nothing of their influence or means. Cannot you, either by direct or indirect action, do something to further me? Do you not know of some parties whom you could induce to give their abolition theories a thoroughly practical shape? I hope this will prove to be the last time I shall be driven to harass a friend in such a way. Do you think any of my Garrisonian friends, either at Boston, Worcester, or in any other place, can be induced to supply a little "straw," if I will absolutely make "bricks"?

I have written George L. Stearns, Esq., of Medford, and Mr. F. B. Sanborn of Concord: but I am not informed as to how deeply-dyed abolitionists those friends are; and must beg of you to consider this communication strictly confidential, unless you know of parties who will feel and act, and hold their peace. I want to bring the thing about during the next sixty days. Please write N. Hawkins, care William J. Watkins, Esq., Rochester, N.Y.

Very respectfully your friend,

JOHN BROWN.

Letters of similar purport, adapted to the supposed character of the men he was addressing, were written to T. W. Higginson, G. L. Stearns, and F. B. Sanborn. The noble and beautiful letter addressed on Feb. 24 to Mr. Sanborn from Peterborough, N.Y., and by him sent to Mr. Parker, among whose papers it was found, — the letter printed on the fifty-third page of "The Atlantic Monthly" for July, 1872, — reads like the message to a trusted but younger and less-experienced soldier than Parker. They all spoke of an important undertaking, — "*by far* the most important undertaking of my whole life" is the expression he uses to Mr. Higginson, — but furnished no precise clew to its character, and awakened no suspicion of it. On the 12th of February Brown wrote again, asking an interview at a friend's house in Central New York. He dared not pass through Massachusetts to come to Boston; dared not be seen in places where he might be recognized, as he would be in Springfield. He was, for good reasons, in hiding. His friends in Kansas knew nothing of his whereabouts. He did not venture to visit his wife and children, so anxious was he to remain concealed. To go to Central New York in mid-winter on such a summons, for a purpose so undefined, was impossible for Mr. Stearns or Mr. Parker. Mr. Higginson also found it inconvenient to go; and Mr. Sanborn went alone, hoping and expecting to receive a full explanation of the charges brought by Hugh Forbes, "the Garibaldian drill-master," but scarcely anticipating any thing more momentous. There, on the evening of Washington's birthday (Feb. 22), in a retired spot, beneath a perfectly loyal roof, to a few tried and trusty people the Virginia scheme was unfolded in all its parts, the locality illustrated, the provisions and contingencies explained, the movements detailed, the probable or possible eventualities confronted. The whole evening, and all the next day, the discussion went on between the conspirator on the one side, and his astonished and half-dismayed auditors on the other; the old hero answering questions, meeting objections, quieting doubts, disarming fears, showing himself prepared at all points, and displaying a force of moral conviction and a grandeur of religious confidence that awed and stilled, if they did not convince. If it was impossible to share his enthusiasm, it was impossible to resist its influence.

Sanborn came back to Boston, and lost no time in reporting to Messrs. Parker and Higginson the result of the interview. It was Parker who suggested that Brown, who had come as far as Brooklyn, should come secretly to Boston for an interview. He did so, and registered himself as "J. Brown," on March 4, at the American House in Hanover Street, where he staid in strict privacy four days; not even calling on Mr. Parker in Exeter Place on Sunday evening, as he had done before. One of the first to call on him, and promise aid, was Parker, who afterwards met there in consultation Messrs. Howe, Higginson, Sanborn, and Stearns; the latter the largest supplier of material aid. The substance of those deliberations at the American House has never been divulged, and perhaps never will be. That Brown's representations made a deep impression on his friends is evident from the fact that they agreed among them to raise a thousand dollars for him: and that he was himself encouraged appears from a letter to Theodore Parker, written at his hotel, and conveyed by a friend to Exeter Place, — a letter printed in Weiss (ii. p. 164), begging him to prepare an address to the officers and soldiers of the United-States army, appealing to their feelings of humanity and their sense of right; and a "similar short address, appropriate to the peculiar circumstances, intended for all persons, old and young, male and female, slaveholding and non-slaveholding, to be sent out broadcast over the entire nation." Mr. Parker never, so far as is known, put his hand to this work. But his intercourse with him was confidential: he lent him helpful books, and gave him the benefit of his vast information. It is believed that he was intrusted by Brown with incidents of his plan which were not revealed to others, and were contemplated rather than decided on by the leader himself. All seemed to be going well: the greater part of the promised money was collected, enlistments of men were getting forward, the meditated blow was about to be struck, when the "Garibaldian drill-master" interposed again, — this time with more formidable demonstration. He had learned some things he did not know before; among these, the complicity of members of the Boston Kansas Committee with Brown: and he insisted that the enterprise should be stopped; that confidence should be taken from Brown, and transferred to him; otherwise what he knew should be given to the public. The committee were staggered. Of the five men composing it, three — Parker, Sanborn, and Stearns — were of the opinion that the blow must be deferred. Dr. Howe was doubtful. Higginson alone sided squarely with Brown, who was not afraid of any thing Forbes could do; disbelieved in the extent and accuracy of his information; and was inclined, on the whole, to think that the vague excitement caused by his disclosure would favor, rather than otherwise, his undertaking. Parker was ready for extreme measures, accepted Brown's ideas, sympathized with him in his moral feelings, was expectant of uprisings on the part of the slaves, would have been glad to see them, had no scruples in aiding them, but doubted the success of any first attempt to incite them to revolt. In his judgment, there must be several such before one succeeded; and he was not enough of a military man to share the old hero's conviction that Hugh Forbes would do more to make the enterprise prosper than to make it fail.

Brown supposed that all he needed was a few hundred dollars. Of the equipment of arms he felt sure; for were not the rifles of the committee in his possession? They were, but still under the committee's ultimate control, to be used only for purposes which they approved of. And when Forbes gave information, in a general way, to Senators Hale, Seward, and Wilson, of Brown's plans, and the complicity of members of the committee with them, and Wilson wrote to Dr. Howe, strongly protesting against the scheme, deprecating any association of the committee with it, and urging the consideration that they would lay themselves open to the charge of bad faith if they persisted, affairs came to a pause. The rifles did not then actually belong to the committee, though it was supposed they did; and, as Brown's use of them for his private raid would, in the public estimation, have compromised them, it was decided that operations must be suspended. Notice was sent to Brown that the rifles must be used only in the defence of Kansas; and postponement became inevitable. This obstacle of the arms was soon after removed by George L. Stearns, their actual owner, who formally put Brown in possession of them as his private agent; thus releasing the committee from all responsibility for their use. Brown was now anxious as before to push his measures to a conclusion: but his friends hung back, thinking postponement wiser; and 1859 was mentioned as the better time.

But the plan was not abandoned, nor was sympathy withheld. More money was promised; the arms were fairly made over in a way to relieve the committee of all embarrassment; and John Brown was left with the sole responsibility of the enterprise, deferring to nobody, consulting nobody, obliged to report to nobody, at liberty to keep his designs secret even from those who thus far had been most in his confidence. In the mean time, it was judged best that he himself should appear to have abandoned his scheme, and should throw Forbes off the scent by returning to Kansas. Thither he went forthwith, and performed great feats there in the way of border warfare; closing the whole by an incursion into Missouri, and bringing away a party of slaves, whom he carried through Kansas, Nebraska, Iowa, Illinois, to Detroit in Michigan, whence he easily despatched them into Canada. It was a great exploit, that made the country ring. This was early in 1859. In May his erect form was seen in the streets of Boston, calmly walking about, unconscious of the stir of the city, like a man absorbed in a high purpose, with long white beard and slow tread, observed by all who had leisure to observe, known of all who cared to know him, unmolested by the authorities, fearless, and apparently careless, but mindful of the price that had been set on his head, and armed against assault. He was there to see his friends, collect resources, and make final preparations for the enterprise on which his whole heart had been set for twenty years. Theodore Parker was then in the West Indies; the house in Exeter Street was closed: but whether at Boston, at Santa Cruz, Montreux, Rome, the brave old man was never forgotten by his friend. "Tell me," he asks from Rome, "how our little speculation in wool goes on, and what dividend accrues therefrom." No one more eagerly looked for tidings of the bold adventure; no one more sincerely regretted its failure; no one more faithfully bore witness to the magnanimity of the martyred man, more frankly confessed his friendship for him, or his approval of his deed. Had he been at home, Music Hall would have been filled with another crowd such as listened to the sermon on "The New Crime against Humanity," and they would have listened to another thrilling chapter on the same theme. How he wished he were there! How he fretted under the conditions that forbade his speaking his word, and standing by his deed, and sharing the fortunes of his friends! The Americans about him gladdened his heart by expressions of approval of the gallant attempt; but they only intensified his desire to unfold its deep lessons to his countrymen at home, confused and staggered, and needing more than ever to be reminded of eternal principles.

"No American has died in this century whose chance of earthly immortality is worth half so much as John Brown's. The ex-governors of Massachusetts are half forgotten before they are wholly dead; rhetoricians and sophists are remembered while they are talking: but a man who crowns a noble life with such a glorious act as John Brown's at Harper's Ferry is not forgotten in haste. The red martyr must be a precious man.

"The effect is not over, nor ever will be. Brown's little spark was not put out till it had kindled a fire which will burn down much more than far-sighted men look for. The Northern sky is full of lightning long treasured up: Brown was one bright, clear flash into the Southern ground. The thunder rattles all over the Union now: there will be other strokes by and by."

The year 1857 was marked by a tremendous financial convulsion, that covered the surface of the commercial world with costly ruins. Mr. Parker was not an unmoved spectator of the calamity; but he was a clear-headed and sound-hearted one. The distress afflicted him: but he was more interested in the causes of it than in the effects;

and the causes he found in the general decay of personal honor incident to the want of great religious ideas. Society, to his view, was a unit, an organized whole, rejoicing and suffering equally, because sympathetically, in all its parts. The community which rejected the idea of a higher law in politics could not be expected to acknowledge it in trade; nor could the men who apologized for slavery in order to secure the profits of the Southern market be counted on to observe the highest rules of conscience in their commercial struggle for the wealth they prized so highly. The "panic," like the strife in Kansas and the suppressed war in Washington, was the result of false ideas of God and man. The coming of it was inevitable, and might have been predicted: the lesson of it was wholesome; the effect of it would be good; but the spectacle of it was awful. On the 19th of October, 1857, he writes to Miss Hunt,—

". . . Now a word about Boston and its affairs. There was never so much mental suffering in any two months as in the last five weeks. Think of men who never thought of want, except as the *proud* angels think of suffering,—as something fit only for the 'lower classes,'—now left without a dollar! The man who refused thirty thousand dollars for his house in Temple Place, when he wanted to sell before he went to Europe, saw it knocked down at auction for nineteen thousand dollars. Michigan State bonds, seven per cent, have gone down from a dollar twenty-five to sixty-six cents. Our banks have been forced to suspend specie payments. All property is depreciated. My income will not be half this year what it was last. But 'I still live;' only I shall buy no books; and it makes a great gap in my charities. Some banks will lose much on failed paper. After a kite has been broken to pieces, the shreds are not worth much. I believe scarcely any house has failed in Boston which ought not to have failed before. One firm had a nominal capital of two million dollars; but four hundred thousand dollars was never paid in, and they owed that to the banks, and never paid, but kept renewing their notes. Another had only five hundred thousand dollars, but business to the amount of three million or four million dollars, it is said. It is not fair to fly other men's paper on so frail a kite.

"Business stops: that is the great calamity. It is hard to see great estates thus changing hands; but, though it impoverishes John to enrich Timothy, it leaves the *nation* just as rich as before. But the nation itself grows poor when its *labor* stops. The property of Massachusetts is, say, at the inflated prices of last July, one billion dollars, — a tenth part of the worth of all the real and personal property of the Union: her annual earnings are, at least, a third as much, — three hundred and thirty-three million dollars. To stop the mills and shops, you see how soon we should be poor. Trade languishes. Waterman, the dealer in kitchen-furniture, commonly sells a hundred dollars' worth in a day, in this month; but, in the six days of last week, he took only fifty-nine dollars. A friend of mine, a jeweller, clears commonly from four thousand to five thousand dollars a year; but last week there were three days in which he did not take a dollar. In Lawrence there were three thousand five hundred, in little Taunton one thousand five hundred, in Natick, in one week, two hundred *men* without work. A few years ago, none would have thought it possible that a grand-daughter of old —— and a grandson of old —— would have been prevented from marriage by poverty; but now, after the ——s and the ——s have both fallen in, the River Pactolus has not water enough to float the little shallop with two lovers in it, — children of the streams, — 'he this side, and she that.' So the little skiff goes down the Pactolus empty and whelmed over, while the lovers crawl to land wet and cold, — 'he this side, and she that side.' Hundreds of marriages will thus cruelly be prevented. Paper-money has a good deal to answer for; for it is that which causes most of the mischief. There is a hundred million dollars' worth of French goods now in New York which will be taken back to Paris. No market for your flowers now, Mr. Crapaud. The artificial flowers in the man-milliner's windows, corner of Summer and Chauncy Streets, look wilted: there is no gum or starch will keep their spirits up in these times.

"But no more of this. The country is full of bread and cloth. We have two hundred and fifteen millions of bank-bills, fifty-three millions of specie in the banks, and perhaps a hundred and sixty millions more of specie in private hands. By and by all the prostrate 'firms' will be up; money will be easy; business will begin again; Pactolus will rise; the lover will swim out and right the little skiff, and take the maiden in; and then the two will row the shallop together for many a happy day, — so they will. God bless them!

" . . . 'Defalcations' continue, of course; for the doctrine of no 'higher law' must produce its effects. *You can never escape the consequences of a first principle.* I think you have heard me say that before. What a terrible logic there is in human affairs! No reasoner is so consequential as mankind. I think we shall learn much from this crisis; and to the community it will be worth all it costs the individuals. But it is painful to see the soldiers who get wounded in this battle of industry. Often these are the best men in the community. There is ——, the founder of Warren-street Chapel, 'has done more,' a merchant told me, 'for the rising generation, than any ten churches in Boston;' and at the age of sixty he is left without a cent."

In another letter to the same correspondent, dated Boston, Nov. 16, 1857, he moralizes on the event in his usual comprehensive and exhaustive manner: —

". . . Great pains will be taken to do all that charity can do. Impostors are already abroad to feed their lazy bones on the *charity* of self-denying, honest people. I hate lazy people, and should (perhaps) see an idle Irishwoman *starve and die* with no compunction at all. But to those who would earn, and spare also, I open my heart. We have the old charitable societies acting with new vigor, and also a committee of gentlemen who are to devise new experiments. Yankees are ingenious. What we want is work. This time of trouble will make some men consider of the chaotic condition of our social system, this *antagonistic competition* in place of *co-operative industry;* and by and by a better state of things will come. Man is not yet far enough advanced to work in an harmonious organization: only self-love can now command the labor of this savage animal. But he grows wiser and better. Now not a word more of this.

What an odds you must find between the Italians and the Germans! This difference of race appears in all the action of a people, — in its literature, art, architecture, music, painting, sculpture, science, and especially in its government.

"There are inferior races which have always borne the same ignoble relation to the rest of men, and *always will.* For two generations, what a change there will be in the condition and character of the Irish in New England! But, in twenty generations, the negroes will stand just where they are now; that is, if they have not disappeared. In Massachusetts there are no laws now to keep the black man from any pursuit, any office, that he will: but there has never been a rich negro in New England; not a man with ten thousand dollars, perhaps none with five thousand dollars; none eminent in any thing except the calling of a waiter. Now imagine two thousand average Yankees set down in Constantinople or Canton with entire freedom for all manner of activities, — all the prizes of commerce, literature, art, science, politics, before them. How long do you think Jonathan would be a bootblack or a waiter? How long before the Turkish or Chinese money would be in Jonathan's pocket, and all the prizes of civilization in his hands? Not two generations would pass over before this terrible Yankee superiority would appear in the facts of history. That is the strongest case which can be found of national difference. But Germany and Italy present a striking example of it. The blue-eyed Germans have been masters in Italy for nearly eleven hundred years. I mean Rome has been subject, more or less, to Germany, ever since the Gothic conquest and Odoacer's sack of Rome in A.D. 476. The two people have been side by side, running the race of power. What an odds between them! In those Italian countries where the Germans mixed their blood with the old populations, there came up adventurous mariners, who opened the way to the new worlds of the East and the West; and Gothic architecture got planted there. But at Venice, Florence, Milan, the religious tree of the Germans could never reach the vast height and wonderful proportions it shot up to, spontaneous, in its native North, where the breath of the people gave life to its great stem, and individuality to every leaf. The rich buildings of these cities are a compromise of the German and the Italian mind.

"At the time of the revival of letters, say 1400 to 1500, see what a different turn the two nations took! The classic authors of Greece and Rome came back to both. The Italians took to art, painting, sculpture, and rested in objective beauty. It satisfied them, or most of them. Michael Angelo was never content with that: all he ever did (except his David) indicates a yearning after something higher and better than objective art. But quite soon that uplifting of the soul which appears in old Italian art; that struggle with the flesh, and yearning after God, so apparent in the pre-Raphael artists, and which they had caught from their contact with the austere spirit of mediæval Christianity hovering over the land, — all this disappears. Italy settles down into content with objective, actual beauty. No more deep thinkers; no more grand poets; not a great preacher in the Italian Church. The spread of knowledge woke nothing deeper: it provoked no revival of religion; nay, it woke no love of liberty, which once created great men. All her great minds — they were born fast enough — turned off to material science, and then did not dare claim the great freedom they knew was their birthright. Galileo, on his knees confessing a lie to men who also knew it was a lie he confessed, is a representative picture of Italy.

"Now look at the Germans. Charlemagne, a great German, a Frank, sought to found schools. Rabanus Maurus begins to organize popular education among his countrymen in 804. The spark they kindled became a fire which always smouldered in the German forest, and sometimes broke out into a light blaze. By and by a German has invented printing; and, before long, there are presses in all the great German towns; yes, Germans printing in all the great *Italian* towns, and some of the little ones, like Aquila and Soncino. When the revival of letters takes place in Germany, there is a revival of religion along with it. Men turn inward their eye, and ask not mere beauty, but also *truth* and *piety*.

"Since then — say since 1517 — what a difference in Italy and Germany! One believes in salvation by the *masquerading of the Church*, by the ritual which the priests say over in Latin; the other in salvation through *faith in Christ*, — an internal matter, personal to each believer. There is vicarious suffering, but no *vicarious faith*.

"Luther was a good type of Germany, — immensely strong in power of instinct, reflection, will, but rough and uncultivated; Leo. X. a good type of Italy, — of noble birth, supple, astute, deceitful, given to lies, licentious, atheistic, effeminate in all things, an amateur even in his lust, not capable of strong, manly love.

"Since then, look at the men who have come of the Teutonic stock! — Bacon, Leibnitz, Newton, Locke, Hume, Kant, Hegel, Shakspeare, Milton; not to name their equals, but in other departments of thought. What has Italy to show? Look at the mass of the Teutonic people in Germany, Scandinavia, Anglo-Saxondom, and compare them with the fifteen million Italians. Compare the light wit of the two nations, — the *Pasquinades* of Italy with the *Reineke Fuches* and the *Narren Schiffs* of old time, or the *Punch* and *Kladderadatsch* of our own day; and in these little grimaces of the people you see the frivolity of the Italian slave, and the grim earnestness of the Teutonic freeman.

"Look at the Italians and Germans in America, and see what a difference! The Italian is a trader, a musician; while the German is a professor in the college. How deeply rooted these things are! Ineffaceable is the difference.

"I like not much the modern German art: it is rich in technical skill; poor in artistic life. It is an imitation of an imitation. I refer to the Düsseldorf school as the typical example. But go back to the German art which came out of the less-cultivated men, like Albrecht Dürer, Cranach, and the like, and you see these men, all full of the yearning after noble things, with their pencil seek to translate the instinct of the people into artistic expression.

"Compare Beethoven's or Mozart's music with Rossini's or Verdi's, and you hear and feel what elsewhere you see and think.

"The Germans just now are charged with atheism: so are the men of science in England and America; that is, the men who think. Certainly they are full of *doubt.* But what a difference between the atheism of grim, resolute thought, and that of easy indifference! — nay, between the atheism which is only the failure of a great, earnest endeavor, and the '*belief*' of a man who don't care enough to think whether the priest tells truth or no! The *credo* of a fool is not worth the *abnego* or *dubito* of a man."

When, two years later (in 1859), the Pemberton Mill at Lawrence, Mass., — a vast structure many stories high, — fell, causing great loss of life, he reflected thus on the catastrophe in a letter from Rome to his friend Mr. Manley: —

"What a ghastly affair was that at Lawrence! — nearly as many killed and wounded as the Americans lost at Bunker Hill. These battles of industry, also, have their victims. I see they had a day of religious observance at Lawrence on the occasion, and am glad of it. It is natural for us in our sorrow, as in our joy, to flee to the Infinite for consolation and hope. But, alas! how few ministers there are who can see and tell the causes of this disaster in human ignorance and cupidity; its function to tell us of the error we commit, and warn us against repeating it; and its consequence, full of beneficence and man's triumph over the elements! These hundreds of innocent people died, not one of them forgotten before God: they slept in heaven instead of a factory boarding-house; and woke next morning, not to the sharp ring of the mill-bell, but to the gladsome call, 'Come, ye beloved! enter ye into the joy of your Lord!'

"But their death is not in vain on earth: they fell as the New-England soldiers fell in our defeats at Bunker Hill and White Plains, and many another fatal battle-field; but all helps to the great victory which is to come. Harsh words are said against the mill-owners, builders, &c. They did the best they knew, risking their money and reputation on the factory. They certainly constructed ill. The walls of this house I live in are thicker in the fifth story than the Pemberton Mills in the first, and *solid* too. Americans are careless, and must suffer unti they learn prudence. Conform to natural law, and it shall be well with thee: that is the language of all 'accidents.'"

In this general connection we may read another letter to Miss Hunt, from Boston, bearing date June 3, 1858: —

"DEAR SARAH, — I have just read your sweet little letter of May 13, full of profound and just remarks on English and

American people. I quite assent to all you say of the English. Their national pride is *immense;* so is their *personal* pride: but, unlike the French and the Americans, they have little national vanity, little personal. *Insolent* they truly are as a nation and as individuals, *incapable of appreciating other nationalities and individualities.*

"But, with all the faults of the Islanders, I like the creatures. We are of the same stock, and have the same great problems to work out in the civilization of mankind; viz.: 1. To organize the powers of Nature for the service of man; 2. To organize the social powers of humanity, so as to have national unity of action; 3. To develop the individual man into a great variety of forms. These are the three great problems of civilization. England and America work thereat side by side, both unconscious that they are factors in this great product of humanity. I love the Germans. As a family of men, they do immense service to mankind. They are not diffusive, but deep, — wells dark, cool, mysterious (you can see stars from their bottom at noonday), never-failing; while the English are a wide lake, full of green islands, varied in form, green with life, but *not deep;* and the Americans are a river, never still, noisy and turbulent, dirty, but bearing fertility in this very mud which troubles the stream; now spreading into rich lakes bigger than the island which holds that British pond; now laughing in waterfalls, which one day will turn the mills of all the world; then flattening out into dull lagunes, where only the alligator and the snapping-turtle can live, and watering marshes which reek with slavery; then, anon, gathering its waters into one deep, wide channel, where, laden with the fleets of commerce going out and coming in, it flows tranquil on to the ocean, whence all wells, lakes, and rivers are at first supplied, and whither they all at last return.

"I don't like to judge Russia by the counts I meet at watering-places, with their seal-rings of Siberian gold on their forefingers, drinking the finest brandy, and passing their nights in unmentionable riot, after buying flowers for some modest English or French or German or Italian maiden they have talked with by day in her own language, not well, but plain. I would not measure Judæa by the Hebrew peddlers on the Rue de Pots de Fée at Paris, or on the Exchange at London, Leipsic, or Amsterdam; and they are *peddlers* in all these places, whether they cry, '*Marchand de drap!*' or loan money by the million to Austria and France. I would not judge France, England, Germany, America, by the creatures you meet at hotels, theatres, and watering-places, &c. But I look and see what Russia has done in two centuries: what Judæa was in her glory, when Rachel bore patriarchs and prophets, — a Moses, a David, an Isaiah, a Jesus, and a Paul; nay, what she has done when all other nations have hated her. I see what Germany has done and is doing: I look at gunpowder, the printing-press, the deepest service, the richest literature, the most symbolic and suggestive art, in the world; a religion which produces a Luther, a Böhme, a Schleiermacher, which comes out in Leibnitz, Kant, Hegel, Humboldt. I see what England has done for human liberty and human law in a thousand years: I see the immense spread of her stock in America, — we are bone of her bone, flesh of her flesh, soul also of her soul, — in Asia, Africa, and all the islands of the deep. I look at France, and see what she once did for civilization from 700 to 1600, and her influence since in making the deep truths of science intelligible to all thoughtful men, and her skill in all that pertains to the terrible art of war and the graceful arts of pleasure: for France is a CAT, the genteelest of all animals, with her *pas de velours;* and the most ferocious, with her deceitful *griffe*, and her wonderful power of centralizing thought, law, and all authority. And for these things I judge all nations. Poor Italy! poor Spain! theirs is the fate of Asia Minor, of Egypt, — the dead nation: no resurrection can lift *it* up.

"If England or France should possess Italy, there would be a renewing life; but it would not be Italian, only *in* Italy. As when a young man, poor and vigorous, but with no honest scruple, or with nature too much for conscience and will, marries an old rich woman, bed-ridden, but with wealthy crutches to hold her up for the benediction of the priest (not to the fire of the lover), she sees new life around, and hears the laugh, ere long, of children *not her own;* so will it one day be with Italy, so with Spain. It is a curious law of nature, — the strong displaces the weak.

"In New England there are two natural grasses for the open field, — the red-top and the white clover, both equally strong and vivacious. The farmer sows two other grasses together, — red clover and herds-grass, — the first a weak grass, the last a strong one. The first year the field is red with clover, the herds-grass does not appear; next year there are but bunches of red clover here and there; the third year the strong herds-grass has killed it all. But little by little the native grasses, stouter than what he scattered there, come up, and in a few years have killed out all the other from the soil. Thus the white man kills out the red man and the black man. When slavery is abolished, the African population will decline in the United States, and die out of the South as out of Northampton and Lexington. It is just so with youth and age in the market. Let a man of seventy and a boy of twenty go into business in the same city, with the same little capital: in five years the young man will run him out of the market, and get away all his customers. So is it with the nations."

The problem of American destiny was forever on his mind: —

"I don't know but these Paddies are worse than the Africans to the country. We made a great mistake in attracting them here, and allowing them to vote under less than twenty-one years of quarantine. Certainly it would take all that time to clean a Paddy, — on the *outside*, I mean: to clean him inwardly would be like picking up all the sands of Sahara. There would be nothing left when the sands were gone.

"It is amazing, the corruption of America! Power is always abused in Church or State. One of the most sensible men I know said to me the other day, 'It makes me think we have made a mistake; that we had better have a nobilitary class, who are above these bitter squabbles about office and money, and also a queen-bee in the hive, as still in England:' but added, '*if they would do any better*.' But our safety consists in going *through* this Red Sea of transition, not turning back to Egypt. We shall go through, not without manifold trouble. Guizot says, 'God has made the terms of national welfare more difficult than any nation is willing to believe.' How true it is! But these are yet the easiest conditions which are possible to infinite perfection. . . . Sumner never took so deep an interest in America, was never so regardless of personal consequences, as now." (This was written in December, 1857.) "The age never needed him more. I seldom covet any man's position: I am quite satisfied with my own. But I should like to be in the United-States Senate this winter. I should like to make four speeches, — on Kansas and its affairs, on the national conduct towards feeble States, on the Dred Scott decision, and on the general conduct of the Federal Government for the last dozen years. But I should rather Sumner would do it than I; rather *any one* would do it. I want it done; and, lacking a better, would do my possible. Don't think I desire such a place, or would accept it were it offered. There is only one position in fancy which I should prefer to the present one; that is, a great quiet house in the country a few miles off, where I could write the books which still burn in my brain. Perhaps I shall have it one day; but who knows? I think 'circumstances' are wiser than I; certainly stronger."

As early as 1844, he wrote from Rome to a friend, Mr. J. H. Billings of West Roxbury, —

"I think we live in a time when it is a man's DUTY to attend to political affairs. If good men neglect their country, the bad will have it all to themselves, and a sad time we shall have of it. We certainly have much to fear; not so much from a tariff party or an anti-tariff party as from an ignorant people and corrupt leaders. The strength of the country is such, and the energy of the people so great, where such opportunities are left for individual freedom and enterprise, that neither John Tyler nor John Calhoun could do us any great harm in four years; but, unless we become a *wiser* people and a *more moral* people, we may give over the dream of governing ourselves, and be ruled by *bayonets and a despot.* The little I can do to aid the country, therefore, will be rather in attempting to promote *education — intellectual, moral, and religious education* — everywhere, and for all men, than in joining in the measures of either party."

To Miss Hunt.

MARCH 23, 1858.

. . . The Devil of slavery now manifests himself in great wrath because he knows that his power is short. Banks says there is not a politician he knows in the South who thinks slavery will last forty years in any slave State. But how the government fights for it! how the hunkers at the North! No foolish mother ever more seriously turned off her only son, and cuddled her monkey close to her breast. If we behave well, by the 4th of July, 1876, we shall extirpate slavery from South Carolina, its last stronghold. I don't believe we shall ever see another slavery President.

JULY 12, 1858.

. . . The slave power pushes things on rapidly. In Virginia the court decides that a slave has no legal rights to *choice*. A woman left money to her slaves on condition that they would be emancipated by *their consent*. The court decided against the will: so the slaves get neither freedom nor money. Louisiana has just passed a law forbidding free blacks to come in, and banishing all who are there now against the law. If they are found after July, 1859, they are to be sold as *slaves forever*. Soon they will attempt to re-enslave all the free blacks. Great efforts are making to restore the African slave-trade. Hundreds of American vessels are in it now: the government does nothing against them; will do nothing. THE END DRAWS NEAR. But some contingency may alter things. In 1856 we were quite close to a civil war. Had the governor of Kansas done as he was bid, and *not* resigned, and taken the free-State side, the war would have begun then. I think we shall never see another slave President. Still I may easily be mistaken. I should like, of all things, to see an insurrection of the slaves. It must be tried many times before it succeeds, *as at last it must*.

He was thinking, when he penned that sentence, of John Brown and his enterprise, of which he thinks a good deal, but dares say nothing, even to these most intimate of his friends in Europe. In all his letters the name is not once mentioned; nor would any suspect that his thoughts were so full of the man from whom he hoped so much. Parker knew how to keep a secret.

From the Journal.

"We understand a little of the evils of war; only a little: the evils of wicked legislation in times of peace we know less of. The English corn-laws in thirty years retarded the progress of mankind in that country more than all the wars of Napoleon. In America the legal continuance of the slave-trade for twenty years, from 1787 to 1808, cost more lives than all our wars for a hundred years. The wicked compromise made by the Constitution in 1787 has more retarded the nation than all other causes put together. It has cost more lives than all the wars of Napoleon; yet what good did men purchase by it?"

"Men wonder I am ill: I marvel not;
For the sad sense of human woe is deep
Within my heart, and deepens daily there.
I see the want, the woe, the wretchedness,
Of smarting men, who wear, close pent in towns,
The galling load of life. The rich, the poor,
The drunkard, criminal, and they that make
Him so, and fatten on his tears and blood, —
I bear their sorrows, and I weep their sins:
Would I could end them! No: I see before
My race an age or so; and I am sent
For the stern work, to hew a path among
The thorns, — I take them in my flesh, — to tread
With naked feet the road, and smooth it o'er
With blood. Well, I shall lay my bones
In some sharp crevice of the broken way.
Men shall in better times stand where I fell,
And journey, singing on in perfect bands,
Where I have trod alone, no arm but God's,
No voice but his. Enough! — his voice, his arm."

CHAPTER XVII.

FAILING HEALTH.

THE accumulation of work on Theodore Parker had by this time become immense; for the new tasks never displaced old ones. All he had done he continued doing, quickening his speed as the road lengthened, and bracing his shoulders as the burden increased. The studies were continued, and under less merciful conditions. The books went in a satchel with him to the trains. All day he read in the jostling car, the motion and noise whereof caused an unnatural irritability of brain; and at night, by the help of a little apparatus he had, the scholar's toil was continued. The sermons were written as conscientiously, and under severer sense of responsibility. His lectures, which were meant to edify and instruct, never to amuse, cost him a world of labor in preparation, and great fatigue in delivery. The parish-work — visiting the sick, comforting the afflicted, burying the dead — was done faithfully, with broken heart of spikenard, very precious, poured out on the feet of the humblest. To weep with the weeping, and rejoice with the rejoicing, was to him a ministerial privilege he never wished to forego, or delegate to others; and his parish included, beside those who regularly attended service at Music Hall, a multitude of strangers who had no claim on him but that of their need, and who hastened to lay their loads, not at his feet, but on his shoulders. He considered himself appointed "minister at large of all fugitive slaves in Boston." How he discharged that ministry we have seen. In special cases his attention was unremitted. Hours were set apart every day for offices of help and sympathy. He multiplied himself with multiplying cares; he spread himself with the spreading field.

It is a common opinion that Mr. Parker sank exhausted from overwork. This is incidentally, but only incidentally, true. But for terrible overwork, he might have lived to be an old man. But for the exposure to which a part of his work (lecturing, for instance) subjected him, he probably would have reached seventy-five or eighty. Still his arch-enemy was not toil: he worked easily. Intellectual labor was a joy to him: it cost him more to suspend it than to pursue it. Toil was a necessity of his being, a law of his constitution. To stop his engines damaged them. Then — after he reached mature life at least — his habits were mainly wholesome. He was temperate, but no ascetic, in eating or drinking. He did not keep inordinately late hours. He was fond of walking; and, in the season for it, took long walks, — made journeys on foot into the country and to the mountains. His animal spirits were high: he could laugh and jest to the last. The blood was swift in his veins. In his youth he had great strength: he was always powerful in his arms and legs. In the postscript to a note to his friend T. W. Higginson, dated March, 1858, he says, —

"Let the saints (at Worcester) always keep good bodies. Do you know I could once *carry a barrel of cider* in my hands? I don't mean a glass at a time, — I could do that now, — but a *barrel* at a time. I have worked (not often, though) at farm-work *twenty hours* out of the twenty-four, for several days together, when I was eighteen or twenty. I have often worked from twelve to seventeen hours a day in my study for a considerable period; and could do that *now:* so you were not wholly wrong in putting me among the able-*bodied* men."

Still there was a radical source of weakness: there was inherited disease. His mother was consumptive. The climate of his birthplace was unhealthy. He grew up amid the disadvantages of poverty, — insufficient and unsuitable food and clothing, privation, and premature labor. His boyish strength was frightfully overtaxed. He knew and was told nothing of the necessity of sleep, exercise, recreation: so that he grew up thoughtless of the simplest conditions of physical health; so ignorant of them, that he fancied he could live at Cambridge on two crackers a day, and actually tried to live on something like it. It is no wonder that his latent foes were re-enforced: that the citadel held out so long is the marvel. Confessions of ill health appear early in the journal. The trouble was mainly in the head, though sometimes in the side. He calls it dyspepsia, "or something else." He complains of useless days and weeks when he could do nothing. Among the letters to Miss Stevenson I find this one, dated Feb. 23, 1846: —

"I was sorry the moment that I mentioned my complaint to you the other day; for I saw that it gave you more trouble than me. I don't often tell my friends that I am ill: then, I know not how, I felt it would be *wrong* not to tell *you*. I have done no work that I could avoid. I have been idle this winter, till my conscience rebuked me sternly, and does now. I am passing my best days, and doing but very little. My troubles are not the result of any *immediate* overdoing, but of causes that go back to my childhood. I have often done two days' work in one; for I was *obliged* to do it. It cost me a struggle, alone and single-handed, to gain an education. The foundation of my present troubles, I have no doubt, was laid more than fifteen years ago, — before I came to Boston as a teacher. Since that, my life has been one of care and anxiety, not diminished since my marriage. You know the cause. I don't know what to do. So long as I can stand upright, I do well: the moment I resolve to lean *a little*, I go plumb down; for there is nothing for me to lean upon: therefore I never fall till the last minute.

I will be as careful as I can be, considering the circumstances of the case. I can't go off a fortnight, though I gladly would. We are just putting the *social meeting* into action: and I feel that I had better be here; though, perhaps, I had better not. Then, too, whom can I get to bend my own bow? — not a long one, not a tough one, perhaps, but one that others don't like to handle. I don't know whether I am destined to a long life or not. Of my seven father Parkers this side the ocean, all but one have lived to be nearly eighty. My candle stands in a current of air, and so, I suppose, will burn away faster than if all about it was still. I don't know that I need *rest:* I think I need *fun*, which I can't easily get. I should like to spend one evening in the week, for three months, with 'good fellows,' who sang, —

'We won't go home till morning!'

However, give yourself no more concern about me; for this week I am a good deal better. Last week I did nothing at all, — not even write a sermon; for an old one took its place the *stormy* Sunday: and so the ill wind actually blew me a sermon. Ah, Hannah! a great many ill winds have blown *me* good.

"Now, you child, I might turn round and caution *you*, who need the advice more than I do, but won't follow it half so much, you good-for-nothing! 'Physician, heal thyself;' take thine own doses. There is no preaching like practice. Cure up Margaret as fast as you can, and I'll take care of my head; and it will last a good while yet, and bear some hard knocks. The spring will soon come; and its freshness of leaves and blossoms will do as much good to all of us as to the bluebird and thrasher. Be a good girl, and don't trouble yourself about

"YOUR GRANDFATHER."

In September, 1849, he constructs a health-scale, thus: —

"When able to write the sermon Monday morning, A.
" " " " " " evening, $\frac{A}{2}$.
" " " " " Tuesday morning, B.
" " " " " " evening, $\frac{B}{2}$.
And so on, — C, D, E, F. If not at all, o."

From the Journal.

Saturday, Sept. 8. — Have done little all the week. Health $\frac{F}{2}$: this is too near an approach to 0 for this season of the year. I have not begun this month so ill for some years. If I had one of the usual *humdrum* parishes, I would leave it for a year, and go off to Europe; but this is a parish which I cannot leave. I feel as if I had squandered a fortune; for, at the age of thirty-nine, I am ill, and lose more than half my time. For the next six months I will take especial care of my health, making all else bend to that, and that to nothing.

Saturday, Sept. 22. — Health about B.

The journal of Aug. 24, 1853, contains a birthday record: —

"I am this day forty-three years old. I used to think I should live as long as my fathers; but certain admonitions of late warn me that I am not to be an old man. The last three years have made great alterations in my health and vigor. I walk and work now *with a will*; then by the spontaneous impulse which once required the will to check it. I neither grieve nor rejoice at the thought of departure; but I will try to set my affairs in such a condition, that I can at any time go over to the other side when summoned, and leave affairs in no perplexity."

Already he had begun to count his chances. He bethought himself of his ten brothers and sisters, all of whom, save one, attained mature years; all of whom, save one, died from forty-four to forty-seven. He kept his eye on that critical period, doubting whether he should pass it; confident that, if he did, he should live to be an old man.

The journal of April, 1856, has another record: —

"Last night I was to lecture at New Bedford, and tried to speak; but was so ill, that I could not hear or see or speak well. I left the room, and went out with Mr. Robeson, and walked a few minutes. Went to an apothecary's, and drank about a spoonful and a half of sherry wine, which helped me. Spoke, but with great difficulty. Am better to-day, but slenderly and meanly. *I take this as a warning,* — not the first."

To Miss Hunt, on the 30th of November of the same year, he writes, —

"I hope that Sarah does not stay a prisoner in her room. There are two admirable doctors; to wit, Dr. SUN and Dr. AIR. Both, I think, will do that little maiden a deal of good; and she need not take their prescription *homœopathically.* I preached two Sundays: —

"1. On needless sickness, &c.

"2. On the progress of the Anglo-Saxons in three hundred years (a sermon on the three-hundredth anniversary of Queen Elizabeth's accession to the British throne). It is a great triumph we have made since that day.

"Then the Catholics had the hall for a fair; and we must shut up on Thanksgiving Day and last Sunday. It happened famously this time; for I was not able to preach. I strained the muscles of my right thigh in getting into the railroad-cars on Wednesday, the day before Thanksgiving; and came home in a bad condition. I have not been down stairs since Thanksgiving morning to breakfast, but stay here; wear the Bear's petticoats, &c.; but am mending, and shall preach next Sunday on the progress which the foremost ideas of humanity will make in the next three hundred years. The last sermon was one of memory and gratitude: the next will be of duty and hope.

"Many thanks for all your kind words, both of you, and your kind wishes. I am the most submissive of all mortals. I do just what the doctor (Cabot) and Bear and Hannah tell me. I am transfigured into a spaniel, a turnspit, a poodle, or some other puppy-dog, with no self-moving principle in him. So don't advise Bear to consult RAREY. She could teach *him* many a lesson in the art of man-taming. I never expect to name myself again.

"My health is good; but I can't walk much, and have a cough, — *not pulmonic,* — which is going off. I can preach without any difficulty; but I don't go about much. Have been in State Street but once for nine weeks, and made but one parish visit for nine, — then to see the sister of Mrs. Fisher: the old lady has moved up and on. So, of course, I have not seen Cabot, who has taken his wife out to Brookline; nor Mr. Waterston. Just now I can't *write* much: so you get little, and others nought.

"Willie writes a nice German *Wunder*-story; but I had rather hear that he had knocked down a Dutch boy of twelve, and could throw any boy in his class. The lad wants *bowels*, *legs*, *arms*, and *chest;* not a head. I tremble at the thought of that school, — thirty-four boys in the class, and he fourth or fifth! I wish he was tending cows somewhere, and not studying so much. . . .

"The cod-liver oil from the Laffoden Isles is rancid before it reaches us. The best we get is made at Provincetown — which lasts from March to September — and at Labrador, which is made in October, and keeps through the winter. None is good more than four or five months. I am taking the Labrador. All the house is well, and we all send love.

"God bless you! "T."

This, then, is his condition in the thick of the Kansas strife, with all that pressure of anxiety on his mind. To Miss Hunt he writes again on the 17th of December, —

"I am as busy as the apostle who had 'no leisure; no, not so much as to eat.' I wonder if St. Peter had not some dear little family off in Siberia or Australia, with a hippopotamus in it, which he must write to by the next steamer from Joppa, or by the Turkish mail-line, or the Jerusalem and Kamtschatka express?

"I am lecturing all the time: twenty-five lectures since the 1st of November, and perhaps fifty more under contract. All this keeps me up late, and makes me work hard, which you know I dislike. In January and February I shall go several times to New-York State, having some twenty or more applications. So, perhaps, I shall continue to do till I am *fifty;* and after August, 1860, I intend no longer to live such an apostolical, nomadic, and unchristian life, but to sit down and write my books, which cry out for me to make them ready. But who knows?

It is not in man that walketh to direct his steps. Some accident may stop the lecturing to-day, or something else make it necessary to continue the toil till I am a hundred. Poverty, like an armed man, may come upon me in my old age as on Pierpont, and stir me up to work when I would rather lie down and sleep. But, as the sky now promises no such storm (I should have said *threatens*), I lay plans of a different sort. 'There's nothing sure but death and rates,' say the Scotch: so who knows that 1860 will bring the long-coveted opportunity to write my books?"

It would seem as if he were determined it should not: for, early in this very year (1856), he undertook to preach on Sunday afternoons to an independent society in Watertown that had no minister; and he did it for a year, with no other compensation than the thanks of the people and the amount of his bill at the stable. The service he enjoyed, and he wrote no new sermon; but the journey in all weathers he had no right to submit to, and the duty was a tax on his conscientiousness. "Work while it is day" was the rule he went by, forgetting that too much work brought on the night before its time. To friends who remonstrated with him he would reply, "Look at the condition of the country to-day! — the slaveholders clamoring for more and more power; the government disposed to yield all they ask; the South united and arrogant; while the North is divided, and disposed to be submissive. I CANNOT stand idly by, a silent witness of this deadly demoralization. I must exert every power I possess to avert the awful evils that slavery threatens, to the slaves first, but also to the whole people; and, if my life must be sacrificed, it cannot be sacrificed in a better cause than that of opposition to this dreadful sin."

To a faithful soul who came to see him not long before he broke down he said with emotion, —

"I am glad *you* have come; for I know *you* won't scold at me. People come here and scold at me for doing what I can't help doing. I feel that the fate is upon me. God has intrusted me with certain powers, and I must use them in the service of my fellow-men. Here are four millions of my brothers and sisters who are literally dumb. They are not allowed to speak; and they hold up their hands to me in earnest entreaty, saying, 'Speak for us!' and I must do for them all I can. I have looked the matter carefully over, and think I can go through the winter safely, and do my work. I come of a long-lived stock, and hope with care to survive; but it matters little whether I go through or go under, if I do my duty as I ought."

"Never," said his friend, "did I see any one so thoroughly aware of the fact that he was laying his life on God's altar."

Still he did the best he could, or thought he could. The summer of 1856 was spent delightfully in the near neighborhood of very dear friends whom he was not to see for three years, but whom he met himself in Europe before they had expired. Many an evening of that summer he passed on the lawn with them, and was in his happiest vein. Every star as it came out in the heavens, the stray odors from the ground, the chirp of cricket and grasshopper, the cry of the startled bird in the chestnut-grove, all sights and sounds, were noted by his quick senses, and woven into his wonderful talk. On the last evening, as he said "Good-by!" he begged for the "Moorish cushion" he had sat on these moonlight or starlight evenings, and took it away as a memorial, and to sit on "sacramentally" after his friends had gone. A touch of his heartstrings always revived him.

In the August of this same summer (1856) he writes to Miss Stevenson, —

"For now a week I have had time — the first for a year or two — to read for general instruction and for immediate delight. Guess how I enjoyed it! Kuno Fischer, Diotima (a 'Treatise on Beauty'), and half a dozen volumes of Vogt, with a 'Vie de Pierre Ramus' by Waddington, and a (very stupid and hypocritical) work on 'La Vie Future' by M. Martin, with divers others, have been the results thus far. Here is unbounded stillness and repose ; nothing to molest."

Light reading to rest the mind!

About this time he amused himself with making translations from German poets; his favorite being Heine, the most difficult of all to render. It was his habit, late on the Sunday afternoons of a single winter and spring, to go to a friend's house in Mt. Vernon Street to hear and read the translations. He took great pains with these trifles; wrote them over and over again; seemed never tired of improving them; prided himself more on their artistic perfection than on much better work; desired that the choicest of them should be preserved, with his name attached to them. Specimens of this light work Mr. Weiss has printed in his second volume. The very best of all I venture to reprint here: —

Oh! knew but the blossoms, the wee things,
  How deep I am wounded at heart,
They'd mingle their tears with my weeping,
  And charm away my smart.

And did but the nightingales know it
  That I'm sad and sick so long,
They would joyfully come and sing me
  A life-awakening song.

And if they could know all my sorrows,
  The dear gold-starlets we see,
They would all come away from their glory,
  And comfort speak to me.

But all of them can't understand it:
  One only she knows of my smart;
For it was she herself rent asunder,
  Asunder rent, my heart.

This is pretty: —

I.

On the pinions of the Muses,
  My dearest, thee I bear
To the banks of holy Ganges,
  Where I know the spot most fair.

II.

A rosy blooming garden
  Lies in still moonlight there:
The lotus-flowers are waiting
  Their little sister dear.

III

The violets are billing and cooing,
  And look to the stars above;
In secret the roses whisper
  Their fragrant story of love.

IV.

There comes to leap and listen
  The shy and cunning gazelle;
And far on the holy river
  The waters rush and swell.

V.

There 'neath a palm we'll lay us,
  Beside the holy stream,
And drink of love and quiet,
  And dream a blessed dream.

The following version of "The Midnight Review" compares fairly with the usual renderings of that famous poem, and shows what he could do: —

I.

About the hour of midnight
  The drummer leaves his grave;
Makes with the drum his circuit;
  Goes up and down so brave;

II.

And with his arm all fleshless
  Goes drumming through and through:
He beateth many a roll-call,
  Reveillé, and tattoo.

III.

The drum resoundeth strangely;
  It has a heavy sound:
The old deceasèd soldiers
  Waken thereat in the ground.

IV.

They who in high Northland,
  All stiff in ice and snow;
Those in Italia sleeping,
  The ground too rich below;

V.

They whom the Nile slime covers,
  And the Arabian sand, —
They rise from out their war-graves,
  And their weapons take in hand.

VI.

About the hour of midnight
  The trumpeter leaves his grave,
And bloweth on his trumpet,
  And up and down rides brave.

VII.

Those serving on airy horses,
  The riders dead, behold!
The bloody ancient squadrons
  With weapons manifold.

VIII.

There the white skulls all grinning
  Beneath the helms appear;
And hands of bone and sinew
  Long troopers' swords uprear.

IX.

About the hour of midnight
  The commander leaves his grave:
From far he cometh hither:
  Round him his staff rides brave.

X.

He wears a little *chapeau;*
  A simple dress he wears;
Also a little straight sword
  At his left side he bears.

XI.

The moon, her light, pale yellow,
  Shines on the long, wide plain:
The man in the small *chapeau*
  Looks on his troops again.

XII.

The ranks present saluting,
  And shoulder then no gun:
With playful sound of trumpet
  The whole host marches on.

XIII.

The generals and marshals
  Around him form a ring:
To the nearest the commander
  A word is whispering.

XIV.

That word goes round the circuit,
  Resounding near and far:
And "France!" is now the watchword;
  The countersign, "St. Helena!"

XV.

This is the mighty muster
  In the Elysian Plain,
Which at the hour of midnight
  The emperor holds again.

To Miss Hunt.

BOSTON, Sept. 4, 1857.

MY DEAR SARAH,—My summer vacation draws nigh its end. I shall begin to preach again Sept. 6.

I have spent the last seven weeks in the most strenuous attempts to be intellectually idle. It is true, I have not all the common helps thereto. I don't drink to excess, or drive fast horses. More than morally, I am materially opposed to smoking, with a constitutional objection to the laziness-producing weed. I keep no bad company. I don't sit in easy-chairs or rocking-chairs. What helps could I have? I have industriously read the Boston newspapers,—the "Courier," "Journal," "Traveller," "Transcript," &c.; and three times have attended church on Sundays. The result is, I never lived so many weeks with so little thought. I have done what I could to effect a cure. If I fail, it must be a vice of my nature, no sin of my will. The doctors (and doctoresses) recommended total abstinence from thought. I have come as near it as the "carnal reason" of my "fallen nature" will allow.

Now I shall begin to think a little, and gradually come back to a little more, and so on. I shall lecture but little this winter; never when I am forced to ride all night, or sleep in a bad bed. There is a deal of writing to be done; and this winter I shall attend to that partly, and partly to acquiring firm and robust health. My nature never consented to this nomadic life of a lecturer, running all over the country, and sleeping in other men's beds (or in no beds, and often not sleeping). But it gave me the means of charity, and an opportunity to publish certain thoughts which I think of value to the people. Hereafter I shall be content with the pulpit and the press, and let the lecture go; at least, for a time.

The visit to Central New York was fatal. It was made in February, 1857. Thus he tells the story:—

"Feb. 9th, I was to lecture at Waterford; 10th, at Syracuse; 11th, at Utica; 12th, at Rochester; and then return, and reach Boston at midnight of 14th–15th. I should pass every night in my bed, except that of the 12th. But, on the contrary, things turned out quite otherwise. The railroad-conductor left us in the cars all night at East Albany, in the midst of the inundation. Common New-England prudence and energy would have taken us all over the river. I had no dinner, no supper, except what I had in my wallet (dried fruit and biscuit); no breakfast the next morning, save a bit of tough beef in an Irish boarding-house. When I awoke on the morning of the 10th, I felt a sharp pain in my right side, not known before. I got to Syracuse that night (10th) *viâ* Troy; lectured at Utica the 11th; and at eleven, P.M., took the cars for Rochester, and rode all night till five or six the next morning, when I got into damp sheets at Rochester, and slept an hour. I was ill all that day, and at night had all the chills of an incipient fever. But I lectured; took the cars at two or three, A.M., having waited for them three or four hours in the dépôt; and reached Albany in time for the four, P.M., train, Friday; and got to Boston about two, A.M., on Saturday; having had no reasonable meal since noon, Thursday. Sunday I preached at Boston and Watertown, as my custom was. The next week I was ill, but lectured four times; so the next and the next; until, in March, I broke down utterly, and could do no more."

To Miss Hunt.

BOSTON, April 7, 1857.

MY DEAR SARAH,—I have written but one letter with my own hand for more than three weeks; and now my pen will *wabble* a little, do the best I can.

What a queer thing for me to be sick! I don't know that I

ought to call it *sick*, though. But I was ailing a month before I finally broke down. For a while I lay horizontally twenty-two hours out of the twenty-four, then twenty-one, then twenty, then nineteen, eighteen, seventeen, sixteen, fifteen; and yesterday I was out of the horizontal line eleven hours. I made up my mind that one of the best medicines would be the usual service of Sunday. The doctors all of them said "No!" all the laical and clerical friends said "No!" and, with even more emphasis, all the women.

But I thought, out of ten chances, there are seven that it will do me good; only three for harm. So I made ready an old sermon of *integrity*, adding a deal of new matter thereto. A coach took Bear and me to the door; and with her help and a cane I crawled into the house, and walked as bravely as I could to the pulpit. I felt a little sinking of the heart as I looked at the congregation, — about two thousand. But all the preliminary services went off without difficulty. I apologized for being sick, and showed that it was not wholly my fault; but the *nervous poison* I took in at East Albany had done the work.

Then came the sermon. I spread out my feet as far apart as I could (old men and little children always *straddle*) to make a wide basis, and kept my hand always on the desk, so that I need not fall over. Only two or three times did I venture to lift both hands at once. The services over, Mr. Manley and others put on my coat; and Bear and Dr. Geist helped me out and into the coach, and I rode home. My pulse is commonly about sixty-four: it stood at seventy-six to eighty-four till about three o'clock; then went down. I felt a little doubtful of the experiment for a while: but at five the tide had begun to turn; and at six I said I would not *crow* till I was out of the woods; and at nine it was clear that the experiment had prospered; and Monday morning, spite of the southerly rain, which held all day, it was plain to all that I was saved by the "foolishness of preaching." To-day I am a deal better, and shall be as careful and prudent as the most cautious can desire.

The parish-meeting was last Sunday, at twelve. They raised my salary from sixteen hundred to two thousand five hundred dollars; and offered me six months' vacation to go to Europe, they supplying the pulpit. I shall not take two thousand five hundred, only two thousand dollars; and shall decline the generous offer of a vacation. The kindly offer effects a cure; and so I need not take all the medicine. I make day-dreams and night-dreams of the visit, and so get a good deal of solid satisfaction out of it. But I don't need the relaxation, and so shall not take it. This recent illness is a warning which I shall carefully heed. I never came quite so near the edge of the precipice before. I might have had either a brain-fever or a lung-fever: I am let off with this trifle of a slow *typhoidal*. Men seldom have the *typhoid* twice. I had mine at twelve, and lay at Death's door a good while, but was not taken in.

At this juncture, his strength failing him, he was subjected to a fresh assault on his theological position. Hitherto his ecclesiastical foes had mainly been members of the Unitarian sect. His theological war had been waged within the limits of a small denomination, which the great religious world of New England had come to overlook as a Boston clique, a local peculiarity too insignificant to be regarded with alarm. Beyond an occasional twitting of the Unitarians with their responsibility for Mr. Parker, there was little serious concern taken in the family quarrel. But now the case was altered. Parker had a national reputation. He lectured and preached throughout the Northern States. His printed sermons were sold by the thousand, and read by the ten thousand. Strangers from afar came to hear him, and carried his thoughts all over the land. His name was spoken in the places of power by men who had the political and social destinies of the country in their charge, — by statesmen, senators, governors of States. Reformers confessed him their leader; philanthropists acknowledged him their fellow in good works. He was a formidable person in the community, an invidious influence on the globe, quite worthy the attention of those who had in their keeping the souls of men. Had not such been faithless to their duty in allowing him to run wild so long? Was it not time that his course should be checked? Had he not lived long enough, yea, too long, for the welfare of the elect? To assassinate him was, of course, out of the question. But if the Lord might only be moved to take him to himself, sanctified or not! Might He not be moved by entreaty? A "providential intervention" would be as effectual as "carnal" methods used to be, and would be edifying beside. Why should such interventions be discontinued?

The great "revival" of 1858, resulting from the commercial ruin of 1857, gave the desired opportunity for an experiment. New England was in a convulsion of religious emotion, torn between ecstasies of devotion and agonies of penitence. Pious whippers-in plied all their arts on the weak, the nervous, the superstitious. Praying bands went from town to town, galvanizing the moribund into spasms of supplication. Churches were open all day, and relays of ministers kept the evangelical car in swift motion towards the kingdom. Posters in the streets announced the time and place of special meetings for intercession. The drama of redemption was exhibited with new scenery, and more imposing stage-effects. The good people who had persuaded themselves that the reign of vulgar superstition was at an end, at all events in Boston, were confounded when they saw the well-worn imagery of the Apocalypse start into life, and the faded pictures of damnation glow once more on the walls of modern meeting-houses. The fetishism they thought obsolete was rampant still in high places. Men in black coats and white neck-ties beat the tomtom as vigorously as New-Zealanders, and called on their idol as lustily as the priests of Baal.

Now, then, was the time to get rid of Parker. He was weak, ailing, prostrate. A combined assault at this juncture, by the combined spirits of earth and heaven, might, perchance, overthrow him. The word was given; the faithful were ready; a simultaneous movement upon the Holy Seat was made. That all the forces might be used, and no atom of momentum lost, it was recommended that men and women, wherever they might be, — in the shop or on the street, — should pray for Mr. Parker daily when the clock struck one. A few samples of these "addresses to the throne of grace" will tell better than any description the method and spirit of the evangelical tacticians. They are taken from the journal, where Mr. Parker had preserved them in connection with one or two other specimens of the superstition of the nineteenth century.

"O Lord! send confusion and distraction into his study this afternoon, and prevent his finishing his labors for to-morrow; or, if he shall attempt to desecrate thy holy day by attempting to speak to the people, meet him there, Lord, and confound him, so that he shall not be able to speak."

"O Lord! put a hook in this man's jaws, so that he may not be able to speak."

"O Lord! meet this infidel on his way, who, like another Saul of Tarsus, is persecuting the Church of God; and cause a light to shine around him, which shall bring him trembling to the earth, and make him an able defender of the faith which he has so long labored to destroy."

"O Lord! if this man will still persist in speaking in public, induce the people to leave him, and to come up and fill this house instead of that."

"Lord, we know that we cannot argue him down; and, the more we say against him, the more will the people flock after him, and the more will they love and revere him. O Lord! what shall be done for Boston if thou dost not take this and some other matters in hand?"

The following prayer was offered by Elder Burnham, who, in an afternoon sermon, said, —

"Hell never vomited forth a more wicked and blasphemous monster than Theodore Parker; and it is only the mercies of Jesus Christ which have kept him from eternal damnation already."

After such an outburst, the petition that follows has a savor of tenderness: —

"O Lord! if this man is a subject of grace, convert him, and bring him into the kingdom of thy dear Son; but, if he is beyond the reach of the saving influence of the gospel, remove him out of the way, and let his influence die with him."

There were some who looked on the strong man's sickness as a judgment on him for his impiety; and some, it is rumored, regarded it as an anticipative answer to the prayers.

Mr. Parker took the nonsense pleasantly, so far as it concerned himself. In a letter, after speaking of it, he lets his thoughts run in other channels: —

"The robins have come; the blue-birds long ago. Give my love to the pope. Don't tell the pope this (about the prayers); for I fear I shall miss the cardinalship, and my black hat is almost worn out. I think the robes will come over in 'The Leviathan.'"

But, as a sign of the times, the "revival" made him sad, and stirred up within him the theological zeal, which never had wholly slept, but which had temporarily yielded to a more practical "enthusiasm of humanity." The two sermons, "A False and True Revival of Religion," and "The Revival of Religion which we Need," showed the old fires still burning, their heat as fierce, their splendor as awful, their beauty as fascinating, as ever, — fires of wrath, and flames of prophecy, at once angering some, and kindling others with hope.

The same spirit animated the four remarkable discourses which he delivered before the Progressive Friends, in Chester County, Pennsylvania, in June, 1858. They are among his most characteristic efforts: —

1. Of the Progressive Development of the Conception of God in the Bible.

2. Of the Ecclesiastical Conception of God, and its Inadequacy to meet the Wants of Science and Religion.

3. Of the Philosophical or Natural Idea of God, and its Fitness for all the Wants of Science and Religion.

4. Of the Soul's Normal Delight in the Infinite God.

By this time it had become plain, that, if Mr. Parker would not take care of himself, his friends must take care of him. In August, a new but already intimate friend, alarmed by the danger, invited him to take a wagon journey of two or three weeks. It is thus described in a letter to his friends, Mrs. Apthorp and Miss Hunt, in Europe: —

PALAZZO BABY SQUEAL, PIAZZA PADDY SMELL,
NEWTON CORNER, MASS., Last Sunday in
Dog Days, 1858.

DEAREST SALLIE AND LIZZIE, — I shall put the two sisters in one letter this day, the last of my vacation.

You think "fleas the only troubles," do you? What if you had flies biting, baby squealing, mother yelling, and doors slamming, all at the same time? "But there is no life without its inconveniences," as the toad said while under the harrow, or might have said if his tongue had been loosed.

Don't think you are the only voyagers on earth, or that Europe is the only country fit to travel in. Have not I, also, had my journey? I returned on Thursday afternoon from a little ride of seven hundred miles with Joseph Lyman. You know Joseph Lyman, Judge Lyman's son, of your own town, — a fine fellow, one of the most gentlemanly of men, "the best traveller in the world," thoroughly eupeptic, and of course good-natured (the stomach is the organ of good temper), conversable, and highly intelligent. Hannah calls him "the lover," — not *hers*, not *Bear's*, but *mine*. (He does come over, sometimes, Sunday night; and takes me to ride, &c.) Didn't we have a good time? His "wagon" is a wonderful "one-hoss shay" on four wheels, which cost four hundred and fifty dollars. Thomas Goddard made it; but for modesty it is called the "wagon." We rode about thirty miles a day, at the rate of from three to five miles an hour: so we were always ten or twelve hours a day in the open air. Beautiful weather all the time. We never staid in a great town — save one night in Albany, which we could not avoid. Here is our route: To Concord (Mass.); through Lancaster, Princeton, Fitzwilliam, to Keene (N.H.); to Charleston, Windsor (Vt.), Comstock, Sherburne, Montpelier, and Burlington, to Lake Saranac in the Adirondack Mountains (New York); down Lake Champlain, and by Fort Ticonderoga and Fort Edward to Saratoga, Troy, Albany; down the Hudson to Newburg; thence through the whole length of Connecticut to Dudley in Massachusetts; thence, *viâ* Hopkinton Springs, home again, — seven hundred miles in twenty-one days, with no accident, no delay. Now, we saw no kings, only *would-bes;* and no queens, only *supposed-to-bes;* and no pope, not even a *cardinal.* Oh! where *is* my cardinal's hat? What faithless friends you are, not to have extorted from the pope this dream of my life, and consummation of all my hopes, — the cardinal's hat! Only think how I should sit on the platform of the Music Hall, with my red hat and my robes! How I should sit in my brass coach with my *Bruschi* horses, and be called Eminence, and high and mighty Prince! I don't quite forgive you. Surely a *woman* could get round the pope, if she would. But you don't care any thing about me; that is clear. If I should die suddenly, be sure the "crowner's verdict" would be, "Lack of a cardinal's hat."

But we did see such neatness, thrift, comfort, and well-diffused wealth, as no other land in all the world can offer. If a Southern slaveholder could ride where we went, and see what he must, he would at once be convinced that his miserable system was a wretched failure. We went in by-roads, lived all the time in small towns, rested at the little country taverns, and not once saw a ragged American, and but one American at all affected by drink. Yet there is a great difference in the various places. The superiority of New-England civilization over all the rest of America is quite clear. In the north and west of Vermont this is damaged by the Canadian French, who take down the tone of the Yankees. In Western Massachusetts and Connecticut, the Dutch element of New York shows itself in the greater slovenliness of all things. New-Englanders marry Dutch girls; and the housekeeping shows the degeneracy of the breed. Dear old Massachusetts! I never loved her so well. Puritanic New England! it is she that has shaped America, and will one day give her a grander destiny than she dreams of yet. In Italy, France, and Germany you see the power of the few, to whom all else is sacrificed or has been. Much beauty came from that arrangement, — grand palaces, magnificent churches, statues, pictures, and things fair to look on. How they haunt one's dreams years after they have faded from the sight! But in democratic America it is all different: all is for the people, of the people, by the people. The plough is in the hands of its owner. Shoemaker Wilson is one of the ablest men in the American Senate. Blacksmith Banks is the best governor Massachusetts has had since I was born. How we have altered *style* in America! The last Sunday that I preached, Mr. Chase, governor of Ohio, with its three million two hundred and fifty thousand people, sat there with all the rest. I tried to reach him and speak to him after meeting; but so many men and women came to bid me good-by, that I could not accomplish it. Riding home, I met Banks, governor of a million two hundred thousand of Massachusetts, in a common country one-horse wagon, which cost seventy-five or a hundred dollars, going to dine with his brother-governor at a tavern, and talk over the affairs of five millions of people. What if the *Durchlaucht* of Hesse-Homburg, ruler of a hundred and fifty thousand, and the —— of ——, with five hundred thousand, were to meet and dine! How many faults New England has! but, God be thanked, how many blessings! What a present for the people! What a future for all!

One thing struck me with astonishment in the woods of New York; for you must know we went fifty miles bodily into the "forest primeval," "the murmuring pines and the hemlocks:" it was the uncommon fertility of the human race in the log-cabins. They are all crowded with babies. Often the mother, a woman of twenty-eight, perhaps, stood at the door (with a *hoop* on), a baby of six weeks in her arms; another of a year old stood at her side; then one of two, one of three, four, five, six, and more. Really it seemed as if the wood was alive with babies, and the trees spawned as the waters do.

Then the letter runs on with charming personalities, which lack of space alone forbids quoting.

Parker was the most jocund of travellers. He had the merry exuberance of a boy when out of doors in pleasant weather. He greeted the trees by name, and welcomed the familiar flowers, introducing them to his companions, with their family connections, and an account of their pedigree. The landscape was on familiar terms with him. The shape of the country told him the secrets of its flora: he knew what wild flower must be hiding behind the rock, in the meadow, in the intricacies of the "stump fence," in the shade of the grove, beside the brook; and in a moment he was out of the wagon in quest of his prize, pausing to pick the berries on the stalk, — "a feast for the gods." If he passed a stone-quarry, he must needs stop, watch the work, and talk with the men, pointing out to them peculiarities in the formation, which might be availed of to assist their labor and secure the full value of its results. The mower attracts his attention: he examines the scythe, — the handling of which he had not forgotten, — explains the make, and probably drops a piece of information that will be of use to the farmer the next time he has occasion to buy. "What is that man doing? Cradling wheat. I must take a turn at that." So out he jumps, springs over the bars, and invites the man to take a rest while he performs the task. The gentleman in the city coat and hat proves equal to the occasion: the smile of incredulity disappears from the farmer's face in a few minutes; and in half an hour he is convinced that his coadjutor must have been a farmer once. He mingles in the discussions at the country inn; listens to the village oracle, confronts him, puts questions to him he cannot answer, brings forward facts he cannot dispute, and ends by instructing the crowd that had gathered on the true state of the country and the real nature of the issues then pending. The forlorn bear tethered to a tree, or confined within a small enclosure in the tavern-yard, always had his sympathy. He could not pass Bruin by, but watched his motions, fed him, called him by pet names till the last moment. In travelling, the peculiar grotesqueness of the man came out. A friend tells me, that journeying one winter's day from Boston to New York where he was engaged to lecture, and being detained at New Haven, he kept himself warm by jumping Jim Crow on the bridge that spans the gloomy station. The exuberance of life was irrepressible. It made him a great recipient of the exuberant vitality of Nature, which flowed in at all the pores of his being, and quickened to the very last moment the latent vigor of his frame. Contact with Nature always revived him. On a sultry summer's day by the seaside he was seen with a scythe, mowing down the Canada thistle that was threatening to overspread the fields. They should get no farther than the roadside if he could prevent. The idlers at the hotel thought he must be in great want of occupation; but he came from his task more refreshed than fatigued.

But no excursions by water, or expeditions on land in open wagons, are a match for hereditary disease and excessive toil. He could not be idle. On his return from this little trip, forty letters were waiting for him: ten more came in straightway. Work of other kinds had accumulated; and he was not the man to shirk any portion of it. In the autumn, preaching began again, and lecturing, and parish work, and fugitive-slave work, and Kansas work, and work of various unexpected kinds.

From the Journal.

OCT. 5, 1858.

The Music Hall opened three weeks ago, and has been filled with quite large congregations. Our course of lectures begins to-morrow. Mr. Sanborn gives the introductory poem.

This course of lectures, the "Fraternity" course, established by his own friends, gave Mr. Parker his first chance to be heard in Boston as a lecturer. He was not backward to use it. The lectures on historic Americans — Franklin, Adams, Jefferson, Washington — were intended and partially prepared for this season. The Franklin was carefully written out and delivered. The Adams was given, though not fully written out. The others were completed from copious notes by the hand of his devoted friend Mr. Lyman, who cherished his memory as tenderly as he cherished his failing life, and hastened his own decline by his unwearied toil over the literary remains of the man he loved as a brother, and revered as a benefactor. Like all Mr. Parker's work, the lectures were designed to instruct and fortify the American people in the essential ideas of their institutions.

Heroic remedies are not always best even for heroes. The effusion of water on the chest which followed the earlier sickness it took nearly eight months to subdue. In the mean time, during the summer, a fistula developed itself, producing painful and alarming consequences. He lost twenty pounds of flesh; had cough, night-sweats, and other dangerous symptoms. It seemed as if the end was nigh. A surgical operation in October gave relief, and the sick man fancied himself delivered from his tormentors; but, on getting into a railroad-car to attend the funeral of a little boy drowned by accident, — a service rendered from pure humanity, — he strained and wrenched himself in delicate parts of the body. The brave man was not daunted; still professed to think he should live to be seventy or eighty; promised to be more moderate in future; staid in his library; had his meals brought up to him; drove out every day; and had the best medical and surgical advice, which he had too much faith not to take. The anxiety of his friends deepened. Already, in August, many members of his society joined in beseeching him to extend the term of his vacation to the utmost limit that prudence required, and by no means to allow his strong desire to be at his post to override their united wishes and settled convictions. Weakness enforced what consideration would scarcely have granted. As the year drew to a close, work had to be dropped, — all but the preaching, which continued with but few interruptions, and those only when it was physically impossible for him to stand even by grasping the desk.

The journal terminates abruptly now, save for a few jottings in small books which can be carried in his pocket. On Jan. 1, 1859, this entry is made: —

"It is Saturday night, — eve of the first day of the new year. I have finished my sermon for to-morrow; and I have nothing to do but indulge my feelings for a minute, and gather up my soul.

"This is the first New-Year's day that I was ever sick. Now I have been a prisoner almost three months, living in my chamber or my study. I have been out of doors but thrice since Sunday last. The doctor says I mend, and I quote him to my friends; but I have great doubts as to the result. It looks as if this were the last of my New-Year's days on earth. I felt so when I gave each gift to-day; yet few men have more to live for than I. It seems as if I had just begun a great work; yet, if I must abandon it, I will not complain. Some abler and better man will take my place, and do more successfully what I have entered on. The Twenty-eighth will soon forget me: a few Sundays will satisfy their tears. Some friends may linger long about my grave, and be inly sad for many a day."

Three pages later, the last word in the bulky quarto, is a direction for a

MONUMENT.

"When I die, I wish to be buried in the old burying-place in Lexington, where my fathers since 1709 — four generations of them — have laid their venerable bones. I wish to be put near them. At my head let there be a plain blue or green slate-stone, thus [A. | B.], with no ornament, no black paint. I mark the stone as double, in case my wife may also subsequently wish to be laid beside me, as she often says: if not, let it be single. A. may contain this inscription: —

THEODORE PARKER,
(SON OF JOHN AND HANNAH.)
Born Aug. 24, 1810; died —

The sermon, "What Religion may do for a Man," was preached with great difficulty on Jan. 2. He felt that it was the last time; and it was. The next Sunday, this little note, in pencil, was read to the congregation met in Music Hall: —

SUNDAY MORNING, Jan. 9, 1859.

WELL-BELOVED AND LONG-TRIED FRIENDS, — I shall not speak to you to-day; for this morning, a little after four o'clock, I had a slight attack of bleeding in the lungs or throat. I intended to preach on "The Religion of Jesus, and the Christianity of the Church; or, The Superiority of Good-Will to Man over Theological Fancies."

I hope you will not forget the contribution for the poor, whom we have with us always. I don't know when I shall again look upon your welcome faces, which have so often cheered my spirit when my flesh was weak.

May we do justly, love mercy, and walk humbly with our God, and his blessing will be upon us here and hereafter; for his infinite love is with us for ever and ever.

Faithfully your friend,

THEODORE PARKER.

The "slight attack of bleeding" was a serious hemorrhage of the lungs. There was now no time to lose. A meeting of the parish, called on the spot, voted a year's salary to the pastor, more if necessary, to enable him to seek complete repose from every kind of care. Experienced physicians pronounced the case grave. Tubercles had formed, and were increasing. The disease he had inherited had already progressed far. The chances of recovery were declared to be as one in ten. The stout soldier laughs at the odds. "If that is all, I'll conquer.

I have fought ninety-nine against one, — yes, nine hundred and ninety-nine against one, — and conquered. Please God, I will again; *sursum corda.*" It is decided that he must go to the West Indies at once; thence to Europe; thence wherever the chances should look brightest.

I shall leave the reader to imagine the grief of Mr. Parker's friends and parishioners when the truth they had feared broke upon them. Any who will may read the letters that passed between pastor and people. They are printed at length in Mr. Weiss's book. Tender and touching they are, but no more so than was sincerely felt on both sides. Private letters of sympathy and manly or womanly love came in such numbers, that the sufferer printed a card in "The New-York Tribune," excusing himself from replying to them all; a notice that only brought fresh tributes from people who had refrained from writing because unwilling to burden him with the care of answering. Now that they were sure he would not answer, they would speak. These heart-roses covered his sick-bed, and filled him with their fragrance. So much of the odor as he could he wafted back. As he lay in his pain, tender thoughts came to him of all he loved, of many who had not loved him; and in all directions the white doves flew from his window with messages of good will, thanks for old kindnesses, gratitude for confidence and sympathy, generous acknowledgment of smallest services rendered and long forgotten by the doer, sweet reminiscences of past joy, praise for good deeds done and good words spoken for freedom, apologies for imaginary troubles or offences, — all in manly, simple language, without a weak expression of complaint, with the natural submission that belonged to his faith. "If I recover," he says in a parting note to Salmon P. Chase (and it is in the spirit of them all), — "if I recover, — and the doctors tell me I have one chance in ten, — only nine chances against me to one in my favor, — I shall be thankful for the experience of affection and friendship which my illness has brought from all parts of the land: if I do not recover, I shall pass off joyfully, with an entire trust in that Infinite Love which cares more for me than I care for myself."

To S. P. Andrews.

BOSTON, Jan. 27, 1859.

MY DEAR SAM, — I am not well enough to see you: it will make my heart beat too fast. I sail — Bear, and Miss S., and Dr. Howe also — in about ten days for the West Indies; thence to Europe, perhaps, in May. Who knows what the result will be? For complete recovery, the chances in my favor are *one out of ten*. So the doctors say. I don't rate it higher. I am ready for either alternative, but am still full of hope that the human mortal life will hold out long enough for me to hammer over again some of the many irons I have laid in the fire and got ready for the anvil. It does seem to me I shall have time left to finish certain pieces of work. But I will not complain of the dear Mother (who long ago admonished me that I must not cherish long hopes in a short world) if the kind Hand that brought me here shall also soon take me away to that world "which eye hath not seen," &c. You and I have had many a good time together; and I hoped we should enjoy many more. Indeed, I laid out my life to work publicly and hard till sixty, and then have a quiet afternoon till eighty for getting in my hay; but, if my hour strikes at forty-eight, let not you nor me complain.

My wife sends love to your wife; whereto add mine, and believe me

Faithfully, affectionately, and yours,

THEODORE.

To Rev. William R. Alger.

BOSTON, Jan. 28, 1859.

MY DEAR ALGER, — I thank you for the flowers and the yet sweeter fragrance of the note which came with them. They bloom on my table, while it sheds its unseen influence elsewhere. I don't know whether I sail to life or death; but heaven is never a distant port, and one need not complain if he gets there sooner than he laid out for. But I leave a deal of work half done, and more only begun, which I meant to finish, and gladly would. I have rejoiced in your noble words, and make no doubt they will grow nobler yet as you change time into life, and natural talents into lofty character. God bless your brave spirit, and keep you faithful! What could I wish more or better?

Give my regards to your wife, and believe me

Yours faithfully,

THEODORE PARKER.

To Mrs. Lydia M. Child.

BOSTON, Jan. 20, 1859.

MY DEAR, KIND FRIEND, — Many thanks for your welcome letter, which I have strength only thus poorly to reply to. I knew *you* when you did not know *me;* and I have much to thank you for in early as well as in later days. I met you at your brother's in Watertown in 1833; and you then spoke some cheering words to a young fellow fighting his way to education. God bless you for that, and for much more! Remember me kindly to your brave husband.

Yours faithfully,

THEODORE PARKER.

He has not forgotten the sonnet he wrote long before: —

"Through crooked paths Thou hast conducted me,
And thorns oft forced my timid flesh to bleed:
Still I rejoiced my Leader's hand to see,
Trusting my Father in my hour of need.
When in the darkness of my early youth,
Stumbling and groping for a better way,
Through riven clouds streamed down the light of Truth,
And made it morning with refulgent ray,
Along the steep and weary path I trod,
With none to guide, and few to comfort me.
I felt the presence of the eternal God,
That in his hand 'twas blessedness to be,
Finding relief from woes in consciousness of thee."

CHAPTER XVIII.

THE DEPARTURE. — THE SEARCH.

THEODORE PARKER, with his wife, Miss Stevenson, and Mr. George Cabot, left the house in Exeter Place, on the 3d of February, with a resolute determination to use his one chance in ten for health, — too resolute, in fact. He who too fiercely fights his own disease may become its ally. He sat in his room at the Astor House, gaunt and gray, but firm, as if he were the carer, and not the cared-for. He knew the contents of each box and bag, where each package and flask was put. When the little procession moved from the hotel, he staid till the last to see that nothing had been dropped; then walked sturdily to Jersey City, where "The Karnac" lay. All was ready for him on board. A dear friend from afar put flowers — violets and carnations — in his state-room. Dr. and Mrs. Howe were there to greet him with manly sympathy and feminine grace. They were to be his companions on the voyage. To the few friends who came to say farewell he said little; responded gratefully to their expressions of affection, but faintly to their words of hope; was silent and thoughtful, though not dejected. The steamer sailed on the 8th. On the 3d of March it reached its destination, — Fredericksted, West End, Santa Cruz; having touched at Nassau, St. Thomas, Nuevitas, Puerto Plata, and St. John, and tarried four or five days at Havana. The voyage, which rough weather made uncomfortable at starting, was afterwards pleasant. The sea became smooth, the air soft, the sky beautifully tender. Nature did her best for the weary man. He lay on the deck for hours, or sat in cool and shady spots. But the restless mind would not be still. "All my life-schemes lie prostrate." "I stand up to the chin in my grave." "Fourteen years to-day since I rode into Boston to preach at the Melodeon. I enlisted for a thirty-years' war; but am wounded, and driven off the field, before half that time is over." "R. W. Emerson is preaching at the Music Hall to-day." "I wonder if they remembered the anniversary." "Those precious guns in my study — what will become of them? They must be kept in a safe place. They will belong to the Commonwealth when I die." "Mr. Shackford would be a good man to preach." Then came plans of work yet to be done. "I must write out and finish my *last sermon*. I must write my autobiography." He felt and thought out a letter to the Twenty-eighth Congregational Society, and began to compose it. At every stopping-place he went ashore with his note-book, and made the most of his opportunity to pick up bits of knowledge. Night and day, on shipboard, he walked the rounds of his parish in a visionary way, asking himself, "Who is sick? Who is sick no more? How is poor old Mr. Cass, the grape-pruner in Chambers-street Court? I must send him some strawberries in their season."

Arriving at Santa Cruz, hardly able to crawl out of the vessel, he begins to labor like a *savan* on a hurried voyage of exploration, — noting every tree, shrub, plant, flower; classifying the products and minerals; studying the natives and the strangers, the increase of population, pursuits, value of properties; in a word, exhausting the island and everybody in it, and putting all he sees and thinks into most instructive and delightful letters to his friends in America and Europe, — letters betraying no sign of ill health in their texture, though, in an occasional sentence, dropping hints thereof. The hilarious nature rollicks in breezy fun about the boys and girls, the ducks and cockadoodles, negroes, pigs, "long-nosed and grave-looking animals, most of them coal-black, and, like Zaccheus small of stature, looking as if they had been through a revival, and were preparing for the ministry."

His first visit, made the day after his arrival, was to the Protestant burial-ground, — "the *terminus ad quem* I am travelling, it may be. It is not an attractive-looking place: none in New England that I know is less so. There the grass comes 'creeping, creeping, creeping, everywhere:' here only a rugged, coarse, rank sedge comes in tufts to supply its place. The trees look ungenial. The *Bombax ceiba* is the biggest, but not inviting, eaten up with its parasites."

From the Journal.

MARCH 13.

Found the monument of Rev. Henry Walker of Charlestown, Mass.; died 1838. I knew him. He studied in Germany, and brought thence the first copy of Strauss, I think, that came to America. I met him at Ripley's, and borrowed his book in 1836 or 1837. He left his library to Rev. James Walker. Here lie his remains, with many more of such as came here after health, and found only a grave. It is not a pleasant place to lie in, with the sedgy grass growing in bunches as high as my head.

There are three other cemeteries, — one Danish, one American, one Catholic: —

"The Danish looks most inviting. I change my mind, and think I shall prefer the Danish to the dark spot under the *Bombax ceiba* in the English."

But there are more cheerful objects than these: —

"The weather is magnificent. Such clear skies! On the wharf at St. Thomas I could clearly see Santa Cruz, forty miles off. The nights are as splendid almost as the days: the stars are so large! The scintillation is peculiar. Those near the zenith twinkle but little. Oh, if Desor were here, or John L. Russell, or Dr. Cabot!"

Nor is the humanity of the island utterly discouraging. He finds a Rev. Mr. Dubois, "an excellent man, full of kindness and industry. He takes great pains in the noble work of elevating the colored people; but the whites do not help the movement, or much favor it. Mr. Dubois has a friendly society of about three hundred colored people, who pay a little sum each week to aid their needy brethren. The most interesting sight on the island is the street full of colored people on Sunday, going to meeting. Soon as possible, they get shoes and other clothing, and help up their self-respect."

The letters to his male friends are crammed with information in regard to the material and political condition of the island, the imports and exports, productive powers and agencies, classes of the population, number of workmen, soldiers, slaves, the state of personal and social morality, amount of rainfall, interspersed with various comment and speculation on the future prospects of the people. The letters to his physician, Dr. Cabot in Boston, give a painfully-detailed account of the progress of his malady as judged by symptoms, the state of the *abductor muscles*, the *respiratory organs*, the precise character of his cough, the appearances of his eyes, his sensations in different temperatures, with the exact locality of each.

The letters to his female friends bloom with color, and sparkle with wit. The bright birds flit through them; the gorgeous flowers spread their glowing leaves. The English Episcopal service is waggishly taken off; the West-Indian aristocracy is deliciously caricatured, with a fine sense of humor solid with truth. The letters are "works," or would have been to a less irrepressible man. By the 19th of April he has finished the "Letter to the Twenty-eighth Congregational Society," — a volume detailing his experience as a minister. "A sick man's work," he calls it, "written under many difficulties, amid continual interruption besides what weakness occasioned, — written in tears of blood. No work of mine, perhaps, cost me such birth-pangs; for I was too sick to write, and yet must be delivered of my book, and that, too, in such a place!"

How could such a man get well? Nature had no chance with him. His fires were always burning. Thought and feeling perpetually consumed him. He could not be quiet. The incessant nervous irritation wasted his strength away. Between ecstasy and despondency he was always torn. If he could have forgotten himself, stretched himself out on the piazza, or beneath the trees without caring what their botanical name might be, and let the natural influences stream into his frame, he might have lived; but he spent more than he gained.

Then, again, he knew too much about his own condition for a sick man's good. His finger was never off his own pulse; he weighed and counted his breaths; was more intimately acquainted with himself than nurse or doctor; and could not desist from acting as his own medical adviser. This is enough to create the atmosphere of a sick-room anywhere. It is like a doomed man's listening to the erecting of his scaffold.

While at the island, he felt comparatively strong; could walk with tolerable ease; had a good appetite, an excellent digestion; slept, on the whole, well; gained in color, weight, and vigor; rode three or four times a week on a pony; his face was brown and ruddy, his eye clear; but the cough continued. The two months at Santa Cruz wrought on him no essential benefit: the critical symptoms were worse. On the 11th of May he left the island, and returned to St. Thomas to take the steamer of the 16th for Southampton. On the voyage to the latter place he lost seven pounds of flesh. The cough and the expectoration increased. He began to lose faith in his powers of recuperation. Some confidence he had in the reviving influences of civilization, but not much. Even the misery of sea-sickness was subdued by the more terrible malady which kept him prostrate. He was in a poor plight on reaching Southampton, the 1st of June; but, the same evening, he went on to London.

Here less than anywhere could he rest. It was the charmed season in London; crowds of people to visit, crowds of things to see. The eleven days there did duty for thirty. There were letters to be read and written, neither without emotion and pain. He had not been at Radley's Hotel, Blackfriars, forty-eight hours, when an old gentleman was announced, — Mr. Brabant, seventy-nine years old, father-in-law of Mr. Hennell. Miss Winkworth and her sister came, Mr. and Mrs. James Martineau, Prof. H. D. Rogers and his wife. Mr. William H. Seward, then in London, showed him politeness. John Bright got him a place in the House of Commons to hear the great debate which led to the expulsion of the Derby ministry.

A visit that touched Mr. Parker deeply was from a comparative stranger, — Mr. Thomas Cholmondeley, a nephew of Bishop Heber, of Oriel College, Oxford, once a pupil of Arthur Hugh Clough, afterwards a student in Germany. He had been in America five years before; had heard Mr. Parker preach; had called on him at his house; was impressed by his power, and interested in his character: for Cholmondeley himself was a man of high aspirations and intellectual aims, though in religion, albeit of broad views, not a pronounced rationalist; indeed, at the time of his visit to America, he was inclined to Puseyism. His interest, however, was in ideas rather than doctrines. He brought letters to Emerson; was eager to know our foremost men; a man of progress, as was evident from his response to a toast given by a Plymouth man on Forefathers' Day: "May the spirit which brought the Pilgrim Fathers here return again to England! and may we have a commonwealth there, if not as great as yours, at least as happy and as well ordered!" This Mr. Cholmondeley, hearing that Mr. Parker was in London, and apprehending that he might be inadequately supplied with funds for travel and sojourn and medical service, delicately put his purse at the invalid's disposal. The kindness fell on a tender heart, and made a deep impression. It was declined, but with gratitude. Mr. Cholmondeley inherited property later, but soon surrendered it all; for he died in 1864 in the same city where Parker breathed his last, and perhaps mingled his dust with the same soil.

But, of all the visits the pilgrim received, none gave him more delight than that of Ellen Craft, his colored parishioner, whom, nearly ten years before, he had helped away to England for safety from the slave-hunters. It all came back to him, — the danger, the fear, the flight; the journey to Brookline, accompanied by John Parkman and Miss Stevenson, in a close carriage, he himself armed with a hatchet in case of necessity; the bringing the fugitive into the refuge of his own house; the subsequent marriage in the boarding-house on "Nigger Hill" with Bible and sword. For all these years she had been safe, and came now to greet her friend and savior. Such remembrance touched him more than any attention from people of station; strengthened him, but weakened him too.

There were visits to be made as well as received. He was desirous of seeing Henry Thomas Buckle; but the author of "The History of Civilization in England" was not at home. His heart had been set, too, on seeing Frances Power Cobbe, with whom he had corresponded, and whose books he ranked among the greatest written by a woman's pen; but neither was she in London. Invitations to breakfasts, dinners, lunches, were incessant, but had to be declined. Once only he lunched at Rev. James Martineau's, where he met, for the first time, Francis William Newman, John James Taylor, Mr. Ireson, and a few others. Eminent men of the Liberal party, coadjutors of Mr. Bright, he saw under pleasant circumstances, but not as closely as he could have wished.

He was always going about to interesting places, — Westminster Hall, Guildhall, the Tower, Billingsgate, St. George's Yard, the British Museum, the College of Surgeons, the Reform Club. He heard Huxley lecture, and Martineau preach; and listened to a charity-sermon at St. Paul's, where "eight thousand children sat alone, and fainted with hunger while they listened to a wretched sermon on human depravity, or sang the litanies they had been made to commit to memory." He called himself very prudent; went into no damp buildings; was home early in the evening; avoided festive excitement of all kinds. But the cloudy, heavy air of the city, thick with coal-smoke, irritated the cough, and increased the expectorations. On the 12th of June, London was left for Paris; the journey *viâ* Folkestone and Boulogne being made by day in twelve hours.

Scarcely was he settled in his lodgings, Hôtel de Londres, 8 Rue St. Hyacinthe, when Charles Sumner called, — "the same dear old Sumner as he used to be before that scoundrel laid him low." The next day, the two friends drove about the city six hours; and, the drive over, Parker went about on foot for more exercise, while Mr. Sumner went home to rest. Paris was, if possible, a more exhausting field of recovery than London. It were idle to attempt to tell what was seen and done during the short week spent there. Yet he writes to Dr. Cabot in Boston, "I became a mollusk, an oyster, in the West Indies, and exercised a most exclusively those *nerves of vegetation* which you discovered. After writing my 'Letter,' I dropped down into my molluscous condition; and, when I saw one of the actual tenants of the mud at London, I said, 'Am I not a clam and a brother?' I never opened my mouth upon oyster, or even *shrimp*, except to speak to them respectfully, lest I should commit the crime against nature, and devour my own kind. In Switzerland I will be as gentle 'as a child that is weaned of its mother,' and behave myself 'like a sucking child.'"

In Paris he consulted the doctors with the usual satisfaction.

"What different counsel in doctors!" he wrote in 1859. "Last October, Bowditch wanted me to go to the West Indies; Dr. J. Jackson not. For hypophosphates, Dr. Flint of Boston, Dr. Bigelow of Paris; against hypophosphates, Dr. Louis of Paris; indifferent, or doubtful, Drs. Bowditch, Cabot, Moleschott. For cod-liver oil, Cabot (moderate); against cod-liver oil, Drs. Louis and Bigelow. Some think Jongh's is the best preparation of the cod-liver oil: Dr. Moleschott thinks him a humbug and a liar; his oil good for nothing. Bigelow recommends Bordeaux wine; Moleschott, Malaga before Bordeaux; Bigelow and Cabot, Jackson and Bowditch, whiskey, brandy, &c.; Moleschott, pilled barley."

Dr. Samuel Bigelow took him to Louis, who thought little of the cough or the expectoration; thought the greenish-yellowish matter came from the bronchia, not from the decomposition of the tubercles; had no faith in Dr. Winchester's hypophosphates, no more in the disgusting cod-liver oil; recommended *pillules de Blancard* (iodide of iron), — one at breakfast, and one at supper. Both physicians advised, 1. Abstinence from all exertion; 2. As much living in the open air as possible; 3. Abundance of nutritious food, especially ripe vegetables; 4. Bordeaux or Neufchâtel wines. Dr. Louis recommended Ems; but Dr. Bigelow was indifferent. As regarded a winter-residence, Louis thought well of Egypt; but the discomforts there, the chill of the Nile, and want of society, made that look unattractive. His thoughts turned toward Montreux for the autumn, and Rome for the winter. The doctors took a more cheerful view of his case than he did himself. He had thought of Scandinavia, Holland, the Rhine, Germany, plans of travel with Desor; but these fine schemes were abandoned. On the 19th of June he is on the way to Dijon, looking toward the Lake of Geneva and Montreux. There he met his dear friends Mr. and Mrs. Apthorp and Miss Hunt on the 22d. His lodgings were ready for him,—fine rooms, commanding a glorious outlook; the Dent du Midi, ten thousand feet high, snow-covered, towering up before him, twenty miles off. The weather had been wet, but was now delicious. Climate, scenery, accommodations, and, above all, the friendliest of friends, all conspired to aid the sick man's recovery. The apricots hung ripe on the garden-wall; the figs were almost grown; strawberries and cherries were plenty; and the sweetest care brightened every day. The letters from Montreux—printed in Weiss, too many and too long to print here—are full of interest. Mr. Apthorp planned delightful excursions to Vevay, Chillon, Lausanne, Ferney, and the other charming spots in the neighborhood. He could walk five miles without fatigue.

The Italian war was raging: of course he must know all about that; and nothing comes amiss,—newspapers, cheap prints, maps, bulletins, pasquinades. The neighborhood is full of associations historical and romantic: he had them all by heart. The local histories, guide-books, descriptions, are all on his table,—out-of-the-way things he had picked up in obscure shops and stalls by the way as he came along.

Late in July he varies the sweet monotony of his life at Montreux by a visit of a few weeks to his friend Prof. Desor at his mountain *châlet*. It was but a day's journey, on a good road, through pleasant villages and rich vineyards; over passes that commanded glorious views of the high Alps, from the peaks of the Bernese Oberland to Mont Blanc. The *châlet* itself had been a hunting-lodge; but the good, hospitable Desor, to accommodate the scientific men who sought the mountains and each other in the summer, had built another house close by for his guests. A background of fir-trees furnished shelter and balmy fragrance. Little clearings in the wood gave the sunlight room to sport with the green grass and the red berries. The owner had extensive vineyards, which he cultivated, storing the rich juice in his cellar.

Here Parker felt at home. He had his sheltered seat on the edge of the wood, his favorite fir-tree, double-headed, like the pine at Lexington. Here were refreshing excursions to spots famous or beautiful; and trees enough, small and large, for the invalid to try his perilous wood-chopping propensities on, as he did, against the advice of all his friends; *savans* they were too. The summer was an intensely hot one; and there, three thousand feet above the valley, it was warm enough to be out of doors many hours of the day. The invalid made the most of it; soaked in the sunshine; inhaled the balsam of the pines, and the aroma from the meadows; drank the professor's good red wine, and felt his heart revive. His vigor increased; his spirits rose; he gained in weight. It seemed as if an arrest of his disease, at least, was probable.

Not the least invigorating influence was the companionship of intelligent men; some of them distinguished in their specialty; all of them interested in living questions: some of them cordially sympathetic with his views; all of them respecting his character, and appreciative of his mind. There was the noble Lorenz Küchler, whom Theodore learned to love as a brother. The meals were enlivened by discussions on all subjects, scientific, political, philosophical, religious, — discussions that sometimes grew into warm debates, but ended in brotherly good-will.

The visitors at Desor's this summer made an album as a memorial of Parker and Küchler, each *savan* contributing a paper. Parker's piece was a satire on the scientific method of the Bridgewater Treatises, very clever, — "A Bumblebee's View of the Universe." Of course he found time to write letters, and long ones. The best of them — and very good they are — may be read in Weiss. They show how affectionately he bore his friends in mind; how closely he kept the run of home-affairs, public and private; and how much deeper was his concern for great principles in America than for his own health in Europe. "I am only one little spurt of water running into the great ocean of humanity; and, if I stop here, I shall not be at all missed there."

Six weeks were passed in this mountain-retreat, — six weeks which Mr. Parker spoke of as among the most delightful of his sojourn in Europe. On the afternoon of Aug. 22 he left the *châlet*, descended the mountains, and kept his birthday (the 24th) at Montreux. He has now an excellent appetite; his spirits never fail; he coughs less, and feels stronger. He carried more than seventy pounds of baggage from the boat to the cars, at Yverdon, without strain. As the autumn advances, he is still improving. On one of his walks in the neighborhood of Montreux, as he is pushing along, eating grapes, a cheery voice calls out, "Can you tell me the way to Boston meetin'-house?" He turns, and meets the jocund face of J. T. Fields the publisher, who was walking over from Vevay to see him. He steadily gains in weight; reaches, in fact, a hundred and fifty-eight and a third pounds, — more than he had weighed for twenty-nine years.

Autumn draws on fast. Desor has come down from his mountain-perch to his residence in Neufchâtel, and bids his friend to make him a parting-visit there in the vintage-time. The scientific men have returned to their duties in the cities. It is time to think of winter-quarters; to bid good-by to the Dent du Midi, the hills, the lake, the lovely meadows, and find a shelter elsewhere from the cold and wind. After much deliberation, study of climates, forecasting of probabilities, Rome is decided on finally. The party of pilgrims break up their pleasant quarters at Montreux on the 12th of October, and set their faces toward Marseilles by way of Geneva and Lyons. Marseilles is left on the 17th: on the 19th the sombre city lets him in. Again, lines written in other years come to mind: —

"For all the trials of my earlier day,
I thank thee, Father, that they all have been;
That darkness lay about the rugged way
Which I must tread alone. For all I've seen
Of disappointment, sorrow, pain, and loss,
I thank thee for them all. And did I sin,
I grieve not I've been tried; for e'en the cross
Of penitence has taught me how to win.
Yet, of the ills as child or man I've borne, —
My hopes laid waste, or friends sent off by death, —
Remorse has most of all my bosom torn
For time misspent, ill deeds, or evil breath.
But yet, for every grief my heart has worn,
Father, I thank thee, still trusting with hearty faith."

CHAPTER XIX.

THE ETERNAL CITY.

PLEASANT lodgings were found in the Via delle Quatro Fontane, No. 16, on the fourth floor, a hundred and twenty steps from the street; the stairs rising in four flights of thirty steps each. There were four rooms, fourteen or fifteen feet high, well furnished "for Italy," comfortably carpeted, with large windows to the east and south, giving plentiful air and sunshine, when there was any, all day. Dinner was sent in from a German eating-house. The house stood high, in an airy, dry part of the city. From its upper stories it commanded a view of the whole city: below, a magnificent prospect stretched out in every direction. Close by was the Quirinal Palace, its gardens lying between: on the other side was the Pincian Hill, with its fine trees and shrubbery. St. Peter's was in full view from base to dome, standing out against the dark background of the Etruscan Hills. The Palazzo Barberini, where William Story the sculptor lived, was hard by. Nothing could promise better. The Apthorps and Hunts occupied the third floor of the same building, ready at all times with social cheer, and, in case of an emergency, with every thing that lay within reach of human power. Daily existence was laid out on a simple plan, which the weather alone deranged. The needs of the invalid were the care of all: unhappily, the invalid could not, with the very best intentions, care for himself.

The same irritability of brain that made rest impossible in the West Indies made it equally — if it could be, more — impossible in Rome. Before he had got into his apartments, before he had been two days in the city, prowling about, he came across, in a stall, a Dutch book on the Existence of God, — a book he had never before been able to find, — and bought it for half a dollar. In the course of a week, he had begun work enough to employ a well man's days; being nothing less than the study of Rome, — its geology, its flora and fauna, its archæology, its architecture. He carries his Mommsen with him in his mind as he visits daily some of the places famous in legend or history. A vast amount of reading of no light kind is done. His shelves are filled with a long range of learned works, in different languages, on Rome and Italy. All the newspapers he can get are on his table. He keeps the run of political events in Europe and America, following minutely the course of affairs in Church and State, so that he could talk with statesmen about them. His correspondence is unintermitted. Ponderous letters, big as pamphlets, come from his restless pen, which, debarred from writing lectures and sermons, puts the same amount of material into epistolary form. His letters are dissertations, crammed with facts and reflections. Scarcely a note escapes from him that has not passages which only a scholar and thinker could have written. To one friend he writes a summary of the epochs in the history of Rome itself; to another, an account of agriculture in the Papal States; to another he gives an outside and inside view of ecclesiastical institutions there; to yet others, interested in such matters, descriptions of domestic economy, humorous sketches of popular manners, statistics of population or trade, comparative tables illustrating the numerical strength or the social condition of various classes of the people; all done methodically and with conscience. His brain is singularly alive; his observing power keen and swift. Nothing escapes him in the street. Passing a book-shop, his eye takes in the title of every volume displayed in the window; going by a fruit-stall, he notices every unfamiliar nut or berry or plant, and will not pass on till he has learned all about it. His memory does not fail him: his reasoning faculty is ever on the alert. At Mrs. Browning's a pamphlet is mentioned, — "Le Pape et le Congrès," by M. Guerronnière. Mrs. Browning has not seen it, only heard of its general character. Nobody, apparently, knows it but Mr. Parker, who had seen a translation of it in "The London Times." He takes up the book at once; gives a full account of it, — its fundamental positions, its argument, its bearing, — and dilates on its tendency and probable effect in different quarters; his hearers listening with more than interest to the development of ideas as they flow from the eloquent speaker's lips. On another occasion he was breakfasting with William Story in company with Mr. and Mrs. Apthorp, Mr. and Mrs. Twisselton, Mrs. Stowe, Hawthorne, Bryant, Gibson, and Browning. The conversation turned on malarious soils. Mr. Parker, who, up to that point, had said little (the act of talking being painful to him), struck in here; gave an account of malarious regions, their peculiarities, their formation, their influence, and the precautions to be observed in guarding against their poison. "No miasma," he said, "could penetrate through fifteen feet of pure gravel." The old residents in Rome, who might be presumed familiar with the subject, were the most interested and the most astonished at the unexpected wealth of information, and freely expressed their amazement as they left the table; Mr. Browning remarking to Mrs. Apthorp, "What a wonderful man! None of us knew the facts he told us." In this instance the subject was one to which Mr. Parker, from the circumstances of his birthplace, the hereditary disease in his family, and the fact of his own illness, had given particular attention. But the marvel of his information was as great in departments which would seem to lie remote from any interest or study of his. Thus, being in a company with ladies, one of whom had a trimming of beautiful lace on a portion of her dress, and question arising in regard to its manufacture, Mr. Parker was alone able to answer; having, it would appear to a stranger, freshly informed himself on the whole subject of lace-making. Omniscience was his forte: during these last six months in Rome it was his weakness. Every thing about him, the wonderful city, the singular aspect of all things, the strange modes of life, the restlessness attendant on his disease, the effort to forget himself, all conspired to sharpen every mental faculty to the utmost. All actions, even the wisest, were overdone.

He had been advised to pass as much time as he could in the open air. He seemed bent on spending all the daytime there. The bad weather seldom kept him in. In the early autumn (October) he walked six or seven hours a day, though he had lost eight pounds since Combe Varin. He explores the ancient city on foot, searching about in the squares and gardens for the localities of famous deeds, identifying temples and palaces in the Forum, mousing round in the quarter on the other side of the Tiber, examining the gates and walls, searching after the remains of theatres; the inseparable umbrella in his hand, often over his head. He does not know how or where to stop, a preternatural power of endurance holding him up, and pushing him on. In the middle of January, 1860, when he has lost ten or twelve pounds of flesh, looks paler and thinner in the face, weaker in the eyes, and is more nervous and desponding, the power of walking does not abate. In April, but little more than a month before the end came, he rides on a donkey to Frascati and to Tusculum two miles beyond, among the mountains, — in all, some twelve miles distant from Rome;

and every day he must descend and ascend those hundred and twenty steps.

He cannot keep out of churches. The pomps attract, while they disgust him; the antiquities attract. The old churches of Sts. Cosmo and Damien (supposed to be built on ancient sites), the temples of Janus and Ceres, the mausoleum of Augustus, draw him as an archæologist. The Santa Maria Maggiore, the Ara Cœli, the San Lorenzo without the walls, San Carlo, and many another, were, of course, intensely interesting; but they were hardly places which a physician would recommend a consumptive invalid to frequent in ugly weather. He confesses that he catches bad colds, and coughs shockingly, now and then raising blood; but he cannot desist. The places are either curious or amusing: in either case he is taken out of himself; entertained for the hour, if for no longer. In what different spirit, with what different purposes, he went over all that ground fifteen years before, taking in stores of thought that were to serve and cheer him in many future years! now killing weary days, and trying to calm a restless mind which had no more work to do on earth, but wished to get from earth such peace as it could before the great future opened.

Friendship did all for him that friendship could. A devoted care, patient and sweet, was always with him. Dearer hearts than those under the same roof with him there were not in the world. There was the smallest possible friction of temper. The kindest of companions attended him in his walks. The affectionate thoughtfulness of the Storys and Brownings was gratefully acknowledged. Miss Charlotte Cushman did all a good heart prompted to cheer the tiresome days. Dr. Frothingham of Boston, who was spending the winter in Rome with his family, came in and chatted about poetry, the theatre, people. Mr. and Mrs. C. T. Thayer toiled dutifully up the hundred and twenty steps to comfort the sick man.

Artists he saw now and then, — William Page, Harriet Hosmer. Story entertained him with various learning and wit, and kept him employed in his studio while making his bust. But society was tantalizing, at times exasperating; for the invalid could not talk without pain, and to listen without responding did not calm his mind. He avoided social occasions, even of the most attractive sort. "I sit at all entertainments," he says, "like the coffin in the Egyptian feasts."

The climate of Rome, this winter, was cruel to the sick who sought its hospitality, — wet, cold, windy, disagreeable. The summer had been dry and cold. The rainy season set in early, and continued late. It rained when he arrived; it rained for two or three weeks afterward. "For nine or ten weeks, it beat any thing I ever knew in New England for badness;" "Cloudy and foggy;" "Chilly and cold:" these are the records in the journal. "A most fitful climate. I have been here near four months, and have seen no particle of dust till yesterday. It has rained almost all the time; yet out of the one hundred and twenty days there have been but eight when I have not walked out an hour or two." "Rome is the dampest city I was ever in. The walls and roofs are green and yellow with fuci and lichens of various kinds. The Tramontana wind is cold and arid: that makes me cough at once." Invalids, or people who had been invalid, cheered him by telling what Rome had done for them; but its kindly offices are not for him. He writes to Miss Cobbe, "Rome has not used me well this winter, and I shall leave it with but one regret; viz., that I came here at all. I have lost three pounds a month since I left Switzerland, and have gained nothing but a great cough."

The city, too, was more than usually gloomy. There were fewer strangers there; and consequently there was less industry, more complaint, more beggary. "Rome is an ugly old place. The past is all: there is no present but misery, and no future but decay and destruction. It is a fossil city, utterly foreign to me and mine. I abhor its form of religion, which is only ceremony: I despise its theology, and find little to respect in its lying, treacherous, and unreliable inhabitants. It is a city of the dead. It has a threefold past, but no future." The finest of ruins are not cheering to a man who feels his steps tending towards decay.

The memory of the brave young America, where his heart was, deepened the gloom of the old city, and made existence there at times almost unbearable. Through letters and newspapers he was informed of all that went on there in the world of religion, politics, society: the petty sectarian quarrels, the pettier sectarian manœuvres, were all reported to him. With beating heart he followed the fortunes of the deepening fight between liberty and slavery, noting the names of those that battled well and of those that faltered, measuring forces, balancing probabilities, forecasting issues, cheering the combatants, and aching with agony because he could not be where the strife was hottest. The heroic venture of his friend John Brown was made while he was on his way from Switzerland to Italy. Every step of that great exploit he traced with eager emotion, bore in mind tenderly the day of execution, and listened breathlessly for the echoes that came from the hills of the North. Every brave word spoken reached his ear; every responsive act done by roused leaders or indignant people, every movement prophetic of popular uprising, made the blood fly in his veins. It is anguish to be idle and useless when soldiers are needed as never before. He would share the fate of his friends, — Sumner, Wilson, Hale, Seward, Gerritt Smith, Stearns, Howe, the faithful few who dared stand up for principle. "O George!" he cries to his friend Ripley, "the life I am here slowly dragging to an end, tortuous but painless, is very, very imperfect, and fails of much I meant to hit, and might have reached, nay, should, had there been ten or twenty years more left for me. But, on the whole, it has not been a mean life, measured by the common run of men; never a selfish one. Above all things else, I have sought to teach the true idea of man, of God, of religion, with its truths, its duties, and its joys. I never fought for myself, nor against a private foe, but have gone into the battle of the nineteenth century, and followed the flag of humanity. Now I am ready to die, though conscious that I leave half my work undone; and much grain lies in my fields, waiting only for Him that gathereth sheaves. I would rather lay my bones with my fathers and mothers at Lexington, and think I may; but will not complain if earth or sea shall cover them up elsewhere."

To all who had been true to him his feeling was exceedingly tender. He had finished a long letter to his old friend Charles Ellis, when the news came of his death. Immediately a touching letter goes to his widow: "He was one of my oldest friends, one of the faithfullest, one of the nearest and dearest. His friendship never failed; and I never asked him in vain to help another. Let us not complain. Tenderly loved by those who knew him best, widely respected by many whom he worked with in the various duties of the day, at a considerable age he has gone home. He has shaken off a worn-out and broken body continually racked with torturing pains, and risen up a free and unfettered spirit. I think it fortunate for him, for you, for us all, that he was spared that long agony which wearies out the day of many, and makes the road to the grave so rough and difficult. Not long ago, poor Katie went before him, lamenting that she must go alone. Now he is with her. Nay, she went to make ready a place in heaven for her father, who so tenderly prepared a place for her on earth." The wife of another of his well-beloved parishioners, Mrs. George Jackson, passed away; and another message of love and faith flew from his pen: "Who would not wish for so smooth a sail out of this little sea, and into the great wide haven we are all bound to? Most men dread *dying*, but not *death*. I can't think our present deaths natural, or to continue always. If something were not wrong in our mode of life, we should all glide gently out of the world; but we must bear the misfortunes that others entail on us. If it were *fate*, it could not be borne; but when we look on it as providence, the work of an infinite Father and Mother, who looks eternally before, and eternally looks after, and rules all things from love as motive, and for blessedness as end, we can take almost any thing with a smile."

His faith in the eternal present and the immortal future never fainted. He felt that the sky was always blue above the clouds: if the star rose in mist, it cleared itself as it ascended. As the mortal disease gained on him,—as it did, and as he better than anybody knew that it did, for he observed and noted each physical change,—the struggle of nature against dissolution was carried on in every department of his frame. That vigorous organization was not soon reconciled to death. Compactly knitted and sturdily built as if to last a century, it could not consent to break up. It had to be taken to pieces slowly, each part separately detached; and the process made the very seat of the soul tremble. The finest nerves were wrung. The sweetest bells became jangled and out of tune. The mechanism of hope and faith and trust was occasionally disordered, and responded faintly to the bidding of the will. The column was moved on which the telescope rested that used to pick out the tiniest stars in the night heavens, and the fields of light were blurred. The sick man had the sick man's fancies,—was restless and self-tormenting; wanted what he could not have; was capricious about meat and drink and medicine; had the usual unaccountable likes and dislikes. His case being desperate, he would clutch at straws, and try experiments with himself, which varied from day to day; refused all regular treatment. He was never a good subject for nurse or physician: he knew too much; was too self-dependent; call it, if you please, too self-willed. He was subject to extreme physical depression from excessive weakness. At such times, waves of sorrow would roll over the helpless soul. The accumulated weight of former years, which he had kept back by main force before, now crowded in with irresistible power: then, his faith and trust asserting themselves as the billows receded for a moment, his spirit rose with a bound into regions of joyous anticipation, where sorrow seemed impossible, and labor light. Even an apostle felt the strait a close one between living and dying, when, though dying was gain, living was Christ. We will say no more about it. It was nobody's fault that the long, trying sickness was distressing: it had to be. Death seemed unnatural with such a creature. The loving ones who ministered to him knew it, and tenderly forgot what they saw it would grieve him bitterly to have them remember. For them to forget was easy; for pitying affection was uppermost in their hearts, and gratitude was uppermost in his. Indeed, he compelled them to forget by the astonishing vigor of his mind. Only three weeks before he died, as he lay one day in Rome, with one eye closed from feebleness, the whole man apparently in the last stage of prostration, a friend who had been absent in Florence for two weeks came in. "What news?" inquired the patient. The visitor took from her pocket two or three unpublished translations, by Owen Meredith, from the Romance dialect. "Read them to me." As she read, the wan countenance regained its animation; speech returned. He took the papers from her hand, read them himself aloud, explained the obscure lines as he went on, and ended by giving a history of the dialect, and an account of the sources whence the poems were taken, as if that kind of literature had been the study of his life.

As the weeks wore on, and spring came again, hope seemed to revive. He talked of travel. He would go to Naples and see Vesuvius, perhaps to Pæstum, afterwards to Siena, Pisa, Florence, Milan, Venice, thence to Vienna, so into Germany, and round into Switzerland. Of ultimate recovery he had no hope; none of substantial improvement: but he thought he might reach home and die. His longing was for his friend Desor: "Let us see you here soon; for *you* are the medicine I ueed most of all, and may do me just the good thing I need to set me on my legs again." At length Desor came, but too late. The sight of him gave strength for a moment; but his society was exhausting. Still, as this note — the last he ever finished, to Miss Stevenson in Florence — bears witness, his courage did not fail. Perhaps the thought of leaving Rome stirred the embers of hope in him.

Rome, Sunday (Quasimodo), April 15, 1860.

Poo ole Ladye, — It is fine weather to-day; and, before Dr. A. and Desor come here, I will try and write you a little letter. Yesterday was dreadful weather, and I did not go out of doors. I think I have been mending ever since Desor came. But it is too much for him to dine here every day: so he lodges and dines mainly at his hotel; and we *drive* together; and he stays an hour or two or more, and talks to me. I sleep tolerably well, and do not complain. The sore throat seems to be improving.

Wife is as cheerful and happy as you could look for with all her anxieties; the best and tenderest of nurses; not at all fussy. She lies down on the sofa after dinner, and sleeps an hour or so: this both helps her to sleep in the night all the better, and, what is more, to keep cheerful and active in the day. It is what she always needed, but would not take.

Cabot thinks it better for me to come home about Sept. 1; and Desor proposes nice little plans for the summer, — partly of travel, partly of residence at Combe Varin. But all this must depend *on a contingency* which I cannot control: therefore I leave all *undecided.*

We shall travel north with the spring; keeping in warm weather till we come into Switzerland. Next Saturday, Appletons and all of us hope to start in a *vettura* for Florence, *viâ* Perugia. It will take us about six days; and, if you will ask Mrs. M. to take us into two rooms then, you will confer a new favor, especially if we get in. *I can't go up high:* the hundred and twenty steps have been almost fatal to me; and I thank God that I am to ascend them but five times more.

This is all that will run out of my pen this morning, and perhaps the last I shall write you from Rome; for I hate a pen now-a-davs. Good-by!

Boo!

But he had changed sadly since the days of Combe Varin: he looked ten years older; had become an old man. It was plain to everybody, soon it was plain to him, that all travelling was impossible, except, perhaps, what was necessary to take him away from the city, the aspect whereof had become ghastly to him, whose atmosphere was mental poison. Then the desire to get away from Rome and its detestable climate became morbidly intense. He was impatient to go; fretted under the delays caused by the weather; insisted on departing. "Should you fail on the road; should you die in a tavern!"—"I will not die so. I will reach Florence. My bones shall not rest in this detested soil. I will go to Florence; and I will get there, I promise you."

The sad procession set off by *vetturino*, by way of Perugia. The journey was made to last five days,—about thirty miles a day; the patient resting as much as he could, attempting no excursions, but inquisitive in regard to all the others saw. "Tell me," he said, "when we pass the frontier and leave the Papal States behind. If I am asleep, wake me to tell it." The post, newly painted red, white, and green, the colors of the kingdom of Italy, was passed in the daytime. He observed it, and roused himself as if electrified. His eyes burned with enthusiasm. Now, at least, he should die in a free land.

Florence was reached, but hardly. The sick man was more than ready to accept the rest it offered. He welcomed his last bed. There, day after day, he lay quietly, his back to the window, his eyelids quivering, his mind much of the time in a half-conscious state, his thoughts wandering in pleasant places. He was on his way to America; he was at home again among his dear parishioners. "Come, Bearsie, let us go and see our friends." Once he tried to write a note to good John Ayres, the friend of many years: —

FLORENCE, May 3.

MY DEAR JOHN AYRES, — So I shall still call you. Will you come over to-morrow and see us, just after your dinner-time? Bring me a last year's apple if you can, or any new melon.

Yours truly, T. P.

You get into my house not far from good Mr. Cummings's grocery.

His broken talk ran upon his old days and old delights. Grateful messages fell from his murmuring lips: —

"Mr. Gooding's pears! — thank him. Couldn't forget the autumn pears!"

"Love to Aunt Mary: that is all that I can send her."

"Tell the Miss Thayers I would like to see them; that I went away in February, 1859, and came back in July, 1860. I should like to touch them, and tread on Boston Common."

He was in his house, his library. One day he declared that all was confusion there; and it was: the careful housekeeper was sweeping it at the moment, unconscious that the master's exorbitant sensibility was restlessly moving about the room, disturbed by her dust. When the fever-fits were on him, he would rouse himself as if to prepare for a journey. "When is that vessel going? Will it not go soon?" In clearer moments he would be aware of his condition, and bid affectionate adieus to those about him; then, rallying, would talk his old child's talk with his wife and Miss Stevenson, his wasted appearance contrasting singularly with the fresh welling-over of his emotion. In these last days he was never petulant or exacting. His gentlest consideration returned to him: he asked humbly for service, and gratefully thanked those who gave it.

Miss Frances Power Cobbe — one of the truest of his spiritual friends, in whose books he had interested himself when in Boston, with whom he had corresponded, whom he hoped to see in London, but had never met — was in Florence, and impatient to see him. Collecting himself by a great effort, the sick man received her tenderly at his bedside. "It is strange that we should meet thus at last. But you do not see me; only the memory of me. They who wish me well wish me a speedy departure to the other world. Of course, I am not afraid to die; but there is so much to do!" — "But you have done much. You have given your life to God, to his truth and his work, as truly as any old martyr of them all." — "I don't know," was the reply. "I had great powers committed to me: I have but half used them." She gave him flowers, — tea-roses, some lilies of the valley. The gentle touch of nature woke the soul of nature in him. A heavenly smile suffused his face, which made his visitor wonder how any should have thought him homely. His spirit roused, he talked with animation of the flowers of America, then of literature, — the literature of Italy. The veil was lifted; and Miss Cobbe had a glimpse of the man as he was in his prime. "Do not speak of your feeling for me," he said: "it makes me too unhappy to leave you." He wanted to see her every day, but could not: the pleasure was too exciting. When he did, the gleams of light came at intervals across a dreamy waste of mind. The lilies caused a gladness that soon faded. "What day is it?"—"Sunday, a blessed day."—"It *is* a blessed day when one has got over the superstition of it." "I want to tell you something," he said earnestly at one of these interviews. "There are two Theodore Parkers now: one is dying here in Italy; the other I have planted in America. He will live there, and finish my work." Weeks before this there were moments, moments in almost every day, when the shattered mental system responded to no supreme effort at control. The mainspring of the mechanism was fatally weakened; the golden bowl was broken; the silver cord was loosed. Once, in Rome, his wife having left the room, he put a paper into a friend's hand. It contained directions for his funeral in the Music Hall. Rome and Boston were mingled confusedly in his mind. "It is all one," he said. "Phillips and Clarke will come for my sake." Notions of time and space were blurred; but the noble heart was true to its instincts. If his mind wandered, it was in heavenly fields. He would save his wife from the bitterness of his thought. He did his friends the justice to think their love as all-victorious as his own.

At last the curtain fell: a gradual weakness, without pain or distress, pressed down the prostrate frame. Mental action ceased: a soft mist crept over the faculties: physical sensibility became less and less. On the 10th of May he fell asleep, so softly, that the most anxious watchers knew not that the last breath had been drawn. The slumber of a little child was in his case more than a metaphor. The great soul had gone, and a simplicity as of infancy rested on the deserted face.

Three days later, on a Sunday afternoon, the body was taken to the little Protestant cemetery just outside the city, by the Pinti Gate. It was a feast-day in the city. The body was taken to its resting-place through streets that were lined with banners, and rang with rejoicing. In the narrow graveyard, blooming with verdure, it was buried.

The reading of the Beatitudes, and the solemn thoughts of the mourners, made all the service. It was enough. Over few graves could those immortal words be more fitly spoken. A plain slab of gray marble, with the simplest of inscriptions, has told many of his country men and women where to leave their sweetest flowers and their tenderest tears. His own words best express the spirit in which he met his end: —

"Yes, holy one, thou the good Shepherd art,
Enduring hardest service for thy sheep,
Hearing their bleatings with a human heart,
Not losing such as thou wert put to keep;
But feeble wanderers from the field astray
Thou on thy shoulders takest, and dost bear
From hireling thieves and murdering wolves away,
And watchest o'er them with a guardian care.
Thou art the human Shepherd of the sheep,
Leading them forth to pasture all the day;
At night to folds which them in safety keep.
Thou light and life from God, to heaven the way,
And giving, at the last, thy own, thy well-beloved, sleep."

CHAPTER XX.

TRIBUTES.

THE tidings of Theodore Parker's death caused a profound sensation in the places that had known him. At the annual festival of the Unitarian Association, on Anniversary Week, it was alluded to with feeling by men who had disagreed with the preacher and reformer, but who sincerely respected the man. At the session of the New-England Antislavery Society, on Thursday, May 31, resolutions of eulogy were offered by Wendell Phillips, which the president of the society, John T. Sargent, seconded in a few appreciative words, and which Theodore's loving and beloved friend, Samuel J. May, followed with a tribute out of a full heart. I shall not copy at length the addresses that were made here or elsewhere; but a few extracts will be proper, as showing the impression that Mr. Parker left on the strongest minds. The language is, of course, language of eulogium; but it fell from sincere lips, that were not in the habit of speaking idle praise of any, holding truth ever more precious than tenderness to living or to dead.

After some words of introduction, Mr. Phillips said, —

"When some Americans die, when most Americans die, their friends tire the public with excuses. They confess this spot; they explain that stain; they plead circumstances as the half justification of that mistake; and they beg of us to remember that nothing but good is to be spoken of the dead. We need no such mantle for that green grave under the sky of Florence; no excuses, no explanations, no spot. Priestly malice has scanned every inch of his garment: it was seamless; it could find no stain. History, as in the case of every other of her beloved children, gathers into her bosom the arrows which malice had shot at him, and says to posterity, 'Behold the title-deeds of your gratitude!' We ask no moment to excuse: there is nothing to explain. What the snarling journal thought bold, what the selfish politician feared as his ruin, it was God's seal set upon his apostleship. The little libel glanced across him like a rocket when it goes over the vault: it is passed, and the royal sun shines out as beneficent as ever.

"When I returned from New York on the thirteenth day of this month, I was to have been honored by standing in his desk; but illness prevented my fulfilling the appointment. It was eleven o'clock in the morning. As he sank away the same week under the fair sky of Italy, he said to the most loving of wives and of nurses, 'Let me be buried where I fall;' and tenderly, thoughtfully, she selected four o'clock of the same Sunday to mingle his dust with the kindred dust of brave, classic Italy.

"Four o'clock! The same sun that looked upon the half-dozen mourners that he permitted to follow him to the grave, that same moment of brightness, lighted up the arches of his own temple as one whom he loved stepped into his own desk, and with remarkable coincidence, for the only time during his absence, opened one of his own sermons to supply my place; and, as his friend read the Beatitudes over his grave on the banks of the Arno, his dearer friend here read from a manuscript the text, 'Have faith in God.' It is said that in his last hours, in the wandering of that masterly brain, he murmured, 'There are two Theodore Parkers: one rests here, dying; but the other lives, and is at work at home.' How true! At that very moment he was speaking to his usual thousands; at that very instant his own words were sinking down into the hearts of those that loved him best, and bidding them, in this the loneliest hours of their bereavement, 'have faith in God.'

"He always came to this platform: he is an old occupant of it. He never made an apology for coming to it. I remember, many years ago, going home from the very hall which formerly occupied this place. He had sat where you sit, in the seats, looking up at us. It had been a stormy, hard gathering, a close fight; the press calumniating us; every journal in Boston ridiculing the idea which we were endeavoring to spread. As I passed down the stairs homeward, he put his arm within mine, and said, 'You shall never need to ask me again to share that platform.' It was the instinct of his nature, true as the bravest heart. The spot for him was where the battle was hottest. He had come, as half the clergy come, a critic. He felt it was not his place; that it was to grapple with the tiger, and throttle him. And the pledge that he made he kept; for whether here or in New York, as his reputation grew, when that lordly mammoth of the press, 'The Tribune,' overgrown in its independence and strength, would not condescend to record a word that Mr. Garrison or I could utter, but bent low before the most thorough scholarship of New England, and was glad to win its way to the confidence of the West by being his mouthpiece, — with that weapon of influence in his right hand, he always placed himself at our side, and in the midst of us, in the capital State of the empire.

"You may not think this great praise: we do. Other men have brought us brave hearts; other men have brought us keen-sighted and vigilant intellects: but he brought us, as no one else could, the loftiest stature of New-England culture. He brought us a disciplined intellect, whose statement was evidence, and whose affirmation the most gifted student took long time before he ventured to doubt or to contradict. When we had nothing but our characters, nothing but our reputation for accuracy, for our weapons, the man who could give to the cause of the slave that weapon was indeed one of its ablest and foremost champions.

"Lord Bacon said in his will, 'I leave my name and memory to foreign lands, and to my own countrymen *after some time be passed.*' No more fitting words could be chosen, if the modesty of the friend who has just gone before us would have permitted him to adopt them for himself. To-day, even within twenty-four hours, I have seen symptoms of that repentance which Johnson describes: —

> 'When nations, slowly wise and meanly just,
> To buried merit raise the tardy bust.'

"The men who held their garments aside, and desired to have no contact with Music Hall, are beginning to show symptoms that they will be glad, when the world doubts whether they have any life left, to say, 'Did not Theodore Parker spring from our bosom?' Yes, he takes his place, his serene place, among those few to whom Americans point as a proof that the national heart is still healthy and alive. Most of our statesmen, most of our politicians, go down into their graves, and we cover them up with apologies: we walk with reverent and filial love backward, and throw the mantle over their defects, and say, 'Remember the temptation and the time!' Now and then one, now and then one, goes up silently, and yet not unannounced, like the stars at their coming, and takes his place; while all eyes follow him, and say, 'Thank God! It is the promise and the herald: it is the nation alive at its heart. God has not left us without a witness; for his children have been among us, and one-half have known them by love, and one-half have known them by hate, — equal attestations to the divine life that has passed through our streets.'"

Mr. Garrison spoke with little premeditation, but in substance thus: He referred to the mental independence and moral courage which characterized Mr. Parker in respect to all his convictions and acts. He was not technically "a Garrisonian abolitionist," though often upon that platform, but voted with the Republican party, though faithfully rebuking it for its timidity and growing spirit of compromise. He was no man's man, and no man's follower, but acted for himself, bravely, conscientiously, and according to his best judgment.

But what of his theology? Mr. Garrison did not know that he could state the whole of Mr. Parker's creed; but he remembered a part of it: "There is one God and Father over all, absolute and immutable, whose love is infinite, and therefore inexhaustible, and whose tender mercies are over all the works of his hand; and, whether in the body or out of the body, the farthest wanderer from the fold might yet have hope." He believed in the continual progress and final redemption of the human race; that every child of God, however erring, would ultimately be brought back. "You may quarrel with that theology," said Mr. Garrison, "if you please: I shall not. I like it; I have great faith in it; I accept it. But this I say in respect to mere abstract theological opinions,—the longer I live, the less do I care about them, the less do I make them a test of character. It is nothing to me that any man calls himself a Methodist, or Baptist, or Unitarian, or Universalist. These sectarian shibboleths are easily taken upon the lip, especially when the 'offence of the cross' has ceased. Whoever will, with his theology, grind out the best grist for our common humanity, is the best theologian for me.

"Many years ago, Thomas Jefferson uttered a sentiment which shocked our eminently *Christian* country as being thoroughly infidel. 'I do not care,' said he, 'whether my neighbor believes in one God or in twenty gods, if he does not pick my pocket;' thus going to the root of absolute justice and morality, and obviously meaning this: If a man pick my pocket, it is in vain he tells me, in palliation of his crime, 'I am a believer in one true and living God.'—'That may be; but you are a pickpocket nevertheless.' Or he may say, 'I have not only one God, but twenty gods: therefore I am not guilty.'—'Nay, but you are a thief!' And so we always throw ourselves back upon character; upon the fact whether a man is honest, just, long-suffering, merciful; and not whether he believes in a denominational creed, or is a strict observer of rites and ceremonies. This was the religion of Theodore Parker, always exciting his marvellous powers to promote the common good, to bless those who needed a blessing, and to seek and to save the lost, to bear testimony in favor of the right in the face of an ungodly age, and against 'a frowning world.'"

Mr. Garrison said they were there to honor his memory.

How could they best show their estimation of him? By trying to be like him in nobility of soul, in moral heroism, in fidelity to the truth, in disinterested regard for the welfare of others.

"Mr. Parker, though strong in his convictions, was no dogmatist, and assumed no robes of infallibility. No man was more docile in regard to being taught, even by the lowliest. Mr. Phillips had done him no more than justice when he said that he was willing and eager to obtain instruction from any quarter. Hence he was always inquiring of those with whom he came in contact, so that he might learn, if possible, something from them that might aid him in the great work in which he was engaged.

"When the question of woman's rights first came up for discussion, like multitudes of others, Mr. Parker was inclined to treat it facetiously, and supposed it could be put aside with a smile. Still it was his disposition to hear and to learn; and as soon as he began to investigate, and to see the grandeur and world-wide importance of the woman's-rights movement, he gave to it his hearty support before the country and the world.

"How he will be missed by those noble but unfortunate exiles who come to Boston from the Old World from time to time, driven out by the edicts of European despotism! What a home was Theodore Parker's for them! How they loved to gather round him in that home! and what a sympathizing friend, and trusty adviser, and generous assistant, in their times of sore distress, they have found in him! There are many such in Boston and in various parts of our country, who have fled from foreign oppression, who will hear of his death with great sorrow of heart, and drop grateful tears to his memory."

Next came James Freeman Clarke, most loyal and generous of friends, whose theological differences left no trace on his moral or personal affection: —

"I remember meeting him on the cars on that fatal winter which laid the foundation of the disease which took him away. He had a carpet-bag with him, filled with German, Greek, and Latin books, — those old books in vellum of the seventeenth century, — volumes which it is a pain merely to look at, so hard reading do they seem to be. On Monday morning he filled his carpet-bag, and went to the place where he was to lecture Monday night: all day long he studied his books, and at night delivered his lecture. Then on Tuesday he would go to the next place; studying his books all day, and lecturing at night. So he would go on through the week until Friday; when he would be back again to Boston, with his carpet-bag exhausted, with every one of those books gutted of its contents, with the whole substance of them in his brain; so that he knew all about every one of them, and could give a perfect analysis of them all from beginning to end. On Saturday morning he would sit down to write his sermon for the next day; on Saturday afternoon go and visit the sick and bereaved of his society; on Sunday morning preach his sermon, and in the afternoon drive out to Watertown and preach there; and on Sunday evening he would lie on the sofa, and talk to his friends. That was his way of working. I got a letter only yesterday from William H. Channing, an old friend of his, who, speaking in the most tender and affectionate terms of his departure, said that he had, by over-working the intellectual part of his faculties, by too great fidelity in study, killed out, to some extent, another masterly faculty, which he had observed, but of which those who did not know him might be ignorant; namely, his gorgeous imagination. Mr. Channing said that he was a man who had, with all his logical power, with all those reflective faculties, with all those immense powers of grasp and reception, — the powers by which he held on to and retained what he had learned, and the powers by which he brought them into one great system in order to set them before men, — with all this he had the imagination of a poet, but did not let it work, he was so busy studying all the time.

"Now, there were other students along with him when he was a boy: and I have known a great many students; but their way of studying was very different from his. When Parker studied, it was not merely with the concentration of certain faculties, for the sake of working out a certain problem, and there an end of it; or merely to gather together certain things, and put them into his brain, and there an end of it. No: he had a great idea before him all the time; and his study was always instinct with the life of that idea; and every word he uttered was a living word; and all the thoughts that came from him came from him as fresh, glowing thoughts, full of love to God and love to man.

"Now with regard to the second thing which goes to make a man great. What was Parker's way of action? It was a grand way of action. His activity was as large, determined, persistent, complete, and thorough as his intellectual working was. What he did was on a plan reaching through years, on a plan arranged when he was a boy, — the whole of his life mapped out before him, with all he meant to do each year previously arranged, and the reason for it fixed in his own mind: and then he went to his work, and did it; lived to accomplish it. But what sort of work was it? Greatness in work considers the quality of the work as well as the amount and method of accomplishing it. What was the quality of his work? It was simply this: it was to lift man toward God. That was the work which Parker gave himself to do in the world; that was the work for which he gathered together all this knowledge; that the work for which he so trained his intellect to be acute, persistent, and comprehensive. It was to raise men to God. With his eye on God, he turned to man to lift him up; and wherever he found a man who needed to be raised, or a class, a race, or a nation, that needed to be lifted up, there he felt his work to be. On that point I say no more, because it is the least necessary to speak of his work; since that is patent, and known to all.

"But there is one other element of greatness in man. Besides the head and the hand, there is the heart. What was the greatness of heart in Theodore Parker? His habit was, in speaking of the Almighty, not to call him the Almighty. He spoke of the 'Absolute Father' in his philosophy and in his theology; but when he came to speak of him from the pulpit, as a Christian man speaking to Christian men, as a brother talking to brethren and sisters of what they needed, it was 'Father' and 'Mother,' — 'the great Father and Mother of us all.' The tender, feminine heart of Theodore Parker was not satisfied with the name of 'Father' unless he united with it that of 'Mother.' So tender was he, so affectionate was he, that no one was ever near to Parker as a friend, as an intimate companion, without wondering how it was that men could ever think of him as hard, stern, severe, cold, and domineering, because, in all the private relations of life, he was docile as a child to the touch of love; and it was only necessary, if you had any fault to find with any thing that he had said or done, to go to him, and tell him just what your complaint was, or what your difficulty was, and just as likely as not he would at once admit, if there was the least reason in the complaint, that he was wrong. He was as ready to admit himself in the wrong as to maintain his stand for the everlasting right.

"I do not know how to describe—with what figure borrowed from nature or art or history to describe—how Parker seems to me in all this varied and accumulated greatness of mind, of heart, and of hand, better than by telling you the incidents of one day of my life. When I was passing out of Italy once by the St. Gothard route, we were in Italy in the morning, on the Italian side of the mountains, surrounded by Italian voices and by the music of Italian nightingales, and within sight of the opening vineyards. Then we began the ascent of the mountain; and, as we ascended, we passed through the valley of pines, until at last, on that 15th of May, we came to the snow. Then we took the little sleds, and went on upon the snow, higher and higher, until we were surrounded with great fields of snow, dazzling white in the sun; and on one side we saw the fall of a terrible avalanche, with its roar of thunder. So we passed on until we reached the summit of the mountain; and then, descending on the other side, we came at last to where again the snow ceased; and, there taking the diligence, we went on our way down the side of the mountain, through gorges and ravines, and glaciers even, the country around growing more and more green, changing from spring to summer, until at last, when we came down toward the Lake of Lucerne, we passed through orchards full of apple-blossoms, and finally crossed the beautiful lake to the town of Lucerne, there to receive a whole bundle of letters from home—from father, mother, brother, sister, and child—to end the day. When I think of that day's journey,—beginning in Italy, and ending in Germany; beginning under an

Italian sun, at mid-day surrounded by snow-fields and glaciers, and at its close amid the apple-blossoms of Germany, — it seems to me that that varied and wonderful day is a sort of type of the life of our friend Theodore Parker; its youth Italian, all fresh and gushing with ten thousand springs of early, boyish life, and hope and animation, and with all the varied study and activity of the child and youth; its early morning passed in the stern work of climbing up the mountain-side; its mid-day with God's everlasting sun over his head, and the great, broad fields all around, over which his eye looked; and, all through its afternoon-hours, passing on into an ever-increasing affluence of spring and summer, and ending at last in the sweet bosom of affection, gratitude, and love."

At the close of the regular services at the Music Hall on the 3d of June, — on which occasion an appreciative discourse on the character of Mr. Parker was delivered by his friend Samuel J. May, — a meeting of the society was held to express their sense of the loss sustained in their minister's death. Mr. Charles W. Slack, chairman of the standing committee, called the meeting to order; and Mr. Frank B. Sanborn presented the fitting resolutions, which, touching as they were, failed to convey all there was in his friends' thoughts or his own. Two days earlier, on June 1, the Fraternity — an organization composed of members of the society for the purpose of aiding in all suitable ways the minister and standing committee — had met, and adopted resolutions in behalf of its own members.

On Sunday, June 17, exercises in commemoration of the death of Theodore Parker were held by the Twenty-eighth Congregational Society in the Music Hall. The immense audience, many standing, remained patient and attentive through proceedings which lasted upwards of two hours. The stand at which he had so long preached was covered with flowers. A cross of white roses and evergreen hung in front; wreaths of variegated flowers, the rarest and most beautiful of the season, were on either side; on the top stood vases with large bouquets. Lilies of the valley, Mr. Parker's favorite, lay beside the Bible. The services consisted of prayer, the reading of expressive passages from Scripture, the singing of hymns which the minister loved to read, — one of them his own selection for this very occasion, — and addresses by Charles M. Ellis, Ralph Waldo Emerson, and Wendell Phillips, — three men who knew him well, had the discernment to understand him, and the tongues to say what they had to say with as much truth as eloquence. A portion of their words, the portion that is most interesting now, is given.

Mr. Ellis spoke first, he being most intimately associated with Mr. Parker as a parishioner and personal friend. His voice was the voice of the society: —

"The resolve 'that Theodore Parker should have a chance to be heard' was more than the word of a friend, or a protest for religious freedom, or a plan for a free church. Before the South-Boston sermon, it was known who and what was coming in this young preacher, who had said, 'God still lives; man has lost none of his high nature:' and in his parable of Paul, 'I shall walk by God's light, and fear not.' It was thought that the *new truth* would be spread by his voice; perhaps not dreamed that one man could spread it so widely. But that simple resolve, the seed of this society, was dropped in faith that that truth would prevail; the mover of it having a year or two before, in a little book now forgotten, shown how it was the 'basis of all true art, criticism, society, morals, laws, and religion.' But of this society: —

"*First*, We may be content to leave almost all — as to what he *undid*, that is matter of discussion at this day, whilst partisans define their positions, priests their creeds — with a word which covers it all, *vera pro gratis*. If truth be started, let old errors go.

"*Next* let us look to what he created and *did*. He ascended to the sublime heights of philosophy and religion; by thought and study made clear to the intellect the truth that fired his soul, — that 'God is infinite perfection, power, wisdom, justice, love,' — and plainly showed it to the world. He saw and showed how, historically and by nature, man grows in the light of love, and has his eyes opened to spiritual truth, as flowers beneath the sun. He took truth from books and scholars, religion from temples and the priests, and showed them to common men.

"His basis was *man's intuition of God, and direct perception of his laws.* We see that the old theologies were most disturbed by his ideas, as slavery was, of all institutions, most shaken by his labors. Probably time will show that the most positive and complete of his intellectual works was his spiritual theology.

"Calmly, and at length, alas! with labor too great for that failing frame, thinking death near, — as he said, 'up to his shoulders in his grave,' — he reviewed that work. He wished to live to round it off, hoping for the length of years and strength of his ancestors, but ready to pass the golden gates to immortal life. His work is fragmentary in relation to his idea, though so much is in itself complete. He tells us, that, after his discourse of 'Matters pertaining to Religion,' he formed a plan, and prepared for the afternoon and evening of his days, to show the 'History of the Progressive Development of Religion among the Leading Races of Mankind.'

"What a few in the grove of the academies, by the lamp of philosophy, in moments of vision, had seen, had become so clear to him, that he would not only make it plain, and prove it to the reason of men, but would traverse the history of the world, and show its growth; show how, by either method, analysis, or synthesis, this one truth was the culmination of human thought. Well may we leave theologies, christologies, creeds, statutes, societies, governments, to take care of themselves.

"Success! For fifteen years a free church; this truth embodied in labors for the dangerous, perishing, criminal classes, for education, woman, temperance, freedom, peace; its light thrown on the lives of our great men and heroes; put in volumes that will live with the English tongue; put into labors that now move and will move the American Church and State whilst they endure; set forth in a system of religion, a positive spiritual theology, a method of spiritual culture; shadowing a scheme of ethics; containing almost the only fit attempt to state the law of nature, the law of laws, in the language; his thought, his labor, his life, — these are success and triumph enough."

Mr. Emerson followed: —

"He whose voice will not be heard here again could well afford to tell his experiences: they were all honorable to him, and were part of the history of the civil and religious liberty of his times. Theodore Parker was a son of the soil, charged with the energy of New England; strong, eager, inquisitive of knowledge; of a diligence that never tired; upright; of a haughty independence, yet the gentlest of companions; a man of study, fit for a man of the world; with decided opinions, and plenty of power to state them; rapidly pushing his studies so far as to leave few men qualified to sit as his critics. He elected his post of duty, or accepted nobly that assigned him in his rare constitution, — wonderful acquisition of knowledge; a rapid wit that heard all, and welcomed all that came, by seeing its bearing. Such was the largeness of his reception of facts, and his skill to employ them, that it looked as if he were some president of council to whom a score of telegraphs were ever bringing in reports; and his information would have been excessive but for the noble use he made of it, ever in the interest of humanity. He had a strong understanding, a logical method, a love for facts, a rapid eye for their historic relations, and a skill in stripping them of traditional lustres. He had a sprightly fancy, and often amused himself with throwing his meaning into pretty apologues; yet we can hardly ascribe to his mind the poetic element, though his scholarship had made him a reader and quoter of verses. A little more feeling of the poetic significance of his facts would have disqualified him for some of his severer offices to his generation. The old religions have a charm for most minds, which it is a little uncanny to disturb. It is sometimes a question, shall we not leave them to decay without rude shocks? I remember that I found some harshness in his treatment both of Greek and Hebrew antiquity, and sympathized with the pain of many good people in his auditory, whilst I acquitted him, of course, of any wish to be flippant.

"He came at a time, when, to the irresistible march of opinion, the forms still retained by the most advanced sects showed loose and lifeless; and he, with something less of affectionate attachment to the old, or with more vigorous logic, rejected them. It is objected to him that he scattered too many illusions. Perhaps more tenderness would have been graceful; but it is vain to charge him with perverting the opinions of the new generation. The opinions of men are organic. Simply those came to him who found themselves expressed by him; and had they not met this enlightened mind, in which they beheld their own opinions combined with zeal in every cause of love and humanity, they would have suspected their own opinions, and suppressed them, and so sunk into melancholy or malignity, a feeling of loneliness and hostility to what was reckoned respectable. It is plain to me that he has achieved an historic immortality here; that he has so woven himself in these few years into the history of Boston, that he can never be left out of your annals. It will not be in the acts of city councils, nor of obsequious mayors, nor in the State House, the proclamations of governors, with their failing virtue, — failing them at critical moments, — that the coming generations will study what really befell; but in the plain lessons of Theodore Parker in this Music Hall, in Faneuil Hall, or in legislative committee-rooms, the true temper and authentic record of these days will be read. The next generation will care little for the chances of elections that govern governors now; it will care little for fine gentlemen who behaved shabbily: but it will read very intelligently in his rough story, fortified with exact anecdotes, precise with names and dates, what part was taken by each actor; who threw himself into the cause of humanity; who came to the rescue of civilization at a hard pinch, and who blocked its course.

"The vice charged against America is the want of sincerity in leading men. It does not lie at his door. He never kept back the truth for fear to make an enemy. But, on the other hand, it was complained that he was bitter and harsh; that his zeal burned with too hot a flame. It is so difficult, in evil times, to escape this charge! — for the faithful preacher most of all. It was his merit, like Luther, Knox, Latimer, and John Baptist, to speak tart truth when that was peremptory, and when there were few to say it. But his sympathy with goodness was not less energetic. One fault he had: he overestimated his friends, I may well say it, and sometimes vexed them with the importunity of his good opinion, whilst they knew better the ebb which follows exaggerated praise. He was capable, it must be said, of the most unmeasured eulogies on those he esteemed, especially if he had any jealousy that they did not stand with the Boston public as highly as they ought. His commanding merit as a reformer is this, that he insisted beyond all men in pulpits — I cannot think of one rival — that the essence of Christianity is its practical morals: it is there for use, or it is nothing; and if you combine it with sharp trading, or with ordinary city ambitions to gloss over municipal corruptions, or private intemperance, or successful fraud, or immoral politics, or unjust wars, or the cheating of Indians, or the robbery of frontier nations, or leaving your principles at home to show on the high seas or in Europe a supple complaisance to tyrants, it is an hypocrisy, and the truth is not in you; and no love of religious music, or of dreams of Swedenborg, or praise of John Wesley or of Jeremy Taylor, can save you from the satan which you are.

"His ministry fell on a political crisis also; on the years when Southern slavery broke over its old banks, made new and vast pretensions, and wrung from the weakness or treachery of Northern people fatal concessions in the Fugitive-slave Bill and the repeal of the Missouri Compromise. Two days, bitter in the memory of Boston, — the days of the rendition of Sims and of Burns, — made the occasion of his most remarkable discourses. He kept nothing back. In terrible earnest he denounced the public crime, and meted out to every official, high and low, his due portion. By the incessant power of his statement, he made and held a party. It was his great service to freedom. He took away the reproach of silent consent that would otherwise have lain against the indignant minority, by uttering in the hour and place wherein these outrages were done the stern protest. There were, of course, multitudes to censure and defame this truth-speaker. But the brave know the brave. Fops, whether in drawing-rooms or churches, will utter the fop's opinion, and faintly hope for the salvation of his soul: but his manly enemies, who despised the fops, honored him; and it is well known that his great hospitable heart was the sanctuary to which every soul conscious of an earnest opinion came for sympathy, — alike the brave slaveholder and the brave slave-rescuer. These met in the house of this honest man; for every sound heart loves a responsible person, — one who does not in generous company say generous things, and in mean company base things, but says one thing, now cheerfully, now indignantly, but always because he must, and because he sees that whether he speak, or refrain from speech, this is said over him, and history, nature, and all souls testify to the same.

"Ah, my brave brother! it seems as if, in a frivolous age, our loss were immense, and your place cannot be supplied. But you will already be consoled in the transfer of your genius, knowing well that the nature of the world will affirm to all men, in all times, that which for twenty-five years you valiantly spoke; that the winds of Italy murmur the same truth over your grave, the winds of America over these bereaved streets; that the sea which bore your mourners home affirms it, the stars in their courses, and the inspirations of youth; whilst the polished and pleasant traitors to human rights, with perverted learning and disgraced graces, rot and are forgotten with their double tongue, saying all that is sordid for the corruption of man."

Wendell Phillips then laid another manly tribute on the grave of his friend: —

"There is one thing every man may say of this pulpit: it was a live reality, and no sham. Whether tearing theological idols to pieces at West Roxbury, or here battling with the every-day evils of the streets, it was ever a live voice, and no mechanical or parrot-tune; ever fresh from the heart of God, as these flowers, these lilies, — the last flower over which, when eyesight failed him, with his old gesture he passed his loving hand, and said, 'How sweet!' As in that story he loved so much to tell of Michael Angelo, when in the Roman palace Raphael was drawing his figures too small, Angelo sketched a colossal head of fit proportions, and taught Raphael his fault; so Parker criticised these other pulpits, not so much by censure as by creation; by a pulpit proportioned to the hour, broad as humanity, frank as truth, stern as justice, and loving as Christ. Here is the place to judge him. In St. Paul's Cathedral the epitaph says, if you would know the genius of Christopher Wren, 'look around.' Do you ask proof how full were the hands, how large the heart, how many-sided the brain, of your teacher: listen, and you will hear it in the glad, triumphant certainty of your enemies, that you must close these doors, since his place can never be filled. Do you ask proof of his efficient labor, and the good soil into which that seed fell: gladden your eyes by looking back, and seeing for how many months the impulse his vigorous hand gave you has sufficed, spite of boding prophecy, to keep these doors open. Yes, he has left those accustomed to use weapons, and not merely to hold up *his* hands. And not only among yourselves: from another city I received a letter, full of deep feeling; and the writer, an Orthodox church-member, says, —

"'I was a convert to Theodore Parker before I was a convert to ——. If there is any thing of value in the work I am doing to-day, it may, in an important sense, be said to have had its root in Parker's heresy: I mean the habit — without which Orthodoxy stands emasculated, and good for nothing — of independently passing on the empty and rotten pretensions of churches and churchmen, which I learned earliest, and more than from any other, from Theodore Parker. He has my love, my respect, my admiration.'

"Yes, his diocese is broader than Massachusetts. His influence extends very far outside these walls. Every pulpit in Boston is freer and more real to-day because of the existence of this. The fan of his example scattered the chaff of a hundred sapless years. One whole city is fresher to-day because of him. The most sickly and timid soul under yonder steeple, hide-bound in days and forms and beggarly Jewish elements, little dreams how ten times worse and narrower it was before this sun warmed the general atmosphere around. As was said of Burke's unsuccessful impeachment of Warren Hastings, 'Never was the great object of punishment, the prevention of crime, more completely obtained. Hastings was acquitted; but *tyranny and injustice were condemned* wherever English was spoken.' So we may say of Boston and Theodore Parker. Grant that few adopted his extreme theological views, that not many sympathized in his politics: still, that Boston is nobler, purer, braver, more loving, more Christian, to-day, is due more to him than to all the pulpits that vex her sabbath air. He raised the level of sermons intellectually and morally. Other preachers were compelled to grow in manly thought and Christian morals in very self-defence. As

Christ preached of the fall of the tower of Siloam the week before, and what men said of it in the streets of Jerusalem; so Parker rang through our startled city the news of some fresh crime against humanity, — some slave-hunt, or wicked court, or prostituted official, — till frightened audiences actually took bond of their new clergyman that they should not be tormented before their time.

"Men say he erred on that great question of our age, — the place due to the Bible. But William Crafts, one of the bravest men who ever fled from our vulture to Victoria, writes to a friend, 'When the slave-hunters were on our track, and no other minister except yourself came to direct our attention to the God of the oppressed, Mr. Parker came with his wise counsel, and told us where and how to go; gave us money. But that was not all: he gave me a weapon to protect our liberties, and a Bible to guide our souls. I have that Bible now, and shall ever prize it most highly.'

"How direct and frank his style! — just level to the nation's ear. No man ever needed to read any of his sentences twice to catch its meaning. None suspected that he thought other than he said, or more than he confessed.

"Like all such men, he grew daily; never too old to learn. Mark how closer to actual life, how much bolder in reform, are all his later sermons, especially since he came to the city, every year a step

'Forward persevering to the last,
From well to better, daily self-surpassed.'

"There are men whom we measure by their times, content and expecting to find them subdued to what they work in. They are the chameleons of circumstance; they are Æolian harps, toned by the breeze that sweeps over them. There are others who serve as guide-posts and landmarks: we measure their times by them. Such was Theodore Parker. Hereafter the writer will use him as a mete-wand to measure the heart and civilization of Boston. Like the Englishman, a year or two ago, who suspected our great historian could not move in the best circles of the city when it dropped out that he did not know Theodore Parker, distant men gauge us by our toleration and recognition of him. Such men are our nilometers:

the harvest of the future is according to the height that the flood of our love rises round them. Who cares now that Harvard vouchsafed him no honors? But history will save the fact to measure the calculating and prudent bigotry of our times.

"Some speak of him only as a bitter critic and harsh prophet. Pulpits and journals shelter their plain speech in mentioning him under the example of what they call his 'unsparing candor.' Do they feel that the *strangeness* of their speech, their unusual frankness, needs apology and example? But he was far other than a bitter critic; though thank God for every drop of that bitterness that came like a wholesome rebuke on the dead, saltless sea of American life! Thank God for every indignant protest, for every Christian admonition, that the Holy Spirit breathed through those manly lips! But, if he deserved any single word, it was 'generous.' *Vir generosus* is the description that leaps to the lip of every scholar. He was generous of money. Born on a New-England farm in those days when small incomings made every dollar a matter of importance, he no sooner had command of wealth than he lived with open hands. Not even the darling ambition of a great library ever tempted him to close his ear to need. Go to Venice or Vienna, to Frankfort or to Paris, and ask the refugees who have gone back — when here friendless exiles but for him — under whose roof they felt most at home. One of our oldest and best teachers writes me, that telling him once, in the cars, of a young lad of rare mathematical genius who could read Laplace, but whom narrow means debarred from the university, 'Let him enter,' said Theodore Parker: 'I will pay his bills.'"

"No sect, no special study, no one idea, bounded his sympathy; but he was generous in judgment where a common man would have found it hard to be so. Though he does not go 'down to dust without his fame,' though Oxford and Germany sent him messages of sympathy, still no word of approbation from the old grand names of our land, no honors from university or learned academy, greeted his brave, diligent, earnest life. Men can confess that they voted against his admission to scientific bodies for his ideas, feeling all the while that his brain could furnish half the academy; and yet, thus ostracized, he was the most generous — more than just — interpreter of the motives of those about him, and looked on, while others reaped where he sowed, with most generous joy in their success. Patiently analyzing character, and masterly in marshalling facts, he stamped with generous justice the world's final judgment of Webster; and, now that the soreness of the battle is over, friend and foe allow it.

"He was generous of labor. Books never served to excuse him from any the humblest work. Though 'hiving wisdom with each studious year,' and passionately devoted to his desk, as truly as was said of Milton, 'the lowliest duties on himself he laid.' What drudgery of the street did that scholarly hand ever refuse? Who so often and constant as he in the trenches when a slave-case made our city a camp? Loving books, he had no jot of a scholar's indolence or timidity, but joined hands with labor everywhere. Erasmus would have found him good company, and Melancthon got brave help over a Greek manuscript: but the likeliest place to have found him in that age would have been at Zwingle's side on the battle-field, pierced with a score of fanatic spears; for, above all things, he was terribly in earnest. If I might paint him in one word, I should say he was always *in earnest*.

"Fortunate man! he lived long enough to see the eyes of the whole nation turned toward him as to a trusted teacher; fortunate, indeed, in a life so noble, that even what was scorned from the pulpit will surely become oracular from the tomb; thrice fortunate, if he loved fame and future influence, that the leaves which bear his thoughts to posterity are not freighted with words penned by sickly ambition, or wrung from hunger, but with earnest thoughts on dangers that make the ground tremble under our feet, and the heavens black over our head, — the only literature sure to live. Ambition says, 'I will write, and be famous.' It is only a dainty tournament, a sham-fight; forgotten when the smoke clears away. Real books are like Yorktown or Waterloo, whose cannon shook continents at the moment, and echo down the centuries. Through such channels Parker poured his thoughts.

"And true hearts leaped to his side. No man's brain ever made him warmer friends; no man's heart ever held them firmer. He loved to speak of how many hands he had in every city, in every land, ready to work for him. With royal serenity he levied on all. Vassal hearts multiplied the great chief's powers; and at home the gentlest and deepest love, saintly, unequalled devotion, made every hour sunny, held off every care, and left him double liberty to work. God comfort that widowed heart!

"Judge him by his friends. No man suffered anywhere who did not feel sure of his sympathy. In sick-chambers, and by the side of suffering humanity, he kept his heart soft and young. No man lifted a hand anywhere for truth and right who did not look on Theodore Parker as his fellow-laborer. When men hoped for the future, this desk was one stone on which they planted their feet. Where more frequent than around his board would you find men familiar with Europe's dungeons and the mobs of our own streets? Wherever the fugitive slave might worship, here was his Gibraltar: over his mantel, however scantily furnished, in this city or elsewhere, you were sure to find a picture of Parker.

"The blessings of the poor are his laurels. Say that his words won doubt and murmur to trust in a loving God: let that be his record. Say that to the hated and friendless he was shield and buckler: let that be his epitaph. The glory of children is the fathers. When you voted 'that Theodore Parker should be heard in Boston,' God honored you. Well have you kept that pledge. In much labor and with many sacrifices he has laid the corner-stone: his work is ended here. God calls you to put on the top-stone. Let fearless lips and Christian lives be his monument."

Theodore Parker's friends have spared no pains to keep his memory green. Skilful men of letters, themselves teachers and reformers, have analyzed his mental and moral character with rare delicacy. Preachers in sympathy, some with his theology, and some with his religion, have done their best to exhibit him as he was in his positive attitudes toward his generation. The Parker Fraternity have, from winter to winter, invited men who were supposed to know him better than most to call up his image freshly for study and admiration. Samuel Johnson and John Weiss have been among these.

The present biographer is permitted to use the following familiar letters from Prof. Edward Desor, written several years after his beloved friend's decease: —

From Prof. E. Desor.

NEUFCHÂTEL, Feb. 13, 1868.

MY DEAR MRS. PARKER, — This is the second letter which I am able to write these last five weeks. Except one or two days, I cannot complain of severe pains; but it is exceedingly tedious to be deprived of the use of the right arm and hand. Thus every year makes us acquainted with some new misery. What meaning and benefit there is in it, I could not, thus far, ascertain. Still I ought not to complain, since my lot is not of the worst; and I am aware that many consider it as rather enviable. Do you know that I am drawing fast near sixty? Fifty-seven years is no joke. It means that I am an old man, and that I must prepare myself for the great departure.

But life needs not, for that reason, to be void; nor is it. I consider, on the contrary, that I have still somewhat to do in scientific as well as in matters of general improvement. I especially consider as such any thing that is done in the spirit of our dear Theodore Parker. There are some reforms going on in our country — for instance, at Bâle — which would have filled our departed friend with joy. A new church is being formed, quite in the spirit of Parker; and I know that his name is often mentioned there as one of the best authorities. Of course, they have to fight for their cause, as Parker had in Boston, especially against all the so-called respectable people, who are, for the most part, very orthodox. Now the young church has organized a series of public lectures, which are delivered on the critical questions, such as atonement, miracles, sacraments, &c., by the most eminent clergymen of the new school.

But that is not all. After the lecture comes the discussion; the head of the other party being there to defend their thesis. The people, seeing that it was a serious debate, proposed that the discussion should take place in the large hall of the gardeners' guild, in which the same questions were discussed at the time of the Reformation. Of course, they did not convert each other; but, according to what I heard, the discussions bore a serious and solemn character. Every thing went on in a very proper manner; and I do not doubt that it will be for the benefit of the great cause of progress. What I am still more sure is, that, had our dear Parker been among us, he would have done his best to encourage this new church.

What shall I tell you from here? I am sitting on a beautiful morning in the upper floor of my house, with a fine sun that falls into the room, quickening and cheering both my little birds, who are singing as much as they can, and the flowers which Mary has raised for my birthday, — splendid hyacinths, as fine as I ever saw. As to Mary herself, she is still unmarried, and growing old and gray, but still kind and careful. There is not much new in Combe Varin, except that the last storm has broken M. Martin's tall pine-tree along the roadside (I have not yet dared to inform him of the accident); whereas the double-headed Parker tree is still alive, although rather sickly. Lyman's linden, on the contrary, is in full vigor. A new one has been dedicated to friend Lesley.

Your most affectionate

E. DESOR.

Pray go occasionally to Cambridge, and pay a visit to Mrs. Manning for my sake.

From the Same.

NEUFCHÂTEL, Feb. 13, 1869.

MY DEAR MRS. PARKER, — I am just leaving my breakfast-table, which I found decorated with magnificent hyacinths, snow-drops, and other flowers, which Mary has raised during the last months. There was also a mighty cake with my name on it. All that is very neat; but, unfortunately, its true meaning is not very pleasant, because it is a step more towards the dissolution of our body. Well, it does not, after all, matter much, provided the mind preserves some strength and brightness. In this respect, I am happy to say that I have not to complain. And I dare say, if our dear Parker were alive, he would approve of what we have done, and are still doing, in a department which was more especially his; viz., in liberal theology. We are organizing a church, which is very much like his own, — perhaps a little more radical, — and which may resume itself in the following tenets : —

A church without sacerdoce,
A religion without catechism,
A worship without mystery,
A moral without theology,
A God without system.

This doctrine, which disclaims, of course, all sorts of sacraments and of miraculous intervention, was preached a few months ago by a young professor of philosophy ; and caused, as you may imagine, a great disturbance among the orthodox. Still the discussion went on decently ; which would not have been the case some twenty or thirty years ago. Some of the most eminent leaders of the French Rational Church came to second us ; among others a M. Félix Pécaud, well known by several publications, and a great admirer of Parker. You cannot imagine how delighted he was to find around me so many traces of our lamented friend. I showed him his likeness, some of his letters, his works ; which all interested him in the highest degree. Had it not been so cold, I would have brought him to Combe Varin to show him the room, and the pine-tree which bears his name. The latter is still alive, although somewhat weather-beaten ; whereas that of Martin, on the side of the road, has been blown down.

I wish and hope this letter may find you in good health, and that you will not forget to tell me of it. Pray give my very best regards to Miss Shannon, whom I liked very much indeed. What a pity it was that I could not enjoy more her company ! Give also my regards to Miss Stevenson ; and, should you happen to pay a visit to my old Mother Manning at Cambridge, do not forget to remember me in your conversation.

Yours,

E. Desor.

Mary sends her best love. She has not yet found a husband ; but has not yet given it up.

From the Same.

NEUFCHÂTEL, Feb. 13, 1870.

MY DEAR MRS. PARKER, — I will not follow your example; and, rather than suppose that you do not care about this correspondence, I prefer supposing that some accident has prevented you from writing on Parker's birthday. Perhaps you have been absent, or had too much to do; although I am at loss to suppose what business you may have. Let me suppose that you are still enjoying that excellent health which was your privilege thus far. As to myself, I have no reason to complain this year with my health: it has been better than many years before. The rheumatism, especially, has not taken hold of me; and this is an unexpected good fortune. Nor was I less active than in former years. My burden, instead of being lightened, has, on the contrary, been increased; for they have elected me a member of the Swiss Congress, which will oblige me to spend yearly about two months at Berne for the coming three years. My relation with Theodore Parker has also caused me an increase of business, inasmuch as they have created in our canton a liberal church, which has caused a great deal of trouble among the conservatives and fogies of all descriptions. Of course, Parker's friend could not stay away. My house was, on the contrary, frequently the rendezvous of the various preachers and leaders of the movement. This, of course, did not make me very beloved among the fashionable people; but, on the other hand, made me rather popular among the liberal minds of all Switzerland. Among the lecturers who came to us from the various parts of France and Belgium, there was also a M. Bost, preacher at Verviers (Belgium), who gave us an excellent letter about our dear Theodore Parker. The lecturer was listened to with great attention and earnestness; and I dare say this noble life, exposed with great enthusiasm, had a good influence on our public. — Mary sends her kindest regards. She is still the old busy housekeeper, taking great care of every thing, — the animals, the plants, and even the books.

I do not know why neither friend Lyman nor friend Lesley writes to me. I intend to spend a week with Martin in the month of March. We have now a great deal of snow, and sleighing in general.

Your E. DESOR.

From the Same.

NEUFCHÂTEL, Feb. 13, 1872.

MY DEAR MRS. PARKER, — Again a year more; again a large step on the slope that leads to the close of this earthly career: but, instead of being quiet, I am more than ever in the harness, and can hardly, among the pre-occupations of our federal and cantonal revision, find a moment to devote to the absent friends. You will therefore excuse me for being rather brief this time. And still there are many things which I would like to talk over with you, if I could sit quietly down and review the past days. My scientific pursuits led me last autumn to Italy, where there was an international congress of anthropology and prehistoric archæology (at Bologna). I went from Bologna to Rome and Naples, and thought with uncommon interest of the excursion which we once decided to make to the Vesuv with our dear friend Theodore. How he would have enjoyed such excursions with men of science, as were my companions, in the pursuit not only of natural problems, but also of archæological ones, such as are now being discussed everywhere!

It was not our intention to stay at Florence; but, in order to be there a day, I separated from my companions at Pisa, and went to Florence. It was on a fine day. My first and near attraction was the grave in the churchyard, you know. I spent there about an hour in quiet and silence. The tomb was in a proper state of conservation; the rose-bush vigorous, and so the ivy. I took a leaf of the last; which I sent in a letter to one of the heads of our church, one of the greatest admirers of Parker, — Dr. Lang at Zurich. I took also the last bud of the rose, which I keep for a French admirer of Parker, — Mr. Félix Pécaud, one of the finest minds and noblest hearts I have met in this life. You will, perhaps, ask why I did not cut one for you. This was, indeed, my first impression; and I would have done it, had I not considered how many Americans are living at and travelling to Florence, and that it is but natural to think that some of them are anxious of visiting that venerated grave, and provide you with flowers and leaves. Our friend Lyman was also present before my mind when I sat on the margin of the beloved grave. Pray tell his wife, Mrs.

Lyman, that I understand how every thing and every word that reminds her husband must be interesting to her. There was never a nobler character than his.

I had the misfortune of missing, last summer, the visit of Dr. Samuel Cabot and his wife. It was a great disappointment for me. Were I not so short of time, I would have written long ago. My old Mary asks me to remember her to good Mrs. Parker, and to say that she has not yet found a husband. She is growing old.

Your most sincerely,

E. DESOR.

From the Same.

NEUFCHÂTEL, April 6, 1873.

MY DEAR MRS. PARKER, — It is for the first time that I am late with my writing to you on my birthday. Strange! the older I am growing, the more have I to work in all directions; so that I am obliged to neglect those duties which I ought above all to fulfil. It is a peculiar feature of our small republics, that, when a man has some good will and some leisure for working, he soon gets overburdened. That is my case; and I trust that you will take it into consideration, and not be angry with me on account of my neglect.

I need not to say that I have not in the least lost sight of the happy days when I used to enjoy your and our dear Parker's company, and delight in his noble deeds. Could I forget the benefit which I derived from this intercourse, the interesting reforms which are going on in religious matters would suffice to recall our beloved friend to my memory. I do not know how they think of him and of his labors in the United States: the fact is, that no important step is taken in our religious affairs without the name of Parker being quoted. I know more than one of our Unitarian ministers who has no greater aim than to follow his footsteps. Were you to attend our meetings, you would frequently hear him quoted as one of the most prominent preachers of the present age. There is especially one of our Unitarian ministers, Dr. Lang of Zurich, now the leading man among the Swiss Unitarians, who considers him almost as a prophet.

I had, some months ago, the occasion of making the acquaintance of another admirer of Parker, — Miss Carpenter, — who felt very thankful when I gave her a little seal with Parker's head, which I had at the time made at Florence. This noble woman is, as I hear, about to start for Boston, in spite of her seventy years, for the sake of organizing refuge-houses for the liberated criminals and abandoned children, after the model of the English institutes of that kind. Should you happen to meet her, I pray you to remember me kindly to her, and to return her friendly remembrance.

Now as to myself and my household. I have nothing particular to say, except that, in spite of the age, I try to keep as active as possible; and, in fact, I far prefer to have too much to do than too little. My public duties call me frequently abroad, to Berne as well as to Zurich. Friend Parker would probably be very much astonished to hear that I am now vice-president of the Swiss House of Representatives. My household is pretty much the same. There is old Mary, still active and devoted, August, and partly, also, Benj, although the latter is married. Mary has given up marrying. I intend to start, towards the end of next month, for the World's Exhibition at Vienna. Now please let me know how you are, and believe me ever

Your faithful

E. DESOR.

After this, it may seem unnecessary, to say the least, for the writer of this biography to add any words of his own descriptive of Theodore Parker; for though the language quoted above, as well as much of that referred to, is the language of eulogy, still it is the language of wise and discriminating men, who praise thoughtfully, and judge while they praise. But the familiar daily converse with private journals and letters makes on the mind a peculiar impression quite different from that left by study of published writings, or observations of an open career; and which may be worth preserving. The careful biographer sees traits that are concealed from even the discerning eye of companion or onlooker, and detects mental qualities which are overlaid by the deposits of outward life. Parker had a habit of confiding secrets to his journal; of laying bare the processes by which his results were reached; and so revealing, as it were, the texture of his faculties, the intellectual "protoplasm," if I may use the word, which afterward took forms of life. To one who has been privileged to examine this, much of what has been said by way of commendation and of censure is aside from the truth. The student of these private papers is confirmed in an assurance of the man's simple genuineness, of his honesty, sincerity, faithfulness, more than that, of his strict dealing with himself, his humility, modesty, unpretentiousness, lowliness, and purity of spirit. Anybody who would might see that he was a good deal of a hero: his biographer knows that he was a good deal of a saint. His power to assert his will was apparent to all, painfully evident to some. His power to resign his will they only knew who knew him intimately: they knew, too, from what self-submission his self-assertion sprang. Men are ready to tell of the wilfulness he exhibited: they cannot tell of the wilfulness he suppressed. His individuality looked aggressive, and doubtless it was: but it must be said that he was as jealous of others' individuality as of his own; laid on himself a solemn vow never to infringe on the sacred personality of enemy or friend; and piously abstained from crushing when he could not lead. The efforts he made to keep himself down appear in every volume of the journal, and make passages of it as touching as the confessions of St. Augustine or the soliloquies of Paul.

He was fond of roughly classifying the human faculties for practical purposes, thus: 1. The religious; 2. The moral; 3. The affectional; 4. The intellectual. WORSHIP OF THE ABSOLUTE PERFECTION: that was chief. ALLEGIANCE TO ETERNAL LAW: that came next. Subordinate only to these were LOVING FIDELITY TO HUMAN RELATIONS, POWER OF UNDERSTANDING. Mental power, in its several phases, majestic and important as it is, must be placed last. Saint, hero, lover, thinker, — this was the order of his human hierarchy. The classification may have reflected his own nature: whether it did or not, his own nature illustrated the classification.

With him the religious sentiment was supreme. It had roots in his being wholly distinct from its mental or sensible forms of expression, — completely distinguished from theology, which claimed to give an account of it in words; and from ceremonies, which claimed to embody it in rites and symbols. Never evaporating in mystical dreams, nor entangled in the meshes of cunning speculation, it preserved its freshness and bloom and fragrance in every passage of his life. His sense of the reality of divine things was as strong as was ever felt by a man of such clear intelligence. His feeling for divine things never lost its glow; never was damped by misgiving, dimmed by doubt, or clouded by sorrow. The intensity of his faith in Providence, and of his assurance of personal immortality, seems almost fanatical to modern men who sympathize in general with his philosophy. His confidence in the latter faith particularly, not all theists share. Yet to him it was native, instinctive (in the sense of spontaneous and irresistible), born of reverence, aspiration, trust, affection, which were ineradicable qualities of his being. So far from dreading to submit his faith to tests, he courted tests; was as eager to hear the arguments against his belief as for it; was as fair in weighing evidence on his opponent's side as on his own. "Oh that mine adversary had written a book!" he was ready to cry, not that he might demolish it, but that he might read it. He knew the writings of Moleschott, and talked with him personally. The books of Carl Vogt were not strange to him. The philosophy of Ludwig Büchner, if philosophy it can be called, was as familiar to him as to any of Büchner's disciples. He was intimate with the thoughts of Feuerbach. He drew into discussion every atheist and materialist he met; talked with them closely, confidentially; and rose from the interview more confident in the strength of his own positions than ever. Darwin's first book "On the Origin of Species," which was brought to him in Rome, contained nothing that disturbed him. He thought it unsupported in many of its facts, and hasty in its generalizations; but the doctrine itself was not offensive to him. Science he counted his best friend; relied on it for confirmation of his faith; and was only impatient because it moved no faster. All the materialists in and out of Christendom had no power to shake his conviction of the infinite God and the immortal existence; nor would have had, had he lived till he was a century old: for, in his view, the convictions were planted deep in human nature, and were demanded by the exigencies of human life. The service they rendered to mankind would have been their sufficient justification, had he found no other; and in this aspect they interested him chiefly. He used them daily, as man, as minister, as reformer, — used them in the closet, the study, the house of mourning, the arena of strife; and, finding them suitable for all emergencies, accepted them as heavenly provisions for them. If more worked their faiths as he did, fewer would assail them. Moleschott respected Parker; Desor was his confidential friend; Feuerbach would have taken him by the hand as a brother.

It has been said that Parker accomplished nothing final as a religious reformer; that if he thought of himself as the inaugurator of a second reformation, a reformation of Protestantism, the leader of a new "departure," as significant and momentous as that of the sixteenth century, he deceived himself. Luther, it is said, found a stopping-place, a terminus, and erected a "station," where nearly half of Christendom have been content to stay for three hundred years, and will linger, perhaps, three hundred years longer. Parker stretched a tent near what proved to be a "branch-road," where a considerable number of travellers will pause on their journey, and refresh themselves, while waiting for the "through-train." That Parker thought otherwise, that he believed himself sent to proclaim and define the faith of the next thousand years, merely gives another illustration of the delusions to which even great minds are subject. Already thought has swept beyond him; already faith has struck into other paths, and taken up new positions. The scientific method has supplanted the theological and sentimental, and has carried many over to new regions of belief. Parker is a great name, was a great power, will be a great memory; but it is doubtful if he did the work of a Voltaire or a Rousseau: that he did not do the work of a Luther is not doubtful at all.

There is much truth in this; but is it the whole truth? That Parker did not inaugurate a second reformation is frankly conceded. The conditions of a second reformation were not given. In Luther's day there was no science as there is now, no general intelligence, no widespread literature, no awakened thought. Christendom included civilized and intelligent mind: Romanism stood for Christendom. It was a solid mass: Luther broke it in two, and of one part made a separate dominion; which can never be done again. Luther's "terminus" was not for all time, but only for so long as the human mind remained in essentially the same condition of dependence in which he found it. Protestantism has been decomposing ever since it began its career, and is, by this time, pretty thoroughly demoralized. The translation of the Bible into the popular speech, on which Luther relied for the establishment of his reform, did as much as any thing to scatter its force. Had Luther lived in the nineteenth century, he could have effected no more than Parker did. Henceforth it will be impossible to handle masses of men by the power of a single will or a single idea.

Certainly Parker was not a discoverer. He originated no doctrine; he struck out no path. His religious philosophy existed before his day, and owed to him no fresh development. But he was the first great popular expounder of it; the first who undertook to make it the basis of a faith for the common people; the first who planted it as the corner-stone of the working-religion of mankind, and published it as the ground of a new spiritual structure, distinct from both Romanism and Protestantism.

Some of his special beliefs have been dropped already. Jesus no longer, in radical thought, holds the place that Parker gave him. The ethics of the New Testament have fallen into some discredit in the esteem of scientific moralists. The conception of Christianity, in its essence, has been greatly modified, and is destined to yet further modification. But these are incidental points, that do not affect the strength of his general position. His peculiarity was, that, assuming man to have a spiritual nature, he went directly to that for the revelations of truth and the inspirations of duty. The Romanist appealed to the Church; the Protestant, to the Bible; Parker, to the soul. *The intuitive philosophy was his stronghold.* That philosophy is not obsolete. It has lived several thousand years. It was old when Plato was a child; and it will endure several thousand years yet to come. Parker's basis, therefore, is permanent. Others may build upon it different structures; for it is common ground, wide enough for whole cities to stand upon: but the structure which Parker built — so ample, comfortable, hospitable, convenient, easy of access, commanding in site, stately at once, and democratic — will be the welcome home of multitudes who are wanderers in the intellectual world, and unable to construct heavenly mansions for themselves. The few educated, cultivated, self-reliant, must be left out of the account. Romanism never included everybody.

Lutheranism was pronounced unsatisfactory by the best thinkers of the reformer's own day. This will be the case, even more, with "Parkerism." For all that, "Parkerism" may deserve to be regarded as a form of religion; and Parker may merit the name of founder, — not of a sect, certainly; he never dreamed of that: nor of a church; for he believed more in ideas than in institutions: say, then, that he merits the name of *crystallizer;* for he supplied the statement about which many floating thoughts gathered. If he did not make a terminus, he laid a new track, along which many will travel towards the one central terminus, — the truth.

The ethics of Theodore Parker grew from the same root as his religion, and were part of the same system. These, too, rested on the spiritual philosophy, — the philosophy of intuition. He believed that to the human conscience was made direct revelation of the eternal law; that the moral nature looked righteousness in the face. He was acquainted with the objections to this doctrine. The opposite philosophy of utilitarianism, whether as taught by Bentham or by Mill, was well known to him, but was wholly unsatisfactory. Sensationalism in morals was as absurd, in his judgment, as sensationalism in faith. The Quaker doctrine of the inner light was nearer the truth, as he saw it, than the experience doctrine of Herbert Spencer. Experience might assist conscience, but create it never. Conscience might consult even expediency for its methods; but for its parentage it must look elsewhere. Conscience for him was authority, divine, ultimate. What that voice commanded — and he did not go to Pennsylvania Avenue or Wall Street to learn what it commanded — he obeyed, even if it commanded the cutting off of the right hand, or the plucking out of the right eye. He would not compromise a principle, wrong a neighbor, injure a fellow-creature, take what was not fairly his, tell a falsehood, betray a trust, break a pledge, turn a deaf ear to the cry of human misery, for all the world could give him. At the heart of every matter there was a right and a wrong, both easily discernible by the simplest mind. The right was eternally right; the wrong was eternally wrong; and eternal consequences were involved in either. Philosophers might find fault with his psychology: they did find fault with it. He answered them if he could; if he could not, he left them answerless: but for himself he never doubted, but leaned against his pillar. A cloudy pillar it certainly was: both base and capital were lost in the mist of eternity; but, so long as it bore up the moral universe, he cared not what it was made of. No casuist he. The school of fidelity was for him the school of wisdom. The journal makes note of a long talk with a friend who doubted the infallibility of conscience under any circumstances, seemed phrenologically inclined, denied the will of man; and the writer says ingenuously, "I could shed no light on the subject at all. He took the ground of Owen, that every thing is forecast in the mental or physical structure of the man. He will have a *motive* for all things, and makes action the result of the balance of forces inclining this way or that. He will outgrow this. It can only be lived down. I have passed through the same stage." This occurred early in his career, when he was in West Roxbury; but his position did not change essentially as he grew older.

The strength of Parker's affections helped to confirm his faith in conscience, and give intensity to his moral instinct. He was a mighty lover. His friends were all glorified by his feeling, till they hardly knew themselves. He lavished on them terms of endearment; had pet names for them all; kept their anniversaries; loved to have memorials of them about him. But his affectionateness by no means confined itself to his friends. His heart was human: its humanity was as remarkable as its tenderness. Love gave him insight, knowledge, prophetic vision; taught him to see the soul of truth in things erroneous, the soul of good in things evil. That he never forgot a kindness, never failed to reciprocate an act of friendliness, never neglected an opportunity of rendering service, is not all: his readiness to forgive those who hated him was as remarkable as his devotion to those who loved him. Beauty attracted him; grace charmed him; gifts gained his admiration; but human qualities commanded his heart. Handsome or otherwise, graceful, accomplished, witty, learned, or otherwise, his love of qualities was the same, knowing no distinction of persons. Yet no man or woman ever breathed a whisper of suspicion against his constancy. No ardor of feeling softened to weakness the texture of his truth.

The controversy is over Theodore Parker's intellectual character. Was he a philosopher, an original thinker, an exact scholar, a man of genius? Whether he was or not is of much less consequence than is suspected; for the power of his life and character lay in other departments. Some, perhaps, have claimed too high a place for him in the ranks of thinkers: possibly he himself overrated his intellectual endowment. If by "philosopher" be meant a man of *pure reason*, he was not one; for with him reason, affection, and conscience went inseparably together: but if by "philosopher" be meant a "rational man," he deserves to be called one. He had the prime quality of mental integrity: he was a sincere lover of the truth; would neither deceive himself nor others, if it could be avoided; was no diplomatist of ideas, no politician of thoughts, no juggler with speech. He desired the ultimate fact. The charge of intellectual pretence or affectation cannot, without malignity, be brought against him. He was a devoted "lover of wisdom," and therefore, by definition, a philosopher.

His mental endowments were extraordinary. What power of acquisition! What power of retention! Was there ever such a memory? It never lost a fact. In 1857, thirteen years after his visit to Europe, he wrote to a friend in Venice, "Please look at the 'Viaggi da Giovanni Gabota' (or Gabotti, or Gabbotti) in the Ducal Library, and give me the exact title. It used to be the corner book in the corner of the library, next the *Canale Grande*, on the lowest shelf. The book is in no catalogue in America; and men say there is no such." One day he recited, without hesitancy, a comic song of more than a dozen verses; and said, when asked where he had learned it, "I never read it in my life; but, when I was twelve years old, my brother brought me to Boston, to the Museum, and a man sang it there." He was then forty years of age. Dr. Nathan Lord of Dartmouth, an apologist for slavery in the days when slavery had apologists among divines, stated in a lecture, as a fact, that "the black Africans were largely descended from the Canaanites, whose name was derived from Cain, the first murderer; whence he assumed it to be quite *probable* that the blackness was a brand set on them, a mark of reprobation. A friend, being in Mr. Parker's study, asked him where Dr. Lord could have found the fact that the black Africans were descended from the Canaanites. "He got it," said Parker, "from Grotius' 'De Veritate;'" and went to the shelf to verify the statement. The book was not there, but a narrow empty space where it usually stood. "Miss Stevenson must have lent the book: I have not. The statement you refer to occurs in that volume. Then he proceeded to say how far along in the book it was, how far down the page, and on which page it was printed. "Have you read the book lately?" asked the friend. "No; not for many years: I never read it but once." — "Is the passage in question associated with any incident in your experience, that you recall it so readily?" — "No: I recollect it simply as a part of the contents of the book." The passage was afterwards found where Parker's memory indicated.

Such a power of holding distinctly great masses of miscellaneous facts, literary and other, will make a man pass for a genius when he is none; but it endangers exactness of thought, by, in a measure, dispensing with it. Distinctness of recollection passes for nicety of discrimination. Nothing may be lost; but nothing may have been, in the best sense, gained. A great deal has been said, every now and then something is said again, about the inexactness of Parker's scholarship; and people make the charge who ought to know what they allege, and ought to be above making rash or ill-natured assertions. If the charge is true, — and I do not believe it is true to any thing like the extent claimed, — the inaccuracy must have been due, partly to the difficulty of combining delicacy of touch with immensity of grasp, the nice analytic power with the power of wielding masses of thought, and partly to the lack of severe training. Self-taught scholars are rarely nice scholars, not having been subjected to the sharp criticism which brings the faculties down to delicate discriminations. It certainly was not due to heedlessness or looseness of mind.

Parker was a thorough workman: he left no stone unturned beneath which might lie a fact. He slighted no authorities. As a member of the Oriental Society, a company of eight or ten persons who met in a parlor on Anniversary Week, he was to read an essay on Mohammed. By way of preparation for the task, he renewed his acquaintance with the Arabic and Spanish languages in order to obtain original materials. Then he collected all the books he could find relating to Mohammed, till, standing with their titles up, side by side, they — folios, 12mos, and all — covered a length of twelve feet on his library floor. These books he read, extracted the pith from them one by one, and then felt qualified to write the essay. The inaccuracies of such a man, supposing his work done conscientiously, are not like the inaccuracies of the careless, who are satisfied with slight preparation; or of the dishonest, who use their materials treacherously. That he was not a scholar after the German type he admitted himself; but as certainly was he not a scholar of the loose, conceited American type. Scholarship with him was not primary, but secondary. He thought in masses, aimed to produce broad effects, and prevailed by virtue of his power to hurl mountains of material on the points he wished to carry. Of course he was thoughtful in regard to the quality of his material; chose it with care; handled it with skill; never used what was unfit: at the same time, he was less dainty in his choice of special bits than a more fastidious critic would have been. His inaccuracies, however annoying they may be to the mental precisian, did not impair the substantial value of his work. Indeed, one may suspect that the prodigious bulk of his acquirements has encouraged some to conjecture their inexactness. It is certain that all who have made the accusation are not the persons to substantiate it. Sectarians have made it to break the force of his assaults; dogmatists have made it as a substitute for argument; sciolists have made it, jealous of his reputation; pedants have made it, failing to perceive the true points at issue, and mistaking the dropping of an *iota* for the omission of an idea.

We need not be anxious to defend Mr. Parker's reputation for scholarship: that must plead its own cause at the bar of scholarship itself. I have said so much, partly to account for the insinuations against it, but more to guard against allowing to them an undue weight in the estimate of his intellectual work. It is admitted that his receptive powers were enormous: it is admitted that they were only matched by his power to retain what he received. These two admissions, if they do not render suspicion of grave errors unreasonable, do, at least, suggest caution in regard to its indulgence.

For the rest it may as well be confessed frankly, that the

æsthetic department of his mind was imperfect. True, the absorption of his life in the business of social reform might have suppressed the æsthetic element, even had it been strong. But this did not suppress the theological bent of his mind, which must, therefore, have been stronger. He may have deliberately sacrificed it on the altar of practical utilities: but then it should have appeared, and given promise of fair proportions, before the pressure of practical utilities came; and this it never did. He read poetry, but was not an artist in verse; he examined works of painting and of plastic art, but was not a connoisseur. By his own confession, made when he first visited the Old World, and during his last visit in Rome, the fine arts interested him less than the coarse arts, which fed, clothed, housed, and comforted mankind. "I should rather," he wrote from Rome in 1859, "be such a man as Franklin than a Michael Angelo; nay, if I had a son, I should rather see him a great mechanic who organized use like the late George Stephenson in England, than a great painter like Rubens, who only copied beauty: in short, I take more interest in a cattle-show than in a picture-show. I love beauty, — beauty in nature, in art, in the dear face of man and woman; but, when a nation runs after beauty to the neglect of use, alas for that people!" He had no sympathy with those who lamented the "absence of art" in America. The useful arts more than made amends. "There is not a saw-mill in Rome!" he cries.

He had a better eye for form than for color; a better eye for moral expression than for either. He admired most what expressed the highest sentiment in the most pathetic manner. As might have been expected, music gave him but little delight. He used to call it "the least intellectual of the fine arts." Jewels and plate interested him, more from their human associations, as heirlooms or appendages to certain family estates, than as works of art: their richness and preciousness, fineness of shape, and delicacy of carving, were blended with something of history, with records of service, or memories of social joy. The diamonds in Dresden delighted him: but the diamonds in Dresden had belonged to great houses, played a part in pageants, decorated beautiful women, shone in coronets and belts, graced royal occasions; thus they suggested to the gazer a brilliancy not their own.

In poetry, it was again the earnest, human quality that gave him deepest satisfaction. He loved the field-flowers of literature best, — the homely ballads, the songs of the people, full of nature, warm with feeling. The German legend of Tannhaüser was familiar to him in every language and dialect. He traced the romantic story of Hero and Leander through the whole range of literature. His admiration for Mrs. Browning's poetry was not unqualified. "Aurora Leigh" he did not care to read a second time. Verses that had a sentiment in them, a smile, or, better still, a tear, lingered longest in his memory. He was fond of quoting poetry in sermons; but it was chiefly of a didactic or sentimental character. The following lines from Lowell's "Ghost Seer" were recited as many as half a dozen times in two years, so deep was the impression they made on him: —

"Hark that rustle of a dress
Stiff with lavish costliness!
Here comes one whose cheek would blush
But to have her garment brush
'Gainst the girl whose fingers thin
Wove the weary broidery in,
Bending backwards from her toil
Lest her tears the silk might soil,
And in midnight's chill and murk
Stitched her life into the work,
Shaping from her bitter thought
Heart's-ease and forget-me-not,
Satirizing her despair
With the emblems woven there."

49

Shakspeare he knew, of course: but it would hardly be suspected from his writings; for, though he did once or twice recommend the study of him to young people, he rarely quoted him, and seldom spoke of his plays with enthusiasm. The Sonnets pleased him most, because saturated with personal feeling. He once thought of editing the Sonnets. As compared with Homer and Sophocles, Shakspeare was nothing to him as a resource in weary hours: he was less than Milton, or than Wordsworth even, as a companion. A passage in the journal gives the impression, that in moral qualities, superiority to the religious and social prejudices of his time, courage to expose popular follies and fashionable vices, Shakspeare was, in his judgment, greatly inferior to Molière. Playfully, yet half in earnest too, he said one day, "Shakspeare, if he were living now, would be a hunker and a snob." This absence from his mind of the fine artistic quality accounts for the something like crudeness that mars occasionally his treatment of the poetical side of ancient religions, their scriptures and their dogmas; and even helps to explain certain inaccuracies, which sprang from a defect in æsthetic perception oftener than from infidelity to literal facts.

The thing of most moment to say of Parker is, that he was pre-eminently a man of uses. His gifts, natural and acquired, he held in trust for his fellow-men. The higher the gifts, the deeper the responsibility. The gifts, as he could not but be aware, were great: the sense of duty was, therefore, incessant; in a less capable man it would have been excessive. But his keen enjoyment of life, and the ease with which he performed his tasks, deprived the burden of service of its apparent weight. "Let him that is greatest among you be your minister, and him that is chief among you be the servant of all," was perpetually in his heart, but not as it is with the ascetic or the self-immolator. His gifts were so rooted in the common earth, had such a strong savor of the ground, derived such fragrance and color from the soil of humanity, it seemed to cost so little to grow them, that their ceaseless consumption by pilgrims, wayfarers, and cattle even, caused no thought of waste, but rather suggested the inexhaustible resources of the nature from which they grew. Pure religion, noble institutions, just laws, humane customs, sweet morals, lovely manners, all slept in the common sods of humanity, and needed but gracious air and sunshine to ripen like flowers of paradise. To supply the air and sunshine he felt to be a privilege, not a toil; and, when the labor became more severe, — the blasting of rocks, the felling of trees, the breaking-up of fallow ground, the ploughing deep furrows across stubborn fields, — he was cheered in it by the vision of the fertility that was to follow.

Faith in humanity — this was his secret; love for humanity — this was his inspiration; sympathy with humanity — this was his consoler. This faith was his key to literature, art, philosophy, society. Had he lived to be an old man, he would have illustrated his principle more amply: he could not have more forcibly demonstrated it.

He was a worker, — he lived for uses; a reformer, who spent his life in efforts to make society more shapely. Every thing he had was turned instantly to service. No gift was folded in a napkin; no pot of gold was buried in the cellar; no fine accomplishment was hung up as ornament, or kept on the centre-table for the entertainment of visitors. He was no dilettante. His conscience, if nothing else, would have made it impossible for him to be a mere scholar toying with books. He could never respect Goethe; he disliked Margaret Fuller; he detested Rousseau. The great work which was the dream of many years was conceived, not in the interest of literature, but in the interest of mankind. We recur once more to C. A. Bartol's impressions of him: —

"Right or wrong, I could not recognize in him genius poetic, philosophic, or metaphysic, but only immense talent, and a conscience since Luther unsurpassed. He was a power, not in the realm of imagination, but of fact; the sheriff of ideas, the translator of knowledge into deed. It was the fault of some of his contemporaries to be too content with the beautiful perceptions, and his merit to insist on putting all the poetry into prose. He was not a master to set the ball in motion, but a loyal follower or ally to keep the motion up till every error and sin fell before it in the way; not an organic and incarnate revolutionizer, or instaurator of opinion, like Swedenborg, but moral from the first brain-cell to his fingers' ends. Having the eternal principles in charge, he used the timely opportunity to set them in gear; and, in such zeal and ability, he transcended those who were otherwise his superiors or peers.

"Parker was scientific in not admitting the entity of sin. Jesus did not admit it, though he was conscious of it, if we mean by sin the rebuke of the ideal on all the facts of life: but he did not dwell on or profess it; was no *professor of sin.* Why talk of the sickness of the mind more than of the body? But who ever more bravely than this son of a soldier fought the Devil, and moved more immediately on his works? How finer seers lagged behind this terrible doer! His great grotesque figure was a Yankee reminder of the Greek Socrates; and those of us who discounted aught from his dimensions on the score of any disproportion of temper or taste, shall, in any revise of our proofs, witness his steady growth in our reverence and esteem."

The above passage is cited as the testimony of a keen and friendly critic to the fact of Parker's eminence in the domain of use; which is the point I am insisting on. That Dr. Bartol does less than justice to his intellectual greatness as a thinker and initiator, as I believe, does not detract from the value of his testimony to the man's essential grandeur, — that of being an adorer of the Infinite Perfection, and a devoted lover of his kind. The "originality" of religious reformers must not be severely scrutinized. Jesus borrowed the material he used. His ideas existed before he did: his genius lay in his use of them. It was the genius of character. He made himself a focus for the solar rays which had been wandering through the atmosphere for ages. The thoughts of Paul were lying loosely about on the surface of his theologic world: he had the genius to combine and apply them. Swedenborg is called a seer; but the substance of his vision had been seen by many a fine soul before his eye was blessed by it. That Theodore Parker was the peer of either of these is by no means claimed; but they that bring against him, as if it were a damning fault, that he lacked genius, must consider how far their accusation reaches. The highest genius is that which creates uses; and of this he did possess something. The world at large felt that he did; and the testimony of the popular consciousness, though not finely discriminating, is sound. He is probably not destined still to ascend in the ranks of scholars, philosophers, men of letters, or men of pure thought; but that he is destined to hold a nobler place in the regards of mankind may be anticipated.

The influence of his thought has been very great, not more in the realm of opinion than in the realm of character; and it is destined to be still greater. A gentleman of intelligence, who, in the days of the Unitarian controversy, had left his church and minister because he had exchanged with Theodore Parker, resumed his old connection some time during the war. It occurred one day to his minister to ask pleasantly the reason of his return. He replied, "I went away because I could not bear the smallest seeming of encouragement to Theodore Parker; but, when I saw the influence of his mind on our soldiers, I was forced to make a different estimate of the man." The youth of America needs the influence of that mind to-day, and will need it for many days to come.

Theodore Parker looked the man he was, — sturdy, strong in legs and arms, with a muscular grip of the hand that knit one to him at once, and a planted foot that asserted a whole man's title to stand on the planet. The lower portion of his face was not good, — strong and firm, but a little grim in expression. His lip curled easily ; and a slightly Socratic nose had possibilities of sarcasm which the stranger might find repellent. The glory of the head was the massive dome, smooth and lofty, which suggested the man of thought ; and underneath it the clear, frank blue eye, that invited confidence, but had in it the gleam of a sword to pierce through hypocrisy, and cleave falsehood to the ground. Not a handsome man, seraphic, poetic ; not the ideal of the philosopher, the saint, or even the prophet ; a man of the people rather ; a working-man, to look at him, but a working-man with such tools as prophets, philosophers, and saints use ; a true American if there ever was one ; the best working-plan of an American yet produced.

INDEX.

D.

E.

F.

G.

H.

I.

J.

K.

L.

www.ingramcontent.com/pod-product-compliance
Lightning Source LLC
LaVergne TN
LVHW021223110826
845150LV00002B/228

* 9 7 8 1 4 2 5 5 6 4 4 7 6 *